THE BARBOUR
COLLECTION
OF CONNECTICUT TOWN
VITAL RECORDS

THE BARBOUR COLLECTION OF CONNECTICUT TOWN VITAL RECORDS

WINDHAM 1692–1850

Compiled by
Carole Magnuson

General Editor
Lorraine Cook White

INTRODUCTION

As early as 1640 the Connecticut Court of Election ordered all magistrates to keep a record of the marriages they performed. In 1644 the registration of births and marriages became the official responsibility of town clerks and registrars, with deaths added to their duties in 1650. From 1660 until the close of the Revolutionary War these vital records of birth, marriage, and death were generally well kept, but then for a period of about two generations until the mid-nineteenth century, the faithful recording of vital records declined in some towns.

General Lucius Barnes Barbour was the Connecticut Examiner of Public Records from 1911 to 1934 and in that capacity directed a project in which the vital records kept by the towns up to about 1850 were copied and abstracted. Barbour previously had directed the publication of the Bolton and Vernon vital records for the Connecticut Historical Society. For this new project he hired several individuals who were experienced in copying old records and familiar with the old script.

Barbour presented the completed transcriptions of town vital records to the Connecticut State Library where the information was typed onto printed forms. The form sheets were then cut, producing twelve small slips from each sheet. The slips for most towns were then alphabetized and the information was then typed a second time on large sheets of rag paper, which were subsequently bound into separate volumes for each town. The slips for all towns were then interfiled, forming a statewide alphabetized slip index for most surviving town vital records.

The dates of coverage vary from town to town, and of course the records of some towns are more complete than others. There are many cases in which an entry may appear two or three times, apparently because that entry was entered by one or more persons. Altogether the entire Barbour Collection--one of the great genealogical manuscript collections and one of the last to be published--covers 137 towns and comprises 14,333 typed pages.

ABBREVIATIONS

ae.------------age
b. ------------born, both
bd.-----------buried
bf.------------born of
B.G.---------Burying Ground
d.------------died, day, or daughter
dea.----------deacon
decd.--------deceased
f.-------------father
h.-------------hour or husband
J.P.-----------Justice of Peace
m.------------married, month, or minister
page#+*-----* = 1/2, example: 125* = page 125 1/2
res.-----------resident
s.-------------son
st.------------stillborn
w.------------wife
wid.----------widow
wk.-----------week
y.------------year

THE BARBOUR
COLLECTION
OF CONNECTICUT TOWN
VITAL RECORDS

WINDHAM VITAL RECORDS
1692 - 1850

	Vol.	Page
ABBE, Abatha, d John & Mary, b Sept. 16, 1736	1	148
Abigail, m. Daniel **SABEN**, Mar. 18, 1701	A	30
Abigail, d Obadiah & Elizabeth, b Oct 25, 1709	A	18
Abigail, d. Ebenezer & Mary, b. Aug. 1, 1724	1	35
Abigail, m. Benj[amin] **COREY**, Nov. 10, 1743	1	252
Abigail, w. John, d. Oct. 16, 1766	1	148
Abner, s. Ebenezer & Abigail, b. Aug 26, 1737	1	121
Abner, s. [Isaac & Eunice], b. Nov. 5, 1758	2	74
Alfred, twin with unnamed son, s. [Elisha & Jerusha], b. Aug. 19, 1779; d. Apr. 13, 1781	2	195
Allice, d. [Joshua, Jr & Tryphenia], b. Nov. 21, 1773	2	168
Anna, d. [Isaac & Eunice], b. Mar. 14, 1757	2	74
Anne, m. Jeremiah **LINKON**, Sept. 20, 1775	2	202
Antionette Charlotte, d. [Lucius, Jr & Mary B.], b. Nov. 11, 1814	3	72
Bela, s [Elisha & Jerusha], b Dec. 18, 1777	2	195
Betsey, d. [Phinehas & Mary], b. Nov. 2, 1771; d. Dec. 21, 1774	2	136
Betsey, d. [Elisha & Jerusha], b. Dec. 13, 1775	2	195
Betsey, d. [Shubael & Lucy], b. Jan 25, 1787	2	229
Betsey, m. Abner **LATHROP**, Oct. 1, 1796	3	46
Caroline, of Windham, m Marvin **SPAFFORD**, of Spaffordville, Jan. 6, 1839, in St. Paul's Church, by Rev. John W Woodward	3	188
Charles, s. [Phinehas & Susannah], b. Jan. 17, 1783	2	136
Chester, twin with Lucretia, s. [Shubael & Lucy], b Jan. 12, 1782	2	229
Christopher, s [Shubael & Lucy], b Oct. 12, 1789	2	229
Ebenezer, m. Mary **ALLEN**, Oct. 28, 1707	1	34
Ebenezer, s. Ebenezer & Mary, b. July 27, 1708	1	35
Ebenezer, m. Abigail **SAVAGE**, Feb. 22, 1729/30	1	121
Ebenezer, s Eb[eneze]r, Jr & Abigail, b. Jan. 10, 1739	1	121
Ebenezer, d. Dec. 5, 1758	1	64
Elisha, s. [Josh[ua] & Mary], b. May 15, 1753	1	161
Elisha, m Jerusha **WEBB**, Oct 27, 1774	2	195
Elisha, s. [Joshua, Jr. & Tryphenia], b. June 25, 1794	2	168
Elizabeth, d. Obadiah & Elizabeth, b. Apr. 1, 1706	A	18

1

	Vol.	Page

ABBE, (cont.)

	Vol.	Page
ABBE, (cont.)		
John, m. Mary **PALMER**, Mar. 12, 1723	1	37
John, s. Eb[eneze]r, Jr. & Abigail, b. Aug. 22,		
1743	1	121
John, s John & Lois, b Jan 10, 1755	1	319
John, s. John, Jr. & Lois, b. Jan. 10, 1755	2	62
John, m. Abigail **RIPLEY**, Apr 23, 1757	1	148
John, d. Jan. 16, 1770	1	148
John, Jr., m. Lois **MANSON**, [ ]	1	319
John Tainton, s. Geo[rge] W., b. Aug. 8, 1819	3	111
Joseph, s. Obadiah & Elizabeth, b. May 28, 1714	A	17
Joseph, s. Obadiah & Elizabeth, b. May [ ], 1714	1	39
Joseph, s. Obadiah & Elizabeth, b. Jan. 16, 1718/19	A	18
Joseph, d. Jan. [ ], 1717/18	A	18
Joseph, s. Solem[on] & Sarah, b Apr. 6, 1752; d.		
Sept. 6, 1754	1	313
Joseph, s [Isaac & Eunice], b. June 5, 1763	2	74
Joshua, s. Ebenezer & Mary, b. Jan. 20, 1710/11	1	35
Joshua, m. Mary **RIPLEY**, Apr 14, 1736	1	161
Joshua, s. [Josh[ua] & Mary], b. Jan. 9, 1751	1	161
Joshua, Jr., m. Tryphenia **BASS**, Nov. 19, 1771	2	168
Joshua, s. [Phinehas & Mary], b. Feb. 15, 1775	2	136
Louisa, of Windham, m Joshua B. **CASWELL**, of North		
Stonington, Oct. 12, 1823	3	22
Lucius, [twin with Moses Cleveland], s. [Phinehas &		
Susannah], b. Nov. 16, 1785	2	136
Lucius, s. [Shubael & Lucy], b Oct. 6, 1786; d. Dec		
6, 1786	2	229
Lucius, s [Shubael & Lucy], b. Apr. 3, 1792	2	229
Lucius, Jr., m. Mary B. **YOUNG**, Apr. 18, 1813	3	72
Lucretia, d. Josh[ua] & Mary, b. Mar. 18, 1749	1	161
Lucretia, m. Edmund **BADGER**, Dec. 15, 1765	2	121
Lucretia, twin with Chester, d. [Shubael & Lucy], b		
Jan. 12, 1782	2	229
Lucretia, m Zephaniah **RIPLEY**, Apr. 12, 1804	3	52
Lucy, d. [Phinehas & Mary], b. Oct. 16, 1768; d. Dec.		
13, 1774	2	136
Lucy, d. [Isaac & Eunice], b. Feb. 4, 1769	2	74
Lucy, d. [Phinehas & Mary], b. Dec. 30, 1776	2	136
Lucy, d. [Shubael & Lucy], b. May 21, 1778	2	229
Lucy, m. Rev. Elijah **WATERMAN**, Nov 18, 1795	2	54
Lucy, m. Rev. Elijah **WATERMAN**, Nov. 18, 1795	3	1
Lucy, d. [Joshua, Jr & Tryphenia], b. July 3, 1797	2	168
Lucy E., housework, b. Franklin, res. Windham, d.		
May 25, 1860, ae. 26	4	161
Lydia, d. John & Hannah, b. May 21, 1696	A	19
Lydia, m Benjamin **BADCO[C]K**, Sept 4, 1722	1	61
Lydia, d. Sol[omon] & Sarah, b. July 6, 1757	1	313

4 BARBOUR COLLECTION

Vol Page

ABBE, (cont.)
Richard, s. John & Hannah, b. Feb 9, 1682/3; d.
   July 10, 1737, ae. 54   A   19
Richard, m. Mary **GEN[N]INGS**, Nov. 16, 1703   A   23
Richard, s John, b Feb. 1, 1683; m. Mary
   GENNINGS, Nov. 16, 1703; d. July 10, 1737   1   227
Richard, s. Obadiah & Elizabeth, b May 15, 1716   A   17
Richard, s. Obadiah & Elizabeth, b. May 16, 1716   1   39
Richard, s John & Mary, b. July 1, 1730   1   59
Richard, s. John, b. Feb. 1, 1683; d. July 10, 1737   1   227
Ruth, d Obadiah & Elizabeth, b Sept. 15, 1712   A   17
Samuell, m. Hannah **SALSBEY**, Mar. 15, 1710   1   22
Samuell, s. Samuell & Hannah, b Oct. 12, 1712   1   22
Sam[ue]ll, s. Sam[ue]ll & Hannah, d. Mar. 11, 1714   1   22
Samuell, s Ebenezer & Mary, b. Oct 30, 1717; d. Mar
   [ ], 1718   1   35
Sam[ue]lll, s. Ebenezer & Mary, b. Apr 24, 1719   1   35
Sam[ue]ll, d. Jan. 15, 1736/7, ae. 61   1   22
Samuel, s. [Ebenezer, Jr. & Abigail], b June 21, 1745   1   121
Sam[ue]ll, s. [Phinehas & Susannah], b. June 7, 1789   2   136
Sarah, d John & Hannah, b Mar 11, 1699   A   12
Sarah, d. Solomon & Sarah, b. Jan. 26, 1754; d. Sept.
   12, 1754   1   313
Sarah, d. Sol[omon] & Sarah, b. Aug. 9, 1755   1   313
Sarah, d. [Isaac & Eunice], b Mar 4, 1771   2   74
Sarah, d. [Joshua, Jr. & Tryphenia], b. Feb. 13, 1772   2   168
Sarah, m. Elisha **WHIPPLE**, Feb. 23, 1800   3   48
Shubael, s. Josh[ua] & Mary, b. Nov. 9, 1744   1   161
Shubael, m Lucy **CHESTER**, Jan. 26, 1774   2   229
Shubael, s. [Shubael & Lucy], b. Feb. 26, 1794; d. Apr.
   4, 1794   2   229
Shubael, d. Apr. 16, 1804, in the 60th y. of his age   2   229
Solomon, s. Ebenezer & Mary, b. [ ] 30, 1730   1   64
Solomon, s. Ebenezer & Mary, b. May 29, 1730   1   113
Solomon, s Gid[eo]n & Mary, b. May 9, 1745   1   182
Solomon, m. Sarah **KNIGHT**, June 17, 1751   1   313
Sophia, d. [Joshua, Jr. & Tryphenia], b Sept 6, 1791   2   168
Susan Brown, m. Andrew **FRINK**, Jr., Sept. 23, 1833.
   "Recorded in Chaplin"   3   98
Susannah, d. [Isaac & Eunice], b. Nov. 15, 1760   2   74
Susannah, twin with Phinehas, [d. Phinehas & Susannah],
   b. Dec. 6, 1784; d. [ ], lived 9 weeks.   2   136
Sybel, d [Joshua, Jr & Tryphenia], b Mar 15, 1785   2   168
Sybbel, m. Lucius **FITCH**, [ ], 1805   3   7
Tabitha, m. Charles **RIPLEY**, Nov. 16, 1758   2   34
Thomas, d. Apr. 1, 1700   A   12
Thomas, s [Phinehas & Susannah], b. Oct. 22, 1779   2   136
Tryphena, m. Abner **ASHLEY**, Jr., May 24, 1781   2   255

	Vol.	Page
ABBE, (cont.)		
Zeruiah, d. Ebenezer & Mary, b. Mar. 17, 1720/21	1	35
Zeruiah, m. Elihu **MARSH**, May 10, 1736	1	170
Ziruiah, d. Joshua & Mary, b. June 11, 1737	1	161
Zeruiah, d. Joshua & Mary, b Jan. 7, 1743	1	161
Zerviah, d. [Isaac & Eunice], b. Apr. 10, 1762	2	74
Zerviah, m. Nathaniel **WEBB**, May 15, 1768	2	137
Ziba, m. Jonathan **WALES**, May 19, 1757	2	40
----, s. Sol[omon] & Sarah, b Aug. 29, 1759; d. Aug. 30, 1759	1	313
----, s. Sol[omon] & Sarah, b. Aug. 12, 1760; d same day	1	313
----, twin with Alfred, s [Elisha & Jerusha], b Aug. 19, 1779; d. same day	2	195
ABBOTT, ABBOT, Abael, s. Phillip & Abigail, b. Mar. 3, 1726	1	62
Abial, m. Abigail **FENTON**, June 5, 1750	1	300
Abiel, m. Abigail **FENTON**, June 5, 1750; d. May 21, 1772	2	142
Abial, s Abial & Abigail, b Nov. 28, 1754	1	300
Abiel, s. [Abiel & Abigail], b. Nov. 28, 1754	2	142
Abiel, m. Ruth **HOVEY**, Nov. 13, 1777	2	223
Abiel, s. [Abiel & Ruth], b. Aug. 15, 1778, in East Windsor	2	223
Abigail, d. [Abial & Abigail], b. Feb. 21, 1763	1	300
Abigail, d. [Abiel & Abigail], b. Feb. 21, 1763	2	142
Abigail, d. [John & Alice], b. Dec. 15, 1764	2	151
Abigail, wid. Abiel, m John **CHAMBERLAIN**, of Amenia Precinth York State, [ ]; d. Aug. 14, 1776	2	142
Alice, d. [John & Alice], b. Apr. 17, 1763	2	151
Amelia, d. [Philip & Anna], b July 1, 1777; d Oct. 11, 1777	2	208
Anna, d. [Abial & Abigail], b. Sept 18, 1765	1	300
Anna, d. [Abiel & Abigail], b. Sept. 18, 1765	2	142
Anna, d. [Philip & Anna], b Apr 27, 1776	2	208
Asa, s. [William & Hannah], b. June 8, 1778, in Ashford	2	228
Asa, m. Sarah **FULLER**, Feb. 7, 1782	2	247
Aurelia, d. [Philip & Anna], b. Apr. 28, 1779	1	208
Benj[ami]n, s. Paul & Elizabeth, b. July 25, 1724	2	71
Betsey, d. [William & Hannah], b. Jan. 8, 1780	2	228
Colbe, s. [Abiel & Ruth], b. May 21, 1783, in Willington	2	223
Daniel, s. James & Hannah, b Oct 25, 1778	2	216
Darius, s. Paul & Elizabeth, b. Oct. 16, 1734	1	138
Elijah, s. [James & Hannah], b [ ]	2	216
Elizabeth, d. Paul & Elizabeth, b. Feb. 5, 1725/6	1	71
Elizabeth, d Paul & Elizabeth, d Aug 29, 1736	1	138
Elizabeth, d. Paul & Elizabeth, b. July 20, 1737	1	138

	Vol	Page
ABBOTT, ABBOT, (cont)		
Geo[rge], farmer, ae. 24, m. Lydia **COGEL**, ae. 20,		
July [ ], [1850], by Rev Bankwell (Bushnell?)	4	116
Hannah, d. Phillip & Abigail, b. Mar. 16, 1730	1	62
Hannah, d Paul & Elizabeth, b Feb 13, 1739/40; d		
Sept. 18, 1740	1	194
Hannah, d. Paul & Elizabeth, b June 20, 1741	1	194
Hannah, m. Samuel **UTLY**, Aug. 1, 1748	1	269
Hannah, d. Benj[ami]n & Mary Ann, b. Jan. 10, 1759	2	52
Hannah, w. James, d. Jan. 17, 1784	2	216
Isaac, s. Paul & Elizabeth, b Aug 25, 1732	1	71
James, s. Abial & Abigail, b. Mar. 9, 1753	1	300
James, s. [Abiel & Abigail], b. Mar. 9, 1753	2	142
James, m. Hannah **DENISON**, Jan. 1, 1778	2	216
Jemima, m John **WALDOE**, Mar. 14, 1750/51	1	306
John, s. Phillip & Abigail, b. July 12, 1724	1	62
John, s. Phillip & Abigail, d. July 18, 1740	1	133
John, s. Phillip & Abigail, b. Sept. 27, 1741	1	133
John, m. Alice **FULLER**, Nov. 4, 1762	2	151
John, s. [Abiel & Ruth], b. May 27, 1781, in Willington	2	223
Joseph, s. Phillip & Abigail, b Feb. 14, 1734/5	1	133
Louisa, d. Benj[ami]n & Mary Ann, b. Dec. 24, 1762	2	52
Mary, d Paul & Elizabeth, b. Mar. 3, 1727/8	1	71
Mary, d. Phillip & Abigail, b. July 6, 1732	1	62
Mary, m. Joshua **HOLT**, Jr., June 28, 1749	1	299
Mary, m. Stephen **FULLER**, Jr., Oct. 17, 1751	1	323
Mary, m Stephen **FULLER**, Jr., Oct. 17, 1751	2	129
Mary, d. Benj[ami]n, b. Aug. 4, 1754	1	188
Mary, d. Benj[ami]n & Mary Ann, b Aug 4, 1754	2	52
Mary, m. Lemuel **HOLT**, Dec. 9, 1778	2	234a
Mary, m Thomas **ADAMS**, Mar. 17, [ ]	2	251a
Nathan, s. Paul & Elizabeth, b. Apr. 11, 1721	1	71
Nathan, m. [E]unice **MASH**, Nov. 24, 1742	1	223
Phillip, m. Abigail **BIGFORD**, Oct. 8, 1723	1	62
Phillip, s. Abial & Abigail, b. Mar 23, 1751	1	300
Philip, s. [Abiel & Abigail], b. Mar. 23, 1751	2	142
Philip, m. Anna **HEWATS**, July 6, 1775	2	208
Philip, s. [Philip & Anna], b. Apr. 14, 1781	2	208
Pliney, of Vienna, N.Y., m Laura M. **LASELL**, of Wind-		
ham, [ ], by Rev. Jesse Fisher	3	167
Polly, d. [Asa & Sarah], b. Nov. 13, 1783	2	247
Sam[ue]l, s. John & Elizabeth, b. Sept. 18, 1726	1	52
Sam[ue]ll, s. John & Elizabeth, b. Sept. 18, 1726	1	84
Sarah, d. Paul & Elizabeth, b. Oct. 16, 1730	1	71
Stephen, s. Phillip & Abigail, b. Apr. 21, 1728	1	62
Stephen, m. Freelo[ve] **BURGESS**, Jan. 3, 1750	1	320
Susannah, d. Stephen & Freelo[ve], b Oct. 23, 1752	1	320
Tryphenia, d. Benj[ami]n & Mary Ann, b. Sept. 22, 1760	2	52

	Vol.	Page
ABBOTT, ABBOT, (cont.)		
William, s. Paul & Elizabeth, b. Feb. 18, 1722/3	1	71
William, m. Hannah **SNOW**, July 8, 1777	2	228
Zabadiah, d. Dec. 2, 1731	1	62
ABEL, Joseph, m. Jenette F **TREADWAY**, b. of Willimantic,		
May 6, 1838, by Rev. Silas Leonard	3	186
ADAMS, Abigail, m. Jeremiah **DURKEE**, Mar 25, 1747	1	284
Anne, m. Azor **ALLEN**, Nov. 20, 1783	2	224
David, Dr., m. Lucy **FITCH**, Oct. 29, 1761	2	88
David Augustus, s. [Dr. David & Lucy], b. Jan. 16,		
1764	2	88
Elizabeth, m. Samuell **WHITING**, Sept. 14, 1696	A	25
Elizabeth, m. Sam[ue]ll **WHITING**, Sept. 14, 1696	1	167
Hannah, m. Abraham **BURNAP**, Apr. 12, 1722	1	62
James, m. Eliza **ORMSBY**, Feb. 10, 1828, by Rev. Jesse		
Fisher	3	152
Jane Eliza, d. [James & Eliza], b Feb. 28, 1829	3	152
John C., [s. Thomas L. & Maria], b. Apr. 8, 1841	3	195
John F., s. Thomas S., painter, ae. 38, & Mariah, ae.		
33, b. Oct. 9, 1847	4	4
Lucy, d. [Dr David & Lucy], b. Aug 7, 1762	2	88
Lydia, d. [Dr. David & Lucy], b. Oct. 16, 1768	2	88
Mary, d. [Dr. David & Lucy], b. Dec. 10, 1771	2	88
Medusa, child of John Q., carpenter, ae. 27, of Willim-		
antic, b Sept. 27, [1849]	4	9
Nancy, of Gotham, m. Miner **SPAFFORD**, of Windham, Nov.		
11, 1835, by Rev Jesse Fisher	3	176
Nancy Maria, [d. Thomas L. & Maria], b. July 5, 1843	3	195
Oliver, s. [James & Eliza], b May 10, 1830	3	152
Ruth, m. Amos **KINGSLEY**, June 12, 1723	1	64
Thomas, m. Mary **ABBOTT**, Mar. 17, [ ]	2	251a
Thomas L., m. Maria **WARNER**, b. of Windham, Nov. 9,		
1840, by Rev. O.C. Whiton, of Scotland Society	3	195
W[illia]m B., of Franklin, m. Mary Ann **WRIGHT**, of		
Windham, Sept 20, 1838, by Rev. Otis C. Whiton, of		
Scotland Society	3	188
William P , of Brooklyn, m. Abigail A. **RIPLEY**, of Wind-		
ham, Oct. 7, 1844, by Rev. John E. Tyler	3	217
——, child of John, ae. 21, b [July] 27, [1849]	4	6
ADGATE, Rebeckah, m. Joseph **HUNTINGTON**, b. of Norwich,		
Nov 28, 1687	2	59
ADIE, Alexander F., of Providence, R.I., m. Almira J.		
PERKINS, of Windham, Dec 2, 1840, by Rev. J E		
Tyler	3	195
AHERN, Mary, of Willimantic, d July 30, 1859, ae. 5 m	4	159-0
AIM, George, m. Abigail **LINKARN**, July 6, 1770	2	157
Ortman, s George & Abigail, b Oct 8, 1772	2	157
Susannah, d. [George & Abigail], b. Dec. 2, 1770	2	157

ALLEN, ALLIN, ALLYN, Aaron, m Tryphenia **STRONG**, Mar
    30, 1809   3   24
Abner, s Amos & Ann, b. Dec. 30, 1757   1   188
Abner, m. Roxalaney **HIB[B]ARD**, June 10, 1778   2   45
Abner Harvey, s [Abner & Roxalaney], b Apr 7,
    1783   2   45
Abner W., m Cynthia **PALMER**, Oct 18, 1807   3   61
Amelia, d. [Amos, Jr. & Anna], b. June 10, 1765   2   105
Amos, m. Ann **DENISON**, Nov 8, 1739   1   188
Amos, s. Amos & Ann, b. Nov. 8, 1744   1   188
Amos, Jr., m. Anna **BADCOCK**, July 13, 1764   2   105
Amos, m. Jerusha **FRINK**, Nov. 14, 1776   2   105
Amos, d. Mar 28, 1788   2   105
Amos D., m. Lydia **TRACY**, Aug. 18, 1796   2   26
Amos D., m. Lydia **TRACY**, Aug 18, 1796   3   76
Amos Denison, s. [Amos, Jr. & Anna], b. Mar. 13, 1774   2   105
Ann, d. John & Mary, b Nov. 23, 1701   A   20
Anne, d. [Amos, Jr. & Anna], b. Feb. 10, 1772   2   105
Anne, w. Amos, d. Oct [ ], 1775   2   105
Asa Witter, s. [Enoch & Betsey], b. June 3, 1795   2   145
Asahel, s. Joseph & Rebeckah, b. Nov. 16, 1742   1   237
Asahel, m. Desire **AMES**, Jan. 24, 1765   2   106
Asahel, twin with Desire, [s Asahel & Desire], b
    Mar. 19, 1774, at Canterbury   2   106
Asher, [triplet with two sons], s [Asahel & Desire],
    b. Jan. 24, 1785 [only Asher living]   2   106
Axa, d [Asahel & Desire], b Aug. 15, 1770   2   106
Azer, s. [Joseph, Jr. & Rebeckah], b. Feb. 11, 1762   2   75
Azor, m Anne **ADAMS**, Nov 20, 1783   2   224
Barnabus, m. Elizabeth **FULLER**, Apr. 21, 1752   1   262
Bebe, d [Joseph, Jr. & Rebeckah], b. Feb. 14, 1769   2   75
Bela, s. [Amos, Jr. & Anna], b. May 23, 1767   2   105
Bela, m Naomi **PHELPS**, May 19, 1793   2   83
Betty, d. Joseph & Rebeckah, b. Nov. 25, 1734   1   237
Chester, s. [Amos & Jerusha], b. May 30, 1788   2   105
Clinton, s. Edward & Abby, b. Apr. 1, 1848   4   2
Daniel, m. Sarah **ALLEN**, Oct. 6, 1731   1   286
Daniel, s. Daniel & Sarah, b. Apr. 21, 1732   1   286
Daniel, d Nov 11, 1794, ae 90   1   286
David Ames, s. [Enoch & Betsey], b. Aug. 10, 1809   2   145
Denison Elderkin, s [Erastus & Charlotte], b. Jan. 29,
    1826   3   56
Desire, twin with Asahel, [d. Asahel & Desire], b. Mar
    19, 1774, at Canterbury   2   106
Desire, m Eleazer **BASS**, Dec. 18, 1794   2   201
E.B., Dr., of Belchartown, Mass., m. Abby C. **TINGLEY**,
    of Windham, Oct. 25, 1840, by Rev John E Tyler   3   194
Edward, twin with Edwin, [s. Amos D. & Lydia], b. Mar.

	Vol.	Page
ALLEN, ALLIN, ALLYN, (cont)		
27, 1811	3	76
Edward, of Windham, m. Abigail **SEGAR**, of Lebanon,		
Feb. 7, 1847, by Rev. John Cooper, Willimantic	3	234
Edwin, twin with Edward, [s Amos D & Lydia], b		
Mar. 27, 1811	3	76
Eleazer, m. Mercy **CASE**, Mar 8, 1717/18	1	22
Eliashib Tracy, s. [Azor & Anne], b. Mar 28, 1786	2	224
Eliza, d. [Erastus & Charlotte], b. May 18, 1817	3	56
Eliza, d. [Enoch & Betsey], b. [ ]; d.		
[ ], ae. 20 m	2	145
Eliza Maria, d. [Aaron & Tryphenia], b. Feb. 15, 1814	3	24
Elizabeth, m. Joseph **WARNER**, June 4, 1722	1	166
Elizabeth, d. Joseph & Mary, b. Aug. 21, 1728	1	134
Enock, s. [Asahel & Desire], b. May 23, 1768	2	106
Enoch, m. Betsey **WITTER**, Apr. 14, 1794	2	145
Ephraim, s. [Timothy & Mary], b. Nov. 7, 1776	2	206
Erastus, s. Asael & Desire, b. Nov. 6, 1783	2	68
Erastus, s. [Asahel & Desire], b. Nov. 6, 1783	2	106
Erastus, of Windham, m. Charlotte **FULLER**, of Lisbon,		
Jan 15, 1807	3	56
Ethan, s. Levi, joiner, ae. 45, & Laura, ae. 40, b.		
Sept. 15, 1850	4	13
Eunice, d. [Joseph, Jr. & Rebeckah], b. Feb. 13, 1771	2	75
Eunice, d. [Bela & Naomi], b. Aug. 8, 1796	2	83
Ezra, s. [Joseph, Jr. & Rebeckah], b. Oct. 21, 1775	2	75
Fanny, d. [Abner & Roxalaney], b. Apr. 25, 1785	2	45
Fanny, m. John **FRENCH**, Dec. 7, 1806	3	58
Fedelia, d. [Erastus & Charlotte], b Nov 28, 1820	3	56
Festus, s. Asael & Desire, b. Aug. 12, 1779	2	68
Festes, s. [Asahel & Desire], b. Aug. 12, 1779	2	106
Ffinias, d. Joseph & Mary, b. Apr. 17, 1730	1	134
Frederick, s. [Amos D. & Lydia], b Sept. 11, 1799	3	76
Harriet, d. [Joseph, 3d, & Sarah], b. Nov. 18, 1813	3	70
Henry, s [Amos D & Lydia], b. Oct. 31, 1807	3	76
Henry Boardman, s. [Lyman & Charlotte], b. Mar. 6,		
1839	3	176
Ja[me]s R., m. Susan M. **LASELE**, b. of Windham, Oct. 4,		
1846, by Rev Thomas L. Greenwood	3	230
Jerusha, d. Daniel & Sarah, b. July 22, 1742	1	286
Jerusha, d [Amos & Jerusha], b. Jan. 10, 1786	2	105
John, m. Mary **FARGO**, June 20, 1700	A	20
John, s. Daniel & Sarah, b. Mar. 23, 1737	1	286
John, s. [Amos & Jerusha], b. Jan. 25, 1782	2	105
John, s. [Enoch & Betsey], b. Sept. 21, 1797	2	145
John P., m. Abba **BOTTOM**, b. of Windham, Mar. 31, 1833,		
by Rev. Jesse Fisher	3	165
Joseph, m. Mary **UTLEY**, Jan. [ ], 1723/4	1	134

	Vol	Page
ALLEN, ALLIN, ALLYN, (cont.)		
Joseph, s. Joseph & Rebeckah, b. Apr. 9, 1739	1	237
Joseph, Jr., m. Rebeckah **ROBINSON**, Mar. 11, 1761	2	75
Joseph, s. [Joseph, Jr. & Rebeckah], b. June 23,		
1763	2	75
Joseph, d. Jan. 1, 1777, ae. 76	2	211
Joseph, Jr , m. Louisa **TRACY**, Jan. 12, 1786	2	87
Joseph, 3rd, m. Sarah **PENVER**, Feb. 15, 1813	3	70
Joshua, d Dec 27, 1699	A	12
Julia, d. [Aaron & Tryphenia], b. Oct. 10, 1810	3	24
Leora, d. [Erastus & Charlotte], b May 16, 1823	3	56
Leora, see also Lora		
Levi, of Windham, m. Anne **CHASE**, of Plainfield, Dec		
11, 1828, by Rev. Jesse Fisher	3	134
Levi, m. Laura **FLINT**, Nov 28, 1833, by Rev Roger		
Bingham	3	166
Lora, d [Amos, Jr. & Anna], b Feb. 8, 1770	2	105
Lora, m. Joshua **SMITH**, Jan. 29, 1790	3	39
Lora, see also Leora		
Lucretia, d. [Erastus & Charlotte], b. Mar. 28, 1814	3	56
Lucretia, of Windham, m. Lemuel A. **CHESTER**, of Hart-		
ford, Nov. 1, 1841, by Rev. Joseph Avery, Jr., of		
Lisbon	3	199
Lucy, d. [Amos & Jerusha], b. Jan. 2, 1780	2	105
Lucy, d [Amos D & Lydia], b. Jan. 17, 1806	3	76
Lucy, m. Stephen H. **KIMBALL**, b. of Willimantic, Oct.		
10, 1836, by Rev Philo Judson, at Willimantic	3	179
Lydia, m. Jonathan **SILSBEY**, Mar. 1, 1715	2	44
Lydia, d. [Amos D. & Lydia], b. Dec. 10, 1801	3	76
Lydia, m. Elisha **HOLMES**, Dec. 4, 1823	3	115
Lydia, d. Sept. 20, [1851], ae. 75	4	157
Lydia E., d. Levi, ae. 42, & Laura, ae. 36, b. Nov. 10,		
[1848]	4	8
Lyman, s. [Erastus & Charlotte], b. Nov. 22, 1809	3	56
Lyman, m. Charlotte **LILLIE**, Dec 1, 1835, by Rev. Jesse		
Fisher	3	176
Marcy, m. Nehemiah **RIPLEY**, June 17, 1736	1	149
Martin, s. [Enoch & Betsey], b. Aug. 25, 1807	2	145
Mary, m. William **MORE**, July 17, 1700	A	10
Mary, m. Ebenezer **ABBE**, Oct. 28, 1707	1	34
Mary, d. Joseph & Rebeckah, b. Nov. 24, 1736	1	237
Mary, m. George **HOLT**, Jr., July 4, 1743	1	236
Mary, m Timothy **ALLEN**, Oct. 6, 1772	2	206
Mary, d. [Amos D. & Lydia], b. Apr. 30, 1809	3	76
Mary, m. Selden **DENISON**, May 12, 1830, by Rev Richard		
F. Cleveland	3	145
Mary Ann, tailoress, b. Ashford, res Willimantic, d		
Nov. [ ], 1848, ae. 31	4	153

	Vol	Page
ALLEN, ALLIN, ALLYN, (cont.)		
William Fitch, s. [Abner W. & Cynthia], b. July 28, 1808	3	61
—, d. [Azor & Anne], b. May 31, [1784]; d. June 6, 1784	2	224
—, 2 s., triplets with Asher, the only one living, b Jan. 24, 1785 [children of Asahel & Desire]	2	106
ALLERSON, Alice, d. Isaac & Lucy, b. May 23, 1765	2	108
ALLWORTH, Rosannah, m Nath[anie]l **MOSELEY**, Jr., Sept. 29, 1768	2	146
AMES, [see also **EAMES**], Desire, m. Asahel **ALLEN**, Jan. 24, 1765	2	106
AMIDON, AMEDOWN, A.C., child of F.S , mechanic, ae. 26, b Mar. 2, [1849]	4	11
Francis S., m Jane D. **KINGSLEY**, Nov. 3, 1845, by Andrew Sharp	3	225
ANDERSON, Margaret, b. Ireland, res Willimantic, d Apr. 1, 1860, ae. 49	4	159-0
ANDREWS, [see also **ANDRUS**], Judeth, m. Joseph **CARRABEE***, Nov. 24, 1720 (*correction **LARRABEE** handwritten in original manuscript)	1	86
Thomas, s. Thomas & Mary, b. Mar. 1, 1723/4	1	69
ANDRUS, ANDRAS, ADRAS, [see also **ANDREWS**], Abiah, d. Isaac & Eliz[abeth], b. May 7, 1758, in Norwich	2	59
Anna, m. Caleb **WOODARD**, July 18, 1727	1	105
Jeremiah, s. Isaac & Eliz[abeth], b. Jan. 15, 1756	2	59
Joseph, s. Isaac & Elizabeth, b May 16, 1754, in Norwich	2	59
Mary A.S , d. Patrick, mechanic, ae. 30, b. Apr. 18, [1850]	4	11
ANNIBALL, Barnabus, m. Mary **WEBB**, Dec 27, 1759	2	61
Nathaniel, s. [Barnabus & Mary], b. Aug. 31, 1760	2	61
ANTIZEL, ANTIZELE, Fear, d Larrance & Mary, b Mar 9, 1741/2	1	218
Simon, s. Larrance & Mary, b June 10, 1740	1	218
Thankfull, m. Luke **HOVEY**, Oct. 31, 1754	2	23
APES, Eunice, of Groton, m. Aaron **BURRELL**, of Windham, Dec 5, 1825, by Rev. Cornelius B. Everest	3	42
APLEY, Mary Ann, of Chaplin, m Waterman **PINNEY**, of Griswold, Aug. 17, 1842, by Rev. N.C. Wheat	3	202
ARMS, Jonathan, 3rd, s. Zerviah Norwood, b Oct 20, 1764	2	74
ARMSTRONG, Abigail, d. Stephen & Hannah, b. May 1, 1712	1	15
Cha[rle]s, of Franklin, m. Eunice **TRACY**, of Windham, May 28, 1843, by Rev. J.E. Tyler	3	209
Eliza[be]th, m Luke **HOVEY**, May 26, 1757	2	23
Hannah, d. Stephen & Hannah, b. Dec. 1, 1710	1	15
Hannah, d. Stephen & Hannah, d Mar 14, 1711	1	16
Hannah, d. Stephen & Hannah, b. Mar. 23, 1714	1	15

	Vol.	Page
ARMSTRONG, (cont)		
Jerusha, d. Stephen & Hannah, b. Aug. 26, 1715	1	15
Leander, m. Elizabeth **BACKUS**, June 4, 1843, by Rev		
Andrew Sharp	3	209
Mary, d. Stephen & Hannah, b. Feb. 19, 1719/20	1	15
Sarah, d. Stephen & Hannah, b. June 21, 1717	1	15
W[illia]m S , painter, ae. 48, m. Emily **WEBB**, ae 27,		
Dec. 30, [1849], by Rev. J.M. Phillips	4	114
ARDSLY(?), Adeline, ae 30, m. Dennis **DAILEY**, laborer, ae		
28, Jan. 5, 1849, by A. Sharp	4	113
ARNOLD, Betsey, m. Nathan **HOPKINS**, Nov 29, 1832, by Rev		
Alva Gregory	3	162
Bowle, m. Elizabeth **LOTHROP**, Sept. 24, 1702	A	33
Eleanor, m. John **SPENCER**, Jan. 24, 1750/51	1	102
Joel R., lawyer, ae. 26, m. Susan **SPAFFORD**, ae 22,		
Oct. 23, [1849], by Mr. Brownley	4	113
John, m. Elizabeth **CROSS**, Apr. 8, 1702	A	22
Lafayette, m. Mary Ann **STEPHENS**, b. of Providence,		
R.I., Feb 20, 1842, by Rev. Andrew Sharp	3	200
Mary, m. Peter **BACKUS**, Feb. 7, 1728/9. Witnesses:		
Sam[ue]ll Brek, Ephraim Crefoot	1	103
ASHLEY, Abner, s. Sam[ue]ll & Elizabeth, b. May 10, 1722	1	19
Abner, m. Mary **CROSSLEY**, Mar. 5, 1745/6	1	303
Abner, s. [Abner & Mary], b. Jan. 19, 1754	1	303
Abner, Jr , m. Tryphena **ABBE**, May 24, 1781	2	255
Abner, s. [Abner, Jr. & Tryphena], b. May 2, 1782	2	255
Ann, d. [Joseph & Sarah], b July 13, 1754	1	223
Bainsford, s. [Daniel], b. Oct. 4, 1787	2	158
Benney, s. [Daniel], b. Feb. 11, 1784	2	158
Betsey, d. [Daniel], b. Aug. 25, 1785	2	158
Billey, s [Daniel], b. Aug 25, 1789	2	158
C[h]loe, d. [Joseph & Zerviah], b. Oct. 2, 1768	1	223
Daniel, s [Abner & Mary], b. Jan 28, 1758	1	303
Daniel, s. [Daniel], b. Feb. 25, 1794	2	158
Ebenezer, s [Joseph & Zerviah], b. Feb. 17, 1775	1	223
Elijah, s. [Abner, Jr. & Tryphena], b. July 28,		
1784	2	255
Eliza Ann, d. [Luther & Eliza], b. Feb. 27, 1811	3	88
Elizabeth, d Abner & Mary, b May 18, 1750	1	303
Elizabeth, w. Sam[ue]ll, d. Aug. 21, 1750	1	194
George, s. [Luther & Eliza], b Mar. 20, 1819	3	88
Gilbert, m. Frances **DROWN**, Apr. 23, 1845, by Henry		
Greenslit	3	221
Hannah, d. [Abner & Mary], b. Dec. 29, 1760	1	303
Henry, s. [James & Achsah], b Nov. 9, 1816	3	88
James, s. [Jonathan & Lydia], b. Aug. 13, 1783	2	205
James, m. Achsah **BURNHAM**, Jan 18, 1816	3	88
James, d. Sept. 13, 1817, ae. 34 y.	3	88

	Vol.	Page
ASHLEY, (cont.)		
James, s. [James & Achsah] b. Mar. 23, 1818	3	88
John Humphrey, s. [Luther & Eliza], b Jan 28, 1817	3	88
Jonathan, s. Sam[ue]ll & Elizabeth, b. Aug. 4, 1737;		
d. June 13, 1740	1	194
Jonathan, s. Abner & Mary, b. Mar. 2, 1746/7	1	303
Jonathan, m. Lydia **HUMPHREY**, June 13, 1773	2	205
Jonathan Humphrey, s. [Jonathan & Lydia], b. Feb. 15,		
1794	2	205
Joseph, s. Sam[ue]ll & Elizabeth, b. June 1, 1728	1	194
Joseph, m. Sarah **CRESSY**, Nov. 5, 1751	1	223
Joseph, m. Zerviah **LYON**, Apr. 25, 1764	1	223
Joseph, m. Rachal **ALLEN**, Apr 10, 1783	2	251a
Josiah, s. [Joseph & Sarah], b. July 21, 1756	1	223
Julia, b. June 18, 1790; m. Erastus **MARTIN**, Jan 11,		
1816	3	125
Loue, d. Sam[ue]ll & Elizabeth, b. July 19, 1731	1	194
Love, d. [Joseph & Sarah], b. Mar. 3, 1758	1	223
Lucy, d [Abner & Mary], b. Apr 13, 1762	1	303
Luther, s. [Jonathan & Lydia], b. June 14, 1781	2	205
Luther, m. Eliza **HUMPHREY**, Sept 20, 1809	3	88
Lydia, d. [Jonathan & Lydia], b. June 18, 1790	2	205
Lydia Diana, d. [Luther & Eliza], b Aug. 18, 1814	3	88
Mary, d. Abner & Mary, b. Aug. 17, 1748	1	303
Polly, d. [Daniel], b. May 18, 1792	2	158
Roxana, d. [Jonathan & Lydia], b. Apr. 11, 1788	2	205
Roxana, d [Luther & Eliza], b. Oct. 2, 1812	3	88
Ruth, d. [Abner & Mary], b. Jan. 21, 1752	1	303
Sally, d. [Jonathan & Lydia], b. Feb 22, 1777; d Oct.		
24, 1778	2	205
Sally, d. [Jonathan & Lydia], b May 11, 1779	2	205
Sam[ue]ll, s. Sam[ue]ll & Elizabeth, b. Nov. 27, 1720	1	19
Samuell, Jr , m. Ruth **CRESSY**, Nov 23, 1746	1	283
Sam[ue]ll, s. [Abner & Mary], b. Jan. 25, 1756	1	303
Samuel, d Feb 12, 1771, in the 83rd y of his age	1	194
Sarah, d. [Joseph & Sarah], b. Nov. 2, 1752	1	223
Sarah, w. Joseph, d. Sept. 11, 1762	1	223
Sarah, m. Peter **INGALLS**, Apr. 20, 1775	2	205
Susannah, d Sam[ue]ll & Elizabeth, b. June 5, 1724	1	19
Susannah, m. John **HOVEY**, Nov. 8, 1742	1	283
Susannah, d. [Joseph & Zerviah], b. Dec. 31, 1776	1	223
Thomas, s. [Joseph & Zerviah], b. Oct. 25, 1765	1	223
Walter, m. Martha **PERRY**, Feb 15, 1829, by Rev. Roger		
Bingham	3	142
Zerviah, w Joseph, d May 5, 1781	1	223
ASPINWALL, Hannah, m. Capt. Samuel **MORGAN**, Apr. 28, 1802	2	13
Lydia, m. Gurdon **ROBINSON**, Nov 9, 1809	3	62
ATWOOD, Charles Warren, [s. Warren & Harriet], b. July 10,		

	Vol	Page
ATWOOD, (cont.)		
1844	3	182
Emily C , of Mansfield, m W[illia]m H **BRANCH**, of		
Willimantic, Nov. 19, 1844, by Rev. Charles Noble,		
Willimantic	3	218
John, 2d, m. Julia Ann **BARROWS**, Oct. 11, 1840, by Rev.		
John B. Guild, Willimantic	3	196
Warren, m. Harriet **BALDWIN**, Jan. 31, 1837, by Rev.		
Philetus Greene, Willimantic, Windham	3	182
AUSTIN, AUSTEN, Agnes, m. Nath[anie]l **LINCOLN**, Dec. 21,		
1757	2	37
John, m. Susaney **HALL**, b. of Willimantic, Jan. 12,		
1834, by Rev. Alva Gregory	3	168
Lois, of Canterbury, m. W[illia]m D. **CADY**, of Monson,		
Mass., Oct 16, 1839, by Rev. Otis C Whiton, of		
Scotland Society	3	192
Mary, m Sam[ue]ll **LINKION**, Mar. 14, 1758	1	83
May, d. Jan. [ ], 1850, ae. 72	4	156
Phillis, m. Sam[ue]l **LINKON**, Jr., Mar. 9, 1758	1	271
Thomas, s. B.H., manufacturer, ae. 37, b. Nov. 28,		
[1849]	4	9
AVERELL, AVEREL, Avery, s. Mary **PRESTON**, b. Dec. 3, 1771	2	181
Barsheba, d. Stephen & Sarah, b. Sept. 22, 1759	1	318
Elizabeth, d. William & Ruth, b. Feb. 17, 1725	1	65
Elizabeth, m. Jonathan **BURNAP**, Apr 21, 1747	1	276
Ephraim, s. William & Ruth, b. July 3, 1722*; d. Aug.		
8, 1743 (*Conflicts with date of birth of James)	1	65
Frederic, s. [Stephen & Sarah], b. Oct. 24, 1761	1	318
James, s. William & Ruth, b. Oct. 2, 1722*; d. Dec		
3, 1722 (*Conflicts with date of birth of Ephraim)	1	65
James, s. William & Ruth, b. Feb 23, 1734/5	1	65
Josiah, s. [Stephen & Sarah], b. Nov. 3, 1763	1	318
Mary, d. William & Ruth, b. May 24, 1724	1	65
Ruth, d. William & Ruth, b. July 25, 1733	1	65
Ruth, w [William], d. Oct. 20, 1749	1	95
Ruth, m. John **LOOMIS**, Jan. 20, 1758	1	228
Ruth, d. [Stephen & Sarah], b. Dec. 3, 1767	1	318
Sarah, d. Stephen & Sarah, b. Sept. 26, 1757	1	318
Stephen, s William & Ruth, b. Aug. 24, 1729; d. Nov		
8, 1729	1	65
Stephen, s. William & Ruth, b Oct. 28, 1730	1	65
Stephen, m. Sarah **HENDEE**, June 18, 1752	1	318
Stephen, s Stephen & Sarah, b June 11, 1753	1	318
William, m. Ruth **BEMIS**, Oct. 13, 1721	1	64
William, d Nov 14, 1748	1	95
William, s. Stephen & Sarah, b. Apr. 19, 1765	1	318
AVERY, Anson A , m. Celia L **KENYON**, b of Willimantic, May		
8, 1837, by Philo Judson, at Willimantic	3	182

	Vol.	Page
AVERY, (cont)		
Arthur D., s. John G., merchant, ae. 25, & Eliza,		
ae. 22, b. Aug. 5, 1850	4	14
Elizabeth, ae. 27, b. Voluntown, res. Willimantic, m.		
Cha[rle]s W **PERKINS**, papermaker, ae. 27, b.		
Manchester, res. Willimantic, Sept. 8, 1850, by		
Rev. J. H. Farnsworth	4	117
Geo[rge] W., s. Christopher W., farmer, ae. 24, b.		
Nov. 23, [1849]	4	9
Harriet, b. Franklin, res. Windham, d May 24, 1851,		
ae 24	4	158
Harriet Elizabeth, [d. Horatio N.], b. Aug. 16, 1842	3	104
Henry D., s. Alfred, laborer, ae. 27, & Permelia, ae		
20, of Willimantic, b. Sept. 3, 1850	4	12
Lucy, m George B. **FISK**, Mar. 12, 1843, by Ella Dunham,		
Elder	3	208
Mary Delia, [d Horatio N.], b Aug. 2, 1838	3	104
Miranda, m. Christopher **CHAMPLAIN**, Feb. 24, 1831, by		
Rev. Roger Bingham	3	151
Nancy, m. William **CAPEN**, b. of Windham, Jan. 25, 1841,		
by Rev. P T. Kenney, Willimantic	3	195
Nancy O., m. Charles H. **FARNHAM**, Nov. 29, 1839	3	97
Nelson H., m Nancy S. **JENNER**, b. of Willimantic		
Village, June 25, 1837, by Rev. B. Cook, Jr.	3	182
Sarah, m. John **BURNAP**, Mar. 30, 1786	2	59
Susan, d. Nov. 29, [1851], ae. 18	4	157
Susan D., of Windham, m Isaac N **PRIOR**, of Hartford,		
Aug. 20, 1833, by Rev. S H. Corson	3	165
Susan Margaret, [d. Horatio N], b. July 23, 1840	3	104
W[illia]m B., s. W[illia]m A., ae. 26, & Caroline, ae.		
36, by Apr 6, [1848]	4	7
——, child of J.G., merchant, of Willimantic, b. Aug.		
5, [1850]	4	10
AYER, AYRES, Abby, d. May 14, 1850, ae. 26	4	155
Buenos, d Sept. 10, 1849, ae. 6 m	4	154
Burrus, s. W[illia]m & Abby, b. Sept. 20, 1849	4	7
Dorrance A., s William, iron moulder, of Willimantic,		
b. Apr. 9, [1850]	4	10
Florinda, m. John N. **CHAMPLAIN**, Oct. 10, 1816	3	33
John P., merchant, ae. 22, m. Laura S. **MAINE**, ae. 24,		
Mar 4, 1849, by Rev. Mr Robinson	4	113
W[illia]m D., d. Nov. 27, 1848, ae. 4 wk.	4	151
BABCOCK, BADCOK, BADCOCK, Abigail, w. Caleb, d. Apr. 21,		
1719, in the 31st y. of her age	1	28
Abigail, d. [Joseph & Ann], b. July 18, 1756; d.		
Sept. 7, 1775	2	113
Abigail, m. Joseph H. **CHENEY**, Oct. 12, 1818	3	104
Abijah, s. [Joseph & Ann], b. Jan. 18, 1749	2	113

	Vol.	Page
BABCOCK, BADCOK, BADCOCK, (cont)		
Albert Frederick, s. Daniel, b. May 26, 1816	3	107
Anna, m. Joseph **PAYN[E]**, Feb. 26, 1723/4	1	81
Anna, m. Amos **ALLEN**, Jr., July 13, 1764	2	105
Anne, d [Joseph & Ann], b Nov 27, 1745	2	113
Anne, d. [Joseph, Jr. & Molly], b. Jan. 18, 1784	3	37
Augustus Wood, s. [Lemuel & Ruth], b. Apr 17, 1832	3	80
Benjamin, [twin with Joseph], s. James & Mary, b. July 24, 1711	1	30
Benjamin, m. Lydia **ABBE**, Sept. 4, 1722	1	61
Benj[ami]n, d (s.?) Benj[ami]n & Lidia, b. July 10, 1725	1	61
Betsey, d. [Joseph, Jr & Molly], b. Oct. 12, 1792	3	37
Betsey, m. Henry **LEFFINGWELL**, Oct. 19, 1831, by Rev. Roger Bingham	3	155
Caleb, m. Abigail **MORE**, Jan. 21, 1712/13	1	28
Caleb, m. Susannah **GLOVER**, May 18, 1721	1	28
Caleb, m. Meriam **SIMONS**, May 7, 1728	1	92
Caleb, s. Jonathan & Mary, b Aug. 28, 1729, d. Nov 5, 1729	1	92
Caleb, d. Aug. the last, 1741, ae. 64 y	1	92
Charles, m. Julia P. **SWIFT**, b. of Windham, Jan. 20, 1829, by Rev. Dennis Platt	3	134
Charles H., of Lebanon, m. Elizabeth M. **WILCOX**, of Windham, [ ] 12, 1843, by Rev Ebenezer Robinson, Willimantic	3	214
Daniel, m. Sarah **ALLYN**, Oct. 23, 1717	1	41
Daniel, s. [Joseph & Ann], b. Apr. 17, 1762	2	113
Deliverance, of Richmond, m. Elijah **KIMBALL**, of Windham, Mar. 8, 1780	2	233
Dorothy, m. Joshua **MORE**, Mar. 3, 1774	1	19
Dyer, s. [Joseph, Jr. & Molly], b. Apr. 8, 1790	3	37
Ebenezer, m Mehitable **BURT**, Sept. 14, 1725	1	63
Elijah, s. [Joseph & Ann], b. Apr. 28, 1750	2	113
Elizabeth, m Seth **CUTLER**, Oct. 22, 1734	1	225
Elizabeth, d. [Lemuel & Ruth], b. June 6, 1825	3	80
Ellen, d. [Lemuel & Ruth], b Sept 18, 1827	3	80
Hannah S., m. Lucian **CLARK**, Nov. 17, 1836, by Rev. William A Curtis	3	181
Harriette, d. [Joseph, Jr. & Molly], b. Jan. 31, 1786	3	37
Huldah, m. Isreal G. **ROBINSON**, b. of Windham, Feb. 2, 1840, by Rev. John E. Tyler	3	192
James, s. Benj[ami]n & Lidia, b Jan 3, 1726/7; d Mar. 29, 1728	1	61
James, s. Benj[ami]n & Lidia, b. Oct. 28, 1728	1	61
James C., of Columbia, m. Louisa **HOVEY**, of Willimantic, Mar. 8, 1846, by John Cooper	3	228
Jerusha, d. [Joseph & Ann], b. May 10, 1764	2	113

	Vol	Page
BABCOCK, BADCOK, BADCOCK, (cont)		
Jerusha, m. Jonathan **WALES**, Jr. Apr. 13, 1794	2	132
John, s John & Martha, b. June 22, 1726	1	80
John, m. Wid. Elizabeth **BARKER**, July 1, 1729	1	114
John, s. Benj[ami]n & Lydia, b. Oct. 28, 1730/31	1	61
John, d. Aug. 15, 1731	1	114
Jonathan, s. Caleb & Abigail, b. June 10, 1718	1	28
Jonathan, m. Mary **HIB[B]ARD**, Oct. 19, 1719	1	37
Jonathan, s. John & Elizabeth, b. Dec. 16, 1731	1	225
Jonathan, m. Susannah **JACOBS**, Sept. 16, 1741; d.		
Aug. 22, 1781	1	125
Jonathan, d. Aug. 22, 1781	1	125
Joseph, [twin with Benjamin], s. James & Mary, b.		
July 24, 1711	1	30
Joseph, m. Ann **CRANE**, Nov. 8, 1744	2	113
Joseph, s. [Joseph & Ann], b. May 26, 1752	2	113
Joseph, Jr., m. Molly **McCALL**, May 1, 1782	3	37
Josiah, s. John & Martha, b. Aug. 14, 1724	1	80
Lemuel, m. Ruth **WOOD**, Feb 23, 1820, by Rev. Jesse		
Fisher	3	80
Lena, d. [Joseph, Jr & Molly], b Feb. 9, 1788	3	37
Lena, m. Aaron **GAGER**, Jan. 29, 1835, by Rev. Roger		
Bingham	3	172
Lydia, m. Alfred **HURLBUTT**, Jan. 11, 1786	2	205
Martha, d. John & Martha, b. May 10, 1728	1	80
Martha, w. John, d. May 18, 1728	1	80
Mary, d. James & Mary, b Mar. 8, 1707/8	1	30
Mary, d. Caleb & Abigail, b. Apr. 22, 1716	1	28
Mary, w. Jonathan, d. Mar. 28, 1719, in the 64th y. of		
her age	1	28
Mary, m. Joshua **SIMONS**, Mar 27, 1733	1	112
Mary, m. Justin **EDGERTON**, Apr. 23, 1832, by Rev. Alva		
Gregory, Willimantic	3	160
Mary, of Willimantic Village, m. Geo[rge] B. **TINGLEY**,		
Apr 3, 1836, by Rev Philo Judson, Willimantic	3	177
Nathan, s. [Joseph & Ann], b. Jan. 31, 1760	2	113
Nathan, m. Susannah **WALES**, Mar. 21, 1780	2	37
Nath[anie]ll, s. John & Elizabeth, b. Mar. 13, 1730	1	114
Ralph, s. [Nathan & Susannah], b. Aug. 9, 1781	2	37
Robert, s. Jonathan & Mary, d. May 11, 1728	1	92
Sarah, d Caleb & Abigail, b. Nov. 19, 1713; d. Nov.		
19, 1713	1	28
Sarah, d Benj[ami]n & Lidia, b. Nov 24, 1723	1	61
Sarah, d. [Joseph & Ann], b. May 6, 1768	2	113
Sarah, m. Fred **CAMPBELL**, b. of Willimantic, Sept. 13,		
1835, by Rev. Philo Judson, at Willimantic	3	174
Sarah A., m. Isaac L. **PALMER**, b. of Windham, Sept. 26,		
1841, by Rev. John E. Tyler	3	198

	Vol.	Page
BABCOCK, BADCOK, BADCOCK, (cont)		
Sarah Ann, d. [Lemuel & Ruth], b. Nov. 27, 1820	3	80
Sumner, s [Nathan & Susannah], b July 24, 1784	2	37
Susannah, w. Caleb, d. Sept. 1, 1727	1	28
William, s Ebenezer & Mehitable, b July 17, 1726	1	63
William, s. [Joseph & Ann], b. June 30, 1754; d.		
Sept. 21, 1775	2	113
William, s [Lemuel & Ruth], b. Aug. 15, 1822	3	80
W[illia]m, carpenter, ae. 26, of Windham, m Mary W.		
FULLER, ae. 19, Oct. 1, [1849], by Tho[ma]s		
Robinson	4	113
Zadoc D., m. Mary E. **SPENCER**, b. of Windham, Nov. 14,		
1841, by Rev Nathan Wildman, of Lebanon	3	199
Zebulon, s. James & Mary, b. Dec. 19, 1713	1	30
Zeruiah, d James, b Jan 18, 1705	A	24
Zeruiah, d James & Mary, b. June 18, 1705	1	30
BACKER, John , m Marcy **CARY**, Dec 17, 1744	1	247
John, s. John & Mary, b Sept. 27, 1748	1	247
Mary, d John & Mary, b. Sept 15, 1749	1	247
Susannah, d. John & Marcy, b. Feb. 17, 1745/6	1	247
BACKUS, Abigail, d William & Mary, b. July 5, 1693, d.		
Sept. 26, 1793* (*Probably 1693)	A	3
Abigail, d. John & Mary, b July 2, 1701	A	2
Abigail, m. Elijah **HURLBUTT**, Aug. 18, 1725	1	75
Abigail, d. Sam[ue]ll & Sarah, b. June 18, 1731	1	103
Albert H., m. Jane C. **WELCH**, b. of Windham, Mar. 12,		
1847, by Rev B M Alden, Jr	3	234
Albert Henry, s. [Henry & Susan D.], b Mar. 25,		
1821	3	86
Alfred, s. [Ebenezer & Mercy], b. Mar. 12, 1770; d.		
[ ]	2	73
Ann, d. John & Mary, b. Jan. 15, 1695	A	2
Ann, d Sam[ue]ll & Sarah, b. Oct. 14, 1735	1	103
Anna, m. John **GENNINGS**, Jr., Dec 11, 1758	2	46
Anne, d William, Jr. & Sarah, b June 1, 1732	1	185
Bela, s. [Ebenezer & Mercy], b. Aug. 24, 1763	2	73
Bela, m Fanny **FITCH**, Aug 29, 1782	2	133
Bela, of Windham, m. Fanny **FITCH**, d. Col. Eleazer, of		
Windham, Aug 29, 1782	3	43
Betsey, 2d w. Luther, d. June 2, 1827	3	4
Betsey Lucina, d [Luther & Betsey], b Mar. 28, 1827	3	4
C.A., d. Dec. 13, [1851], ae. 2 d.	4	157
Calvin, s [Dilauna & Olive], b Oct 1, 1817	3	54
Calvin, m. Sophia L. **RUSSELL**, b of Chaplin, Nov. 4,		
1840, by Rev. John E Tyler	3	194
Celinda, d. [Whiting & Sarah], b. Nov. 10, 1769	2	199
Charles, s John & Sybell, b Aug. 15, 1753	1	159
Charles, s. [Dilauna & Olive], b. Mar. 15, 1815	3	54

	Vol.	Page
BACKUS, (cont.)		
Charles Clark, s. [Luther & Zerviah], b. May 29, 1807	3	4
Charlotte, d. [Luther & Zerviah], b. Sept. 21, 1813	3	4
Charlotte, m Isaac **WILLSON,** b of Windham, Jan. 20, 1833, by John Baldwin, J.P.	3	163
Chute*, s. [Henry & Susan D.], b. Dec. 20, 1832 (*correction "Chute" crossed out and "Chester" handwritten in margin of original manuscript)	3	86
Colaty, d. Ephraim & Colaty, b. June 8, 1736	1	142
Daniel, s. William & Mary, b Oct. 27, 1696	A	3
Debauna, s. John & Sibble, b. Oct. 2, 1744	1	158
Debauna, see also Dilauna		
Delacoria, s. [Ebenezer & Mercy], b. July 30, 1773	2	73
Demetrius, s Ephraim & Colaty, b. May 31, 1745	1	142
Demetrius, m. Lydia **BACKUS,** Apr. 30, 1767	2	125
Dilauna, m. Olive **SIMONS,** of Hampton, Jan 5, 1811	3	54
Dilauna, see also Debauna		
Dionijah*, s. Samuell & Sarah, b. July 11, 1725 (*correction "Adonijah (per Mrs. Philip Andover)" handwritten in margin of original manuscript.	1	39a
Ebenezer, s. John & Sibble, b. May 31, 1740	1	158
Ebenezer, m. Mercy **EDWARDS,** Nov 25, 1760, by Rev Mr. Eells, at Middletown	2	73
Ebenezer, of Norwich, m Elizabeth **FITCH,** d Col Eleazer, of Windham, Jan. 7, 1767	3	43
Edgar H , s. Albert & Cornelia, b. July 26, 1849	4	7
Elijah, s. [Nath[anie]ll & Elizabeth], b. July 23, 1755	1	321
Eliza Elizabeth, d. [Henry & Susan D.], b. Mar. 12, 1826	3	86
Elizabeth, d. John, Jr. & Sibel, b. Feb. 17, 1731/2	1	72
Elizabeth, d. John & Sibble, d. Oct 21, 1747	1	158
Elizabeth, d. [Silvanus & Elizabeth], b. Nov. 25, 1765	2	43
Elizabeth, d. [Luther & Zerviah], b. Sept. 22, 1815	3	4
Elizabeth, m. Leander **ARMSTRONG,** June 4, 1843, by Rev Andrew Sharp	3	209
Ellen M., d Albert, farmer, ae. 27, & Cornelia, ae. 26, of Willimantic, b. Apr. 1, 1848	4	1
Ephraim, s. William & Mary, b. May 25, 1708	A	9
Ephraim, m. Colaty **VINING,** Oct. 10, 1734	1	142
Eunice, d. [Silvanus & Elizabeth], b. Jan. 16, 1769	2	43
Evaline Joan, d. Albert H., farmer, ae. 30, & Cornelia, ae. 21, b. Apr. 14, 1851	4	14
Fanny, d. [Whiting & Sarah], b. May 19, 1775	2	199
Frederick Palmer, s. [Dilauna & Olive], b. Mar. 15, 1819	3	54

	Vol.	Page
BACKUS, (cont.)		
Freelove, d. [Luther & Zerviah], b. Oct. 21, 1805	3	4
George, m. Lama **DYER**, b. of Windham, Mar 23, 1836,		
by John Baldwin, J.P. (Perhaps "Laura"?)	3	177
Geo[rge] Abbe, s. [Henry & Susan D], b Nov. 11,		
1836	3	86
Gurdon, s. [Ebenezer & Mercy], b. Feb. 12, 1762	2	73
Hannah, d. William & Mary, b. Nov. 1, 1699	A	3
Hannah, d Eph[rai]m & Collata, b. Oct 16, 1750	1	151
Harriet, d. [Luther & Zerviah], b. Oct. 26, 1796	3	4
Harriet J., m. Charles **FITCH**, Dec. 2, 1821	3	120
Henry, s. [Luther & Zerviah], b. Oct. 1, 1795	3	4
Henry, m. Susan D. **SAWYER**, Jan 3, 1819, by Rev.		
C. B. Everest	3	86
Huldah, d. [Nath[anie]ll & Elizabeth], b. Mar 14,		
1757	1	321
Huldah Maria, d. [Henry & Susan D.], b. Aug. 3,		
1824	3	86
Jerusha, d. John & Mary, b. Sept. 29, 1704	A	2
Jerusha, m. Daniel **STOUGHTON**, Oct. 20, 1742	1	224
Jerusha, d. [Luther & Zerviah], b. Oct. 25, 1802	3	4
Joel W. s. [Luther & Malinda], b. Sept. 19, 1840	3	4
John, m Mary **BINGHAM**, Feb. 17, 1692	A	2
John, s. John & Mary, b. Mar. 5, 1697; d. Mar. 5.,		
1697	A	2
John, s. John & Mary, b. Jan. [ ], 1698	A	2
John, Jr., m Sibel **WHITING**, Jan. 15, 1725	1	72
John, s. John, Jr. & Sibel, b. Mar. 23, 1728	1	72
John, d. Mar 27, 1744, ae. above 82	1	4
John, d. Mar. 27, 1744 (Written "John **BARKUS**")	1	267
John, s Silva[nus] & Eliz[abeth], b. Feb 25, 1759	2	43
John C. Avery, s. [Henry & Susan D.], b. June 6, 1822	3	86
Joseph S , painter, of Chaplin, m. Mary L. **CLARK**, Aug		
1, 1848, by Rev. John Tyler	4	112
Julia Ann, d. [Henry & Susan D.], b. Oct 23, 1819	3	86
Laura, d. [Luther & Zerviah], b. Feb. 2, 1800	3	4
Lemuel, s Sam[ue]ll & Sarah, d. June 11, 1748, at		
Kinderhook	1	103
Lucretia, d. John, Jr. & Sibel, b. Feb. 22, 1733/4	1	72
Lucretia, d. [Ebenezer & Mercy], b. Feb. 20, 1765; d.		
Jan. 4, 1768	2	73
Luther, m. Zerviah **CLARK**, [ ], 1795	3	4
Luther, m. Betsey **LYMAN**, [ ]	3	4
Luther, m. Malinda **LYMAN**, [ ]	3	4
Luther Edwin, s. [Luther & Malinda], b. Sept 22, 1833	3	4
Luther Finis, s. [Henry & Susan D.], b. Mar. 5, 1828	3	86
Lydia, m. Thomas **DYAR**, Oct. 24, 1717	1	18
Lydia, m. Thomas **DYAR**, Oct. 24, 1717	1	39a

	Vol	Page
BACKUS, (cont.)		
Lydia, d. John & Sibble, b. July 15, 1736	1	158
Lydia, d [William & Mary], b. Mar. 28, 1745	1	234
Lydia, w. [John], d. Feb. 19, 1747 (Written "Lydia		
BARKUS")	1	267
Lydia, m. Demetrius **BACKUS**, Apr. 30, 1767	2	125
Lidia, d. [Whiting & Sarah], b. June 22, 1773	2	199
Lydia Louisa, d. [Dilauna & Olive], b. Feb. 25, 1823	3	54
Marcia, d. Sept 18, 1847, ae 14	4	151
Maria, d. [Luther & Zerviah], b. Apr. 9, 1798	3	4
Mary, d John & Mary, b. Nov. 8, 1693	A	2
Mary, d. William & Mary, b. Dec. 22, 1694	A	3
Mary, m. Joshua **RIPLEY**, Dec. 8, 1712	1	39
Mary, d. Samuell & Sarah, b. Oct. 7, 1720	1	39a
Mary, d Sam[ue]ll & Sarah, d. May 23, 1737	1	103
Mary, d. Ephraim & Colaty, b. Sept. 4, 1740; d. Dec.		
15, 1748	1	142
Mary, d. John & Sibble, b. Apr. 5, 1742; d. May 8,		
1744	1	158
Mary, d. Eph[rai]m & Collata, b. Feb. 19, 1747/8	1	151
Mary, d. [Luther & Zerviah], b Apr. 17, 1810	3	4
Mary M., d. [Henry & Susan D.], b. Dec. 3, 1830	3	86
Nancy, d. [Luther & Zerviah], b. Mar. 12, 1812	3	4
Nancy, m. Henry **KENYON**, Aug. 3, 1840, by Rev. John B.		
Guilde, Willimantic	3	196
Nathaniel, s. John & Mary, b. Jan. 10, 1712; d. Aug.		
15, 1720	1	4
Nathaniell, s. John, Jr. & Sibel, b. Feb. 5, 1726/7; d.		
Nov. 29, 1727	1	72
Nath[anie]ll, s. Sam[ue]ll & Sarah, b. Jan. 13, 1728/9	1	103
Nath[anie]ll, m Elizabeth **HEB[B]ARD**, Oct. 7, 1753	1	321
Olive J., of Chaplin, m. Jos[eph] R. **BILLS**, of Union,		
Jan. 13, 1845, by Rev Henry Greenslit	3	220
Peter, s. William & Mary, b. Apr. 25, 1701	A	3
Peter, m. Mary **ARNOLD**, Feb. 7, 1728/9 Witnesses:		
Sam[ue]ll Brek, Ephraim Crefoot	1	103
Polly, d. [Ebenezer & Mercy], b. Mar. 18, 1767	2	73
Rufus, s. Ephraim & Colaty, b. Oct. 15, 1742	1	142
Rufus, d May 4, 1774	1	142
Salmon, s. [Dilauna & Olive], b. Apr. 17, 1813	3	54
Samuell, s. William & Mary, b July 5, 1693	A	3
Samuell, m. Sarah **GARD**, Dec. 2, 1712	1	39a
Samuel Whiting, s. [Ebenezer & Marcy], b Jan [ ],		
1769; d. Feb. [ ], 1769	2	73
Sanford H., s [Luther & Zerviah], b Nov 21, 1819	3	4
Sarah, m. Isaac **BINGHAM**, July 6, 1732	1	120
Sarah, d. William, Jr. & Sarah, b Aug. 15, 1736	1	185
Sarah, d. [Ebenezer & Mercy], b. July 29, 1777	2	73

	Vol.	Page
BACKUS, (cont)		
Shubael, s. [Demetrius & Lydia], b. Dec. 1, 1779	2	125
Silvanus, s. John & Sibble, b. July 5, 1738	1	158
Silvanus, m. Elizabeth **GAMBLE**, Apr. 12, 1758	2	43
Simon, s. Silva[nus] & Eliz[abeth], b Oct 20, 1761	2	43
Soffia, d [Whiting & Sarah], b. July 10, 1771	2	199
Stephen, s. William & Mary, b. Mar. 12, 1704	A	4
Stephen, s. William, Jr. & Sarah, b. May 27, 1734	1	185
Stephen, s. [Demetrius & Lydia], b. Mar. 10, 1768	2	125
Sibel, d. John, Jr. & Sibel, b. Mar. 1, 1729/30	1	72
Sybel, m. Benj[amin] **LATHROP**, Jr., July 8, 1751	1	306
Sybbel, m. Benjamin **LOTHROP**, Jr., July 8, 1751	2	120
Sibel, w. John, Jr., d. Aug. 7, 1755	1	72
Sibil, d. [Silvanus & Elizabeth], b. June 14, 1764; d. June 13, 1766	2	43
Virgal, s. Samuell & Sarah, b Sept. 21, 1722	1	39a
Whiting, m. Sarah **BINGHAM**, Feb. 15, 1769, in Hebron	2	199
Whiting [Broke*], s. John & Sibble, b Dec 28, 1747 (*correction Broke crossed out in original manuscript)	1	158
William, m. Mary **DUNTON**, Aug. 31, 1692	A	3
Will[iam], s William & Mary, b. Apr. 1, 1697	A	3
William, s. William & Mary, b. Apr. 4, 1702	A	4
William, d. Jan 25, 1707/8	A	4
William, m. Sarah **BENNIT**, Mar. 24, 1708	A	9
William, m. Mary **DIMMOCK**, Nov. 3, 1742	1	234
William, d. Mar. 5, 1776	1	234
William Fitch, s. [Bela & Fanny], b. Aug. 10, 1784	2	133
Zerviah, d. John & Mary, b. Aug. 10, 1709	1	4
Zeruiah, d. Ephraim & Colaty, b. May 17, 1738	1	142
Zerviah, m. John **ROUSE**, Mar. 13, 1763	2	80
Zerviah, w. Luther, d. May 3, 1825	3	4
——, d. [Nath[anie]ll & Elizabeth], b. Aug. 14, 1754; d Oct. 7, 1754	1	321
——, child of Albert H., farmer, ae. 31, & Cornelia, ae. 22, b July 6, 1852	4	14
——, child of [Bela & Fanny], b. [ ]; d. 3 days after birth	2	133
BACON, Benjamin, s. John & Ruth, b. July 17, 1743	1	222
Darius, of Southbridge, Mass., m. Mariah **ROBINSON**, of Windham, Mar. 26, 1844, by Rev. Isaac H. Coe	3	213
Elizabeth, m Nathaniel **KNOWLES**, Apr. 25, 1717	1	32
BADGER, BADGE, Abigail, w. Sam[ue]ll, d. Oct. 13, 1775	2	203
Albert, m. Asenath **CROSBY**, of Mansfield, Jan. 16, 1821	3	96
Albert Allen, s. [Edmond & Amelia], b. Jan. 16, 1801	3	95
Albert Murry, s. [Albert & Asenath], b Dec. 16, 1821	3	96
Anna, d. [Edmund & Lucretia], b. Oct. 29, 1776	2	121

	Vol.	Page
BADGER, BADGE, (cont)		
Bela, s. [Edmund & Lucretia], b. Feb. 6, 1768	2	121
Betsey, d. [Edmund & Lucretia], d. Apr. 24, 1781	2	130
Charles Taintor, s. [Edmond & Amelia], b. Sept. 14, 1819	3	95
Edmund, m. Lucretia **ABBE**, Dec. 15, 1765	2	131
Edmond, s [Edmund & Lucretia], b Feb. [ ], 1779	2	231
Edmond, m. Amelia **DYER**, Aug. 20, 1798	3	95
Edmond, s. [Edmond & Amelia], b. July 20, 1806; d. Aug. 3, 1806	3	95
Edmond, s. [Edmond & Amelia], b Aug. 16, 1817	3	95
Elizabeth, d. [Edmund & Lucretia], b. Feb. 11, 1774	2	121
Elizabeth Mary, d. [Edmond & Amelia], b. Nov. 10, 1815	3	95
Fanny, d. [Edmund & Lucretia], b Feb 12, 1785	2	121
Francis Amelia, d. [Edmond & Amelia], b. Aug. 7, 1804	3	95
George, s. [Edmund & Lucretia], b. Mar. 24, 1770	2	121
George Dyer, s. [Edmond & Amelia], b. Nov. 23, 1807	3	95
Gideon Flint, s. [Joseph & Prudence], b. Aug. 1, 1778	2	188
Henry Dyer, s. [Edmond & Amelia], b. Mar. 18, 1810	3	95
Jedediah, s. [Joseph & Prudence], b. Feb. 19, 1773	2	188
Jerusha, d. [Joseph & Prudence], b. Oct. 11, 1785	2	188
Joseph, m. Prudence **FLINT**, Sept. 24, 1772	2	188
Lucretia, d. [Edmund & Lucretia], b. May 5, 1772	2	121
Lucretia, d. [Edmund & Lucretia], b. Mar. 17, 1781	2	121
Lucretia Ann, d. [Edmond & Amelia], b. Oct. 14, 1821	3	95
Ruth, m. Asa **BREWSTER**, May 28, 1760	2	119
Samuel, Jr., m. Loisa Rachal **ELDERKIN**, Sept. 26, 1776	2	213
Samuel, s. [Edmund & Lucretia], b. Dec. 6, 1786	2	121
Samuel, father of Edmund, d. Apr. 9, 1797, in the 87th y. of his age	2	121
Sarah, m. Roswell **LOTHROP**, Oct. 22, 1772	2	187
Thomas, s [Edmund & Lucretia], b. June 28, 1766	2	121
Thomas Dyer, s. [Edmond & Amelia], b. Oct. 14, 1799; d. Oct 8, 1818	3	95
Wallace, s. [Edmond & Amelia], b. Mar. 18, 1812	3	95
William, s. [Edmond & Amelia], b. Sept. 10, 1802	3	95
William B., of Hartford, m. Salome **SNOW**, of Ashford, May 10, 1831, by Rev. Alva Gregory, Willimantic	3	156
BAILEY, Betsey, m. Ezra **CHAPMAN**, May 1, 1796	3	54
Dwight, m. Marah A. **BROWN**, Mar. 20, 1848	4	112
BAKER, Abigail, m. Stephen **DOWNING**, Nov. 17, 1763	2	100
Addonijah, s. [Sam[ue]l, Jr & C[h]loe], b Apr. 29, 1777	2	92
Andrew, m. Dianthe **CAREY**, Oct. 24, 1806	3	37
Anna, d. Sam[ue]ll & Prudence, b. May 20, 1746	1	260
Benj[ami]n, s. Sam[ue]ll & Prudence, b. June 15, 1751	1	260
Benjamin, m. Lucy **BOTTOM**, Nov. 25, 1773	2	192

	Vol.	Page
BALCOM, BALKCOM, Caroline Frances, of Windham, m. Charles Augustus **CONVERSE**, of Norwich, Feb. 24, 1845, by Rev. Giles W. Dunham	3	220
Edwin G., m. Emma **McGOWTY**, b. of Windham, Apr. 5, 1835, by Rev L.H Corson	3	172
Henry A., [s. Edwin G. & Emma], b. July 26, 1836	3	172
Horrace, s. [Socrates & Amie], b. July 9, 1811	3	69
Horace E., [s. Edwin G. & Emma], b. Apr. 10, 1841	3	172
Laura, m. Alvin C. **SMALL**, Feb. 1, 1846, at Willimantic, by John Cooper	3	227
Sarah, m. Nathan **SIMONS**, Oct. 29, 1741	1	203
Socrates, m. Amie **BINGHAM**, Aug. [ ], 1810	3	69
BALDEN, [see also **BALDWIN** and **BOLWIN**], Florence, d. John, merchant, ae. 45, & Ann, ae. 30, b. Sept. 3, [1847]	4	3
BALDWIN, [see also **BALDEN** and **BOLWIN**], Alice S., of Canterbury, m. Lewis **WALDO**, of Windham, Feb. 26, 1834, by Rev. Otis C. Whiton	3	169
Arba, child of Geo[rge], ae. 33, b. Feb. 7, [1849]	4	6
Celia, b. Aug. 11, 1850	4	13
Daniel, s. Daniel & Anna, b. May 16, 1754	1	298
Elisha, s. Daniel & Anna, b. May 16, 1756	1	298
Emily G., d. Aug. 31, [1849], ae. 43	4	155
Emily M., m. Nath[aniel] R. **LILLIE**, b. of Windham, June 8, 1836, by Rev. Philo Judson, at Willimantic	3	178
Eunice, m. Harry **BOSS**, b. of Windham, May 21, 1837, by Rev. Winslow Ward	3	189
Harmey, ae. 24, m. Clark **McTHURSTON**, farmer, ae. 24, of Stafford, Aug. 20, 1847, by Rev. Daniel Dorchester	4	111
Harriet, m. Warren **ATWOOD**, Jan. 31, 1837, by Rev. Philetus Greene, Willimantic, Windham	3	182
John, Jr., m. Elizabeth **McGOUTY**, July 7, 1822, by Samuel Perkins, Esq.	3	105
John, layer, d. Mar. 27, 1850, ae. 78	4	156
John Huntington, m. Abby Eleanor **FRINK**, b. of Windham, Nov. 2, 1846, by Rev. A. Ogden, Jr.	3	233
Mary, of Canterbury, m. Septimies **BAKER**, Mar. 30, 1811	3	37
Mary R., m. Martin B. **BRANARD**, Nov. 12, 1841, by Rev. Andrew Sharp	3	199
Samuel L., s. Samuel, b. Feb. 9, 1815	3	78
Seth, of Brooklyn, Conn., m. Phebe H. **MARTIN**, of Windham, Nov. 27, 1845, by Rev. Henry Coe	3	225
Thomas, of Chaplin, m. Lucia **BIBBINS**, of Windham, Mar. 7, 1830, by Henry Huntington, J.P.	3	145
BALLARD, Abner, s. Humphrey & Hannah, b. June 6, 1731; d. June 22, 1731	1	122
David, s. Humphrey & Hannah, b. Apr. 1, 1723	1	10
Humphrey, m. Hannah **BROUGHTEN**, Nov. 6, 1717	1	10

	Vol.	Page
BALLARD, (cont.)		
Humphrey, d. May 22, 1735	1	122
Jeremiah, s. Humphrey & Hannah, b. Jan. 19, 1733/4	1	122
John, s. Humphrey & Hannah, b. Jan. 17, 1720	1	10
Joseph, s. Humphrey & Hannah, b Aug. 20, 1727	1	10
Sarah, m. Col. Jonathan **KINGSBURY**, Jan. 14, 1761	2	95
Sarah, m. Lieut. Jon[a]th[a]n **KINGSBURY**, Jan. 14, 1761	2	127
Zebulon, s. Humphrey & Hannah, b. Nov. 5, 1718	1	10
BARBER, BARBOUR, Jane, black, b. Lebanon, res. Windham,		
d. Apr. 14, 1850, ae. 65	4	156
John D., merchant, ae. 31, b. W. Springfield, res.		
Springfield, m. Eliza H. **SKINNER**, ae. 19, b.		
Bolton, res. Springfield, Nov. 19, 1850, by Rev.		
Jno. Cady	4	118
Sally, of Canterbury, m. William H. **GREEN**, of		
Griswold, Sept. 13, 1840, by Rev. Otis C. Whiton	3	194
William, of Hebron, m. Ann **SWEET**, of Hampton, Feb.		
26, 1839, at Willimantic, by Rev. Philo Judson	3	188
BARKER, Chloe, m. John P. **GAGER**, [ ] 28, 1808	3	64
Elizabeth, Wid., m. John **BADCOCK**, July 1, 1729	1	114
Hannah, w. Eph[rai]m, d. July 29, 1765	2	86
Hannah, m. Capt. Joseph **GINNINGS**, June 21, 1779	2	194
Mary, d. Nath[anie]l & Elizabeth, b. Mar. 29, 1728	1	225
Nath[anie]ll, d. Aug. 27, 1727, ae. about 34 y.	1	80
——, s. [Ephraim & Hannah], b. Mar. 19, 1763; d.		
Mar. 20, 1763	2	86
BARNAM, [see also **BURNHAM**], Abigail, d. Josh[ua] & Abigail,		
b. Jan. 18, 1747/8	1	298
Daniel, [twin with Josiah, s. Eb[enezer] & Martha],		
b. Mar. 21, 1753	1	295
Daniel, m. Martha **SMITH**, Apr. 20, 1780	2	14
Dorothy, d. Josh[ua] & Abigail, b. Nov. 9, 1749/50	1	298
Dorothy, m. William **HEB[B]ARD**, Oct. 16, 1750	1	291
Ebenezer, m. Martha **HEBBARD**, Jan. 1, 1745/6	1	295
Eben[ezer], s. Eb[eneze]r & Martha, b. Feb. 17, 1747/8	1	295
Eleazer, s. Eben[eze]r & Martha, b. Aug. 9, 1757	1	295
Eleazer, s. [Daniel & Martha], b. Oct. 2, 1780	2	14
Elias, s. [Daniel & Martha], b. Sept. 7, 1785	2	14
Eliphaz, s. [Ebenezer & Martha], b. Mar. 17, 1766	1	295
Hannah, d. Eb[enezer] & Martha, b. Nov 27, 1746	1	295
James, s. Eben[eze]r & Martha, b. Aug. 21, 1759	1	295
Jedediah, s. Eben[ezer] & Martha, b. Dec. 17, 1761	1	295
John, s. Eben[ezer] & Martha, b. Dec. 20, 1749	1	295
Joshua, s. Josh[ua] & Abigail, b. Mar. 8, 1745/6	1	298
Josiah, [twin with Daniel], s. Eb[enezer] & Martha,		
b. Mar. 21, 1753	1	295
Lucy, d. Josh[ua] & Abigail, b. Sept. 10, 1751	1	298

30 BARBOUR COLLECTION

	Vol.	Page
BARNAM, (cont.)		
Lydia, d. [Daniel & Martha], b. Feb. 16, 1783	2	14
Mary, d. [Ebenezer & Martha], b. Sept. 14, 1755	1	295
Sarah, d. Joshua & Abigail, b. Sept. 2, 1742	1	298
BARNES, BARNS, Deborah, d. Gideon & Mehetable, b. Apr. 2, 1739	1	197
Nathaniell, s. Nathaniell & Hannah, b. Mar. 10, 1714	1	34
BARRADEL, Mary, m. Benony **PHILLIPS**, June 12, 1712	1	43
BARRETT, Borden P., m. Frances H. **CAREY**, b. of Windham, Oct. 22, [1837], by Rev. Otis C. Whiton, of Scotland Society, Windham	3	184
Mary, m. William **FRANKLIN**, b. of Willimantic, Sept. 4, 1843, by Rev. Henry Bromley	3	211
BARROWS, Amasa P., m. Ann W. **WILLIAMS**, Dec. 15, 1841, by Rev. Andrew Sharp	3	200
Ann, m. Francis **SHALLIESS**, Aug. 19, 1781	2	243
Delia, b. Sept. 21, 1814; m. John **TRACY**, Apr. 14, 1835, in Mansfield, by Rev. S. S. Atwood	4	22
Emeline J., b. Windham, res. Willimantic, d. June 16, 1860, ae. 52	4	161
Frances, s. [Sylvanus, Jr. & Triphena], b. Sept. 4, 1787	2	231
Francis, s. [Sil[vanus] & Ruth], b. Feb. 13, 1758; d. Sept. 24, 1781	2	12
Frederick F., m. Harriet **HARRIS**, Mar. 29, 1847, by Rev. Andrew Sharp	3	235
Ginda, of Decatur, N.Y., m. Sabina **WHIPPLE**, of Willimantic, Oct. 2, 1836, by Rev. Philo Judson, at Willimantic	3	179
Hannah, of Willimantic, m. Jabez **BROWN**, of Vernon, N.Y., Dec. 27, 1836, by Rev. Philo Judson, at Willimantic	3	180
Jane, ae. 18, m. Asa **WHITNEY**, blacksmith, ae. 22, b. Stafford, res. Windham, July 3, 1848, by Andrew Sharp	4	111
Josephine, d. Walter, minister, ae. 45, & Hannah, ae. 40, b. May 16, 1850	4	13
Julia Ann, m. John **ATWOOD**, 2d, Oct. 11, 1840, by Rev. John B. Guild, Willimantic	3	196
Leonard Hensley, s. [Sylvanus, Jr. & Triphena], b. Feb. 5, 1795	2	231
Lydia, d. [Sylvanus, Jr. & Triphena], b. May 5, 1790	2	231
Martha, m. Joseph H. **BROWN**, Apr. 17, 1791	2	58
Mehetable, d. Sil[vanus] & Ruth, b. Mar. 29, 1756	2	12
Mehitable, m. Joseph **JOHNSON**, June 19, 1783	2	25
Ruth, m. Benjamin **HOLLAND**, Apr. 26, 1778	2	223
Sybell, m. John **BROWN**, Dec. 22, 1763	2	110

	Vol.	Page
BARROWS, (cont)		
Sylvanus, Jr., m. Triphena **WEBSTER**, Sept. 14, 1786	2	231
BARSTOW, Bethiah, m. Ephraim **PALMER**, Feb. 4, 1806	3	40
Mary, m. Elisha **PALMER**, Oct. 22, 1807	3	100
Sarah L, of Windham, m. Horace **THAYER**, of Thompson, May 7, 1840, by Rev. Otis C. Whiton	3	194
Sarah Larnard, d. Ebenezer & Lucy, b July 20, 1814	3	73
BARTLETT, Edward A., b. Honesdale, Pa., res. Willimantic, d. Nov. 3, 1850, ae. 15 m.	4	157
Mary E., b. Stafford, res. Willimantic, d. June 14, [1849], ae. 44	4	153
Noah, ae. 24, m. [ ], Jan. [ ], [1848], by Andrew Roberts	4	113
W[illia]m H., d. Mar. 7 [1849], ae. 1	4	153
----, child of Noah, laborer, ae. 23, of Willimantic, b. Dec. 26, 1849	4	10
BASS, [see also **BOSS**], Abisha, m. Phebe **COOK**, Mar. 16, 1772	2	169
Adonijah, s. Henry & Elizabeth, b. Sept. 13, 1744	1	147
Avena, d. [Abisha & Phebe], b. Dec. 18, 1784	2	169
Bela, s. [Ebenezer & Ruth], b. Jan. 16, 1776	2	150
Benjamin, s. [John & Mary], b. Feb. 26, 1768	1	312
Betsey, w. John, d. Jan. 9, 1837	3	74
Bridget, d. [Abisha & Phebe], b. Apr. 7, 1774	2	169
Bridget, d. [Joshua & Phebe], b. Apr. 9, 1774	2	201
Charles, s. [Nathan & Nancy], b. Jan. 15, 1825	3	103
Charlotte, d. [Ebenezer, Jr. & Sarah], b. Aug. 2, 1833	3	71
Clinton, s. [Ebenezer, Jr. & Sarah], b. Mar. 14, 1828	3	71
Cornelia, d. [John & Betsey], b. Dec. [ ], 1825	3	74
Cornelia, ae. 23, m. George **HOVEY**, farmer, ae. 24, of Windham, July 10, 1848, by Rev. Henry Coe	4	112
Cuff, m. Sarah **SMITH**, Sept. 1, 1785	2	15
Damaries, d. [Joshua & Phebe[, b. Sept. 4, 1775	2	201
Damaras, d. [Abisha & Phebe], b. Sept. 4, 1775	2	169
Dorothy, d. Thomas & Dorothy, b. Oct. 29, 1736	1	82
Dorothy, w. Tho[ma]s, d. July 12, 1778, in the 78th y. of her age	1	218
Ebenezer, s. Henry & Elizabeth, b. Oct. 26, 1746	1	147
Ebenezer, m. Ruth **WALDO**, Dec. 13, 1769	2	150
Ebenezer, s. [Ebenezer & Ruth], b. July 1, 1784	2	150
Ebenezer, Jr., m. Sarah **McCURDY**, Mar. 27, 1811	3	71
Edgar, [s. John & Betsey], b. Sept. 13, 1834	3	74
Edwin, s. [Ebenezer, Jr. & Sarah], b. Jan. 28, 1816	3	71
Egbert, s. [John & Betsey], b. Jan. 29, 1828	3	74
Eleazer, s. [Sam[ue]ll & Hannah], b. Apr. 15, 1767; d. [ ]	2	126
Eleazer, s. [Ebenezer & Ruth], b. Sept. 4, 1770	2	150
Eleazer, m. Desire **ALLEN**, Dec. 18, 1794	2	201
Elisha, s. Thomas & Dorothy, b. Aug. 1, 1745	1	218

	Vol.	Page
BASS, (cont.)		
Elizabeth, m. John **KINGSLEY**, Dec. 25, 1717	1	46
Elizabeth, d. Thomas & Dorothy, b. Mar. 1, 1730/31	1	82
Ellen, ae. 19, m. W[illia]m **BURNHAM**, farmer, ae.		
23, Nov. 24, 1849, by Henry Coe	4	113
Ellen, d. [John & Betsey], b. [ ]	3	74
Esther, d. [John & Mary], b. Sept. 14, 1756; d.		
Jan. 11, 1759	1	312
Eunice, d. [Ebenezer & Ruth], b. Aug. 9, 1780	2	150
Eunice, w. John, d. Nov. 12, 1820	3	74
Eunice, d. [John & Betsey], b. Feb. 25, 1822	3	74
Eunice, d. [John & Betsey], b. Feb. 25, 1822	3	103
Eunice, of Windham, m. Nathan **MORSE**, of Woodstock,		
Aug. 25, 1844, by Rev. Thomas Tallman, Scotland	3	216
George, twin with Ruth, [s. Ebenezer, Jr. & Sarah],		
b. Nov. 15, 1813	3	71
George, m. Mary L. **CAREY**, b. of Windham, Apr. 9, 1840,		
by Rev. Tubal Wakefield	3	193
Hannah, d. John & Elizabeth, b. May 27, 1711	1	5
Hannah, m. Zebulon **HEB[B]ARD**, Mar. 30, 1737 (sic)	1	165
Hannah, d. [John & Mary], b. Aug. 30, 1758	1	312
Harriet, d. [Ebenezer, Jr. & Sarah], b. Apr. 20, 1826	3	71
Henry, m. Elizabeth **CHURCH**, Dec. 10, 1735	1	147
Henry, d. Dec. [ ], 1783	1	147
Henry, s. [Ebenezer, Jr. & Sarah], b. Nov. 24, 1817	3	71
Jason Gager, s. [Joseph & Lucy], b. Mar. 2, 1802	2	185
Jemima, d. [Sam[ue]ll & Hannah], b. Sept. 10, 1768	2	126
Jerusha, d. [Abisha & Phebe], b. June 12, 1783	2	169
Joab, s. Thomas & Dorothy, b. Dec. 9, 1739	1	82
Joab, s. Tho[ma]s, d. Nov. 6, 1759	1	218
Joel, s. [Ebenezer & Ruth], b. Mar. 4, 1774	2	150
Joel, m. Polly **MARTIN**, Dec. 22, 1796	2	112
John, s. John & Elizabeth, d. Jan. 7, 1719	1	5
John, s. Thomas & Dorothy, b. Sept. 14, 1727	1	82
John, d. Oct. 10, 1733, in his 80th y.	1	5
John, m. Mary **PAIN**, Dec. 23, 1751	1	312
John, s. [Ebenezer & Ruth], b. Oct. 22, 1786	2	150
John, m. Eunice **TRACY**, Sept. 18, 1814	3	74
John, m. Betsey **MARTIN**, Apr. 25, 1821	3	74
John, m. Betsey **MARTIN**, Apr. 25, 1821	3	103
John, s. [John & Betsey], b Aug. [ ], 1832; d. Dec.		
24, 1833	3	74
John, m. Maria **TRACY**, b. of Windham, Feb. 11, 1838, by		
Rev. Otis C. Whiton	3	185
Jonathan, s. Tho[ma]s & Dorothy, b. Dec. 31, 1741	1	218
Jonathan, m. Hannah **PAIN[E]**, June 2, 1761	2	101
Jonathan, s. [Jonathan & Hannah], b. Nov. 7, 1761; d.		
Dec. 7, 1764	2	101

	Vol.	Page
BASS, (cont.)		
Joseph, s. Henry & Eliza[beth], b. Oct. 13, 1750	1	147
Joseph, s. [Ebenezer & Ruth], b. Apr. 17, 1772	2	150
Joseph, m. Lucy **GAGER**, Dec. 30, 1795	2	185
Joshua, s. Tho[ma]s & Dorothy, b. Mar. 6, 1748/9	1	218
Joshua, m. Phebe **COOK**, Mar. 11, 1772	2	201
Lavira, d. [Abisha & Phebe], b. Feb. 3, 1787	2	169
Levi, s. Abisha & Phebe, b. May 6, 1778	2	169
Lina, d. [Abisha & Phebe], b. Nov. 10, 1781	2	169
Lucian, s. [Ebenezer, Jr. & Sarah], b. Mar. 15, 1830	3	71
Lydia, d. Thomas & Dorothy, b. Apr. 15, 1738	1	82
Lydia, d. [John & Mary], b. Jan. 10, 1763	1	312
Lydia, d. [John & Eunice, b. Nov. 4, 1817	3	74
Lydia, m. Epaphras **SAFFORD**, Apr. 3, 1836, by Rev. Jesse Fisher	3	177
Maria, d. [John & Eunice], b. Feb. 22, 1816	3	74
Maria, m. Rob[er]t W. **ROBINSON**, b. of Windham, Sept. 18, 1837, by Rev. Otis C. Whiton, of Scotland Society, Windham	3	184
Martha, d. John & Elizabeth, b. June 6, 1715	1	5
Mary, d. Thomas & Dorothy, b. June 20, 1729	1	82
Mary, d. John & Mary, b. Dec. 30, 1760	1	312
Mary, w. John, d. Feb. 12, 1769	1	312
Mary, d. [Joseph & Lucy], b. Apr. 6, 1798	2	185
Nancy, d. [John & Betsey], b. Dec. 21, 1823	3	74
Nathan, s. Henry & Elizabeth, b. Oct. 10, 1740	1	147
Nathan, s. [Ebenezer & Ruth], b. Apr. 15, 1782	2	150
Nathan, m. Nancy **CLIFT**, Mar. 27, 1822	3	103
Nathan, s. [Ebenezer, Jr. & Sarah], b. Feb. 14, 1824	3	71
Nathan, m. Laura **FISHER**, b. of Windham, Mar. 28, 1838, by Rev. Otis C. Whiton, of Scotland Society, in Windham	3	185
Priscilla, d. John & Elizabeth, b. Apr. 13, 1713; d. Sept. 1, 1714	1	5
Priscialla, m. Eldad **KINGSLEY**, June 20, 1733	1	121
Prudence, d. [John & Mary], b. June 22, 1765	1	312
Rachal, d. Tho[ma]s & Dorothy, b. Aug. 20, 1750	1	218
Rachel, m. Lemuel **ROBBINS**, Apr. 30, 1769	2	192
Rodman, m. Prudence **SPENCER**, Apr. 29, 1844, by Rev. John B. Guild, Willimantic	3	214
Ruth, twin with George, [d. Ebenezer, Jr. & Sarah], b. Nov. 15, 1813	3	71
Samuel, s. Henry & Elizabeth, b. Nov. 15, 1738	1	147
Sam[ue]ll, m. Hannah **WOODARD**, Oct. 2, 1766	2	126
Sarah, d. John & Mary, b. June 24, 1753	1	312
Sarah, d. [Joseph & Lucy], b. Dec. 14, 1799	2	185
Sarah Ann, d. [Ebenezer, Jr. & Sarah], b. Dec. 1, 1821	3	71

	Vol.	Page
BASS, (cont.)		
Sarah Ann, m. William L. **GAGER**, b. of Windham, May		
16, 1842, by Rev. John E. Tyler	3	201
Susan, d. [John & Eunice], b. July 6, 1819	3	74
Susan, d. [Ebenezer, Jr. & Sarah], b. Sept. 30, 1819;		
d. Sept. 15, 1822	3	71
Susan, m. Dwight **CAREY**, b. of Windham, Nov. 15, 1843,		
by Rev. H. Slade	3	212
Sybel, d. Henry & Elizabeth, b Sept. 18, 1748	1	147
Sibbel, m. Eleazer **FITCH**, 3d., Apr. 23, 1769	2	150
Tabitha, d. [Ebenezer & Ruth], b. Apr. 2, 1778	2	150
Talitha, m. Rufus **BURNHAM**, Dec. 14, 1797	3	22
Thomas, m. Dorothy **PARISH**, Nov. 9, 1726	1	82
Thomas, d. Jan. 8, 1787, in the 86th y. of his age	1	82
Tryphenia, d. Henry & Eliza[beth], b. Mar. 6, 1753	1	147
Tryphenia, m. Joshua **ABBE**, Jr., Nov. 19, 1771	2	168
Wealthy, d. [Jonathan & Hannah], b. Sept. 1, 1763	2	101
William McCurdy, s. [Ebenezer, Jr. & Sarah], b. Jan.		
10, 1812	3	71
Zebulon, s. John & Elizabeth, b. May 22, 1718; d. Feb.		
4, 1719	1	5
Zebulon, s. Henry & Elizabeth, b. July 26, 1737	1	147
BASSETT, BASSET, Azariah, s. Ezra, b. May 18, 1779	2	74
Ebenezer, s. Nathaniel & Johannah, b. May 4, 1699; d.		
May 4, 1699	A	14
Ebenezer, s. Nathaniel & Johannah, b. Apr. 2, 1701; d.		
Apr. 5, 1701	A	14
Ezra, s. [Ezra], d. Oct. 1, 1778	2	74
Johannah, d. Nathaniel & Johannah, b Sept 24, 1697	A	14
Joseph C., m. Ann W. **HEBBARD**, Aug. 29, 1842, by Rev.		
Andrew Sharp, Willimantic	3	203
Nathaniel, m. Johannah **BORDEN**, Dec. 10, 1695	A	14
——, child of J.C., machinist, ae. 40, of Williman-		
tic, b. July 28, [1850]	4	10
BATES, Archibald, m. Dorcas **ROBINSON**, Nov., 20, 1826, by		
Elder Allen Barnes	3	128
Asa, of Sterling, m. Jerusha **LINCOLN**, Apr. 20, 1823	3	108
George P., m. Dorcas **OTIS**, Jan. 31, 1830, by Rev.		
Roger Bingham	3	143
Jerusha, of Windham, m. Lucius **INGRAM**, of Columbia,		
Aug. 27, 1843, by Rev. Henry Greenslit	3	211
Lydia, d. John, b. Dec. 4, 1749	1	295
Maria, ae. 25, m. W[illia]m C. **CAYEL**, painter, ae. 27,		
Oct. 22, [1849], by A. Sharp	4	115
BATTELL, BATTELLE, BATTLE, Eliza, d. Ziba B., laborer, ae.		
46, & Mary E., ae. 43, b. Nov. 14, 1847	4	2
Maria, operative, b. Mass., res. Windham, d. Aug. 9,		
1847, ae. 12	4	151

	Vol.	Page
BATTELL, BATTELLE, BATTLE, (cont.)		
Mary, d. John, laborer, ae. 21, b. Oct. 28, [1849]	4	9
BAXTER, Charlotte, A., m. Edward L. **FLINT**, July 4, 1847,		
by Rev. Andrew Sharp	3	236
BEACH, Catherine M., m. George S. **ESTUS**, Oct. 13, 1843, by		
Rev. Andrew Sharp	3	211
BEAMONT, Lydia, m. Elnathan **WARNER**, May 9, 1781	2	248
William, m. Sarah **EVERETT**, Dec. 29, 1747	1	275
BECKWITH, Ambrose, s. Chester, blacksmith, ae. 23, &		
Marinda, ae. 20, b. Mar. 20, 1851	4	13
Ambrose, d. Apr. 11, [1851], ae. 3 w.	4	158
Chester H., blacksmith, ae. 24, of Windham, m. Minerva		
H., **BILLINGS**, ae. 20, b. Penn., res. Windham, Sept		
1, [1850], by E. W. Barrows	4	118
Hannah, ae. 48, m. James **BECKWITH**, carpenter, ae. 50,		
of Windham, Apr. 16, 1848, by Eld. Henry Greenslit	4	112
James, carpenter, ae. 50, of Windham, m. 2d w. Hannah		
BECKWITH, ae. 48, Apr. 16, 1848, by Eld. Henry		
Greenslit	4	112
Laura, m. Lyman **LORDEN**, Aug. 11, 1844, by Rev.		
Cha[rle]s Noble, Willimantic	3	216
Leonard, of Waterford, m. Amanda **WITTER**, of Windham,		
Jan. 3, 1847, by Rev. B. M. Alden, Jr	3	233
Mary, of Windham, m. Alexander **CRANDELL**, of Franklin,		
Apr. 14, 1836, by Rev. M. Dwight	3	177
Sally M., m. Abner **REID**, [ ]	3	83
Sophia, of Windham, m. Norman **MAL[L]ORY**, of Canterbury,		
Sept. 10, 1845, by John Crocker	3	223
Thomas, m. Sally **STAUNTON**, Feb. 2, 1823	3	109
Thomas S., m. Betsey M. **CROSS**, b. of Windham, Sept. 9,		
1844, by Rev. J.E. Tyler	3	216
W[illia]m E., m. Sophia **HEWITT**, Nov. 29, 1835, by Rev.		
Moseley Dwight, Willimantic	3	176
William E., m. Rebecca T. **HOLLOWAY**, b. of Windham,		
June 15, 1840, by Rev. R. Ransom	3	193
BEEBE, John W., m. Permelia A. **DAVIS**, Oct. 10, 1842, by		
Andrew Sharp	3	204
BEFINGS*, Sarah, m. Return **MES[S]ENGER**, Apr. 16, 1713		
(*correction F in **BEFINGS** is crossed out in the		
original manuscript)	1	4
BEMIS, Ephraim, m. Lydia [ ], Oct. 1, 1736	1	155
James, s. Ephraim & Lydia, b. Aug. 6, 1737	1	155
Mary, d. Ephraim & Lydia, b. May 15, 1739	1	155
Ruth, m. William **AVEREL**, Oct. 13, 1721	1	64
BENCHLEY, Henry A., m. Emily **PALMER**, b. of Willimantic,		
Apr. 28, 1839, at Willimantic, by Rev. B. Cook,		
Jr., of Willimantic	3	189
James B., b. July 15, 1841	3	181

	Vol.	Page
BENCHLEY, (cont.)		
John B., b. Sept. 16, 1835	3	181
Joseph, s. Henry, laborer, ae. 31, & Emily, ae. 30, of Willimantic, b. May 11, [1847]	4	5
Mary A., m. Edward F. **MOULTON**, June 21, 1846, by Rev. Andrew Sharp	3	229
Nathan T., m. Olive S. **COX**, b. of Windham, Sept. 8, 1834, by Rev. Philo Judson, Willimantic	3	169
Olive S., m. Solomon F. **PLACE**, June 9, 1844, by Rev. Andrew Sharp	3	215
BENJAMIN, David, of Preston, m. Cornelia **SMITH**, of Windham, Mar. 23, 1835, by Rev. Jesse Fisher	3	173
Joanna, m. Ebenezer **FARNAM**, Mar. 3, 1773	2	179
Judah, s. Joseph & Hannah, b. July 8, 1755	2	9
Mary, m. Andrew **DURKEE**, Jan. 28, 1762	2	73
Peleg, s. Joseph & Hannah, b. Mar. 5, 1752	2	9
Sam[ue]l, s. Joseph & Hannah, b. Dec. 8, 1749	2	9
William, s. Joseph & Hannah, b. June 18, 1748	2	9
BENNETT, BENNET, BENNIT, BENET, Clarrissa, d. [Isaac & Sarah], b. June 24, 1780; d. July 4, 1780	2	90
Daniel, of Preston, m. Delight **PALMER**, Feb. 28, 1782	2	95
Delia B., d. Julia, ae. 26, of Willimantic, b. Aug. 1, 1848	4	1
Elizabeth, d. [William], d. Mar. 20, 1765, ae. 21	2	1
Elizabeth, d. [Isaac & Sarah], b. Apr. 18, 1766	2	90
Eunice, m. Solomon **SMITH**, Nov. 27, 1760	2	63
Francis, s. [Stephen], b. Feb. 4, 1786	2	61
George B., of Brooklyn, m. Julia **WILLSON**, of Windham, June 8, 1840, by Rev. Nathan Wildman, of Lebanon	3	193
Hannah, d. [Isaac & Sarah], b. Jan. 5, 1775	2	90
Isaac, m. Sarah **CADY**, Nov. 2, 1763	2	90
Isaac, s. [Isaac & Sarah], b. Jan. 5, 1782	2	90
Isaac, Dr., m. Margaret **PAIN**, Sept. 9, 1784	2	90
Jacob, m. Nancy **FOLLETT**, Dec. 30, 1834, by Rev. Marvin Root	3	171
James, m. Harriet D. **WEBB**, Oct. 18, 1835, by Rev. Jesse Fisher	3	176
Jane, m. Andrew **BURNHAM**, May 11, 1757	2	36
Jane, d. W[illia]m A., physician, ae. 35, & Jane, ae. 31, of Willimantic, b. June 29, 1851	4	12
Jared, s. [Isaac & Sarah], b. Aug. 23, 1768	2	90
Jonathan, of Pomfret, m. Catharine L. **WEBB**, of Windham, Apr 12, 1829, by Rev. Jesse Fisher	3	135
Joseph T., m. Julia W. **BILL**, Sept. 8, 1844, by Rev. Cha[rle]s Noble, Willimantic	3	216
Lois, d. John & Sarah, b. May 23, 1755	1	288
Luce, m. Joseph **BURNAM**, Dec 11, 1740	1	264
Lucy, d. [Isaac & Sarah], b. Oct. 29, 1776	2	90

	Vol	Page
BENNETT, BENNET, BENNIT, BENET, (cont.)		
Lydia, m. Joseph **MARSH**, June 20, 1754	1	230
Lidia, d. [Isaac & Sarah], b. Dec. 5, 1772	2	90
Maria, ae. 22, m. Geo[rge] **BROWN**, farmer, ae. 23,		
Oct. [1849], by Rev. H. Bromley	4	115
Mary, d. John & Sarah, b. Apr. 22, 1753	1	288
Mary, Wid., m. Jehiel **ROBBINS**, Nov 18, 1758	2	63
Sally, m. Seymour **SCOTT**, Jan. 7, 1833, by Rev. A.		
Gregory, Willimantic	3	163
Sarah, m. William **BACKUS**, Mar. 24, 1708	A	9
Sarah, m. John **HOWARD**, Jr., Jan. 8, 1740	1	232
Sarah, d. [Isaac & Sarah], b. Aug. 5, 1770	2	90
Sarah, w. Dr. Isaac, d. July 17, 1782	2	90
Walter, s. Sterry, weaver, ae. 40, & Susan, ae. 30,		
of Willimantic, b. Mar. 12, 1847	4	1
William, s. [Isaac & Sarah], b. Aug. 14, 1764	2	90
William, d. Sept. 3, 1764	2	1
W[illia]m A., m. Jane S. **HOSMER**, June 20, 1844, by		
Rev. Andrew Sharp	3	215
W[illia]m Henry, s. [James & Harriet D.], b. June 10,		
1839	3	176
——, child of Origen, farmer, ae. 32, b. June 3,		
1850	4	11
BENNING, Henry T., of Meriden, m. Nancy M. **ROBINSON**, of		
Windham, Sept. 22, 1833, by Rev. Ella Dunham	3	165
BENTLEY, Lucy, of Windham, m. Frank W. **TAYLOR**, of North		
Stonington, [Sept.] 5, 1830, by Rev. Chester		
Tilden, Willimantic	3	147
BENTON, Harriet, m. Frederick **HASLER**, b. of Windham, Sept		
16, 1838, at Willimantic, by Rev. B. Cook, Jr.,		
of Willimantic	3	187
BEVINS, See **BEFINGS*** (*correction entire entry **BEVINS**, see		
BEFINGS handwritten in original manuscript)		
BIBBINS, BIBENS, BEBINS, BIBBIN, BIBBONS, BEBENS,		
BIBBENS, Abigail, d Arther, Jr. & Abigail, b. July		
8, 1738	1	133
Abigail, m Moses **SPAFFORD**, May 24, 1763	2	90
Abigail, d. [William & Louisa], b. Jan. 16, 1771	2	158
Abigail, wid. [Arther, Jr.], d. Mar. 19, 1784	1	133
Allatheah, d. [Elijah & Amy], b. May 1, 1768	3	8
Alethea, m. Owen **ORMSBY**, Jan. 5, 1793	3	58
Amos, s. Arther & Elizabeth, b. May 14, 1736	1	130
Amos, s Art[h]er & Elizabeth, d. July 16, 1757, at		
Fort Edward	1	42
Amy, w Elijah, d. Mar. 4, 1799	3	8
Ann, d. Arther & Elizabeth, b. Mar. 21, 1737/8	1	130
Arther, m. Elizabeth **EAM[E]S**, May 26, 1731	1	130
Arther, Jr., m. Abigail **FFOLLETT**, Nov. 8, 1732	1	133

	Vol.	Page
BIBBINS, BIBENS, BEBINS, BIBBIN, BIBBONS, BEBENS, BIBBENS, (cont.)		
Arther, Jr., d. [ ], at Ashford	1	133
Belia, m. Elizabeth **FARNUM**, May 29, 1796	3	25
Benj[ami]n, s. Arther, Jr. & Abigail, b. July 3, 1736	1	133
Benjamin, [s. Arther, Jr. & Abigail], d. Dec. 27, 1756	1	133
Benjamin, S. [Elijah & Amy], b. May 10, 1765	3	8
Benjamin, m. Clarissa **CAREY**, Dec. 31, 1789	3	23
Clarissa, d. [William & Louisa], b. Nov. [ ], 1769	2	158
Clarissa, d. [Benjamin & Clarissa], b. Sept. 12, 1792	3	23
Clarissa, m. Henry **HUNTINGTON**, Feb. 23, 1823	3	110
Clarissa, housekeeper, of Windham, d. Jan. 19, 1860, ae. 93	4	159-0
Clark, d Aug. [ ], 1848, ae. 65	4	152
Ebenezer, s. Arther & Experience, b. Feb. 1, 1714/15	1	130
Eben[eze]r, s. Eben[eze]r & Susannah, b. Feb. 11, 1747	1	217
Eben[eze]r, d. Nov. 19, 1761, in the 47th y. of his age	1	217
Elijah, s. Arther, Jr. & Abigail, b. Sept. 18, 1740	1	133
Elijah, s. [Elijah & Amy], b. Apr. 7, 1767; d same day	3	8
Elijah, m. Amy **HILL**, Oct. [ ], 1762	3	8
Elijah, m. Silence **FRENCH**, Nov. 3, 1799	3	8
Elijah, m. Margaret **WELLS**, Aug. 16, 1819, at Colchester; d. Mar. 28, 1820	3	8
Elizabeth, d. Arther & Elizabeth, b Nov. 20, 1733	1	130
Elizabeth, d. Ebenezer & Susannah, b. Aug. 1, 1758	1	217
Elizabeth, d Art[h]er & Elizabeth, d. Feb. 15, 1768	1	42
Erastus, m. Phila **KINGSBURY**, Jan. 1, 1799	3	94
Erastus, m. Bethiah **FORD**, Mar. 21, 1806	3	94
Eunice, d. Art[h]er & Elizabeth, b. Dec. 24, 1742; d. Dec. 9, 1756	1	42
Experience, d. Arther & Elizabeth, b. Apr. 6, 1722; d. Nov. 12, 1729	1	130
Experience, w. Arther, d. May 7, 1730	1	130
Experience, d Arther & Elizabeth, b. June 10, 1732	1	130
Israel, s. Art[h]er, Jr. & Abigail, b. Jan. 18, 1747/8	1	133
Israel, m. Mary **ROBINSON**, Sept. 12, 1799	3	38
Jacob, s. Arther & Experience, b. Oct. 2, 1717	1	130
Jacob, s. Ebenezer & Susannah, b. Apr. 26, 1742	1	217
Jerusha, d. [Sanford & Anne], b. Apr. 1, 1797	3	21
Jerusha, m. William A. **LATHROP**, Mar. 28, 1824	3	119
John, s. Eben[eze]r & Susannah, b. Mar. 16, 1750	1	217
John, s. Art[h]er, Jr. & Abigail, b. June 14, 1750; d		

	Vol	Page
BIBBINS, BIBENS, BEBINS, BIBBIN, BIBBONS, BEBENS, BIBBENS, (cont.)		
Nov. 1, 1754	1	133
Laura, m Samuel **TRIPP**, Mar. 28, 1830, by Rev. Roger Bingham	3	141
Lucia, of Windham, m Thomas **BALDWIN**, of Chaplin, Mar. 7, 1830, by Henry Huntington, J.P.	3	145
Lucius, s. [Erastus & Bethiah], b. Mar. 27, 1815	3	94
Lucius, m. Lydia Caroline **EWEING**, b. of Windham, Apr. 14, 1843, by Rev. Henry Bromley	3	208
Lydia, m. Lucius **DENISON**, [ ] 27, 1834, by Dexter Bullard, Hampton	3	168
Lydia Davidson, d. [Erastus & Bethiah], b. May 3, 1808	3	94
Maria, d. [Benjamin & Clarissa], b. Aug. 18, 1797	3	23
Molle, d. Eben[eze]r & Susannah, b. Jan. 30, 1745	1	217
Molly, m. Robert **COBURN**, Feb. 24, 1771	2	162
Nathaniel C., [s. Benjamin & Clarissa], b. May 7, 1800	3	23
Nath[anie]l C., teamster, of Windham, d. Jan. 25, 1848, ae. 48	4	151
Patience, d. Arther, Jr. & Abigail, b. Oct. 23, 1733	1	133
Patience, m. Mannassah **FARNAM**, Jr., Apr. 19, 1758	2	47
Patience, d [Elijah & Amy], b. June 13, 1770	3	8
Patience, m. Oliver **SMITH**, June 23, 1791	3	35
Phebe, d Ebenezer & Susannah, b. Oct. 25, 1756	1	217
Phila, d. [Erastus & Phila], b. Aug. 25, 1803	3	94
Phila, w. Erastus, d. Feb. 3, 1804	3	94
Phila, m. Royal **LINCOLN**, Oct. 12, 1823	3	71
Rebeckah, d. Arther & Elizabeth, b. Apr. 17, 1740	1	130
Samuell, s. Arther, Jr. & Abigail, b. Dec. 12, 1742	1	133
Samuel, s. [Elijah & Amy], b. July 23, 1775; d. same day	3	8
Sanford, s. [Elijah & Amy], b. June 20, 1773	3	8
Sanford, m. Anne **WELCH**, Oct. 27, 1796	3	21
Sarah, d. Ebenezer & Susannah, b. May 24, 1754	1	217
Selinne, d. [Benjamin & Clarissa], b. Apr. 1, 1795	3	23
Silence, w. Elijah, d. Aug. 15, 1818	3	8
Stowell, s. [Erastus & Phila], b. Apr. 22, 1800	3	94
Susan, d. [Erastus & Bethiah], b. May 26, 1820	3	94
Thankfull, [d. Art[h]er & Elizabeth], b. Mar. 24, 1746	1	42
Thankfull, m. Benjamin **FOLLET**, Jr., Mar. 8, 1769	2	158
Tryphenia, d. [Elijah & Amy], b. Aug. 10, 1763; d. Dec. 15, 1764	3	8
William, s. Art[h]er, Jr. & Abigail, b. Nov. 23, 1745	1	133
William, m Louisa **SIMONS**, Apr. 23, 1769	2	158
William, s. [Erastus & Bethiah], b. Dec. 13, 1806; d. Sept 9, 1808	3	94

	Vol.	Page
BIBBINS, BIBENS, BEBINS, BIBBIN, BIBBONS, BEBENS,		
BIBBENS, (cont.)		
William Henry, s. [Erastus & Bethiah], b. Jan. 1, 1813	3	94
Zerviah, d. [Benjamin & Clarissa], b. Jan. 10, 1791;		
d. May 12, 1791	3	23
BIDLAKE, BIDLOCK, Amos, s. John & Mary, b. May 19, 1754;		
d. Aug. 23, 1777	2	2
Asa, s. [Jonathan & Hannah], b. Oct 9, 1771	2	131
Benjamin, d. Feb. 23, 1740/41	1	184
Benjamin, m Edeth **SPALDEN,** Nov. 11, 1742	1	238
Bethia, d. Benjamin & Lydia, b. May 22, 1738	1	184
Bethia, m. Christopher **DAVIDSON,** June 24, 1756	2	48
Christopher, d. Feb. 23, 1740/41, ae. about 80 y.	1	184
Edeth, m. Joshua **READ,** Apr. 7, 1756	2	36
Edeth, d. [Jonathan & Hannah], b. Jan. 22, 1780	2	131
Eunice, d. [Jonathan & Hannah], b. Feb. 9, 1768	2	131
Hannah, d. Benj[amin] & Lydia, b. Aug. 26, 1741	1	184
John, s. John, d. Aug. 8, 1776	2	2
Jonathan, s. Benj[amin] & Edith, b. Nov. 19, 1744	1	238
Jonathan, m. Hannah **CUTLER,** Apr. 22, 1767	2	131
Jonathan, s. [Jonathan & Hannah], b. Sept. 19, 1776	2	131
Lydia, d. Benjamin & Lydia, b. Jan. 8, 1736/7	1	184
Lydia, m. Asa **FARNAM,** Mar. 2, 1756	2	21
Mary, m Ebenezer **GEN[N]INGS,** Dec 16, 1713	1	39a
Mary, d. Benj[amin] & Lydia, b. July 29, 1732; d.		
Feb 27, 1732/3	1	108
Mary, d. Benj[amin] & Lydia, b. Dec. 4, 1733	1	108
Mary, d. Jonathan & Hannah], b. Apr. 27, 1773	2	131
Olive, d. [Jonathan & Hannah], b. Dec. 1, 1769	2	131
Oliver, s. [Jonathan & Hannah], b Apr. 29, 1778	2	131
Ralph, s. [Jonathan & Hannah], b. Oct. 2, 1774	2	131
Ruth, d. Benj[ami]n & Edeth, b. Feb 14, 1746/7; d		
Jan. 7, 1751	1	238
Sarah, w. Christopher, d. Nov. 25, 1739, ae 74 y	1	184
Sarah, m. Nath[anie]ll **FLINT,** Jr., June 16, 1742	1	219
Sarah, m. Nath[anie]ll **FFLINT,** June 16, 1742	1	231
Sarah, d. Benj[ami]n & Edeth, b. Nov. 29, 1748; d.		
Jan. 15, 1751	1	238
Sarah, m. Stephen **FULLER,** Jr., [ ];		
"lived at Westmoreland"	2	247
BIGALOW, Aaron, of Colcheser, m. Joanna **PEVEY,** of Willi-		
mantic, Sept. 27, 1846, by Rev John Cooper	3	230
BIGBEE, Mary, m. Eben[eze]r **LAMB,** Jan. 17, 1748/9	1	288
BIGFORD, Abigail, m. Phillip **ABBOT[T],** Oct. 8, 1723	1	62
BILL, BILLS, Betsey E., m. Isaac **CHAMPLAIN,** Nov. 24, 1845,		
by Andrew Sharp	3	225
Delight A., m. Silas **JAGGER,** b. of Windham, Aug. 27,		
1837, by Rev. Silas Leonard	3	183

	Vol	Page
BILL, BILLS, (cont)		
Eleazer, m. Emily **BINGHAM,** b. of Windham, Jan. 10,		
1847, by Rev. B M. Alden, Jr.	3	233
Emily S., d. Eleazer, mason, ae. 65, of Willimantic,		
b Jan. 2, [1850]	4	10
Esther, m. Elijah **WOLCUTT,** May 8, 1758	2	41
Eunice, d. [Roswell & Rebeckah], b Jan. 17, 1779	2	221
Jos[eph] R., of Union, m. Olive J. **BACKUS,** of Chaplin,		
Jan. 13, 1845, by Rev. Henry Greenslit	3	220
Julia W., m. Joseph T. **BENNETT,** Sept. 8, 1844, by Rev.		
Cha[rle]s Noble, Willimantic	3	216
Mary, m. Hezekiah **COBURN,** Jan. 17, 1771	2	221
Roswell, m. Rebeckah **BURGE,** Nov. 20, 1777	2	221
——, st. b. child of Eleazer & Emily, b. Nov. 30,		
[1848]	4	6
BILLINGS, Ambrose, farmer, d. July 16, 1849, ae. 17	4	154
Bethiah, d. William & Bethiah, b. Nov 4, 1727	1	69
Bethyah, m. Rev. Samuell **MOSELEY,** July 4, 1734	1	144
Gilbert, m. Emily **FOLLETT,** b. of Windham, Dec 13,		
1835, by Rev. Edward Harris	3	175
Hannah, d. William & Bethiah, b Nov. 8, 1729	1	69
Lucian, m. Nancy **BUCK,** Mar. 20, 1834, by Rev. Roger		
Bingham	3	168
Maria, m. Lewis L. **DAVIS,** manufacturer, of Windham,		
Feb 10, [1849], by Rev. J.M Phillips	4	114
Minerva H., ae. 20, b. Penn., res. Windham, m. Chester		
H. **BECKWITH,** blacksmith, ae. 24, of Windham, Sept		
1, [1850], by E.W. Barrows	4	118
Olive M., ae. 24, m. Servis **DAVIS,** wagonmaker, ae. 23,		
Feb. 9, [1850], by Rev. Phillips	4	114
Patience, d William & Bethiah, b. June 3, 1731	1	69
William, s. William & Bethiah, b. Mar. 18, 1725/6	1	69
BINGHAM, Abel, s Abel & Elizabeth, b. June 17, 1704, at		
Stratfield	1	36
Abel, m. Abigail **MOULTON,** Mar. 1, 1725/6	1	73
Abel, s. Abel & Abigail, b. May 24, 1741	1	148
Abel, d. Mar 25, 1745, ae. 76 y	1	148
Abel, m. Betty **PHELPS,** Oct. 13, 1752	1	148
Abigail, d. Abel & Elizabeth, b. June 7, 1696, at		
Stratfield	1	36
Abigail, d. Joseph & Abigail, b. Nov 2, 1716	1	38
Abigail, d. Abel & Abigail, b. Jan. 15, 1726/7	1	73
Abigail, d. Samuel & Elizabeth, b. July 18, 1736	1	142
Abigail, d. Sam[ue]ll & Elizabeth, b. July 18, 1736	1	147
Abigail, w. Joseph, d. Mar 30, 1741	1	38
Abigail, d. Elijah & Theodosay, b. Oct. 26, 1746	1	154
Abigail, d. Abel & Abigail, d. Sept. 17, 1750	1	148
Abishai, s. Sam[ue]ll & Ffaith, b. Jan. 29, 1718/9	1	3
Abisha, m Ann **SAWYER,** Feb [ ], 1755	2	161

	Vol.	Page
BINGHAM, (cont.)		
Abner, s. [Benjamin & Sarah], b. Jan. 23, 1761	2	49
Adonijah, s. Isaac & Sarah, b. Aug 23, 1737; d.		
Oct. 27, 1745	1	120
Alexander, s. Nath[anie]l & Martha, b June 11,		
1757	2	25
Alfred, s. [Ebenezer & Amey], b. Aug. 9, 1762	2	63
Alfred, m. Zerviah **YOUNG**, Nov. 24, 1787	2	50
Alice, d. [Jeremiah, Jr. & Est[h]er], b. Oct. 12,		
1772	2	167
Almantha, d [Gamaleel & Betsey], b. May 18, 1821	3	46
Almantha M., m. William **CUNNINGHAM**, b. of Windham,		
Sept. 21, 1845, by Rev. Isaac H. Coe	3	222
Almira, m. Charles **LILLIE**, Feb. 13, 1825, by Alfred		
Young, Esq.	3	60
Amanda, m. Charles **LARRABEE**, Mar. 23, 1846, by Rev.		
J E. Tyler	3	109
Amey, d. [Benjamin & Sarah], b. Sept. 21, 1767, in		
Salisbury	2	49
Amey, d. [Ebenezer & Amey], b. Mar. 17, 1770; d. Sept.		
28, 1775	2	63
Amie, m. Socrates **BALKCOM**, Aug. [ ], 1810	3	69
Amie, b. Jan. 1, 1784; m. Socrates **BOLWIN**, Aug. 19,		
1810	3	91
Ann, m. Hezekiah **MASON**, June 7, 1699	A	32
Ann, d. Abel & Elizabeth, b. Sept. 13, 1706, at		
Stratfield	1	36
Ann, m. Sam[ue]ll **FFOLSOM**, May 3, 1739	1	193
Ann, w. Capt. Sam[ue]ll, d Sept. 6, 1792	2	148
Anna, d. [Gideon & Mary], b. [ ], 1751; d. May		
[ ], 1752	1	145
Anna, d. [Gideon & Mary], b. Apr. [ ], 1753	1	145
Anna, d. [Jedediah & Elizabeth], b Jan 8, 1783; d		
same day	2	228
Anna, d. [Jedediah & Elizabeth], b. May 16, 1786	2	228
Anne, d. Sam[ue]ll & Ffaith, b. Nov. [ ], 1716	1	3
Anne, d. Lemuel & Hannah, b Sept 12, 1750	1	162
Anne, d. [Abisha & Ann], b. Oct. 7, 1772	2	161
Anson H., s. Elias, b. Oct. 21, 1814	3	87
Asa, s. [Silas], b. Aug. 22, 1772	2	185
Asahel, s [Abisha & Ann], b. May 15, 1765	2	161
Augustus Whealock, s. [Joseph, Jr. & Sarah], b. Feb.		
13, 1764	2	128
Bennajah, s. [Ebenezer & Amey], b. Nov. 3, 1779	2	63
Benjamin, m. Sarah **STEWART**, of Norwich Landing, Oct		
15, 1754	1	324
Benjamin, m. Sarah **STEWART**, of Norwich, Oct. 15, 1754	2	49
Benjamin, s. Benj[ami]n & Sarah, b. June 5, 1757	1	324

	Vol.	Page
BINGHAM, (cont.)		
Benjamin, s. [Benjamin & Sarah], b. June 5, 1757	2	49
Betsey, d. [Maltiah & Mercy], b. Jan. 4, 1776; d.		
Mar. 8, 1779	3	18
Betsey, d. [Maltiah & Mercy], b. Sept. 22, 1780	3	18
Betty, w. Abel, d. May 8, 1771	1	148
Bial, s. Benj[ami]n & Sarah, b. June 29, 1755	1	324
Calista, d. [Gamaleel & Betsey], b. Dec. 5, 1805	3	46
Calvin, s. Elij[ah] & Sarah, b. July 30, 1762	2	11
Calvin, s. [Thomas & Amy], b. Mar. 16, 1770; d.		
Sept 8, 1802	2	117
Ceazer, m. Bridget **FAGIN**, June 5, 1823	3	50
Celende, d. [Joseph, Jr. & Sarah], b. Feb. 23, 1762	1	233
Celinda, d. [Joseph, Jr. & Sarah], b. Feb. 23, 1762	2	128
Charles A., m. Phebe **HELLEN**, July 11, 1830, by Rev		
Chester Tilden, Willimantic	3	147
Charlotte, d. [Alfred & Zerviah], b. Oct. 11, 1793	2	50
Charlotte, d. George, manufacturer, ae. 39, & Mary,		
ae. 38, of Willimantic, b. Aug. 27, 1847	4	1
Charlotte Y., b. Oct. 11, 1793; m. John **PALMER**, Nov.		
8, 1820, by C B Everest	3	116
Chester, s. Joseph & Sarah, b. Sept. 7, 1748	1	233
Chester, [s. Joseph, Jr & Sarah], b. Sept. 7, 1748	2	128
Clarina, d. [Samuel, Jr. & Aletheah], b. Nov. 18,		
1785	3	56
Daniel, s. Abel & Elizabeth, b. Sept. 12, 1714	1	36
Daniel, m. Hannah **CONANT**, Jan. 13, 1747/8	1	277
Daniel, s. [Elij[ah] & Sarah], b. Apr. 10, 1769	2	11
Deborah, m. Stephen **TRACY**, Jan. 26, 1707	1	11
Deborah, d. Sam[ue]ll & Elizabeth, b. May 4, 1729	1	69
Delight, d Abel & Abigail, b. Aug. 4, 1739	1	148
Dorothy, m. Josiah **KINGSLEY**, Dec. 10, 1718	1	28
Ebenezer, m Amey **WOOD**, Apr. 15, 1761	2	63
Ebenezer, s. [Ebenezer & Amey], b. Aug. 12, 1776	2	63
Egbert, s. [Gamaleel & Betsey], b Feb. 8, 1808	3	46
Eleazer, s. Stephen & Rebeckah, b. July 13, 1718	1	34
Elias, s. Gideon & Mary, b May 14, 1744; d Apr		
20, 1745	1	145
Elias, s. Lemuel & Hannah, b Sept. 28, 1753	1	162
Elias, s. [Abisha & Ann], b. Dec. 10, 1756	2	161
Elias, of Scotland, m. Vashti **ELDERKIN**, Nov. 28,		
1776	2	115
Elias, s [Elias & Vashti], b. July 22, 1779	2	115
Elias, Jr., m. Alice **BROUGHTON**, Mar. 15, 1781	2	248
Elias, s. [Jedediah & Elizabeth], b. Jan 31, 1792	2	228
Elijah, s. Joseph & Abigail, b. Jan. 1, 1719	1	38
Elijah, m Theodosay **CRANE**, Mar. 2, 1738/9	1	154
Elijah, s. Elijah & Theodosay, b. Nov. 24, 1739	1	154

	Vol.	Page
BINGHAM, (cont.)		
Elijah, m. Sarah **JACKSON**, July 19, 1752	1	154
Eliphalet, s. Gideon & Mary, b. May 4, 1740	1	145
Elisha, s. Jonathan, Jr., & Sarah, b. July 13, 1740	1	207
Elizabeth, d. Abel & Elizabeth, b Mar. 27, 1702,		
at Stratfield	1	36
Elizabeth, d. Sam[ue]ll & Elizabeth, b. Dec 14, 1722;		
d. Dec. 26, 1722	1	69
Elizabeth, d. Abel & Abigail, b Mar. 27, 1729	1	73
Elizabeth, d. Isaac & Sarah, b. May 19, 1743; d. Nov.		
30, 1745	1	120
Elizabeth, d. Abel & Abigail, d. Sept. 2, 1747	1	148
Elizabeth, d. Isaac & Sarah, b. Dec. 5, 1748	1	220
Elizabeth, wid. Sam[ue]ll, d. Mar. 27, 1780	1	69
Elizabeth, d. [Jedediah & Elizabeth], b Mar 23, 1781	2	228
Elizabeth, w. Jedediah, d. Jan. 22, 1803	2	228
Elizabeth, d. [Gamaleel & Betsey], b Aug 6, 1815	3	46
Elizabeth, m. Lucius **LINCOLN**, b. of Windham, June 12,		
1838, by Rev O.C. Whiton	3	186
Emily, m. Eleazer **BILL**, b. of Windham, Jan. 10, 1847,		
by Rev. B.M. Alden, Jr.	3	233
Emily A., of Windham, m. John **BLIVEN**, of Westerly,		
R I., May 22, 1834, by Rev Jesse Fisher	3	169
Erastus, twin with Ralph, s. [Jedediah & Elizabeth], b.		
Dec 15, 1795	2	228
Eunice, d. Isaac & Sarah, b. May 25, 1735	1	120
Eunice, d Elij[ah] & Sarah, b June 18, 1756	2	11
Eunice, d. [Silas], b. Mar. 6, 1769; d. Mar. 6, 1769	2	185
Eunice, d [Gideon & Ruth], b Feb 4, 1773	2	46
Eunice, d. [John & Eunice], b. May 16, 1789	2	45
Ffaith, w Sam[ue]ll, d. Feb. 11, 1720/21	1	3
Fanny, d. [Benjamin & Sarah], b. Nov. 25, 1762, in		
Salisbury	2	49
Gamaleel, s. Isaac & Sarah, b. Sept. 7, 1739; d. Dec.		
4, 1745	1	120
Gamaliel, s. [Jeremiah, Jr. & Est[h]er], b. May 17,		
1775	2	167
Gamaleel, m. Betsey **ROBINSON**, Aug. 5, 1800	3	46
George, s. [John & Eunice], b. July 11, 1781	2	45
George, s. [Gamaleel & Betsey], b. Feb. 6, 1801	3	46
George, m. Marcy **DENISON**, Oct. 22, 1809	3	58
George, m. Judeth **RIPLEY**, Feb. 20, 1825, by Rev. Jesse		
Fisher	3	119
George Dunham, [s. Thomas, Jr. & Lyma], b. Dec. 20,		
1824	3	68
Gideon, s. Joseph & Abigail, b. July 3, 1714	1	38
Gideon, m. Mary **CARY**, June 13, 1734	1	145
Gideon, s. Gideon & Mary, b. Dec. 5, 1735	1	145

	Vol	Page
BINGHAM, (cont.)		
Gideon, m. Ruth **WARNER**, Nov. 15, 1761	2	46
Gideon, d. Mar. 19, 1791, ae 55 y	2	46
Gideon, s. [Roger & Nancy], b. Sept. 20, 1816	3	87
Hannah, w. Abel, Jr & Abigail, b. Dec 27, 1734	1	148
Hannah, d. Lemuel & Hannah, b. Apr. 26, 1738	1	162
Hannah, d. Daniel & Hannah, b Nov. 8, 1748	1	277
Hannah, m. Joshua **LASSAL**, Jan. 20, 1757	2	33
Hannah, m Nathaniel **FORD**, July 7, 1763	2	87
Hannah, d. [Gideon & Ruth], b. Mar. 19, 1767	2	46
Hannah, d. [Jedediah & Elizabeth], b July 24, 1784	2	228
Hannah, wid. Lemuel, d. Oct. 21, 1793	1	162
Harris, s. Elij[ah] & Sarah, b. Nov 17, 1763	2	11
Harry, s. [Samuel, Jr. & Aletheah], b. Oct. 18, 1782	3	56
Henry Laurens, s. [George & Marcy], b. Apr 1, 1814	3	58
Herbert C., s. Samuel, ae. 36, & Ann, ae. 30, b.		
[1848]	4	7
Hoel, s. [Silas], b. Aug. 16, 1770; d. Dec. 3, 1771	2	185
Huldah, d. Jer[emiah] & Mary, b. Mar. 27, 1757	1	208
Irena, d. [Abisha & Ann], b. July 29, 1767	2	161
Isaac, s. Nathaniell & Sarah, b. July 1, 1709	1	37
Isaac, m. Sarah **BACKUS**, July 6, 1732	1	120
Ithemer, s. John & Mary, b. Sept 7, 1724	1	79
Jabez, Jr., m. Mary **WHEELOCK**, Dec. 29, 1746	1	264
Jabez, s Jab[ez] & Mary, b. Feb. 13, 1748/9	1	264
Jabez, s. [Ebenezer & Amey], b. June 25, 1765	2	63
Jabez, s [Alfred & Zerviah], b. Aug. 17, 1788	2	50
James, s. Gid[eon] & Mary, b. Jan. [ ], 1749; d.		
[ ], 1753	1	145
James, s. Elij[ah] & Sarah, b. Apr. 23, 1758	2	11
James, s. [Thomas & Amy], b Oct. 28, 1772	2	117
James, s. [Maltiah & Mercy], b. Jan. 24, 1774; d. Aug.		
29, 1778	3	18
James, s. Uriah & Eunice, b. May 26, 1782	2	235
James, s. [Oliver & Lucy], b. Nov. 28, 1784	2	140
James, m. Maria **HUNTINGTON**, Dec. 30, 1829, by Rev.		
Roger Bingham	3	144
Jedediah, s. Lemuel & Hannah, b. Mar. 3, 1747/8	1	162
Jedediah, m. Elizabeth **WEBB**, Apr. 29, 1779	2	228
Jedediah, s. [Jedediah & Elizabeth], b. Feb. 22, 1790	2	228
Jedediah, m. Mary **TRACY**, Sept. 12, 1810	2	228
Jemima, d. Abel & Elizabeth, b. Oct. 24, 1708	1	36
Jemima, m. Ebenezer **GEN[N]INGS**, Aug. 10, 1726	1	54
Jeremiah, s. Nathaniell & Sarah, b. Jan. 27, 1715/16	1	37
Jeremiah, m. Mary **LILLEY**, Sept. 25, 1740	1	208
Jeremiah, s. Jeremiah & Mary, b. Aug. 24, 1748	1	208
Jeremiah, m. Mehitable **CRAFT**, Oct 12, 1769	2	146
Jeremiah, Jr., m. Est[h]er **PALMER**, Jan. 15, 1772	2	167

	Vol.	Page
BINGHAM, (cont.)		
Jeremiah, d. Sept. 4, 1784, in the 69th y. of his		
age	1	208
Jeremiah, s. [Uriah & Eunice], b. Feb. 13, 1786	2	235
Jerusha, d Sam[ue]ll & Ffaith, b Feb 2, 1708	1	3
Jerusha, m. Benj[amin] **ROBINSON**, Mar. 4, 1728/9	1	110
Jerusha, d. John & Mary, b. Aug. 22, 1733	1	79
Jerusha, d. Abel, Jr. & Abigail, b. Apr. 24, 1737	1	148
Jerusha, d. Joseph, Jr & Sarah, b Oct. 15, 1743	1	233
Jerusha, d. [Joseph, Jr. & Sarah], b. Oct. 15,		
1743	2	128
Jerusha, d. [Lemuel & Hannah], b. July 3, 1756; d.		
July 10, 1756	1	162
Jerusha, m. Rev. Sam[ue]ll **HILLARD**, Sept. 20, 1769	2	173
John, s Abel & Elizabeth, b. Feb. 9, 1700, at		
Stratfield	1	36
John, m. Mary **MOULTON**, Dec. 6, 1721	1	79
John, s. [Gideon & Mary], b. Nov. 26, 1755	1	145
John, m. Eunice **WARNER**, May 1, 1777	2	45
John, s. [John & Eunice], b. Dec. 27, 1793	2	45
John, m. Diana **STEARNES**, Dec. 31, 1822, by Samuel		
Perkins, Esq.	3	106
John, m. Jerusha **FRINK**, Sept. 20, 1829, by Rev. Roger		
Bingham	3	143
John, 2d, m. Julia Ann **INGRAM**, July 4, 1830, by Rev		
Chester Tilden, Willimantic	3	147
Jonathan, m Ann **HUNTINGTON**, Oct. 28, 1697	A	21
Jonathan, s. Abel & Elizabeth, b. Aug. 17, 1712	1	36
Jonathan, s. Samuel & Elizabeth, b. Mar. 19, 1733/4	1	142
Jonathan, m. Mary **ABBE**, May 9, 1734	1	144
Jonathan, s. Jonathan & Mary, b Feb 20, 1734/5	1	144
Jonathan, m. Sarah **VINTON**, June 7, 1735/6	1	144
Jonathan, Jr., d Feb. 16, 1800, in the 88th y. of his		
age	1	207
Joseph, m. Abigail **SCOT[T]**, Dec. 14, 1710	1	38
Joseph, s. Joseph & Abigail, b. Aug. 10, 1721	1	38
Joseph, m. Rachel **HUNTINGTON**, Nov 30, 1742, in		
Norwich; d. Sept. 4, 1765, in the 78th y. of his		
age	1	38
Joseph, Jr., m. Sarah **WHEALOCK**, Dec. 1, 1742	2	128
Joseph, Jr., m Sarah **WHEELOCK**, Dec 21, 1742	1	233
Josiah, s. John & Mary, b. May 25, 1731	1	79
Josiah, s. Abel & Abigail, b. Sept. 22, 1743; d. Dec		
5, 1746	1	148
Julia, d [John & Eunice], b. Apr. 6, 1787; d. May 15,		
1789	2	45
Julia, d [George & Marcy], b. Aug. 16, 1810	3	58
Laura, d. [John & Eunice], b. Nov. 24, 1795	2	45

	Vol	Page
BINGHAM, (cont.)		
Laura, Mrs., d. Apr. 24, [1849], ae. 53 (Entered		
among births)	4	6
Lemuel, s. Sam[ue]ll & Ffaith, b. Sept. 20, 1713	1	3
Lemuel, m. Hannah **PIRKENS**, Apr 28, 1737	1	162
Lemuel, s. [Elias & Vashti], b. Mar. 23, 1781	2	115
Lemuel, d. Nov. 3, 1788	1	162
Lemuel, s. [Jedediah & Elizabeth], b. Jan. 7, 1794	2	228
Levi, s. [Abisha & Ann], b. July 14, 1762	2	161
Levi, s. [Elias, Jr. & Alice], b. Jan. 8, 1782	2	248
Lois, d. [Gamaleel & Betsey], b. Dec 9, 1802	3	46
Lora, d. [Silas], b. Feb. 20, 1768	2	185
Lucian, s. [Samuel, Jr. & Aletheah], b Apr. 22, 1794	3	56
Lucretia, d. [Abisha & Ann], b. July 3, 1760	2	161
Lucretia, m. Benjamin **MILLARD**, Jan. 19, 1784	2	71
Lucee, d. John & Mary, b. Nov. 23, 1728	1	79
Lucy, d. Lemuel & Hannah, b. Sept 14, 1742; d Feb.		
7, 1777	1	162
Lucy, d [Elij[ah] & Sarah], b. Feb. 26, 1767	2	11
Lucy, d. [Gideon & Ruth], b. Oct. 15, 1774	2	46
Lucy, d. [Jedediah & Elizabeth], b. Feb. 14, 1780	2	228
Lucy, d. [Roger & Nancy], b. Nov. 17, 1824	3	87
Lucy Mary, d. [Abisha & Ann], b. Aug. 23, 1770	2	161
Luther, s. [Elias & Vashti], b. Apr. 5, 1778	2	115
Lydia, d. Joseph & Abigail, b Feb. 9, 1711/12	1	38
Lydia, m. Elias **FFRINK**, June 3, 1731	1	122
Lydia, d. Jerem[iah] & Mary, b. Dec. 10, 1745	1	208
Lydia, d. Sam[ue]ll, Jr. & Lydia, b. Sept. 3, 1749;		
d. July 5, 1787	1	282
Lydia, w. Sam[ue]ll, Jr., d. Jan. 15, 1768	1	282
Lydia, m. Josiah **LAS[S]EL**, Sept. 29, 1768	2	141
Lydia, d. [Gideon & Ruth], b. Apr. 13, 1771	2	46
Lydia, d. [Uriah & Eunice], b. Aug. 31, 1788	2	235
Lydia, m. John **STANIFORD**, Jan. 21, 1816	3	65
Lyman, d Apr 21, [1849], ae 63	4	154
Malatiah, s. Jonathan & Sarah, b. May 5, 1738	1	144
Maltiah, m. Mercy **WRIGHT**, Feb 14, 1771	3	18
Marah, d. Sam[ue]ll & Ffaith, b. Feb. 10, 1720/21; d.		
Feb. 22, 1727	1	3
Marcy, d. [Gamaleel & Betsey], b. Sept. 12, 1813	3	46
Marshall, s. [Jeremiah, Jr. & Ester], b Aug 28, 1781;		
d. Mar. 1, 1812	2	167
Martha, d. Sam[ue]ll, Jr & Lydia, b. Sept. 7, 1751	1	282
Martha, d. Sam[ue]ll, Jr. & Lydia, b. June 7, 1755	1	282
Mary, m John **BACKUS**, Feb. 17, 1692	A	2
Mary, d. Abel & Elizabeth, b. Dec. 17, 1697, at		
Stratfield	1	36
Mary, w. Stephen, d. Dec. 6, 1714	1	34

	Vol.	Page
BINGHAM, (cont)		
Mary, m. John **ABBE**, Nov. 7, 1717	1	37
Mary, d John & Mary, b. Aug 28, 1723; d Sept 13, 1724	1	79
Mary, w. Dea. Thomas, d. Aug. 5, 1726, ae. about 78 y	1	37
Mary, d. John & Mary, b. Sept. 28, 1726	1	79
Mary, d. Sam[ue]ll & Elizabeth, b. Oct. 18, 1731	1	69
Mary, w. Jonathan, d. Mar. 4, 1734/5	1	144
Mary, d. Jona[than] & Sarah, b Nov 14, 1736	1	144
Mary, d. Jeremiah & Mary, b. Aug. 22, 1743	1	208
Mary, m Eleazer **PALMER**, Jr., May 5, 1756	2	10
Mary, w. Gideon, d. Dec. 22, 1758	1	145
Mary, d. [Gideon & Ruth], b Mar 13, 1765; d Mar 3, 1776	2	46
Mary, d. [Thomas & Amy], b. Feb. 20, 1767	2	117
Mary, m. Phinehas **ABBE**, Dec. 7, 1767	2	136
Mary, w. Jeremiah, d Aug 9, 1768	1	208
Mary, d. [Ralph & Hannah], b. Oct. 14, 1783	2	244
Mary, m Nath[anie]l D. **FISHER**, b. of Windham, Nov 13, [1837], by Rev. Otis C. Whiton, of Scotland Society, Windham	3	184
Mary, d. Sept. 14, [1849], ae. 82	4	156
Mary W., d. Wallace, ae. 32, & Mary P., ae 32, b Feb 3, [1849]	4	7
Mary W., d. June 23, 1849, ae 4 m.	4	154
Mason, s. [Samuel, Jr. & Aletheah], b. Feb. 14, 1779	3	56
Mehetabel, d. Nathaniell & Sarah, b. Nov. 21, 1713	1	37
Nancy, m. Jairus **SMITH**, Oct. 18, 1818	3	92
Nancy Maria, d. [Roger & Nancy], b. Oct 17, 1821	3	87
Nancy Merrick, m. Henry **McCALLUM**, Dec. 25, 1845, by Rev. Abel Nichols	3	226
Naomi, d. Jonathan, Jr. & Sarah, b. May 13, 1744	1	207
Naoma, [twin with Ruth], d. Isaac & Sarah, b. Aug. 16, 1751	1	220
Nathan, s. Elij[ah] & Sarah, b Jan. 4, 1760	2	11
Nathan, s. Elijah & Sarah, d. July 8, 1760	2	11
Nathan, s. Elij[ah] & Sarah, b. Apr 4, 1761	2	11
Nathaniell, m. Sarah **LOBDIL**, July 25, 1705; d. Dec. 16, 1754, in the 74th y. of his age	1	37
Nathaniel, m. Sarah **LOBDIL**, July 25, 1705	A	26
Nath[anie]ll, s. Isaac & Sarah, b. May 12, 1733	1	120
Nath[anie]ll, Dea., d. Dec. 16, 1754, in the 74th y. of his age	1	37
Nath[anie]l, m. Martha **BAKER**, Jan. 2, 1757	2	25
Olive, d [Benjamin & Sarah], b. Mar 8, 1759	2	49
Oliver, s. [Gideon & Ruth], b. Dec. 28, 1763	2	46
Oliver, m Lucy **MOULTON**, Nov. 13, 1783	2	140
Ozias, s. Jos[eph] & Sarah, b. June 12, 1750	1	233

	Vol.	Page
BINGHAM, (cont)		
Ozias, s. [Joseph, Jr. & Sarah], b. June 12, 1750	2	128
Parthenia, d. [Silas], b Oct 1, 1766; d. Mar 28,		
1767	2	185
Phebe, d. Jonathan, Jr & Sarah, b. Apr. 26, 1742	1	207
Polina, d. [Jedediah & Elizabeth], b. June 14,		
1788	2	228
Polina, m. Daniel **GAGER**, Nov. 2, 1808	3	81
Polly, d. [John & Eunice], b. Aug. 4, 1784	2	45
Priscilla, m. Amaziah **FISK**, Jan. 3, 1771	2	165
Ralph, s. Joseph, Jr. & Sarah, b Oct. 12, 1755	1	233
Ralf, s. [Joseph, Jr. & Sarah], b. Oct. 12, 1755	2	128
Ralph, m. Hannah **SHATTUCK**, June 26, 1776	2	244
Ralph, twin with Erastus, s. [Jedediah & Elizabeth],		
b. Dec. 15, 1795	2	228
Rebeckah, d. Stephen & Rebeckah, b. Nov. 28, 1720	1	34
Rial, s [Benjamin & Sarah], b. June 20, 1755 (see		
also Bial)	2	49
Roger, s. [Gideon & Ruth], b June 23, 1768	2	46
Roger, m. Nancy **WALDO**, Sept. 1, 1815	3	87
Rosewell, s Elijah & Sarah, b. Apr. 27, 1754; d		
Nov. 6, 1754	1	154
Roswell, s. [Thomas & Amy], b Jan. 22, 1775	2	117
Royal, s. [Maltiah & Mercy], b. Mar. 30, 1772; d. Aug.		
31, 1778	3	18
Rufus, s. W[illia]m, farmer, ae. 25, & Ellen, ae. 22,		
b. Feb. 14, 1851	4	13
Rune, d. [Maltiah & Mercy], b. Aug. 6, 1778	3	18
Ruth, [twin with Naoma], d. Isaac & Sarah, b Aug. 16,		
1751	1	220
Ruth, d [Ebenezer & Amey], b. Mar [ ], 1773	2	63
Ruth, w. Gideon, d. Apr. 21, 1817, ae. 84 y.	2	46
Salome, d. [Joseph, Jr. & Sarah], b. Apr 11, 1760	2	128
Salome, d. [Joseph, Jr. & Sarah], b. Apr. [ ], 1760	1	233
Salomy, d. [Gideon & Ruth], b. June 3, 1778; d. Aug.		
12, 1809, ae. 31	2	46
Samuell, m. Ffaith **RYPLEY**, Jan 5, 1708	1	3
Samuel, m. Elizabeth **MANNING**, Nov. 23, 1721	1	3
Sam[ue]ll, s. Sam[ue]ll & Elizabeth, b. Nov. 11, 1723	1	58
Sam[ue]ll, s. Sam[ue]ll & Elizabeth, b. Nov. 11, 1723	1	69
Sam[ue]ll, Jr., m Lydia **MIDGE**, Nov 10, 1748	1	282
Samuell, s. Sam[ue]ll, Jr. & Lydia, b. Mar. 24, 1753	1	282
Samuel, Capt., d Mar 1, 1760, ae 74	1	142
Sam[ue]ll, Capt., m. Ann **RIPLEY**, May 17, 1769	2	148
Samuel, Jr., m. Aletheah **HEB[B]ARD**, Jan. 1, 1778	3	56
Samuel, Capt., d. July 25, 1805, in the 82nd y. of his		
age	2	148
Samuel, s. [Roger & Nancy], b. Dec. 21, 1818	3	87

	Vol.	Page

BINGHAM, (cont)

Samuel, m. Ann Robinson **CUSHMAN**, b. of Windham, Dec. 24, 1840, in St Paul's Church, by Rev. Henry Beers Sherman — 3 — 195

Samuel Bishop, s. Erastus, b Nov. 26, 1822 — 3 — 81

Samuel Paine, s. [Thomas, Jr. & Lyma], b. Sept. 3, 1812 — 3 — 68

Sarah, m. Joseph **WALDEN**, Jan. 16, 1723/4 — 1 — 76

Sarah, d. Abel & Abigail, b. Sept. 16, 1732 — 1 — 73

Sarah, d. Jeremiah & Mary, b. June 29, 1741 — 1 — 208

Sarah, d. Joseph & Sarah, b. June [ ], 1747; d same day — 1 — 233

Sarah, d. [Joseph, Jr & Sarah], b. June 14, 1747; d. same day — 2 — 128

Sarah, m. Asher **FLINT**, Aug. 20, 1752 — 1 — 314

Sarah, d. [Abisha & Ann], b. July 24, 1758 — 2 — 161

Sarah, m. A[a]ron [ ], Mar. 3, 1763 — 2 — 80

Sarah, w. Dea. Nath[anie]ll, d. June 28, 1763, ae. 80 y. — 1 — 37

Sarah, d. [Benjamin & Sarah], b. June 9, 1765, in Salisbury — 2 — 49

Sarah, m. Whiting **BACKUS**, Feb. 15, 1769, in Hebron — 2 — 199

Sarah, m. Adriel **SIMONS**, Mar. 8, 1781 — 2 — 241

Sarah E., m. Henry **WEBB**, b. of Windham, Feb. 13, 1842, by Rev. John E. Tyler — 3 — 200

Sarah Jane, d. [Roger & Nancy], b. Dec. 26, 1826 — 3 — 87

Septor, s. [Uriah & Eunice], b Oct. 29, 1792; d. Aug 4, 1794 — 2 — 235

Silas, s Elijah & The[o]dosay, b. Dec. 3, 1742 — 1 — 154

Silas, m. [ ] **HIBBARD**, Dec. 10, 1765 — 2 — 185

Silas, s. [Silas], b. Sept. 18, 1771 — 2 — 185

Silvanius, s. Isaac & Sarah, b. May 7, 1741; d. Nov. 19, 1762 — 1 — 120

Sophia, d. [Ralph & Hannah], b. May 29, 1777; d. Mar. 21, 1778 — 2 — 244

Stephen, m. Mary **KINGSBERY**, Dec. 11, 1712 — 1 — 34

Stephen, m. Rebeckah **BISHOP**, Nov. 30, 1715 — 1 — 34

Stephen, s. Joseph & Sarah, b. Sept. 15, 1745 — 1 — 233

Sybal, d. Abel & Abigail, b Sept. 20, 1730 — 1 — 73

Sybel, m. Shubael **PALMER**, Aug. 20, 1752 — 1 — 314

Tabitha, d. Elijah & Sarah, b. June 24, 1755 — 1 — 154

Temperance, d. Jerem* & Sarah, b. Jan. 26, 1745/6 (*Isaac?) — 1 — 220

Theodosay, w. Elijah, d. Apr. 6, 1751 — 1 — 154

Thomas, m. Sarah **HUNTINGTON**, Apr 23, 1724 — 1 — 79

Thomas, s. Sam[ue]ll & Elizabeth, b. Sept. 12, 1725; d. July 9, 1726 — 1 — 69

Thomas, s. Sam[ue]ll & Elizabeth, b. June 20, 1727 — 1 — 69

	Vol.	Page
BINGHAM, (cont.)		
Thomas, Dea., d. Jan. 16, 1729/30, ae. about 88 y.	1	37
Thomas, s. Gideon & Mary, b. July 3, 1742	1	145
Thomas, m. Amy **SMITH**, Feb. 13, 1766	2	117
Thomas, s. [Ebenezer & Amey], b. Jan. 20, 1768	2	63
Thomas, s. [Thomas & Amy], b. Apr. 1, 1782	2	117
Thomas, m Charlotte **FLINT**, May 17, 1795	3	50
Thomas, Jr., m. Lyma **PAINE**, Nov. 29, 1809	3	68
Thomas Hulford, s. [Ralph & Hannah], b Sept. 29, 1779	2	244
Truman, s. [Elij[ah] & Sarah], b. Feb. 17, 1771	2	11
Tryphenia, d. [Joseph, Jr. & Sarah], b. Sept. 15, 1745	2	128
Uriah, s. Jerem[iah] & [Mary], b. Nov. 10, 1751	1	208
Uriah, m. Eunice **WEBB**, Apr. 26, 1781	2	235
Vine, s. Elij[ah] & Sarah, b. May 27, 1765	2	11
Waldo, s. [Roger & Nancy], b May 3, 1817	3	87
Waldo, m. Mary P. **WEST**, b. of Windham, Sept. 8, 1840, by Rev. Henry Beers Sherman	3	194
Warren, s. [Gamaleel & Betsy], b. Aug. 13, 1810	3	46
William, s. Gid[eon] & Mary, b. Mar. 6, 1737/8	1	145
William, s. [Thomas & Amy], b. June 18, 1777	2	117
Zephaniah, s. [Uriah & Eunice], b. Mar. 24, 1784	2	235
Zeruiah, d. Lemuel & Hannah, b. Mar. 5, 1740	1	162
Zerviah, m. Oliver **SMITH**, Sept. 27, 1764	2	200
Zerviah, w. Alfred, d. May 26, 1796	2	50
----, child of Samuel, cashier of bank, ae. 31, b June 22, 1851	4	13
----, 2 s. of Gid[eon] & Mary, b. Dec 3, 1738; d Dec. 5 & 6, [1738]	1	145
----, s. [Gideon & Ruth], b Oct 7, 1762; d. same day	2	46
----, d [Ralph & Hannah], b Aug 10, 1778; d. Aug. 10, 1778	2	244
BIRCHARD, Calistia H , of Norwich, m. Walter **NIMOCK**, of Carthage, Jefferson County, N.Y., Apr. 27, 1843, by Rev Henry Bromley	3	208
BIRGE, [see under **BURGE**]		
BISHOP, Mary, m. Sidney S. **BREWSTER**, b of Willimantic, Nov 20, 1837, by Rev. Philo Judson, at Willimantic	3	184
Mercy, m. Joshua **LUCE**, Oct. 17, 1733	1	116
Rebeckah, m. Stephen **BINGHAM**, Nov. 30, 1715	1	34
Sarah, m. Thomas **BROWN**, Oct. 20, 1748	1	201
Susannah, m. James **TRACY**, May 26, 1748	1	278
BISSELL, Amelia, d [Hez[ekia]h & Anne], b. May 2, 1765	2	109
Anna, m. Stephen **COY**, Nov. 11, 1762	2	64
Anne, d. [Hez[ekia]h & Anne], b. July 5, 1770	2	109
George Elderkin, s. [Hez[ekia]h & Anne], b. Mar. 5,		

	Vol.	Page
BISSELL, (cont.)		
1781; d. Mar. 26, 1782	2	109
George Malmedy, s [Hez[ekia]h & Anne], b. Feb. 9,		
1777; d. Nov. 26, 1777	2	109
Hez[ekia]h, m. Anne **ELDERKIN**, Mar. 18, 1765	2	109
Hezekiah Woodbridge, s. [Hez[ekia]h & Anne], b.		
Nov. 29, 1772	2	109
Katharine, d. [Hez[ekia]h & Anne], b. Jan. 16, 1779	2	109
Mary, d. [Hez[ekia]h & Anne], b. Feb. 9, 1775	2	109
Myra, d. [Hez[ekia]h & Anne], b. July 29, 1787; d.		
Sept 10, 1788	2	109
Theophilas Oliver, s. [Hez]ekia]h & Anne], b. Jan.		
18, 1783	2	109
Wealthian, d. [Hez[ekia]h & Anne], b. Apr. 6, 1768	2	109
BLACK, W[illia]m, s W[illia]m, painter, ae. 25, & Sarah,		
ae. 24, of New York, b. Aug. 10, 1850	4	13
BLACKMAN, Alathea, m. Samuel **FLINT**, 2d, Mar 31, 1835	3	89
Elethe, m. Samuel **FLINT**, b. of Windham, Mar. 31, 1835,		
by Rev. Dexter Bullard	3	172
Alathea, m. Samuel **FLINT**, 2d, Mar. 31, 1835, by Rev.		
Dexter Bullard	3	185
Sarah, m. Samuel **FLINT**, Jan. 9, 1781	2	232
BLANCHER, Alpheas, s. [John & Lois], b Apr 1, 1764	2	12
Betty, d. [John & Lois], b. Oct. 4, 1771	2	12
Clarrie, d. [John & Lois], b. Oct. 16, 1777	2	12
Daniell, s. Sam[ue]ll & Mercy, b. Feb. 15, 1728/9	1	121
Darius, s [John & Lois], b. Mar. 12, 1766	2	12
Elias, s. John, b. June 1, 1757, in Pomfrett	2	12
Jedediah, [twin with Mary], s. Samuel & Mercy, b.		
Jan. 21, 1731/2	1	121
John, s. John & Lois, b. Apr. 16, 1762	2	12
Lois, d. [John & Lois], b. Jan. 11, 1768	2	12
Mary, [twin with Jedediah], d Samuel & Mercy, b Jan		
21, 1731/2	1	121
Mercy, d Samuel & Mercy, b. July 4, 1734	1	121
Percy*, d. John, b. Oct. 7, 1759, in Pomfrett		
(*Perhaps "Perly")	2	12
Sally, d. [John & Lois], b. Jan. 22, 1775	2	12
Sam[ue]l, m. Mercy **RICHARDSON**, Mar. 27, 1727	1	121
Sam[ue]ll, s. Sam[ue]ll & Mercy, b. Nov. 4, 1727	1	121
BLISH, [see also **BLISK** and **BLISS**], Dwight F., s. Francis		
H., manufacturer, ae. 24, & Sally, ae. 22, of		
Willimantic, b Dec 29, 1847	4	1
Hannah Maria, m. Chipman **YOUNG**, b. of Windham, May		
16, 1847, by Rev. Tho[ma]s Dowling, Willimantic	3	235
BLISK, see also **BLISH** and **BLISS**], Henry F., m. Sally		
FREEMAN, b of Willimantic, Oct 13, 1844, by		
C. Noble	3	217

Vol. Page

BLISS, [see also BLISH and BLISK], Elijah Worthington,
  of Sharbourne, N.Y., m. Lucy RIPLEY, of Windham,
  May 24, 1815   3   26
  Henry Worthington, [s. Elijah Worthington & Lucy],
  b Nov. 24, 1821   3   26
BLIVEN, BLIVIN, Alice M., d. John M., machinist, ae. 23,
  & Julia E., ae 22, of Willimantic, b. Apr. 15,
  [1851]   4   12
  Cha[rle]s, mechanic, ae. 23, m. Laura HARRINGTON, ae
  20, May 10, [1850], by Rev. Bromley   4   116
  Cha[rle]s S., machinist, ae. 23, m Louisa HARRINGTON,
  ae. 20, Apr. 28, 1850, by Rev. Bromley   4   115
  Charlotte E , w. Joseph Barber, d. Sept. 29, 1855   4   23-4
  Charlotte Levina, d. [Joseph Barber & Charlotte
  Elizabeth], b. Oct. 4, 1844; d. Sept. 3, 1877   4   23-4
  Elizabeth, ae. 23, m. J.W. FOX, papermaker, ae. 25,
  May [ ], 1850, by Rev. Farnsworth   4   115
  Emma Perry, d. [Joseph Barber & Charlotte Elizabeth],
  b. Oct. 20, 1848; d Oct. 21, 1848   4   23-4
  Harriet Weston, d. [Joseph Barber & Charlotte
  Elizabeth], b Sept. 8, 1851; d. [Sept.] 18,
  [1851]   4   23-4
  J. Vincent, b. Oct. 2, 1835, at Willimantic, Windham   3   180
  John, of Westerly, R.I., m. Emily A. BINGHAM, of
  Windham, May 22, 1834, by Rev. Jesse Fisher   3   169
  John N., merchant, ae. 23, b. Westerly, res. Willi-
  mantic, m Julia E. MAY, ae 22, b. Westerly, res.
  Willimantic, Oct. [ ], 1851, by Rev. J. H.
  Farnsworth   4   117
  Joseph B., m. Charlotte LUMMIS, b. of Windham, July 3,
  1839, by Rev. Windslow Ward   3   189
  Joseph Barber, m. Charlotte Elizabeth LOOMIS, July 3,
  1839, in Willimantic, by Rev. Windsor Ward   4   23-4
  Lotta, [d. Joseph Barber & Charlotte Elizabeth], d.
  Sept. 3, 1877   4   23-4
  Mary W., d. John, farmer, & Emily, b. Jan. 26, 1848   4   3
  Samuel B., s. John, manufacturer, ae 42, of Willim-
  antic, b. Feb. 8, [1850]   4   10
  ——, child of Joseph, of Willimantic, d Oct 20,
  [1848]   4   153
BOAB, Bridget, ae. 22, m. John O'NEIL, blacksmith, ae 30,
  Nov. 29, [1850], by Rev. Brady   4   115
BOLWIN, [see also BALDWIN and BALDEN], Alfred, s [Socrates
  & Amie], b. Oct. 15, 1814   3   91
  Caroline, d. [Socrates & Amie], b. [   ]   3   91
  Edward, s. [Socrates & Amie], b. June 14, 1817   3   91
  Edwin, s. [Socrates & Amie], b Mar. 20, 1813   3   91
  Horace, s. [Socrates & Amie], b. July 11, 1811   3   91

	Vol.	Page
BOLWIN, (cont.)		
Julian, s. [Socrates & Amie], b. May 28, 1819	3	91
Socrates, b. Jan. 11, 1786; m Amie **BINGHAM**, Aug.		
19, 1810	3	91
BOND, Eliza, b. England, res Windham, d. Aug. 11, 1847,		
ae. 20	4	152
Eliza J., s. Henry, ae 26, b. Aug 1, [1849]	4	6
Henry, m. Nancy Ann **JORDAN**, b. of Windham, July 12,		
1846, by Rev. John Cooper, Willimantic	3	229
John, m. Prudence **SAWYER**, Aug. 29, 1759	2	151
Mary Ann, m. Charles **LINCOLN**, b. of Windham, Feb 5,		
1837, by John Baldwin, J.P.	3	181
Mary E., d. Henry, operative, ae. 28, & Lucinda, ae		
25, b. Apr. 30, 1851	4	12
Prudence, [w John], d. Dec. 25, 1769, in the 59th y		
of her age	2	151
Prudence, d Dec 25, in the 58th y. of her age.		
[Entered in the record of Jacob Sawyer's family]	2	157
Rachal, w. John, d. Nov. 27, 1758, in the 69th y. of		
her age	1	128
Robert, Jr., m. Sara A. **FISK**, Aug 11, 1844, by Rev J.		
B. Guild, Willimantic	3	215
Rachel, m. John **DEAN**, Jan. 22, 1745/6* (*correction		
entire entry handwritten at the end of the names		
for **BOND**)	1	266
BOONE, BOON, Enoch G., m. Mary P. **SMITH**, b. of Windham,		
Jan. 31, 1841, by Rev. P.T. Kenney, Willimantic	3	196
Mary M., m. Jonathan A. **TURNER**, Dec. 15, 1844, by Rev.		
Andrew Sharp, Willimantic	3	218
Sarah L., m. Charles **LILLIE**, b. of Willimantic, Feb.		
15, 1846, by H. Slade	3	226
W[illia]m C., mechanic, d. Dec. 4, [1849], ae. 65	4	155
BOOTH, Mary Jane, d. W[illia]m S., ae 42, & Sarah B., ae		
52, b. Sept. 24, [1848]	4	7
BORDEN, Johannah, m Nathaniel **BASSETT**, Dec. 10, 1695	A	14
BOSS, [see also **BASS**], Eunice, d. [1850], ae. 34	4	155
Harry, m. Eunice **BALDWIN**, b. of Windham, May 21, 1837,		
by Rev. Winslow Ward	3	189
Harry, spinner, ae. 37, b Hampton, res Willimantic,		
m. 2d w. Isabella **SESSION**, ae. 28, b. Mansfield,		
res. Willimantic, Mar. 3, 1851, by Rev. S G		
Williams	4	118
Sarah, d. Sept. 24, 1850, ae 61	4	158
BOTTOM, BOTTON, Abba, m. John P. **ALLEN**, b. of Windham,		
Mar. 31, 1833, by Rev. Jesse Fisher	3	165
Appolas, [s. Joshua], b. [ ], 1789	2	193
Asa, m. Elizabeth **FARNAM**, Apr. 7, 1774	2	25
Asa, s. [Asa & Elizabeth], b. Nov. 2, 1791	2	25

	Vol.	Page
BOTTOM, BOTTON, (cont)		
Charles, s. [Asa & Elizabeth], b. Jan. 2, 1775, in		
Norwich	2	25
David, s. [Asa & Elizabeth], b. Feb. 12, 1784	2	25
Elizabeth, d [Asa & Elizabeth], b. Sept. 5, 1788	2	25
Hannah, [d. Joshua], b. [ ], 1787	2	193
Jairus, s. [Asa & Elizabeth], b. Jan 2, 1779	2	25
John, [s. Joshua], b. [ ], 1785	2	193
Joshua, [s Joshua], b. [, 1782	2	193
Joshua, s. [Asa & Elizabeth], b. Sept. 9, 1786	2	25
Lucy, m. Benjamin **BAKER**, Nov. 25, 1773	2	192
Lucy, [d. Joshua], b. [ ], 1791	2	193
Sally, m. Jeremiah **WHITE**, Oct. 1, 1801	3	20
Samuel A., m. Sarah A. **STORRS**, b. of Mansfield, Mar.		
10, 1842, at North Windham, by Elder R V Lyon,		
of Ashford	3	201
Sarah, d. Asa & Eliz[abe]th, b. Nov 18, 1776	2	25
Septa, s. [Asa & Elizabeth], b. Jan. 17, 1795	2	25
Walter, s. [Asa & Elizabeth], b. Oct. 29, 1781	2	25
William Fairwell, [s. Joshua], b. [ ], 1794	2	193
BOURN, Alice, m. Sam[ue]ll **PHILLIPS**, Feb. 20, 1745	1	125
Elizabeth, m. John **PHILLIPS**, Feb. 2, 1737/8	1	180
BOWEN, Amey, m. Col. Eleaz[e]r **FITCH**, [ ]	2	26
Benj[amin], s. George & Elizabeth, d. Jan. 14,		
1741/2	1	50
Cranston, m. Betsey **YOUNG**, Feb. 11, 1824	3	15
Elizabeth, w. George, d. Feb. 6, 1741/2	i	50
Huldah, of Providence, m. Elip[h]alet **DYAR**, May 9,		
1745	1	251
BRADFORD, Hannah, m. Joshua **RIPLEY**, Nov. 28, 1682	A	16
Sophronia A., m Thomas A. **WEDGE**, Dec. 10, 1826, by		
Rev. Jesse Fisher	3	127
BRADLEY, Mary, m. Isaac **STILES**, Apr. 17, 1751	1	313
BRALEY, Amos, m. Amelia **RATHBURN**, Dec. 9, 1829, by Rev.		
Chester Tilden, Willimantic	3	140
BRAMAN, Michael, laborer, ae. 24, m. Catharine **HEVNIA**(?),		
ae. 24, May [ ], [1850], by Rev. Cady	4	114
BRANCH, Desire, m. Ebenezer **MORGAN**, June 24, 1745.		
Certified by Hez[ekiah] Lord	1	254
Mary, m. John **READ**, Mar. 14, 1711	1	45
W[illia]m H., of Willimantic, m. Emily C. **ATWOOD**, of		
Mansfield, Nov. 19, 1844, by Rev. Charles Noble,		
Willimantic	3	218
BRANNARD, BRANARD, Martin B., m. Mary R. **BALDWIN**,		
Nov 12, 1841, by Rev. Andrew Sharp	3	199
——, child of Calvin, laborer, ae. 28, & Sarah, ae.		
22, b. July 11, [1849]	4	5
BRANNON, BRANAN, [see also **BRENHANE**], Catharine, b.		

	Vol.	Page
BRANNON, BRANAN, (cont.)		
Ireland, res. Willimantic, d. Aug. 5, [1849],		
ae 70	4	153
Catharine, d. Aug. 7, [1849], ae. 60	4	155
James, s. John, laborer, ae. 22, & Julia, ae. 24, of		
Willimantic, b. Mar. 31, 1851	4	12
BRENHANE, [see also **BRANNON**], Bridget, ae. 20, m Daniel		
CALLIHAN, laborer, ae. 22, res. Ireland, Jan.		
27, 1848, by Rev. Andrew Sharp	4	111
BRETTAL, Claudius, s. Claudius & Alethea, b. Sept. 15, 1761	2	9
BREWSTER, Abigail, d. [Asa & Ruth], b. Oct. 28, 1775	2	119
Ann, d. Jonah & Joannah, b. Feb. 12, 1748/9	1	243
Asa, m. Ruth **BADGER**, May 28, 1760	2	119
Augustus, s. [John & Mary], b. May 30, 1768	2	62
Benjamin, s. W[illia]m & Esther, b Feb 6, 1753	1	282
Benjamin, m. Susannah **GREENE**, Sept. 8, 1786	2	80
Bethiah, m. William **PARRISH**, May 23, 1738	1	67
Bowen, s. W[illia]m & Esther, b. Apr. 19, 1773	1	282
Chaunc[e]y, s. Joseph, ae. 26, & Sarah J., ae 25, b		
Sept. 5, [1849]	4	7
Cynthia, d. W[illia]m & Esther, b. July 25, 1762	1	282
Cyrus, s. W[illia]m & Esther, b. Aug. 5, 1769	1	282
David, s James & Faith, b. Dec 21, 1753	1	263
Drusilla, m. William **ELY**, Oct. 12, 1766	2	122
Edmond, s. [Asa & Ruth], b. Jan. 12, 1767	2	119
Elijah, s. Jonathan & Mary, b. Mar. 12, 1731	1	172
Elizabeth, d. W[illia]m & Esther, b. Jan 19, 1759	1	282
Erastus, s. [Asa & Ruth], b. Mar. 15, 1773; d. Oct. 15,		
1775	2	119
Esther, d. W[illia]m & Esther, b. Dec. 22, 1756	1	282
Eunice, d. [Jonathan & Eunice], b Jan. 8, 1770	2	135
Ezekiel, s. Jonah & Joannah, b. July 19, 1747	1	243
Ffaith, d. James & Ffaith, b May 30, 1742	1	160
Faith, d. James, d. Sept. 28, 1745	1	263
Faith, d. James & Faith, b. Nov. 18, 1746	1	263
Grace, m. Nathaniel **WALES**, 3d, Feb. 9, 1755	1	326
Hannah, d W[illia]m & Esther, b Oct 26, 1754	1	282
James, m. Ffaith **RIPLEY**, Mar. 15, 1738/9	1	160
James, s. James & Faith, b. Jan 8, 1748/9	1	263
James, Capt., d. Oct. 2, 1755, ae. 40 y. last May	1	263
Jerusha, m. Zebulon **RUDD**, June 4, 1741	1	217
Joan[n]a, d. [Jonathan & Eunice], b. July 29, 1775	2	135
John, m. Mary **DURKEE**, Nov. 6, 1760	2	62
John, s. [John & Mary], b. May 30, 1766	2	62
Jonah, m Jenna **WALDO**, Jan. 25, 1743/4	1	243
Jonah, d. June 3, 1750	1	243
Jonah, s. Jonah & Joannah, b Sept 1, 1750	1	243
Jonathan, s. Jonathan & Mary, b. May 5, 1737	1	172
Jonathan, s. Jonah & Jenna, b. Aug 25, 1744	1	243

	Vol	Page
BREWSTER, (cont.)		
Jonathan, d. Nov. 24, 1753	1	172
Jonathan, m. Eunice **KINGSLEY**, Feb 12, 1767	2	135
Jonathan, s. [Jonathan & Eunice], b. Oct. 17,		
1781	2	135
Lydia, d. James & Ffaith, b. Mar. 18, 1739/40	1	160
Lydia, m. William **RIPLEY**, Jan. 11, 1757, by Rev.		
Eben[eze]r Devotion	2	24
Lydia, d. [Jonathan & Eunice], b Jan. 2, 1779	2	135
Margaret, d. [Benjamin & Susannah], b. Nov. 12,		
1794	2	80
Mary, m. R[e]uben **LILLY**, Feb. 14, 1733/4	1	139
Mary, d. James & Faith, b June 30, 1751	1	263
Mary, d. [John & Mary], b. Sept. 9, 1762	2	62
Mary, w. Dr. John, d. June 4, 1783	2	62
Nathan, s. Jonah & Joannah, b. Jan. 31, 1745/6	1	243
Ohel, s. [Jonathan & Eunice], b. Aug. 28, 1771	2	135
Olive, d. James & Ffaith, b. June 18, 1744	1	160
Oliver, s [Asa & Ruth], b. Mar. 17, 1769	2	119
Oramal, s. [Jonathan & Eunice], b. Oct. 31, 1773	2	135
Orson, s. [Jonathan & Eunice], b. Aug. 30, 1767	2	135
Royal, s. [John & Mary], b. July 13, 1770	2	62
Sidney S., m. Mary **BISHOP**, b. of Willimantic, Nov.		
20, 1837, by Rev. Philo Judson, at Willimantic	3	184
William, s. [John & Mary], b. June 17, 1764	2	62
William, s. [W[illia]m & Esther], b. Jan. 21, 1765	1	282
----, d. [Jonathan & Eunice], b. Jan. 25, 1769; d		
Feb. 9, 1769	2	135
BRIDGMAN, Lydia, m. Andrew **DODGE**, Jan. 27, 1725/6	1	89
BRIGGS, Albert, of Willimantic, d. May 26, 1860, ae. 5	4	161
Albert J., s G.W., manufacturer, ae. 33, b. Nov.		
7, [1849]	4	9
Albert J., of Willimantic, d Aug. 20, 1850, ae. 10 m	4	157
Cha[rle]s W., of Lebanon, m. Delia F. **GAGER**, of		
Franklin, Feb. 8, 1843, by Rev Nathan Wildman,		
Lebanon	3	207
----, child of Geo[rge], machinist, ae 38, of		
Willimantic, b. June 27, [1850]	4	10
BROAD, Hannah, d. [William & Anne], b. July 29, 1778	2	211
William, m. Anne **HEBBARD**, July 28, 1777	2	211
BROADBANK, Mary, ae. 21, b. England, res. Mansfield, m.		
Lafayette **DODGE**, farmer, ae. 25, of Mansfield,		
Jan. 29, [1850], b. E W. Barrows	4	118
BROADSTREET, Andrew, s. John & Rebeckah, b. Mar. 28, 1722	1	99
Mary, d. John & Rebeckah, b. Feb. 16, 1723/4	1	99
Mercy, d. John & Rebeckah, b. Jan. 29, 1726/7	1	99
Susannah, d John & Rebeckah, b. Mar. 16, 1724/5	1	99
BRO[A]DWAY, Thomas, s. Edward, spinner, ae. 24, b. Apr.		

58   BARBOUR COLLECTION

	Vol.	Page

BRO[A]DWAY, (cont.)

26, [1850] — 4, 11

BROMLEY, Calvin B , m. Mary Ann **TYLER**, b. of Windham,
Oct. 11, [1837], by Rev. Otis C. Whiton, of
Scotland Society, Windham — 3, 184

E.M., d. Sept. 20, 1847, ae. 1 m. — 4, 151

----, child of J., d. Aug. 7, [1849], ae 3 1/2 — 4, 153

----, female, of Willimantic, d. Aug. 24, 1860,
ae. 6 m. — 4, 161

----, female, of Willimantic, d. Aug. 25, 1860,
ae. 6 m — 4, 161

BRONTSON, Fanny, of Mass., m. James **ROBINSON**, Jr., Oct.
28, 1810 — 3, 51

BROOKS, Asenath, m. Marvin **LINCOLN**, b. of Windham, Jan.
1, 1837, by Rev. Alfred Burnham — 3, 181

John, of Roxbury, Mass., m. Thankfull L. **DOWNER**, of
Windham, May 4, 1841, by Rev. Nathan Wildman — 3, 197

BROUGHTON, BROUGHTEN, BROGHTON, Abigail, d. John &
Hannah, b. Apr. 15, 1705 — A, 13

Alice, d. Tho[ma]s & Adrea, b. Jan. 27, 1753 — 1, 193

Alice, m. Elias **BINGHAM**, Jr., Mar 15, 1781 — 2, 248

Amos, s. John & Tabatha, b. May 23, 1718 — 1, 26

Atkeson, s. Samuell & Martha, b. Aug 24, 1719 — 1, 24

Delight, d. Thomas & Adrea, b. Apr. 16, 1747 — 1, 186

Elizabeth, d. John & Tabatha, b. Mar. 9, 1720 — 1, 26

Esther, d. John & Hannah, b. Feb. 10, 1699/1700 — A, 13

Esther, m. James **BROWN**, Mar. 10, 1718 — 1, 16

[E]unice, d. Thomas & Adrea, b. Nov. 28, 1739 — 1, 186

Eunice had s. Eleazer **ROBINSON**, b. Jan. 5, 1762 — 2, 9

Hannah, m. Humphrey **BALLARD**, Nov. 6, 1717 — 1, 10

Jemima, d. Tho[ma]s & Adrea, b. Mar. 25, 1751 — 1, 193

Jemime, m. Jacob **SAWYER**, June 22, 1778 — 2, 141

Johannah, d Thomas & Andrea, b. Oct 12, 1741; d.
Mar. 14, 1741 — 1, 186

John, m. Tabithy **KINGSLEY**, May 10, 1709 — 1, 26

John, s. Samuel & Martha, b. Jan. 16, 1717 — 1, 24

John, d Jan. 1, 1730/31, ae. 77 — A, 13

John, m. Anne **LAMPHERE**, Sept. 23, 1745 — 1, 255

Keziah, d. Thomas & Adrea, b. July 20, 1744 — 1, 186

Lydia, d. Thomas & Adrea, b. Sept. 12, 1742 — 1, 186

Margaret, d Sam[ue]ll & Martha, b. Oct. 6, 1724 — 1, 67

Martha, d. Sam[ue]ll & Martha, b. Jan. 15, 1715 — 1, 24

Martha, w. Samuell, d Oct. 24, 1759 — 1, 24

Mary, d. John & Hannah, b. June 17, 1697 — A, 13

Mary, d. John & Hannah, d. Sept. 11, 1707 — 1, 18

Mary, d. John & Tabatha, b. June 12, 1710 — 1, 26

Mary, m. Stephen **WALCOT[T]**, Nov 15, 1737 — 1, 178

Mehitabel, d. John & Hannah, b. Mar. 8, 1703 — A, 13

	Vol	Page
BROUGHTON, BROUGHTEN, BROGHTON, (cont.)		
Phebe, d. John & Tabatha, b. Mar. 15, 1721	1	26
Phebe, m. Ichabod **PALMER,** Nov. 22, 1738	1	174
Prudence, d. Tho[ma]s & Adrea, b. Mar. 5, 1748/9	1	193
Prudence, m. Nathan **SIMONS,** Apr. 15, 1773	2	197
Sam[ue]ll, m. Martha **LILLY,** May 2, 1711	1	24
Samuel, s. Samuell & Martha, b Dec. 15, 1711	1	24
Sarah, d. Samuell & Martha, b. Jan. 27, 1721/22	1	24
Sarah, m. Sam[ue]ll **DEAN,** Dec. 1, 1743	1	229
Tabitha, d. John & Tabatha, b. Jan. 9, 1712	1	26
Thomas, s John & Hannah, b. Aug. 8, 1707	1	17
Thomas, m. Adrea **CRANE,** Nov. 15, 1738	1	186
William, s. Sam[ue]ll & Martha, b. Mar 20, 1727	1	67
Zerviah, d. Sam[ue]ll & Martha, b. July 5, 1729	1	67
BROWN, Abby S., ae. 18, m. Cha[rle]s **LEE,** hatter, ae. 22, Nov. 29, [1850], by Rev. Bromley	4	115
Abigail, d. Stephen & Abigail, b. Nov. 2, 1731	1	135
Abigail, w. Stephen, d. Nov. [ ], 1731	1	135
Abigail, d. Thomas & Elizabeth, b. Feb. 7, 1739/40; d. Feb. 13, 1739/40	1	201
Abigail, d. Tho[ma]s & Sarah, b. Oct. 19, 1755	1	201
Abigail, d. [Henry & Sarah], b. Sept. 16, 1769	2	101
Abigail, m. Jeduthan **SPENCER,** Aug. 13, 1776	2	218
Abigail, m. Eleazer **WELCH,** May 20, 1784	2	14
Albert B , m Marcia T. **DUNHAM,** b. of Windham, Mar 15, 1840, by Rev. Ella Dunham, Willimantic	3	192
Ambrose, s. [Stephen, Jr. & Mary], b Dec. 31, 1775; d. [ ]	2	58
Anne, d. [Henry & Sarah], b. Dec 1, 1780	2	101
Athea, ae. 26, m. Minor **PERKINS,** laborer, ae. 22, Jan. 1, [1850], by Rev. Bromley	4	115
Bridget, ae. 20, m. Pat **RILEY,** laborer, ae. 35, May 10, [1850], by Rev. Brady	4	115
Caroline, d. [Jerome & Lucy], b. Aug. 10, 1803; d. Nov. 22, 1802	3	60
Caroline Elizabeth, d. [Stephen, Jr. & Jerusha], b. Sept. 24, 1808	3	6
Cha[rle]s, s. Sanford, farmer, b. June 26, [1850]	4	11
Cornelia E., m. Horace **CAREY,** June 14, 1847, by Rev. B.M. Alden, Jr.	3	235
Danforth, of Worcester, Mass., m. Jane M. **PARKHURST,** of Scotland, Conn., Sept. 6, 1846, by Rev. Thomas Tallman, of Scotland	3	230
Daniel, s. Tho[ma]s & Sarah, b. Jan. 13, 1748/9	1	201
Dorothy, m. George **MARTIN,** Jr., June 7, 1764	2	109
Edward, m. Jerusha **RIPLEY,** Sept. 9, 1744	1	253
Edward, d. July 28, 1791	1	253
Elijah, s. [Stephen, Jr. & Mary], b. June 10, 1780	2	58

	Vol.	Page
BROWN, (cont.)		
Elizabeth, d. Thomas & Elizabeth, b. Nov. 20, 1741	1	201
Elizabeth, w. Thomas, d Dec. 12, 1742	1	201
Eunice, d. [Stephen, Jr. & Mary], b. Apr. 13, 1761; d. Dec 30, 1764	2	58
Eunice, d. [John & Sybell], b. Mar. 16, 1772	2	110
Auniss, d. [Stephen, Jr. & Mary], b. Apr. 31, 1791	2	58
Fanny, d. [Joseph H. & Martha], b. Jan. 16, 1792	2	58
Geo[rge], farmer, ae 23, m. Maria **BENNETT**, ae. 22, Oct. [1849], by Rev. H. Bromley	4	115
George Washington, s. [Stephen, Jr. & Jerusha], b. Sept. 30, 1798	3	6
Grace, d. [Henry & Sarah], b. July 15, 1776	2	101
Hannah, d. [Stephen, Jr. & Mary], b. July 9, 1765	2	58
Harry, s. [Joseph H. & Martha], b. Dec. 9, 1797	2	58
Henry, m. Sarah **MARTIN**, May 5, 1762	2	101
Henry, s. [Henry & Sarah], b. Apr. 26, 1772	2	101
Henry, m. Sophia **CUSHMAN**, Apr. 15, 1832, by Rev. R.T. Crampton	3	160
Hezekiah P., Jr., m. Cordelia M. **CUMMINGS**, b. of Mansfield, Oct 25, [ ], by Rev. B. M. Alden	3	236
Horace E., m. Eunice **FLINT**, b. of Windham, Nov. 16, 1846, by Rev. John E. Tyler	3	231
Hubbard, s. Edw[ar]d & Jerusha, b. Dec. 11, 1745. "Supposed to have been lost at sea in the year 1779".	1	253
Jabez, of Vernon, N.Y., m. Hannah **BARROWS**, of Willi- mantic, Dec. 27, 1836, by Rev. Philo Judson, at Willimantic	3	180
James, m. Ester **BROUGHTON**, Mar. 10, 1718	1	16
James, s. James & Esther, b. Jan. 29, 1720/21	1	16
Jearam, s. [Stephen, Jr. & Mary], b. Mar. 17, 1778	2	58
Jerome, m. Lucy **SIMONS**, Mar. 14, 1802	3	60
Jerusha, wid. Edward, d. Oct. 8, 1792, in the 88th y. of her age	1	253
John, s. Stephen & Mary, b. June 18, 1742	1	135
John, m. Sybell **BARROWS**, Dec. 22, 1763	2	110
John, s. [John & Sybell], b. Nov. 16, 1769	2	110
John, s. [Henry & Sarah], b. June 14, 1774	2	101
John, Jr., m. Olive **MARTIN**, Oct. 10, 1793	3	19
John, m. Nancy **FITCH**, [Oct.] 13, 1839, by Rev. R Ransom, Willimantic	3	190
John, b. Mansfield, res. Windham, d. Nov. 27, [1851], ae. 57	4	158
John M., m Harriet E. **CAREY**, Aug. 30, 1846, by Rev B.M. Alden, Jr.	3	233
Joseph, Jr., m. Nancy A. **LYMAN**, Nov 2, 1826, by Rev. Cornelius B. Everest	3	74

	Vol.	Page
BROWN, (cont)		
Stephen, s. Stephen & Mary, b. Aug. 27, 1735	1	135
Stephen, Jr m Mary **SHATTUCK**, Dec. 3, 1760	2	58
Stephen, s. [Stephen, Jr. & Mary], b. Sept. 14, 1770	2	58
Stephen, Jr., m. Jerusha **JACOBS**, Dec. 12, 1790	3	6
Susan M., ae. 23, b. Mansfield, res. Chaplin, m Cha[rle]s **MOULTON**, farmer, ae. 24, b. Chaplin, res. Chaplin, Oct 25, 1850, by Rev Knight	4	118
Susannah, d. Tho[ma]s & Sarah, b. Oct. 15, 1750	1	201
Susannah, m. Phinehas **ABBE**, Dec. 2, 1778	2	136
Sylvester, s. [Stephen, Jr. & Jerusha], b. Aug. 24, 1791	3	6
Thomas, m. Sarah **BISHOP**, Oct. 20, 1748	1	201
Thomas, d Jan. 10, 1773	1	201
Thomas, s. [Henry & Sarah], b. Oct. 24, 1778	2	101
Warren, s. [Jerome & Lucy], b. June 1, 1806	3	60
Washington, s. [Joseph H. & Martha], b. Mar. 2, 1794	2	58
William H H., m. Philomela **HALL**, b. of Willimantic, Jan. 25, 1835, by Rev. Philo Judson	3	171
BROWNLEY, BRONLEY, Jane, d. Stephen, operative, ae 36, & Julia, ae. 35, of Willimantic, b. Sept. 14, 1850	4	12
Stephen D., m. Julia **FITCH**, Oct. 12, 1842, by Andrew Sharp	3	204
BUCK, Abby, black, b. Lisbon, res. Willimantic, d. Dec. 2, 1850, ae. 42	4	157
Almira, m. John **DENISON**, Jan. 16, 1831, by Rev. Rich[ar]d F. Cleveland	3	150
Betsey, d. [Daniel & Tryphenia], b. Aug. 24, 1768	2	120
Bradford, s. [Daniel & Tryphenia], b. Feb. 2, 1785	2	120
Bradford, m. Betsey **ROBINSON**, Feb. 11, 1806	3	53
Catherine, d. [Daniel & Tryphenia], b Sept. 2, 1782	2	120
Daniel, m. Tryphenia **MANNING**, Jan. 15, 1766	2	120
Daniel, s. [Daniel & Tryphenia], b. Apr. 4, 1773; d Oct. 14, 1775	2	120
Daniel, s. [Daniel & Tryphenia], b Aug. 15, 1780	2	120
Elizabeth Proby, d. [Henry & Sarah], b. May 17, 1794	2	208
Frederick, s. [Daniel & Tryphenia], b. Apr. 11, 1776	2	120
Henry, s. [Daniel & Tryphenia], b. Nov. 21, 1770	2	120
Henry, m. Sarah **YOUNG**, Nov. 30, 1791	2	208
Julia H., of Windham, m. Alonzo B. **CHAPIN**, of Spring-field, Oct. 16, 1843, by Rev. Giles H. Desham	3	212
Margaret, m. Solomon **FULLER**, b. of Chaplin, Oct. 21, 1835, by Rev. L. H. Corson	3	175
Mary, m. Marvin **FOLLETT**, b. of Windham, Feb. 8, 1829, by Rev. Dennis Platt	3	135
Mary Wetmore, d. [Henry & Sarah], b. Aug. 19, 1792	2	208

	Vol.	Page
BUCK, (cont.)		
Nancy, m. Lucian **BILLINGS**, Mar. 20, 1834, by Rev.		
Roger Bingham	3	168
Polly, d. [Daniel & Tryphenia], b. June 1, 1778	2	120
Polly, m. Thomas **ELDERKIN**, Aug. 27, 1797	3	36
Polly, d. [Bradford & Betsey], b. Sept. 28, 1806	3	53
Sally Young, d. [Henry & Sarah], b. Aug. 30, 1796	2	208
Wealthy, d. [Daniel & Tryphenia], b. Apr. 27, 1766	2	120
Wealthy Miranda, d. [Henry & Sarah], b. Sept. 2, 1798	2	208
——, child of Edwin & Experience, b. May 5, [1848]	4	7
BUCKBANK, John, carpenter, ae 22, m. Mary **CHAPPELL**, ae.		
20, Jan. 30, 1850, by Rev. E.W. Barrows	4	114
John, carpenter, ae 22, m. Mary **CHAPPELL**, ae. 20,		
June 23, [1850], by Rev. Barrows	4	116
BUCKINGHAM, Charles H., of Franklin, m. Olive **FLINT**, of		
Windham, Mar. 31, 1845, by Rev. John H. Tyler	3	220
Mary, m. Solomon **HUNTINGTON**, Oct 31, 1727	1	91
BUEL, W[illia]m, butcher, b. Marlborough, Ct., res.		
Willimantic, d Feb. 15, 1860, ae. 49	4	159-0
BUGBEE, Esther, m. Caleb **JOHNSON**, Jr., Feb. 6, 1745/6	1	258
BULL, Harriet, d. William, butcher, ae. 40, of Willimantic,		
b. Dec. 19, 1849	4	10
Nancy, d Geo[rge] A., blacksmith, ae. 37, & Mary, ae		
41, of Willimantic, b. June 24, [1851]	4	12
BULLEN, Joseph, s. John & Sarah, b. Aug. 30, 1716	1	18
Mary, d. John & Sarah, b. June* 8, 1721 (*Perhaps		
"Jan.")	1	55
BUNDY, BUNDE, Abigail, m. Joel **MANNING**, Mar. 1, 1782	2	194
[E]unice, m. Theodore **PRESTON**, Jan. 29, 1741/2	1	232
——, m. Joel Manning, [ ]	3	32
BURBANK, Mehitable, m. Eben **RIPLEY**, June 11, 1752	2	11
BURDICK, ——, d. Eliza Ann, laborer, ae. 16, b. July		
30, [1851]	4	13
——, s. Eliza Ann, ae. 17, b. July 30, 1851	4	14
BURGE, BURGEE, Eunice, m. Jeduthan **ROGEN**, Oct 4, 1772		
(**ROGERS**?)	2	69
Freelove, m. Amos **GEER**, June 3, 1784	3	11
Lydia, m. Salmon **KINGSLEY**, Jan. 24, 1743	1	240
Martha, m. Sam[ue]ll **STORRS**, Oct. 31, 1700	A	32
Mary, m. George **LILLIE**, Nov. 12, 1751	2	27
Rebeckah, m. Roswell **BILL**, Nov. 20, 1777	2	221
BURGESS, Asa N., m. Mary Ann **PERRY**, b. of Windham, Nov.		
29, 1841, by Rev. Nathan Wildman	3	200
Benjamin, m. Hannah **HOLT**, Mar. 26, 1760; d. Nov. 28,		
1762	2	2
Eliphal, d. [William & Eunice], b. July 24, 1767	2	56
Eunice, d. [William & Eunice], b Oct. 1, 1760	2	56
Freelo[ve], m. Stephen **ABBOT[T]**, Jan. 3, 1750	1	320

	Vol.	Page
BURGESS, (cont.)		
Freelove, d. [William & Eunice], b. July 14, 1763	2	56
Rebeckah, d. [William & Eunice], b. Aug 11, 1758	2	56
Susannah, w. Benj[ami]n, d. Feb. 9, 1767	2	2
William, s. Benj[ami]n & Susannah, b. Mar. 7, 1733/4	1	143
William, m. Eunice **PUTNAM**, Dec. 23, 1756	2	56
William, s. Benj[ami]n & Susannah, b. Mar. 7, 1773	2	2
William, d [ ]	2	56
BURK, Abigail, m. Jonathan **WOLCOTT**, Mar. 1, 1798	3	67
Catharine, m. Joseph **DINISON**, Jan. 8, 1804	3	73
BURLEY, Mary, m. Nathan **HUNTINGTON**, Oct. 2, 1752	1	310
BURNAP, BURNUP, Abigail, d. Jacob, & Abigail, b. May 8, 1739	1	174
Abigail, m. Archippus **PARISH**, Mar. 10, 1763	2	81
Abigail, wid. Jacob, d. Oct. 2, 1796	1	174
Abraham, m. Hannah **ADAMS**, Apr. 12, 1722	1	62
Anne, d. [John & Sarah], b. Sept. 19, 1789	2	59
Beby, d. Jacob & Abigail, b. Feb 8, 1740/41; d July [ ], 1741	1	174
Benj[ami]n, s. Jona[than] & Elizabeth, b Feb. 21, 1753	1	276
Benjamin, m. Elizabeth **COBURN**, Feb. 16, 1775	2	217
Benjamin, s. [Benjamin & Elizabeth], b. Mar. 23, 1777	2	217
Bishop, s. [Benjamin & Elizabeth], b Dec 22, 1779	2	217
Calvin, s. [Jonathan & Elizabeth], b. May 18, 1760	1	276
Catharine, d. [Jonathan & Elizabeth], b. Mar. 31, 1762	1	276
Chloe, d. [Benjamin & Elizabeth], b. Nov. 13, 1775	2	217
Elizabeth, d. Jacob & Abigail, b. Dec. 17, 1741	1	174
Elizabeth, m. John **WARREN**, Mar. 6, 1760	2	108
Esther, d. [Jonathan & Elizabeth], b. Aug. 13, 1767	1	276
Isaac, s. Jacob & Abigail, b. Feb. 10, 1747	1	174
Jacob, m. Abigail **CLARK**, Feb. 3, 1735/6	1	174
Jacob, s. Jacob & Abigail, b. Feb. 20, 1761	1	173
Jacob, d Aug 31, 1771, in the 68th y. of his age	1	173
Jacob, d. Aug. 31, 1771, in the 68th y. of his age	2	1
James, s Jacob & Abigail, b. Feb. 20, 1749; d. Oct. 31, 1754	1	173
James, s. Jacob & Abigail, b. Mar. 21, 1755	1	173
James, s. [Jonathan & Elizabeth], b. Apr. 5, 1756	1	276
John, s. Jacob & Abigail, b. Apr 28, 1757	1	173
John, s. [Jonathan & Elizabeth], b. June 7, 1766; d. Aug. 14, 1768	1	276
John, m. Sarah **AVERY**, Mar. 30, 1786	2	59
Jonathan, m. Elizabeth **AVERELL**, Apr. 21, 1747	1	276
Jonathan, s. Jona[than] & Elizabeth, b. June 8, 1749	1	276
Luther, s. [Jonathan & Elizabeth], b. Feb. 14, 1764	1	276
Lydia, d. Jacob & Abigail, b. Mar. 10, 1742	1	174

	Vol	Page
BURNAP, BURNUP, (cont.)		
Lydia, d. Jacob, d. Feb. 10, 1754	1	173
Martha, d. [Jonathan & Elizabeth], b Mar 6, 1758	1	276
Mary, m. Joshua **LASSAL,** Dec. 14, 1714	1	10
Mary, d. Jacob & Abigail, b. Apr 13, 1737	1	174
Mary, mother of Jacob, d. Dec. [ ], 1741, ae. 80 y.	1	174
Mary, m Samuell **HEB[B]ARD,** Sept. 27, 1748	1	185
Mary, m. John **KINGSLEY,** Feb. 19, 1755	1	322
Mary, m John **KINGSLEY,** Feb. 19, 1755	2	212
Naoma, d. Jacob & Abigail, b. Apr. 11, 1753	1	173
Ruth, d. Jonathan & Elizabeth, b. Feb. 3, 1747/8	1	276
Sybel, d. Jacob & Abigail, b. Apr. 10, 1750	1	173
William, s. [Jonathan & Elizabeth], b. Sept. 17,		
1769	1	276
William, s. Jonathan & Elizabeth, b. Apr. 27, 1751;		
d. July 15, 1769	1	276
BURNES, [see also **BYRNE**], Laura, housekeeper, b Coventry,		
Ct., res. Windham, d. June [ ], [1848]	4	151
W[illia]m, d. Ireland, res. Willimantic, d. June 17,		
[1849], ae. 19	4	153
BURNETT, BURNET, Clarre, d [James], b June 20, 1781	2	243
Isaac, Ensigne, d. Dec. 20, 1740, ae. 47	1	174
Martha, m. Perez **HEB[B]ARD,** Dec. 2, 1784	3	33
Nancy, d. Aug. 22, 1860, ae. 57	4	161
BURNHAM, BURNAM, BURMAN, [see also **BARNAM**], A.,		
child of Elisha, storeman, ae. 40, & [ ],		
ae. 38, b. Mar. [ ], 1848	4	2
Abby, of Windham, m. James **PAYNE,** of Astatan (?), Wis.,		
Sept. 25, 1845, by Rev. J E. Tyler	3	222
Abigail, m. Ichabod **HYDE,** Jan. 24, 1771	2	177
Achsah, m. James **ASHLEY,** Jan. 18, 1816	3	88
Adonijah, s. [Andrew & Jane], b. July 25, 1770	2	36
Adonijah, m. Abigail **FULLER,** Jan. 9, 1800	3	60
Alfred, m. Lois **FULLER,** Mar. 18, 1827, by Elder Elias		
Thorp	3	129
Amanda, m. Charles **LARRABEE,** b. of Windham, Mar. 23,		
1846, by Rev. J.E. Tyler	3	227
Andrew, m. Jane **BENNET,** May 11, 1757	2	36
Andrew, s. Andrew & Jane, b. Jan. 15, 1760	2	36
Anson, s. [Adonijah & Abigail], b. Mar. 24, 1805	3	60
Asa, s. [Adonijah & Abigail], b. Aug. 28, 1802	3	60
Augustus, s. [James & Tammy], b. June 9, 1795	2	50
Charles, s [John & Tryphena], b. Aug. 11, 1791	2	211
Charles Lucius, [s. Lucius & Lorinda], b. Oct. 12,		
1834	3	11
Clirama, d. [Isaac & [E]unice], b. Mar. 24, 1760	1	279
Dorothy, m. William **WEBB,** Oct. 16, 1750	1	313
Dorothy, m. Eliphas **PARISH,** Nov. 1, 1770	2	178

	Vol.	Page
BURNHAM, BURNAM, BURMAN (cont)		
Easter, see under Esther		
Ebenezer, Jr., m. Sibbell **GREENSLITT**, Jan. 29, 1771	2	178
Ebenezer, s. [John & Tryphena], b. June 4, 1780	2	211
Elisha, s. [William & Lois], b. July 17, 1792; d.		
May 19, 1793	3	14
Elisha, 2d, s. [William & Lois], b. Aug. 24, 1794	3	14
Elisha, of Windham, m. Leander **MEACKIM**, of Hebron,		
Sept. 28, 1842, by Rev. A.C. Wheat	3	203
Eliza A., of Windham, m. Frederick T. **COE**, of Ashford,		
Aug. 14, 1843, by Rev. Isaac H. Coe	3	210
Elizabeth, d. [Andrew & Jane], b Dec. 27, 1765	2	36
Elizabeth Lorinda, d. [Lucius & Lorinda], b. Mar. 20,		
1829	3	11
Esther, m. Ens. Nath[anie]l **RUDD**, Apr. 18, 1728		
(Written "Esther **BURMAN**")	1	48
Easter, m. Lemuel **PETTINGILL**, Jan. 26, 1758	2	65
Eunice, d. [Isaac & [E]unice], b. Aug. 26, 1754	1	279
Eunice, m. Andrew **FULLER**, Jan. 18, 1770	2	152
Hannah, m. Nathaniel **COBURN**, Nov. 29, 1764	2	168
Harriet Cornelia, d. [Lucius & Lorinda], b. May 27,		
1837	3	11
Isaac, m. [E]unice **HOLT**, Mar. 22, 1747	1	279
Isaac, s. [Isaac & [E]unice], b. Mar. 8, 1765	1	279
Jacob, s. Isaac & [E]unice, b. Apr. 19, 1748; d. Apr.		
20, 1749	1	279
James, m. Tammy **HOLT**, Nov. 24, 1784	2	50
James, s. [James & Tammy], b. Dec. 12, 1791	2	50
Jesse, s. [John & Tryphena], b. July 12, 1797	2	211
Job., s. Andrew & Jane, b. Feb. 13, 1758	2	36
John, m. Tryphena **ROBINSON**, Oct. 23, 1777	2	211
John, s. [John & Tryphena], b. Aug 9, 1778	2	211
Joseph, m. Luce **BENNET**, Dec. 11, 1740	1	264
Joseph, s. [Isaac & [E]unice], b. Apr. [ ], 1752	1	279
Joshua, m. Abigail **MANARD**, Apr. 19, 1740 (See under		
BARNUM for children)	1	298
Laura, m. Amos **PALMER**, b. of Willimantic Falls, Dec.		
11, 1836, by Rev. Benajah Cook, Jr	3	180
Lorinda, m. Lucius **BURNHAM**, Nov. 16, 1826, at Hampden,		
Conn	3	11
Lucinda, d. [James & Tammy], b. July 31, 1787	2	50
Lucius, s. [William & Lois], b. Dec. 12, 1803	3	14
Lucius, m. Lorinda **BURNHAM**, Nov. 16, 1826, at Hampden,		
Conn.	3	11
Lucy, m. Abner **FOLLETT**, Jr., Feb. 16, 1823, by Rev.		
Cornelius B Everest	3	111
Lucy Ann, m. Wolcott **CAREY**, b. of Windham, Oct. 26,		
1842, by Rev. Isaac H. Coe	3	205

	Vol.	Page
BURNHAM, BURNAM, BURMAN, (cont.)		
Luther, s. [Adonijah & Abigail], b. Nov. 2, 1800	3	60
Luther, m. Marcelia **LINCOLN**, Apr. 29, 1827, by Rev.		
Alfred Burnham	3	130
Lydia, m. Dr. Luther **MANNING**, Jr., Jan 10, 1810	3	61
Lyman, s. [Adonijah & Abigail], b. Apr. 2, 1808	3	60
Maran, s. [William & Lois], b. July 27, 1806	3	14
Maran, s. [William & Lois], b. Jan. 5, 1809	3	14
Marcia, d. Feb. 24, 1848, ae. 48	4	151
Marcy, d. [Andrew & Jane], b. Sept. 29, 1772	2	36
Mariah, ae. 53, m. John **DAY**, ae. 65, of Killingly,		
Mar. 26, [1849], by Rev. Phelps	4	113
Martha Amelia, [d Lucius & Lorinda], b. Nov. 11, 1830	3	11
Mary A., m. Frank M. **LINCOLN**, Nov. 22, 1846, by Rev.		
Isaac H. Coe	3	232
Mary Caroline, d. Geo[rge] & Miranda, b. July 23, 1849	4	7
Nancy, d. [John & Tryphena], b. Nov. 26, 1794	2	211
Parmelia, d. [John & Tryphena], b. Nov. 9, 1782; d.		
Nov. 25, 1782	2	211
Parmelia, d. [John & Tryphena], b. Nov. 22, 1783; d.		
July 12, 1788	2	211
Ralph, s. [John & Tryphena], b. Sept. 6, 1786; d. Nov.		
24, 1787	2	211
Ralph, s. [John & Tryphena], b. Jan. 26, 1789	2	211
Roxwell, s. [Isaac & [E]unice], b. Nov. 15, 1761	1	279
Rufus, m. Talitha **BASS**, Dec. 14, 1797	3	22
Rufus, s. [William & Lois], b. Jan. 25, 1799	3	14
Sarah, d. [Isaac & [E]unice], b. Aug. 21, 1750	1	279
Sarah, m. John **GREENSLITT**, Nov. 20, 1765	2	138
Sarah, d. [Andrew & Jane], b. Sept. 28, 1767	2	36
Sarah, m. John **LEACE**, Nov. 3, 1789	2	60
Septimus, s. [James & Tammy], b. Oct. 17, 1785; d. Nov.		
20, 1787	2	50
Septimus, s. [James & Tammy], b. Sept. 21, 1789	2	50
Sibbell, [w. Ebenezer, Jr.], d. Nov. 30, 1772	2	178
Sophia, m. Charles L. **SMITH**, Sept 11, 1826, by Rev.		
Jesse Fisher	3	127
Sybil, see under Sibbell		
Tryphosa, d. [Isaac & [E]unice], b. Aug. 21, 1767	1	279
Urijah, s. [Ebenezer, Jr. & Sibbell], b. Nov 14, 1772	2	178
William, s. Andrew & Jane, b. Mar. 5, 1764	2	36
William, m Lois **GROW**, Dec. 2, 1790	3	14
William, s. [William & Lois], b. Aug. 20, 1796	3	14
W[illia]m, farmer, ae. 23, m. Ellen **BASS**, ae. 19, Nov.		
24, 1849, by Henry Coe	4	113
W[illia]m, d Apr. 13, 1840, ae. 25 y	4	157
——, twins of [Ebenezer, Jr. & Sibbell], b. Sept. 30,		
1771; d. same day	2	178

	Vol.	Page
BURRELL, Aaron, of Windham, m. Eunice **APES**, of Groton, Dec. 5, 1825, by Rev. Cornelius B. Everest	3	42
BURROWS, Francis, m. Eliza **GRANNIS**, Oct 11, 1805	3	61
Henry Abbe, s. [Francis & Eliza], b. July 28, 1807	3	61
Tryphena, d. [Francis & Eliza], b Feb. 25, 1810	3	61
BURT, Mehitable, m. Ebenezer **BADCO[C]K**, Sept. 14, 1725	1	63
BURY, Seth, s. Joseph & Thankfull, b May 31, 1744	1	243
BUSHNELL, Abigail, m. Joseph **CARY**, July 4, 1711	1	42
Benj[amin] P , m. Fanny **SIMPSON**, Nov. 28, 1839, by Rev. Reuben Ransom	3	191
Harriet, m. Martin **SAFFORD**, Nov. 7, 1831, by Henry Hall, J.P.	3	155
BUTLER, Abigail, d. Thomas & Abigail, b. Jan 10, 1743	1	250
Abigail, w. Thomas, d. Jan. 11, 1743	1	250
Abigail, d. Daniel & Hannah, b. Nov. 12, 1755	1	257
Abigail, m. Joseph **MARTIN**, Jr. June 2, 1774	2	203
Adonijah, s. Dan[ie]ll & Hannah, b. Apr. 15, 1768; d. May 15, 1768	2	163
Benjamin, s Thomas & Abigail, b. Apr 21, 1739	1	250
Daniel, m. Hannah **PARKER**, Dec. 5, 1744	1	257
Daniel, s. Daniel & Hannah, b July 25, 1749; d. June 22, 1750	1	257
Daniel, s. Daniel & Hannah, b. Oct. 8, 1751	1	257
Daniel, m. Hannah **READ**, Feb. 24, 1774	2	204
Daniel, s. [William & Lora], b May 1, 1797	3	48
Deborah, [w. Thomas], d. Mar. 3, 1748/9	1	250
Deborah, d. Tho[ma]s & Thankfull, b. Mar. 22, 1753	1	250
Eleizer, s. Thomas & Abigail, b. Sept. 24, 1736	1	250
Eleazer, m. Lydia **DURKEE**, Jan 11, 1758	2	40
Elisha, s. [William & Lora], b. Aug. 17, 1801	3	48
Fanny, d. [William & Lora], b. Jan. 9, 1794	3	48
Hannah, d. Dan[ie]l & Han[n]ah, b. Dec. 10, 1747; d. June 12, 1750	1	257
Hannah, d. Daniel [& Hannah], b. July 8, 1750; d. Oct. 25, 1750	1	257
Hannah, d. Tho[ma]s & Thankfull, b. Feb. 2, 1756	1	264
Hannah, d [Daniel & Hannah], b. June 22, 1761	1	257
Hipsibeth, d. Dan[ie]l & Han[n]ah, b. Apr. 12, 1746	1	257
Hipsibeth, [d. Daniel & Hannah], d Sept. 30, 1754	1	257
Hisibeth, d. Daniel & Hannah, b. Sept. 19, 1757	1	257
Josiah, s. [Daniel & Hannah], b Jan 20, 1775	2	204
Lois, d. [Eleazer & Lydia], b. Nov. 27, 1758	2	40
Mary, d Tho[ma]s & Thankfull, b Sept 2, 1750	1	250
Mary, d. [Daniel & Hannah], b. Aug. 15, 1763	1	257
Rufus, s. [Daniel & Hannah], b. Jan. 10, 1778	2	204
Sarah, d. Tho[ma]s & Thankfull, b. Mar. 14, 1760	1	264
Stephen, s. [Tho[ma]s, Jr & Eliz[abeth], b. Aug. 28, 1757	2	35

	Vol	Page
BUTLER, (cont.)		
Thankfull, m. Barzillai **HENDEE**, Dec. 18, 1739	1	201
Thomas, m Abigail **CRAFT**, Mar 9, 1732	1	250
Thomas, s. Thomas & Abigail, b. June 23, 1734	1	250
Thomas, m. Deborah **MEACHAM**, Feb 7, 1744/5	1	250
Thomas, m. Thankfull **LUCE**, June 19, 1749	1	250
Tho[ma]s, Jr , m Eliz[abeth] **HOLT**, Jan 19, 1757	2	35
William, s. Tho[ma]s & Thankfull, b. Feb. 27, 1754	1	264
William, s Daniel & Hannah, b Aug. 6, 1759; d Oct. 16, 1760	1	257
William, s. Daniel & Hannah, b. Sept 7, 1765	2	163
William, m. Lora **HUNTINGTON**, Oct. 2, 1788	3	48
William, s. [William & Lora], b Aug 8, 1799	3	48
Zebediah, s. [Tho[ma]s, Jr. & Eliz[abeth], b. Apr. 13, 1759	2	35
BUTTON, Anna, [twin with Deborah], d. Daniell & Anna, b. May 2, 1727	1	104
Betsey, m Miner **ALLEN**, b. of Willimantic Falls, Mar. 8, 1835, by Rev. Benajah Cook	3	175
Daniell, s. Daniell & Anna, b. July 22, 1724	1	104
Deborah, [twin with Anna], d. Daniell & Anna, b. May 2, 1727	1	104
Elizab[et]h, m. Amos **MAINARD**, Apr. 20, 1769	2	144
Thankfull, d. Daniell & Anna, b. Mar. 9, 1731/32	1	104
BYRNE, [see also **BURNES**], Abby, of Windham, m Dea W[illia]m **ROGERS**, of Norwich, [ ], by Rev. John Starrs	3	166
Betsey, d. [John & Anne], b. Nov. 11, 1785, at New London	3	3
Charlotte Gray, d. [Samuel H. & Mary], b. Feb. 28, 1816; d Feb 6, 1819	3	89
George, s. [John & Anne], b. May 7, 1796	3	3
Harriet G , m William **SWIFT**, b of Windham, May 3, 1847, by Rev. J.E. Tyler	3	235
John, b Dec 6, 1760, m. Anne **POWERS**, Nov 14, 1784	3	3
John, s. [John & Anne], b May 26, 1792	3	3
John, s. [Samuel H. & Mary], b. Aug. 31, 1821	3	89
Nancy, d [John & Anne], b Sept 12, 1794; d Oct 16, 1795	3	3
Olive H., m Jeremiah **RIPLEY**, Sept 15, 1825	3	92
Sally, d [John & Anne], b. Mar. 28, 1787	3	3
Samuel Gray, s [Samuel H & Mary], b Nov 11, 1818	3	89
Samuel H., m. Mary **GRAY**, Mar. 5, 1815	3	89
Samuel Hazard, s [John & Anne], b Feb 8, 1789	3	3
CADY, Fidelia, m. Andrew **TRACY**, Mar. 25, [1849], by Mr. Bray	4	113
Kingsbury, of Hartford, m. Rachal M. **MARTIN**, of		

	Vol.	Page
CADY, (cont.)		
Windham, Jan. 10, 1847, by H. Slade	3	233
Lucius, of Canterbury, m Lucy F. **JONES**, of Windham,		
Apr. 3, 1834, by Rev. Jesse Fisher	3	169
Sarah, m. Isaac **BENNET**, Nov. 2, 1763	2	90
Tameezen, m. Capt. Joseph **GINNINGS**, Dec. 22, 1774	2	194
W[illia]m D., of Monson, Mass., m. Lois **AUSTIN**, of		
Canterbury, Oct. 16, 1839, by Rev. Otis C.		
Whiton, of Scotland Society	3	192
CALKINS, CAULKINS, Abigail, m. Ephraim **ROBINS**, May 5,		
1771	2	190
Cook, s. [Nathaniel Skiff & Leah], b. Oct. 26, 1783	2	189
Eunice, d [Nathaniel Skiff & Leah], b. Sept. 21, 1780	2	189
Fanny Caroline, d. [Nathaniel Skiff & Leah], b. July		
9, 1791	2	189
John R.H., b. Dec. 26, 1810	3	52
Lucius, s. [Nathaniel Skiff & Leah], b. Oct. 26, 1787	2	189
Nancy, d. [Nathaniel Skiff & Leah], b. Jan. 26, 1782	2	189
Nathaniel, s [Nathaniel Skiff & Leah], b. Aug. 3, 1778	2	189
Nathaniel Skiff, m. Leah **COOK**, Oct. 12, 1777	2	189
CALLEY, Dennis, s. James, laborer, ae 34, b. Dec. 6, 1850	4	12
CALLIHAN, Daniel, laborer, ae. 22, res. Ireland, m. Bridget		
BRENHANE, ae. 20, Jan 27, 1848, by Rev Andrew		
Sharp	4	111
CALSE, Sarah, d. [Stephen & Elizabeth], b. Oct 12, 1783	2	252
Stephen, m. Elizabeth **TOURS**, Nov. 1, 1782, by Mr.		
Justice Belnap, at Newburgh, N.Y.	2	252
CAMPBELL, Fred, m. Sarah **BABCOCK**, b. of Willimantic, Sept.		
13, 1835, by Rev Philo Judson, at Willimantic	3	174
George, s. Jefferson, stonemason, ae. 44, & Mary, ae.		
37, b. Feb. 25, 1848	4	2
Harriet, d. Frederick, storekeeper, ae. 42, & Sally,		
ae. 40, b Oct 10, 1847	4	2
Harriet O., d. Mar. 17, [1850], ae. 2 1/2	4	155
Jefferson, m Mary A. **PALMER**, b of Windham, Mar 3,		
1839, by Rev. Otis C. Whiton, of Scotland Society	3	189
Mary A , d Aug 29, 1849, ae 34	4	155
William S., s. Peter & Caroline, b. Dec. 29, 1847	4	2
CANADA, CANNADA, Algernon Sidney, s. [Isaac & Meriam], b.		
Dec. 19, 1775	2	50
Alvah, s [Daniel & Ruamah], b. July 26, 1770	2	154
Beky, d. [Daniel & Ruamah], b. Aug. 21, 1773	2	154
Betsey, m Jacob **LINKON**, Nov 26, 1805	3	21
C[h]loe, d. [Daniel & Ruamah], b. Sept. 19, 1766	2	154
Clarinda, d. [Isaac & Meriam], b Oct. 19, 1761	2	60
Clarrissa, d. [David & Lucy], b. Sept. 8, 1786	2	65
Daniel, s. David & Margret, b. June 19, 1730	1	108
Daniel, m. Ruamah **PRESTON**, Nov. 16, 1763	2	154

	Vol	Page
CANADA, CANNADA, (cont.)		
Daniel, s. [Daniel & Ruamah], b. Sept. 24, 1764	2	154
David, m. Margaret **LAMBART**, Nov 5, 1718	1	21
David, s. David & Margaret, b. Mar. 28, 1728	1	21
David, d Nov 18, 1732	1	108
David, m. Deborah **GENNINGS**, Jan. 10, 1749/50	1	301
David, s. David & Deborah, b. Jan. 20, 1755	1	301
David, m. Lucy **WEDGE**, Mar. 11, 1784	2	65
Deborah, d [David & Deborah], b. Aug. 12, 1770	1	301
Elizabeth, d. David & Margaret, b. June 4, 1726	1	21
Elizabeth, m. Ezra **GEERS**, Nov. 7, 1745	1	281
Erastus, s. [David & Lucy], b. Nov. 4, 1788	2	65
Eunice, d. [Isaac & Meriam], b. Jan. 10, 1783	2	60
Festus, s. [David & Lucy], b. Apr. 10, 1800	2	65
Hadassah, d. [David & Deborah], b. May 22, 1775	1	301
Hannah, d. David & Margaret, b. Mar. 30, 1723	1	21
Hannah, m. Robert **COBURN**, Nov. 9, 1726	1	95
Hannah, m. Jonathan **ORMS**, Jan. 17, 1749/50	1	312
Hannah, d. David & Deborah, b. Aug. 20, 1752	1	301
Harriet, d. [Isaac & Meriam], b. Sept. 16, 1769	2	60
Isaac, m. Phebe **LENARD**, Jan. 21, 1729/30	1	94
Isaac, m. Phebe **CONARD**, Jan. 21, 1729/30 (Probably		
"**LENARD**")	1	116
Isaac, s. Isaac & Phebe, b. Dec. 23, 1732	1	116
Isaac, m Meriam **FITCH**, Feb. 26, 1761	2	60
Jerusha, d. [Isaac & Meriam], b. Feb. 25, 1763	2	60
John, s. David & Margret, b Nov. 18, 1732	1	108
John, s. David & Deborah, b. Jan. 8, 1761; d. May 12,		
1765	1	301
John, s. [David & Deborah], b. May 7, 1765	1	301
Leonard, s. [Isaac & Meriam], b. Mar. 3, 1767	2	60
Lucy Fitch, d. [Isaac & Meriam], b. Sept. 20, 1779	2	60
Margaret, d. David & Deborah, b. Sept 8, 1757	1	301
Margaret, m. Elijah **SIMONS**, Apr. 6, 1780	2	232
Nathan, s David & Deborah, b June 24, 1763	1	301
Nath[anie]ll, s. [David & Deborah], b. Feb. 4, 1768	1	301
Pamela, d. [David & Lucy], b Sept 13, 1784	2	65
Peerly, s. [Daniel & Ruamah], b. July 4, 1768	2	154
Rachel, d. [Isaac & Meriam], b. Mar. 20, 1765	2	60
Rufus, s. [David & Lucy], b. Jan. 23, 1791	2	65
Ru[h]amah, d. [Daniel & Ruamah], b Oct. 19, 1775	2	154
Samuel Kennedy, s. Isaac & Phebe, b. Apr. 10, 1739	1	116
Sarah, d. David & Margaret, b. Oct 13, 1720	1	21
Sybel, d. [David & Deborah], b. Oct. 5, 1750	1	301
Sybbel, m Thomas **DEAIUS**, b. of Windham, Mar. 24,		
1774	2	193
Thomas, s. [Isaac & Meriam], b. Nov. 11, 1771	2	60
William, s. [Daniel & Ruamah], b. Oct. 19, 1778	2	154

	Vol.	Page
CANNAWAY, Mary, m. Benjamin **PHILLIPS**, Feb. 2, 1737/8	1	180
CAPEN, Abby D., d. Mar. 2, [1849], ae. 38	4	155
Charles A., s John H., manufacturer, ae. 41, b Nov. 8, [1849]	4	9
Charles H., s. Randall, farmer, ae. 24, & Julia A , b. Oct. 11, [1849]	4	9
John H., m. Abby D. **COOK**, b. of Windham, Feb. 6, 1832, by Rev. R.T. Crampton	3	157
John H., manufacturer, ae. 41, m. Mary J. **FRINK**, ae. 38, July 22, [1850], by Rev. J.H. Farnsworth	4	115
Josephine, d. Aug. 31, 1851, ae 11 m	4	157
Philip A., of Windham, m. Temperance **SCOVILLE**, of Bozrah, Apr. 25, 1841, by Rev. John E. Tyler	3	197
Sarah, b. July 25, 1725, in Dorchester; m. Nath[anie]l **MOSELEY**, Aug. 17, 1742	2	66
William, m. Nancy **AVERY**, b. of Windham, Jan. 25, 1841, by Rev P T. Kenney, Willimantic	3	195
CAPRON, George, of Palmyra, N.Y., m. Tabitha F. **STODDARD**, of Windham, Oct. 20, 1841, by Rev J.E. Tyler	3	198
Josephine, d. Tho[ma]s W., merchant, ae. 28, b. Sept. 22, [1849]	4	9
Sarah, m. Nath[anie]l **MOSELEY**, [ ]	1	249
CAPWELL, Joseph, s. Allen, farmer, ae. 28, & Mary **MENNIREAU***, ae. 20, b. May 29, 1848 (*Probably "**CAPWELL**")	4	4
CARD, Averell H.C., m. Rebecca **NICHOLS**, Dec. 24, 1826, by Rev Jesse Fisher	3	126
Laura A., m. William **WITTER**, b. of Windham, Apr. 5, 1846, by Rev. B.M. Alden	3	228
CAREY, [see under **CARY** and **COREY**]		
CARGILL, W[illia]m L., s W[illia]m P , dresser tender, ae 29, & Maria, ae. 27, of Willimantic, b. Nov. 5, 1850	4	12
CARPENTER, Allen, farmer, ae. 20, of Windham, m. Mary M. **MUNSEAR**, ae 23, Mar. 12, 1847, by Alfred Brewster	4	111
Elizabeth, d. John & Sarah, b. May 16, 1733	1	107
Huldah, m. John **SILSBURY**, May 12, 1746	1	257
Lois, m. Zeb[ulon] **PALMER**, Apr. 25, 1746	1	258
Orra, m. Sarah **GURLEY**, b. of Willimantic, Sept 24, 1838, at Willimantic, by Rev. Philo Judson	3	187
Sarah, d. John & Sarah, b Mar. 20, 1730	1	107
——, child of John D., ae. 37, & Catharine, ae. 38, b. Nov 25, [1848]	4	6
CARR, Jane, d. Jan. [1849], ae. 34	4	155
John, laborer, ae 29, m Margaret **MURR[A]Y**, ae. 25, Jan. 29, [1850], by Rev. Brady	4	115
Mary J., d. John, laborer, ae 29, of Willimantic, b Jan. [1850]	4	10

	Vol.	Page
CARY, CAREY, (cont)		
Allatheah, d. [William, Jr. & Irena], b. Dec. 9, 1773	2	169
Alatheah, d. [John & Sybel], b. Aug. 14, 1812	3	74
Alfred, s. [Jonathan & Martha], b. June 29, 1781	2	145
Ann, m. Nathan **DENISON**, Apr. 1, 1736	1	153
Ann B., d. Dwight, farmer, ae 30, & Susan B., ae 28, b. Feb. 24, 1848	4	4
Anna, d. Benajah & Deborah, b. Feb. 4, 1745/6; d. June 19, 1763	1	223
Anne, d. [Phinehas & Mary], b. Oct. 26, 1771	2	151
Anson, s. [Nath[anie]l & Jerusha], b. Mar. 15, 1762	2	20
Benajah, s. John & Hannah, b. Mar. 7, 1718/9	1	17
Benajah, m. Deborah **PERKINS**, Feb. 11, 1741/2	1	223
Benjamin, s. Jabez & Hannah, b. Jan. 25, 1741/2; d. same day	1	63
Betsey, d. [Luther & Rispah], b Dec. 7, 1797	3	32
C[h]loe, d. [William, Jr. & Irena], b. Jan. 20, 1776	2	169
Clarissa, m. Benjamin **BIBBENS**, Dec. 31, 1789	3	23
Daniel, s. Seth & Mary, b. Feb. 22, 1733/4	1	68
Daniel Allen, s. [Luther & Rispah], b. June 12, 1795	3	32
Deborah, d. Benajah & Deb[orah], b. Feb. 17, 1747/8	1	223
Diantha, d. [Ezekiel & Zerviah], b. July 14, 1768	2	97
Dianthe, m. Andrew **BAKER**, Oct. 24, 1806	3	37
Dumont Ripley, s. [Waldo & Freelove], b Nov 21, 1819	3	75
Dwight, s. [Sanford & Caroline], b. Feb. 24, 1817	3	77
Dwight, m. Susan **BASS**, b. of Windham, Nov. 15, 1843, by Rev. H. Slade	3	212
Eleizer, Jr., m Jerusha **WALES**, Jan. 29, 1735/6	1	156
Eleizer, s. Eleizer, Jr. & Jerusha, b. Aug 7, 1737	1	156
Elizer, Jr., d. July 24, 1754	1	156
Eleazer, Dea., d. July 28, 1754, in the 76th y. of his age	1	52
Eleazer, s. [William & Eunice], b Apr. 23, 1757	2	32
Eleazer, m. Wid. Marcy **FITCH**, July 19, 1767	2	136
Eleazer, m. Matilda **PARISH**, Nov. 21, 1792	3	34
Eleazer, m. Lois **ROBINSON**, Apr. 13, [1835?], by Rev. Roger Bingham	3	173
Elijah, s. [William, Jr. & Irena], b. Oct. 4, 1780	2	169
Elisha, s. [Phinehas & Mary], b. Aug 12, 1775	2	151
Elizabeth, d. Joseph & Hannah, b. Apr. 14, 1700	A	11
Elizabeth, m. Seth **PALMER**, Apr. 19, 1720	1	5
Elizabeth, d. Seth & Mary, b. Apr. 25, 1727	1	68
Elizabeth, m. Joshua **WHITTE**, July 4, 1728	1	97
Ellen, washwoman, b. Ireland, res. Willimantic, d. Jan. 1, 1860, ae. 65	4	159-0
Elliott, s. [William & Eunice], b. Dec. 28, 1763	2	32

	Vol	Page

CARY, CAREY, (cont.)

Erving, see under Irving

Easther, d. [John, Jr. & Rebeckah], b. May 14, 1756;
d. July 16, 1777 — 1, 209

Esther B., of Windham, m. Havilah **MOREY**, of Bozrah-
ville, Aug. 30, 1836, by Rev. Jesse Fisher — 3, 179

Eunice, [triplet with Will[ia]m & James], d. William
& Eunice], b. Jan. 4, 1767 — 2, 32

Eunice, d. [Roger & Eunice], b. Dec [ ], 1787 — 2, 239

Ezekiel, s. John, Jr. & Rebeckah, b. Dec. 7, 1741 — 1, 209

Ezekiel, m. Zerviah **SKIFF**, Mar. 15, 1764 — 2, 97

Ezekiel, d. May 14, 1782 — 2, 97

Ezekiel W., m. Harriet M. **FIELD**, May 16, 1830, by Rev
Roger Bingham — 3, 145

Fanny, d. [Jonathan & Martha], b. July 26, 1791 — 2, 145

Fidelia, w. Waldo, d. Dec. 22, 1813 — 3, 67

Frances H , m. Borden P **BARRETT**, b. of Windham, Oct
22, [1837], by Rev. Otis C. Whiton, of Scotland
Society, Windham — 3, 184

Frances Harriet, d. [John & Sybel], b. Nov. 12, 1810 — 3, 74

Frank W , s. Dwight, farmer, b. June 9, [1850] — 4, 11

Frederick, s. [Jonathan & Martha], b. Feb. 14, 1786 — 2, 145

George Thomas, operative, of Willimantic, d. Apr. 20,
1860, ae. 18 — 4, 159-0

Giles, s. [John], b. May 10, 1821 — 3, 98

Hannah, d. Joseph & Hannah, b. Mar. 7, 1693 — A, 11

Hannah, d. Jabez & Hannah, b July 6, 1725; d. Dec. 25,
1741 — 1, 63

Hannah, d. Seth & Mary, b. June 25, 1739 — 1, 150

Hannah, d. John & Rebeckah, b. Nov. 15, 1745 — 1, 209

Hannah, d. Joseph & Phebe, b. July 11, 1748 — 1, 269

Harriet, d. [Eleazer & Matilda], b. Dec. 29, 1799 — 3, 34

Harriet, m. Oliver **LATHROP**, Feb. 23, 1817 — 3, 63

Harriet E., m. John M. **BROWN**, Aug. 30, 1846, by Rev.
B.M. Alden, Jr. — 3, 233

Henry Hudson, s. [Sanford & Caroline], b. July 2, 1814 — 3, 77

Henry Lucius, s [Eleazer & Marcy], b. Oct. 18, 1769 — 2, 136

Horace, m. Cornelia E. **BROWN**, June 14, 1847, by Rev.
B.M. Alden, Jr. — 3, 235

Irena, d. [Nath[anie]l & Jerusha], b Oct. 2, 1757; d.
Jan 7, 1777 — 2, 20

Irene, d. [Jonathan & Martha], b. Aug. 17, 1777 — 2, 145

Erving Wales, s. John, b. Oct. 22, 1815 — 3, 98

Jabis, s. Joseph & Hannah, b. July 12, 1691 — A, 11

Jabez, m. Hannah **HANDY**, Nov 15, 1722 — 1, 63

Jabez, s. Jabez & Hannah, b. July 30, 1727 — 1, 63

James, s. Benajah & Deborah, b Nov. 27, 1750 — 1, 223

James, [triplet with Eunice & Will[ia]m, s. [William &

	Vol.	Page
CARY, CAREY, (cont.)		
Eunice], b. Jan. 4, 1767; d. Jan. 9, 1767	2	32
Jerusha, d. Eleizer, Jr. & Jerusha, b. Jan. 14, 1755	1	156
Jerusha*, m Capt. James **LAS[S]AL**, Jan. 19, 1758 (*Mrs.)	2	40
Jerusha, m. R[e]uben **WELCH**, May 1, 1776	2	219
Joannah, d. Seth & Mary, b. Dec. 28, 1731	1	68
Joannah, m. John **FRAME**, Aug. 16, 1757	1	265
Joannah, m. John **FRAME**, Aug. 16, 1757	1	309
John, s. Joseph & Hannah, b. June 25, 1695	A	11
John, s. John & Hannah, b. Apr. 12, 1717	1	17
John, m. Hannah **THOMASTON**, Jan 15, 1726	1	13
John, Jr., m. Rebeckah **RUDD**, Nov. 13, 1740	1	209
John, s [Ezekiel & Zerviah], b. June 7, 1766	2	97
John, d. Jan. 11, 1776, in the 81st y. of his age	1	128
John, s. John, Jr. & Rebeckah, b. Aug. 9, 1751; d. Sept. 22, 1776, at East Chester, ae. 25 y.	1	209
John, s. [William, Jr & Irena], b. Mar. 18, 1778	2	169
John, m. Sybel **GAGER**, Feb. 11, 1810	3	74
John, paper maker, b. Ireland, res. Willimantic, d Jan. 1, 1849, ae. 35	4	153
Jonathan, s. John & Hannah, b. Aug. 24, 1729; d. Feb. 10, 1742/3	1	13
Jonathan, s. John, Jr. & Rebeck[ah], b June 5, 1749	1	209
Jonathan, m. Martha **HURLBUTT**, Sept. 21, 1775	2	145
Jonathan, s. [Jonathan & Martha], b. Nov 26, 1783	2	145
Joseph, s. Joseph & Hannah, b. May 3, 1689	A	11
Joseph, m. Abigail **BUSHNELL**, July 4, 1711	1	42
Joseph, s. Joseph & Abigail, d. Dec. 10, 1715	1	42
Joseph, Lieut , d Jan. 10, 1721/22	1	54
Joseph, Lt., d. June 29, 1722	A	11
Joseph, s. John & Hannah, b. Aug. 4, 1723	1	17
Joseph, s. Jabez & Hannah, b. Sept. 28, 1723	1	63
Joseph, m Phebe **MARSH**, July 1, 1747	1	269
Joseph, m. Abigail **HEB[B]ARD**, Dec. 10, 1747	1	202
Joseph, s. [Nath[anie]l & Jerusha], b. Aug. 19, 1760	2	20
Joseph, s. [Roger & Eunice], b. July 4, 1783	2	239
Josiah, s. Seth & Mary, b. Jan 18, 1729/30	1	68
Julia, d. [Waldo & Fedelia], b. Nov. 1, 1796; d. Dec. 21, 1813	3	67
Julia E., of Windham, m. William **WRIGHT**, of Chatham, Aug 12, 1838, by Rev. John E. Tyler	3	187
Julia Elizabeth, d. [Waldo & Freelove], b. Oct. 10, 1816	3	75
June, d. [Sanford & Caroline], b. Sept. 8, 1823	3	77
Lavina, d. [Nath[anie]l & Jerusha], b. Sept. 23, 1765	2	20
Lucia, d. [Eleazer & Matilda], b. Jan. 2, 1794; d.		

	Vol.	Page
CARY, CAREY, (cont)		
Feb. 27, 1795	3	34
Lucia, d. [Eleazer & Matilda], b June 16, 1795	3	34
Lucina W., of Windham, m. George H. **GRISWOLD,** of		
Milford, Mass., Mar. 29, 1847, by Rev. Z.W		
Howe	3	235
Lucius Henry, m. Mary **HARRISS,** Sept 27, 1812	3	72
Lucretia S., m. Collins **YORK,** Dec. 8, 1822	3	109
Luther, m. Rispah **ALLEN,** Nov. 11, 1792	3	32
Lydia, m. David **RIPLEY,** Mar. 21, 1720	1	61
Lydia, d. Eleizer & Jerusha, b. Dec. 26, 1751; d.		
Sept. 17, 1754	1	156
Lydia, wid. Dea. Eleazar, d. June 12, 1761, in the		
75th y. of her age	1	52
Lydia, d. [William & Eunice], b. Feb. 19, 1769; d		
May 12, 1770	2	32
Lydia, m. John **WEARE*,** July 13, 1823 (*Perhaps		
"WEAVE[R]")	3	113
Marcy, wid. Dea. Joseph, d Jan. 23, 1740/41, ae.		
about 84 y.	1	150
Marcy, m. John **BACKER,** Dec. 17, 1744	1	247
Margarette M., d. Mar. 21, 1848, ae. 2	4	152
Martha, d. Benajah & Deb[orah], b. May 18, 1755; d.		
June 2, 1762	1	223
Martha, d. [Nath[anie]l & Jerusha], b. Jan. 13, 1764	2	20
Marthaette, d. Mar. 18, 1848, ae. 2	4	152
Mary, d. Seth & Mary, b. Oct. 20, 1723	1	68
Mary, d. John & Hannah, b. Oct. 21, 1725	1	17
Mary, m. Gideon **BINGHAM,** June 13, 1734	1	145
Mary, d. Jabez & Hannah, b. Nov. 17, 1739	1	63
Mary, m. James **MOLTEN,** Jr., July 2, 1745	2	49
Mary, d. [William & Eunice], b. Feb. 20, 1759	2	32
Mary, d. [Phinehas & Mary], b. Mar. 20, 1770	2	151
Mary L., m. George **BASS,** b. of Windham, Apr. 9, 1840,		
by Rev. Tubal Wakefield	3	193
Mercy, m. John **BAKER,** Jr., Dec. 17, 1744	2	144
Moses, s. Seth & Mary, b. Dec 15, 1740	1	150
Nancy, d. [Luther & Rispah], b. Oct. 10, 1800	3	32
Nathan, s. Eleizer, Jr. & Jerusha, b Jan. 17, 1739/40	1	156
Nath[anie]l, s. Jabez & Hannah, b. Oct. 23, 1729	1	63
Nath[anie]ll, s. John & Hannah, b. Nov 1, 1731	1	128
Nath[anie]l, m. Jerusha **DOWNER,** Jan. 6, 1757	2	20
Nath[anie]l, Capt., d. Nov. 22, 1776	2	20
Nathaniel, s. [Roger & Eunice], b. Sept. 16, 1780	2	239
Olivet, s. [William & Eunice], b Oct 20, 1761	2	32
Phebe, d. John & Hannah, b. July 22, 1721	1	17
Phebe, d. John & Hannah, d Oct. 10, 1738	1	128
Phebe, d. John, Jr. & Rebeckah, b. Nov. 17, 1743	1	209

	Vol.	Page
CARY, CAREY, (cont)		
Phebe, d. Joseph & Phebe, b. Jan. 6, 1749/50	1	269
Philomela, d. [Nath[anie]l & Jerusha], b Mar. 2, 1767	2	20
Philomela, m. Isaiah **GEER**, Nov. 27, 1788	2	116
Pheneas, s. Eleizer & Jerusha, b. Oct. 7, 1746	1	156
Phinehas, m. Mary **HURLBUTT**, Feb. 26, 1769	2	151
Polly, d. [Luther & Rispah], b. Feb. 21, 1793	3	32
Prudence, d. Eleizer & Jerusha, b Mar. 26, 1749; d July [ ], 1750	1	156
Ralph, s. [Jonathan & Martha], b. June 2, 1788	2	145
Rebeckah, d. John, Jr. & Rebeckah, b. Dec. 29, 1753	1	209
Rebeckah, m. Walter **BAKER**, Dec. 21, 1775	2	98
Roger, s. [Nath[anie]l & Jerusha], b. Jan. 7, 1759	2	20
Roger, m. Eunice **PARISH**, Jan. 27, 1780	2	239
Sam[ue]ll, s. John & Hannah, b. June 13, 1734	1	128
Sanford, m. Caroline **TRACY**, May 16, 1811	3	77
Sarah, d. Eliazar & Lydia, b. Apr. 10, 1720	1	52
Sarah, [d Eliazar & Lydia], d. May 4, 1726	1	52
Seth, s. Joseph & Hannah, b. July 23, 1697	A	11
Seth, m Mary **HIB[B]ARD**, Apr 17, 1722	1	68
Seth, s. Seth & Mary, b. July 12, 1725	1	68
Seth, m. Hannah **GENNINGS**, Apr 9, 1752	1	314
Sophronia, d. Waldo & Fedelia, b. Oct. 14, 1794	3	67
Susannah, d. Eleizer, Jr. & Jerusha, b. Apr 22, 1742	1	156
Susannah, d. Eleizer & Jerusha, d. July 25, 1754	1	156
Susannah, d. William & Eunice, b Dec. 11, 1754	1	323
Susannah, d. [William & Eunice], b. Dec. 11, 1754	2	32
Susannah, d. W[illia]m & Eunice, d. July 30, 1757	2	32
Susannah, d. [William & Eunice], b. Apr. 14, 1771	2	32
Thomas Hurlbutt, s. [Jonathan & Martha], b. July 8, 1779	2	145
Thomas Storrs, s. [Eleazer & Matilda], b. Mar. 21, 1792	3	34
Waldo, s. [Ezekiel & Zerviah], b. Apr. 13, 1772	2	97
Waldo, m. Freelove **DUMONT**, Dec. 8, 1814	3	75
Waldo, s. [Ezekiel W. & Harriet M.], b. Jan. 27, 1833	3	145
William, s Eliazar & Lydia, b. Mar. 4, 1721/22; d May 2, 1726	1	52
William, s. John & Hannah, b. Dec 12, 1727; d. Dec 9, 1742/3	1	13
William, s. Eliazar & Lydia, b Oct 28, 1729	1	52
William, s. John, Jr. & Rebec[kah], b. Oct. 25, 1747	1	209
William, m. Eunice **WEBB**, Feb. 19, 1754	1	323
William, m. Eunice **WEBB**, Feb. 19, 1754	2	32
Will[ia]m, [triplet with Eunice & James], s. [William & Eunice], b. Jan. 4, 1767	2	32
William, Jr , m Irena **MANNING**, May 16, 1771	2	169
William, s. [William, Jr. & Irena], b. Dec. 10, 1782	2	169

	Vol.	Page
CARY, CAREY, (cont)		
W[illia]m H., s. Horace, ae. 29, & Emeline, ae. 22,		
b. Nov. 2, [1848]	4	8
Wolcott, s. [Sanford & Caroline], b. June 29, 1819	3	77
Wolcott, m. Lucy Ann **BURNHAM**, b. of Windham, Oct. 26,		
1842, by Rev. Isaac H. Coe	3	205
Zerviah, d. Joseph & Abigail, b. May 22, 1718	1	42
Zillah, d. Benajah & Deborah, b. Dec. 5, 1743	1	223
Zillah, m. James **LUCE**, Jr., May 13, 1762	2	89
——, child of Horace, carpenter, ae. 34, b. Mar.		
[ ], 1850	4	11
CASE, Abigail, d. Barnard & Abigail, b. Apr. 8, 1720	1	32
Abigail, w. Barnard, d. Apr. 10, 1722	1	32
Alexander W[illia]m, s. [Pardon P. & Priscelia], b.		
Dec. 29, 1813	3	103
Almira, d. [Pardon P. & Priscelia], b. Mar. 25, 1822	3	103
Angeline, d. [Pardon P. & Priscelia], b. Oct. 19, 1829	3	103
Barnard, s. John & Desire, b. Oct. 29, 1688, in		
Martha's Vineyard; m. Abigail **RUDD**, May 22, 1712	1	32
Barnard, m. Abigail **CLARKE**, Oct. 17, 1722	1	32
Benj[ami]n, s. John & Desire, b Dec. 4, 1703, at		
Martha's Vineyard	1	95
Benj[ami]n, m. Mary **MANNING**, Apr. 25, 1728	1	95
Elizabeth, m. Benj[amin] **DUFFEY**, Feb. 23, 1715/16	1	50
Elizabeth, d. Barnard & Abigail, b. Jan. 31, 1725/6	1	32
Geo[rge] Seaman, s. [Pardon P. & Priscelia], b. Feb.		
14, 1818	3	103
Gilbert Mott Lafayette, s. [Pardon P. & Priscelia], b.		
Sept. 22, 1824	3	103
Hester, d. Seth & Sarah, b. Sept. 26, 1737	1	187
Ichabod, s. Seth & Sarah, b. Apr. 10, 1741	1	187
Jonathan, s. Barnard & Abigail, b. May 16, 1718	1	32
Joseph, s. Barnard & Abigail, b. Apr. 26, 1714; d.		
Apr. 29, 1714	1	32
Josephine, d. [Pardon P. & Priscelia], b Feb. 24, 1827	3	103
Luce, d. William & Luce, b. Nov. 22, 1739	1	187
Lydia, d. [Pardon P. & Priscelia], b. Feb 7, 1820	3	103
Mary Ann, d. [Pardon P. & Priscelia], b. Apr. 30, 1816	3	103
Mercy, m Eleazer **ALLYN**, Mar. 8, 1717/18	1	22
Pardon P., m. Priscelia **WESTGATE**, Mar. 28, 1812	3	103
Pardon Phipps, s. [Pardon P. & Priscelia], b. Nov. 6,		
1831	3	103
Seth, s. Barnard & Abigail, b. Jan. 26, 1712/13	1	32
Seth, m. Sarah **GRIGGS**, Nov. 11, 1736	1	187
Susannah, d. Seth & Sarah, b. Apr 15, 1739	1	187
William, s. Barnard & Abigail, b. Feb. 7, 1715/16	1	32
William, m. Luce **TRACY**, Nov. 11, 1736	1	187
William, s. William & Luce, b. Nov. 25, 1737	1	187

80 BARBOUR COLLECTION

	Vol.	Page
CASEY, Roswell Randal[l], m. Mary **ROBINSON**, July 22, 1828, by Hon. John Baldwin	3	130
CASHMAN, Susannah, m Robert **HOWE**, [ ], 1805	3	38
CASSAL, CASSALL, CASAL, CASSEL, [see under **LASSELL**]		
CASWELL, Ezra, m Mercy **WILLSON**, b of Windham, Jan 27, 1833, by John Baldwin, J.P.	3	163
Joshua B., of North Stonington, m. Louisa **ABBE**, of Windham, Oct. 12, 1823	3	22
CATLIN, Geo[rge] Smith, m Mary M **TINGSLEY**, b of Windham, June 12, 1834, by Rev. L.H. Corson	3	171
Mary Mayne, d. Oct 17, 1849, ae 33	4	156
CAULKINS, [see under **CALKINS**]		
CAYEL, W[illia]m C , painter, ae. 27, m Maria **BATES**, ae 25, Oct 22, [1849], by A. Sharp	4	115
CHAFFEE, Zelotes E , m Hannah S **SNELL**, Mar 8, 1841, by Rev. Andrew Sharpe, Willimantic	3	196
CHAMBERLAIN, Abigail, [w. John], d Aug 14, 1776	2	142
Ann, m. Dan **HARDOCK**, Mar. 31, 1762	2	83
John, of Amenia Precinth, York State, m. Abigail [**ABBOTT**], wid. of Abiel, [ ]	2	142
CHAMPION, John, of Leroy, N.Y , m Myra **WHITE**, of Windham, May 5, 1834, by L.S. Corson, Rector	3	170
CHAMPLAIN, Christopher, m Miranda **AVERY**, Feb 24, 1831, by Rev. Roger Bingham	3	151
Christopher G , of Willimantic Falls, m Amanda A. **PARKER**, of Mansfield, Aug. 8, 1836, by Rev. B. Cook, Jr., at Willimantic Falls	3	178
Isaac, m. Betsey E. **BILL**, Nov. 24, 1845, by Andrew Sharp	3	225
John N., m Florinda **AYERS**, Oct. 10, 1816	3	33
Maria, of Lebanon, m. Andrew **PHILLIP**, of Hebron, June 6, 1847, by Rev Daniel Dorchester, Willimantic	3	235
Noyes Edwin, s. [John N. & Florinda], b. Sept. 22, 1817	3	33
Prudence, of Windham, m Lester **WEBSTER**, of Rochester, N.Y., Jan. 24, 1830, by Rev. Richard F. Cleveland	3	140
CHANDLER, Mehitable, m. Paul **HOLT**, Jan. 20, 1741/2	1	228
CHAPIN, Alonzo B , of Springfield, m Julia H **BUCK**, of Windham, Oct. 16, 1843, by Rev. Giles H. Desham	3	212
CHAPLIN, CHAPLAIN, Daniel, s Joseph & Sarah, b. July 10, 1761	2	10
Eunice, m Zebediah **TRACY**, Jan 10, 1788	2	222
John, s. Joseph & Sarah, b. Nov. 30, 1756	2	10
Joseph, s. Joseph & Sarah, b Apr 10, 1750	2	10
Joseph, m. Sarah **STEDMAN**, June 13, 1754	1	317
Joseph, s. Joseph & Sarah, b Apr 10, 1755	1	317
Joseph, m. Sarah **STEDMAN**, [ ]	2	10
Nath[anie]ll, s Joseph & Sarah, b Mar 20, 1759, d Jan. 6, 1763	2	10

	Vol.	Page
CHAPLIN, CHAPLAIN, (cont.)		
Nath[anie]ll, s. [Joseph & Sarah], b. May 1, 1764	2	10
Sarah, d. [Joseph & Sarah], b. Oct. 22, 1766	2	10
Sarah, m. James **HOWARD**, Dec. 4, 1782	2	249
CHAPMAN, Almira, m. Cyrus **ELLSWORTH**, b. of Windham,		
Mar. 23, 1837, by Stowell Lincoln, J.P.	3	188
Deborah, m. Israel **ROBINSON**, Feb. 21, 1748/9	1	81
Elijah, of Tolland, m. Emily C. **SWIFT**, of Windham,		
June 23, 1830, by Rev. Richard F. Cleveland	3	146
Ezra, m. Betsey **BAILEY**, May 1, 1796	3	54
Harriet, d. [Ezra & Betsey], b. May 9, 1801	3	54
Hezekiah, m. Chloe **FLINT**, June 4, 1778	2	240
Mary, d. [Ezra & Betsey], b. Jan. 25, 1797	3	54
William Ward, s. [Ezra & Betsey], b. Feb. 27, 1799	3	54
——, child of Lafayette, lawyer, ae. 26, & Mary J.,		
ae. 19, b. July 9, 1848	4	2
CHAPPELL, Caroline, d. W[illia]m, laborer, ae. 51, of		
Willimantic, b. Dec. 21, 1849	4	10
Charles W., of Lebanon, m. Hannah A. **LAMB**, of Franklin,		
Oct. 3, 1837, by Rev. B. Cook, Jr., at Willimantic		
Falls	3	183
Edward, m. Abigail **LYON**, Sept. 25, 1831, by Rev.		
Rich[ar]d F. Cleveland	3	154
Elizabeth, of Willimantic, d. July 9, [1849], ae. 2	4	153
Frank N., s. Geo[rge], laborer, ae. 48, & Sarah, ae.		
45, b. Jan. 12, 1851	4	14
George, m. Sally **CRANDALL**, Nov. 5, 1826, by Rev. Roger		
Bingham	3	142
Harriet, m. Alvin **TRIMM**, Apr. 11, 1830, by Rev. Roger		
Bingham	3	144
Mary, ae. 20, m. John **BUCKBANK**, carpenter, ae. 22, Jan.		
30, 1850, by Rev. E.W. Barrows	4	114
Mary, ae. 20, m. John **BUCKBANK**, carpenter, ae. 22, June		
23, [1850], by Rev. Barrows	4	116
Susan, m. Simeon T. **GAVITT**, Feb. 26, 1832, by Rev.		
Roger Bingham	3	158
Susan, ae. 22, m. Edwin **GROW**, press tender, ae. 19, of		
Mansfield, Apr. 22, 1849, by Mr. Robinson	4	113
William, m. Betsey **CRANDALL**, Nov. 15, 1829, by Rev		
Roger Bingham	3	141
CHASE, Anne, of Plainfield, m. Levi **ALLEN**, of Windham, Dec.		
11, 1828, by Rev. Jesse Fisher	3	134
CHEDLE, Benj[ami]n, m. Sarah **GREENSLIT**, Jan. 19, 1762	2	114
Benj[amin], s. [Benj[ami]n & Sarah], b. May 17, 1762	2	114
Martha, d. [Benj[ami]n & Sarah], b Mar. 17, 1764	2	114
CHEETS, Alexander, s. [Ce[a]sar & Electa], b. Dec. 25, 1796	2	71
Ce[a]sar, m. Electa **RAND**, Nov 14, 1793	2	71
Ceasar, d. July [ ], 1816	2	71

	Vol.	Page
CHEETS, (cont.)		
Charlotte, d. [Ce[a]sar & Electa], b. Aug. 27,		
1800	2	71
Electa, d. [Ce[a]sar & Electa], b. Jan. 13, 1815;		
d June 23, 1815	2	71
Hannah, d. [Ce[a]sar & Electa], b. Feb. 10, 1803	2	71
Joseph, s. [Ce[a]sar & Electa], b. Aug. 26, 1805	2	71
Louisa, d. [Ce[a]sar & Electa], b. Mar. 1, 1811;		
d. July 17, 1812	2	71
Susan, d. [Ce[a]sar & Electa], b. Mar. 26, 1808	2	71
Susan, m. Jacob **HEELMES**, of Greenfield, N Y., Dec.		
4, 1823 (Perhaps "Jacob **HOLMES**"?)	3	14
Wealthy, d. [Ce[a]sar & Electa], b. June 29, 1794	2	71
Wealthy, m. Thomas **FOSTER**, July 18, 1814	2	71
CHENEY, CHEENEY, Adeline, d. Marvin, ae 35, & Adeline,		
ae. 33, b. Mar. 15, 1848	4	3
Bethiah, m Benj[ami]n **FLINT**, Apr. 12, 1770	2	191
Edward, s. [Joseph H. & Abigail], b. Mar. 29, 1822	3	104
Edward, painter, ae. 28, of Windham, m Emeline		
FRANKLYN, ae. 22, July 3, 1848, by Mr. Catharn	4	111
Joseph H., m. Abigail **BADCOCK**, Oct. 12, 1818	3	104
Mary C., b. Norwich, res. Willimantic, d. Feb. 20,		
[1849], ae. 22	4	153
Nathan, s. [Joseph H. & Abigail], b. Sept. 7, 1819	3	104
Susan S , of Willimantic, m Lucius W. **ELLSWORTH**, of		
East Windham, Sept. 21, 1845, by Rev. Z. Baker,		
Willimantic	3	222
Susan Sumner, d. [Joseph H. & Abigail], b. Apr. 12,		
1824	3	104
William, shoemaker, ae. 28, of Windham, m. Lucretia		
ELLSWORTH, ae 22, Jan. 25, 1848, by Rilander		
Sharp	4	111
CHESTER, Frederick Manning, s. [Jonathan & Polly], b. Aug		
2, 1811	3	90
Jonathan, m. Polly **MANNING**, Oct 6, 1810	3	90
Lemuel A., of Hartford, m. Lucretia **ALLEN**, of Windham,		
Nov. 1, 1841, by Rev. Joseph Avery, Jr., of Lisbon	3	199
Lucy, m. Shubael **ABBE**, Jan. 26, 1774	2	229
Lucy, m. Lewis **MANNING**, Feb 18, 1812	3	63
Nancy, m. William T. **DORRANCE**, Mar. 18, 1827, by Rev.		
Cornelius B. Everest	3	126
CHILD, CHILDS, Clarissa, m. William C. **SMITH**, Feb. 19, 1812,		
by Isaac Ticknor, J.P.	3	42
Edward, laborer, ae. 24, b. Woodstock, res. Rockville,		
m. Mariah **CHILDS**, operative, ae. 19, b. Willington,		
res. Rockville, Apr. 6, 1851, by Rev. Miner	4	117
Jerusha, ae. 17, m. George **SHARP**, operative, ae. 19,		
Aug. 10, 1848	4	111

	Vol	Page

CHILD, CHILDS, (cont)

Julia, operative, ae. 26, b. Keene, N.H., res.
Albany, m. Leman **OSBORN**, engraver, ae. 31, res
Albany, Jan. 13, 1851, by Rev. Miner — 4 — 117

Mariah, operative, ae. 19, b Willington, res.
Rockville, m. Edward **CHILDS**, laborer, ae. 24, b.
Woodstock, res Rockville, Apr. 6, 1851, by Rev.
Miner — 4 — 117

CHITTENDEN, Samuel, of Boston, m. Sally B. **DAVIS,** of
Windham, Apr. 7, 1833, by Rev. Alva Gregory — 3 — 164

CHOATE, Anne, of Chebacco in Ipswich, m. George **MARTIN**, Jr ,
Nov. 29, 1706 — 1 — 116

CHURCH, Bethiah, m. Andrew **ROBINSON**, Apr. 16, 1820 — 3 — 28

Elizabeth, m. Henry **BASS**, Dec. 10, 1735 — 1 — 147

Eunice, m Isaac **ABBE**, Mar. [ ], 1753 — 2 — 74

Lydia, m. Andrew **ROBINSON**, Mar. 17, 1813; d. Oct. 12,
1819 — 3 — 28

Mason, ae. 46, b. Mansfield, res. Chaplin, m. 2d w.
Julia **POLK**, ae. 37, Feb. 13, 1848, by W[illia]m
Lamb — 4 — 112

Michael, laborer, b. Chaplin, res. Windham, d. Apr. 22,
1849, ae. 49 — 4 — 154

Phebe, m Luther **KIDDER**, Sept. 25, 1789 — 2 — 51

Zalmon A., of Mansfield, m. Nancy **HUNTINGTON**, of
Windham, Mar. 27, 1842, by Rev. J. E Tyler — 3 — 201

CLACK, [see also **CLARK**], Sarah Louisa, m. John Thompson
READ, b. of Washington, D.C., [Oct. 8, 1845], by
Rev. Abel Nichols — 3 — 224

CLAP[P], Anne, d. Thomas & Mary, b May 13, 1734; d. Apr.
[ ], 1735 — 1 — 88

Jonathan, m. Ann **HIB[B]ARD**, Feb 26, 1728/9 — 1 — 106

Mary, d. Thomas & Mary, b. Apr. 21, 1729 — 1 — 88

Mary, w. Thomas, d. Aug. 9, 1736 — 1 — 88

Sophronia, of South Hampton, Mass., m. Calvin **ROBINSON**,
of Windham, Apr. 1, 1832, by Rev Anson S. Atwood,
Mansfield — 3 — 159

Temperance, d. Thomas & Mary, b. Apr. 21, 1731; d June
4, 1731 — 1 — 88

Temperance, d Thomas & Mary, b. Apr. 29, 1732 — 1 — 88

Thomas, m. Mary **WHITING**, Nov. 23, 1727 — 1 — 88

CLARK, CLARKE, [see also **CLACK**], Abel, s [Amos &
Abigail], b. Oct. 18, 1756 — 2 — 31

Abigail, m Barnard **CASE**, Oct 17, 1722 — 1 — 32

Abigail, m. Jacob **BURNAP**, Feb. 3, 1735/6 — 1 — 174

Abigail, d. [Amos & Abigail], b. Apr. 11, 1758 — 2 — 31

Abner Oliver, s. [Amos], b. Aug. 29, 1786 — 2 — 256

Alfred, s. Lem[ue]ll, b. Aug 30, 1780 — 2 — 168

Allen, m. Elisa **READ**, b. of Windham, Nov. 15, 1842, by

	Vol.	Page
CLARK, CLARKE, (cont)		
Rev. J.E. Tyler	3	205
Amanda, d [Dr John & Abigail], b. Oct. 12, 1794	2	240
Amasa, s. [Jeremiah & Hannah], b. Aug. 11, 1764	1	316
Amie, [w. Jabez], d. July 2, 1838, at Utica, N Y	2	212
Amos, s. John & Ruth, b. Sept. 19, 1729	1	53
Amos, m. Abigail **UTLEY**, Oct 23, 1755	2	31
Amos, s. [Amos & Abigail], b. May 6, 1762	2	31
Amos, m. [ ], Jan. [ ], 1785	2	256
Amy, see under Amie		
Anne, d. Nathan & Abigail, b. July 15, 1758	2	45
Anne, d. [Amos & Abigail], b. Dec. 23, 1767	2	31
Anne, d. [Jabez & Amie], b. Apr. 6, 1792	2	212
Bertha, b. Norwich, res Willimantic, d May [ ],		
1849, ae. 10	4	153
Caleb, s. Nathan & Abigail, b. July 14, 1760	2	45
Charles, s. [Jabez & Amie], b. Mar. 6, 1788; d. Oct.		
22, 1788	2	212
Charlotte E., m. Samuel H. **PERKINS**, [ ]	3	120
Charlotte Elderkin, d [Jabez & Amie], b. Oct. 30,		
1798	2	212
Chester, m. Julia **CUSTUS**, Oct. 24, 1831, by Rev.		
Rich[ar]d F. Cleveland	3	155
Cynthia, b. Lebanon, res. Windham, d Apr. 10, 1848,		
ae. 77	4	151
Daniel, s. John & Ruth, b. Nov. 27, 1722	1	53
Daniel, s. John & Elizabeth, b. Oct. 17, 1750	1	280
Daniel, s. [Amos & Abigail], b. Feb. 22, 1760	2	31
Daniel, m. Mehetable **SLATE**, Oct. 19, 1780	2	250
Daniel, s. [Daniel & Mehetable], b. Aug 28, 1781	2	250
David, s. John & Ruth, b. July 14, 1724	1	53
David, s. [Amos & Abigail], b. Apr 2, 1764	2	31
David, s. [Jeremiah, Jr. & Hannah], b. Apr. 26, 1781	2	213
Ebenezer, s [John & Elizabeth], b. June 7, 1754	1	280
Ebenezer, m. Eunice **MARTIN**, Jan. 12, 1778	2	218
Ebenezer, s. [Ebenezer & Eunice], b Feb. 17, 1779	2	218
Edward, s. [Jabez & Amie], b. Feb. 24, 1796	2	212
Edward, m. Harriet **PERKINS**, May 28, 1823	3	113
Elijah, m. Emily **PALMER**, b. of Windham, [ ],		
1833, by Rev. John Storrs	3	167
Eliza, ae. 22, m. John **SPENCER**, shoemaker, ae. 27, b.		
Montville, res. New Jersey, Mar. 15, 1848, by		
Tho[ma]s Dowling	4	111
Eliza, of Mansfield, m. [ ] **WHITON**, of		
Willington, [ ], by Rev. Henry Greenslit	3	227
Eliza Ann, m. W[illia]m T. **ESSEX**, of Windham, Nov 10,		
1839, by Rev. Otis C. Whiton, of Scotland Society	3	192
Eliza J., b. Chapin, res. Willimantic, d Feb. [ ],		

	Vol.	Page
CLARK, CLARKE, (cont.)		
1851, ae. 24	4	157
Elizabeth, d [Jeremiah & Hannah], b Apr. 7, 1762	1	316
Elizabeth, d. [Jabez & Amie], b. Oct. 29, 1789	2	212
Elizabeth, d. of Jabez, m. Walter **KING**, of Utica,		
N.Y., Nov. 13, 1810; d. [ ], at Utica,		
[N.Y.]	3	24
Esther, m. James **GALLUP**, Sept. 15, 1822	3	106
Eunice, d. [Jeremiah & Hannah], b. Feb. 17, 1754	1	316
Eunice, m. Eliphalet **MARTIN**, May 15, 1799	2	87
Eunice, m. Samuel **FLINT**, Jan. [ ], 1812	3	19
Fanny, d. [Stephen & Hannah], b. Sept. 22, 1756	1	238
George Montame, b. Oct. 5, 1844	3	90
Hannah, d. John & Ruth, b. Dec. 14, 1727	1	53
Hannah, d. [Stephen & Hannah], b. Feb. 22, 1749/50	1	238
Hannah, m. Jonathan **KINGSBURY**, Jan. 9, 1750/51	1	309
Hannah, m Jon[a]th[an] **KINGSBURY**, Jan 9, 1754 [sic]		
[1751]	2	127
Hannah, d. [Jeremiah & Hannah], b. Dec. 29, 1757	1	316
Hannah, d. [Jeremiah, Jr. & Hannah], b. Aug. 20, 1774	2	213
Hannah, m. Phinehas **FLINT**, Feb. 24, 1780	2	207
Hannah, d. [Dr. John & Abigail], b. Sept. 14, 1797	2	240
Henry, s. [Jeremiah, Jr. & Hannah], b Mar. 31, 1785	2	213
Henry V., s. Edward, lawyer, ae. 53, & Harriet, ae. 48,		
b. Oct. 2, [1849]	4	9
Isaac, s. John & Ruth, b. June 18, 1736	1	53
Isaac, Gen , of Castleton, m. Anne **TEMPLE**, of Windham,		
Mar. 25, 1790	2	59
Isaac, of Vermont, m. Amie **TEMPLE**, wid. William, late		
of Boston, & d. Col. Eleazer **FITCH**, Mar. 29, 1790	3	43
Isaac, of Canterbury, m. Susan **TRACY**, of Windham, Apr		
12, 1826	3	121
Jabez, m. Amie **ELDERKIN**, Apr. 4, 1787	2	212
Jabez, d. Nov. 11, 1836	2	212
James W., of South Kingston, R.I., m. Susan **HEB[B]ARD**,		
of Windham, Jan. 11, 1829, by Tho[ma]s Gray, J.P.	3	134
Jeremiah, s. John & Ruth, b. Mar. 16, 1726	1	53
Jeremiah, m. Hannah **GOOLD**, May 3, 1750	1	316
Jeremiah, s. [Jeremiah & Hannah], b. Mar. 14, 1751	1	316
Jeremiah, Jr., m. Hannah **FLINT**, Feb. 18, 1773	2	213
Jeremiah, s. [Jeremiah, Jr. & Hannah], b Nov 15, 1776	2	213
Jerusha, d. [Jabez & Amie], b. Mar. 26, 1794	2	212
John, s. John & Ruth, b. Aug. 14, 1719	1	53
John, m. Elizabeth **PARKER**, Nov. 12, 1747	1	280
John, m. Jerusha **HUNTINGTON**, Nov 7, 1751	1	311
John, s. John & Elizabeth, b. Mar. 16, 1756; d. June		
19, 1771	1	280
John, Dr., m. Abigail **MOSELEY**, Dec. 13, 1781	2	240

	Vol.	Page

CLARK, CLARKE, (cont.)

John Moseley, s. [Dr. John & Abigail], b. July 2,
1788; d. Oct. 22, 1788 — 2 — 240
Jonathan, s. John & Ruth, b. Sept. 12, 1734 — 1 — 53
Jonathan, m. Martha **FARNAM,** Apr. 6, 1759 — 2 — 50
Jonathan, s. [Jeremiah & Hannah], b. Sept. 17, 1773 — 1 — 316
Lias, d. Aug. 20, 1849, ae. 63 — 4 — 154
Louice, d. [Stephen & Hannah], b. Feb. 25, 1765 — 1 — 238
Lucian, m. Hannah S. **BABCOCK,** Nov. 17, 1836, by Rev
William A. Curtis — 3 — 181
Lucinda, m. Stephen **ROOT,** Nov. 24, 1835, by Rev. S R.
Cook, at Willimantic — 3 — 175
Lydia, m. Arastus **STANDISH,** Nov. 24, 1835, by Rev
S.R. Cook, at Willimantic, Windham — 3 — 176
Mary, d. John & Ruth, b. Aug. 16, 1731; d July 29,
1753 — 1 — 53
Mary, d. [Jeremiah & Hannah], b. June 19, 1752 — 1 — 316
Mary, d. [Dr. John & Abigail], b. June 17, 1792 — 2 — 240
Mary, m. Franklin **COBB,** Oct. 28, 1845, at Willimantic,
by John Cooper — 3 — 224
Mary, m. Jabez N. **LINCOLN,** Jan. 4, 1846, by Rev. Abel
Nichols — 3 — 226
Mary L., m. Joseph S. **BACKUS,** painter, of Chaplin, Aug.
1, 1848, by Rev. John Tyler — 4 — 112
Mehetable, d. [Daniel & Mehetable], b. Oct. 24, 1783 — 2 — 250
Nabby, d. [Dr. John & Abigail], b. Nov. 30, 1789; d.
Aug. 22, 1807 — 2 — 240
Nancy P., m. W[illia]m **WALES,** b. of Windham, Apr. 8,
1837, by Rev. W[illia]m A. Curtis — 3 — 182
Nathan, s. [Amos & Abigail], b. Dec. 30, 1769 — 2 — 31
Olive, d. Stephen & Hannah, b. Mar. 14, 1762 — 1 — 238
Oliver, s. [Amos & Abigail], b. Mar. 20, 1766 — 2 — 31
Polly, d. [Jeremiah, Jr. & Hannah], b. May 26, 1779 — 2 — 213
Ruth, d. Stephen & Hannah, b. May 21, 1746 — 1 — 238
Sally, d. [Jeremiah, Jr. & Hannah], b. Feb 2, 1783 — 2 — 213
Sarah, d. John & Elizabeth, b. Apr. 1, 1752 — 1 — 280
Sarah, d. John, d. July 3, 1778 — 1 — 280
Sarah, of Willimantic, m. Rufus **BROWN,** of Coventry,
Feb. 22, 1834, by Rev. Alva Gregory — 3 — 168
Sarah Louisa, m. John Thompson **READ,** b. of Washington,
D.C., Oct. 8, 1845, by Rev. Abel Nichols — 3 — 224
Silas F., m. Elizabeth L. **WOODWORTH,** June 9, 1842, by
Rev. Andrew Sharp — 3 — 202
Sophia, d. [Dr. John & Abigail], b. Sept. 24, 1782 — 2 — 240
Stephen, s. John & Ruth, b. May 16, 1721 — 1 — 53
Stephen, m. Hannah **DORKEE,** Feb. 1, 1742/3 — 1 — 238
Stephen, s. Stephen & Hannah, b. July 25, 1744 — 1 — 238
Stephen, s. Stephen & Hannah, b. Jan. 28, 1752 — 1 — 238

	Vol	Page
CLARK, CLARKE, (cont)		
Susannah, d. [Jeremiah & Hannah], b. Mar. 22, 1756	1	316
Theodore, shoemaker, b. Chaplin, res Windham, d		
Aug. 2, 1848, ae. 27	4	151
Titus, s John & Elizabeth, b. Jan 25, 1758	1	280
Tryphena, d. [Dr. John & Abigail], b. May 17, 1786	2	240
William, s. Stephen & Hannah, b. Feb. 7, 1754	1	238
W[illia]m, s. W[illia]m, farmer, ae. 31, & Mercy		
Ann, ae. 34, b Oct. 5, [1849]	4	9
William Moseley, s. [Dr. John & Abigail], b. Mar.		
23, 1803	2	240
Zaccheas D., of Springfield, Mass., m. Mary **NACY**,		
of Willimantic, Nov. 16, 1845, by B.M. Alden,		
Willimantic	3	224
Zerviah, m. Luther **BACKUS**, [ ], 1795	3	4
CLEVELAND, Abel, s. [Moses & Tabitha], b. Jan. 25, 1770	2	99
Abigail, m. Samuel **HOVEY**, Sept. 29, 1763	2	98
Abigail, m. Sam[ue]l **HOVEY**, Dec. 29, 1764	2	104
Abijah Perkins, s. [Mason & Eliza Maria], b. Dec		
8, 1822	3	97
Ann, w Benjamin, d Oct. 21, 1754	1	160
Ann, d. Benj[amin], Jr. & Mary, b. May 9, 1755	2	38
Ann, d. [Richard F. & Ann], b. July 9, 1830	3	153
Asa, s. [Moses & Tabitha], b. Mar. 13, 1763	2	99
Benjamin, s. Benjamin & Ann, b. Aug 30, 1733	1	160
Benjamin, Jr., m. Mary **ELDERKIN**, Jr., Feb. 20,		
1754	2	38
Charlotte, of Mansfield, m. Nathaniel **WEBB**, Jr.		
of Windham, Apr 15, 1792	2	129
C[h]loe, d. Benjamin & Ann, b. May 30, 1744	1	160
C[h]loe, m. William **YERRINGTON**, Sept. 28, 1763	2	102
Clark, s. [Moses & Tabitha], b. Mar. 12, 1768	2	99
Dyer, s. [Moses & Tabitha], b. Oct. 22, 1772	2	99
Easther, see under Esther		
Eliphaz, s. [Moses & Tabitha], b. Feb. 13, 1761	2	99
Esther, m. John **PALMER**, May 18, 1749	1	294
Easther, d. [Moses & Tabitha], b. June 7, 1765	2	99
Franklin, s. [Eph[rai]m & Mary], b. Aug 13, 1779	2	9
James, s. [Moses & Tabitha], b. Dec. 14, 1775	2	99
Joanna, m. Robert **HEB[B]ARD**, May 12, 1760	1	115
Martin Luther, s. [Benj[amin], Jr. & Mary], b. Jan.		
23, 1759	2	38
Mary, d. [Benj[amin], Jr. & Mary], b. May 16, 1761	2	38
Mary, d. Eph[rai]m & Mary, b. Mar 30, 1768	2	9
Mason, m. Eliza Maria **PERKINS**, of Lisbon, Feb. 19,		
1822	3	97
Moses, s. Benjamin & Ann, b. July 20, 1736	1	160
Moses, m. Tabitha **SPENCER**, May 31, 1759	2	99

88 BARBOUR COLLECTION

	Vol.	Page
CLEVELAND, (cont.)		
Olive, d. [Benj[amin], Jr. & Mary], b. Jan. 23, 1763	2	38
Parmelia, m. Samuel **GRIFFIN**, Jr., May 31, 1782	2	255a
Phocelenia, d. Benj[amin], Jr. & Mary, b. Feb. 14, 1757	2	38
Richard F., m. Ann **NEAL**, Sept. 16, 1829, by Rev. Nelson Read, in the Methodist Episcopal Church, Baltimore, Md.	3	153
William Neal, s. [Richard F. & Ann], b. Apr. 7, 1832	3	153
CLIFT, Hannah, m. Henry **WEBB**, June 1, 1794	2	55
Hannah, m Henry **WEBB**, June 1, 1794	3	2
Lucia, m. Nathan **KINNE**, Mar. 24, 1824, by Rev. Cornelius B. Everest	3	118
Nancy, m. Nathan **BASS**, Mar. 27, 1822	3	103
COBB, COBBES, Edward T., of Lebanon, m. Huldah **SPENCER**, of Willimantic, Apr. 19, 1846, by Jacob Bakin	3	229
Franklin B., m. Mary **CLARK**, Oct. 28, 1845, at Willimantic, by John Cooper	3	224
H.A , ae. 21, m. A.D. **PORTER**, laborer, ae. 20, Nov. 29, [1848], by Mr. Bray	4	113
Michael, operative, ae 21, b East Lyme, res. Windham, m. Mary A. **STORY**, ae. 19, Jan. 7, 1848, by Abel Nelson	4	111
Sarah, d. [William & Huldah], b. Oct. 30, 1772, in Norwich	2	176
William, m. Huldah **NORTON**, Dec. 22, 1768	2	176
William, s. [William & Huldah], b. Sept. 18, 1769, in Norwich	2	176
W[illia]m, operative, ae. 19, m. S.E **IDEY**, ae. 21, July 9, 1848	4	111
COBURN, [see also **COLBON** and **COLBURN**], Abigail, d [Edward & Prudence], b. Dec. 15, 1754	1	258
Amanda, d. Jonathan, b. Mar. 8, 1802	3	49
Amaziah, s. [Zebadiah & Eliz[abeth], b. Jan. 14, 1768	2	21
Asa, s. [Cornelius & Abigail], b. Oct. 25, 1763; d Feb. 8, 1764	2	35
Chloe, d [Zebadiah & Eliz[abeth], b. May 8, 1760	2	21
Clarrissa, d. [Cornelius & Abigail], b. Nov. 3, 1770; d. Aug. 18, 1776	2	35
Clyma, d. [Hezekiah & Mary], b. Feb. 2, 1786	2	221
Cornelius, s. Sam[ue]ll & Elizabeth, b. Jan. 1, 1733/4	1	89
Cornelius, m. Abigail **GREENSLIT**, Apr. 20, 1757	2	35
Cornelius, m Rachal **ROBINSON**, Apr. 5, 1780	2	227
Daniel, s. [Robert & Mary], b. May 19, 1759	1	297
Dinah, d. Sam[ue]ll & Eliza[beth], b. Sept 20, 1746	1	235
Doetty, d. [Robert & Mary], b. Oct. 27, 1764	1	297
Edward, s Sam[ue]ll & Elizabeth, b. Apr 5, 1730	1	89
Edward, m. Prudence **WEEKLY**, Oct. 17, 1751	1	258

	Vol.	Page
COBURN, (cont.)		
Edward, s. Edward & Prudence, b. Oct. 9, 1757	1	258
Edward, m. Sarah **WYMAN**, Feb 22, 1774	2	60
Eleazer, s. [Nathaniel & Hannah], b. Aug. 19, 1778	2	168
Elip, s. Cornelius & Abigail, b. Jan. 2, 1758	2	35
Eliphalet, s. [Hezekiah & Mary], b. Apr. 25, 1781	2	221
Eliphalet, m. Lois **TRACY**, Oct. 28, 1781	2	153
Eliphaz, s. [Cornelius & Abigail], b. Apr. 11, 1767; d. [ ]	2	35
Eliphaz, [s. Cornelius & Abigail], d. Aug. 16, 1771	2	35
Elizabeth, d. [Zebadiah & Eliz[abeth], b. Nov 12, 1754	2	21
Elizabeth, d. [Cornelius & Abigail], b. Dec 29, 1764	2	35
Elizabeth, m Benjamin **BURNAP**, Feb 16, 1775	2	217
Esther, d. [Hezekiah & Mary], b. Oct. 24, 1783	2	221
Eunice, d. [Cornelius & Abigail], b. Aug. 4, 1760	2	35
George, s. Sam[ue]ll & Elizabeth, b. Sept. 4, 1737	1	89
Hannah, d. Robert & Mary, b. Oct. 11, 1750	1	297
Hannah, m. Oliver **ROGERS**, Feb. 11, 1770	2	211
Hezekiah, m. Mary **BILL**, Jan. 17, 1771	2	221
Ithamer, s. [Robert & Mary], b. May 1, 1768	1	297
Joel, s. [Hezekiah & Mary], b. Sept 22, 1774	2	221
Jonathan, s. [Robert & Mary], b. Mar. 22, 1765	1	297
Jonathan, s. [Hezekiah & Mary], b. Sept 17, 1771; d. Aug. 18, 1772	2	221
Jonathan, s. [Hezekiah & Mary], b. Dec. 3, 1772	2	221
Judeth, d. Sam[ue]ll & Judeth, b. Nov. 17, 1751	1	308
Laura, d. Sylvanus, b. Mar. 31, 1803	2	161
Lucy, d. [Edward & Prudence], b. Oct. 9, 1763	1	258
Lydia, d. [Edward & Prudence], b Oct. 19, 1769	1	258
Martha, d. [Nathaniel & Hannah], b. May 27, 1771	2	168
Mary, d. Sam[ue]ll & Elizabeth, b. Apr [ ], 1740	1	89
Mary, d. [Robert & Mary], b. Nov. 25, 1752	1	297
Mary, m. William **NEFF**, Aug. 28, 1761	2	72
Mary, w. [Robert], d. Dec. 27, 1769	1	297
Mary, d [Hezekiah & Mary], b. Oct. 26, 1778	2	221
Nabby, d. [Cornelius & Abigail], b. Oct. 22, 1780	2	35
Nathaniel, s. Sam[ue]ll & Elizabeth, b. Apr. 28, 1742	1	88
Nathaniel, s. [Zebadiah & Eliz[abeth], b. Dec. 8, 1762	2	21
Nathaniel, m. Hannah **BURNAM**, Nov. 29, 1764	2	168
Olive, d. [Zebadiah & Eliz[abeth], b. Aug. 1, 1758	2	21
Olivia, d. [Nathaniel & Hannah], b. Jan. 31, 1780	2	168
Phylura, d. [Nathaniel & Hannah], b. Sept. 24, 1773	2	168
Prescilla, d Sam[ue]ll & Eliza[beth], b. Sept. 16, 1748	1	235
Prescilla, d. Edward & Prudence, b. Sept. 21, 1752	1	258
Prudence, d. [Edward & Prudence], b. Apr. 27, 1760	1	258

	Vol.	Page
COBURN, (cont)		
Prudence, d. Oct. 19, 1772	1	258
Prudence, w. Edward, d. Oct 19, 1772	1	258
Robert, m. Hannah **CANADA**, Nov. 9, 1726	1	95
Robert, s. Robert & Hannah, b. Apr. 15, 1728	1	95
Robert, Jr., m. Mary **GENNINGS**, Nov. 7, 1749	1	297
Robert, s. [Robert & Mary], b. Apr. 17, 1763	1	297
Robert, m. Molly **BIBBINS**, Feb. 24, 1771	2	162
Roswell, s. [Hezekiah & Mary], b. Nov. 11, 1776	2	221
Sam[ue]ll, m. Elizabeth **HOLT**, Nov. 16, 1727	1	89
Sam[ue]ll, s. Sam[ue]ll & Elizabeth (**HOLT**), b. Sept. 29, 1728	1	89
Sam[ue]ll, Jr., m. Judeth **WEBSTER**, Jan 29, 1750/51	1	308
Samuel, s. [Edward & Prudence], b. Oct. 25, 1762; d. same day	1	258
Sarah, d. Sam[ue]ll & Elizabeth, b. Apr. 17, 1736	1	89
Sibbel, see under Sybil		
Silvanus, s. [Robert & Mary], b. July 23, 1757	1	297
Stephen, s. [Zebadiah & Eliz[abeth], b. Nov. 13, 1764	2	21
Susannah, d. [Edward & Prudence], b. Jan. 27, 1767	1	258
Susannah, m. Elle **RUD[D]**, Sept. 9, 1789	3	42
Sibbel, d. [Cornelius & Abigail], b. Oct. 30, 1773	2	35
Tryphenia, d. [Robert & Mary], b. Apr. 13, 1761	1	297
Tryphosa, of Windham, m. Benjamin **KEACH**, of Mansfield, Feb. 24, 1822, by Elder Elias Sharp	3	66
William, s. [Edward & Prudence], b. Oct 9, 1756; d. Oct. 16, 1756	1	258
Zebadiah, s. Sam[ue]ll & Elizabeth, b. Feb. 26, 1731/2	1	89
Zebadiah, m. Eliz[abeth] **DURKEE**, Jan. 22, 1754	2	21
Zebadiah, s. [Zebadiah & Eliz[abeth], b. Oct. 29, 1756	2	21
COE, Frederick T., of Ashford, m. Eliza A. **BURNHAM**, of Windham, Aug. 14, 1843, by Rev. Isaac H Coe	3	210
COFFIN, Mary, d. Michael, laborer, ae. 32, b. Sept 18, [1849]	4	9
COGEL, Lydia, ae. 20, m. Geo[rge] **ABBOTT**, ae. 24, July [ ], [1850], by Rev. Bankwell* (*Bushnell?)	4	116
COGSWELL, William H., m. Mary L. **FULLER**, Feb. 23, 1824	3	15
COLBON, [see also **COLBURN** and **COBURN**], Elizabeth, d. Sam[ue]ll & Elizabeth, b. Aug. 27, 1743	1	235
Lydia, d. Sam[ue]ll & Eliza[beth], b. Apr 13, 1745	1	235
COLBURN, [see also **COLBON** and **COBURN**], Royal S., m. Sarah Ann **SHERMAN**, Mar. 18, 1833, by Rev. Alva Gregory	3	164
COLE, Amanda, b. Providence, R.I., res Windham, d. Nov. 25, 1848, ae. 14	4	154
Benjamin, of Warwick, R.I., m. Marcia **WEEKS**, of Windham, Oct. 18, 1832, by Rev. Ella Denham	3	161

	Vol.	Page
COLE, (cont.)		
Eliza Ann, ae. 32, m. Lucius H. **CROSS**, farmer, ae.		
30, Nov. 19, 1849, by Rev. Henry Brownley	4	114
Sophia, tailoress, b. Killingly, res. Windham, d.		
Aug. 1, 1860, ae 71 y. 6 m.	4	161
COLEMAN, Joanna, m. Isaac **ROBINSON**, Jr., Oct. 26, 1775	2	172
Merian, m. Solomon **LORD**, Apr. 3, 1766	2	165
Mindwell, m. Jonathan **JENNINGS**, July 17, 1782	2	245
Phebe, m. Nathaniel **ROBINSON**, Aug. 13, 1778	2	20
COLLINS, Augustus, s. Augustus P., merchant, ae. 24, &		
Harriet P., ae. 22, b. Sept. 14, 1847	4	1
Augustus, b. Willimantic, res. Windham, d. Sept. 18,		
1847, ae. 5 d.	4	151
Hannah, m. Ichabod **WARNER**, Apr. 2, 1798	3	49
Mary, m. Samuel **GIFFORD**, Nov. 1, 1693	A	20
Mary, m. Ebenezer **HOLT**, [ ]	2	184
Phebe, m. Stephen **ORMSBY**, Nov. 9, 1786	2	252
Seth, of Columbia, m. Lydia **PENRE**, of Willimantic,		
Feb. 10, 1846, at Willimantic, by John Cooper	3	227
W[illia]m A., ae. 51, m. Sarah A. **ELLIOTT**, ae. 32,		
Apr. 16, [1849], by Rev. J.M. Phillips	4	114
COLLSON, John, s. [Moses & Sarah], b. July 6, 1770	2	121
Moses, m. Sarah **SILSBY**, Apr. 10, 1766	2	121
William, s. [Moses & Sarah], b. July 26, 1766; d.		
Aug. 16, 1766	2	121
William, s. [Moses & Sarah], b. June 26, 1768	2	121
COMINS, [see under **CUMMINGS**]		
CONADY, Catharine, d. Feb. [1850?], ae. 1 1/2	4	155
CONANT, CONNENT, Benajah, s. Caleb & Hannah, b Feb. 13,		
1716/17	1	23
Caleb, m. Hannah **CRANE**, Aug. 23, 1714	1	23
Elizabeth, m. Richard **HENDE[E]**, Oct. 17, 1695	A	6
Hannah, m. Daniel **BINGHAM**, Jan. 13, 1747/8	1	277
Henry M., of Hampton, m. Mary **HUTCHINS**, of Windham,		
Sept. 28, 1845, Willimantic, by John Crocker	3	223
Joseph, m. Eunice C. **WILLIAMS**, Apr. 13, 1845, by		
Rev. James W. Woodward	3	221
Josiah, m. Joanna **DIMMOCH**, Oct. 6, 1709	1	12
Josiah, s. Caleb & Hannah, b. Dec. 9, 1724	1	23
Malachi, s. Caleb & Hannah, b. June 12, 1715	1	23
Mary, d. Caleb & Hannah, b. Jan. 5, 1722/3	1	23
Ruth, d. Caleb & Hannah, b. Oct. 28, 1720	1	23
Sarah, w. Lieut. Ebenezer, d. Dec. 4, 1718	1	12
Sarah, d. Caleb & Hannah, b. Dec. 20, 1718	1	23
Shubael, s. Josiah & Joanna, b. July 15, 1711	1	12
CONARD, Phebe, m. Isaac **CANADA**, Jan. 21, 1729/30	1	116
CONDY, Thady(?), laborer, d. [1849], ae 30	4	155
CONGDON, Andrew J., m. Emily **LINCOLN**, b. of Willimantic,		

	Vol.	Page
CONGDON, (cont.)		
Sept. 23, 1839, by Rev. B. Cook, Jr., of		
Willimantic	3	190
Eliza Abby, of Willimantic Falls, m. Emery B. **RAY**,		
of Haddam, Nov. 26, 1835, by Rev. Benajah Cook	3	175
George, of Norwich, m. Ellen **HAVENS**, of Jewett City,		
Aug. 8, 1847, by Rev. D. Dorchester, Willimantic	3	236
George, s. John, stone-mason, ae. 29, & Fanny, ae.		
28, b. Dec. 20, 1847	4	1
Martha, of Windham, m. George **GORHAM**, of New London,		
Nov. 24, 1829, by Rev. Eseck Brown, of Lebanon	3	139
Martha, m. Benjamin **SEGAR**, Mar. 29, 1830, by Elder		
Babcock, at Pomfret	3	157
Mary, m. Ezra **SELDEN**, Dec. 7, 1806	3	41
Stephen, m. Phebe **GUIANT**, Nov. 29, 1810	3	66
William Henry, s. [Stephen & Phebe], b. Oct. 11, 1811	3	66
CONNELL, Daniel, s. Tho[ma]s, boiler maker, of Willimantic,		
b. June 22, [1850]	4	10
CONNER, Sarah, m. Joshua **FLINT**, Aug. 12, 1742	1	242
CONTER, Eleazer Welch, s. Betsey, b. May 3, 1821	3	49
CONVERSE, Charles Augustus, of Norwich, m. Caroline Frances		
BALCOM, of Windham, Feb. 24, 1845, by Rev. Giles		
W. Dunham	3	220
COOK, Abby D., m. John H. **CAPEN**, b. of Windham, Feb. 6,		
1832, by Rev. R. T. Crampton	3	157
Catharine, of Windham, m. James **SPAULDING**, of Norwich,		
Jan. 5, 1829, by Rev. Dennis Platt	3	133
Daniel, s. Sam[ue]ll & Leah, b. Aug. 25, 1732	1	105
Ellen E., d. Edwin, ae 25, b. Apr. 28, [1849]	4	6
Harriet, m. William **NEWCOMB**, b. of Windham, Nov. 27,		
1828, by Rev. Dennis Platt	3	133
James, m. Abigail **ROBBINS**, July 16, 1778	2	17
James, s. [James & Abigail], b. Mar 23, 1780	2	17
Jerusha, d. Sam[ue]ll & Leah, b. Feb. 20, 1721	1	38
John, s Abigail **ROBBINS**, b. June 9, 1777; d Sept. 9,		
1778	2	17
John B., of Willimantic, d Apr. 22, 1860, ae. 3	4	159-0
Leah, m. Nathaniel Skiff **CALKINS**, Oct. 12, 1777	2	189
Mary, d. Sam[ue]ll & Leah, b. July 25, 1729	1	105
Phebe, m. Joshua **BASS**, Mar. 11, 1772	2	201
Phebe, m. Abisha **BASS**, Mar 16, 1772	2	169
Phinehas, s. Sam[ue]ll & Leah, b. Dec. 6, 1716	1	38
Phine[h]as, [s. Sam[ue]ll & Leah], d. Jan. 22, 1728/9	1	38
Phine[h]as, s. Sam[ue]ll & Leah, b. June 7, 1736	1	105
Rebeckah, d. Sam[ue]ll & Leah, b. Nov. 26, 1718	1	38
Sam[ue]ll, m. Leah **RIPLEY**, Mar. 14, 1716	1	38
Samuell, m. [E]unice **WEBB**, Mar. 31, 1751	1	311
Samuel, s. [Sam[ue]ll & [E]unice], b. Feb. 18, 1754	1	311

	Vol	Page
COOK, (cont.)		
Samuel, m. Jemima **HEBARD**, Mar. 28, 1776	2	210
Samuel, s. [Samuel & Jemima], b. Feb. 12, 1777; d.		
Feb. 19, 1778	2	210
Samuel, s. [Samuel & Jemima], b. June 25, 1778	2	210
Sybell, d. Sam[ue]ll & [E]unice, b. Sept. 3, 1751	1	311
Welthian, d. Sam[ue]ll & Leah, b Aug 20, 1724	1	38
CORBIN, CORBEN, Louisa W., twin with W[illia]m, d.		
W[illia]m, clerk, ae 37, & Louisa W., ae 24,		
b. Apr. 26, 1848	4	2
Richard A., b. Apr. 24, 1848	4	2
Richard A., d. Sept. 23, [1849], ae. 1 1/2	4	155
William, m. Loisa W. **PERRY**, Jan. 11, 1847, by Rev		
John Cooper, Willimantic	3	234
W[illia]m, twin with Louisa W., s. W[illia]m, clerk,		
ae. 37, & Louisa W., ae. 24, b. Apr. 26, 1848	4	2
William, merchant, d. Sept. 23, [1849], ae. 27	4	155
COREY, [see also **CARY**], Benj[amin], m. Abigail **ABBE**, Nov.		
10, 1743	1	252
John, s. Benj[amin] & Abigail, b. Mar. 9, 1746	1	252
John, m. Nancy **ROUSE**, Jan 1, 1837, by Rev. Philetus		
Greene	3	180
Mary, d. Benj[amin] & Abigail, b. Aug. 12, 1744	1	252
CORGALL, Catharine, ae. 21, m. Royal C. **NEAL**, operative,		
ae. 22, b. Ireland, res. Windham, Feb. 4, 1848, by		
a Catholic Priest	4	111
CORNING, Sabra, of Bolton, Conn., m. Joshua **FRINK**, of		
Coventry, Conn., June 28, 1836, by Rev. Philo		
Judson, at Willimantic	3	178
COSTELLO, Mat[t]hew, paper maker, ae. 24, m. M. **McCARTY**,		
ae. 22, Sept. [ ], [1850], by Rev. Brady	4	115
COVEL, Lues, m. Ann **SIMONS**, May 30, 1745	1	140
Thomas, s Lues & Ann, b. Mar. 10, 1745/6	1	140
COX, Mary A., m. Lucius W. **SPENCER**, b. of Windham, Feb. 19,		
1838, at Willimantic, by Rev B. Cook, Jr.	3	185
Olive S., m. Nathan T. **BENCHLEY**, b. of Windham, Sept.		
8, 1834, by Rev. Philo Judson, Willimantic	3	169
Sarah F., m. John **WILLSON**, Mar. 15, 1846, by Andrew		
Sharp	3	228
COY, Elizabeth, m. Joseph **MARTIN**, Jan. 3, 1765	2	116
Elizabeth, d. [Joseph & Jerusha], b. Feb. 14, 1769	2	130
Jerusha, d. [Joseph & Jerusha], b. June 1, 1772	2	130
John, s. [Joseph & Jerusha], b. Sept. 1, 1780	2	130
Joseph, m. Jerusha **SAWYER**, Dec. 31, 1767	2	130
Joseph, s [Joseph & Jerusha], b. May 23, 1770; d.		
[ ]	2	130
Lewis, s. [Joseph & Jerusha], b. Nov. 13, 1774	2	130
Sarah, d. [Joseph & Jerusha], b. Feb. 23, 1779	2	130

	Vol.	Page
COY, (cont.)		
Stephen, m. Anna **BISSELL,** Nov. 11, 1762	2	64
Susannah, d. [Joseph & Jerusha], b. May 26, 1782	2	130
CRAFT, Abigail, m. Thomas **BUTLER,** Mar. 9, 1732	1	250
Mehitable, m. Jeremiah **BINGHAM,** Oct 12, 1769	2	146
CRAGIN, Peter, paper maker, ae. 26, b. Dublin, m.		
Catharine **MELLIN,** ae. 19, Aug 29, [1848], b		
Rev. And. Robinson	4	113
CRANDALL, Alexander, of Franklin, m. Mary **BECKWITH,** of		
Windham, Apr. 14, 1836, by Rev. M. Dwight	3	177
Betsey, m. William **CHAPPELL,** Nov. 15, 1829, by Rev.		
Roger Bingham	3	141
Edward R., m. Sarah **ELY,** Mar. 9, 1835, by Rev. Roger		
Bingham	3	172
Hannah, m Benjamin **HOXSIE,** b. of Windham, Mar 26,		
1838, by Rev. B. Cooke, Jr., of Willimantic	3	186
Sally, m. George **CHAPPELL,** Nov. 5, 1826, by Rev.		
Roger Bingham	3	142
CRANE, CRAIN, CREAN, Abel, s. John & Sarah, b Mar 27,		
1748	1	173
Abia, s. John & Sarah, b Oct. 12, 1710	1	24
Abigail, d. Jonathan & Deborah, b. Feb. 15, 1701	A	4
Abigail, m. David **KNIGHT,** Dec. 24, 1718	1	41
Airei*, d. Isaac & Ruth, b. July 25, 1720 (*Adrea?)	1	132
Adrea, m. Thomas **BROUGHTON,** Nov. 15, 1738	1	186
Adrie, d. [Isaac & Eunice], b. July 7, 1770	2	83
Ama, ae. 20, m. Antony **HOFERING,** laborer, ae. 24,		
Dec. [1850], by Rev. Brady	4	115
Ann, m. Joseph **BADCOCK,** Nov. 8, 1744	2	113
Ann, ae. 26, m. Ansel **HEVNIA**(?), laborer, ae. 27,		
Feb. 9, [1850], by Rev. Brady	4	114
Anna, d. Jonathan & Mary, b. May 24, 1711	1	13
Anna, d. [Isaac & Eunice], b. Apr 3, 1776	2	83
Anne, d. Isaac & Ruth, b. Feb. 1, 1723/4	1	132
Card M., of Mansfield, m. Lucy **RISING,** of Windham,		
Jan. 3, 1833, by Henry Hall, J.P.	3	162
Deborah, twin with Elizabeth, d. Jonathan & Deborah,		
b. "beginning of" Feb. 1698; d. aged 3 d.	A	4
Deborah, d. Isaac & Ruth, b. July 28, 1729	1	132
Dina*, d. Humphrey & Hannah, b. Dec. 10, 1737**		
(*correction **CRAM** handwritten in margin next to		
Dina in the original manuscript;**correction m.		
Thomas Park **ROOD** handwritten after birthdate in		
the original manuscript)	1	151
Elizabeth, twin with Deborah, d Jonathan & Deborah,		
b. "beginning of" Feb. 1698; d. aged 3 ds.	A	4
Eunice, d. John & Sarah, b May 12, 1712	1	24
Eunice, d. [Isaac & Eunice], b. Oct. 19, 1765	2	83

	Vol.	Page
CRANE, CRAIN, CREAN, (cont.)		
Hannah, d. Jonathan & Deborah, b. Mar. 7, 1692	A	4
Hannah, m. Caleb **CONANT**, Aug. 23, 1714	1	23
Hannah, d. Humphrey & Hannah, b. Apr. 12, 1733	1	151
Harvey, of Hartford, m. Laura **SIMPSON**, of Willi-		
mantic, Dec. 2, 1834, by Rev. Philo Judson,		
in Willimantic	3	171
Humphrey*, s. Humphrey & Hannah, b. Mar. 12, 1735/6		
(*correction **CRAM** handwritten next to Humphrey		
in margin of original manuscript)	1	151
Isaac, s. Jonathan & Deborah, b. Apr. 2, 1694	A	4
Isaac, m. Ruth **WALDO**, Aug. 12, 1716	1	132
Isaac, s. Isaac & Ruth, b. July 27, 1726	1	132
Isaac, m. Eunice **WALCUTT**, May 8, 1763	2	83
Isaac, s. [Isaac & Eunice], b July 1, 1772	2	83
Isaac, d. Oct. 10, 1777, in the 52nd y. of his age	2	83
John, m. Sarah **SPENCER**, Sept. 16, 1708	1	24
John, s. John & Sarah, b. July 31, 1709	1	24
John, m. Rebeckah **HUNTINGTON**, Jan. 24, 1733/4	1	148
John, m. Sarah **HUTCHINSON**, Nov. 11, 1742	1	173
John, s. [Isaac & Eunice], b. Apr. 21, 1774	2	83
John Nelson, s. Fanny **FRANCIS**, b. May 1, 1802	3	49
Jonathan, m. Mary **HIB[B]ARD**, July 31, 1705	1	13
Jonathan, s. Jonathan & Mary, b. July 6, 1715	1	13
Joseph, s. Jonathan & Deborah, b. May 17, 1696	A	4
Mary, d. Jonathan & Mary, b. Apr. 13, 1709	1	13
Mary, m. Jacob **SIMONDS**, Apr 4, 1710	1	44
Michael, b. Canaan, res. Willimantic, d. Dec. [ ],		
1850, ae. 18 m.	4	157
Ruth, d. Isaac & Ruth, b. Apr. 12, 1718	1	132
Ruth, m. Ebenezer **WEBB**, Dec 3, 1740	1	210
Sarah, m. Nathaniel **HEBARD**, Apr. 16, 1702	A	22
Sarah, m. Nathaniell **HIB[B]ARD**, Apr. 16, 1702	1	1
Sarah, d. Jonathan & Mary, b. May 11, 1707	1	13
Sarah, w. John, d. Sept. 15, 1715	1	24
Sarah, d. [Isaac & Eunice], b. Jan. 24, 1764	2	83
Theodosay, m. Elijah **BINGHAM**, Mar 2, 1738/9	1	154
Zebulon, s. Jonathan & Mary, b. Apr. 26, 1713	1	13
Zebulon, s. Jonathan & Mary, d. Oct. 6, 1714	1	46
CRANSTON, Gardiner, farmer, ae. 38, b. R.I., res. Windham,		
m. Eliza **MINER**, ae. 48, Nov 24, 1847, by Rev A		
Sharp	4	111
Rhoda, of Willimantic, m. Zaccheas **PARKER**, of Mans-		
field, Mar. 8, 1846, by John Cooper	3	228
CRAWFORD, CREWFIELD, Lucretia, d. July [ ], 1850, ae 17	4	155
Richard, laborer, b. Ireland, res. Willimantic, d.		
Aug. 2, 1851, ae 43	4	157
Samuel, s. Richard, laborer, ae. 41, b. June 25, [1849]	4	11

	Vol.	Page
CUMMINGS, COMMINS, COMINS, CUMMINS, CUMINS, (cont.)		
Cordelia M., m. Hezekiah P. **BROWN**, Jr., b. of Mansfield, Oct. 25, [ ], by Rev. B.M. Alden	3	236
John, of Southbridge, Mass., m. Marietta **HEB[B]ARD**, of Windham, Oct. 10, 1833, by Rev. Jesse Fisher	3	167
Patrick, laborer, b. Ireland, res. Willimantic, d. Feb 28, 1860, ae 35	4	159-0
Pattey, d. [Stephen & Martha], b. Dec. 5, 1772	2	204
Polly, d. [Stephen & Martha], b. Dec. 18, 1773	2	204
Stephen, m. Martha **FARNAM**, May 3, 1769	2	204
Stephen, s. [Stephen & Martha], b. Sept. 6, 1775	2	204
William, m. Huldah **DYER**, Apr. 12, 1827, by Rev. Cornelius B. Everest	3	123
CUNNINGHAM, Ann Amelia, d. [Thomas W. & Wealthy Ann], b. June 1, 1837	3	92
Annabana, d. Tho[ma]s & Martha, b. May 17, 1750	1	277
Brunetta, d. Robert, laborer, ae. 28, of Willimantic, b. Aug. 31, [1850]	4	10
Dennis, s. Dennis, laborer, ae. 34, b. Sept. [ ], [1849]	4	9
George, s. [Thomas W. & Wealthy Ann], b. Apr. 10, 1829; d. Aug. 22, 1829	3	92
Hannah, d. [Robert & Hannah], b. Oct. 2, 1795	2	55
Hannah, [w. Robert], d. Aug. 4, 1838	2	55
Issac Sawyer, s. [Robert & Hannah], b. Mar 28, [ ]	2	55
Joel, s. [Robert & Hannah], b. Aug. 15, 1788; d. Aug. 24, 1796	2	55
Lucy, d. [Robert & Hannah], b. Apr. 8, 1784	2	55
Michael, s. Robert, laborer, ae. 38, & Meeney, ae 28, of Willimantic, b. June 30, 1851	4	12
Robert, s. Tho[ma]s & Martha, b. July 8, 1748	1	277
Robert, m. Hannah **SAWYER**, Sept. 10, 1783	2	55
Robert, d. Apr. 10, 1825	2	55
Robert, s. Dennis, laborer, ae. 38, & Catharine, ae. 30, b. Jan. 20, 1851	4	12
Thomas, m. Martha **GENNINGS**, Nov. 3, 1747	1	277
Thomas, d. Mar. [ ], 1751	1	277
Thomas, s. [Robert & Hannah], b. Feb. 2, 1786; d. Aug. 15, 1796	2	55
Thomas W., m. Wealthy Ann **WILLSON**, Dec. 3, 1827, by Rev. Chester Tilden	3	92
Thomas W., m. Sophia S. **PORTER**, June 5, 1843, by Rev. Andrew Sharp	3	209
Thomas Willson, s. [Robert & Hannah], b. Dec. 18, 1797	2	55
William, m. Almantha M. **BINGHAM**, b of Windham, Sept. 21, 1845, by Rev. Isaac H. Coe	3	222

	Vol.	Page
CURRIN, Webster, b. Coventry, res. Willimantic, d. Dec.		
6, 1849, ae. 13	4	153
CURRY, Kate, operative, ae. 23, b. Ireland, res. Williman-		
tic, m. W[illia]m **JUDGE**, laborer, ae. 26, b.		
Ireland, res. Willimantic, July 9, 1851, by Rev.		
Smith	4	117
CURTIS, Caroline, m. Capt. William S. **JILLSON**, b. of		
Windham, Dec. 26, 1831, by Rev. R.T. Crampton	3	157
Jesse, of Coventry, m Ann **WEAVER**, Oct. 6, 1825, by		
Rev. C.B. Everest	3	114
Zachi, of Chaplin, m. Selina **RIPLEY**, of Windham, Feb		
10, 1845, by Rev. J.E. Tyler	3	220
CUSHMAN, Ann Robinson, m. Samuel **BINGHAM**, b. of		
Windham, Dec. 24, 1840, in St. Paul's Church, by		
Rev. Henry Beers Sherman	3	195
Pamela, of Windham, m. Fanning **TRACY**, of Canterbury,		
May 11, 1829, by Rev. Jesse Fisher	3	136
Sophia, m. Henry **BROWN**, Apr. 15, 1832, by Rev. R.T.		
Crampton	3	160
CUSTUS, Julia, m. Chester **CLARK**, Oct. 24, 1831, by Rev.		
Rich[ar]d F. Cleveland	3	155
CUTLER, Daniel, m. Mary **WOODARD**, July 9, 1736	1	179
Daniel, s. Daniel & Mary, b. Jan. 22, 1742/3	1	179
Dinah, d. Seth & Elizabeth, b. Nov. 12, 1740	1	225
Eleizer, s. Daniel & Mary, b. Nov. 20, 1739; d. Aug.		
1, 1759	1	179
Elizabeth, d. Seth & Elizabeth, b. July 19, 1735	1	225
Eunice, d. [Samuel & Eunice], b. Oct. 7, 1774	2	177
Hannah, d. Seth & Elizabeth, b. Mar. 30, 1737; d		
Jan. 13, 1742/3	1	225
Hannah, d. Seth & Elis[abeth], b. Feb. 17, 1742/3	1	225
Hannah, m. Jonathan **BIDLAKE**, Apr. 22, 1767	2	131
Hannah, m. Asa **WHITE**, Apr. 7, 1805	2	45
Jarah, d. Daniel & Mary, b. Jan. 30, 1737/8	1	179
Joannah, d. Seth & Elis[abeth], b. Mar. 20, 1745/6	1	225
John, s. Seth & Elizabeth, b. Jan. 17, 1738	1	225
Mary, d. Daniel & Mary, b. Oct. 8, 1746	1	179
Mary, m. William **HUNTINGTON**, Feb. 15, 1770	2	162
Nathaniel, s. [Samuel & Eunice], b. Mar 17, 1772	2	177
Olive, d. Seth & Elis[abeth], b. Jan. 27, 1747/8	1	225
Samuel, s. Daniel & Mary, b. Feb. 6, 1744/5	1	179
Samuel, m. Eunice **SIMONS**, Nov. 23, 1769	2	177
Sarah, d Seth & Elis[abeth], b July 18, 1750	1	225
Seth, m. Elizabeth **BADCO[C]K**, Oct. 22, 1734	1	225
Seth, d. Feb. 9, 1750/51	1	225
Vine, s. [Samuel & Eunice], b. May 25, 1770	2	177
DAILEY, DAYLEY, David, s. [James & Zerviah], b. Dec 4,		
1767	2	74

	Vol.	Page

DAILEY, DAYLEY, (cont.)
Dennis, laborer, ae. 28, m. Adeline **ARDSLY**(?),
   ae. 30, Jan. 5, 1849, by A. Sharp — 4 — 113
James, m. Zerviah **NORWOOD**, Aug. 19, 1766 — 2 — 74
Zerviah, m. Joseph **MARTIN**, Apr 11, 1776 — 2 — 202
DANIELS, DANIEL, Enoch M., m. Emily **JAMES**, June 20,
   1830, by Rev. Chester Tilden, Willimantic — 3 — 146
Jesse F., of Lebanon, m. Esther M. **PEASE**, of
   Windham, Jan. 5, 1845, by Rev. Charles Noble — 3 — 219
Mary, m. Israel **SHAW**, Sept. 20, 1734 — 1 — 171
DAVENPORT, Abraham, m. Elizabeth **HUNTINGTON**, Nov. 15,
   1750 — 2 — 1
Delia, d. Oct 14, [1849], ae. 47 — 4 — 155
Geo[rge] N., d. Aug. 11, 1848, ae. 8 m. — 4 — 151
Sayman, merchant, ae. 43, m. Charlotte **WOODWORTH**,
   ae. 42, his 2d w., Jan. 27, [1850], by Rev.
   A.H. Robinson — 4 — 115
DAVIS, DAVISS, DEAIUS, DAVICE, Abby, of Willimantic, m.
   Henry H. **KEIRER**, of Hampton, Jan. 22, 1837, by
   Rev. P. Judson, at Willimantic — 3 — 181
Ann C., d. Isaac P., machinist, b. Dec. 16, [1849] — 4 — 9
Anne, m. Isaac **WARNER**, Oct. 11, 1739 — 1 — 197
Chloe, m. W[illia]m **DEAN**, Dec. 26, 1830, by Rev.
   Roger Bingham — 3 — 149
Deborah, housekeeper, b. Mansfield, res. Windham,
   d. July 28, 1848, ae. 82 — 4 — 151
Desire, m Royal **GENNINGS**, May 27, 1816 — 3 — 89
Elizabeth, m. William **SHAW**, Oct. 9, 1725 — 1 — 104
Emily, d. Isaac P & Sally, b. Sept. 15, 1847 — 4 — 2
Haddrie, m. Daniel **WOODBURY**, Nov. 24, 1775 — 2 — 188
Henrietta, m. James **WILLSON**, May [ ], 1812 — 3 — 86
Jerusha Allen, d. [Samuel & Parmela], b. Feb. 10,
   1821 — 3 — 90
John, operative, ae. 22, b. Tolland, res. Windham,
   m. Sarah **WILLSON**, ae 19, Nov. 25, 1847, by
   Tho[ma]s Dowling — 4 — 111
Lewis L., manufacturer, of Windham, m Maria **BILLINGS**,
   Feb. 10, [1849] by Rev. J.M. Phillips — 4 — 114
Lydia, d. Zephaniah & Susannah, b. Mar. 12, 1755 — 1 — 319
Lydia, d. [Thomas & Sybbel], b. Nov. 5, 1778 — 2 — 193
Mary, m. Nathaniell **FFLINT**, May 2, 1727 — 1 — 91
Mary Jane, of Willimantic, d. Sept. [ ], [1848], ae. 7 — 4 — 153
Permelia A., m. John W. **BEEBE**, Oct. 10, 1842, by Andrew
   Sharp — 3 — 204
Sally B., of Windham, m Samuel **CHITTENDEN**, of Boston,
   Apr. 7, 1833, by Rev. Alva Gregory — 3 — 164
Samuel, m. Parmela **ORMSBY**, Apr. 30, 1820 — 3 — 90
Sam[ue]l, d. Feb. 13, [1851], ae. 82 — 4 — 158

	Vol	Page
DAVIS, DAVISS, DEAIUS, DAVICE, (cont.)		
Servis, wagonmaker, ae. 23, m. Olive M. **BILLINGS,**		
ae. 24, Feb. 9, [1850], by Rev. Phillips	4	114
Thomas, m. Sybbel **CANNADA,** b. of Windham, Mar. 24,		
1774	2	193
Zephaniah, m. Susannah **DURKEE,** July 16, 1752	1	319
DAVISON, Ann Mariah, d W[illia]m, manufacturer, ae. 49,		
& Calista, ae. 42, b. July 21, 1848	4	4
Asa, s [Christopher & Lydia], b. Apr. 1, 1756	1	328
Benjamin, s. [Zephaniah & Susannah], b. Oct. 19,		
1761	2	32
Christopher, m. Lydia **HOVEY,** June 5, 1755	1	328
Christopher, m. Bethia **BIDLOCK,** June 24, 1756	2	48
Daniel, s. [Christopher & Bethia], b. Nov. 9, 1757;		
d. Dec. [ ], 1757	2	48
Deborah, m. Sam[ue]ll **WEBB,** July 2, 1746	1	259
Eliz[abe]th, d. [Zephaniah & Susannah], b Mar. 16,		
1753	2	32
Lydia, d. [Zephaniah & Susannah], b Mar. 12, 1755	2	32
Lydia, w. Christopher, d. Apr. 8, 1756	1	328
Lydia, m. Amos **FORD,** May 25, 1761	2	68
Tho[ma]s, s. [Zephaniah & Susannah], b. June 7, 1757	2	32
William, s. [Zephaniah & Susannah], b. Sept. 9, 1759	2	32
Zephaniah, m. Susannah **DURKEE,** July 16, 1752	2	32
DAY, John, ae. 65, of Killingly, m. Mariah **BURNHAM,** ae. 53,		
Mar. 26, [1849], by Rev. Phelps	4	113
DEAIUS, [see under **DAVIS**]		
DEAN, DEANS, Aaron, s. Nathan & Sarah, b. Jan. 21, 1758	2	42
Abigail, w. Ox[enbridge], d. Sept. 30, 1772	1	202
Abigail, m. Zebulon **GENNINGS,** Nov. 16, 1772	1	101
Adah, m. W[illia]m H **YOUNG,** Nov. 10, 1831, by Rev.		
Ralph S. Crampton	3	156
Asa, s. Benajah & Mary, b. Dec. 9, 1746	1	140
Chester, m. Caroline **POTTER,** b. of Willimantic, Oct. 1,		
1838, at Willimantic, by Rev. P. Judson	3	187
Ebenezer, s. Ebenezer & Deborah, b. Sept. 30, 1739	1	202
Ebenezer, d May 22, 1753	1	56
Ebenezer, s. John & Rachel, b. July 28, 1756	1	266
Elizabeth, d. [Zachariah & Elizabeth], b. June 18, 1761	2	64
Experience, m. James **SPAULDING,** May 22, 1797	3	31
Hannah, d. Ebenezer & Mercy, b. Aug. 9, 1722	1	56
Hannah, d. Feb. 18, 1746/7	1	266
Hannah, of Norwich, m. Henry **DEWITT,** [ ], 1772	3	80
James Luddington, s. [Zachariah & Elizabeth], b. Feb.		
29, 1764	2	64
John, s. Ebenezer & Mercy, b. June 29, 1724	1	56
John, m. Rachel **BOND,** Jan. 22, 1745/6	1	266
John, s. John & Rachel, b. Jan. 6, 1748/9; d. June 30,		

	Vol.	Page
DEAN, DEANS, (cont.)		
1750	1	266
John, s. John & Rachel, b. Apr. 27, 1751	1	266
Josiah, s. Ebenezer & Deborah, b. Mar. 27, 1741	1	202
Josiah, Jr., m. Fanny **YOUNG**, Apr. 11, 1831, by Rev. Rober Bingham	3	152
Lemuel, s. [Zachariah & Elizabeth], b. Sept. 23, 1762	2	64
Lemuel, m. Abiah **HARRIS**, Dec. 11, 1784	2	21
Lydia, d. Nathan & Sarah, b. Mar. 8, 1754	2	42
Mary, d. Benajah & Mary, b. Aug. 11, 1735	1	140
Mercy, d. John & Rachel, b Mar. 14, 1754	1	266
Mercy, d. [Zachariah & Elizabeth], b. Jan. 13, 1768	2	64
Meriam, d. Benajah & Mary, b. June 30, 1737; d Sept 12, 1742	1	140
Meriam, 2d, d Benajah & Mary, b. Jan. 13, 1742/3	1	140
Nancy, d. [Lemuel & Abiah], b. Sept. 26, 1785	2	21
Nathan, s. Nathan & Sarah, b. May 11, 1752; d. Oct 26, 1752	2	42
Nathan, s. Nathan & Sarah, b. Mar. 16, 1756	2	42
Oxenbridge, m. Mary **HUMPHREY**, Dec. 15, 1772	1	202
Rachel, d. John & Rachel, b. Feb. 5, 1746/7	1	266
Sam[ue]ll, m. Sarah **BRO[U]GHTON**, Dec. 1, 1743	1	229
Sarah, d. Benajah & Mary, b. Mar. 22, 1740	1	140
Silence, d. [Zachariah & Elizabeth], b. Jan. 9, 1770	2	64
Solomon, s. Benajah & Mary, b. Aug. 15, 1733	1	140
Thomas, s. Oxenbridge & Abigail, b. Jan. 23, 1753	1	202
Wealthe, d. [Zachariah & Elizabeth], b. Jan. 26, 1766	2	64
William, s. John & Rachel, b. Nov. 11, 1758	1	266
W[illia]m, m. Chloe **DAVIS**, Dec. 26, 1830, by Rev. Roger Bingham	3	149
Zachariah, m. Elizabeth **LUDDINGTON**, June 18, 1760	2	64
Zurviah, d. Ebenezer & Mercy, b. Mar. 31, 1720	1	56
DECKER, Abigail, d. Joseph & Thankfull, b. July 25, 1724	1	31
Abigail, d. Joseph & Thankfull, d. Mar. 28, 1740	1	173
Ebenezer, s. Joseph & Thankfull, b. Aug. 19, 1722; d. Sept. 14, 1722	1	31
John, s. Joseph & Thankfull, b. Feb. 25, 1713/14	1	31
John, m. Martha **WOODIN**, Apr 26, 1742 "Divorced"	1	230
Joseph, Sergt., d. Dec. 31, 1755, in the 71st y. of his age	1	173
Martha, m. Samuell **PHILLIPS**, Mar. 27, 1751	1	125
Mary, d. Joseph & Thankfull, b. Nov. 5, 1716	1	31
Mary, m. John **FULLER**, Jr., Dec. 24, 1755	2	20
Mary, d. Joseph & Thankfull, d. Dec. 12, 1737	1	173
Thankfull, d. Joseph & Thankfull, b. Apr. 25, 1719	1	31
Thankfull, wid. Sergt. Joseph, d. Apr. 26, 1761, in the 76th y. of her age	1	173

	Vol.	Page
DECKER, (cont)		
Thankfull, d. Sergt. Joseph, d. Mar. 25, 1766, in the		
46th y. of her age	1	173
DeLEE, James, farmer, black, d. [1850], ae. 41	4	156
DEMING, Elizer, m. Asenath **PARSONS**, Jan. 2, 1826	3	122
DENISON, DENNISON, DINISON, Amos, s. Nathan & Ann, b.		
May 31, 1749; d. Sept. 19, 1753	1	153
Ann, m. Lieut. Jeremiah **RIPLEY**, July 16, 1734	1	100
Ann, m. Amos **ALLEN**, Nov. 8, 1739	1	188
Ann, d. Nathan & Ann, b. Nov. 19, 1742	1	153
Ann, w. Nathan, d. May 16, 1776, in the 60th y. of		
her age	1	153
Anna, d. [Eleazer & Susannah], b. Dec 25, 1773	2	170
Anne, m. Solomon **HUNTINGTON**, Mar. 28, 1762	2	75
Charles Lee, twin with George Washington, s. [Eleazer		
& Susannah], b. Dec. 21, 1776	2	170
Charlotta, d. [Eleazer & Susannah], b. Apr. 20, 1772	2	170
Charlotte, m. Dan **SAWYER**, Feb. 4, 1795	3	23
Daniel, m. Hannah **CROCKER**, Dec 6, 1727	1	101
Daniel, s. Daniel & Hannah, b. Sept. 5, 1730	1	101
Daniel, d. Sept 24, 1732, ae. about 30 y.	1	101
Daniel, m. Lydia **PEARL**, Nov. 27, 1753	1	320
Daniel, s. Daniel & Lydia, b. Jan. 25, 1755	1	320
Diah, s. [Thomas & Eunice], b. May 10, 1773	2	163
Dyer, s. Daniel & Lydia, b. Oct. 25, 1767; d Jan. 13,		
1772	1	320
Eleizer, s. Nathan & Ann, b. Dec. 24, 1744	1	153
Eleazer, m. Susannah **ELDERKIN**, Mar. 27, 1769	2	170
Eleazer, s. [Eleazer & Susannah], b. Jan. 10, 1770	2	170
Eleazer, s. [Thomas & Eunice], b. May 22, 1778	2	163
Elizabeth, d Daniel & Hannah, b Sept. 5, 1728	1	101
Elizabeth, d. [Thomas & Eunice], b. Dec. 25, 1768, at		
Palmer	2	163
Emeline, d. [Joseph & Catharine], b. June 24, 1806	3	73
Eunice, d [Thomas & Eunice], b. Aug. 13, 1782	2	163
Fernandas, d. [Eleazer & Susannah], b. [ ]	2	170
George Washington, twin with Charles Lee, s. [Eleazer		
& Susannah], b. Dec. 21, 1776	2	170
Hannah, d. Daniel & Hannah, b. Feb. 22, 1731/2	1	101
Hannah, d. Dan[ie]l & Lydia, b. Mar. 18, 1757	1	320
Hannah, m. James **ABBOT[T]**, Jan. 1, 1778	2	216
John, m. Almira **BUCK**, Jan. 16, 1831, by Rev. Rich[ar]d		
F. Cleveland	3	150
Joseph, s. Nathan & Ann, b. Nov. 2, 1738	1	153
Joseph, m. Catharine **BURK**, Jan. 8, 1804	3	73
Joseph, s. [Eleazer & Susannah], b. [ ]	2	170
Lucius, s. [Joseph & Catharine], b. Jan. 27, 1813	3	73
Lucius, m. Lydia **BIBBON**, [ ], 27, 1834, by		

	Vol	Page
DENISON, DENNISON, DINISON, (cont)		
Dexter Bullard, Hampton	3	168
Lydia, d Nathan & Ann, b. Apr. 27, 1747	1	153
Lydia, m. Joshua Booth **ELDERKIN**, Oct. 16, 1769	2	159
Marcy, m. George **BINGHAM**, Oct. 22, 1809	3	58
Mary, d. [Eleazer & Susannah], b. [ ]	2	170
Nathan, m. Ann **CARY**, Apr. 1, 1736	1	153
Nathan, s. Nathan & Ann, b. Sept. 17, 1740	1	153
Nathan, m. Hannah **FULLER**, Mar. 16, 1778	1	153
Orrilla, of Windham, m. W[illia]m M. **WELLS**, of Lyme,		
July 6, 1831, by Henry Huntington, J.P.	3	153
Polly, d. [Thomas & Eunice], b. May 2, 1780	2	163
Prudence, m. Nathaniell **WALES**, Jr , Dec. 27, 1726	1	85
Prudence, d. Nathan & Ann, b. Feb. 11, 1736/7	1	153
Prudence, twin with Susannah, d. Eleaz[er] &		
Susannah, b. Dec. 27, 1770	2	170
Rebeckah, d. [Eleazer & Susannah], b. Feb. 25,		
1775	2	170
Roswell, s. Tho[ma]s & Eunice, b. Mar. 7, 1771	2	163
Selden, m. Mary **ALLEN**, May 12, 1830, by Rev.		
Richard F. Cleveland	3	145
Susannah, twin with Prudence, d. Eleaz[er] &		
Susannah, b Dec. 27, 1770	2	170
Thomas, m. Eunice **HUTCHINSON**, Dec. 4, 1766	2	163
Thomas, s. [Thomas & Eunice], b. Apr 3, 1775	2	163
William, s. [Joseph & Catharine], b. May 22, 1804	3	73
DENNER, Sylvester, farmer, d. Feb. 18, [1850], ae 74	4	156
DENNY, Tamerin, of Leicester, m. Peter **WEBB**, of Windham,		
June 5, 1783	2	50
DERBY, Susanna, Wid., of Canterbury, m. Joshua **HOLT**, Jr.,		
Apr. 26, 1770	2	165
DEVINE, Daniel, operative, of Willimantic, d. Mar. 15,		
1860, ae. 28	4	159-0
John, of Willimantic, d. Mar. 26, 1860, ae. 3	4	159-0
DEVINEY, Michael, m. Altheah **PARISH**, b of Windham, July		
28, 1844, by Rev. Alfred Burnham	3	215
DEVOTION, Ann, m. John **WEBB**, July 30, 1746	1	261
Betsey, d. [Jonathan & Roxana], b. July 8, 1798	3	28
Ebenezer, m. Martha **LOTHROP**, July 25, 1738	1	216
Ebenezer, s. Ebenezer & Martha, b. Aug. 10, 1740	1	216
Ebenezer, Jr., m. Eunice **HUNTINGTON**, [ ], 1764	2	189
Ebenezer, s. [Ebenezer, Jr. & Eunice], b. Sept. 27,		
1764	2	189
Ebenezer, Rev., d. July 16, 1771, in the 59th y. of		
his age	1	216
Elizabeth, d. Ebenezer & Martha, b. Feb. 28, 1752	1	216
Elizabeth, d. [Ebenezer, Jr & Eunice], b. Dec. 28,		
1773; d. same day	2	189

	Vol	Page
DEVOTION, (cont.)		
Eunice, d. [Ebenezer, Jr. & Eunice], b. Sept. 6,		
1770	2	189
Eunice, m. Ebenezer **WALDO**, Aug. 22, 1797	3	17
Eunice H., m. Henry **MANNING**, Nov. 30, 1823	3	114
Francis R., m. Lee **LATHROP**, Oct. 16, 1831, by Rev.		
Rich[ar]d F. Cleveland (Scotland)	3	155
Hannah, d. Ebenezer & Martha, b. Jan. 11, 1742/3	1	216
Harriet S., of Windham, m. John S. **ROSS**, of Chaplin,		
Dec. 23, 1833, by Rev. Jesse Fisher	3	168
John, s. [Ebenezer, Jr. & Eunice], b. Dec. 26, 1766	2	189
Jonathan, s. [Ebenezer, Jr. & Eunice], b. Jan. 10,		
1769	2	189
Jonathan, m. Roxana **HOUSE**, Oct. 7, 1797	3	28
Louis, s. [Ebenezer, Jr. & Eunice], b. Nov 17, 1776	2	189
Lucy, d. Eb[enezer] & Martha, b. Feb. 12, 1754	1	216
Martha, d. Ebenezer & Martha, b. June 3, 1739	1	216
Martha, d. [Ebenezer, Jr. & Eunice], b. Jan. 25, 1773	2	189
Mary, d. Ebenezer & Martha, b. Nov 20, 1747	1	216
DEWEY, Alatheah, d. [Alpheas & Lydia], b. Aug. 24, 1788	2	101
Alpheas, m. Lydia **FRINK**, Nov. 29, 1787	2	101
Freeman, m. Dolly **HEB[B]ARD**, Mar. 31, 1796	2	63
Freeman, d. Aug. 12, 1807	2	63
George Rudd, s. [Alpheas & Lydia], b. Nov. 26, 1795	2	101
Henry Freeman, s. [Freeman & Dolly], b. Aug 17, 1800	2	63
Jonathan, s. [Freeman & Dolly], b. Apr. 7, 1803	2	63
Lucy, d. [Freeman & Dolly], b. May 24, 1797	2	63
William Pitt, s. [Alpheas & Lydia], b. Aug. 27, 1798	2	101
DEWITT, Charles, [s. Henry & Hannah], b Sept. 29, 1795	3	80
Hannah, d. [Henry & Hannah], b. Nov. 6, 1776	3	80
Henry, m. Hannah **DEAN**, of Norwich, [ ], 1772	3	80
Henry, s. [Henry & Hannah], b. June 15, 1792	3	80
Jabez, s. [Henry & Hannah], b. Nov. 6, 1774; d. Oct.		
[ ], 1777	3	80
Jabez Dean, [s. Henry & Hannah], b. May 11, 1779	3	80
Jacob, [s. Henry & Hannah], b. Sept. 17, 1785	3	80
Mariah, [d. Henry & Hannah], b. May 24, 1790	3	80
Martha, [d. Henry & Hannah], b. May 13, 1798	3	80
Mary, [d. Henry & Hannah], b. July 10, 1783	3	80
Mary Fenbrook, [d. Henry & Hannah], b. Mar. 30, 1781;		
d Oct. [ ], 1782	3	80
Nabby, [d. Henry & Hannah], b. Aug. 24, 1787; d. Nov.		
[ ], 1814, in Boston	3	80
Nancy, d. [Henry & Hannah], b. Feb. 19, 1773	3	80
DEXTER, William L., m. Alma **LINCOLN**, b. of Windham, June 6,		
1836, by Rev. Dexter Bullard	3	178
DICKENS, Mary, black, ae 23, had s. George **SPAFFORD**, b.		
May 6, 1848	4	3

	Vol.	Page
DILWORTH, DILLWORTH, Norris, s Norris, ae. 42, b.		
June 15, [1849]	4	6
Norris, shoemaker, b. Penn., res. Willimantic, d.		
May 1, 1851, ae. 44	4	157
DIMMOCK, DIMMICK, DEMMUCK, DIMUCK, DIMMOCH, DIMMICH, Austin, machinist, d. Dec. 12, [1849],		
ae. 18	4	155
Daniel, m. Mary **TERREL**, Nov. 23, 1732	1	140
Deidamia, m. Perez **TRACY**, Mar. 31, 1765	2	130
Joanna, m. Josiah **CONANT**, Oct. 6, 1709	1	12
Lydia, m. Joseph **MEACHAM**, Jr., Nov. 27, 1760	2	65
Mary, m. William **BACKUS**, Nov. 3, 1742	1	234
Mehitable, m David **LUCE**, May 24, 1759	2	9
Phebe, d. Daniel & Mary, b. Dec. 8, 1733	1	140
Rebeckah, m Jeduthan **SIMONDS**, Oct. 19, 1756	2	24
Thankfull, m. Edward **WALDO**, June 28, 1706	1	29
DINGLEY, Abigail, d. [John & Mary], b. May 2, 1772	2	142
John, s. Joseph & Katherine, b. Dec. 8, 1718	1	41
John, s. Joseph, d. Aug. 14, 1726	1	55
John, s. Jos[eph] & Zerviah, b. Dec. 12, 1748	1	210
John, m. Mary **FITCH**, Apr. 12, 1769	2	142
Joseph, m. Catharine **WALDO**, Nov. 2, 1702	A	33
Joseph, s. Joseph & Katharine, b. Oct. 18, 1708	1	41
Joseph, Jr., m. Zerviah **RIPLEY**, Apr. 25, 1739	1	210
Josiah, s. [Joseph, Jr. & Zerviah], b. July 12, 1751;		
d. Oct. 22, 1767	1	210
Katharine, w Joseph, d Sept. 15, 1747, in the 61st		
y. of her age	1	41
Mary, d. Joseph & Katharine, b Nov 12, 1712	1	41
Mary, m. Ephraim **UPTON**, Dec. 31, 1731	1	154
Mary, m. Josiah **MANNING**, May 6, 1742	1	234
Mary, d. Joseph, Jr. & Zerviah, b. July 31, 1745	1	210
Rebeckah, d. Joseph & Catharine, b. Dec. 12, 1703	A	33
Rebeckah, d. Joseph & Katharine, d. Mar. 17, 1712/13	1	41
Tryphenia, d. Jos[eph] & Zerviah, b. July 2, 1753	1	210
Trypheny, m. Shubael **FITCH**, Nov. 17, 1774	2	197
Zerviah, d. Joseph, Jr. & Zerviah, b June 22, 1742	1	210
DODGE, Abel, s. Andrew & Lydia, b. Feb. 9, 1735/6	1	139
Amos, m. Mary **WEBB**, Oct. 14, 1713	1	42
Amos, s. Amos & Mary, b. Nov. 27, 1714	1	42
Amos, d. Mar. 28, 1765, in the 67th y of his age	1	111
Andrew, m. Lydia **BRIDGMAN**, Jan. 27, 1725/6	1	89
Andrew, s. Andrew & Lydia, b. Feb. [ ], 1726/7; d.		
Feb. [ ], 1726	1	89
Andrew, s. Andrew & Lydia, b Apr 4, 1732; d. Apr 4,		
1732	1	89
Andrew, s Andrew & Lydia, b. Feb. 21, 1734/5; d. Feb.		
22, 1734/5	1	139

	Vol	Page
DODGE, (cont.)		
Andrew, s. Andrew & Lydia, b. Feb. 14, 1738/9	1	139
Elizabeth, d. Amos & Mary, b. Aug. 7, 1722	1	42
Hannah, d. Andrew & Lydia, b. Apr. 12, 1728	1	89
Irena, d. Andrew & Lydia, b. Mar. 29, 1729	1	89
Isaac, s. Andrew & Lydia, b. Feb. 25, 1739/40	1	139
Isaac, m. Sarah **UTLEY**, Oct. 28, 1762	2	84
Joel, m. Dorcas **SMITH**, June 18, 1753	1	322
John, s. Amos & Mary, b. June 14, 1724	1	42
Lafayette, farmer, of Mansfield, ae. 25, m. 2d w.		
Mary **BROADBANK**, ae 21, b. England, res		
Mansfield, Jan. 29, [1850], by Rev. Coe	4	118
Lydia, d. Andrew & Lydia, b May 23, 1730	1	89
Martha, d. Amos & Mary, b. July 25, 1720	1	42
Martha, m. Paul **HEB[B]ARD**, Apr. 30, 1741	1	224
Mary, d. Amos & Mary, b. Sept. 23, 1717	1	42
Phineas, s Amos & Mary, b. June 14, 1734; d. July		
11, 1773, in the 40th y. of his age	1	111
Rufus, s. Andrew & Lydia, b. Mar. 22, 1734	1	139
Ruth, d. Amos & Mary, b. Feb. [ ], 1727/8	1	111
Sam[ue]ll, s Amos & Mary, b. Apr 3, 1731	1	111
Sam[ue]ll, m. Hannah **PALMER**, May 18, 1767	2	64
Sarah, d. Andrew & Lydia, b Mar. 10, 1736/7	1	139
Zebulon, s. Amos & Mary, b. Mar. 20, 1716	1	42
DONE, [see under **DUNN**]		
DONOHUE, DONIHUE, DUNIHOE, John, s. Michael, ae. 30, &		
Ann, ae. 28, b. Aug. 17, 1849	4	8
John, d. May [1849], ae. 1	4	155
Thomas, s. Michael, manufacturer, ae. 25, & Bridget,		
ae. 26, b. Nov. 27, 1848	4	3
Tho[ma]]s, s. Cha[rle]s, laborer, ae 35, b Mar. 18,		
[1849]	4	11
DORAN, Daniel, m. Sophia **GETCHELL**, b of Windham, Nov 23,		
1828, by Rev. Chester Tilden	3	131
DORRANCE, [see also **LARRANCE**], Amey B , m. Niles		
POTTER, b. of Willimantic, Nov. 17, 1833, by Rev.		
A. Gregory	3	166
Eunice, m. Ralph **WEBB**, Dec. 31, 1815	3	83
Margaret, m. Ashbell **WELCH**, Oct. 15, 1795	3	38
Mary, m. Thomas **WEBB**, Jan. 20, 1822	3	93
Mary Rebecca, d. Alexander & Mary C., b Sept 19,		
1840	3	113
Orissa, of Willimantic, m Mason **KINNEY**, of Norwich,		
Aug. 7, 1843, at Willimantic, by Rev. J.B. Guild	3	210
William R., m. Mary Ann **FRINK**, Nov. 8, 1830, by Rev		
Jesse Fisher	3	149
William T., m. Nancy **CHESTER**, Mar. 18, 1827, by Rev		
Cornelius B. Everest	3	126

	Vol.	Page
DUBBLEDAY, Elizabeth, d Joseph & Eliza, b. Apr. 26, 1764	2	17
DOW, Rufus, of Coventry, m. Betsey B. **FULLER**, of Columbia, Nov. 25, 1831, by Rev. Peter Griffin	3	156
DOWN, Ann, b. Stonington, res. Windham, d. Sept. [ ], 1850, ae 69	4	158
Martha, b. Stonington, res. Windham, d. Oct. 11, 1850, ae 45	4	158
Sam[ue]ll F., d. Mar. [ ], 1851, ae. 36	4	158
DOWNER, Achsah, of Lebanon, m. William **FRINK**, of Stonington, Apr. 13, 1834, by Rev. Roger Bingham	3	169
[E]unice had s. Jona[than] **CARVER**, b. Dec. 18, 1741 Reputed father Jonathan **CARVER**	1	125
Jerusha, m. Nath[anie]l **CARY**, Jan. 6, 1757	2	20
Shubael, b. Lisbon, res. Windham, d. Mar. [ ], 1851, ae. 74	4	158
Simeon Palmer, m. Lucy **LEE**, Apr. 8, 1830, by Rev. Roger Bingham	3	144
Thankfull L., of Windham, m. John **BROOKS**, of Roxbury, Mass., May 4, 1841, by Rev. Nathan Wildman	3	197
DOWNING, Abner, s. [Henry & Mary], b. Sept. 12, 1778	2	196
Diantha C., of Windham, m. Samuel L. **HATCH**, of Norwalk, O., Sept. 22, 1844, by H. Slade, Scotland Society	3	217
Elizabeth, d. [Ichabod & Abigail], b. May 24. 1744	1	88
Henry, m. Mary **WEBB**, Aug. 15, 1774	2	196
Henry, s. [Henry & Mary], b. Nov. 23, 1775	2	196
Ichobod, s. Ichabod & Abigail, b. Mar. 1, 1741; d. Nov. 27, 1742	1	88
Ichabod, d. Dec. 26, 1742	1	88
Ichabod, d. Apr. 29, 1768	2	48
Martha, d. Ich[abod], & Abigail, b. Mar. 27, 1749	1	88
Mary, d. [Henry & Mary], b. Mar 22, 1777	2	196
Mason, s. [Henry & Mary], b. Mar. 1, 1780	2	196
Nathan, s [Henry & Mary], b. Nov. 18, 1774	2	196
Nathaniel, d. Aug. 10, 1766	2	48
Sarah, d. Ich[abod] & Abigail, b. Oct. 10, 1746	1	88
Stephen, m. Abigail **BAKER**, Nov. 17, 1763	2	100
DRAPER, Geo[rge], of Attleboro, Mass., m. Harriet **LEE**, of Windham, June 3, 1829, by Rev. Jesse Fisher	3	136
DROWN, Frances, m. Gilbert **ASHLEY**, Apr. 23, 1845, by Henry Greenslit	3	221
DUDINGTON, [see also **LUDDINGTON**], Phebe, m. Samuel **GEER**, Dec. 10, 1765	3	16
DUFFEY, Benj[amin], m. Elizabeth **CASE**, Feb. 23, 1715/16	1	50
Desire, d. Benj[amin] & Elizabeth, b. July 8, 1717	1	50
Elizabeth, d. Benjamin & Elizabeth, b. Nov 21, 1719	1	50
Ma[r]g[a]ret, d. Benjamin & Elizabeth, b. Feb. 13, 1722/3	1	50
DUMONT, Eunice, m. Hezekiah **RIPLEY**, Apr. 29, 1784	3	1

	Vol.	Page
DUMONT, (cont.)		
Freelove, m. Waldo **CAREY**, Dec. 8, 1814	3	75
DUNHAM, Almira, m. Joseph E. **WEAVER**, b. of Windham, Oct		
6, 1839, by Rev. Ella Dunham, Willimantic	3	191
Edwin H , m. Betsey C. **HALL**, Sept. 21, 1846, by		
Rev. Andrew Sharp	3	231
Elijah H , m. Susan **ROBERTSON**, b. of Windham, Jan.		
1, 1833, by Dexter Bullard	3	163
Eliza, housework, b. Norwich, res. Willimantic, d		
Apr. 13, [1849], ae. 21	4	153
Hannah B., m. Daniel **POTTER**, Dec. 9, 1841, by Rev.		
Andrew Sharp	3	199
Jemima, m. Sam[ue]ll **HUNTINGTON**, Jr., Jan 3, 1740	1	227
Josephine M., d. Joseph M., manufacturer, ae. 27, b.		
Sept. 5, [1849]	4	9
Leonard R., of Mansfield, m. Fanny R. **ROBINSON**, of		
Windham, Apr. 2, 1833, by Rev. Henry Mayo, Windsor	3	164
Marcia T., m. Albert B. **BROWN**, b. of Windham, Mar. 15,		
1840, by Rev Ella Dunham, Willimantic	3	192
Philena, m. Elnathan **WARNER**, Feb. 5, 1815	2	248
Sarah A., m. Marvin B. **WEAVER**, b. of Willimantic Falls,		
July 3, 1836, by Rev. Benajah Cook, Jr.	3	178
Submit M., m. George L. **WEAVER**, July 11, 1835, by Rev		
Ella Dunham	3	173
DUNN, DONE, Eunice, m. Hezekiah **RIPLEY**, Apr. 29, 1784	2	253
Huldah, ae. 25, b. Coventry, res. Rockville, m.		
Leonard **ROSELE**, farmer, ae. 30, b. Windham, res		
Rockville, Sept. 15, [1850], by Rev. E.W. Barrows	4	118
Tho[ma]s, s. cutter, b. Ireland, res. Willimantic, d		
Feb. [ ], 1851, ae. 22	4	157
DUNTON, Mary, m. William **BACKUS**, Aug. 31, 1692	A	3
DURANT, Elizabeth, ae. 29, m. John **LITTLEFIELD**, merchant,		
ae 31, Sept 1, 1849, by Rev. Hicks	4	115
DURKEE, DURKE, DURGEE, DURGE, DURGEY, DIRKE, **DORKEE, DUKE, DURKEY**, Abba, s [Joseph & Elizabeth], b. Aug. 18, 1772 (See also Alba **DURKEE**)	2	183
Abial, s. [Henry, Jr. & Sarah], b. Mar. 14, 1774; d. Feb 8, 1778	2	148
Abiel, s. [Henry, Jr. & Sarah], b. May 27, 1781	2	148
Abigail, d. William & Abigail, b. Apr. 14, 1734	1	137
Abigail, d. Henry & Releaf, b. July 7, 1745	1	242
Abigail, d. Jeremiah & Abigail, b. Aug. 1, 1747	1	284
Abigail, m. Josiah **HAMMOND**, Jr., Nov. 19, 1751	1	317
Abigail, d. Joseph & Elizabeth, b Feb. 11, 1756	1	258
Abigail, d. Jos[eph] & Elizabeth, b. Feb. 11, 1756	2	183
Abigail, m Benjamin **DURKEE**, Jan. 21, 1762	2	55
Abigail, m. Joel **UTLEY**, Jan. 7, 1768	2	131

	Vol.	Page
DURKEE, DURKE, DURGEE, DURGE, DURGEY, DIRKE,		
DORKEE, DUKE, DURKEY, (cont.)		
Abigail, m. Abiel **HOLT**, July 18, 1776	2	222
Alba, s. [Joseph & Elizabeth], b. July 1, 1772		
(See also Abba **DURKEE**)	1	258
Alecta, d. [Jeremiah & Abigail], b. Mar. 2, 1764	1	284
Amasa, s. Stephen & Lois, b. Oct 7, 1747	1	118
Amasa, s. [Stephen & Lois], b. Oct. 7, 1747; d.		
Sept. 21, 1754	1	225
Amasa, s. [Stephen & Jerusha], b. Mar. 14, 1777	2	153
Ame, d. Thomas & Rebeckah, b Apr. 10, 1731	1	92
Amelia, d. [Robert & Sarah], b. Aug. 3, 1772	2	18
Amhurst, s. [Robert & Sarah], b. Aug. 20, 1768	2	18
Amy, see under Ame		
Andrew, s. Thomas & Elizabeth, b. Feb. 2, 1715	1	20
Andrew, s. Stephen & Lois, b. Nov 24, 1737	1	118
Andrew, m. Mary **BENJAMIN**, Jan. 28, 1762	2	73
Anna, m. Samuel **PALMER**, Dec. 6, 1827 [1727?]	1	84
Anna, d. [Andrew & Mary], b. Apr. 19, 1766	2	73
Asel, s [Benjamin & Abigail], b. Dec. 11, 1765	2	55
Benjamin, s. William & Elizabeth, b. Oct. 18, 1744	1	219
Benjamin, m Abigail **DURKEE**, Jan. 21, 1762	2	55
Benjamin, s. [Benjamin & Abigail], b. Dec. 12, 1779	2	55
Benjamin, m. Lora **MARTIN**, Aug 26, 1804	3	55
Betsey, d. [Benjamin & Abigail], b. Feb. 6, 1770	2	55
Cynthia, d. [Andrew & Mary], b. Feb 18, 1772	2	73
Diadama, d. Joseph & Elizabeth, b. Feb. 6, 1758	1	258
Diadama, d. Joseph & Eliz[abe]th, b Feb. 6, 1758	2	183
Ebbe, s. [Joseph & Elizabeth], b. July 26, 1768	2	183
Eben, s. [Andrew & Mary], b Nov. 26, 1769	2	73
Electa, see under Alecta		
Eliphalet, s. [Henry], b. Aug. 6, 1762	2	66
Elizabeth, m. David **FFISKE**, Dec. 25, 1723	1	70
Elizabeth, w. Thomas, d. July 28, 1727	1	92
Elizabeth, [twin with Hannah], d. Nath[anie]ll &		
Mary, b. Feb. 6, 1728/9	1	99
Elizabeth, d William & Elizabeth, b. Nov. 28,		
1737	1	55
Elizabeth, d. William & Abigail, b. Nov. 28, 1737		
("Sd. Elizabeth belongs to Dea. Durge")	1	137
Eliz[abeth], m. Zebadiah **COBURN**, Jan. 22, 1754	2	21
Elizabeth, wid., m. Jacob **WOODWARD**, Mar. 28, 1754	1	204
Elizabeth, d. Joseph & Elizabeth, b. June 13, 1754	1	258
Elizabeth, d. Joseph & Elizabeth, b. June 13, 1754	2	183
Eunice, d. [Henry & Releaf], b. Feb. 18, 1754	1	242
Eunice, d. [Stephen & Jerusha], b. Apr. 28, 1772	2	153
Eunice, d [Henry, Jr. & Sarah], b. June 10, 1779	2	148
Ezra, s. [Joseph & Elizabeth], b. July 26, 1768	1	258

	Vol	Page
DURKEE, DURKE, DURGEE, DURGE, DURGEY, DIRKE, DORKEE, DUKE, DURKEY, (cont.)		
Hannah, [twin with Elizabeth], d. Nath[anie]ll & Mary, b. Feb. 6, 1728/9	1	99
Hannah, d. William & Abigail, b. Jan. 26, 1738/9	1	137
Hannah, d. Stephen & Lois, b. May 2, 1742	1	118
Hannah, m. Stephen **CLARKE**, Feb. 1, 1742/3	1	238
Hannah, m. William **FOSTER**, May 27, 1755	2	10
Hannah, m. William **FOSTER**, May 27, 1755	2	17
Hannah, m. Nathan **UTLEY**, Apr. 27, 1762	2	140
Henry, [s. William & Rebeckah], b. Jan. 18, 1718	1	25
Henry, s. Henry & Releaf, b. June 29, 1740	1	242
Henry, [s. Henry & Releaf], d. Apr 28, 1745	1	242
Henry, s. Henry & Releaf], b. Sept. 29, 1749	1	242
Henry, Jr., m. Sarah **HOLT**, Nov. 16, 1769	2	148
Henry, s. [Henry, Jr. & Sarah], b. Aug. 25, 1770	2	148
Henry, Jr., m. Sarah **LOOMIS**, Apr. 23, 1778	2	148
Henry, d. Sept. 6, 1785, in the 68th y. of his age	2	66
Heastar, d. Robert & Heastar, b Apr. 14, 1739	1	191
Heastar, d. May [ ], 1739	1	191
Huldath, d. William & Rebeckah, b. Jan. 17, 1720	1	25
Huldah, m. Sam[ue]ll **STILES**, Oct. 7, 1735	1	142
Ipsaba, d. William & Elizabeth, b. Dec. 8, 1742	1	222
James, s. Thomas & Elizabeth, b. June 3, 1721	1	20
Jannette, [d. William & Rebeckah], b. Jan. 14, 1824 [1724?]	1	25
Jedeiah, s. [Oliver & Mary], b. Mar 13, 1780	2	104
Jeremiah, s. John & Elizabeth, d. Jan. 5, 1724/5	1	73
Jeremiah, s. William & Susannah, b. Jan 21, 1726/7	1	55
Jeremiah, m. Abigail **ADAMS**, Mar. 25, 1747	1	284
Jeremiah, s. Jerem[ia]h & Abigail, b. May 7, 1754	1	284
Jeremiah, d. Nov. 29, 1775	1	284
Jerusha, d. William & Rebeckah, b. Aug. 12, 1710	1	25
Jerusha, m. Ebenezer **MARTIN**, Apr. 1, 1729	1	76
Jerusha, d. [Stephen & Jerusha], b. Nov. 6, 1769	2	153
John, s. William & Susannah, b. Dec. 11, 1728	1	55
John, d. Sept 11, 1739, ae. about 75 y	1	188
John, s. [Joseph & Elizabeth], b. July 2, 1762	1	258
John, s. [Joseph & Elizabeth], b. July 2, 1762	2	183
John, s. [Benjamin & Abigail], b. Apr. 9, 1784	2	55
Joseph, s. [Joseph & Elizabeth], b. May 8, 1778	2	183
Joseph, m. Elizabeth [ ]	2	183
Levi, of Norwich, m. Julia G. **SPAULDING**, of Windham, Oct. 8, 1829, by Rev. Dennis Platt	3	138
Lois, d. Stephen & Lois, b. Mar 1, 1739/40	1	118
Lora, d. [Benjamin & Lora], b. June 26, 1805	3	55
Luce, [d. William & Rebeckah], b. Jan. 6, 1728	1	25
Luce, m. Ezekiel **HOLT**, Nov. 5, 1745; d. Aug. 11, 1747	1	270

	Vol.	Page
DURKEE, DURKE, DURGEE, DURGE, DURGEY, DIRKE, DORKEE, DUKE, DURKEY, (cont.)		
Lucy, d. Henry & Releaf, b. Aug 9, 1747	1	242
Lucy, d. [Joseph & Elizabeth], b. Aug. 21, 1766	1	258
Lucy, d. [Joseph & Elizabeth], b. Aug 21, 1766	2	183
Lucy, twin with Luther, [d. Shubael], b. Nov. 10, 1795	2	243
Luther, twin with Lucy, [s. Shubael], b. Nov. 10, 1795	2	243
Lydia, d. Stephen & Lois, b. Aug. 3, 1735	1	118
Lydia, m. Eleazer **BUTLER**, Jan. 11, 1758	2	40
Lydia, d. Jeremiah & Abigail, b. Nov. 7, 1759	1	284
Lydia, d. [Stephen & Jerusha], b. May 16, 1783	2	153
Martha, d. William & Rebeckah, b. Dec. 11, 1705	1	25
Martha, m. John **HIB[B]ARD**, Sept 22, 1725	1	93
Martha, wid., d. Jan. 11, 1726/7, ae. about 87	1	20
Mary, d. Thomas & Rebeckah, b. Feb. 28, 1728/9	1	92
Mary, d. William & Abigail, b. Nov. 29, 1741	1	137
Mary, m. John **BREWSTER**, Nov. 6, 1760	2	62
Mary, d. [Andrew & Mary], b. Jan. 11, 1763	2	73
Mary, d. Henry & Releaf, b. Sept. 30, 1765	1	243
Mary, m. Nathaniel **FULLER**, Jr., Aug. 8, 1780	2	245
Mary, d. [Henry, Jr. & Sarah], b Nov. 26, 1784	2	148
Mehitable, d. William & Susannah, b. Feb. 10, 1730/31	1	55
Nabby, d. [Benjamin & Abigail], b. Oct. 4, 1774	2	55
Nathan, s. Thomas & Elizabeth, b. Dec. 27, 1725	1	20
Nath[anie]ll, m. Mary **BAKER**, Aug. 21, 1727	1	99
Nath[anie]ll, s Nath[anie]ll & Mary, b. Dec. 10, 1730	1	99
Olive, d [Henry], b. June 12, 1761	2	66
Oliver, s. William & Elizabeth, b. Apr. 30, 1741	1	219
Oliver, s. William & Elizabeth, b. Apr. 30, 1741	1	222
Oliver, m. Mary **HIDE**, June 21, 1764	2	104
Perles, d. [Joseph & Elizabeth], b. July 1, 1770	2	183
Persas, d. [Joseph & Elizabeth], b. July 1, 1770	1	258
Phineas, s. Stephen & Lois, b. Sept 16, 1730	1	118
Rebeckah, [d. William & Rebeckah], b. June 11, 1722	1	25
Releaf, d. Henry & Releaf, b Apr. 3, 1743	1	242
Robert, s. Thomas & Elizabeth, b. Dec. 10, 1713	1	20
Robert, s. Stephen & Lois, b. Nov. 26, 1733	1	118
Robert, m. Heastar **WARREN**, Apr. 25, 1738	1	191
Robert, m. Sarah **DURKEE**, Nov. 21, 1754	2	18
Robert, s. [Robert & Sarah], b. Aug. 6, 1766	2	18
Robert, Capt., d July 3, 1778 "Was killed by the enemy at Westmoreland, Forty Fort, near Fort Durkee"	2	18
Robert, s. [Stephen & Jerusha], b. Mar. 11, 1779	2	153

	Vol	Page
DURKEE, DURKE, DURGEE, DURGE, DURGEY, DIRKE,		
DORKEE, DUKE, DURKEY, (cont.)		
Ruby, d. Jerem[ia]h & Abigail, b Feb. 4, 1762	1	284
Saben, s. William & Susannah, b. Mar. 12, 1732/33	1	55
Samuel, s. [Oliver & Mary], b Feb 25, 1774	2	104
Sarah, d. William & Rebeckah, b. Mar. 3, 1714	1	25
Sarah, d. William & Abigail, b Aug. 31, 1736	1	137
Sarah, m. George **MARTIN**, Jr., May 12, 1737	1	150
Sarah, d. William & Elizabeth, b. Aug. 23, 1739	1	55
Sarah, d. William, Jr. & Abigail, d. June 15, 1742	1	137
Sarah, d Henry & Releaf, b. Jan. 16, 1752; d		
Sept. 17, 1754	1	242
Sarah, m. Robert **DURKEE**, Nov. 21, 1754	2	18
Sarah, d. [Robert & Sarah], b. Mar. 5, 1755	2	18
Sarah, d Henry & Releaf, b. Aug. 21, 1756	1	242
Sarah, d. [Henry, Jr. & Sarah], b. Jan. 18, 1777	2	148
Sarah, w. Henry, Jr, d Apr 7, 1777	2	148
Shubael, s. [Stephen & Jerusha], b. May 12, 1767	2	153
Solomon, s. William & Elizabeth, b. Apr. 28, 1748;		
d. Sept. 3, 1754	1	222
Solomon, s. [Benjamin & Abigail], b. Sept 13, 1762	2	55
Stephen, m. Lois **MOULTEN**, Mar. 19, 1729/30	1	118
Stephen, s. Stephen & Lois, b Oct. 14, 1745	1	225
Stephen, m. Jerusha **SIMONS**, May 15, 1766	2	153
Stephen, s. [Stephen & Jerusha], b Apr 26, 1774	2	153
Susannah, [w. William], d. Feb. 8, 1734/5	1	55
Susannah, d William & Elizabeth, b. Aug 14, 1736	1	55
Susannah, d. [Jeremiah & Abigail], b. Jan. 4,		
1749/50	1	284
Susannah, m. Zephaniah **DAVISS**, July 16, 1752	1	319
Susannah, m. Zephaniah **DAVISON**, July 16, 1752	2	32
Sybil, d. Stephen & Lois, b. Jan. 10, 1731/2	1	118
Sybel, m. William **HOLT**, May 14, 1752	1	221
Sybel, d. [Stephen & Jerusha], b. Apr. 12, 1781	2	153
Tamma, d. William & Elizabeth, b June 23, 1746	1	222
Tama, d. [Oliver & Mary], b. Aug. 22, 1765	2	104
Tamma, m. Shubael **SIMONS**, Apr. 6, 1769	2	156
Thomas, s. Thomas & Elizabeth, b. Dec. 14, 1717	1	20
Thomas, s. John & Elizabeth, d. Dec 26, 1724	1	73
Thomas, m. Rebeckah **LAMB**, June 26, 1728	1	92
Thomas, s Jeremiah & Abigail, b. Apr. 5, 1752	1	284
Timothy, s. [Joseph & Elizabeth], b. May 18, 1776	2	183
Tryphenia, d. [Joseph & Elizabeth], b Oct. 21, 1759	1	258
Tryphena, d. [Joseph & Elizabeth], b. Oct. 21, 1759	2	183
Tryphenia, m. Thomas **HODKINS**, Jr, June 22, 1780	2	234a
Vine, s. [Oliver & Mary], b. Mar. 26, 1768	2	104
Waitstill, d. Jeremiah & Abigail, b. May 19, 1757	1	284
Wilkes, s. [Andrew & Mary], b. July 25, 1768	2	73

	Vol.	Page

DYER, DYAR, (cont.)

Lama, m. George **BACKUS**, b. of Windham, Mar. 23,
    1836, by John Baldwin, J.P. (Laura?) — 3 — 177

Laura, d. [Dr. Benjamin & Mary], b. Sept. 17, 1789 — 2 — 250

Lucy, d. [Dr. Benjamin & Mary], b. Jan. 15, 1795 — 2 — 250

Lydia, d. Thomas & Lydia, b. July 12, 1724 — 1 — 39a

Lydia, m. Sam[ue]ll **GRAY**, Nov. 7, 1742 — 1 — 205

Lydia, m. Samuel **GRAY**, Nov. 7, 1742 — 2 — 6

Lydia, w. Thomas, d. Mar. 12, 1750 — 1 — 39a

Lydia, m. Elisha **WHITE**, Jr., Sept. 10, 1815 — 3 — 77

Lydia, m. James **LINDSEY**, Dec. 31, 1836, by Rev.
    Philetus **GREENE** — 3 — 180

Maria, d. [Dr. Benjamin & Mary], b. July 18, 1785 — 2 — 250

Maria, m. Nathaniel **HOWES**, Jan. 1, 1811 — 3 — 35

Maria, m. Nathaniel **HOWES**, Jan. 1, 1811 — 3 — 76

Mary, d. Thomas & Lydia, b. Jan. 31, 1718/19 — 1 — 39a

Mary, m. Rev. Stephen **WHITE**, Sept. 2, 1741 — 1 — 226

Mary, m. Rev. Stephen **WHITE**, Sept. 2, 1741 — 2 — 174

Mary, of Willimantic, m James **HOUSTON**, of Norwich,
    Sept. 12, 1841, by Rev. Andrew Sharpe — 3 — 198

Mehetable, [w. Col. Thomas], d. Nov. 1, 1753 — 1 — 92

Oliver, s. Elip[halet] & Huldah, b. Dec. 22, 1755; d.
    June 6, 1778 — 1 — 251

Susan, m. William H. **HOSMER**, July 14, 1842, by Rev.
    Andrew Sharp, Willimantic — 3 — 202

Thomas, m. Lydia **BACKUS**, Oct. 24, 1717 — 1 — 18

Thomas, m. Lydia **BACKUS**, Oct. 24, 1717 — 1 — 39a

Thomas, s. Elip[halet] & Huldah, b. Nov. 22, 1747 — 1 — 251

Thomas, Col., m. Mehetable **GARDINER**, Oct. 10, 1752 — 1 — 92

Thomas, Col., m. Sarah **WALDEN**, Oct. 5, [ ]; d. May
    27, 1766 — 2 — 1

Thomas, m. Elizabeth **RIPLEY**, May 6, 1771 — 2 — 166

Thomas, s. [Thomas & Elizabeth], b. Jan. [ ], 1773 — 2 — 166

William Bowen, s. [Dr. Benjamin & Mary], b. Feb. 17,
    1799 — 2 — 250

——, Capt., had Dinah, b. to Hager, servant maid,
    June [ ], 1736; d. Dec. 25, 1736 — A — 32

——, Capt., had negro Dinah, d. Hager, b. June 2,
    1736; d. Dec. 25, 1736 — 1 — 170

EAMES, EAMS, [see also **AMES**], Elizabeth, m. Arther **BEBENS**,
    May 26, 1731 — 1 — 130

Lydia, m. John **PALMER**, Oct. 28, 1755 — 2 — 105

EATON, Albert, s. Calvin R., coachman, ae. 32, & Julia,
    ae. 35, b. Oct. 15, [1849] — 4 — 9

Caleb, of Norwich, m. Hannah F. **ROBINSON**, of Windham,
    Oct. 9, 1842, by Rev. Isaac H. Coe — 3 — 204

Henry C., s. Caleb, shoemaker, ae. 47, of Willimantic,
    b. Jan. 20, [1850] — 4 — 10

	Vol.	Page
EATON, (cont.)		
Joseph, s. Joseph & Hannah, b. Aug. 7, 1723	1	60
Mary, m. Eleazer **PALMER**, Jr., Nov. 8, 1770	2	10
Merchant, s. Joseph & Hannah, b. Dec. 3, 1725	1	60
EDGERTON, EDGARTON, Abby, d. [Andrew & Nancy], b. Sept.		
6, 1806	3	35
Andrew, m Nancy **WEBB**, Oct. 16, 1794	3	35
Anne, m. Eliel **WALES**, June 28, 1792	2	108
Edward, s. [Andrew & Nancy], b. Jan. 16, 1800	3	35
Justin, m. Mary **BABCOCK**, Apr. 23, 1832, by Rev.		
Alva Gregory, Willimantic	3	160
Mary Ann, d. [Andrew & Nancy], b. July 26, 1795, at		
Burlington, N Y.	3	35
EDMONDS, L.H., painter, b. Sutton, Mass., res. Willimantic,		
d. Aug. 4, [1849], ae. 43	4	153
Rosannah E., d. Dan[ie]l, painter, ae. 44, & Betsey,		
ae. 37, of Willimantic, b. Oct. 4, [1848]	4	5
William H., b. Tolland, res. Windham, d. July 18,		
1848, ae. 7	4	151
EDSON, ——, s. [ ], soap maker, ae. 25, &		
[ ], ae. 21, b. Mar. 20, 1848	4	2
EDWARDS, Anna, m. Jeremiah **PHILLIPS**, Sept. 29, 1821, by		
Rev. C B. Everest	3	120
Daniel, m. Elizabeth **MORE**, Feb. 27, 1700	A	8
Daniell, s. Daniell & Elizabeth, d. Mar. 7, 1704	A	29
Daniell, s. Daniell & Elizabeth, b. Jan. 3, 1705/6	1	25
Daniel, see also David		
David*, s. David* & Elizabeth, b. Mar. 21, 1704		
(*Probably Daniel)	A	8
Elizabeth, d. Daniell & Elizabeth, b. Apr. 28, 1708	1	25
Elizabeth, m. Jabez **HUNTINGTON**, June 30, 1724	1	78
Hannah, d. Daniell & Elizabeth, b. July 22, 1713	1	25
Jane, m. Thomas **HARRIS**, Mar. 5, 1700	A	8
Loring, painter, b. Millbury, Mass., res. Windham,		
d. Aug. 5, 1848, ae. 42	4	151
Mary, d. Daniel & Elizabeth, b. Nov. 18, 1716	1	25
Mercy, m. Ebenezer **BACKUS**, Nov. 25, 1760, by Rev.		
Mr. Eells, at Middletown	2	73
Thomas, s. Daniell & Elizabeth, b. July 16, 1711	1	25
Will[iam], s. David & Elizabeth, b. Nov. 12, 1703	A	7
William, s. Daniell & Elizabeth, b. Nov. 12, 1703	1	25
ELDERKIN, Alatheah, m. Jairus **LITTLEFIELD**, Nov. 23, 1805	3	54
Alfred, s. Jed[ediah] & Anna, b. Jan. 4, 1759	1	247
Alfred, s. [Jedediah & Anne], b. Jan. 4, 1759	2	233
Alfred, m. Sarah **BROWN**, Jan. 27, 1779	2	219
Amy, d. Jed[ediah] & Anna, b. Mar. 5, 1761	1	247
Amey, d. [Jedediah & Anne], b. Mar. 5, 1761	2	233
Amie, m. Jabez **CLARK**, Apr. 4, 1787	2	212

	Vol.	Page
ELDERKIN, (cont.)		
Amie, d. [Bela & Philena], b. Nov. [ ], 1789	3	41
Anne, d. Jed[ediah] & Anne, b. Oct. 30, 1747	1	247
Anne, d. [Jedediah & Anne], b. Oct. 30, 1747	2	233
Anne, m. Hez[ekia]h **BISSELL**, Mar. 18, 1765	2	109
Anthony Yeldat, s. [Bela & Philena], b. Dec. 9, 1786	3	41
Bela, s. [Jedediah & Anne], b. Dec. 10, 1751	2	233
Bela, s. [Vine & Lydia], b. Feb. 3, 1770	2	128
Bela, m. Philena **FITCH**, d. Col. Eleazer, Mar. 18, 1773	3	41
Bela, s. [Bela & Philena], b. Sept. 30, 1782	3	41
Billy, s. Jed[ediah] & Anna, b. Dec. 10, 1751	1	247
Bishop, s. [Alfred & Sarah], b. Feb. 16, 1784	2	219
Charlotte, d. [Jedediah & Anne], b. Oct. 23, 1764; d. Dec. 13, 1897 [1797?]	2	233
Charlotte, m. Sam[uel] **GRAY**, July 2, 1788	2	137
Eleazer, s. [Bela & Philena], b. June 28, 1775	3	41
Fanny, d. [Alfred & Sarah], b. Nov. 22, 1781	2	219
George, s. [Bela & Philena], b. Nov. 2, 1784	3	41
George, s. [Thomas & Polly], b. Nov. 14, 1797	3	36
Hannah, d. [Joshua & Rachel], b. Apr. 24, 1750, at Haddam; d. Aug. 17, 1750	2	19
Hannah, d. Josh[ua] & Rachel, d. Aug. 17, 1750	2	19
Hannah Huntington, d. [Joshua & Rachel], b. Feb. 26, 1764	2	19
Harriet, d. [Vine & Lydia], b. Oct. 4, 1768	2	128
Henry, s. [Bela & Philena], b. Aug. 2, 1780	3	41
Jedediah, m. Anne **WOOD**, Aug. 31, 1741	2	233
Jedediah, s. [Bela & Philena], b. Jan. 1, 1774	3	41
Joshua, m. Rachel **WETMORE**, July 31, 1749	2	19
Joshua Booth, s. [Joshua & Rachel], b. June 14, 1751; at Haddam	2	19
Joshua Booth, m. Lydia **DENISON**, Oct. 16, 1769	2	159
Judeth, d. [Jedediah & Anne], b. Mar. 2, 1743, in Norwich	2	233
Judeth, m. Jabez **HUNTINGTON**, Aug. 6, 1760	2	57
Judeth, d. [Alfred & Sarah], b. Aug. 2, 1788	2	219
Julia, m. Timothy **STANIFORD**, Nov. 14, 1795	3	29
Louisa Rachal, d. [Joshua & Rachel], b. May 31, 1753	2	19
Loisa Rachal, m. Samuel **BADGER**, Jr., Sept. 26, 1776	2	213
Lora, d. Jed[ediah] & Anna, b. Nov. 30, 1753	1	247
Lora, d. [Jedediah & Anne], b. Nov. 30, 1753	2	233
Lora, d. [Alfred & Sarah], b. Feb. 20, 1786	2	219
Mary, Jr., m. Benjamin **CLEVELAND**, Jr., Feb. 20, 1754	2	38
Mary, d. [Joshua Booth & Lydia], b. July 16, 1770	2	159
Mary Ann, d. [Vine & Lydia], b. Dec. 18, 1771	2	128

	Vol.	Page
ELDERKIN, (cont.)		
Mira, d. [Bela & Philena], b. Jan. 19, 1793	3	41
Philena, w. Bela, d. Dec. 8, 1796	3	41
Polly, w. Tho[ma]s, d. Sept. 13, 1799	3	36
Sally, d [Alfred & Sarah], b. Aug. 8, 1779	2	219
Stephen White Head, s. [Vine & Lydia], b. Sept. 12, 1773	2	128
Susannah, d. [Joshua & Rachel], b. Nov. 7, 1760	2	19
Susannah, m. Eleazer **DENNISON**, Mar 27, 1769	2	170
Susannah, m. Roger **HUNTINGTON**, Aug. 10, 1780	2	229
Thomas, m. Polly **BUCK**, Aug. 27, 1797	3	36
Thomas Mason Fitch, s. [Bela & Philena], b. Oct. 5, 1778	3	41
Vashti, m. Elias **BINGHAM**, of Scotland, Nov. 28, 1776	2	115
Vine, s. Jedediah & Anna, b. Sept. 11, 1745	1	247
Vine, s. [Jedediah & Anne], b. Sept. 11, 1745	2	233
Vine, m. Lydia **WHITE**, Nov. 23, 1767	2	128
Wealthy, d. Martha **HILL**, b. Jan. 8, 1769	2	153
——, s. Jed[ediah] & Anna, b. Apr. 24, 1756; d. May 1, 1756	1	247
——, s. [Jedediah & Anne], b. Apr. 24, 1756; d. May 1, 1756	2	233
ELDRIDGE, Anna, m. Benjamin **HIDE**, Jan. 30, 1766	2	124
ELICE, Mary, m. David **READ**, Dec. 28, 1746	1	263
ELLIOT, ELLOT, Ann Mariah, d. Warren, laborer, ae. 31, b. Mar. 27, 1851	4	13
Geo[rge] W., s. Warren, ae. 29, & Ann, ae. 25, b. Nov. [ ], 1848	4	7
Mary, d. Nancy **JONES**, b. Jan. 12, 1806	3	73
Sarah A., ae. 32, m. W[illia]m A **COLLINS**, ae. 51, Apr. 16, [1849], by Rev. J.M. Phillips	4	114
Warren B , m. Ann P. **SQUIRES**, b. of Windham, Aug. 18, 1844, by Rev. S.B. Paddock, of Norwich	3	216
ELLSWORTH, Cyrus, m. Almira **CHAPMAN**, b of Windham, Mar. 23, 1837, by Stowell Lincoln, J.P.	3	188
Lucius W., of East Windham, m. Susan S **CHEENEY**, of Willimantic, Sept. 21, 1845, by Rev. Z. Baker, Willimantic	3	222
Lucretia, ae. 22, m. William **CHEENEY**, shoemaker, ae. 28, of Windham, Jan. 25, 1848, by Rilander Sharp	4	111
ELY, Sarah, m. Edward R. **CRANDALL**, Mar. 9, 1835, by Rev. Roger Bingham	3	172
William, m. Drusilla **BREWSTER**, Oct. 12, 1766	2	122
ENSWORTH, Horace, of Hartford, m Jerusha A. **LASSELL**, of Windham, Apr. 19, 1840, by Rev. Otis C. Whiton	3	193
ESSEX, Elizabeth C., m. Daniel W. **HADDAM**, Oct. 15, 1843, by Rev. Andrew Sharp	3	211

	Vol	Page
ESSEX, (cont.)		
W[illia]m T., m. Eliza Ann **CLARK,** b. of Windham,		
Nov. 10, 1839, by Rev. Otis C. Whiton, of		
Scotland Society	3	192
Zerviah E., m. Gardiner **HALL,** Nov. 29, 1832, by		
Rev. Alva Gregory	3	162
ESTUS, George S., m. Catherine M. **BEACH,** Oct. 13, 1843, by		
Rev. Andrew Sharp	3	211
EVERETT, EVERET, EVERIT, Israel, Jr., m. Hannah **WEST,**		
Feb. 11, 1739/40	1	202
Israel, s. Israel, Jr. & Hannah, b. Jan. 14, 1740/41	1	202
Sarah, d. Israel & Sarah, b. Apr. [ ], 1720	1	17
Sarah, d. Israel & Sarah, b. May 28, 1721	1	17
Sarah, m. William **BEAMONT,** Dec. 29, 1747	1	275
EWEING, Lydia Caroline, m. Lucius **BIBBONS,** b. of Windham,		
Apr. 14, 1843, by Rev. Henry Bromley	3	208
FAGIN, Bridget, m Ceazer **BINGHAM,** June 5, 1823	3	50
FAIRBANKS, Reuben G., m. Lucy L. **WEBB,** Mar. 11, 1831, by		
Rev. Rich[ar]d F. Cleveland	3	152
FALES, Edward, ironsmith, of Windham, d. May 16, 1849, ae.		
22	4	154
FANNING, Thomas, Capt., m. Phebe **HURLBUTT,** Jan. 16, 1772	2	181
FARGO, Mary, m. John **ALLEN,** June 20, 1700	A	20
FARNHAM, FFARNUM, FARNAM, FFARNAM, FARNUM,		
A[a]ron, s. Nath[anie]ll & Hannah, b. May 30, 1742	1	171
Annah, d. William & Annah, b. Oct. 27, 1723	1	53
Anne, d. Nath[anie]ll & Hannah, b Apr. 2, 1726	1	171
Anne, d. Nath[anie]l & Hannah, b. Apr. 26, 1726	1	18
Anne, m. Nehemiah **HOLT,** Nov. 25, 1745	1	259
Anne, m. Jeduthan **ROGERS,** Oct. 21, 1747	1	281
Art[h]er Benjamin, s. [Mannassah, Jr. & Patience], b		
Jan. 7, 1759	2	47
Asa, s. Nathaniell & Hannah, b. Nov. 11, 1731	1	94
Asa, m. Lydia **BIDLAKE,** Mar. 2, 1756	2	21
Calven, s. [Zebediah & Mary], b. Oct. 22, 1763	2	8
Caroline M., d. Charles, ae. 35, & Nancy, ae. 28, b.		
Apr. 27, 1848	4	3
Charles H., m. Nancy O. **AVERY,** Nov. 29, 1839	3	97
Daniel, s. [Zebediah & Mary], b. July 19, 1752; d		
Jan. 9, 1777	2	8
Daniel, s. [Ebenezer & Joanna], b. Jan. 5, 1779	2	179
Eben, s. [Zebediah & Mary], b. Dec. 17, 1750	2	8
Ebenezer, m. Joanna **BENJAMIN,** Mar. 3, 1773	2	179
Eliah*, Henry & Phebe, b. July 24, 1731 (* correc-		
tion "Eliab" handwritten in margin of original		
manuscript)	1	131
Elijah, s. William & Annah, b. Jan. 10, 1728/9	1	53
Elijah, s. [Zebediah & Mary], b. Dec. 16, 1759	2	8

	Vol.	Page
FARNHAM, FFARNUM, FARNAM, FFARNAM, FARNUM, (cont.)		
Mannassah, s. Mannassah & Kezia, b. July 29, 1739	1	196
Mannassah, Jr., m. Patience **BIBBINS**, Apr. 19, 1758	2	47
Martha, d. Nath[anie]ll & Hannah, b. Dec. 17, 1736	1	171
Martha, m. Jonathan **CLARK**, Apr. 6, 1759	2	50
Martha, m. Stephen **COMMINS**, May 3, 1769	2	204
Mary, d. Joseph & Lydia, b. Jan. 28, 1729/30	1	117
Mary, d. Zeb[ediah] & Mary, b. July 19, 1744; d. June 22, 1745	1	235
Mary, d. [Zebediah & Mary], b. July 19, 1744	2	8
Mary, d. Zeb[ediah] & Mary, d. June 22, 1745	2	8
Mary, d. [Zebediah & Mary], b. Aug. 21, 1757	2	8
Mary Emily, d. [Charles H. & Nancy O.], b. Feb. 19, 1843	3	97
Nath[anie]l, s. Nath[anie]l & Hannah, b May [ ], 1720	1	18
Nath[anie]ll, s. Nath[anie]ll & Hannah, b. May 9, 1720	1	171
Nath[anie]ll, d. July 9, 1760, ae. 65 y.	1	171
Nathaniel, m. Hannah **KNOWLTON**, Nov. 18, 1762	2	107
Olive, d. [Zebediah & Mary], b. Nov. 12, 1765	2	8
Olive, m. Philip **SEARL**, Oct. 25, 1780	2	199
Phebe, d. Henry & Phebe, b. July 4, 1713	1	131
Rebeckah, d. Nath[anie]l & Hannah, b. Apr. 7, 1730	1	18
Rebeckah, d. Nath[anie]ll & Hannah, b. Apr. 12, 1730	1	171
Rebeccah, m. John **ROB[B]INS**, Jan. 21, 1748/9	1	293
Sarah, d. Nath[anie]l & Hannah, b. Mar. 27, 1724	1	18
Sarah, d. Nath[anie]ll & Hannah, b. Mar. 27, 1724	1	171
Sarah, m. David **FISK**, Mar. 26, 1747	1	278
Sarah, d. Josh[ua] & Sarah, b. Mar. 27, 1749; d Aug. 26, 1758	1	279
Sarah, m. Sam[ue]l **BAKER**, Jr., Dec. 23, 1794	2	92
Sarah Elizabeth, [d. Charles H. & Nancy O.], b. July 29, 1841	3	97
Solomon, s. Nath[anie]l & Hannah, b. June 10, 1727	1	18
Sollomon, s. Nathaniell & Hannah, b. Jan 10, 1727/8	1	94
Stephen, s. Henry & Phebe, b. Mar. 27, 1728	1	131
Thomas, s. [Zebediah & Mary], b. Nov. 19, 1754	2	8
William, m. Martha **FFULLER**, June 23, 1742	1	230
William, d. Mar. 14, 1777, in the 32nd y. of his age	2	1
Zebediah, m. Mary **FULLER**, July 27, 1743	1	235
Zebediah, m. Mary **FULLER**, July 27, 1743	2	8
Zebediah, s. Zeb[ediah] & Mary, b. Jan. 10, 1745	1	235
Zebediah, s. [Zebediah & Mary], b. Jan. 10, 1746	2	8
Zebediah, Jr., m. Mary **HEBBARD**, Nov. 9, 1763	2	95
Zebediah, s. Zeb[edia]h & Mary, b. Feb. 1, 1765	2	95

	Vol.	Page
FARNHAM, FFARNUM, FARNAM, FFARNAM, FARNUM, (cont.)		
Zebulon, s. William & Annah, b. June 18, 1721	1	53
FAY, Geo[rge] W., of Marlborough, Mass., m. Amanda A. **WARD**, of Willimantic, Windham, Oct. 5, 1835, by Rev. Benajah Cook, Jr	3	174
Ruth, m. Samuel **SHELDON**, July 26, 1829, by E. Lee Brown, Willimantic	3	137
FEHENE, Mary, b. Ireland, res. Windham, d. Oct. 9, 1859, ae 48	4	159-0
FELCH, [see also **FITCH**], Mariot, m. Dean **SLADE**, Aug. 12, [1832], by Rev. Alva Gregory	3	160
[FENNO], **FFENNO**, [see also **FENTON**], Elizabeth, m. John **WALDO**, Oct. 3, 1706	1	19
FENTON, FFENTON, [see also **FENNO**], Abigail, m. Abial **ABBOTT**, June 5, 1750	1	300
Abigail, m. Abiel **ABBOTT**, June 5, 1750	2	142
Beridget, d. Robert & Dorit[h]y, b. Aug. 14, 1695	A	26
Dorrit[h]y, d. Robert & Dorrit[h]y, b. Sept. 14, 1700	A	26
Jacob, s. Robert & Dorit[h]y, b. Apr. 1, 1698	A	26
Phebe, m. Sam[ue]l **LINKON**, Jr., Oct. 1, 1747	1	271
Rebeckah, m. John **LINKION**, [ ]	2	40
FERGUSON, Christopher, m. Charlotte Ann **SMITH**, b. of Windham, May 28, 1838, by Rev. John E. Tyler	3	186
FIELD, Geo[rge], manufacturer, ae 25, m. Elizabeth **RYAN**, ae. 25, Sept. 25, 1849, by Rev. J.E. Tyler	4	114
Harriet M., m. Ezekiel W. **CAREY**, May 16, 1830, by Rev. Roger Bingham	3	145
FINNAN, Bridget, d. Michael, laborer, ae 28, & Catharine, ae. 22, of Willimantic, b. [1848]	4	5
Henry, s. Patrick, laborer, ae 37, & Ellen, ae 29, of Willimantic, b. Mar. 24, [1848]	4	5
FINNEY, [see under **PHINEY** and **PINNEY**]		
FISH, Caroline, b. R.I., res. Windham, d. Mar. 10, [1851], ae. 45	4	158
David, s. [Jonathan & Sarah], b. June 9, 1770	2	206
Delos, m Fanny L. **MOSELEY**, b. of Willimantic, Nov 16, 1846, by Rev. John E. Tyler	3	231
Francis A., s. Delos, carpenter, ae. 26, & Fanny, ae. 23, of Willimantic, b. Aug. 21, 1850	4	12
George, of Willimantic, d. July 21, 1851, ae 7 m.	4	157
Giles L., s. Nathan, mechanic, ae. 30, & Sarah, ae. 26, of Willimantic, b Dec 18, 1850	4	12
Jonathan, m. Sarah **LEACH**, Mar. 18, 1762	2	206
Lucy, m. Aseriah **LATHROP**, June 8, 1845, by Andrew Sharp	3	223
Margary, d. [Jonathan & Sarah], b. Oct. 9, 1763	2	206
Nathan, s. [Jonathan & Sarah], b. Oct 7, 1772	2	206

	Vol.	Page
FISH, (cont.)		
Nathan A., m. Sarah A. **HOVEY**, b. of Windham,		
[ ], by John Cooper	3	225
Richard, b. Norwich, res. Windham, d. July [ ],		
1860, ae. 1 y. 3 m.	4	161
Sybel, tailoress, b. Canterbury, res. Willimantic,		
d. Sept. 1, 1850, ae. 87	4	157
—, child of William, mule tender, ae. 26, &		
Sarah, ae. 23, b. July 25, 1848	4	2
—, child of Nathan, d. Aug. 6, 1848, ae. 2 w.	4	151
—, st. b. child of Delos & Fanny, b. Oct 28,		
[1848]	4	6
FISHER, Laura, m. Nathan **BASS**, b. of Windham, Mar. 28,		
1838, by Rev. Otis C. Whiton, of Scotland Society,		
in Windham	3	185
Nath[anie]l D., m. Mary **BINGHAM**, b. of Windham, Nov.		
13, [1837], by Rev. Otis C. Whiton, of Scotland		
Society, Windham	3	184
FISK, FISKE, FFISKE, Amaziah, s. David & Elizabeth, b.		
Feb. 15, 1741/2; d. Aug. 19, 1745	1	152
Amaziah, m. Priscilla **BINGHAM**, Jan. 3, 1771	2	165
Asa, s. David & Elizabeth, b. May 28, 1733	1	70.
Asa, m. Elizabeth [ ], Mar. 19, 1755	1	327
Asa, s. [Asa & Elizabeth], b. Dec. 21, 1757	1	327
David, m. Elizabeth **DURGE**, Dec. 25, 1723	1	70
David, s. David & Elizabeth, b. Nov. 3, 1724; d.		
Nov. 24, 1724	1	70
David, s. David & Elizabeth, b. Dec. 17, 1726	1	70
David, m. Sarah **FERNAM**, Mar. 26, 1747	1	278
David, d. Mar. 25, 1748	1	152
David, s. Jonath[an] & Elizabeth, b. May 29, 1752;		
d. Nov. [ ], 1754	1	302
David, s. David & Sarah, b. Aug. 12, 1754	1	152
David, s. [David & Sarah], b. Aug. 12, 1754	1	278
David, s. [David & Sarah], d. July 24, 1775	1	278
David, s. [Amaziah & Priscilla], b. Feb. 8, 1776	2	165
David H., m. Nancy E **SUMNER**, Oct 22, 1835, by Rev.		
Roger Bingham	3	175
Ebenezer, s. David & Sarah, b. Oct. 6, 1747	1	278
Elizabeth, d. David & Elizabeth, b. Mar. 6, 1735/6	1	152
Eliza[be]th, m. Samuell **WEBB**, May 14, 1752	1	15
Eliz[abet]h, d. Jonath[an] & Elizabeth, b. Jan. 22,		
1761	1	302
Elizabeth, w. Jonath[an], d. Feb. 15, 1761	1	302
Eunice, d. [Amaziah & Priscilla], b Oct 23, 1771	2	165
Ezra, s. [Amaziah & Priscilla], b. Apr. 13, 1778	2	165
George B., m. Lucy **AVERY**, Mar. 12, 1843, by Ella		
Dunham, Elder	3	208

Vol.   Page

FISK, FISKE, FFISKE, (cont.)
  H.L., doctor, ae. 27, b. Stafford, res. Willi-
    mantic, m. Sarah A. PATT*, dressmaker, ae.
    26, b. Scituate, R.I., res. Willimantic,
    May 11, 1851, by Rev. S.G. Williams (*Perhaps
    POTT?)   4   117
  Hannah, d. [Asa & Elizabeth], b. Aug 1, 1759   1   327
  Hannah, d. [David & Sarah], b. July 29, 1766   1   278
  Hannah, m. Joseph MILLARD, Nov. 24, 1791   2   100
  Hez[ekiah], s. [Asa & Elizabeth], b. June 2,
    1756   1   327
  John, s. David & Elizabeth, b. Aug. 27, 1729   1   70
  John, s. David & Elizabeth, d. Mar. 3, 1734/5   1   137
  John, s. David & Elizabeth, d. Mar. 3, 1734/5   1   152
  John, s. David & Elizabeth, b. Apr. 17, 1738; d.
    May 31, 1742   1   152
  John, m. Elizabeth CROSS, Apr. 15, 1832, by Rev
    Alva Gregory, Willimantic   3   160
  Jonathan, s. David & Elizabeth, b. July 4, 1731   1   70
  Jonathan, m. Elizabeth SCOTT, Aug. 9, 1750   1   302
  Jonathan, s. Jonathan & Elizabeth, b. Dec. 18, 1750;
    d. Oct. [ ], 1754   1   302
  Jonathan, s. Jonath[an] & Elizabeth, b. Aug. 15, 1755   1   302
  Lucy, d. [David & Sarah], b. Apr. 27, 1760   1   278
  Lydia, d. [Amaziah & Priscilla], b. Sept 15, 1773   2   165
  Mary, d. Jonathan & Elizabeth, b. Feb. 17, 1758; d.
    July 29, 1760   1   302
  Sarah, d. David & Sarah, b. Apr. 13, 1749   1   152
  Sarah, d. [David & Sarah], b. Apr. 13, 1749   1   278
  Sarah A., m. Robert BOND, Jr., Aug. 11, 1844, by Rev.
    J.B. Guild, Willimantic   3   215
  ——, Col., m. Lucy HARVEY, Jan. 18, 1835, by James
    Littlefield, J P.   3   171
FITCH, FFITCH, [see also FELCH], Abner, s. [Eleazer &
    Zerviah], b. Dec 16, 1753; d. Apr. 6, 1754   1   183
  Alice, m. John FFITCH, Jr., Jan. 25, 1730/31   1   119
  Alice, d. John, Jr & Alice, b Oct. 7, 1734   1   119
  Alice, d. John, Jr. & Marcy, b. Jan. 1, 1755   1   326
  Amey, d. [Col. Eleaz[e]r & Amey], b. Jan. 20, 1751;
    at Lebanon   2   26
  Ann, d. [Col. Eleaz[e]r & Amey], b. Apr. 18, 1747, at
    Providence   2   26
  Ann Eliza, d. [Charles & Harriet J.], b. Dec. 29,
    1834   3   120
  Anna, d. Rev. Mr. WHITING, d. Sept. 18, 1778   1   54
  Anne, d. [Jabez & Mary], b. June 15, 1764   2   37
  Anne, d. [James & Anne], b. Oct 16, 1765   2   91
  Anne, d. Col. Eleazer, of Windham, m. Ebenezer WHITING,

	Vol.	Page
FITCH, FFITCH, (cont)		
of Norwich, Nov. 29, 1767	3	43
Anne, d. Col Eleazer, of Windham, m William		
TEMPLE, of Boston, Apr. 12, 1781	3	43
Asa, s. Stephen & Elener, b Dec 18, 1752	1	172
Asenath, d. [Shubael & Asenath], b. Sept. 10, 1794	2	197
Bela, s [Eleazer, 3d, & Sibbel], b June 2, 1774	2	150
Betsey, d. [Jabez, Jr. & Olive], b. May 19, 1777	2	186
Bridget, d Eleazer & Zerviah, b Feb 14, 1747/8;		
d Oct. 4, 1759	1	183
Charles, s [Eleazer, 3d, & Sibbel], b Aug 28,		
1770	2	150
Charles, m Harriet J **BACKUS,** Dec 2, 1821	3	120
Christopher, s. [Col. Eleaz[e]r & Amey], b. Apr. 23,		
1763	2	26
Christopher, m. Lydia **RIPLEY,** Apr 29, 1784	2	149
Clarissa, d [John & Clarissa], b May 10, 1788	2	230
Cinthia, d. Ebenezer & C[h]loe, b. Nov. 19, 1761	2	68
Cynthia, m Naniah **PALMER,** May 23, 1782	2	62
Daria, child of Harden, farmer, ae. 33, b. Sept. 27,		
[1849]	4	9
Delia C., m. Huntington F. **KENNEY,** b of Windham,		
Nov. 21, 1843, by Rev. Giles H. Desham	3	212
Delia Caroline, d. [Charles & Harriet J.], b. May 29,		
1823	3	120
E.A., d. Sept. 25, [1850], ae. 36	4	157
Ebenezer, s John, Jr. & Alice, b Nov 3, 1736	1	119
Ebenezer, m. C[h]loe **KINGSBURY,** May 4, 1760	2	68
Eben[eze]r, d [ ], at Salisbury	2	68
Edward, m. Luara **HOVEY,** Apr. 3, 1822 (Laura?)	3	101-2
Edward Perkins, s [Charles & Harriet J], b Aug 31,		
1825	3	120
Eleizer, m Zerviah **WALES,** May 11, 1738	1	183
Eleazear, s. Eleazear & Zerviah, b. Apr. 20, 1743	1	183
Eleazer, 3d, m. Sibbel **BASS,** Apr 23, 1769	2	150
Eleaz[e]r, Col , m. Amey **BOWEN,** [ ]	2	26
Elener, w Stephen, d July 13, 1791	1	172
Elijah, s. John & Alice, b Jan. 8, 1745/6	1	119
Elijah, s. [Ebenezer & C[h]loe], b. Dec 10, 1763	2	68
Elijah, m. Hannah **FULLAR,** Apr 17, 1766	2	133
Elijah Lord, s [Elijah & Hannah], b. Dec 12, 1766	2	133
Elizabeth, d. Lt. John & Elizabeth, b. June 1, 1696	A	15
Elizabeth, d John & Elizabeth, b. June 1, 1696	1	33
Elizabeth, m. Nathaniell **WEBB,** Apr. 24, 1718	1	33
Elizabeth, d John, Jr & Alice, b. Oct 9, 1743	1	119
Elizabeth, d. [Col. Eleaz[e]r & Amey], b. Feb 12,		
1749, at Lebanon	2	26
Elizabeth, w Capt. John, d. June 25, 1751	1	119

	Vol.	Page
FITCH, FFITCH, (cont.)		
Elizabeth, m. Sanford **KINGSBURY**, Jan. 9, 1766	2	118
Elizabeth, d. Col. Eleazer, of Windham, m.		
Ebenezer **BACKUS**, of Norwich, Jan. 7, 1767	3	43
Elizabeth, d. [Eleazer, 3d, & Sibbel], b July 2,		
1772; d. Nov. 11, 1775	2	150
Elizabeth, d. [Eleazer, 3d, & Sibbel], b. Jan. 3,		
1783	2	150
Elizabeth, m. Elisha **STARKWEATHER**, Sept. 1, 1822,		
by Rev. Cornelius B. Everest	3	108
Emily Elizabeth, d. [Charles & Harriet J.], b.		
Jan. 27, 1833	3	120
Erastus, m. Betsey **HOVEY**, Nov. 28, 1814	3	100
Esther Ripley, d. [Christopher & Lydia], b. May 9,		
1792	2	149
Eunice, d. John & Alice, b. [ ]	1	119
Fanny, d. Jabez, Jr. & Olive],b. Jan. 11, 1776	2	186
Fanny, m. Bela **BACKUS**, Aug. 29, 1782	2	133
Fanny, d. Col. Eleazer, m. Bela **BACKUS**, b. of Windham,		
Aug. 29, 1782	3	43
Frances, d. [Col. Eleaz[e]r & Amey], b. Aug. 27, 1765	2	26
George, s. [Col. Eleaz[e]r & Amey], b. Mar. 7, 1768	2	26
George, s. [Joseph D. & Betsey], b. Mar. 31, 1812	3	59
Hardin, s. [Erastus & Betsey], b. Nov. 28, 1817	3	100
Hardin H., m. Julia A. **RUSS**, Nov. 9, 1842, by Rev.		
Andrew Sharp, Willimantic	3	205
Harriet, m. William **MORRISON**, May 3, 1847, by Rev.		
Andrew Sharpe	3	235
Henry, s. [Col. Eleaz[e]r & Amey], b. Oct 12, 1757	2	26
Henry, s. [Eleazer, 3d & Sibbel], b. Feb. 15, 1780	2	150
Henry, s. [Luther & Bethiah], b. Apr. 3, 1783	2	96
Henry, s. [Christopher & Lydia], b. Mar. 15, 1787	2	149
Henry, s. [Erastus & Betsey], b. July 2, 1820	3	100
Henry, m. Amelia **RUSS**, Jan. 8, 1843, by Rev. Andrew		
Sharp, Willimantic	3	206
Henry C., m. Charlotte E. **SAWYER**, Feb. 16, 1823	3	110
Hez[ekiah], s. Eliza[be]th **GRAY**, b. Feb. 5, 1772	2	1
Jabez, s. Stephen & Elener, b. Dec. 2, 1737	1	172
Jabez, s. John & Alice, b. Mar. 2, 1747/8	1	119
Jabez, m. Mary **HUNTINGTON**, Jan. 5, 1758	2	37
Jabez, s. [Jabez & Mary], b. Jan. 30, 1767	2	37
Jabez, Jr., m. Olive **RIPLEY**, Oct. 7, 1773	2	186
James, s. John, Jr. & Alice, b. Apr. 9, 1739	1	119
James, m. Anne **HURLBUTT**, May 23, 1763	2	91
James, s. [James & Anne], b. Mar. 11, 1767	2	91
James, s. [John & Clarissa], b. Apr. 18, 1781; d.		
Apr. 19, 1781	2	230
Jerusha, d. [Eleazer & Zerviah], b. Aug. 2, 1761	1	183

	Vol.	Page
FITCH, FFITCH, (cont.)		
Jerusha, m. Matthais **SAWYER**, July 11, 1802	2	231
Jesse, s. Stephen & Elener, b. Jan. 21, 1757	1	172
Jesse, m. Huldah **WARNER**, Apr. 29, 1779	2	230
John, s. James & Prescilla, b. Jan. [ ], 1667/8;		
m. Elizabeth **WATTERMAN**, July 10, 1695	1	33
John, Lt., m. Elizabeth **WATTERMAN**, July 10, 1695	A	15
John, s. John & Elizabeth, b. Mar. 18, 1704	1	33
John, s. John & Elizabeth, b. Mar. 18, 1704/5	A	15
John, Jr., had negro Phineas, s. Jobe **HALE** &		
Blos[s]om, b. Aug. 12, 1728; d. Oct. [ ],		
1741; Blos[s]om, w. Jobe **HALE**, d. Feb. [ ],		
1729; Patience, d. Jobe **HALE**, & Blos[s]om,		
d. Jan. [ ], 1730/31	1	170
John, Jr., m. Alice **FFITCH**, Jan. 25, 1730/31	1	119
John, s. John, Jr. & Alice, b. July 14, 1732	1	119
John, Capt., d. May 24, 1743, ae. about 76 y.	1	119
John, Jr., m. Marcy **LATHROP**, Nov. 7, 1753	1	326
John, Jr., d. June 25, 1755, in the 23rd y. of his		
age	1	326
John, s. John, Jr. & Marcy, b. Jan. 11, 1756, in		
Canterbury	1	326
John, Capt., d. Feb. 19, 1760, ae. 54 y. 11 mo.	1	119
John, s. [Jabez, Jr. & Olive], b. Jan. 5, 1779	2	186
John, m. Clarissa **WALES**, Feb. 24, 1780	2	230
John, s. [John & Clarissa], b. Sept. 14, 1783	2	230
John, s. [Lucius & Sybbel], b. May 5, 1806	3	7
Joseph D., m. Betsey **JOHNSON**, Oct. 25, 1807	3	59
Joseph Dingley, s. [Shubael & Tripheny], b. Oct. 6,		
1780	2	197
Julia, d. [Erastus & Betsey], b. Sept. 30, 1815	3	100
Julia, m. Sheffield **LEWIS**, Nov. 30, 1837, at		
Willimantic, by Rev. Philo Judson	3	184
Julia, m. Stephen D. **BROWNLEY**, Oct. 12, 1842, by		
Andrew Sharp	3	204
Lora M., m. Joseph **MARSH**, Jr., of Norwich, Dec. 28,		
1823	3	116
Lucius, s. [John & Clarissa], b. Mar. 11, 1786	2	230
Lucius, m. Sybbel **ABBE**, [ ], 1805	3	7
Lucius, s. [Lucius & Sybbel], b. Sept. 30, 1808	3	7
Lucy, d. John & Alice, b. Mar. 26, 1753	1	119
Lucy, m. Dr. David **ADAMS**, Oct. 29, 1761	2	88
Lucy, d. [Col. Eleaz[e]r & Amey], b. May 20, 1771	2	26
Lucy, d. [Jabez, Jr. & Olive], b. Nov. 9, 1783	2	186
Lucy, m. Libbeas **LARRABEE**, Oct. 5, 1788	2	46
Lucy, d. Col. Eleazer, m. Lebbeus **LARRABEE**, b. of		
Windham, Oct. 5, 1788	3	43
Lucy, d. [Christopher & Lydia], b. July 7, 1789	2	149

	Vol.	Page
FITCH, FFITCH, (cont.)		
Lucy, d. [Lucius & Sybbel], b. Mar. 14, 1814	3	7
Luther, s. [Eleazer & Zerviah], b. Dec 9, 1757	1	183
Luther, m. Bethiah **HOWES**, [ ], 1782	2	96
Luther, s. [Shubael & Tripheny], b. Dec. 26, 1784	2	197
Marcy, wid., m. Eleazer **CAREY**, July 19, 1767	2	136
Maria, d. [Joseph D. & Betsey], b. May 1, 1808	3	59
Mariott, see under Mariott **FELCH**		
Mary, d. [Eleazer & Zerviah], b May 17, 1751	1	183
Mary, d. [Col. Eleaz[e]r & Amey], b. Nov. 22, 1761	2	26
Mary, m. John **DINGLEY**, Apr. 12, 1769	2	142
Meriam, d. Lt. John & Elizabeth, b. Oct. 17, 1699	A	15
Miriam, d. John & Elizabeth, b. Oct. 17, 1699	1	33
Meriam, m. Hezekiah **RIPLEY**, Oct. 16, 1740	1	205
Meriam, d. John, Jr. & Alice, June 9, 1741	1	119
Meriam, m. Isaac **CANNADA**, Feb. 26, 1761	2	60
Nancy, d. [Eleazer, 3d & Sibbel], b. July 16, 1785	2	150
Nancy, m. John **BROWN**, [Oct.] 13, 1839, by Rev. R.		
Ransom, Willimantic	3	190
Nathan, d. Jan. 24, 1764	2	1
Nathan, s. [Eleazer, 3d, & Sibbel], b. July 29,		
1776	2	150
Nathaniel, s. Eleazer & Zerviah, b. Aug. 9, 1745	1	183
Nathaniel, s. [Jesse & Huldah], b. Apr. 14, 1780	2	230
Newton, s. [Joseph D. & Betsey], b June 10, 1810	3	59
Newton, m. Eunice H. **JILLSON**, of Pelham, Mass., Apr.		
20, 1834, by Rev. Jesse Fisher	3	169
Olive, d. [Eleazer & Zerviah], b. June 5, 1755	1	183
Olive, d. [Jabez, Jr. & Olive], b. Sept. 26, 1780	2	186
Olive, m. John **WELCH**, Jr., Sept. 19, 1782	2	251
Philena, d. [Col. Eleaz[e]r & Amey], b July 4, 1755	2	26
Philena, d. Col. Eleazer, m. Bela **ELDERKIN**, Mar. 18,		
1773	3	41
Priscilla, d. John & Elizabeth, b. Feb. 5, 1702	A	15
Priscilla, d. John & Elizabeth, b Feb 5, 1702	1	33
Rosewell, s. Jabez & Mary, b. Dec. 20, 1758	2	37
Sarah, d. [Col. Eleaz[e]r & Amey], b. Jan. 18, 1760	2	26
Sarah, d. Col. Eleazer, of Windham, m. Hezekiah		
PERKINS, of Norwich, Mar. 4, 1784	3	43
Shubael, s. [Eleazer & Zerviah], b. Feb. 22, 1750	1	183
Shubael, m. Tripheny **DINGLEY**, Nov. 17, 1774	2	197
Shubael, s. [Shubael & Tripheny], b. July 8, 1776	2	197
Shubael, m. Asenath **WELCH**, July 4, 1793	2	197
Sibbel, w. Eleazer, 3d, d. July 8, 1786, in the 38th		
y. of her age	2	150
Stephen, m. Elener **STRONG**, Jan. 25, 1736/7	1	172
Stephen, s. Stephen & Elener, b. Sept. 2, 1750	1	172
Sybil, see under Sibbel		

	Vol.	Page
FLINT, FFLINT, (cont.)		
Benjamin, s. Nath[anie]l, Jr. & Sarah, b. Sept.		
27, 1743	1	219
Benj[ami]n, m. Bethiah **CHENEY**, Apr. 12, 1770	2	191
Betsey, d. [John & Philena], b. July 12, 1783	2	234
Charles, s. [John & Sarah], b. Aug. 20, 1780	2	190
Charlotte, d. [Benj[ami]n & Bethiah], b. Apr. 19,		
1774	2	191
Charlotte, m. Thomas **BINGHAM**, May 17, 1795	3	50
C[h]loe, d. James & Jemima, b. July 26, 1752	1	316
Chloe, d. [Benj[ami]n & Bethiah], b. May 10, 1772	2	191
Chloe, m. Hezekiah **CHAPMAN**, June 4, 1778	2	240
Christian, w. John, d. Sept. 27, 1721	1	6
Christian, d. Rufus & Mary, b. Jan. 19, 1740/41	1	211
Daniel, s. Nath[anie]ll, Jr. & Mary, b. Dec. 7,		
1761	1	219
Deborah, d. Joshua & Sarah, b. Oct. 1, 1742	1	242
Diah, s. [Sam[ue]ll, Jr. & Lucy], b. Mar. 26, 1771	2	139
Edward L., m. Charlotte A. **BAXTER**, July 4, 1847, by		
Rev. Andrew Sharp	3	236
Eli, s. James & Jemima, b. Aug. 21, 1764	1	316
Elijah, s. Rufus & Mary, b. Jan. 16, 1749/50	1	211
Elijah, s. Abner & Patience, b. Feb. 23, 1757; d.		
Mar. 14, 1757	2	12
Elijah, s. Abner, d. Mar. 14, 1757	2	12
Elijah, s. [Luke & Mary], b. Dec. 7, 1777	2	135
Eliphalet, s. Joshua & Deborah, b. July 18, 1734	1	98
Elisha, s. [Asher & Lucy], b. Oct. 12, 1763	1	314
Elisha, s. Nath[anie]ll, Jr. & Mary, b. Nov. 25,		
1763	1	219
Elisha, s. [James & Jerusha], b. Apr. 3, 1774; d.		
Apr. 16, 1774	2	191
Elisha, s. [Benj[ami]n & Bethiah], b. Aug. 30, 1781	2	191
Elizabeth, d. Joshua & Deborah, b. May 29, 1730	1	98
Elizabeth, d. Joshua & Sarah, b. Jan 24, 1743/4	1	242
Elizabeth, d. James & Jemima, b. Dec. 1, 1755	1	316
Elizabeth, [d. James & Jemima], d. Oct. 11, 1776, in		
Newark, N.J.	1	316
[E]unis, d. Nath[anie]l & Sarah, b. Dec. 15, 1726;		
Dec. 25, 1726	1	91
[E]unice, d. Sam[ue]ll & Mary, b. Mar. 10, 1748	1	157
Eunice, m. Aaron **MARTIN**, Nov. 13, 1766	2	126
Eunice, d. [Abner & Patience], b. Aug. 8, 1775	2	12
Eunice, m. Horace E. **BROWN**, b. of Windham, Nov. 16,		
1846, by Rev. John E. Tyler	3	231
Fana, d. [Bartholomew & Mary], b. Aug. 21, 1765; d.		
May 24, 1766	2	5
Fanny Maria, [d. Jacob & Hannah], b. Apr. 2, 1817	3	68

	Vol.	Page
FLINT, FFLINT, (cont.)		
Fred A., d. July [ ], 1848, ae. 56	4	151
Gideon, s. John & Lydia, b. July 25, 1729	1	110
Gideon, m. Sara **WALCUTT**, Nov. 5, 1753	1	321
Gideon, d. Mar. 12, 1764	1	321
Gideon, s. [John & Philena], b. Oct. 26, 1781	2	234
Hannah, d. Samuel & Mary, b. Aug. 10, 1756	2	15
Hannah, d. [Benj[ami]n & Bethiah], b. Aug. 16, 1770	2	191
Hannah, m. Jeremiah **CLARK**, Jr., Feb. 18, 1773	2	213
Hannah Jefforts, d. [Jacob & Hannah], d. Sept. 1, 1821	3	68
Horace, s. [Jacob & Hannah], b. June 16, 1809	3	68
Horace, m. Fanny **YOUNG**, Mar. 23, 1832, by Rev. Roger Bingham	3	159
Huldah, d. Joshua & Deborah, b. June 24, 1728	1	98
Huldah, m. Asa **SPAFFORD**, Dec. 16, 1746	1	275
Jabez, s. [Asher & Lucy], b. May 2, 1756	1	314
Jacob, s. [John & Sarah], b. Nov. 25, 1780 [sic]	2	190
Jacob, m. Hannah **HOLT**, Nov. 6, 1806	3	68
Jacob Holt, s. [Jacob & Hannah], b. Oct. 22, 1807	3	68
James, s. Joshua & Deborah, b. July 26, 1722	1	98
James, s. Samuel & Mary, b. Aug. 10, 1751	1	157
James, m. Jemima **GENNINGS**, Aug. 27, 1751	1	316
James, 3rd, m. Jerusha **LILLIE**, Apr. 22, 1773	2	191
James Clark, s. [Samuel & Eunice], b. Jan. [ ], 1815	3	19
James Lassel, s. Abner & Patience, b. Feb. 23, 1757; d. Jan. 22, 1759	2	12
James Lassel, s. Abner, d. Jan. 22, 1759	2	12
James Lassel, s. Abner & Patience, b. Oct 12, 1759	2	12
Jeremiah, s. [Phinehas & Hannah], b. Nov. 17, 1784	2	207
Jerusha, d. [James & Jerusha], b. Aug. 4, 1775	2	191
Jerush[a], m. Jonathan **LEE**, Apr. 19, 1795	3	2
John, m. Christian **READ**, May 5, 1709	1	6
John, s. John & Christian, b. Jan. 23, 1714	1	6
John, m. Lydia **GENINGS**, Mar 14, 1721/2	1	6
John, s. Sam[ue]ll & Mary, b. Sept. 8, 1749	1	157
John, s. [Gid[eon] & Sarah], b. Feb. 13, 1760	1	321
John, m. Sarah **TILDEN**, of Norwich, Dec. 30, 1772	2	190
John, s. [John & Sarah], b. July 17, 1777; d. Aug 30, 1778	2	190
John, m. Philena **FLINT**, Nov. 30, 1780	2	234
John, s. [John & Sarah], b. Mar. 3, 1786	2	190
John, m. Sophia **ROB[B]INS**, Nov 5, 1829, by Rev. Roger Bingham	3	142
Jonathan, twin with Nathan, s. John & Lydia, b July 10, 1725	1	6

	Vol.	Page
FLINT, FFLINT, (cont.)		
Jonathan, s. Rufus & Mary, b. Nov. 13, 1747	1	211
Jonathan, s. Nath[anie]ll, Jr & Mary, b. Mar 29, 1754; d. Apr. 14, 1754	1	219
Jonathan, s. Nath[anie]ll, Jr. & Mary, b. Nov. 22, 1755	1	219
Joseph, s John & Lydia, b. Sept. 13, 1725 [sic] (1723?)	1	6
Joshua, s. Joshua & Deborah, b. Feb. 26, 1720	1	98
Joshua, m. Sarah **CONNER**, Aug. 12, 1742	1	242
Josiah, s. [Luke & Mary], b. Aug. 21, 1784	2	135
Laura, m. Levi **ALLEN**, Nov. 28, 1833, by Rev. Roger Bingham	3	166
Laura, see also Lorry		
Leonard, s. [John & Sarah], b. Apr. 29, 1782	2	190
Levina, d Barth[olomew] & Lydia, b. Oct 4, 1755; d. Oct. 28, 1756	2	5
Lorry, d. [Samuel & Eunice], b. Mar. [ ], 1813	3	19
Lorry, see also Laura		
Loxa, d. [Bartholomew & Mary], b. Apr. 4, 1767	2	5
Lucius, s. [Jacob & Hannah], b. June 12, 1813	3	68
Luce, s. Nath[anie]ll, Jr. & Mary, b. Dec. 20, 1752	1	219
Lucy, d. [Asher & Lucy], b. Sept. 2, 1757	1	314
Lucy, d. [Silas & Abigail], b. Aug. 21, 1762	2	34
Lucy, d. [Nath[anie]ll, 3d, & Lucy], b. July [ ], 176[ ]	2	123
Lucy A., of Windham, m. Charles C **JOHNSON**, of Franklin, Mar. 22, 1847, by Rev. J.E. Tyler	3	234
Lucy Ann, d. [Samuel & Eunice], b. Apr 23, 1824	3	19
Luke, m. Mary **SLATE**, June 6, 1776	2	135
Lydia, d. John & Lydia, b. June 4, 1735	1	110
Lydia, w. Barth[olomew], d. Oct. 26, 1756	2	5
Lydia, d. [Gid[eon] & Sarah], b. Mar. 28, 1757, d. May 30, 1761	1	321
Lydia, m. Nath[anie]l **WALCUTT**, Nov. 4, 1764	2	107
Lydia H., tailoress, ae. 42, of Hampton, m. Joel W. **SEARLES**, shoemaker, ae 50, of Hampton, Jan. 21, 1851, by Rev. Henry Greenslit	4	118
Mary, d. John & Christian, b Apr. 12, 1710; d Aug. 23, 1716	1	6
Mary, d. Joshua & Deborah, b. Jan. 13, 1718	1	98
Mary, w. Nath[aniell], d. Feb. 22, 1727/28	1	91
Mary, d. John & Lydia, b. Feb 15, 1731/2	1	110
Mary, d. Sam[ue]ll & Mary, b. Nov. 26, 1738	1	157
Mary, m. Asa **HENDEE**, Jan. 31, 1738/9	1	177
Mary, w. Sam[ue]ll, d. Jan. 1, 1743/4	1	157
Mary, d. John, d. Oct. 22, 1746, ae. 15 y	1	110
Mary, w. Rufus, d. [ ], 1752	1	211

	Vol.	Page
FLINT, FFLINT, (cont.)		
Mary, m. Daniel **ROBINSON**, Mar. 29, 1758	2	81
Mary, d. Nath[anie]ll, Jr. & Mary, b. Apr. 28,		
1765	1	219
Mary, m. John **HUNTINGTON**, Apr. 15, 1770	2	23
Mary E., m. Ezra **STARKWEATHER**, May 1, 1833, by		
Rev. Roger Bingham	3	164
Mary Eliza, d. [Jacob & Hannah], b. May 26, 1815	3	68
Mason, s. [Bartholomew & Mary], b. Aug. 29, 1763	2	5
Mehit[able], d. Samuel & Mary, b. June 18, 1753	1	190
Mehetable, d. Samuel & Mary, b. June 18, 1753	2	15
Mehetable, m. Jacob **PARRISH**, Feb. 2, 1772	2	194
Mehetable, d. [John & Sarah], b. Nov. 3, 1787	2	190
Mercy, w. Nath[anie]l, d. Dec. 5, 1771	1	91
Naomi, d. Rufus & Mary, b. Mar. 24, 1745	1	211
Nathan, twin with Jonathan, s. John & Lydia, b.		
July 10, 1725	1	6
Nathan, s. [Gid[eon] & Sarah], b. Apr. 17, 1762	1	321
Nathan, s. [Luke & Mary], b. Jan. 15, 1780	2	135
Nath[anie]ll, s. Nath[anie]ll & Sarah, b. Sept.		
5, 1720	1	28
Nathaniell, m. Mary **DAVICE**, May 2, 1727	1	91
Nathaniell, m. Mercy **ABBE**, Dec. 11, 1734; d. June 3,		
1766	1	91
Nath[anie]ll, Jr., m. Sarah **BIDLARK**, June 16, 1742	1	219
Nath[anie]ll, m. Sarah **BIDLAKE**, June 16, 1742	1	231
Nath[anie]ll, s. Nath[anie]ll & Sarah, b. July 11,		
1745	1	231
Nath[anie]ll, s. Nath[anie]ll, Jr. & Sarah, b. July		
15, 1745	1	219
Nath[anie]ll, Jr., m. Mary **HENRY**, July 3, 1751	1	219
Nath[anie]l, d. June 3, 1766	1	91
Nath[anie]ll, 3rd, m. Lucy **MARTIN**, May 23, 176[ ]	2	123
Olive, d. [Sam[ue]ll, Jr. & Lucy], b. Sept. 11, 1768	2	139
Olive, of Windham, m. Charles H. **BUCKINGHAM**, of		
Franklin, Mar. 31, 1845, by Rev. John H. Tyler	3	220
Oliver, s. Abner & Patience, b. Oct. 16, 1762	2	12
Orran, s. [John & Sarah], b. Aug. 29, 1794	2	190
Patience, d. [Phinehas & Hannah], b. Nov. 28, 1780	2	207
Philena, d. [Bartholomew & Mary], b. Apr. 4, 1762	2	5
Philena, m. John **FLINT**, Nov. 30, 1780	2	234
Phinehas, s. Nath[anie]ll, Jr. & Mary, b. Feb. 23,		
1757	1	219
Phineas, s. [Silas & Abigail], b. July 1, 1770	2	34
Phinehas, m Hannah **CLARK**, Feb. 24, 1780	2	207
Phinehas, s. [Phinehas & Hannah], b. Aug. 17, 1782	2	207
Polly, d. [John & Sarah], b Apr. 20, 1793	2	190
Prudence, d. Gid[eon] & Sarah, b. Sept. 6, 1754	1	321

	Vol.	Page
FLINT, FFLINT, (cont.)		
Prudence, m. Joseph **BADGER**, Sept. 24, 1772	2	188
Royal, s. James & Jemima, b. Jan. 12, 1754	1	316
Rufus, s. John & Christian, b. Oct. 29, 1716	1	6
Rufus, m. Mary **JONES**, Mar. 13, 1739/40	1	211
Rufus, s. [Silas & Abigail], b. Apr. 3, 1768	2	34
Rufus, d. [ ], at Attleborough	1	211
Samuell, s. John & Christian, b. Apr. 9, 1712	1	6
Sam[ue]ll, m. Mary **LAMPHERE**, Apr. 13, 1736	1	157
Sam[ue]ll, m. Mary **HALL**, Apr. 11, 1745	1	157
Sam[ue]ll, s. Samuel & Mary, b. Oct. 25, 1746	1	157
Sam[ue]ll, Jr., m. Lucy **MARTIN**, Dec. 17, 1767	2	139
Samuel, m Sarah **BLACKMAN**, Jan. 9, 1781	2	232
Samuel, s. [John & Sarah], b. July 25, 1789	2	190
Samuel, s. [Jacob & Hannah], b. Dec. 8, 1810	3	68
Samuel, m. Eunice **CLARK**, Jan. [ ], 1812	3	19
Samuel, 2d, m. Alathea **BLACKMAN**, Mar. 31, 1835	3	89
Samuel, 2d, m. Alathea **BLACKMAN**, Mar. 31, 1835, by Rev. Dexter Bullard	3	185
Samuel, m. Elethe **BLACKMAN**, b. of Windham, Mar. 31, 1835, by Rev. Dexter Bullard	3	172
Samuel, 2d, d. July 20, 1850	3	89
Sarah, d. Joshua & Deborah, b. June 21, 1716	1	98
Sarah, d. Nathaniell & Sarah, b. Jan. 12, 1717/18	1	28
Sarah, w. Nath[anie]l, d. Dec. 20, 1726	1	91
Sarah, m. Zebadiah **HOLT**, Aug. 14, 1732	1	123
Sarah, m. Joshua **SAWYER**, Nov. 5, 1735	1	149
Sarah, d. Nath[anie]ll, Jr. & Sarah, b. Apr. 28, 1747	1	219
Sarah, w. Nath[anie]ll, Jr., d. Sept. 5, 1749	1	219
Sarah, d. [Asher & Lucy], b. Oct. 6, 1760	1	314
Sarah, d. [Nath[anie]ll, 3d, & Lucy], b. Sept. 2, 1769	2	123
Sarah, d. John & Sarah, b. Nov. 29, 1773	2	190
Sarah, d. [Benj[ami]n & Bethiah], b. Apr. 14, 1776; d. Apr. 28, 1776	2	191
Sarah, d. [Benj[ami]n & Bethiah], b. June 2, 1777	2	191
Seldon Blackman, s. [Samuel, 2d, & Alathea], b. Apr. 26, 1836	3	89
Seldon Blackman, s. [Samuel, 2d, & Alathea], d. Apr. 20, 1838	3	89
Seldon Blackman, s. [Samuel, 2d, & Alathea], b. Apr. 26, 1836; d. Apr. 20, 1838	3	185
Silas, s. Sam[ue]ll & Mary, b. Mar. 19, 1736/7	1	157
Silas, m. Abigail **ROBINSON**, Apr 19, 1762	2	34
Silas, s. [Silas & Abigail], b. Apr. 20, 1774	2	34
Sophia, d. [James & Jemima], b. May 6, 1770; d. Aug 29, 1771	1	316

	Vol.	Page
FOLLETT, FFOLLETT, FOLLET, FFOLETT, (cont)		
Elizabeth, d. [Hez[ekiah] & Hannah], b. Mar. 6, 1751	1	239
Emily, d. [Oliver & Elizabeth], b. Jan. 21, 1812	3	30
Emily, m. Gilbert **BILLINGS**, b. of Windham, Dec. 13, 1835, by Rev. Edward Harris	3	175
Ephraim, s. [Oliver & Elizabeth], b. Dec. 24, 1805	3	30
Erastus, m. Sophia **WILLOBY**, Jan. 2, 1825	3	109
Eunice, d. [Benjamin, Jr. & Hannah], b. Feb. 4, 1744; d. Apr. 13, 1747	1	200
Eunice, twin with Amos, d. Joseph & Hannah, b May 31, 1759	1	236
Frederick, s. Benj[ami]n & Easther, b. Mar. 10, 1761	2	39
George, s. [Abner, Jr. & Lucy], b. Feb. 10, 1825	3	111
Geo[rge], s. Geo[rge], machinist, ae. 22, & Elizabeth, ae. 26, b. Sept. 20, 1850	4	13
George, d. June 4, 1851, ae. 26	4	158
Hannah, d. Benjamin & Patience, b. Nov. 15, 1716	1	50
Hannah, m. Joshua **READ**, Dec. 26, 1745	1	255
Hannah, d. Joseph & Hannah, b. Nov. 17, 1748, st. b.	1	236
Hannah, d. [Hez[ekiah] & Hannah], b. Sept. 27, 1752	1	239
Hannah, w. Benj[ami]n, d. May 2, 1757	1	200
Hannah, w. Joseph, d. Oct. 9, 1762	1	239
Hannah Ellen, d. [Benjamin & Hannah M.], b. Feb. 3, 1830	3	143
Hezekiah, m. Hannah **READ**, Jan. 8, 1743/4	1	239
Hezekiah, m. Susannah **HEATH**, Nov. 30, 1764	2	115
Hezekiah, s. [Hezekiah & Susannah], b. Aug. 15, 1768	2	115
Hezekiah, d. Aug. 31, 1782, ae. 63	2	115
Irena, d. [Hez[ekiah] & Hannah], b. Mar. 13, 1755	1	239
Isaac, s. Joseph & Hannah, b. Nov. 30, 1756	1	236
Jerusha, d. Hez[ekiah] & Hannah], b. Oct. 29, 1744	1	239
John, s. Hez[ekiah] & Hannah, b. Mar. 5, 1746	1	239
Joseph, s. Benjamin & Patience, b. Apr. 21, 1723	1	50
Joseph, m. Hannah **HEB[B]ARD**, Nov. 9, 1743	1	236
Joseph, s. Joseph & Hannah, b. Sept. 11, 1747, stillborn	1	236
Joseph, s. Joseph & Hannah, b. Dec. 3, 1751	1	236
Levi, s. [Benjamin, Jr. & Hannah], b. Aug. 16, 1756; d. June 12, 1757	1	200
Lovina, d. [Hez[ekiah] & Hannah], b. Mar. 26, 1757	1	239
Lydia, d. Benj[ami]n & Easther, b. Dec. 17, 1759	2	39
Maria, d. [Oliver & Elizabeth], b. Jan. 31, 1800	3	30
Maria, m. Martin **HARRIS**, Dec. 6, 1821, by Rev. Cornelius B. Everest	3	36
Marvin, s. [Oliver & Elizabeth], b. Nov. 28, 1801	3	30
Marvin, m. Mary **BUCK**, b. of Windham, Feb. 8, 1829, by Rev. Dennis Platt	3	135

	Vol	Page
FOLLETT, FFOLLETT, FOLLET, FFOLETT, (cont.)		
Mary, d. Benjamin & Patience, b. Mar. 23, 1711	1	50
Mary, m. Ezra KINGSLEY, Nov. 10, 1743	1	7
Mary, d. Joseph & Hannah, b. July 18, 1744; d.		
Apr. 11, 1745	1	236
Mary, d. Joseph & Hannah, b. Dec. 2, 1745	1	236
Mary, d. Benj[ami]n & Easther, b. Dec. 4, 1758	2	39
Nancy, m. Jacob BENNETT, Dec. 30, 1834, by Rev.		
Marvin Root	3	171
Nathan, s. Benj[amin], Jr. & Hannah, b. Aug. 27,		
1739; d. July 18, 1744	1	200
Nathan, s. [Benjamin, Jr. & Hannah], b. Feb. 11,		
1748; d. Jan. 9, 1776	1	200
Nathan, s. [Benj[amin] & Easther], b. Jan. 23,		
1765; d Nov. 25, 1766	2	39
Oliver, s. [Hezekiah & Susannah], b. Nov. 1, 1766	2	115
Oliver, m. Elizabeth STOEL, Mar. 29, 1798	3	30
Oliver, s. [Oliver & Elizabeth], b. Jan. 31, 1810;		
d. Jan. 21, 1814	3	30
Oliver, s. [Oliver & Elizabeth], b. Apr. 8, 1814	3	30
Rebeckah, d. Benjamin & Patience, b. Aug. 23, 1719	1	50
Roger, s. Benj[ami]n & Easther, b. Aug. 9, 1763	2	39
Susannah, d. Benjamin & Patience, b Dec. 13, 1712	1	50
Susannah, d. Hez[ekiah] & Hannah, b. Oct. 31, 1749	1	239
Timo[thy], s. Joseph & Hannah, b. Sept. 22, 1754	1	236
Waterman, s. [Oliver & Elizabeth], b. Feb. 15, 1808	3	30
William, s. [Abner, Jr. & Lucy], b. [ ]	3	111
[FOLSOM], FFOLSOM, Ann, d. Sam[ue]ll & Ann, b. Aug. 19,		
1740	1	193
Sam[ue]ll, m. Ann BINGHAM, May 3, 1739	1	193
Sam[ue]ll, s. Sam[ue]ll & Ann, b. May 10, 1742	1	193
FORD, FFORD, Abigail, d. Joseph & Elizabeth, b. June 12, 1719	1	26
Abigail, twin with Jacob, [d. Abraham & Abigail], b.		
Apr. 7, 1766	2	94
Abigail, b. Hampton, res. Windham, d. Sept. 4, 1847,		
ae. 39	4	151
Abraham, s. Nathaniell & Diner, b. Aug. 29, 1744	1	111
Abraham, m. Abigail WOODWARD, Nov. 8, 1763	2	94
Abraham, s. [Abraham & Abigail], b. May 15, 1764	2	94
Alice, d. [Abraham & Abigail], b. Mar. 20, 1769; d.		
May 18, 1784	2	94
Amos, s. Nathaniell & Diner, b. Aug. 2, 1742	1	111
Amos, m. Lydia DAVISON, May 25, 1761	2	68
Amos, s. Amos & Lydia, b. Aug. 24, 1763	2	68
Anna R., d. Samuel, carpenter, ae. 26, b. June 7,		
[1849]	4	11
Bethiah, m. Erastus BIBBINS, Mar. 21, 1806	3	94
C[h]loe, d. [Abraham & Abigail], b. Aug. 1, 1773	2	94

	Vol.	Page
FORD, FFORD, (cont)		
Diner, d. Nathaniell & Diner, b. Sept. 17, 1735	1	111
Dinah, m. Daniel **PRESTON**, Mar. 4, 1756	2	14
Dinah, w. Nath[anie]ll, d. Jan. 12, 1763	1	112
Dinah, d. [Abraham & Abigail], b. Oct. 5, 1770;		
d. June 1, 1778	2	94
Dinah, d. [Abraham & Abigail], b. July 27, 1780	2	94
Dyer, s. [Abraham & Abigail], b. Jan. 31, 1772	2	94
Elisha, s. [Abraham & Abigail], b. Jan. 5, 1785	2	94
Elizabeth, d. Joseph & Elizabeth, b. Dec. 20, 1712	1	26
Elizabeth, d. Nathaniell & Diner, b. June 4, 1733	1	111
Elizabeth, m. William **DURKEE**, Aug. 5, 1735	1	55
Elizabeth, d. John & Mary, b. June 7, 1743	1	163
Elizabeth, m. Joseph **MARTIN**, Oct. 17, 1751	1	307
Eliz[abeth], mother of Nath[anie]ll, d. Sept. 10,		
1754	1	112
Elizabeth, d. [Amos & Lydia], b. Aug. 12, 1769	2	68
Elle, d. [Abraham & Abigail], b. Apr. 6, 1775	2	94
Eunice, d. Nath[anie]ll, d. Aug. 21, 1754	1	112
Eunice, d. [Amos & Lydia], b. Nov. 17, 1771	2	68
George, s. Nath[anie]ll & Diner, b. Mar 7, 1748/9;		
d. July 14, 1750	1	111
Hannah, d. Joseph & Elizabeth, b. Sept. 9, 1723	1	51
Hannah, m. Josiah **ROGERS**, Mar. 1, 1742/3	1	276
Hannah, d. [Abraham & Abigail], b. May 22, 1776	2	94
Jacob, twin with Abigail, [s. Abraham & Abigail],		
b. Apr. 7, 1766	2	94
John, [twin with Mary], s. Joseph & Elizabeth, b.		
Apr. 1, 1717	1	51
John, [twin with Mary], s. Joseph & Elizabeth, b.		
Apr. 6, 1717	1	27
John, m. Mary **SEAS***, Aug. 5, 1735 (*correction		
PEASE handwritten in original manuscript)	1	163
John, s. John & Mary, b. June 2, 1737; d. Sept. 6,		
1737	1	163
John, s. John & Mary, b. Oct. 29, 1739	1	163
John, s. [Amos & Lydia], b. Oct. 10, 1774	2	68
Jonathan, s. Nath[anie]ll & Diner, b. Sept. 20, 1746	1	111
Joseph, s. Joseph & Elizabeth, b. Jan. 20, 1705	1	26
Joseph, m. Hannah **GRAVES**, Apr. 22, 1730	1	112
Joseph, m. Sarah **GREENSLIT**, Apr. 23, 1755; d. June 18,		
1758	1	269
Joseph, d. June 18, 1758	1	269
Julia A., ae. 17, b. Hampton, res. Windham, m. Warren		
S. **LILLIE**, farmer, ae. 23, of Windham, [ ],		
1851, by Rev. Henry Greenslit	4	118
Kezia, d. Joseph & Elizabeth, b. Mar. 27, 1721	1	51
Kezia, m. Mannassah **FFARNAM**, Apr. 23, 1739	1	196

	Vol.	Page
FORD, FFORD, (cont)		
Lucy, d. Amos & Lydia, b. Oct. 23, 1762	2	68
Lucy, m. William **NEFF**, Jr., Nov. 1, 1781	2	240
Lydia, d. [Amos & Lydia], b. Oct. 26, 1776	2	68
Mary, [twin with John], d. Joseph & Elizabeth,		
b. Apr. 1, 1717	1	51
Mary, [twin with John], d. Joseph & Elizabeth,		
b. Apr. 6, 1717	1	27
Mary, d. John & Mary, b. Nov. 7, 1735	1	163
Mary, m. John **PRESTON**, Jr., Dec. 9, 1736	1	179
Nathaniell, s. Joseph & Elizabeth, b. June 3,		
1707	1	26
Nathaniell, m Diner **HOLT**, Apr. 1, 1730	1	111
Nathaniell, s. Nathaniell & Diner, b. Nov. 7, 1739;		
d. Oct. 9, 1758, at Green Bush	1	111
Nathaniel, m. Hannah **BINGHAM**, July 7, 1763	2	87
Nathaniel, s. [Amos & Lydia], b. July 11, 1765	2	68
Nath[anie]ll, d. Oct. 25, 1779, in the 70th y. of		
his age	1	112
Phinie, d. Nathaniell & Diner, b. May 25, 1737	1	111
Phineas, s. Nath[anie]ll & Dinah, b. Mar. 26, 1753	1	112
Sally, d. [Abraham & Abigail], b. Nov. 27, 1767	2	94
Samuel B., m. Esther T. **HENRY**, Oct. 5, 1846, by Rev		
Andrew Sharp	3	231
Sarah, d. Joseph & Elizabeth, b. Mar. [ ], 1710; d.		
Sept. [ ], 1713	1	26
Sarah, d. Joseph & Elizabeth, b. Dec. 20, 1714	1	26
Sarah, m. Joshua **FARNAM**, June 6, 1748	1	279
Sarah, d. John & Mary, b. Dec. 9, 1747; d. Dec 13,		
1750	1	163
Sarah, d. Nath[anie]ll & Dinah, b. July 2, 1751	1	112
Thiah, d. [Amos & Lydia], b. Aug. 7, 1780	2	68
Tryphenia, d. [Amos & Lydia], b. June 15, 1767	2	68
FORSHEY, W[illia]m A., of Ashford, m. Elizabeth **WHITE**, of		
Palmer, Mass., June 16, 1846, by Zeph[ania]h		
Palmer, J.P.	3	229
FOSS, Lydia, d. John, pedler, ae. 35, & [ ], ae		
32, b. Oct. 8, 1847	4	2
Lydia, d. Oct. [ ], [1849], ae. 2	4	155
FOSTER, Daniel, m. Keziah **SAWYER**, Apr. 1, 1765	2	112
Fanny, d. [Daniel & Keziah], b. Oct. 26, 1765	2	112
Lois, m. Elihu **PALMER**, Jr., Aug. 11, 1752	1	319
Lucy, d. [Thomas & Wealthy], b. Dec. 15, 1814	2	71
Mehetable, m. Silas **LILLIE**, Nov. 10, 1763	2	95
Nabby, m. John **WEBB**, Jr., Oct. 2, 1817	3	83
Sam[ue]l A., carpenter, ae. 42, b. Hebron, res.		
Hebron, m. Isabella D. **McNALLY**, ae. 25, b		
Windham, res. Windham, Nov. 25, 1850, by Rev.		

	Vol.	Page
FOSTER, (cont.)		
Sam[ue]l G. Williams	4	117
Sarah, m. Jacob **PRESTON**, Jr., Sept. 21, 1730	1	118
Thomas, m. Wealthy **CHEETS**, July 18, 1814	2	71
William, m. Hannah **DORKEE**, May 27, 1755	2	10
William, m. Hannah **DURKEE**, May 27, 1755	2	17
FOX, Abigail, m. Ransom **PERRY**, Jan. 13, 1833, by		
Henry Hall, J.P.	3	163
David, m. Wid. Eunice **PALMER**, May 22, 1814, by		
Jesse Fisher; d. Sept. 6, 1826	3	54
Eunice, d. Aug. 26, 1848, ae. 84	4	152
Hannah J., operative, ae. 18, b. Hopkinton, res.		
Willimantic, m Consider S. **WEEDEN**, farmer,		
ae. 20, b. Hopkinton, res. Willimantic, Mar.		
29, 1851, by Rev. Brush	4	117
J.W., papermaker, ae. 25, m. Elizabeth **BLIVEN**, ae.		
23, May [ ], 1850, by Rev. Farnsworth	4	115
Jabez, m. Jerusha **PERKINS**, Feb. 26, 1777	2	212
Jerusha, d. [Jabez & Jerusha], b. Dec. 15, 1777; d.		
Feb. 24, 1778	2	212
Joanna, of Windham, m. Eleazer **SMITH**, of Canterbury,		
Dec. [ ], 1832, by Rev. John Storrs	3	162
Sally, m. Joel W. **WHITE**, of Bolton, June 24, 1824	3	16
FRAME, FFRAME, John, m. Lydia **JOHNSON**, Oct. 19, 1746	1	265
John, m. Joannah **CARY**, Aug 16, 1757	1	265
John, m. Joannah **CARY**, Aug. 16, 1757	1	309
John, s. John & Joannah, b. June 21, 1758	1	265
Lydia, m. William **SHAW**, Jr., Oct. 15, 1749	2	20
Lydia, [w. John], d. [ ]	1	265
Mary, m. Joseph **PRESTON**, 2d, Apr. 8, 1738	1	173
FRANCIS, Fanney, d. [Manning & Sarah], b. Sept. 12,		
1777	2	184
Fanny had s. John Nelson **CRANE**, b. May 1, 1802	3	49
Festus, s. [Manning & Sarah], b. Mar. 30, 1775	2	184
Filander, d. [Manning & Sarah], b Oct. 20, 1782	2	184
Fimelia, d. [Manning & Sarah], b. Sept. 25, 1779	2	184
Loro, d. [Manning & Sarah], b Mar 17, 1785; d.		
Dec. 17, 1785	2	184
Manning, m. Sarah **GINNINGS**, Apr. 1, 1772	2	184
Philander, see under Filander		
Sarah, d. [Manning & Sarah], b May 13, 1773	2	184
FRANKLIN, FRANKLYN, A.H., ae. 25, m. [ ],		
Apr. 8, [1848], by Andrew Roberts	4	113
Emeline, ae. 22, m. Edward **CHENEY**, painter, ae. 38,		
of Windham, July 3, 1848, by Mr. Catham (?)	4	111
Harriet, of Willimantic, m. Washburn N. **MATSON**, of		
South Glastonbury, Mar. 24, 1844, by Rev Ziba		
Loveland	3	213

	Vol.	Page
FRANKLIN, FRANKLYN, (cont.)		
Lucia Ann, m. Marvin **HILLS**, b. of Willimantic,		
Sept. 15, 1844, by Rev. Charles Noble,		
Willimantic	3	217
Warren, s. Geo[rge], ae. 29, & Harriet, ae. 21,		
b. Jan. 22, 1849	4	7
William, m. Mary **BARRETT**, b. of Willimantic,		
Sept. 4, 1843, by Rev. Henry Bromley	3	211
FREEMAN, Charlotte, ae. 22, m. John H. **MOULTON**,		
druggist, ae. 21, May 12, 1850, by Rev. J.H.		
Farnsworth	4	115
Frances J., m. Josiah **HARRINGTON**, b. of Windham,		
Nov. 29, 1838, by Rev. Windser Ward	3	187
Henry, machinist, b. Colchester, res. Windham, d.		
Apr. 12, 1848, ae. 19	4	151
Sally, m. Henry F. **BLISK**, b. of Willimantic, Oct.		
13, 1844, by C. Noble	3	217
FRENCH, FFRENCH, Amos, s. Jonathan & Mary, b. Aug. 30,		
1748	1	282
Elkanah, s. John & Elizabeth, b. Apr. 19, 1768	2	175
Frederick, s. Joshua & Hannah, b. Oct. 15, 1772	2	95
John, m. Fanny **ALLEN**, Dec. 7, 1806	3	58
John W., s. John C., farmer, ae. 31, & Margaret, ae.		
30, b. Jan. 19, [1851]	4	13
John William, s. [John & Fanny], b. Oct. 31, 1807	3	58
Jonathan, m. Sarah **WALCUT**, Dec. 15, 1725	1	71
Jonathan, s. Jonathan & Sarah, b. Jan. 19, 1726/7	1	71
Mary, m. Asa **ROBINSON**, Oct. 25, 1749	1	292
Miriam, d. Jona[tha]n & Sarah, b. Mar. 22, 1733	1	71
Rachel, d. Jonathan & Sarah, b. Feb. 19, 1730/31	1	71
Ruth, d. [John & Elizabeth], b Aug. 29, 1772	2	175
Sam[ue]ll, d. Apr. 20, 1727	1	6
Sarah, d. Jonathan & Sarah, b. June 13, 1729	1	71
Silence, m. Elijah **BIBBONS**, Nov. 3, 1799; d. Aug.		
15, 1818	3	8
Zephaniah, s. [John & Elizabeth], b. Oct. 19, 1769	2	175
——, st. b. child of John c., farmer, of Willi-		
mantic, b. Jan. 17, [1850]	4	10
FRINK, FFRINK, Abby Eleanor, m. John Huntington **BALDWIN,**		
b. of Windham, Nov. 2, 1846, by Rev. A. Ogden, Jr.	3	233
Alathea, d [Andrew & Jerusha], b. Sept. 4, 1763	2	45
Alfred B., m. Marcy **PAGE**, Apr. 8, 1822; by John		
Baldwin, Esq.	3	34
Amanda, d. [Andrew & Phila], b. Jan. 21, 1803	3	51
Amanda, m. Edwin **SMITH**, Oct. 16, [1828], by Rev		
Dennis Platt, Willimantic Falls	3	132
Amos, s. Elias & Lydia, b. Feb. 25, 1749/50	1	122
Andrew, s. Elias & Lydia, b. Oct. 26, 1738	1	122

	Vol.	Page
FRINK, FFRINK, (cont.)		
Andrew, m. Jerusha **RUDD**, May 26, 1762	2	45
Andrew, s [Andrew & Jerusha], b. Jan. 28, 1769	2	45
Andrew, m. Lydia **SAWYER**, Oct. 9, 1770	2	45
Andrew, s. [Andrew & Lydia], b. July 7, 1777	2	45
Andrew, m. Phila **STOWELL**, Oct. 12, 1801	3	51
Andrew, s. [Andrew & Phila], b. July 20, 1812	3	51
Andrew, Jr., m. Susan Brown **ABBE**, Sept. 23, 1833.		
"Recorded in Chaplin"	3	98
Bela, s. [Andrew & Lydia], b. May 30, 1771	2	45
Bela, m. Lydia **ROBINSON**, Apr. 15, 1795	2	192
Calvin, s. [Elijah & Ruth], b. Oct. 13, 1769	2	50
C[h]loe, d. [Elijah & Ruth], b. Dec. 28, 1761	2	50
Edward Huntington, s. [Silas & Mary], b. Oct. 21,		
1805	3	44
Edwin Smith, s. [Andrew, Jr. & Susan Brown], b.		
Sept. 22, 1842	3	98
Elias, m. Lydia **BINGHAM**, June 3, 1731	1	122
Elias, s. Elias & Lydia, b. May 3, 1745	1	122
Elias, Jr., d. Sept. 29, 1756	1	188
Elijah, s. Elias & Lydia, b. May 28, 1735	1	122
Elijah, m. Ruth **HIBBARD**, June 21, 1758	2	50
Elijah, s. [Elijah & Ruth], b. Oct. 3, 1765	2	50
Eunice, d. [Elijah & Ruth], b. Apr. 11, 1759	2	50
Fanny, d. [Andrew & Lydia], b. Dec. 11, 1781	2	45
Fanny, m. Gurdon **HEB[B]ARD**, Jr., Mar. 30, 1799	3	45
George Abbe, s. [Andrew, Jr. & Susan Brown], b.		
Aug. 10, 1836; d. Sept. 29, 1836	3	98
Henry, s. [Bela & Lydia], b. Jan. 16, 1796	2	192
Irena, d. [Andrew & Lydia], b. May 19, 1775	2	45
Irena, m. Gurdon **HEB[B]ARD**, Nov. 27, 1796	3	5
Jane, d. Aug. 9, 1847, ae. 1	4	152
Jerusha, d. Elias & Lydia, b. June 21, 1752	1	122
Jerusha, w. Andrew, d. Feb. 8, 1769	2	45
Jerusha, d. [Andrew & Lydia], b. Oct. 4, 1773	2	45
Jerusha, m. Amos **ALLEN**, Nov. 14, 1776	2	105
Jerusha, m. John **BINGHAM**, Sept. 20, 1829, by Rev.		
Roger Bingham	3	143
John, s. Elias & Lydia, b. May 6, 1743	1	122
John, s. Charles, carpenter, ae. 31, & Caroline,		
ae. 26, b. Dec. 3, 1847	4	4
Jonathan Stowell, s. [Andrew & Phila], b. Oct. 7,		
1805	3	51
Joseph, s. Elias & Lydia, b. Mar. 16, 1741	1	122
Joseph, m. Sarah **LATHROP**, [ ], 1763	2	93
Joshua, of Coventry, Conn., m. Sabra **CORNING**, of		
Bolton, Conn., June 28, 1836, by Rev. Philo		
Judson, at Willimantic	3	178

	Vol.	Page
FRINK, FFRINK, (cont.)		
Julia M., m. W[illia]m P. **GATES**, Oct. 7, 1834, by		
Rev. Marvin Root	3	93
Julia M., m. William P. **GATES**, Oct. 7, 1834, by		
Rev. Marvin Root	3	170
Julia Maria, d. [Andrew & Phila], b. Apr. 4, 1815	3	51
Laura, d. L H., b. Nov. 4, 1847	4	3
Lucretia F., of Windham, m. John S. **HAZEN**, of New		
York, Aug 7, 1833, by Rev. Jesse Fisher	3	165
Lucy, d. [Elijah & Ruth], b. Nov. 14, 1762; d. May		
21, 1764	2	50
Luther, s. [Elijah & Ruth], b. July 30, 1767	2	50
Lydia, d. Elias & Lydia, b. Dec. 6, 1747	1	122
Lydia, d. [Andrew & Jerusha], b. Oct. 13, 1765	2	45
Lydia, m. Alpheas **DEWEY**, Nov. 29, 1787	2	101
Mary, b. Mansfield, res. Scotland, d. Apr. 28, [1849],		
ae. 68	4	153
Mary Ann, d. [Silas & Mary], b. Oct. 25, 1808	3	44
Mary Ann, m. William R **DORRANCE**, Nov. 8, 1830, by		
Rev. Jesse Fisher	3	149
Mary J., ae. 38, m John H. **CAPEN**, manufacturer, ae		
41, July 22, [1850], by Rev. J.H. Farnsworth	4	115
Nathan, s. Elias & Lydia, b. June 20, 1733	1	122
Nathaniel Lathrop, s. [Joseph & Sarah], b. Dec. 26,		
1763; d. Feb. 24, 1814	2	93
Rebecca, m. Jabez **GILBERT**, Oct. 9, 1826, by Rev. Jesse		
Fisher	3	129
Silas, s. Elias & Lydia, b. Aug. 22, 1754	1	122
Silas, s. [Andrew & Lydia], b Oct. 24, 1779	2	45
Silas, m. Mary **STOWELL**, Nov. 11, 1804	3	44
William, of Stonington, m. Achsah **DOWNER**, of Lebanon,		
Apr. 13, 1834, by Rev. Roger Bingham	3	169
William Baldwin, s. [Andrew & Phila], b. Dec. 6, 1808	3	51
William F., merchant, of Windham, d. Sept. 19, 1847,		
ae. 39	4	151
——, st. b. child of John C., ae. 32, & Margaret,		
ae. 24, b. May 5, [1848]	4	7
——, d. Amanda, ae. 26, b. July 9, [1851]	4	13
FULLER, FFULLER, Aaron, s. Nathaniell & Ann, b. Oct. 30,		
1706	1	5
Aaron, s. Stephen & Hannah, b. Jan. 26, 1733/4	1	136
Arron, s. Stephen & Hannah, b. Jan. 26, 1734/5	1	183
Aaron, m. Sarah **HOLT**, Mar. 15, 1755	2	53
Aaron, s. [Aaron & Sarah], b. Nov. 10, 1757, in		
Canterbury	2	53
Aaron Frances, [s. David L. & Hadassah], b. Dec. 21,		
1839	3	56
Abby Ann, [d. David L. & Hadassah], b. Mar. 15, 1833	3	56

	Vol.	Page
FULLER, FFULLER, (cont.)		
Abigail, d. Stephen & Hannah, b. Sept. 6, 1728	1	80
Abigail, m. John **HAMMOND**, Dec. 19, 1749 "Yet to		
be certified".	1	310
Abigail, d. Stephen, Jr. & Mary, b. Jan. 3, 1752	1	323
Abigail, d. [Stephen, Jr. & Mary], b. Jan. 3, 1752	2	129
Abigail, d. [Thomas & Sarah], b. Oct. 12, 1770	2	51
Abigail, d. [Abijah & Abigail], b. May 22, 1778	2	236
Abigail, m. Adonijah **BURNAM**, Jan. 9, 1800	3	60
Abijah, s. David & Hannah, b. Aug. 5, 1753	1	206
Abijah, s. David & Hannah, b. Aug. 5, 1753	2	7
Abijah, m. Abigail **MEACHAM**, May 15, 1777	2	236
Albert, s. [David L. & Hadassah], b. Sept. 20, 1818	3	56
Alice, d. Stephen & Hannah, b. [ ] 22, 1741	1	183
Alice, m. John **ABBOTT**, Nov. 4, 1762	2	151
Alice, d. [Nathan & Susannah], b. Apr. 3, 1802	2	212
Alpheas G., s. [David L. & Hadassah], b. June 23,		
1822	3	56
Andrew, s. David & Hannah, b. Sept. 30, 1747	1	206
Andrew, s. David & Hannah, b. Sept. 30, 1747	2	7
Andrew, m. Eunice **BURMAN**, Jan. 18, 1770	2	152
Andrew, s. [Andrew & Eunice], b. Oct. 20, 1770	2	152
Andrew, d. Apr. 17, 1782, in the 36th y. of his age	2	152
Ann, m. James P. **HOWES**, b. of Windham, Dec. 9, 1840,		
by Rev. Andrew Sharpe, Willimantic	3	195
Arthur Lee, s. [Abijah & Abigail], b. Mar. 27, 1780	2	236
Asa, s. David & Hannah, b. Mar. 7, 1751	2	7
Asa, s. David & Hannah, b. Mar. 17, 1751	1	206
Bathsheba, d. Daniell & Mary, b. Nov. 6, 1708	A	26
Betsey, d. [Andrew & Eunice], b. Oct. 6, 1780	2	152
Betsey B., of Columbia, m. Rufus **DOW**, of Coventry,		
Nov. 25, 1831, by Rev. Peter Griffin	3	156
Caroline, of Windham, m. Andrew M. **LITCHFIELD**, of		
Hampton, Dec. 30, 1829, by Rev. Jesse Fisher	3	140
Charlotte, of Lisbon, m. Erastus **ALLEN**, of Windham,		
Jan. 15, 1807	3	56
Daniell, s. Daniell & Mary, b. Mar. 1, 1702	A	26
Daniel, s. [Aaron & Sarah], b. June 25, 1775, in		
Canterbury	2	53
Daniel Luce, s. [Nathan & Susannah], b. Sept. 10,		
1788	2	212
David, m. Hannah **FFULLER**, May 17, 1741	1	206
David, m. Hannah **FULLER**, May 17, 1741	2	7
David, s. David & Hannah, b. Aug. 4, 1744	1	206
David, s. David & Hannah, b. Aug. 4, 1744	2	7
David, s. David & Hannah, d. Sept. 14, 1762, at		
Hanvannah	2	7
David, s. [Andrew & Eunice], b. Mar. 15, 1772	2	152

	Vol.	Page
FULLER, FFULLER, (cont.)		
David, Sr., d. Apr. 26, 1774	2	7
David L., m. Hadassah **GAY**, Nov. 27, 1817, by Rev.		
Roswell Wetmore	3	56
David L., s. [David L. & Hadassah], b. Sept. 2,		
1826	3	56
Dwight, [s. Pearly B.], b. Nov. 23, 1837	3	234
Ele[a]nor, d. [Thomas & Sarah], b. Aug. 6, 1768	2	51
Elisha, s. David & Hannah, b. Nov. 11, 1761	2	7
Elizabeth, m. Barnabus **ALLEN**, Apr. 21, 1752	1	262
Elizabeth K., [twin with Sarah C., d. David L. &		
Hadassah], b. Apr. 4, 1829	3	56
Emma Alice, [d. Pearly B.], b. Mar. 4, 1845	3	234
Erastus, s. [Andrew & Eunice], b. Mar. 10, 1778	2	152
Erastus, m. Jerusha G. **MORGAN**, Mar. 24, 1816	3	79
Eunice, d. [Aaron & Sarah], b. May 5, 1773, in		
Canterbury	2	53
Eunice, d. [Andrew & Eunice], b. Nov. 4, 1775	2	152
George, s. [David L. & Hadassah], b. May 9, 1824	3	56
Hannah, d. Nathaniel & Ann, b. Aug. 22, 1704	A	14
Hannah, d. Stephen & Hannah, b. Oct. 30, 1725	1	80
Hannah, m. David **FFULLER**, May 17, 1741	1	206
Hannah, m. David **FULLER**, May 17, 1741	2	7
Hannah, d. David & Hannah, b. Sept. 20, 1755	2	7
Hannah, m. Elijah **FITCH**, Apr. 17, 1766	2	133
Hannah, m. Nathan **DENISON**, Mar. 16, 1778	1	153
Hannah, m. Samuel **STODDARD**, Dec. 2, 1778	2	236
Hannah, d. [Andrew & Eunice], b. Aug. 29, 1782	2	152
Isaac, s. [Aaron & Sarah], b. Oct. 17, 1759, in		
Canterbury	2	53
Jacob, s. [Andrew & Eunice], b. Dec. 4, 1773	2	152
James H., of Mansfield, m. Mary E. **PERRY**, of Windham,		
Apr. 29, 1839, by Rev. Winslow Ward	3	189
Jane, d. [David L. & Hadassah], b. Feb. 19, 1820	3	56
Jared, s. [Nathan & Susannah], b. July 26, 1805	2	212
Jared William, [s. David L. & Hadassah], b. July 31,		
1835; d. Feb. 18, 1839	3	56
John, s. Daniell & Mary, b. Aug. 13, 1706	A	29
John, s. Stephen & Hannah, b. Mar. 13, 1739/40	1	183
John, s. David & Hannah, b. Jan. 30, 1748/9	1	206
John, s. David & Hannah, b. Jan. 30, 1748/9	2	7
John, s. David & Hannah, d. Oct. 25, 1754	2	7
John, Jr., m. Mary **DECKER**, Dec 24, 1755	2	20
John, s. [Stephen, Jr. & Mary], b. Jan. 26, 1762	2	129
John, s. [Nathaniel, Jr. & Mary], b. Nov. 25, 1780	2	245
John M., of Kent, m. Cynt[hi]a **ROUTH**, of Windham,		
Aug. 27, 1825, by Rev Jesse Fisher	3	115
Jonathan, s. [Aaron & Sarah], b. Aug. 29, 1755	2	53

	Vol.	Page
FULLER, FFULLER, (cont.)		
Jonathan, m. Experience **HUNT**, May [ ], 1774	2	167
Jonathan, s. [Jonathan & Experience], b. Dec. 22, 1776	2	167
Josiah, s. David & Hannah, b. Oct. 30, 1762	2	7
Leonard, s. [Aaron & Sarah], b. Oct. [ ], 1781, in Canterbury	2	53
Lois, m. Alfred **BURNHAM**, Mar. 18, 1827, by Elder Elias Thorp	3	129
Lucy, d. [Thomas & Sarah], b. Aug. 8, 1763	2	51
Lucy, d. [Nathan & Susannah], b. Mar. 23, 1792	2	212
Lucy, m. Sylvester **TRACY**, Feb. 27, 1814	3	77
Luther, s. [Nathaniel, Jr. & Mary], b. July 8, 1782	2	245
Luther, [s. Pearly B.], b. June 22, 1847	3	234
Lydia, d. [Nathan & Susannah], b. Jan. 27, 1790	2	212
Marcia M., of Windham, m. Nathan H. **PAYN**, of Brooklyn, May 7, 1838, by Rev. O.C. Whiton	3	186
Maria, d. [Nathan & Susannah], b. July 26, 1794	2	212
Martha, d. Stephen & Hannah, b. Sept. 7, 1724	1	80
Martha, m. William **FFARNAM**, June 23, 1742	1	230
Mary, d. Stephen & Hannah, b. Mar. 9, 1726/7	1	80
Mary, m. Zebediah **FARNAM**, July 27, 1743	1	235
Mary, m. Zebediah **FARNAM**, July 27, 1743	2	8
Mary, m. John **LOOMIS**, Dec. 10, 1747	1	228
Mary, d. Stephen & Mary, b. May 28, 1759	1	323
Mary, d. [Stephen, Jr. & Mary], b. May 28, 1759	2	129
Mary, d. [Nathaniel, Jr. & Mary], b. July 10, 1785	2	245
Mary L., m. William H. **COGSWELL**, Feb. 23, 1824	3	15
Mary W., ae. 19, m. W[illia]m **BABCOCK**, carpenter, ae. 26, of Windham, Oct. 1, [1849], by Tho[ma]s Robinson	4	113
Miranda, m. Payne **ROSS**, May 3, 1835, by Rev. Roger Bingham	3	175
Miriam, d. Nathaniell & Ann, b. Mar. 10, 1708	1	5
Mosess, s. Nathan[ie]ll & Ann, b. Sept. 14, 1702	A	14
Nabby, d. [Nathan & Susannah], b. Sept. 12, 1799	2	212
Nathan, s. [Aaron & Sarah], b. Sept. 3, 1763, in Canterbury	2	53
Nathan, m. Susannah **LUCE**, Mar. 8, 1788	2	212
Nathan, s. [Nathan & Susannah], b. May 19, 1797	2	212
Nathan, Jr , m. Elizabeth **HARRINGTON**, Mar. 8, 1827, by Rev. Jesse Fisher	3	126
Nathaniel, s. [Thomas & Sarah], b. May 14, 1758	2	51
Nathaniel, Jr., m. Mary **DURKEE**, Aug. 8, 1780	2	245
Olive, m. John F. **JUDD**, Sept. 6, 1825, by Elisha Frink, Elder	3	71
Oscar L., farmer, of Hampton, m. Ardelia **WILLIAMS**, b. Hampton, res. Willimantic, Jan. 13, 1851, by		

	Vol.	Page
FULLER, FFULLER, (cont.)		
Rev. S.G. Williams	4	118
Phebe, d. David & Hannah, b. Dec 1, 1759	2	7
Polly, d. [Stephen, Jr. & Sarah], b. Apr. 16,		
1778, at Westmoreland	2	247
R[e]uben, s. [Stephen, Jr. & Mary], b. Feb. 10,		
1769	2	129
Robert B., [s. Pearly B.], b. Apr. 2, 1836	3	234
Rufus, s. [Aaron & Sarah], b. Aug. 30, 1766, in		
Canterbury	2	53
Ruth, m. Peter **ROBINSON**, June 30, 1725	1	77
Sarah, d. [Thomas & Sarah], b. May 14, 1760	2	51
Sarah, d. [Aaron & Sarah], b. Oct. 21, 1768, in		
Canterbury	2	53
Sarah, d. Jona[tha]n & Exper[ien]ce, b. July 11,		
1775	2	167
Sarah, m. Asa **ABBOTT**, Feb. 7, 1782	2	247
Sarah, d. [Nathaniel, Jr. & Mary], b. Nov. 1, 1787	2	245
Sarah, m. Sylvester **LINCOLN**, Aug. 28, 1836, by		
Elias Sharpe, Elder	3	179
Sarah, factory, b. Coventry, res. Willimantic, d.		
Jan. 17, 1849, ae. 19	4	153
Sarah C., [twin with Elizabeth K., d. David L. &		
Hadassah], b. Apr. 4, 1829	3	56
Sarah Esther, [d. Pearly B.], b. Oct. 28, 1843	3	234
Sarah R., of Windham, m. Daniel B. **MARTIN**, of Chaplin,		
Feb. 20, 1833, by Rev. L.S. Hough, of Chaplin	3	163
Siah, s. [Aaron & Sarah], b. Nov. 18, 1770, in		
Canterbury	2	53
Solomon, of Chaplin, m. Margaret **BUCK**, of Chaplin, Oct.		
21, 1835, by Rev. L.H. Corson	3	175
Stephen, m. Hannah **MOULTON**, Jan. 1, 1723/4	1	80
Stephen, s. Stephen & Hannah, b. Nov. 30, 1730	1	80
Stephen, Jr., m. Mary **ABBOT[T]**, Oct. 17, 1751	1	323
Stephen, Jr., m. Mary **ABBOT[T]**, Oct. 17, 1751	2	129
Stephen, s. Stephen & Mary, b. Jan. 22, 1754	1	323
Stephen, s [Stephen, Jr. & Mary], b. Jan 22, 1754	2	129
Stephen, s. [Thomas & Sarah], b. Apr. 21, 1773	2	51
Stephen, Jr., m. Sarah **BIDLOCK**, [ ], "lived		
at Westmoreland"; d. [ ], at Westmoreland	2	247
Susannah, d. Nath[anie]l & Deliverance, b. Oct. 3, 1762	2	141
Thomas, s. Stephen & Hannah, b. June 10, 1732	1	136
Thomas, s. Stephen & Hannah, b. June 10, 1732	1	183
Thomas, m. Sarah **GRIFFIN**, Jan. 19, 1757	2	51
Thomas, s [Stephen, Jr. & Mary], b. Apr. 7, 1757	2	129
Thomas, s. Stephen & Mary, b. May 7, 1757	1	323
Thomas, s. [Thomas & Sarah], b. July 21, 1765	2	51
Thomas Hart, [s. Pearly B.], b. Feb. 22, 1840	3	234

	Vol.	Page
FULLER, FFULLER, (cont.)		
Timothy, s. Daniell & Mary, b. Feb. 29, 1704	A	29
W[illia]m H., s. Sol R., farmer, ae. 34, &		
Margaret, b. Nov. 28, [1849]	4	9
FULLSON, Rachall, d. Israel & Rachall, b. Apr. 29, 1732	1	125
GAGE, Tho[ma]s, m. Mary C. **WEBB**, Sept. 30, 1821, by Rev.		
Cornelius B. Everest	3	117
GAGER, Aaron, s. [Jason & Lucy], b. July 13, 1776	2	156
Aaron, s. [Jason & Lucy], b. Sept. 5, 1778	2	156
Aaron, m. Polly **SMITH**, May 5, 1803	3	99
Aaron, m. Debba **MURDOCK**, June 20, 1805	3	99
Aaron, m. Lena **BABCOCK**, Jan. 29, 1835, by Rev. Roger		
Bingham	3	172
Andrew, s. [Jason & Lucy], b. Feb. 24, 1772	2	156
Charles, s. [John P. & Chloe], b. May 5, 1817	3	64
Chauncey, s. [John P. & Chloe], b. Feb. 4, 1825	3	64
Chauncey, s. John, ae. 28, & Lydia Ann, ae. 29, b		
Sept. 20, 1847	4	4
Chauncey, d. Oct. 7, [1849], ae. 2	4	156
Chloe, w. J[oh]n P., d. June 27, 1834	3	64
Daniel, m. Polina **BINGHAM**, Nov. 2, 1808	3	81
David, s. [Jason & Lucy], b. Oct. 3, 1784	2	156
Delia F., of Franklin, m. Cha[rle]s W. **BRIGGS**, of		
Lebanon, Feb. 8, 1843, by Rev. Nathan Wildman,		
Lebanon	3	207
Eliphalet M., [s. Aaron & Debba], b. May 2, 1814	3	99
Ellen Maria, d. John P., farmer, ae. 30, & Lucy Ann,		
ae. 32, b. Aug. 31, 1849	4	9
Harriet, d. [Jason & Lucy], b. July 25, 1792	2	156
Jason, Jr., m. Esther **WALDO**, Nov. 3, 1806	3	57
John P., m. Chloe **BARKER**, [ ] 28, 1808	3	64
John P., Jr., s. [John P. & Chloe], b. May 22, 1819	3	64
John Peck, s. [Jason & Lucy], b. July 19, 1782	2	156
Lewis, s. [John P. & Chloe], b. Mar. 19, 1815	3	64
Lewis, m Harriet **JENNINGS**, b. of Windham, June 14,		
1841, by Rev. Ansel Nash	3	197
Lucia A., d. W[illia]m S., farmer, ae. 46, of Willi-		
mantic, b. May 1, [1850]	4	10
Lucretia, d. W[illia]m S., farmer, & Sarah, b. Feb.		
12, 1848	4	3
Lucy, d. [Jason & Lucy], b. Apr. 2, 1770; d. Feb. 22,		
1773	2	156
Lucy, d. [Jason & Lucy], b. Jan 31, 1774	2	156
Lucy, m. Joseph **BASS**, Dec. 30, 1795	2	185
Lucy A , [d. Aaron & Debba], b. July 10, 1809	3	99
Lucy A., m. Archa **WILLOBY**, Mar. 2, 1831, by Rev.		
Roger Bingham	3	151
Mary, m. Jeremiah **RYPLEY**, Apr. 7, 1690	A	27

	Vol	Page
GAGER, (cont.)		
Mary H., [d. Aaron & Debba], b. July 10, 1806	3	99
Polly **SMITH**, w. [Aaron], d. May 10, 1804	3	99
Rebecca, d. [Jason & Lucy], b. Nov. 3, 1790	2	156
Rufus Henry, s. [Daniel & Polina], b July 12, 1810	3	81
Samuel B., m. Mary E. **JENNER**, b. of Windham (Scotland Society) Mar. 21, 1836, by Rev. Benajah Cook, Jr., at Willimantic Falls	3	177
Samuel Baker, s. [John P. & Chloe], b. May 23, 1812	3	64
Sarah Ann, d. [John P. & Chloe], b. Oct. 3, 1821	3	64
Sarah Ann, of Windham, m George **PERRY**, of Lisbon, Mar. 12, 1842, by Rev. Joseph Ayer, Jr., of Lisbon	3	201
Sophronia, [d. John P. & Chloe], b. Dec. 19, 1809	3	64
Sophronia, m. Uriah R. **TRACY**, May 16, 1826, by Rev. Jesse Fisher	3	128
Stephen Decatur, s. [Daniel & Polina], b. Oct. 13, 1813	3	81
Sibbel, d. [Jason & Lucy], b. Sept. 5, 1780	2	156
Sybel, m. John **CAREY**, Feb. 11, 1810	3	74
William L., m. Sarah Ann **BASS**, b. of Windham, May 16, 1842, by Rev. John E. Tyler	3	201
GALLAGHER, Thomas, operative, of Willimantic, d. June 28, 1860, ae. 19	4	161
GALLUP, Charles, m Lama* **SIMONS**, Feb. 11, 1838, by Rev. Alfred Burnham (*Laura?)	3	184
Charles A., of Windham, m. Lydia **NICHOLS**, of Mansfield, [Sept.] 4, 1839, by Rev. John E. Tyler	3	191
Edwin, m. Martha **GALLUP**, b. of Sterling, Nov. 26, 1839, by Rev. Otis C. Whiton, of Scotland Society	3	192
Eliza A., m. Henry **STARKWEATHER**, Aug. 27, 1844, at Willimantic by Rev. J.B. Guild	3	216
Emma, ae. 20, m. James B. **SPRAGUE**, farmer, ae. 23, of Windham, Nov. 25, 1848, by Rev. B.M. Allen	4	112
Esther, m. William **GALLUP**, Dec. 18, 1843, at Willimantic, by Rev. J.B. Guild	3	212
James, m. Esther **CLARK**, Sept. 15, 1822	3	106
Martha, m. Edwin **GALLUP**, b. of Sterling, Nov. 26, 1839, by Rev. Otis C. Whiton, of Scotland Society	3	192
William, m. Esther **GALLUP**, Dec. 18, 1843, at Willimantic, by Rev. J.B. Guild	3	212
GAMBLE, Elizabeth, m. Silvanus **BACKUS**, Apr. 12, 1758	2	43
GARD, Judith, m. Jonathan **GININGS**, Dec. 25, 1701	A	29
Sarah, m. Samuel **BACKUS**, Dec. 2, 1712	1	39a
GARDINER, Harriet, d. [Nero & Rose], b Jan. 9, 1799	3	27
Henry, of Hartford, m. Lydia Swift **YOUNG**, of Windham,		

	Vol.	Page
GARDINER, (cont.)		
Apr. 8, 1834, by L.S. Corson, Rector	3	170
Mehetable, m. Col. Thomas **DYAR**, Oct. 10, 1752; d.		
Nov. 1, 1753	1	92
Nero, m. Rose **LARRENCE**, Apr. 9, 1797	3	27
Sanford, s. [Nero & Rose], b. Nov. 8, 1797	3	27
William H., tinner, b. Newport, R.I., res Willi-		
mantic, d. Apr. 13, 1860, ae. 28	4	159-0
GATES, Martha, m George **SHAW**, Dec. 2, 1726	1	97
Susan A., d. [W[illia]m P. & Julia M.}, b. Nov. 14,		
1837	3	93
W[illia]m P., m. Julia M. **FRINK**, Oct. 7, 1834, by		
Rev. Marvin Root	3	93
William P., m. Julia M. **FRINK**, Oct. 7, 1834, by		
Marvin Root, Minister	3	170
W[illia]m P., s. [W[illia]m P. & Julia M.], b.		
Aug. 7, 1836	3	93
GAVIT, GAVITT, Sarah, ae. 19, m. W[illia]m **ROBINSON**,		
operative, ae. 25, of Thompson, Sept 26, 1847,		
by Rev. A. Sharp	4	111
Simeon T., m. Susan **CHAPPELL**, Feb. 26, 1832, by Rev.		
Roger Bingham	3	158
GAVITO, Anna A., of Willimantic, m. Nathaniel C. **PAYNE**, of		
Lebanon, Oct. 4, 1846, by Rev. John Cooper	3	233
GAY, Hadassah, m. David L. **FULLER**, Nov. 27, 1817, by Rev.		
Roswell Wetmore	3	56
GAYLORD, Mary, m. Rev. Sam[ue]ll **MOSELEY**, Apr. 1, 1752	1	328
GEER, GEERS, Aaron, m. Hannah **UTL[E]Y**, July 8, 1755	1	281
Aaron, m. Meriam **SPAFFORD**, Oct. 19, 1758	1	281
Aaron, s. [Isaiah & Philomela], b. Nov. 20, 1804	2	116
Aaron, s. Aaron, mechanic, ae. 46, & Sarah E., ae.		
40, of Willimantic, b. May 22, 1851	4	12
Alathea, d. [Aaron & Meriam], b. Apr. 19, 1764	1	281
Amos, m. Freelove **BURGE**, June 3, 1784	3	11
Anna, m. Jonathan **KINGSBURY**, Jr., Jan. 14, 1768	2	134
Anne, d. [Samuel & Phebe], b. Mar. 13, 1777	3	16
Asaenna, d. [Aaron & Meriam], b. Aug. 23, 1769	1	281
Bela, s. [Samuel & Phebe], b. Apr. 21, 1790	3	16
Betsey, d [Samuel & Phebe], b. Nov. 13, 1785	3	16
Clarissa, d. [Samuel & Phebe], b. July 22, 1766	3	16
Eliphalet, d. [s.?] [Amos & Freelove], b. July 1,		
1787	3	11
Elizabeth, d. [Aaron & Meriam], b. Jan. 25, 1759	1	281
Elizabeth Ostrander, [d. James & Fanny], b. Apr.		
29, 1816	3	82
Ezra, m. Elizabeth **CANADA**, Nov. 7, 1745	1	281
Frances Louisa, d [James & Fanny], b. May 17, 1814	3	82
Frederick Woolcott, s. [John Carey & Mary], b. May		

	Vol	Page
GEER, GEERS, (cont)		
24, 1817	3	81
George Wyllys, s. [Samuel & Phebe], b May 18,		
1779	3	16
H.A. farmer, ae. 37, m. Sally Ann **JILLSON**, ae. 36,		
Nov. 22, 1848, by Rev. J.R. Arnold	4	113
Hannah, d. [Aaron & Hannah], b. Nov. 2, 1755	1	281
Hannah, w. A[a]ron, d. Dec. 25, 1755	1	281
Hannah, m. Stephen **HOLT**, Nov. 22, 1772	2	196
Henry Belcher, s. [Jeptha], b. Feb. 18, 1836	3	107
Irena, d. [Isaiah & Philomela], b. Jan. 2, 1802	2	116
Isaiah, s. [Aaron & Meriam], b. June 25, 1762	1	281
Isaiah, m. Philomela **CAREY**, Nov. 27, 1788	2	116
James, s. [Amos & Freelove], b. July 15, 1785	3	11
James, m. Fanny **SEYMOUR**, Oct. 5, 1813	3	82
Jepthah, m. Mary **HEB[B]ARD**, May 19, 1839	3	107
Jepthar, m. Mary L. **HEBBARD**, b of Windham, May 19,		
1839, by Rev. Otis C. Whiton, of Scotland Society,		
Windham	3	189
John Carey, m. Mary **JOHNSON**, Sept. [ ], 1815	3	81
Joseph, s. [Isaiah & Philomela], b. Feb. 5, 1795	2	116
Juliana, d. [Amos & Freelove], b. Jan. 27, 1796	3	11
Lucy, d. [Samuel & Phebe], b. Apr. 25, 1788	3	16
Lucy A., of Chaplin, m. Reuben A. **RICE**, of Mansfield,		
Aug. 10, 1845, by Rev. Henry Greenslit	3	222
Lydia, d. [Aaron & Meriam], b. Nov. 25, 1766	1	281
Marcy, d. [Samuel & Phebe], b. Feb. 19, 1770	3	16
Nathaniel, s. Ezra & Elizabeth, b. Mar. 27, 1748	1	281
Olive, d. [Samuel & Phebe], b. May 29, 1781	3	16
Olive, w. Jepthah, d. Oct. 24, 1838	3	107
Phebe, d. [Samuel & Phebe], b. July 30, 1783	3	16
Phila, s. [Isaiah & Philomela], b. Jan. 4, 1808	2	116
Phinehas, s. [Samuel & Phebe], b. Oct. 27, 1774	3	16
Ralph, s. [Isaiah & Philomela], b. Aug. 2, 1789	2	116
Ralph Carey, s [John Carey & Mary], b. Mar. 13,		
1816	3	81
Samuel, m Phebe **DUDINGTON**, Dec. 10, 1765	3	16
Samuel Fisher, s. [Samuel & Phebe], b. Nov. 15, 1772	3	16
Sarah, m. Joseph **GEN[N]INGS**, Dec the last, 1707	1	47
Sidney Leonard, s. [Jeptha], b. Sept. 16, 1838	3	107
W[illia]m, dyer, ae. 28, b. N.Y., res. Hopville, m.		
Amelia **DYER**, ae. 29, operative, b. Independence,		
res. Hopville, May 1, 1851, by Rev S.G Williams	4	117
Winthrop, s. [Isaiah & Philomela], b. Aug. 2, 1797	2	116
GENNER, George, s. Elias B., farmer, & Emma, b. Oct. 29,		
1847	4	3
GENNINGS, [see under **JENNINGS**]		
GETCHELL, Sophia, m. Daniel **DORAN**, b. of Windham, Nov. 23,		

	Vol.	Page
GETCHELL, (cont.)		
1828, by Rev. Chester Tilden	3	131
GIBSON, Hannah, wid. Henry, d Apr. 10, [ ]	2	1
GIDDENS, Jasper, m. Elizabeth **SKINNER**, Oct. 9, 1765	2	111
GIFFORD, Hannah, d. Sam[ue]ll & Mary, b. Dec. 23, 1696	A	20
Jeremiah, s. Samuell & Mary, b. Sept. 4, 1699	A	20
Samuel, m. Mary **COLLINS**, Nov. 1, 1693	A	20
Sam[ue]ll, s. Sam[ue]ll & Mary, b. Sept. 23, 1694	A	20
GILBERT, Betsey, m. Abraham **HOXIE**, Oct 21, 1829, by Rev. Richard F. Cleveland	3	139
Eunice, d. Jabez & Mary, b. Nov. 27, 1771; d. July 10, 1773	2	147
George, s. [Jabez & Mary], b. Aug. 10, 1779	2	147
Jabez, m. Mary **READ**, June 8, 1769	2	147
Jabez, m. Rebecca **FRINK**, Oct. 9, 1826, by Rev. Jesse Fisher	3	129
Jabez, d. Dec. 29, 1827	2	147
James, s. Jabez & Mary, b. Mar. 20, 1770	2	147
Lydia, d. Jabez & Mary, b. Sept. 23, 1774; d Oct 23, 1775	2	147
Polly Ellis, d. [Jabez & Mary], b Aug. 19, 1776	2	147
Rebecca, b. New London, res. Windham, d. Dec. 10, 1848, ae. 89	4	154
GILES, Peggy, m. Enoch **MEACHAM**, Apr. 11, 1793	2	164
GILLETT, Benjamin, s. Cornelius & Deborah, b. July 25, 1722	1	86
Mary, d. Cornelius & Deborah, b. Jan. 22, 1726/7; d. Feb. 27, 1726/7	1	86
GINNE, Joe, "the negro", d. Apr. 16, 1700	A	12
GINNINGS, [see under **JENNINGS**]		
GLASS, James, m. Hannah **SUFFORD**, Oct. 28, 1767	2	135
Parthenia, d. [James & Hannah], b. Feb. 23, 1769	2	135
GLOVER, Susannah, m Caleb **BADCO[C]K**, May 18, 1721	1	28
GOAECK, Lewis, m. Susan **HOOPER**, b. of Willimantic Falls, Sept 14, 1837, by Rev. B. Cook, Jr.	3	183
GODFREY, Addison A., merchant, ae. 20, b. S. Coventry, res. Willimantic, m Julia M. **SENVANTO**, ae. 21, b. S. Coventry, res. Willimantic, Oct. 13, 1850, by Rev Henry Bromley	4	117
GOFF, William, m. Harriet **SUMNER**, Oct. 22, 1835, by Rev. Roger Bingham	3	175
GOLD, [see also [**GOULD**], Abigail, d. [John & Abigail], b. Feb. 14, 1760	2	82
John, m. Abigail **KINGSBURY**, Nov. 13, 1759	2	82
John, s. [John & Abigail], b. Aug. 12, 1761	2	82
John, d. Oct. 29, 1764	2	82
Jonathan, s. [John & Abigail], b. Apr. 28, 1763	2	82
Sallah, d. John & Abig[ail], b. July 8, 1765	2	82

	Vol.	Page
GOODSPEED, Cynthia, m. Henry B. HALL, b. of Hampton, Conn., Jan. 7, 1838, by Rev. John E. Tyler	3	184
Harriet, m. Joseph CARTWRIGHT, July 4, 1827, by Elder Chester Tilden	3	129
Isaac, of Southbridge, Mass., m. Emily SMITH, of Windham, June 12, 1837, by Rev. Philo Judson, at Willimantic Village	3	183
Lydia, m. John C. SWEETLAND, May 13, [ ], by Rev. Cornelius B. Everest	3	80
GORDON, Alexander, dyer, m. Rebecca CARTER, May 12, 1850, by Rev. Henry Greenslit	4	114
James, m. Ruba Anne ROBERTS, Apr. 29, 1844, by Rev. John B. Guild, Willimantic	3	214
Martha, of Windham, m. Charles S. GROSVENOR, of Hampton, Mar. 13, 1833, by Rev. Jesse Fisher ("See note under GROSVENOR") is handwritten after entry in the original manuscript.	3	165
GORHAM, George, of New London, m. Martha CONGDON, of Windham, Nov. 24, 1829, by Rev. Eseck Brown, of Lebanon	3	139
GORMLEY, Ann, ae. 21, m. Patrick E. NEAL, ae. 24, Apr 22, [1849], by Mr. Robinson	4	113
GOULD, GOOLD, [see also GOLD], Amie, m Nehemiah RIPLEY, Feb. 24, 1791	2	57
Hannah, m. Jermiah CLARK, May 3, 1750	1	316
Martha, m. Joseph HEB[B]ARD, Jr., Feb. 1, 1742/3	1	245
GRAHAM, Mary Ann, d. John, operative, ae. 45, b. July 1, 1849	4	6
GRANNIS, Eliza, m. Francis BURROWS, Oct. 11, 1805	3	61
GRANT, Andrew M., merchant, ae. 21, b. Ashford, res. Ashford, m. Sarah J. WILLIAMS, ae. 19, b. Mansfield, res Willimantic, Nov 12, 1850, by Rev. Sam[ue]l G. Williams	4	117
GRAVES, GREAVES, Benjamin, m Louisa LATHROP, May 10, 1831, by Rev. Rich[ar]d F. Cleveland	3	153
Hannah, m. Joseph FFORD, Apr. 22, 1730	1	112
Hannah, d. [June] 6, [1850], ae. 65	4	155
Jerusha, d. Jedediah & Jerusha, b. Aug 13, 1736; d. July 30, 1752	1	94
Ruth, m. Jonah LINKON, Feb 13, 1727/8	1	94
——, farmer, ae. 23, m. Phebe KEMPTON, ae. 19, May [1850], by Rev. Calhoun	4	115
GRAY, Abigail, [w. Thomas], d. [ ]	2	179
Adah, d. John & Ann, b. Mar 18, 1733/4	1	106
Ann, d. John & Ann, b. Nov. 18, 1729	1	106
Betsey, d. [Thomas & Abigail], b. [ ]	2	179
Charlotte, d. [Ebenezer & Sarah], b. Mar. 9, 1789	2	215

	Vol.	Page
GRAY, (cont.)		
Charlotte, w. Sam[ue]l, d. Dec. 13, 1797, ae. 33 y,		
2 m.	2	137
Charlotte, d. [Thomas & Lucretia], b. June 14, 1830	3	117
Ebenezer, Dr., s. Samuel & Susannah, b. Oct. 31,		
1697, in Preston; educated at Harvard, practiced		
medicine, spent his days at Easthampton, Lebanon,		
Newport, Windham; d. Sept. 8, 1773, almost 76 y.		
of age	2	2
Ebenezer, s. Sam[ue]ll & Lydia, b. July 26, 1743	1	205
Ebenezer, s. Samuel & Lydia, b. July 26, 1743	2	6
Ebenezer, m. Sarah **STANIFORD**, Mar. 30, 1786	2	215
Ebenezer, m. Sarah **STANFORD**, b of Windham, Mar 30,		
1786, by Rev. Stephen White; d. June 18, 1795	3	110
Ebenezer, s. [Ebenezer & Sarah], b. Aug. 16, 1787	2	215
Ebenezer, Col., d. June 18, 1795	2	215
Eliza[be]th, had s. Hez[ekiah] **FITCH**, b. Feb. 5, 1772	2	1
Hannah, d. [Thomas & Lucretia], b. Sept. 2, 1837	3	117
Harriet, d. [Sam[ue]l & Charlotte], b. Feb 1, 1790	2	137
Henry, s. [Thomas & Lucretia], b. Mar. 13, 1825	3	117
Henry, Dr., physician, ae. 24, m. Sarah A. **KENNEY**, ae		
24, Oct. 4, 1849, by Rev. J.E. Tyler	4	114
James, laborer, ae 20, m. Margaret **RILEY**, ae. 20, Oct.		
[ ], [1850], by Rev. Brady	4	115
Jane Ann, of Lebanon, m. Elliott **VALENTINE**, of Boston,		
Mass., Nov. 6, 1823	3	115
Joseph, s. John & Ann, b. June 12, 1732	1	106
Lucy, d. Sam[ue]ll & Lydia, b. June 27, 1746	1	205
Lucy, d. Samuel & Lydia, b. June 27, 1746; d. Mar. [ ]	2	6
Lucy, d. [Thomas & Abigail], b. [ ]	2	179
Lydia, d. Samuel & Lydia, b. Apr. 17, 1761; d. June 9,		
1761	2	6
Lydia, d. [Thomas & Abigail], b. Mar. 24, 1773	2	179
Lydia, wid. Samuel, d. July 3, 1790	2	6
Mary, d. Sam[ue]ll & Lydia, b Oct. 14, 1744	1	205
Mary, d. Samuel & Lydia, b. Oct. 14, 1744	2	6
Mary, d. [Sam[ue]l & Charlotte], b. May 31, 1792	2	137
Mary, m. Samuel H. **BYRNE**, Mar. 5, 1815	3	89
Mary, d. [Thomas & Lucretia], b. June 11, 1827	3	117
Mary, d. [Thomas & Lucretia], b. Apr. 8, 1838	3	117
Mary C., d. Mar. 16, 1823	3	117
Prudence, d. [Thomas & Abigail], b. [ ]	2	179
Ruth, m. Jacob **SIMONS**, Jr., May 2, 1728	1	103
Sam[ue]ll, m. Lydia **DYAR**, Nov. 7, 1742	1	205
Samuel, m. Lydia **DYER**, Nov. 7, 1742	2	6
Samuel, s. Sam[ue]ll & Lydia, b. June 21, 1751	1	205
Samuel, s. Samuel & Lydia, b. June 21, 1751	2	6
Samuel, had negro Zilpha, d. Phillis, b. Feb. 25,		

	Vol	Page
GRAY, (cont.)		
1767; Pompey McCuff, s. Phillis, b. Dec. 28,		
1768	2	6
Samuel, d. Aug. 3, 1787	2	6
Sam[uel], m. Charlotte **ELDERKIN**, July 2, 1788	2	137
Samuel, s. [Ebenezer & Sarah], b. Sept. 5, 1792	2	215
Samuel, d. Dec. 13, 1836, ae. 85 y.	2	137
Sarah, w. Ebenezer, d. Sept. 29, 1835	3	110
Thomas, s. Sam[ue]ll & Lydia, b. May 22, 1749	1	205
Thomas, s. Samuel & Lydia, b. May 22, 1749	2	6
Thomas, m. Abigail **WALES**, Apr. 9, 1771	2	179
Thomas, d. Feb. [ ], 1792	2	179
Thomas, s. [Sam[ue]l & Charlotte], b Sept. 3, 1794	2	137
Thomas, m. Lucretia **WEBB**, May 11, 1824, by Rev. C.B.		
Everest	3	117
Timothy, farmer, black, d. Aug. [ ], 1849, ae. 50	4	156
GREEN, GREENE, A.B., ae. 25, m. [ ], Nov. 12,		
[1848], by Andrew Roberts	4	113
Alonzo, laborer, ae. 24, m. Susan **SWEETLAND**, ae 23,		
Mar. [ ], [1849], by Mr. Bray	4	113
Elisha, farmer, ae 21, b. Lisbon, res. Windham, m		
Jane **ROBINSON**, b. Lisbon, res. Windham, Sept. [ ],		
1850, by Rev. Henry Greenslit	4	118
Elizabeth, m. Robert **ROUNDING**, Feb. 15, 1726	1	27
Elizabeth, m. Robert **ROUNDYE**, Feb. 15, 1725/6	1	195
Marcy, m. Prince **WILLIAM**, negro man, June 12, 1777	2	237
Orrin, m. Maria **PEIRCE**, Sept. 24, 1828, by Alfred		
Young, J.P.	3	130
Rebecca, m. W[illia]m **HENRY**, b. of Windham, Apr 30,		
1837, by Rev. W[illia]m A. Curtis	3	182
Sarah, d. Elisha N., b. Sept. 11, 1858	3	97
Susannah, m. Benjamin **BREWSTER**, Sept. 8, 1786	2	80
William H., of Griswold, m. Sally **BARBOUR**, of Canter-		
bury, Sept. 13, 1840, by Rev. Otis C. Whiton	3	194
GREENLEAF, Stephen, m. Anna **RIDINGTON**, Sept. 19, 1772	2	186
Wingate Newman, s. [Stephen & Anna], b. Mar. 12, 1773	2	186
GREENMAN, John, d. May 7, 1821	3	27
GREENSLIT, GREENSLITT, Abigail, m. Cornielus **COBURN**,		
Apr. 20, 1757	2	35
David, s. John & Sarah, b. Feb. 5, 1755	1	195
Ebenezer, of Hampton, m. Lucy **WEBB**, of Windham, June 1,		
1826	3	124
Elijah, s. John & Sarah, b. Aug 3, 1743	1	195
Elizabeth, d. John & Sarah, b. Mar. 2, 1747/8	1	195
Elizabeth, d. [John & Sarah], b. Feb. 13, 1766	2	138
James H., b. Sept. 21, 1829	3	101-2
Joel, s. John, Jr. & Sarah, b. Sept. 30, 1745	1	195
John, s. John, Jr. & Sarah, b. June 30, 1741	1	195

	Vol.	Page
GREENSLIT, GREENSLITT, (cont.)		
John, d. Nov. 14, 1760, in the 49th y. of his age	1	195
John, m. Sarah **BURNHAM**, Nov. 20, 1765	2	138
John, s. [John & Sarah], b. June 5, 1767	2	138
John, d. Jan. 7, 1769	2	138
Martha Jane, b. Aug. 15, 1840	3	101-2
Mary, d. John & Sarah, b. Feb. 19, 1761	1	195
Sarah, d. John, Jr. & Sarah, b. May 18, 1739	1	195
Sarah, m. Joseph **FORD**, Apr. 23, 1755	1	269
Sarah, m. Benj[ami]n **CHEDLE**, Jan. 19, 1762	2	114
Sibbel, d. John & Sarah, b. May 23, 1750	1	195
Sibbell, m. Ebenezer **BURNHAM**, Jr , Jan. 29, 1771	2	178
GRIFFIN, GRIFFEN, Artemesia, d. [Ebenezer, Jr. &		
Eliz[abeth], b. Nov. 18, 1765	2	52
Benjamin, s. Ebenezer & Hannah, b. Aug. 7, 1746; d.		
Nov. 11, 1748	1	284
Benjamin, s. Eben[ezer] & Hannah, b. May 10, 1754	1	284
Benjamin, m. C[h]loe **HOWARD**, Feb. 8, 1776	2	209
Benjamin, s. [Benjamin & C[h]loe], b. June 26, 1780	2	209
Betsey, d. [Ebenezer, Jr. & Elizabeth], b. Aug. 24,		
1772	2	52
C[h]loe, w. Benjamin, d. Nov. 16, 1784	2	209
Clarinda, d. [Benjamin & C[h]loe], b. Nov. 16, 1776	2	209
Ebenezer, s. Ebenezer & Hannah, b. July 20, 1734	1	138
Ebenezer, Jr., m. Eliz[abeth] **MARTIN**, Feb. 2, 1757	2	52
Ebenezer, s. [Ebenezer, Jr. & Eliz[abeth], b. Apr. 6,		
1775	2	52
Elisha, s. [Ebenezer, Jr. & Eliz[abeth], b. May 6,		
1777	2	52
Ellevisa, d. [Ebenezer, Jr. & Eliz[abeth], b. Feb. 23,		
1768	2	52
Hannah, d. Ebenezer & Hannah, b. Sept. 11, 1732	1	138
Hannah, m. James **STEDMAN**, Apr. 11, 1751	1	305
Hannah, d. [Ebenezer, Jr. & Eliz[abeth], b. Aug. 1,		
1763	2	52
John Howard, s. [Benjamin & C[h]loe], b. Oct. 29, 1784	2	209
Lucinda P., m. Fitch **STARK**, b of Lyme, Sept. 14, 1830,		
by Rev. Chester Tilden	3	148
Luce, d. Ebenezer & Hannah, b. Apr. 17, 1739	1	138
Lucy, m. Hezekiah **HAMMOND**, Nov. 15, 1758	2	115
Lucy, d. [Ebenezer, Jr. & Eliz[abeth], b. July 21,		
1779	2	52
Mary, [d. Ebenezer & Hannah], b. Mar. 16, 1743/4	1	138
Mehetable, d. Ebenezer & Hannah, b. Nov. 29, 1741	1	138
Mehetable, m. Thomas **STEDMAN**, Jr., Sept. 23, 1760	2	113
Molly, d. [Benjamin & C[h]loe], b. Mar. 7, 1778	2	209
Nath[anie]ll, s. Eben[eze]r & Hannah, b. Aug 23, 1748;		
d. Sept. 7, 1754	1	284

	Vol.	Page
GRIFFIN, GRIFFEN, (cont.)		
Nath[anie]l, s. [Ebenezer, Jr. & Eliz[abeth], b.		
Oct. 13, 1759; d Nov. 25, 1760	2	52
Nath[anie]l, s. [Ebenezer, Jr. & Eliz[abeth], b.		
Oct. 11, 1761	2	52
Olive, d. [Ebenezer, Jr. & Eliz[abeth], b. Apr.		
22, 1770	2	52
Samuel, Jr., m. Parmelia **CLEVELAND**, May 31, 1782	2	255a
Sarah, d. Ebenezer & Hannah, b. Aug. 12, 1736	1	138
Sarah, m. Thomas **FULLER**, Jan. 19, 1757	2	51
Sarah, d. [Benjamin & C[h]loe], b. June 27, 1782	2	209
—am, s. [Samuel, Jr. & Parmelia], b. Mar. 20,		
1783	2	255a
——, s. [Samuel, Jr., & Parmelia], b. Dec. 28,		
1784	2	255a
GRIGGS, Edward, b. Hampton, res. Windham, d. July 15,		
1848, ae. 1 y	4	151
Sarah, m. Seth **CASE**, Nov. 11, 1736	1	187
GRISWOLD, George H., s. [Henry W. & Tryphena], b. Aug. 31,		
1824	3	18
George H , of Milford, Mass., m. Lucina W. **CAREY**, of		
Windham, Mar. 29, 1847, by Rev. Z.W. Howe	3	235
Henry W., m. Tryphena **PAGE**, Feb. 22, 1824	3	18
GROSS, Abiel, d. Isaac & Mary, b. June 16, 1715	1	39
Asahell, s. Isaac & Mary, b. June 4, 1713; d. Feb.		
[ ], 1714/15	1	39
Isaac, d. Mar. 27, 1715	1	39
GROSVENOR, Charles S.*, of Hampton, m. Martha **GORDON**, of		
Windham, Mar. 13, 1833, by Rev. Jesse Fisher		
(*correction - typed note, dated Dec. 4, 1935, was		
attached to original manuscript and reads:		
"**GROSVENOR**, Charles S....According to a letter		
from his grandson, Arthur T. Grosvenor of Abing-		
ton, this entry should read: '**GROSVENOR**, Charles		
I(ngalls), of Hampton, m. Euretta Catherine		
GORDON, of Canterbury, Mar. 13, 1833, by Rev.		
Jesse Fisher.'"	3	165
GROVE, Anna, d. [Thomas & Experience], b. Feb. 15, 1777	2	140
C[h]loe, d. [Thomas & Experience], b. Oct. 18, 1773	2	140
Dillie, d. Thomas & Experience, b. Sept. 14, 1768	2	140
Hannah, d. [Thomas & Experience], b. Aug 31, 1775	2	140
Lois, d. [Thomas & Experience], b. Mar. 6, 1771	2	140
Olive, d. [Thomas & Experience], b. Jan 27, 1770	2	140
Phebe, d. [Thomas & Experience], b. Apr. 2, 1772	2	140
GROW, Edwin, presstender, ae. 19, of Mansfield, m. Susan		
CHAPPELL, ae. 22, Apr. 22, 1849, by Mr. Robinson	4	113
Lois, m. William **BURNHAM**, Dec. 2, 1790	3	14
Polly, d. [William & Prescilla], b. Dec. 31, 1777	2	215

	Vol.	Page
GROW, (cont.)		
Thomas, m. Jerusha **WALES**, Apr. 20, 1831, by Rev.		
Roger Bingham	3	153
William, m. Prescilla **MORSE**, May 30, 1776	2	215
GUIANT, Phebe, m. Stephen **CONGDON**, Nov. 29, 1810	3	66
GUILD, Elizabeth, d. Sam[ue]ll & Sarah, b. Oct. 6, 1716	1	21
Hugh W., d. July 7, [1850], ae. 15	4	155
John Good, s. John B. & Sophronia, b. June 27,		
1840, at Willimantic	3	87
Temperance, m. Joseph **HIBBARD**, Aug. 7, 1755	2	43
GUILE, Hannah, m. William **CROSS**, Oct. 8, 1826, by Rev.		
Cornelius B. Everest	3	122
GUINNICUS, Francis, had s. Cha[rle]s **GROGAN**, b. Oct.		
17, 1848	4	8
GURLEY, Almira, of Windham, m. Joseph **WOODWARD**, of		
Ashford, Apr. 29, 1829, by Rev. Dennis Platt	3	136
Eph[rai]m, m. Hannah **CROSS**, b. of Mansfield, May		
22, 1845, by Rev. Charles Noble, Willimantic	3	221
Harriet, of Windham, m. Charles **LYON**, of Lisbon,		
Sept. 23, 1829, by Rev. Dennis Platt	3	138
Sarah, m. Orra **CARPENTER**, b. of Willimantic, Sept.		
24, 1838, at Willimantic, by Rev. Philo Judson	3	187
HADDAM, Daniel W., m. Elizabeth C. **ESSEX**, Oct. 15, 1843,		
by Rev. Andrew Sharp	3	211
HAGENT, John, Jr , s. John, laborer, ae. 28, of Willimantic,		
b. May 17, [1850]	4	10
HAGGERTY, Michael, s. John, laborer, ae. 27, & Mary, ae 27,		
b. July [ ], [1851]	4	12
HALE, HAIL, Benj[ami]n, s. [Israel & Sarah], b. Dec. 11,		
1758; d. [ ]	1	318
Benj[amin], s. [Israel & Sarah], b. July 10, 1760	1	318
Blossom, w. Job, d. Aug. [ ], 1729	A	32
Gershom, s. [Israel & Sarah], b June 12, 1756	1	318
Israel, m. Sarah **RATHBONE**, Nov. 16, 1752	1	318
Patience, d. Job & Blossom, d. Jan. [ ], 1730/31	A	32
Phinias, s. Job & Blossom, b. Aug. 12, 1728	A	32
Sarah, d. [Israel & Sarah], b. June 9, 1763	1	318
Sybel, d. Israel & Sarah, b. June 17, 1753	1	318
HALL, Betsey C., m Edwin H. **DUNHAM**, Sept. 21, 1846, by		
Rev. Andrew Sharp	3	231
Deborah *, m. Benjamin **PRESTON**, May 5, 1727		
(*correction **HOLT** handwritten in margin of original		
manuscript)	1	90
Esther, d. Isaac & Sarah, b. Feb. 28, 1701	A	8
Gardiner, m. Zerviah E. **ESSEX**, Nov. 29, 1832, by Rev.		
Alva Gregory	3	162
Henry B , m. Cynthia **GOODSPEED**, b. of Hampton, Conn ,		
Jan. 7, 1838, by Rev. John E. Tyler	3	184

	Vol.	Page
HALL, (cont.)		
Horace, m. Jane **MANNING**, June 28, 1829, by Rev.		
Roger Bingham	3	142
Katurah *, m. Joshua **HOLT**, Feb. 16, 1724/5		
(*correction **HOLT** handwritten in margin of		
original manuscript)	1	102
Margaret, m. Charles **WARNER**, Apr. 11, 1827, by Rev.		
Cornelius B. Everest	3	126
Mary, m. Sam[ue]ll **FFLINT**, Apr. 11, 1745	1	157
Nathan, m. Dana **WHITING**, b. of Willimantic, Sept.		
7, 1839, by Rev. B. Cook, Jr. of Willimantic	3	190
Philomela, m. William H.H. **BROWN**, b. of Willimantic,		
Jan. 25, 1835, by Rev. Philo Judson	3	171
Susannah, m. Ebenezer **GINNINGS**, Oct. 10, 1791	2	213
Susan[n]ey, m. John **AUSTIN**, b. of Willimantic, Jan.		
12, 1834, by Rev. Alva Gregory	3	168
Wealthy, of East Haddam, m. Elijah **SELDEN**, Apr. 17,		
1811	3	41
----, m. Elijah **ROBBINS**, [ ], 1762	2	76
HALLET, Isaac, m. Sarah **READ**, Apr. 24, 1700	A	8
HAMMOND, HAMMON, HAMOND, Abigail, d. John &		
Abig[ai]l, b. Aug. 21, 1753	2	30
Abigail, w. John, d. Apr. 12, 1758	2	30
Abigail, d. Josiah, Jr. & Abigail, b. Dec. 23, 1759	1	317
Acsee, d. [Josiah, Jr. & Elizabeth], b. Oct. 4, 1784	2	231
Asail, s. Josiah & Mary, b. July 28, 1727; d. Feb.		
25, 1729/30	1	100
Asail, s. Josiah & Mary, b. Nov. 10, 1731	1	100
Asel, s. [Hezekiah & Lucy], b May 10, 1778	2	115
Chloe, d. [Josiah & Abigail], b. Apr. 15, 1772	2	70
David, s. Josiah & Mary, b. Feb. 22, 1746/7	1	193
Elisha, s. [Hezekiah & Lucy], b. May 28, 1780	2	115
Elisha G., m Olive **JOHNSON**, Nov 25, 1830, by Rev		
Roger Bingham	3	150
Elizabeth, d. [John & Abigail], b. Feb. 10, 1761	2	96
Ellenor, d. [Hezekiah & Lucy], b. May 19, 1775	2	115
Hannah, d. [Josiah & Abigail], b. Feb 10, 1767	2	70
Hezekiah, s. Josiah & Mary, b. Nov. 4, 1733	1	100
Hezekiah, m. Lucy **GRIFFEN**, Nov 15, 1758	2	115
Hezekiah, s. [Hezekiah & Lucy], b. Dec. 8, 1782	2	115
James, s. Caleb & Mary, b. July 11, 1737	1	130
John, s. Josiah & Mary, b. Oct. 13, 1729	1	100
John, m. Abigail **FULLER**, Dec. 19, 1749. "Yet to be		
certified"	1	310
John, s. John & Abigail, b. Aug. 2, 1751; d. May		
25, 1753	1	310
John, s. John & Abig[ai]l, b. May 20, 1757; d Nov.		
14, 1759	2	30

	Vol.	Page
HAMMOND, HAMMON, HAMOND, (cont.)		
John, m. Abigail **MOULTON**, Apr. 7, 1761	2	96
Josiah, Jr , m. Abigail **DURKEE**, Nov. 19, 1751	1	317
Josiah, s. Josiah, Jr. & Abigail, b. Jan. 9, 1760	1	317
Josiah, Jr., m. Elizabeth **MOSELEY**, Sept. 28, 1780	2	231
Lois, d. John & Abig[ai]l, b. Aug. 18, 1755	2	30
Lois, m. Stephen **PRESTON**, Jan. 4, 1773	2	225
Lucy, d. [Hezekiah & Lucy], b. Aug. 30, 1760	2	115
Mary, d. Josiah & Mary, b. Jan. 7, 1735	1	100
Mary, d. [John & Abigail], b. June 16, 1762	2	96
Mary, d. Josiah & Abigail, b. Feb. 23, 1764	2	70
Moses, s. Caleb & Mary, b. May 15, 1739	1	130
Olive, d. [Hezekiah & Lucy], b. July 8, 1764	2	115
Olive, of Windham, d. July 22, 1848, ae. 41	4	151
Robert, s. [John & Abigail], b. Dec. 23, 1763	2	96
Ruth, d. Caleb & Mary, b. July 1, 1735	1	130
Sarah, d. Caleb & Mary, b. Aug. 25, 1740	1	130
Sarah, d. Josiah, Jr. & Abigail, b. Aug. 16, 1753;		
d. Apr. 10, 1755	1	317
Sarah, d. Josiah, Jr. & Abigail, b. Dec. 3, 1755;		
d. Sept 16, 1757	1	317
Sarah, d. Josiah & Abigail, b. Jan. 3, 1762	2	70
Uriel, s. [Josiah, Jr. & Elizabeth], b. July 5, 1781	2	231
William, s. Eleizer & Marg[a]ret, b. Sept. 19, 1735	1	131
William, s. [Josiah & Abigail], b. Dec. 30, 1769	2	70
HANDY, HANDEE, [see also **HENDEE**], Abigail, d. Jonathan &		
Rachel, b July 29, 1725	1	16
Abigail, d. Joshua & Elizabeth, b. Oct. 27, 1745	1	101
Asa, s. Richard & Elizabeth, b. Aug. 25, 1715	1	23
Bareillia*, s. Richard & Elizabeth, b. June 18, 1713		
(*correction "e" in Bareillia was crossed out in		
original manuscript)	1	23
Caleb, s. Richard & Elizabeth, d. Jan. 19, 1725/6	1	23
David, s. Jonathan & Rachel, b. Mar. 12, 1723	1	16
Eleizer, s Joshua & Elizabeth, b. Oct. 27, 1729	1	101
Elizabeth, d. Richard & Elizabeth, b. Apr. 28, 1710	1	23
Elizabeth, d. Joshua & Elizabeth, b. May 13, 1734	1	101
Elizabeth, w. Joshua, d. June 4, 1750	1	101
Elnathan, s. Joshua & Elizabeth, b. Mar. 14, 1730/31;		
d. Mar. 15, 1730/31	1	101
Eunice, d. Joshua & Elizabeth, b. May 20, 1744	1	101
Hannah, m. Jabez **CAREY**, Nov. 15, 1722	1	63
Hannah, d. Jonathan & Rachel, b. Apr. 29, 1728	1	102
Jabez, s. Joshua & Elizabeth, b. Mar. 13, 1732/3	1	101
Jonathan, m. Rachel **KNIGHT**, Mar. 20, 1718	1	16
Joshua, s. Richard & Elizabeth, b. Apr. 25, 1707	1	23
Joshua, m. Elizabeth **WHEELOCK**, Dec. 4, 1728	1	101
Joshua, s. Joshua & Elizabeth, b. July 7, 1748	1	101

	Vol.	Page
HANDY, HANDEE, (cont.)		
Mary, d. Richard & Elizabeth, b. July 6, 1720	1	23
Nathaniell, s. Richard & Elizabeth, b. Aug 14,		
1718	1	23
Rebecka, d. Jonathan & Rachel, b. June 15, 1718	1	16
Ruth, d. Joshua & Elizabeth, b. Dec. 20, 1736	1	101
Sarah, d. Jonathan & Rachel, b. June 21, 1721	1	16
Sarah, m. John **HURD**, Sept. 16, 1725	1	65
Zebulon, s. Jonathan & Rachel, b. Jan. 12, 1719/20	1	16
HANKS, Benjamin, m. Alice [ ]	2	116
Lydia, d. [Benjamin & Alice], b. Dec. 10, 1776	2	116
HANOVER, ——, child of Geo[rge], spinner, ae. 26, b.		
July [1850]	4	11
HARDING, Charles, of Mansfield, m. Sarah **PHILLIPS**, of		
Willimantic, May 27, 1839, at Willimantic, by		
Rev. B. Cook, Jr., of Willimantic	3	189
HARE, Mehetable, m. John **LARRABEE**, Nov. 18, 1779, by		
Samuel Gray, J.P.	2	224
HARDOCK, Dan, m. Ann **CHAMBERLAIN**, Mar. 31, 1762	2	83
HARP, Maria L., ae. 19, m. Edwin **THOMAS**, manufacturer,		
ae. 20, June [ ], [1850], by Rev. J. Cady	4	116
HARRINGTON, Almira, b. Coventry, R.I., res. Willimantic,		
d. July 23, 1860, ae. 71	4	161
Elizabeth, m. Nathan **FULLER**, Jr., Mar. 8, 1827, by		
Rev. Jesse Fisher	3	126
Joanna, d. Daniel, laborer, ae. 36, & Joanna, ae. 28,		
b. June [ ], 1851	4	12
Josiah, m. Frances J. **FREEMAN**, b. of Windham, Nov. 29,		
1838, by Rev. Windser Ward	3	187
Laura, ae. 20, m. Cha[rle]s **BLIVEN**, mechanic, ae. 23,		
May 10, [1850], by Rev. Bromley	4	116
Louisa, ae. 20, m. Cha[rle]s S. **BLIVEN**, machinist, ae.		
23, Apr. 28, 1850, by Rev. Bromley	4	115
HARRIS, HARRISS, Abiah, m. Lemuel **DEANS**, Dec. 11, 1784	2	21
Adeline M., d. Sept. 7, 1860, ae. 3 m.	4	161
Albert, s. [Martin & Maria], b. June 18, 1829	3	36
Anna, b. Mansfield, res. Willimantic, d. Oct. 13,		
[1848], ae. 44	4	153
Edward, farmer, ae. 27, b. Windham, res. Mansfield, m.		
Miss **PORTER**, operative, ae. 27, b. Lisbon, res.		
Mansfield, Oct. 15, 1850, by Rev. Wallace	4	117
Edwin, s. [Martin & Maria], b. Jan. 8, 1825	3	36
Harriet, d. [Martin & Maria], b. July 31, 1827	3	36
Harriet, m. Frederick F. **BARROWS**, Mar. 29, 1847, by		
Rev Andrew Sharp	3	235
Lucretia, m. William **HUNTINGTON**, Nov. 27, 1823	3	14
Martha, ae 19, m. Elihu **PHILLIPS**, manufacturer, ae.		
24, Apr. 14, 1850, by [Rev.] Bromley	4	116

	Vol	Page
HARRIS, HARRISS, (cont)		
Martin, m. Maria **FOLLETT**, Dec 6, 1821, by Rev.		
Cornelius B Everest	3	36
Mary, m. Lucius Henry **CAREY**, Sept. 27, 1812	3	72
Oliver, s. [Martin & Maria], b Oct. 5, 1822	3	36
Oliver F., m. Julia **TRACY**, b. of Windham, Apr. 7,		
1845, by Rev. Tho[ma]s Tallman, Scotland	3	221
Thomas, m Jane **EDWARDS**, Mar. 5, 1700	A	8
-----, of Willimantic, d. Apr 20, 1860, ae. 4 d.	4	159-0
HARTSHORN, Hannah, m. Calvin **PALMER**, Oct. 6, 1791	3	59
Mason, of Hampton, m Marilla **THOMPSON**, May 4, 1826	3	124
HARVEY, Elizabeth J., b. Hampton, res. Willimantic, m.		
George **PHILLIPS**, farmer, b. Hampton, res.		
Willimantic, Feb. 27, 1851, by Rev. S.G. Williams	4	118
Frederick, laborer, ae 24, b N Y., res Windham, m		
Amelia **KENYON**, ae. 16, Feb. 6, 1848, by Daniel		
Dorchester	4	111
Lucy, m. David **MEDBURY**, Mar. 14, 1824	3	118
Lucy, m Col **FISK**, Jan 18, 1835, by James Little-		
field, J.P.	3	171
Susan, m Albert N. **MAINE**, of Bolton, Aug 21, 1843,		
at Willimantic, by Rev. J.B. Guild	3	211
HASLER, Frederick, m Harriet **BENTON**, b. of Windham, Sept		
16, 1838, at Willimantic, by Rev. B. Cook, Jr., of		
Willimantic	3	187
HASTINGS, Ziporah, m. Stephen **UTLEY**, Apr. 28, 1757	2	51
HATCH, Cha[rle]s W , d. Aug 7, 1848, ae 7 wk	4	151
Elizabeth, ae. 21, m. L.W. **JACOBS**, merchant, ae. 32,		
May 10, [1850], by Rev. J Cady	4	116
Heman, s. Heman & Eunice, b. June 14, 1767	2	8
Mary, m. John **LARRABEE**, May 22, 1711	1	28
Samuel L., of Norwalk, O., m. Diantha C. **DOWNING**, of		
Windham, Sept 22, 1844, by H Slade, Scotland		
Society	3	217
HAVEN, HAVENS, Alice, m Edward **KARTWRIGHT**, Dec 28,		
1774	2	63
Ellen, of Jewett City, m. George **CONGDON**, of Norwich,		
Aug. 8, 1847, by Rev. D. Dorchester, Willimantic	3	236
Julia, d. Patrick, laborer, ae 22, & Margaret, ae		
23, of Willimantic, b. Apr. 30, [1849]	4	5
Sam[ue]l, d [Aug.] 29, [1848], ae 1	4	153
HAWKINS, James M., m Julia S. **MILLARD**, b. of Willimantic,		
[Oct.] 28, 1838, by Rev J E Tyler	3	187
HAYDEN, Emera, child of Daniel, cotton manufacturer, ae.		
31, & Elizabeth, ae 27, of Willimantic, b Oct		
22, [1848]	4	5
HAYWARD, Charles C , of Windham, m. Eliza **SWIFT**, of		
Franklin, Dec. 24, 1835, by Rev. L.H. Corson,		

	Vol.	Page
HAYWARD, (cont.)		
Willimantic	3	176
Jane, b. R.I., res Willimantic, d. Aug. 3, [1849],		
ae. 5	4	153
Mary, b. Mass , res. Willimantic, d. Feb. 29, 1860,		
ae. 88	4	159-0
Matilda, d. [Charles C. & Eliza], b. Sept. 1, 1836	3	176
Sarah, m. Timothy **WEBB**, May 26, 1728	1	92
HAYWOOD, Jonas, s. Ralph, laborer, ae. 34, & Maria, ae		
33, of Willimantic, b. July 27, [1848]	4	5
HAZARD, Julian, m. William T. **ROBINSON**, Aug. 5, 1832, by		
Rev. Roger Bingham	3	160
HAZEN, Jacob*, m. Peggy **LORD**, Feb 24, 1785 (*correction		
Jabez, per Windham VR VB-P160, Arnold's error,		
handwritten in original manuscript)	2	160
John S., of New York, m. Lucretia F. **FRINK**, of		
Windham, Aug. 7, 1833, by Rev. Jesse Fisher	3	165
Laura, d. [Jacob* & Peggy], b. Dec. 18, 1788		
(*correction Jacob crossed out in original manu-		
script, as referenced above)	2	160
Lord, s. [Jacob* & Peggy], b June 24, 1786		
(*correction Jacob crossed out in original manu-		
script, as referenced above)	2	160
Mary Ann, d. [Prosper & Hannah E.], b. Jan. 8, 1833	3	112
Nabby, d. [Jacob* & Peggy], b Dec. 20, 1790		
(*correction Jacob crossed out in original manu-		
script, as referenced above)	2	160
Peggy, d. [Jacob* & Peggy], b. Apr. 29, 1793		
(*correction Jacob crossed out in original manu-		
script, as referenced above)	2	160
Peggy, [w. Jacob*], d. July 28, 1793 (*correction Jacob		
crossed out in original manuscript, as referenced		
above)	2	160
Prosper, of Franklin, m. Hannah E. **STANTON**, Mar. 14,		
1825	3	5
Prosper, m. Hannah E. **STANTON**, Mar. 14, 1825, by Rev.		
C.B. Everest	3	112
Prosper, of Franklin, m. Eunice **WILLOBY**, [ ]	3	3
Robert S., s. [Prosper & Hannah E.], b. Aug. 20, 1825	3	112
W[illia]m Webb, s. [Prosper & Hannah E.], b. Apr. 5,		
1829	3	112
——, child of R.W., blacksmith, ae. 33, b. July 24,		
[1850]	4	11
HEARRINE, [see under **HEORRIN**]		
HEATH, Jesse, s. Starbin & Hannah, b. Apr. 17, 1726	1	82
Rachal, m. Gideon **MARTIN**, Jan. 24, 1765	2	124
Susannah, m. Hezekiah **FOLLET**, Nov. 30, 1764	2	115
Sibel, d. Thomas & Waitstill, b. July 18, 1743	1	237

	Vol.	Page
HEBBARD, [see under **HIBBARD**]		
HEELMES*, Jacob, of Greenfield, N.Y., m. Susan **CHEETS**,		
Dec. 4, 1823 (*Perhaps "**HOLMES**"?)	3	14
HELLEN, Phebe, m. Charles A. **BINGHAM**, July 11, 1830, by		
Rev Chester Tilden, Willimantic	3	147
HENDEE, HENDE, HENDY, [see also **HANDY**], Asa, m. Mary		
FLINT, Jan. 31, 1738/9	1	177
Barzillai, m. Thankfull **BUTLER**, Dec. 18, 1739	1	201
Barzillai, s. Barzillai & Thankfull, b Nov. 6,		
1740	1	201
Caleb, s. Richard & Elizabeth, b. Mar. 12, 1704	A	7
Desire, d. Barzillai & Thankfull, b. Nov. 25, 1742	1	201
Eliphalet, s. Asa & Mary, b. Apr. 28, 1743	1	177
Elizabeth, m. David **MARTIN**, May 27, 1756	2	15
Hannah, d. Richard & Elizabeth, b. Dec. 25, 1697	A	6
Jonathan, s. Richard & Sarah, b. Mar. 17, 1694	A	6
Josiah, s. Richard & Elizabeth, b. Mar. 6, 1702	A	6
Lucy, d. Barzillai & Thankfull, b. Jan. 25, 1744/5	1	201
Richard, m. Sarah **SMITH**, Mar. 1, 1693	A	6
Richard, m. Elizabeth **CONNENT**, Oct. 17, 1695	A	6
Richard, Ensigne, d. Feb. 6, 1742/3, ae. about 76 y.	1	201
Sarah, w. Richard, d. Apr. 18, 1694	A	6
Sarah, d. Richard & Elizabeth, b. Apr. 18, 1700	A	6
Sarah, m. Phinehas **MANNING**, June 30, 1748	1	304
Sarah, m. Stephen **AVERELL**, June 18, 1752	1	318
HENDERSON, Elizabeth, d. Tho[ma]s, shoemaker, ae. 27, of		
Willimantic, b. June 29, [1850]	4	10
Mary, ae. 23, m. B. **SULLIVAN**, laborer, ae. 30, Jan. 1,		
[1850], by Rev. Brady	4	115
HENRY, Esther T., m. Samuel B. **FORD**, Oct. 5, 1846, by Rev.		
Andrew Sharp	3	231
Mary, m. Nath[anie]ll **FLINT**, Jr., July 3, 1751	1	219
W[illia]m, m. Rebecca **GREENE**, b. of Windham, Apr. 30,		
1837, by Rev. W[illia]m A. Curtis	3	182
HEORRIN, HEARRINE, Michael, s. Anthony, laborer, ae. 25, &		
Anna, ae. 26, of Willimantic, b. Nov. 8, 1850	4	12
——, st. b., s. Patrick, laborer, ae. 54, & Margaret,		
ae. 50, b. Jan. 20, 1851	4	12
HERRICK, Elizabeth, m. Oliver **YOUNG**, b. of Windham, Oct. 20,		
1836, by Rev. Benajah Cook, Jr.	3	180
Ephraim, cabman, ae. 37, b. Preston, res. Willimantic,		
m. Nabby **ROYAL**, ae. 37, b. Mansfield, res. Willi-		
mantic, Jan. 20, 1851, by Rev. John Cady	4	117
Sarah B., m. Ulyssys **YOUNG**, Nov. 24, 1836, by Rev.		
Philetus Greene	3	180
HERRINGTON, Zephaniah, of Mansfield, m. Hannah H.		
PARKER, of Windham, Mar. 11, 1827, by Rev.		
Cornelius B. Everest	3	125

HERVIE, Mary R., of Windham, m. W[illia]m H **OSBORN**,
    of Columbia, Apr. 28, 1844, by Comfort D.
    Fillmore, Local Deacon   3   214
HEVNIA(?), Ansel, laborer, ae. 27, m. Ann **CREAN**, ae. 26,
    Feb. 9, [1850], by Rev. Brady   4   114
Catharine, ae. 24, m. Michael **BRAMAN**, laborer, ae.
    24, May [ ], [1850], by Rev. Cady   4   114
HEWITT, HEWETT, HEWATS, Anna, m. Philip **ABBOT**, July 6,
    1775   2   208
Benj[amin], m. Ann **PERRY**, June 3, 1829, by Elder
    Esek Brown   3   157
Clarinda, d. Sept. 13, [1849], ae. 73   4   156
Content, m. Stephen **WEBB**, May 22, 1766   2   152
George Jona[than], s. [Benj[amin] & Ann], b. July 7,
    1831   3   157
Henry, s. Frances, carpenter, ae. 48, & Rose, ae. 41,
    b. Jan. 12,]1851]   4   13
Jonas, farmer, d. May 14, [1850], ae. 85   4   156
Mary Ann, of Windham, m. Morgan **SAFFORD**, of Canter-
    bury, Dec. 2, 1832, by Rev. Alva Gregory   3   162
Sophia, m. W[illia]m E. **BECKWITH**, Nov. 29, 1835, by
    Rev. Moseley Dwight, Willimantic   3   176
Zerviah, m. John **HOWARD**, Jr., Nov. 15, 1763   2   94
——, child of Eli & May, b. Sept. [ ], 1849   4   7
HIBBARD, HEBARD, HIBARD, HEBBARD, HOBARD, Abel, s
    [Samuell & Mary], b. Oct. 12, 1749   1   185
Abel, s. [Diah & Zerviah], b. Nov. 26, 1784   2   187
Abigail, d. Joseph & Abigaill, b. Mar. 15, 1699   A   21
Abigail, d. Ebenezer & Margaret, b. June 11, 1724   1   47
Abigail, d. Joseph, Jr. & Ann, b. June 9, 1738   1   96
Abigail, m. Joseph **CARY**, Dec 10, 1747   1   202
Abigail, d. Nathan & Zip[p]orah, b. Apr. 23, 1752   1   191
Abijah, s. Joshua & Ruth, b. Sept 21, 1753   1   214
Ahimaz, s. [Paul & Martha], b. May 31, 1759; d.
    [   ]   1   224
Ahimaz, m. Asenath **MILLARD**, May 24, 1781   2   251a
Aletheir, d. [Nathan & Zip[p]orah], b Oct. 5, 1754   1   191
Aletheah, m. Samuel **BINGHAM**, Jr., Jan. 1, 1778   3   56
Alfred, s. [Diah & Zerviah], b. Sept. 2, 1794   2   187
Alpheas, s. Moses & Hannah, b. Oct. 15, 1754   2   5
Amey, d. Zeb[ulon] & Hannah, b Nov. 15, 1759   1   231
Andrew, s. Nathan & Zip[p]orah, b. Nov. 1, 1748;
    d. Apr. 8, 1773   1   191
Andrew, s. [Jared & Elizabeth], b. Dec. 29, 1777;
    d. Jan. 17, 1778   2   210
Andrew, s. [Gurdon & Irena], b. Dec. 31, 1797   3   5
Andrew Frink, s. [Gurdon, Jr. & Fanny], b. Dec. 14,
    1807   3   45

	Vol.	Page
HIBBARD, HEBARD, HIBARD, HEBBARD, HOBARD, (cont.)		
Ann, m. Jonathan **CLAP[P]**, Feb. 26, 1728/9	1	106
Ann, d. Joseph & Ann, b. July 22, 1730	1	96
Ann, d. John & Martha, b. Aug. 13, 1734	1	93
Ann, w. Joseph, Jr , d. Jan. 31, 1741/2	1	96
Ann W., m. Joseph C. **BASSETT**, Aug. 29, 1842,		
by Rev. Andrew Sharp, Willimantic	3	203
Anna, d. [Josiah & Hannah], b. Mar. 14, 1757	2	31
Anne, d. Nathaniell & Sarah, b. May 30, 1705	1	1
Anne, d. Elisha & Mary, b. Aug. 16, 1747	1	237
Anne, d. [Dan & Anne], b. Jan. 18, 1773	2	183
Anne, m. William **BROAD**, July 28, 1777	2	211
Asa, s. Sam[ue]ll & Mary, b. Oct 3, 1755	1	233
Augustine, s. Joseph & Martha, b. Mar. 27,		
1748	1	245
Augustus, m. Bathsheba **LEARNED**, Mar. 19, 1796	2	63
Averill, s. [Perez & Martha], b. Aug 25, 1798	3	33
Benjamin, s. Joseph, Jr. & Ann, b. Feb. 17,		
1735/6; d. July 28, 1737	1	96
Benjamin, s. [Joseph & Temperance], b. Apr. 8,		
1762, in Lebanon	2	43
Betsey, d. [Diah & Zerviah], b. Mar. 28, 1786	2	187
Beulah, d. Elisha & Mary, b. June 24, 1764	1	237
Bushnall, s. [Nathan & Zip[p]orah], b. Oct. 3, 1758	1	191
Calvin, s. [Perez & Martha], b. Mar. 21, 1788	3	33
Catharine P., m. William L. **TINGLEY**, May 24, 1843,		
by Rev. Andrew Sharp	3	209
Charity, d. Nathan & Zipporah, b. Jan. 6, 1746/7;		
d. Apr. 5, 1759	1	191
Charity, d. Nathan & Zip[pora]h, b. Jan. 4, 1763	1	191
Charles, s. [Augustus & Bathsheba], b. Dec. 18, 1796	2	63
Charlotte Matilda, [d. Ozias & Mary], b. Jan. 20,		
1814	3	84
Chloe, twin with Gurdon, d. [Jabez & Anna], b. Aug.		
21, 1780	2	226
Clarrissa, d. [Joseph & Temperance], b. Dec. 8, 1773	2	43
Clarissa, d. Lyndon & Wealthy, b. Jan. 9, 1791	2	111
Dann, s. Nathan & Zipporah, b. Aug. 18, 1745	1	191
Dan, m. Anne **RIPLEY**, Jan. 2, 1772	2	183
Daniel, s. John & Martha, b. Sept. 29, 1738	1	93
Daniel, s. Robert & Ruth, b. Jan. 29, 1742	1	115
David, s. Robert & Mary, b. Mar. 9, 1716	1	20
David, m. Elizabeth **LEAVENS**, Sept. 15, 1743	1	239
David, s. David & Eliza, b. Dec. 2, 1755	1	239
David, m. Dorcas **THROOP**, June 26, 1763, by Rev Peter		
Reynolds	2	86
Deborah, d. Nathaniell & Sarah, b. May 28, 1707	1	1
Deborah, m. Isaac **ROBINSON**, Dec. 15, 1737	1	203

	Vol	Page
HIBBARD, HEBARD, HIBARD, HEBBARD, HOBARD, (cont.)		
Deborah, w. Jonath[a]n, d. Mar. 4, 1780	2	175
Diah, s. Sam[ue]ll & Mary, b Jan. 29, 1756	1	233
Diah, s. [Zebulon, Jr. & Lucy], b. Dec. 16,		
1782	2	217
Diah, m. Zerivah **HEB[B]ARD**, June 3, 1784	2	187
Diah, see also Dyar		
Dolly, m. Freeman **DEWEY**, Mar. 31, 1796	2	63
Dorcas, d. [David & Dorcas], b. Dec. 12, 1763	2	86
Dyar, s. David & Elizabeth, b. Dec. 18, 1744;		
d. [ ], at Killingly	1	239
Dyar, see also Diah		
Ebenezer, m. Margaret **MORGEN**, Mar. 16, 1709	1	47
Ebenezer, s. Ebenezer & Marg[a]ret, b. Mar 16,		
1720/21	1	47
Ebenezer, s Joshua & Ruth, b. July 15, 1737	1	127
Eben[eze]r, s. Elisha & Mary, b. June 9, 1755	1	237
Eben[eze]r, s. [Nathan & Zip[p]orah], b Oct. 4,		
1756	1	191
Ebenezer, s. [Josiah & Hannah], b. Feb. 19, 1759	2	31
Ebenezer, m. Eunice **LILLIE**, Sept. 30, 1790	2	124
Eleizer, s. John & Martha, b. Aug. 20, 1732	1	93
Eleazer, s. Moses & Hannah, b. July 27, 1747	1	270
Eleazer, s. Moses & Hannah, b. July 27, 1747	2	5
Elias, s. [Elisha & Mary], b. June 29, 1770	1	237
Elijah, s. Robert & Ruth, b. Aug. 27, 1748	1	115
Elijah, s. [Robard & Lydia], b. Nov. 13, 1760	2	46
Elijah, s. [Ahimaz & Asenath], b. Jan. 11, 1782	2	251a
Eliphalet, s. Josh[ua] & Ruth, b. Feb. 15, 1751	1	214
Eliphaz, s. Joseph & Martha, b. June 16, 1744	1	245
Elisha, s. Nathaniell & Sarah, b. Dec. 11, 1719	1	1
Elisha, m. Mary **PALMER**, Aug. 16, 1744	1	237
Elisha, s. Elisha & Mary, b. July 18, 1749	1	237
Elisha, s. [Perez & Martha], b. Sept. 14, 1785	3	33
Eliza, of Windham, m. Anson **JEPSON**, of Springfield,		
Mass., Mar. 11, 1834, by Rev. Alva Gregory	3	168
Eliza Ann, d. [Ozias & Mary], b. Apr. 10, 1812	3	84
Elizabeth, d. Robert & Ruth, b. Aug. 23, 1731	1	115
Elizabeth, d. Nathan & Zip[p]orah, b. Jan. 9, 1743/4;		
d. Jan. 10, 1766	1	191
Elizabeth, d. John & Martha, b. Feb. 15, 1746/7; d.		
Aug. 31, 1748	1	112
Elizabeth, d. John & Martha, b. Mar. 8, 1748/9; d.		
Apr. 6, 1753	1	112
Elizabeth, m. Nath[anie]ll **BACKUS**, Oct. 7, 1753	1	321
Elizabeth, d. Elisha & Mary, b Dec. 26, 1759	1	237
Elizabeth, d. David & Eliza[beth], b. May 6, 1760	1	239
Elizabeth, w. David, d. Feb. 13, 1762	1	239

	Vol.	Page
HIBBARD, HEBARD, HIBARD, HEBBARD, HOBARD, (cont.)		
Eliz[abe]th, m. Gamaliel **RIPLEY**, Dec. 15, 1764	2	84
Elizabeth, d. [Nathan & Irena], b. May 17, 1767	2	103
Enoch, s. Nathan, Jr. & Mehitable, b. May 18, 1761	2	54
Enoch, s. [Zebulon, Jr. & Lucy], b. Mar. 22, 1779	2	217
Eunice, d. Sam[ue]ll & Lydia, b. May 14, 1745	1	185
Eunice, d. [Diah & Zerviah], b. Dec. 26, 1791	2	187
Eunice, d. [Ebenezer & Eunice], b. June 14, 1792	2	124
Fanny, d. [Jared & Elizabeth], b. Feb. 4, 1774; d. July 17, 1775	2	210
Fanny, d. [Jared & Elizabeth], b. July 26, 1780	2	210
Fanny Henrietta, d. [Gurdon, Jr. & Fanny], b. Apr. 2, 1810	3	45
Frances Mehetable, d. Geo[rge] W., b. Aug. 27, 1834	3	106
Frederick Hovey, s. [Shubael & Lucy], b. Nov. 29, 1799	3	26
George, s. Joseph, Jr. & Martha, b. Jan. 1, 1745/6	1	245
George, s. [Diah & Zerviah], b. Aug 30, 1797	2	187
George, m. Harriet **YOUNG**, Jan. 2, 1831, by Rev. Roger Bingham	3	151
Gideon, s. Nathaniell & Sarah, b. Mar. 11, 1721	1	1
Gideon, m. Elizabeth **KINGSLEY**, b Dec. 14, 1749	1	294
Giles, s. [Ahimaz & Asenath], b. Oct. 17, 1785	2	251a
Gurdon, s. [Nath[anie]ll & Mary], b. Oct. 29, 1770	2	161
Gurdon, twin with Chloe, s. [Jabez & Ann], b. Aug. 21, 1780	2	226
Gurdon, m. Irena **FRINK**, Nov. 27, 1796	3	5
Gurdon, Jr., m. Fanny **FRINK**, Mar. 30, 1799	3	45
Hannah, d. Robert & Mary, b. Apr. 22, 1721	1	20
Hannah, d. Zebulon & Hannah, b. Aug. 30, 1741	1	231
Hannah, m. Joseph **FOLLET**, Nov. 9, 1743	1	236
Hannah, d. Moses & Hannah, b. Nov. 10, 1761	2	5
Hannah, m. John **PARRISH**, Apr. 16, 1778	2	30
Harriet, d. [Perez & Martha], b. Jan. 29, 1802	3	33
Harvey, s. [Jabez & Anna], b. Feb. 18, 1782	2	226
Harvey, s. [Gurdon, Jr. & Fanny], b. Dec. 20, 1805	3	45
Henrietta, of Windham, m. Frank **WEBB**, of Hartford, Sept. 17, 1837, by Rev. Dexter Bullard	3	183
Henry, s. [Jonathan & Deborah], b. Nov. 17, 1771; d. Nov. 27, 1772	2	175
Henry, s. [Warner & Polly], b. Oct. 22, 1790	3	15
Henry, s. [Ozias & Mary], b. Dec. 13, 1792; d. Feb. 12, 1797	3	84
Henry, 2d, [s. Ozias & Mary], b. Jan. 12, 1797	3	84
Hezekiah, s. Zeb[ulon] & Hannah, b. Sept. 22, 1756	1	231
Irena, d. Elisha & Mary, b. Feb. 25, 1757	1	237
Ithamer, s. Elisha & Mary, b. June 7, 1745	1	237

	Vol	Page
HIBBARD, HEBARD, HIBARD, HEBBARD, HOBARD, (cont.)		
Ithamar, m. Est[h]er **HOSKINS**, Mar. 8, 1768	2	137
Jabez, s. Zeb[ulon] & Hannah, b. July 2, 1754	1	231
Jabez, s. [Joseph & Temperance], b. Apr. 27,		
1764	2	43
Jabez, m. Anna **SABIN**, Dec. 6, 1779	2	226
James, s. Moses & Hannah, b Jan. 27, 1750	2	5
James, s. Robert & Ruth, b. Aug. 21, 1751	1	115
James Madison, s. [Gurdon, Jr. & Fanny], b. Aug.		
30, 1813	3	45
Jared, s. Josh[ua] & Ruth, b. Aug. 8, 1748	1	214
Jared, m. Elizabeth **PALMER**, Oct. 19, 1774	2	210
Jared, s. [Jared & Elizabeth], b July 2, 1776	2	210
Jedediah, s. John & Martha, b. Oct. 14, 1740	1	93
Jedediah, s. [Josiah & Hannah], b. Jan 14, 1761	2	31
Jemima, d. Joseph & Abigail, b. Aug. 16, 1711	1	21
Jemima, m. Jonathan **MARTIN**, Jan. 19, 1730/31	1	114
Jemima, d. Joseph, Jr. & Ann, b. June 11, 1740	1	96
Jemima, m. Samuel **COOK**, Mar. 28, 1776	2	210
Jemima, d. Joshua & Ruth, b. May 17, 17[ ]	1	127
Jeremiah, s. [Warner & Polly], b. May 16, 1800	3	15
Jerusha, d. Nathan & Zip[p]orah, b. Jan. 8, 1749/50	1	191
Jerusha, d. Zeb[ulon] & Hannah, b. Jan. 24, 1750	1	231
Joanna, d. Joseph & Abigail, b. Jan. 25, 1707	1	21
Joannah, d. Joseph, Jr. & Ann, b. Apr. 4, 1732	1	96
John, s. Robart & Mary, b. Oct. 30, 1704	A	20
John, m. Martha **DURKEE**, Sept. 22, 1725	1	93
John, s. John & Martha, b. Dec. 9, 1727	1	93
John Gilmore, [s. Ozias & Mary], b. June 3, 1807	3	84
Jonathan, twin with Nathaniel, s. Nathaniell & Sarah,		
b. Oct. 23, 1709	1	1
Jonath[an], s. Paul & Martha, b. Apr. 24, 1746	1	224
Jonathan, s. [Josiah & Hannah], b. June 7, 1770; d.		
Dec. 7, 1775	2	31
Jonathan, m. Deborah **SAWYER**, July 18, 1772	2	175
Jonathan, m. Elizabeth Church **LEARNED**, June 19, 1781	2	175
Joseph, m. Abigail **LINDALL**, Apr. 20, 1698	A	21
Joseph, s. Joseph & Abigail, b. Jan. 15, 1703	A	21
Joseph, Jr., m. Ann **HICKLAND***, Oct. 13, 1726		
(*correction **STRICKLAND** handwritten in original		
manuscript)	1	96
Joseph, s. Joseph, Jr. & Ann, b. Sept. 15, 1727; d.		
Oct. 3, 1727	1	96
Joseph, d. Joseph, Jr. & Ann, b. Mar. 15, 1733/4	1	96
Joseph, Jr., m. Martha **GOULD**, Feb. 1, 1742/3	1	245
Joseph, d. Mar. 15, 1751, in the 49th y. of his age	1	245
Joseph, m Temperance **GUILD**, Aug. 7, 1755	2	43
Joseph, s. Joseph & Temperance, b. Mar. 17, 1758	2	43

	Vol.	Page
HIBBARD, HEBARD, HIBARD, HEBBARD, HOBARD, (cont.)		
Joseph, d. Apr. 16, 1774, in the 41st y. of his		
age	2	43
Joshua, s. Robert & Mary, b. Oct. 19, 1713	1	20
Joshua, m. Ruth **ROSS**, Oct. 4, 1733	1	127
Joshua, s. Joshua & Ruth, b. Dec. 21, 1741	1	127
Joshua, m. Hannah **PALMITER**, Dec 2, 1772	2	176
Joshua, s. [Josiah & Hannah], b. Dec. 11, 1775	2	31
Josiah, s. Joseph & Abigaill, b. Feb. 9, 1701;		
d. Aug. 26, 1703	A	21
Josiah, s. Robert & Mary, b. Sept. 30, 1708; d.		
Dec. 19, 1733	1	39a
Josiah, s. Joshua & Ruth, b. June 15, 1735; d		
Mar. 27, 1748, in the 18th y. of his age	1	127
Josiah, s. Joshua [& Ruth], d. Mar. 27, 1748, in		
the 18th y. of his age	1	127
Josiah, m. Hannah **WHITE**, Oct. 12, 1756	2	31
Josiah, d. [ ] or was killed by the enemy		
near New York	2	31
Julia A., of Windham, m. James Harvey **CROCKER**, of		
New York City, June 27, 1847, by H. Slade	3	236
Julian, [d. Ozias & Mary], b. Mar. 31, 1803	3	84
Kezia, d. Ebenezer & Margeret, b. May 19, 1722	1	47
Larned, s. [Augustus & Bathsheba], b. Apr. 24, 1799	2	63
Lora, d. [Jared & Elizabeth], b July 2, 1782 (Laura)	2	210
Laura, d. [Perez & Martha], b. Jan. 31, 1793	3	33
Leslie, d. Aug. 22, 1849, ae 9	4	156
Levi, s. Moses & Hannah, b. Apr. 15, 1759	2	5
Lora, see under Laura		
Lorenzo Dow, s. [Ozias & Mary], b. Apr. 15, 1805	3	84
Lucius, s [Perez & Martha], b. Feb. 13, 1791	3	33
Lucius, m. Catharine **RICHARDSON**, Jan. 12, 1823	3	107
Lucie, d. Sam[ue]ll & Mary, b Jan. 27, 1753	1	233
Lucy, m. Zebulon **HEB[B]ARD**, Jr., Apr. 18, 1776	2	217
Lucy, d. [Ozias & Mary], b. Feb 17, 1801	3	84
Luther, s. [Joseph & Temperance], b. June 2, 1768	2	43
Lydia, d. Zebulon & Hannah, b. Nov. 18, 1737	1	165
Lydia, d. Samuel & Lydia, b. Oct. 20, 1740	1	185
Lydia, w. Sam[ue]ll, d. Apr. 16, 1747	1	185
Lydia, m. Robard **HIB[B]ARD**, Aug. 1, 1758	2	46
Lydia, d. [Nathan & Irena], b. Nov. 9, 1769	2	103
Lydia, d. [Gideon & Elizabeth], b. Dec. 27, 1769	1	294
Lydia, d. [Diah & Zerviah], b. Oct. 6, 1788	2	187
Lydia, d. [Warner & Polly], b. Oct. 12, 1795	3	15
Lydia A., m. Charles F. **MANNING**, b. of Windham, Oct.		
10, 1842, by Rev. J.E. Tyler	3	204
Lyman, of Canterbury, m. Mary L. **KIMBALL**, of Windham,		
Oct. 30, 1831, by Rev. Jesse Fisher	3	158

	Vol	Page
HIBBARD, HEBARD, HIBARD, HEBBARD, HOBARD, (cont.)		
Lyna, d. Sam[ue]ll & Mary, b. June 6, 1760	1	233
Lyndon, s. [Joseph & Temperance], b. Apr. 11, 1766	2	43
Marg[a]ret, d. Ebenezer & Marg[a]ret, b. May 10, 1713	1	47
Maritta, d. [Gurdon, Jr. & Fanny], b. Oct. 8, 1811	3	45
Marietta, of Windham, m John **COMINS**, of Southbridge, Mass., Oct. 10, 1833, by Rev. Jesse Fisher	3	167
Martha, d. Robert & Mary, b. Sept 9, 1718; d. Sept 23, 1718	1	20
Martha, d. John & Martha, b. Dec 21, 1725	1	93
Martha, m. Ebenezer **BARNAM**, Jan. 1, 1745/6	1	295
Mary, m. Jonathan **CRANE**, July 31, 1705	1	13
Mary, d. Robert & Mary, b. Dec. 14, 1711	1	20
Mary, m. Jonathan **BADCO[C]K**, Oct. 19, 1719	1	37
Mary, m. Seth **CARY**, Apr. 17, 1722	1	68
Mary, m. Sam[ue]ll **TARRANCE**, Nov. 6, 1733	1	135
Mary, d. John & Martha, b. Sept. 30, 1736	1	93
Mary, d. Joshua & Ruth, b. Oct. 19, 1739	1	127
Mary, d. Paul & Martha, b. Nov. 15, 1743	1	224
Mary, d. Sam[ue]ll & Mary, b. Nov. 22, 1750	1	233
Mary, d. Elisha & Mary, b. Jan. 22, 1752; d. Mar. 20, [1752]	1	237
Mary, w. [Robert], d. Mar. 7, 1763	1	20
Mary, m. Nathaniel **WARREN**, Jan. 9, 1763	2	111
Mary, m. Zebediah **FARNAM**, Jr., Nov. 9, 1763	2	95
Mary, d. [David & Dorcas], b. Feb. 25, 1768, in Mansfield	2	86
Mary, d. [Ozias & Mary], b Feb. 9, 1799	3	84
Mary, m. Jepthah **GEER**, May 19, 1839	3	107
Mary L , m. Jepthar **GEER**, b of Windham, May 19, 1839, by Rev. Otis C. Whiton, of Scotland Society, Windham	3	189
Metilda, d. [Jared & Elizabeth], b. Aug. 24, 1784	2	210
Mehetable, d. Joseph & Abigail, b Sept. 29, 1713	1	21
Minerva, d. [Perez & Martha], b. July 25, 1795	3	33
Moses, s. Joseph & Abigail, b. Apr. 10, 1719	1	21
Moses, m. Hannah **MURDOCK**, May 31, 1744	1	270
Moses, m. Hannah **MURDOCK**, May 31, 1744	2	5
Moses, s. Moses & Hannah, b. June 20, 1745	1	270
Moses, s. Moses & Hannah, b. June 20, 1745	2	5
Nancy, d. [Ozias & Mary], b. Oct. 10, 1809	3	84
Nathan, s Ebenezer & Marg[a]ret, b Nov. 6, 1715	1	47
Nathan, s. Nathan & Zipporah, b. Jan. 16, 1739/40	1	191
Nathan, Jr., m. Mehetable **CROSBY**, Sept 27, 1759	2	54
Nathan, m. Irena **WARNER**, Dec. 4, 1764	2	103
Nathaniel, m. Sarah **CRANE**, Apr. 16, 1702	A	22
Nathaniell, m. Sarah **CRANE**, Apr. 16, 1702	1	1

	Vol.	Page

HIBBARD, HEBARD, HIBARD, HEBBARD, HOBARD, (cont)

Nathaniel, s. Nathaniel & Sarah, b. Jan. 3, 1703;		
d. May 16, 1704	A	22
Nathaniel, s. Nathaniell & Sarah, b. Jan. 3, 1703	1	1
Nathaniell, s. Nathaniell & Sarah, d. May 11, 1704	1	2
Nathaniell, twin with Jonathan, s. Nathaniell &		
Sarah, b. Oct. 23, 1709	1	1
Nath[anie]ll, Sergt., d. Apr. 26, 1725	1	2
Nathaniel, s. Paul & Martha, b. Jan 18, 1741/2	1	224
Nath[anie]ll, m. Mary **ABBE**, Mar. [ ], 1770	2	161
Olive, d. Nathan, Jr. & Mehitable, b. Oct. 25,		
1762	2	54
Orester, s. [Gurdon, Jr. & Fanny], b. Jan. 10, 1801	3	45
Ozias, s. Paul & Martha, b. June 6, 1749	1	224
Ozias, s. [Paul & Martha], b. Dec. 1, 1763	1	224
Ozias, m. Mary **FLOWERS**, Nov. [ ], 1791	3	84
Ozias, s [Paul & Martha], d. [ ]	1	224
Paul, s. Nathaniell & Sarah, b. Mar. 4, 1712	1	1
Paul, m. Deborah **LARRANCE**, Jan 6, 1735/6	1	152
Paul, m. Martha **DODGE**, Apr. 30, 1741	1	224
Paul, s. [Ahimaz & Asenath], b. Feb. 15, 1784	2	251a
Peggy, d. Joshua & Ruth, b. Sept. [ ], 1757	1	214
Peggy, m. Frederick **OWEN**, Sept. 10, 1778, by Samuel		
Gray, J.P.	2	224
Peninnah, d. [Zebulon & Hannah], b. Feb. 13, 1752	1	231
Perez, s. Gid[eon] & Elizabeth, b. Feb. 21, 1752	1	294
Perez, m. Martha **BURNETT**, Dec. 2, 1784	3	33
Polly, d. [Jonathan & Deborah], b. Sept. 27, 1773	2	175
Prudent, d. Ebenezer & Marg[a]ret, b. Feb 3, 1711	1	47
R[e]uben, s. Ebenezer & Marg[a]ret, b. May 21, 1718	1	47
R[e]uben, s. [Robard & Lydia], b. June 23, 1759	2	46
Robert, m. Mary **READ**, Dec. 3, 1702; d. June 26,		
1742	1	20
Robard, m. Mary **READ**, Dec. 22, 1702	A	1
Robard, s. Robard & Mary, b. Apr. 5, 1706	A	20
Robert, [d.] Apr. 29, 1710, ae. 63 y.	1	21
Robert, Jr., m Ruth **WHEELOCK**, Nov. 6, 1730	1	115
Robert, s. Robert & Ruth, b. Sept. 12, 1737	1	115
Robard, Jr., m. Lydia **HIB[B]ARD**, Aug. 1, 1758	2	46
Robert, m. Joanna **CLEVELAND**, May 12, 1760	1	115
Robert, s. [Jared & Elizabeth], b June 8, 1790	2	210
Roger, s. Moses & Hannah, b. Apr. 4, 1757	2	5
Roxalaney, twin with Tryphenia, d. Joseph &		
Temp[erance], b. Feb. 16, 1760	2	43
Roxalaney, m. Abner **ALLEN**, June 10, 1778	2	45
Royal, s. [Josiah & Hannah], b. July 10, 1763; d.		
June 11, 1767	2	31
Ruth, d. Joseph & Abigail, b. Sept. the last, 1717	1	21

	Vol	Page

HIBBARD, HEBARD, HIBARD, HEBBARD, HOBARD, (cont.)

	Vol	Page
Ruth, d. Robert & Ruth, b. Feb. 20, 1735/6; d.		
Mar. 7, 1735/6	1	115
Ruth, d. Robert & Ruth, b. Aug. 28, 1739	1	115
Ruth, m. Nathaniel **SHATTOCK**, Feb. 16, 1741/2	1	252
Ruth, d. Joshua & Ruth, b. Apr. 13, 1744	1	127
Ruth, w. Robert, d. Apr. 6, 1757	1	115
Ruth, m. Elijah **FRINK**, June 21, 1758	2	50
Ruth, m. Ephraim **ORMSBY**, [ ] 16, 1762	2	76
Ruth, w. Joshua, d. May 27, 1772	1	214
Sally, d. [Ozias & Mary], b. Dec. 30, 1794	3	84
Salome, d. [Joseph & Temperance], b. Apr. 17, 1771	2	43
Samuell, s. Nathaniell & Sarah, b. July 21, 1704	1	1
Samuell, s. Nathaniell & Sarah, b. July 21, 1704	1	2
Sam[ue]l, s. Robert & Mary, b. May 2, 1710	1	20
Samuel, m. Lydia **KINGSLEY**, Jan. 17, 1738/9	1	185
Samuel, s. John & Martha, b. Feb. 8, 1742/3	1	93
Samuell, m. Mary **BURNAP**, Sept. 27, 1748	1	185
Samuel, s. [Zebulon, Jr. & Lucy], b. Dec. 11, 1780	2	217
Samuel Lee, s. [Ozias & Mary], b. May 22, 1817	3	84
Sarah, d. Nathaniell & Sarah, b. Jan 27, 1717	1	1
Sarah, m. Ebenezer **SPENCER**, Sept. 29, 1736	1	153
Sarah, d Zebulon & Hannah, b July 25, 1739	1	165
Sarah, d. John & Martha, b. Feb. 2, 1744/5	1	112
Sarah, d. [Elisha & Mary], b. Mar. 10, 1762	1	237
Selah, s. [David & Dorcas], b. Apr. 5, 1766, in		
Lebanon	2	86
Seth, s. Robert & Mary, b. Apr. 29, 1714	1	39a
Seth, s. [Josiah & Hannah], b. July 14, 1765	2	31
Shuba[e]l, s. Ebenezer & Margaret, b. Aug. 2, 1726	1	47
Shubael, m. Lucy **HOVEY**, Sept. 23, 1798	3	26
Shubael Palmer, s. [Jared & Elizabeth], b. June 21,		
1786	2	210
Shubael Ross, s. [Josiah & Hannah], b. Apr. 11, 1773;		
d. Nov. 12, 1774	2	31
Sibel, see under Sybil		
Silas, s. David & Eliz[abeth], b. May 30, 1758	1	239
Submit, d. Moses & Hannah, b. Dec. 16, 1752	2	5
Susan, of Windham, m. James W. **CLARKE**, of South		
Kingston, R.I., Jan. 11, 1829, by Tho[ma]s Gray,		
J.P.	3	134
Susannah, d. [Gideon & Elizabeth], b. May 17, 1754	1	294
Susannah, m. Phinehas **SPAFFORD**, Mar. 28, 1782	2	225
Sibel, d. [Zebulon & Hannah], b. Oct 29, 1743	1	231
Sebel, d. David & Eliza, b. Feb. 1, 1746/7; d.		
[ ], at Killingly	1	239
Sybel, d. Seth & [E]unice, b. Dec. 5, 1753	1	230
Temperance, d. Joseph & Temperance, b May 24, 1756	2	43

	Vol.	Page
HIBBARD, HEBARD, HIBARD, HEBBARD, HOBARD, (cont.)		
Theode, d. Gid[eon] & Elizabeth, b. Aug. 7, 1750	1	294
Thomas, s. Paul & Martha, b. July 20, 1752	1	224
Thomas, s. [Josiah & Hannah], b. Oct. 29, 1767	2	31
Timothy, s. Joshua & Ruth, b. Nov. 28, 1759	1	214
Timothy Warner, s. [Nathan & Irena], b. Oct. 22, 1764	2	103
Truman, s. [Jared & Elizabeth], b. Apr. 26, 1788	2	210
Tryphenia, twin with Roxalaney, d. Joseph & Temp[erance], b. Feb. 16, 1760	2	43
Uriah, s. David & Elizabeth, b. Mar. 24, 1748/9; d. [ ], at Killingly	1	239
Uriah, s. [Josh[ua] & Ruth], b. Apr. 23, 1753	1	214
Warner, m. Polly **WHITE**, Apr. 2, 1789	3	15
William, s John & Martha, b. Jan 20, 1729/30	1	93
William, m. Dorothy **BARNUM**, Oct. 16, 1750	1	291
William, s. [William & Dorothy], b. July 6, 1751	1	291
William, s. [Sam[ue]ll & Mary], b. Jan. 30, 1762	1	233
William, s. [Diah & Zerviah], b. Nov. 26, 1800	2	187
Zebulon, s. Nathaniell & Sarah, b. Feb. 20, 1714/5	1	1
Zebulon, m. Hannah **BASS**, Mar. 30, 1737 (sic)	1	165
Zebulon, s. Zeb[ulon] & Hannah, b. Feb. 17, 1747/8	1	231
Zebulon, Jr., m. Lucy **HEB[B]ARD**, Apr. 18, 1776	2	217
Zerviah, d. [Gideon & Elizabeth], b. Jan. 23, 1758	1	294
Zerviah, m. Diah **HEB[B]ARD**, June 3, 1784	2	187
Zerviah, d. [Diah & Zerviah], b. Dec. 12, 1790; d. Dec. 14, 1790	2	187
Zilpah, d. Zebulon & Hannah, b. Nov. 20, 1745	1	231
Zipporah, d. Nathan & Zip[p]orah, b Nov. 14, 1741; d. Feb. 28, 1769	1	191
Zip[p]orah, w. Nathan, d. Jan. 9, 1763	1	191
——, d. John & Martha, b. Nov. 26, 1751; d. same day	1	112
——, d. [Nathan, Jr & Mehetable], b. June 17, 1760; d. July 1, 1760	2	54
——, m. Silas **BINGHAM**, Dec 10, 1765	2	185
HICKLAND*, Ann, m. Joseph **HEB[B]ARD**, Jr., Oct. 13, 1726 (*correction typed entry, "**HICKLAND** should be **STRICKLAND**", added to original manuscript)	1	96
HIDE, [see under **HYDE**]		
HILL, HILLS, Aaron, m. Lucinda **ROBINSON**, June 3, 1832, by Rev. Roger Bingham	3	160
Abigail, d. John & Thankfull, b. Mar. 10, 1752	1	256
Abram, s. Abram & Jerusha, b. May 2, 1750	1	298
Amy, m. Elijah **BIBBINS**, Oct. [ ], 1762	3	8
Charlotte, d. John & Thankfull, b. Oct 28, 1763	2	114
Delight, m. Matthais **SAWYER**, Apr. 5, 1778; d. Sept. 10, 1800	2	231
Eunice, d. John & Thankfull, b. Nov. 15, 1759	2	114

	Vol	Page
HILL, HILLS, (cont.)		
Jepthia, s. John & Thankfull, b. July 9, 1761	2	114
Jerusha, w. Abram, d. May 17, 1750	1	298
John, s. John & Thankfull, b. May 17, 1754	1	256
John F., d. Feb 10, 1851, ae. 1 y. 2 m 15 d	4	158
Martha had d. Wealthy **ELDERKIN**, b. Jan. 8, 1769	2	153
Marvin, m Lucia Ann **FRANKLIN**, b of Willimantic,		
Sept. 15, 1844, by Rev. Charles Noble,		
Willimantic	3	217
Mary, m. David **SPENCER**, June 16, 1762	2	24
W[illia]m Nelson, s. Nelson S., laborer, ae. 36,		
& Fanny, b. Aug. 5, 1849	4	9
HILLARD, George Whitfield, twin with John Thornton, s.		
Sam[ue]ll & Jerusha, b. Aug. 17, 1770, at		
Connejoharry	2	173
John Thornton, twin with George Whitfield, s.		
Sam[ue]ll & Jerusha, b Aug. 17, 1770, at		
Connejoharry	2	173
Mary, d. [Sam[ue]ll & Jerusha], b. May 31, 1772;		
d. Oct. [ ], 1772, in Norwich	2	173
Sam[ue]ll, Rev., m. Jerusha **BINGHAM**, Sept. 20, 1769	2	173
HODGKINS, HODGEKINS, HODKINS, Abigail, d. [Tho[ma]s &		
Anna], b. June 21, 1758	2	106
Abigail, m. Thomas **UTLEY**, May 25, 1780	2	242
Anna, d. [Tho[ma]s & Anna], b Apr. 3, 1763; d. Oct.		
5, 1775	2	106
Anne, d. [Thomas, Jr. & Tryphenia], b. Apr. 16, 1781	2	234a
Mary, d. [Nath[anie]l & Jerusha], b. Feb. 11, 1785	2	254
Nath[anie]l, s. [Tho[ma]s & Anna], b. Jan 3, 1761	2	106
Nath[anie]l, m. Jerusha **SPENCER**, Jan. 1, 1784	2	254
Sarah, d. [Tho[ma]s & Anna], b. Sept. 13, 1766	2	106
Thomas, s. Tho[ma]s & Anna, b. June 7, 1756, in Weston	2	106
Thomas, Jr., m. Tryphenia **DURKEE**, June 22, 1780	2	234a
Thomas, s. [Thomas, Jr. & Tryphenia], b. Sept. 8, 1782	2	234a
HOFERING, Antony, laborer, ae. 24, m. Ama **CRANE**, ae. 20,		
Dec. [1850], by Rev. Brady	4	115
HOLBROOK, Elizabeth, m. Phineas **TRACY**, May 29, 1766	2	118
HOLDEN, [see also **HOLDING**], Benj[ami]n, [twin with Joseph],		
s. Ebenezer & Elizabeth, b. May 5, 1725	1	78
Edward, min[ister], ae. 35, b. Dorchester, res.		
Illinois, m. 2d w. Edwin (sic) **PARKER**, ae. 23, b		
Ashford, res. Illinois, July 28, [1850], by E. W.		
Barrows	4	118
Jabez, s. Ebenezer & Elizabeth, b. Sept. 7, 1721	1	78
Joseph, [twin with Benj[ami]n, s Ebenezer & Elizabeth,		
b. May 5, 1725; d. July 2, 1725	1	78
William, s. Ebenezer & Elizabeth, b. Sept. 5, 1723	1	78
HOLDING, [see also **HOLDEN**], Benjamin, m. Rebeckah **LILLIE**,		

	Vol.	Page
HOLDING, (cont.)		
Feb. 3, 1757	2	25
Benjamin, d. Jan. 15, 1777	2	25
C[h]loe, d. Benj[ami]n & Rebeckah, b. Oct. 22, 1757	2	25
Elizabeth, d. [Benjamin & Rebeckah], b. Aug. 22, 1763; d. June 3, 1772	2	25
Jane, d. [Benjamin & Rebeckah], b. Feb. 28, 1760	2	25
Rebeckah, d. [Benjamin & Rebeckah], b. Sept. 25, 1761	2	25
HOLLAND, Benjamin, m. Ruth **BARROWS**, Apr. 26, 1778	2	223
Benjamin, s. [Benjamin & Ruth], b. Nov. 29, 1782	2	223
Francis, s. [Benjamin & Ruth], b. Feb. 20, 1781	2	223
John Henry, s. [Benjamin & Ruth], b. May 23, 1786	2	223
Thomas, s. [Benjamin & Ruth], b. Mar. 12, 1779	2	223
HOLLINGSWORTH, Edwin, of Woodstock, m. Clarissa **LINCOLN**, of Windham, Nov. 24, 1839, by Rev. R. Ransom	3	191
HOLLOWAY, Rebecca T., m. William E. **BECKWITH**, b. of Windham, June 15, 1840, by Rev. R. Ransom	3	193
HOLMES, [see also **HEELMES**], Elisha, m. Lydia **ALLEN**, Dec. 4, 1823	3	115
Joanna, of Willimantic, m. Leonard **WOODWORTH**, of Coventry, Sept. 15, 1834, by Rev. Philo Judson	3	170
Mary, m. Jacob **PRESTON**, Jan. 1, 1752	1	241
Patrick, d. Oct. [ ], [1849], ae. 26	4	156
R[h]oda, b. Stonington, res. Windham, d. Feb. [ ], 1851, ae. 36	4	158
Rhoda Ann, of Windham, m. John L. **STANTON**, of Norwich, Jan. 1, 1846, by Rev. R.V Lyon	3	226
W[illia]m, d. Feb. 23, [1848 or 1849], ae. 12	4	6
----, child of John, laborer, ae. 49, & Bridget, ae. 37, of Willimantic, b. Mar. 20, [1849]	4	5
HOLT, Abial, s. Abial & Hannah, b. Feb. 1, 1726/7	1	71
Abiel, s. W[illia]m & Sibbel, b. July 8, 1755	2	2
Abiel, m. Abigail **DURKEE**, July 18, 1776	2	222
Abigail, [twin with Sarah], d. Robert & Rebeckah, b. Feb. 20, 1722/3	1	56
Abigail, d. Daniel & Abigail, b. Feb. 20, 1732/3	1	120
Abigail, m. Jonathan **KINGSLEY**, Dec. 3, 1736	1	181
Abigail*, m. Jonathan **KINGSBURY**, Dec. 3, 1736 (*correction on note attached to page of original manuscript states "Abigail m. Jonathan **KINGSBURY** is right – not **KINGSLEY**"; also on note in a different handwriting was written: "Authority?")	2	127
Abigail, m David **KINDEL**, Nov 5, 1741	1	249
Abigail, d. [Will[ia]m, Jr. & Mercy], b. Sept. 27, 1774	2	100
Alice, d. William & Hannah, b. Apr. 26, 1747	1	221

	Vol.	Page
HOLT, (cont.)		
Alice, m. Robert **LYON**, Nov. 13, 1764	2	102
Amasa, s. William & Sibel, b. May 24, 1759	2	2
Anna, d. [Nehemiah & Anna], b. July 5, 1765	1	259
Anne, d. Abial & Hannah, b. Jan. 14, 1734/5	1	135
Benj[ami]n, s. George & Mary, b. Sept. 8, 1748	1	236
Bethiah, d. W[illia]m & Sybel, b Aug. 16, 1754;		
d. same day	1	221
Bethiah (**PEABODY**), w. Robert, d. Feb. 6, 1742/3	1	211
Caleb, s. Abial & Hannah, b. Mar. 6, 1728/9; d.		
Oct. 21, 1730	1	71
Chloe, d. [Ebenezer & Mary], b. Apr. 6, 1775; d.		
Apr 7, 1776	2	184
Chloe, d. [Ebenezer & Mary], b. Feb. 24, 1777	2	184
Daniel, m. Abigail **SMITH**, Mar 31, 1730	1	120
Daniel, s. Daniel & Abigail, b. Apr. 5, 1731	1	120
Deborah, twin with Dorothy, d. [Lemuel & Mary],		
b. Oct. 3, 1781* (*1781 was erased from the		
second line of this entry, handwritten and		
added to the end of the first line of entry)	2	234a
*Deborah, m. Benj. **PRESTON**, May 5, 1727 (*Correction		
entire entry handwritten and inserted on the line		
vacated when 1781 was erased and moved to the		
line above. Note: see **PRESTON** entry for volume		
and page number.)		
Dinah, d. Joshua & Katurah, b. Mar. 17, 1725/6	1	102
Diner, m. Nathaniell **FFORD**, Apr. 1, 1730	1	111
Dinah, m. Timothy **PEARL**, Nov. 6, 1746	1	274
Dina[h], d. [Joshua, Jr. & Mary], b. Mar. 22, 1750	1	299
Dorcas, d. [Joshua, Jr. & Mary], b. Mar. 30, 1767	1	299
Dorothy, twin with Deborah, d. [Lemuel & Mary], b.		
Oct. 3, 1781	2	234a
Ebenezer, s. Paul & Mehet[able], b. Feb. 23, 1745/6	1	228
Ebenezer, m. Mary **COLLINS**, [ ]	2	184
Ebenezer, s. [Ebenezer & Mary], b. [ ]	2	184
Eliphalet, s. Nehemiah & Anne, b. Apr. 1, 1749; d.		
Sept. 4, 1754	1	259
Elisha, s. [Stephen & Hannah], b. Oct. 8, 1778	2	196
Elizabeth, d. Abial & Hannah, b. Feb 16, 1724/5	1	71
Elizabeth, m. Sam[ue]ll **COBURN**, Nov. 16, 1727	1	89
Elizabeth, d. Zebadiah & Sarah, b. Jan. 10, 1738/9	1	123
Elizabeth, d. George & Mary, b. May 25, 1751	1	236
Eliz[abeth], m. Tho[ma]s **BUTLER**, Jr , Jan. 19, 1757	2	35
Esther, m. Ezra **LILLIE**, May 29, 1788	2	14
Eunice, d. Zebadiah & Sarah, b. Oct. 8, 1732	1	123
[E]unice, m. Isaac **BURNAM**, Mar. 22, 1747	1	279
Eunice, d. [Zebediah, Jr. & Jemima], b. Dec 17, 1770	2	47
Ezekiel, s. Robert & Rebeckah, b. Apr. 21, 1727	1	56

	Vol.	Page
HOLT, (cont.)		
Ezekiel, m. Luce **DURKEE**, Nov. 5, 1745	1	270
Ezekiel, m. Abiah **SESSIONS**, May [ ], 1748	1	287
Famme, d. [Zebediah, Jr. & Jemima], b. Dec. 25, 1765	2	47
George, Jr., m. Mary **ALLEN**, July 4, 1743	1	236
Geo[rge] N., of Willimantic, d. Feb. 27, [1849], ae. 2	4	153
Hannah, d. Abial & Hannah, b. Apr 17, 1723	1	71
Hannah, d. George & Mary, b. Mar. 11, 1729/30	1	108
Hannah, m. William **HOLT**, July 14, 1742	1	221
Hannah, d. William & Hannah, b. Jan. 26, 1744/5; d. Aug. 30, 1754	1	221
Hannah, m. Jethro **ROGERS**, Oct. 8, 1747	1	271
Hannah, w. William, d. Jan. 25, 1750/51	1	221
Hannah, d. W[illia]m & Sibel, b. Apr. 25, 1755; d. Sept. 10, 1774	2	2
Hannah, m. Benjamin **BURGESS**, Mar. 26, 1760	2	2
Hannah, d. [Joshua, Jr. & Mary], b. May 24, 1764	1	299
Hannah, d. [Stephen & Hannah], b. Nov. 13, 1780	2	196
Hannah, m. Jacob **FLINT**, Nov. 6, 1806	3	68
Huldah, d. [James & Huldah], b. Sept. 9, 1772; d. Sept. 28, 1775	2	149
Isaac, s. Abial & Hannah, b. Mar. 2, 1737/8	1	135
Jacob, s. [Zebediah, Jr. & Jemima], b. Mar. 19, 1760	2	47
James, s. Paul & Mehet[able], b. May 21, 1750	1	228
James, m. Huldah **STILES**, Dec. 31, 1769	2	149
John S., s. George, ae. 27, & Fanny, ae. 24, b. Nov. 28, [1848]	4	6
Jonathan, m. Mary **PARKER**, Apr. 12, 1738	1	189
Jonathan, s Nehem[iah] & Anne, b. Aug. 20, 1750; d Sept. 1, 1754	1	259
Joshua, m Katurah **HALL***, Feb. 16, 1724/5 (*correction **HALL** crossed out and **HOLT** handwritten at end of line in original manuscript)	1	102
Joshua, s. Joshua & Katurah, b. Mar. 19, 1727/8	1	102
Joshua, Jr , m. Mary **ABBOTT**, June 28, 1749	1	299
Joshua, Jr., m. Wid. Susanna **DERBY**, of Canterbury, Apr. 26, 1770	2	165
Josiah, s. Zebadiah & Sarah, b. Nov. 19, 1743	1	123
Josiah, s. Paul & Mehet[able], b. May 28, 1754	1	228
Josiah, s. [Stephen & Hannah], b. May 24, 1786	2	196
*Keturah (**HOLT**), m Joshua **HOLT**, Feb. 16, 1724/5 (*correction entire entry handwritten in original manuscript)		
Keturah, d. Joshua & Keturah, b. Nov. 22, 1729	1	102
Keturah, d. [Joshua, Jr & Mary], b Aug. 21, 1758	1	299
Keturah, w. Joshua, d. Oct. 2, 1781	1	102

	Vol.	Page
HOLT, (cont.)		
Lemuel, s. [Joshua, Jr. & Mary], b. Feb. 28, 1756	1	299
Lemuel, m. Mary **ABBOT**, Dec. 9, 1778	2	234a
Liester, s. [Lemuel & Mary], b. Aug. 27, 1779	2	234a
Lucinda, d. [Philemon], b. Apr. 30, 1775	2	182
Louce, d. Daniel & Abigail, b. Feb. 4, 1739/40	1	120
Luce, [w. Ezekiel], d. Aug. 11, 1747	1	270
Lucy, d. [James & Huldah], b. Jan. 28, 1770	2	149
Marcy, d. Zebadiah & Sarah, b. Feb. 14, 1740/41	1	123
Martha, d. Robert & Rebeckah, b. Apr. 11, 1725	1	56
Martha, m. John **RICHARDSON**, Jr., Jan. 1, 1754	1	322
Martha, d. [Nehemiah & Anna], b. Sept. 22, 1760	1	259
Mary, d. Robert & Rebeckah, b. Feb 7, 1724/5	1	56
Mary, d. Abial & Hannah, b. May 4, 1742	1	135
Mary, d. George, Jr. & Mary, b. Apr. 25, 1746	1	236
Mary, d. [Joshua, Jr. & Mary], b. July 11, 1752	1	299
Mary, w. Joshua, Jr., d. Aug 10, 1769	1	299
Mary A., b. Hampton, res. Windham, d. Feb. 22, 1848, ae. 22 m.	4	151
Matilda, [d. Philemon], b. Feb. 14, 1773	2	182
Mehetable, d. Paul & Mehet[able], b. May 1, 1757	1	228
Mehetable, w. Paul, d. May 10, 1773	1	228
Mercy, m. Will[ia]m **HOLT**, Jr., Sept. 8, 1763	2	100
Mercy, d. [Will[ia]m, Jr. & Mercy], b. Dec. 7, 1766	2	100
Molly, d. [Ebenezer & Mary], b. June 29, 1773	2	184
Nathan, s. Abial & Hannah, b. Apr. 18,. 1733	1	71
Nathaniell, s. George & Mary, b. Mar. 18, 1733/4	1	108
Nathaniel, s. [Nehemiah & Anna], b. Mar. [ ], 1754; d. Sept. 3, 1754 (sic)	1	259
Nehemiah, m. Anne **FARNUM**, Nov. 25, 1745	1	259
Ne[h]amiah, s. Ne[h]amiah & Anne, b. Oct. 24, 1746; d. Sept. 8, 1754	1	259
Nehemiah, s. Nehemiah & Anna, b. Nov. 28, 1756	1	259
Newton M., m. Emmy M. **MOSELEY**, Nov. 5, 1847	4	112
Newton M , harnessmaker, ae. 24, of Hampton, m. Emma F. **MOSELEY**, ae. 22, Nov. 25, 1847	4	111
Paul, s. Paul & Sarah, b. Aug. 21, 1721	1	228
Paul, m. Mehitable **CHANDLER**, Jan. 20, 1741/2	1	228
Paul, Sr., d. May 7, 1742	1	228
Paul, s. Paul & Mehitable, b. Jan. 4, 1742/3	1	228
Paul, Jr., m. Sarah **WELCH**, Aug. 20, 1767	2	145
Paul, m. Mary **SPENCER**, Jan. 4, 1774	2	187
Phebe, d. Joshua & Keturah, b. Aug. 16, 1734	1	102
Philemon, s. Paul & Mehetable, b. June 22, 1744	1	228
Presilla, m. Ic[h]abod **ROGERS**, Nov. 10, 1743	1	235
Rebeckah, [w. Robert], d. May 1, 1727	1	56
Roixanna, d. [Nehemiah & Anna], b Apr. 6, 1762	1	259
Sabra, see under Sebra		

	Vol.	Page
HOLT, (cont.)		
Samuel, s. [Joshua, Jr. & Susanna], b. May 16,		
1771	2	165
Sarah, [twin with Abigail], d. Robert & Rebeckah,		
b. Feb. 20, 1722/3	1	56
Sarah, d. George & Mary, b. Mar. 7, 1731/2	1	108
Sarah, d. Zebadiah & Sarah, b. Feb. 13, 1736/7	1	123
Sarah, w. Paul, d. Aug. 12, 1742	1	228
Sarah, d. William & Hannah, b. June 21, 1748	1	221
Sarah, d. Nehemiah & Anna, b. Aug. 30, 1754; d.		
Aug. 30, 1754 (sic)	1	259
Sarah, m. Aaron **FULLER**, Mar. 15, 1755	2	53
Sarah, d. Neh[emiah] & Anna, b. Oct. 10, 1758	1	259
Sarah, d. [Joshua, Jr. & Mary], b. Oct. 26, 1761	1	299
Sarah, m. Henry **DURKEE**, Jr. Nov. 16, 1769	2	148
Sebra, d. [Nehemiah & Anna], b. Jan. 12, 1768	1	259
Silas, s. Daniel & Abigail, b. Dec. 29, 1735	1	120
Stephen, s. Paul & Mehet[able], b. Mar. 12, 1748	1	228
Stephen, m. Hannah **GEERS**, Nov 22, 1772	2	196
Stephen, s. [Stephen & Hannah], b. Oct. 2, 1775;		
d. Feb. 15, 1779	2	196
Stephen, s. [Stephen & Hannah], b. Sept. 12,		
1783	2	196
Tammy, m. James **BURNHAM**, Nov. 24, 1784	2	50
Tammy, see also Famme		
Thomas, s. Paul & Mehet[able], b. Feb. 25, 1752	1	228
Thomas, s. Paul & [Mehetable], d. Aug. 17, 1754	1	228
Thomas, s. [Paul, Jr. & Sarah], b. Sept. 3, 1768	2	145
Timothy, s. Abial & Hannah, b. Dec. 2, 1739	1	135
Uriah, s. Joshua & Mary, b. Mar. 23, 1754	1	299
Vine, s. [Paul, Jr. & Sarah], b. Feb. 16, 1770	2	145
William, m. Hannah **HOLT**, July 14, 1742	1	221
William, s. William & Hannah, b. July 15, 1743	1	221
William, m. Sybel **DURKEE**, May 14, 1752	1	221
Will[ia]m, Jr., m Mercy **HOLT**, Sept. 8, 1763	2	100
William, s. [Will[ia]m, Jr. & Mercy], b. Nov. 22,		
1764	2	100
Zebadiah, m. Sarah **FFLINT**, Aug. 14, 1732	1	123
Zebadiah, s. Zebadiah & Sarah, b. Sept. 13, 1734	1	123
Zebediah, Jr., m. Jemima **SIMONDS**, Feb. 16, 1758	2	47
Ziba, s. [Paul, Jr. & Sarah], b Aug. 25, 1771	2	145
HOMER, Geo[rge] H., student, d. Mar. 18, 1850, ae. 22	4	156
HOOKER, Jonathan W., of Norwich, m. Sophronia		
RICHARDSON, of Windham, Nov. 11, 1838, by		
Oliver Kingsley, Jr., J.P.	3	187
HOOPER, John C., m. Mary Ann **READ**, b. of Willimantic		
Village, Windham, Apr. 11, 1826, by Rev.		
Benajah Cook, Jr., at Willimantic [1836?]	3	177

	Vol.	Page
HOOPER, (cont.)		
Robert W., m. Susan **PRENTICE**, b. of Willimantic,		
July 19, 1837, by Rev. Philo Judson, at		
Willimantic	3	183
Susan, m. Lewis **GOAECK**, b. of Willimantic Falls,		
Sept. 14, 1837, by Rev. B. Cook, Jr.	3	183
HOPE, Mary Ann, d. Benj[amin], farmer, ae. 35, & Mary,		
ae. 34, b. May 11, [1851]	4	14
HOPKINS, Harriet L., b. Barrington, res. Willimantic,		
d. Sept. 8, 1850, ae. 13 m.	4	157
Moses B., m. Miranda **TAYLOR**, Aug. 22, 1824	3	119
Nathan, m. Betsey **ARNOLD**, Nov. 29, 1832, by Rev.		
Alva Gregory	3	162
——, child of Lyman, laborer, ae. 34, & Harriet,		
ae. 33, of Willimantic, b. May 6, 1851	4	13
HOSKINS, Est[h]er, m. Ithamar **HEBBARD**, Mar. 8, 1768	2	137
HOSMER, HOSMORE, J.K., merchant, ae. 23, m. Maria L.		
HOVEY, ae. 21, Apr. 23, [1850], by Rev.		
Bankwell (Bushnell?)	4	116
Jane S., m. W[illia]m A. **BENNETT**, June 20, 1844, by		
Rev. Andrew Sharp	3	215
John B., m. Julia **SPAFFORD**, Oct. 15, 1826, by Rev.		
Cornelius B. Everest	3	123
Mary E., d. W[illia]m H., farmer, ae. 38, b. Sept.		
2, [1848]	4	6
William H., m. Susan **DYER**, July 14, 1842, by Rev.		
Andrew Sharp, Willimantic	3	202
HOUSE, [see under **HOWES** and **HOWE**]		
HOUSTON, James, of Norwich, m. Mary **DYER**, of Willimantic,		
Sept. 12, 1841, by Rev. Andrew Sharpe	3	198
HOVEY, HOVVEY, HOUEY, HOOVEY, Abel, s. [Nath[anie]ll &		
Ruth], b. Jan. 3, 1763; d. Mar. 9, 1771	1	292
Abel, s. [Jonathan & Eunice], b. Aug. 4, 1773	2	74
Abigail, [twin with Nathaniel], d. Nathaniel &		
Abigail, b. Oct. last day, 1713	1	14
Abigail, m. William **DURGE**, Feb. 8, 1732/3	1	137
Abigail, d. [Samuel & Elizabeth], b. Mar. 9, 1751	2	222
Abigail, d. [Jonathan & Eunice], b. Apr. 21, 1769	2	74
Abigail, w. Nath[anie]ll, d. Dec. 14, 1773, ae. 80 y.	1	107
Achsah, d. Eben[eze]r [& Dorcas], b. Feb. 21, 1766	2	117
Alice, d. [Jonathan & Eunice], b June 2, 1771	2	74
Allen, [s. Benjamin & Fanny], b. Oct. 9, 1842	3	93
Asa, s. [Eben[eze]r & Dorcas], b. May 3, 1769	2	117
Benjamin, s. [Dudley & Polly], b. Dec. 14, 1796	3	44
Benjamin, m. Fanny **BAKER**, Feb. 5, 1822	3	93
Betsey, m. Erastus **FITCH**, Nov. 28, 1814	3	100
Caroline, ae. 30, m Clark M. **SAUNDERS**, weaver, ae.		
32, b. Smithfield, res. Windham, Jan. 2, 1848,		

	Vol.	Page
HOVEY, HOVVEY, HOUEY, HOOVEY, (cont)		
by Thomas Dowling	4	111
Catharine Elizabeth, twin with Edwin Hurley, [d		
Benjamin & Fanny], b. Oct. 1, 1830	3	93
Charles, s. [Dudley & Polly], b. July 17, 1801;		
d. Mar. 2, 1804	3	44
Charles, s. [Benjamin & Fanny], b. Nov. 22, 1822	3	93
Clarrissa, d. [Jonathan & Eunice], b. Sept. 13,		
1781	2	74
Daniel, s. [Sam[ue]l & Abigail], b. July 24, 1764	2	104
Darius, s. Eben[eze]r & Dorcas, b. Mar 24, 1758	1	328
Darius, s. Eben[eze]r [& Dorcas], b. Mar. 24, 1758	2	117
Darius, s. [Jonathan & Eunice], b. Aug. 20, 1779	2	74
David, [twin with Jonathan], s. [Samuel & Elizabeth],		
b. Aug. 5, 1757	2	222
David, m. Anna **ROBINSON**, Aug. 28, 1783	2	133
David, s. [David & Anna], b. Mar. 19, 1784	2	133
Dudley, s. [Samuel & Elizabeth], b. Apr. 2, 1761	2	222
Dudley, m. Polly **MOORE**, Oct. 8, 1795	3	44
Dudley, d. Aug. 14, 1844	3	44
Ebenezer, s. Nath[anie]l & Abigail, b. Apr 9, 1722;		
d. Nov. 29, 1723	1	14
Ebenezer, s. Nath[anie]l & Abigail, b. Feb. 21, 1723	1	14
Ebenezer, s. Nath[anie]ll & [Ruth], b. Oct. 5, 1752	1	292
Ebenezer, m. Dorcas **DWIGHT**, [ ]	2	117
Edwin Hurley, twin with Catharine Elizabeth, [s.		
Benjamin & Fanny], b. Oct. 1, 1830	3	93
Elijah, s. [Jonathan & Eunice], b. Oct. 13, 1765	2	74
Eliza, of Windham, m. Erastus **TUCKER**, of Windham, May		
21, 1829, by Rev. Jesse Fisher	3	136
Eliza, [d. Benjamin & Fanny], b Oct. 28, 1837	3	93
Elizabeth, d. John & Susannah, b. Jan. 15, 1743/4	1	283
Elizabeth, d. [Luke & Eliza[be]th], b. July 9, 1775	2	23
Eunie, d. Eben[eze]r & Dorcas, b. Mar. 12, 1760	1	328
Eunice, d. [Jonathan & Eunice], b. Sept. 4, 1767	2	74
Fanny, d. [Dudley & Polly], b. Jan. 6, 1799	3	44
Fanny, of Windham, m. Mason **MANNING**, of Stonington,		
Nov. 20, 1821	3	92
Fanny, [d. Benjamin & Fanny], b. Mar. 1, 1833	3	93
Frank, s. George, carpenter, ae. 29, b. Mar. 1, [1849]	4	11
Frederick, s. [Luke & Eliza[be]th], b. Dec. 14, 1763	2	23
Frederick, s. [Jonathan & Eunice], b. May 29, 1783	2	74
Frederick, s. [Jacob & Lucy], b. May 1, 1788; d. Oct.		
18, 1793	2	198
George, s. [Benjamin & Fanny], b. July 10, 1824	3	93
George, farmer, ae. 24, of Windham, m. Cornelia **BASS**,		
ae. 23, July 10, 1848, by Rev. Henry Coe	4	112
Hannah, d. [Nathaniel, 3rd], b. Feb. 9, 1776	2	14

	Vol.	Page
HOVEY, HOVVEY, HOUEY, HOOVEY, (cont.)		
Henry, [s. Benjamin & Fanny], b. Dec. 18, 1839	3	93
Hezekiah Manning, s. [Jacob & Lucy], b. Mar. 28,		
1790	2	198
Jacob, s. [Nathanie]ll & Ruth], b. May 16, 1760	1	292
Jacob, s. [Jonathan & Eunice], b. Mar. 23, 1762	2	74
Jacob, m. Lucy **MANNING**, Oct. 30, 1773	2	198
Jacob, s. Jacob & Lucy, b. Feb. 13, 1774; d. Sept.		
30, 1775	2	198
Jacob, s. [Jacob & Lucy], b. Aug. 6, 1776	2	198
Jerusha, d. [Jacob & Lucy], b. Sept. 1, 1780	2	198
Jerusha, m. Dyer **TRE[A]DWAY**, Sept. 28, 1810	3	57
John, s. Nathaniel & Abigail, b. Jan. 16, 1719/20	1	14
John, m. Susannah **ASHLEY**, Nov. 8, 1742	1	283
John, s. Nath[anie]ll & Ruth, b. Jan. 9, 1750/51	1	292
John Dudley, s. [Benjamin & Fanny], b. May 14,		
1826	3	93
Jonathan, s. Nath[anie]l & Abigail, b. Apr. 4, 1728	1	14
Jonathan, s. Nath[anie]ll & Abigail, d. Jan. 7,		
1731/2	1	107
Jonathan, s. Nath[anie]ll & Abigail, b. Dec. 2, 1734	1	107
Jonathan, [twin with David], s. [Samuel & Elizabeth],		
b. Aug. 5, 1757	2	222
Jonathan, s. [Luke & Eliza[be]th], b. Apr. 12, 1758	2	23
Jonathan, m. Eunice **WOODWARD**, Dec. 31, 1761	2	74
Jonathan, s. [Jonathan & Eunice], b. Sept. 21, 1777	2	74
Laura A., m. Noah A. **SMITH**, b. of Willimantic, Sept.		
7, 1846, by Rev. John Cooper	3	230
Lewis, s. [Benjamin & Fanny], b. May 20, 1828	3	93
Lois, d. [Jacob & Lucy], b. Jan. 23, 1785	2	198
Louisa, of Willimantic, m. James C. **BABCOCK**, of		
Columbia, Mar. 8, 1846, by John Cooper	3	228
Lovicy, d. [Luke & Eliza[be]th], b. May 18, 1767	2	23
Lucy, d. [Jacob & Lucy], b. Jan. 27, 1779	2	198
Lucy, m. Shubael **HEB[B]ARD**, Sept. 23, 1798	3	26
Luke, s. Nath[anie]ll & Abigail, b. Feb. last day,		
1729/30	1	107
Luke, m. Thankfull **ANTIZELE**, Oct. 31, 1754	2	23
Luke, m. Eliza[be]th **ARMSTRONG**, May 26, 1757	2	23
Luora, m. Edward **FITCH**, Apr. 3, 1822	3	101-2
Lydia, d. Nath[anie]ll & Abigail, b. Jan. 15, 1736/7	1	107
Lydia, m. Christopher **DAVISON**, June 5, 1755	1	328
Lydia, d. [Samuel & Elizabeth], b. Dec. 16, 1773 [sic]		
(Probably 1753)	2	222
Mariah, m. Henry **WELSON**, b. of Willimantic, Sept. 7,		
1846, by Rev. John Cooper	3	230
Maria L., ae. 21, m. J.K. **HOSMER**, merchant, ae. 23,		
Apr. 23, [1850], by Rev. Bankwell (Bushnell?)	4	116

	Vol.	Page
HOVEY, HOVVEY, HOUEY, HOOVEY, (cont.)		
Marianna, milliner, b. Mansfield, res. Willimantic,		
d. Feb. 22, 1850, ae. 21	4	157
Mary, d. Nathaniel & Abigail, b. May 15, 1726	1	14
Mary, d. [Nath[anie]ll & Ruth], b. July 28, 1758;		
d. Sept. 8, 1762	1	292
Mary, w. Dudley, d. Dec. 21, 1846	3	44
Nathan, s. [Luke & Eliza[be]th], b. Oct. 7, 1761	2	23
Nathaniel, m. Abigail **GEN[N]INGS**, Nov. 25, 1712	1	14
Nathaniel, [twin with Abigail], s. Nathaniel &		
Abigail, b. Oct. last day, 1713	1	14
Nathaniel, s. Nathaniel & Abigail, d. Dec. the last,		
1713	1	14
Nathaniel, s. Nathaniel & Abigail, b. Oct. 23, 1717	1	14
Nath[anie]ll, Jr., m. Ruth **PARKER**, Jan. 21, 1747/8	1	292
Nath[anie]ll, s. [Nath[anie]ll, Jr. & Ruth], b.		
June 14, 1749	1	292
Nath[anie]ll, d. June 26, 1761, ae. about 67	1	107
Nath[anie]l, 3rd, m. [ ], [, 17[ ]	2	14
Olive, d. Eb[enezer] [& Dorcas], b. Nov. 30, 176[ ]	2	117
Olive, d. [Jonathan & Eunice], b. July 4, 1775	2	74
Olive, m. Andrew **ROBINSON**, Mar. 10, 1785	3	28
Orrin, [s. Nath[anie]l, 3rd], b. Feb. 15, 1780, at		
Willington	2	14
Patty, d. Eb[enezer & Dorcas], b. Mar. 12, 1760	2	117
Phineas, s. Nath[anie]ll & Abigail, b. Dec. 6, 1731	1	107
Phinehas, s. [Nath[anie]ll & Ruth], b. Apr. 12,		
1756	1	292
Phineas, s. [Nat[anie]l, 3rd], b. Dec. 22, 1778	2	14
Prescilla, d. [Luke & Eliza[be]th], b. Jan. 8, 1772	2	23
Rensslaer C., m. Lama* **PRENTICE**, b. of Willimantic,		
Oct. 2, 1836, by Rev. Philo Judson, at		
Willimantic (*Laura?)	3	179
Ruth, d. [Nath[anie]ll & Ruth], b. Aug. 28, 1754	1	292
Ruth, m. Abiel **ABBOT**, Nov. 13, 1777	2	223
Salley, d. Eben[eze]r, b. Aug. 1, 1756	1	328
Sally, d. Eben[eze]r [& Dorcas], b. Aug. 1, 1756	2	117
Samuel, m. Abigail **CLEVELAND**, Sept. 29, 1763	2	98
Sam[ue]l, m. Abigail **CLEVELAND**, Dec. 29, 1764	2	104
Sarah, d. Nathaniel & Abigail, b. Nov. 10, 1716	1	14
Sarah, m. Joseph **GIN[N]INGS**, Apr 15, 1735	1	169
Sarah, d. [Luke & Thankfull], b. Nov. 11, 1755	2	23
Sarah, d. [Eben[eze]r & Dorcas], b. Dec. 10, 1763	1	328
Sarah A., m. Nathan A. **FISH**, b. of Windham, [ ],		
by John Cooper	3	225
Simeon, s. Eben[ezer] [& Dorcas], b. Dec. 30, 176[ ]	2	117
Thankful, w. Luke, d. Dec. 11, 1756	2	23
Thankfull, d. [Luke & Eliza[be]th], b. Jan. 15, 1760	2	23

	Vol.	Page
HOWARD, (cont.)		
Vine, s. [John, Jr. & Zerviah], b. Nov. 14, 1769	2	94
William, s. John & Mary, b. Oct. 28, 1736, at		
Ipswich; d. same day	1	184
William, s. John & Sarah, b. Jan. 7, 1748/9	1	232
HOWE, HOW, [see also **HOWES**], Abigail, d. [Robert &		
Susannah], b. June 25, 1811	3	38
Lucinda, of Coventry, R.I., m. John **WEAVER**, of		
Windham, June 12, 1843, by Calvin Hebbard, J.P.	3	209
Mary, m. John **CROWEL**, Jr., Mar. 18, 1747	2	53
Nancy, d. [Robert & Susannah], b. Nov. 1, 1807	3	38
Nancy, of Windham, m. Seth **JACOBS**, of Boston, Mass.,		
Apr. 26, 1829, by John Baldwin, J.P	3	135
Robert, m. Susannah **CASHMAN**, [ ], 1805	3	38
HOWES, HOWS, HOUES, HOUSE, [see also **HOWE**], Alfred, s.		
[Zenas & Eunice], b. July 26, 1780	2	238
Benjamin Dyer, [twin with George Dyer], s [Nathaniel		
& Maria], b. Apr. 5, 1822	3	76
Bethia[h], d. [Zach[ariah] & Bethiah], b. Feb. 20,		
1762	2	56
Bethiah, m. Luther **FITCH**, [ ], 1782	2	96
Bethiah, d. [Zenas & Eunice], b. Feb. 1, 1792	2	238
David, s. Zach[ariah] & Bethiah, b. Feb. 26, 1759	2	56
Eunice, d. [Zenas & Eunice], b. June 1, 1783	2	238
Fanny, d. [Zenas & Eunice], b. Mar. 16, 1790	2	238
Frank, s. James P., machinist, ae. 30, & Ann, ae. 33,		
of Willimantic, b. Sept. 9, [1851]	4	12
George Dyer, [twin with Benjamin Dyer], s. [Nathaniel		
& Maria], b. Apr. 5, 1822	3	76
Huldah Maria, d. [Nathaniel & Maria], b. Dec. 11,		
1819; d. Dec. 21, 1819	3	76
James P., m. Ann **FULLER**, b. of Windham, Dec. 9, 1840,		
by Rev. Andrew Sharpe, Willimantic	3	195
Lucretia T., m. Joshua B. **LORD**, Nov. 2, 1841, by Rev.		
Andrew Sharp	3	198
Lucretia T., d. James P., manufacturer, ae. 27, & Ann,		
ae. 30, b. July 3, 1848, of Willimantic	4	1
Marg[a]ret, m. Daniel **ROSS**, June 5, 1716; d. June 19,		
1724	1	46
Nathaniel, s. [Zenas & Eunice], b. June 12, 1787	2	238
Nathaniel, m. Maria **DYER**, Jan. 1, 1811	3	35
Nathaniel, m. Maria **DYER**, Jan. 1, 1811	3	76
Roxana, m. Jonathan **DEVOTION**, Oct. 7, 1797	3	28
William Bowen, s. [Nathaniel & Maria], b. May 8, 1814	3	76
William Bowen, s. [Nathaniel & Maria], b. May 14,		
1814 (sic)	3	76
William Brown, s. [Nathanial & Maria], b. May 4, 1814	3	35
Zenas, m. Eunice **HUNT**, Dec. 16, 1779	2	238

	Vol.	Page
HOWES, HOWS, HOUES, HOUSE, (cont.)		
Zenas, s. [Zenas & Eunice], b. Jan. 10, 1785	2	238
HOXSIE, HOXIE, Abraham, m. Betsey **GILBERT**, Oct 21, 1829, by Rev. Richard F. Cleveland	3	139
Benjamin, m. Hannah **CRANDALL**, b. of Windham, Mar. 26, 1838, by Rev. B. Cooke, Jr., of Willimantic	3	186
Perry G., s. Benj[amin], ae. 33, & Mary, ae. 32, July 18, 1849	4	8
HUMES, Warren, of Burrillville, R.I., m. Mary **IDE**, of Griswold, Conn., July 2, 1846, by Rev. John E. Tyler	3	229
HUMPHREY, Eliza, m. Luther **ASHLEY**, Sept. 20, 1809	3	88
Lydia, m. Jonathan **ASHLEY**, June 13, 1773	2	205
Mary, m. Oxenbridge **DEANS**, Dec. 15, 1772	1	202
HUNT, Alice, d. [John, Jr. & Asenath], b. Feb. 18, 1804	3	45
Anne, d. [John, Jr. & Asenath], b. Aug. 17, 1793	3	45
Asa, s [John, Jr. & Asenath], b Feb. 28, 1802	3	45
Clarissa, of Bolton, Conn., m. Martin **SMITH**, of Vernon, Conn., Apr 2, 1845, by Rev. Charles Noble, Willimantic	3	221
Elisha, s. [John, Jr. & Asenath], b. Feb. 27, 1800	3	45
Eunice, m. Zenas **HUNT**, Dec. 16, 1779	2	238
Experience, m. Jonathan **FULLER**, May [ ], 1774	2	167
Hannah, m. Asa **THATCHER**, July 22, 1779	2	131
Jabez C., of Norwich, m. Frances A. **LADD**, of Franklin, Oct. 21, 1850, by Rev. Jno. Cady	4	118
John, Jr., m. Asenath **GENNINGS**, Oct. 21, 1792	3	45
Lester, s. [John, Jr. & Asenath], b. Apr. 25, 1814	3	45
Lucretia, d. [John, Jr. & Asenath], b. Feb. 18, 1798	3	45
Polly, d. [John, Jr. & Asenath], b. June 7, 1795	3	45
William, s. [John, Jr. & Asenath], b. Oct. 18, 1808	3	45
HUNTINGTON, Abigail, s. [d.] Nathaniell & Mehetable, b. June 27, 1727	1	74
Abigail, m. Richard **KIMBALL**, Jr., Nov. 7, 1750	1	301
Alathear, d [Solomon & Anne], b. Nov. 29, 1764	2	75
Amanda Anne, d. [Jabez & Judeth], b. Apr. 21, 1764	2	57
Amanda Sarah, d [Jabez & Judeth], b. Jan. 26, 1761	2	57
Ann, m. Jonathan **BINGHAM**, Oct. 28, 1697	A	21
Ann, w. John, d. May 6, 1758	2	23
Anna, m. Prosper **WHITMORE**, July 23, 1747	1	269
Anna, m. Samuel **ROUNDY**, Dec. 23, 1755	2	26
Anna, w. John, d. May 6, 1758	1	190
Anna, d. N[athan] & Mary, b. Jan. 2, 1762	2	13
Anna, twin with Solomon, d. Solomon & Anna, b. Apr. 7, 1770	2	75
Anne, s. [d.] David & Mary, b. Nov. 14, 1730	1	74
Anne, d. Jabez & Sarah, b. Jan. 20, 1739/40	1	126
Anne, d. [John & Mary], b. Jan. 24, 1771	2	23

	Vol.	Page
HUNTINGTON, (cont.)		
Anne, m. Eleazer **RIPLEY**, Jr., Mar. 28, 1802	3	69
Apley, s. Abner & Mary, b. Apr. [ ], 1754	2	28
Asenath, m. Zebadiah **TRACY**, Dec. 14, 1808	3	68
Betsey, d. [Daniel & Martha], b. Sept. 15, 1793	3	29
Charles, m. Cynthia **TRACY**, Mar. 15, 1809	3	22
Charlotte, d. [Jonathan, Jr. & Sarah], b. Nov. 16, 1770	2	59
Christopher T., m. Mary **WEBB**, Sept. 9, 1823	3	112
Daniel, s. [Nathan & Mary], b. Dec. 13, 1763	2	13
Daniel, s. [Abner & Mary], b. May 13, 1769	2	28
Daniel, m. Maria **TRACY**, Apr. 19, 1786	3	29
David, s. Joseph & Rebekah, b. Dec. 6, 1697	A	10
David, m. Mary **MASON**, June 30, 1725	1	74
David, s. David & Mary, b. Oct. 14, 1733; d Oct. 25, 1733	1	74
David, s. David & Mary, b. Feb. 27, 1742/43	1	227
David, s. [Joseph & Rebeckah], b. Dec. 6, 1797 (Probably 1697)	2	59
Dianna, d. [Capt. Ebenezer & Lydia], b. June 14, 1811	3	50
Dorkus, d. William & Mary, b. Sept. 23, 1737	1	158
Eben[ezer], s. [Jonathan, Jr. & Sarah], b. May 1, 1764	2	59
Ebenezer, Capt., m. Lydia **PECK**, of Franklin, Sept. 10, 1810	3	50
Edney, d. N[athan] & Mary, b. Jan. 15, 1760	2	13
Eleazer, s. Thomas & Elizabeth, b. July 28, 1697	A	9
Elijah, s. Nath[anie]ll & Mehet[able], b Feb 7, 1745/6; d. Oct. 21, 1753	1	214
Elijah, s. [Eliphalet & Dinah], b. Nov. 27, 1764	2	78
Elijah D., of Norwich, m. Julia C. **WELCH**, of Windham, Mar. 6, 1843, by Rev. J.E. Tyler	3	207
Eliphalet, s. Joseph & Elizabeth, b. May 15, 1725	1	41
Eliphalet, s. Joseph & Elizabeth, d. Dec. 16, 1726	1	83
Eliphalet, m. Dinah **READ**, Nov. 4, 1762	2	78
Eliphalet, of Lebanon, m. Sally **ALLEN**, of Windham, Nov. 19, 1828, by Rev. Edw[in] Bull	3	133
Eliza, m. Cyrus **PALMER**, Mar. 24, 1844, by Rev. Andrew Sharp	3	213
Elizabeth, d. Thomas & Elizabeth, b. Apr. 17, 1695	A	9
Elizabeth, d. Jabez & Elizabeth, b. Nov. 1, 1725	1	78
Elizabeth, d. Joseph & Elizabeth, b. July 5, 1727	1	83
Elizabeth, d. Nath[anie]ll & Mehetable, b. Apr. 24, 1737	1	74
Elizabeth, d. Jonathan & Elizabeth, b. July 19, 1738	1	134
Elizabeth, d. Jonathan & Elizabeth, d. Oct. 4, 1741	1	220
Elizabeth, d. Simeon & Ame, b. June 12, 1743	1	206

	Vol.	Page
HUNTINGTON, (cont.)		
Elizabeth, m. Abraham **DAVENPORT**, Nov. 15, 1750	2	1
Elizabeth, w. Jonathan, d. Sept. 20, 1751	1	220
Elizabeth, d. [Solomon & Anne], b. Jan. 15, 1767	2	75
Elizabeth, d. [Jonathan, Jr. & Sarah], b. May 23, 1773, at Worthington	2	59
Elizabeth, w. Joseph, d. Jan. 4, 1774	1	83
Elizabeth, d. [John & Mary], b. Jan. 18, 1777	2	23
Elizabeth, d. Joseph & Elizabeth, d. Dec. 22, 1788	1	83
Elizabeth (**EDWARDS**), w. Jabez, d. Sept. 24, 1733	1	78
Enoch, s. Nathaniel & Mehetable, b. Dec. 15, 1739	1	214
Eunice, d. Jonathan & Elizabeth, b. Sept. 11, 1742	1	220
Eunice, d. [Hezekiah & Submit], b. Jan. 3, 1756	2	70
Eunice, m. Ebenezer **DEVOTION**, Jr., [ ], 1764	2	189
Eunice, d. [Eliphalet & Dinah], b. Nov. 17, 1769	2	78
Eunice, m. Ralph **RIPLEY**, Dec. 8, 1774	2	195
Eunice, m. George W. **ABBE**, Apr. 13, 1823	3	111
Gamaliel, s. [Hezekiah & Submit], b. Nov. 28, 1760	2	70
Gurdon, s. [Hezekiah & Submit], b. Apr. 30, 1763	2	70
Gurdon, s. [John & Mary], b. Dec. 21, 1778	2	23
Hannah, d. [Jabez & Judeth], b. Aug. 7, 1765	2	57
Henry, m. Clarissa **BIBBINS**, Feb. 23, 1823	3	110
Henry, s. [Jabez & Judeth], b. [ ]	2	57
Hezekiah, s. David & Mary, b. Oct. 3, 1728	1	74
Hezekiah, Maj., m. Submit **MURDOCK**, Nov. 28, 1754	2	70
Hezekiah, s. [Jabez & Judeth], b. July 24, 1771	2	57
Horatio, s. Jon[atha]n & Sarah, b. June 28, 1755	2	9
Horatio, s., Dr., d. Sept. 17, 1759	2	9
Huldah, d. [Roger & Susannah], b. Nov. 14, 1782	2	229
Jabez, m. Elizabeth **EDWARDS**, June 30, 1724	1	78
Jabez, m. Sarah **WETMORE**, May 21, 1735	1	126
Jabez, Col., d. Sept. 26, 1752, N.S.	1	126
Jabez, m. Judeth **ELDERKIN**, Aug. 6, 1760	2	57
Jabez, s. [Jabez & Judeth], b. Aug. 23, 1767	2	57
Jabez, d. Nov. 24, 1782, in the 45th y. of his age	2	57
James, s. Abner & Mary, b. June 23, 1760	2	28
James, s. [Eliphalet & Dinah], b. Nov. 16, 1767	2	78
Jedediah, s. [Jabez & Judeth], b. Aug. 11, 1769	2	57
Jerusha, d. Jabez & Elizabeth, b. Aug. 24, 1731	1	78
Jerusha, m. John **CLARK**, Nov. 7, 1751	1	311
Jerusha, d. [Hezekiah & Submit], b. Mar. 7, 1780	2	70
John, s. Joseph & Elizabeth, b. Sept. 22, 1720; d. June 17, 1731	1	41
John, s. Joseph & Elizabeth, b. Dec. 22, 1729	1	83
John, s. Sam[ue]ll, Jr. & Jemima, b. Oct. 13, 1741	1	227
John, m. Ann **WRIGHT**, Mar. 11, 1756	2	23
John, m. Mary **FLINT**, Apr. 15, 1770	2	23
John, s. [John & Mary], b. Mar. 16, 1773	2	23

	Vol.	Page
HUNTINGTON, (cont.)		
John, d. Sept. 18, 1791	2	23
John, m. Anna [**WRIGHT**], [ ]	1	190
Jonathan, s. Joseph & Rebekah, b. Oct. 7, 1695	A	10
Jonathan, (Dr.), s. [Joseph & Rebeckah], b.		
Oct. 7, 1695	2	59
Jonathan, s. Nath[anie]ll & Mehetabel, b. May		
17, 1733	1	74
Jonathan, m. Elizabeth **ROCKWELL**, Nov. 7, 1734	1	134
Jonathan, s. Jona[than] & Elizabeth, b. Oct. 11,		
1735; d. Apr. 3, 1738	1	134
Jonathan, s. Jonathan & Elizabeth, b. Aug. 20,		
1745; d. Feb. 15, 1754	1	220
Jonathan, m. Sarah **NORTON**, Aug. 7, 1754	1	220
Jonathan, m. Sarah **NORTON**, Aug. 7, 1754	2	9
Jonathan, Jr., m. Sarah **HUNTINGTON**, Oct. [ ], 1757	2	59
Jonathan, s. [Eliphalet & Dinah], b. Nov. 17, 1771	2	78
Jonathan, Hon., d. Sept. 15, 1773	2	9
Jonathan, s. [Jonathan, Jr. & Sarah], b. Aug. 24,		
1778, at Worthington	2	59
Jonathan, Dr , d. Apr. [ ], 1781, at Worthington	2	59
Jonathan, s. [Roger & Susannah], b. May 11, 1781;		
d. July 14, 178[ ]	2	229
Joseph, m. Rebeckah **ADGATE**, b. of Norwich, Nov. 28,		
1687	2	59
Joseph, s. [Joseph & Rebeckah], b. Aug. 29, 1688, at		
Norwich	2	59
Joseph, m. Elizabeth **RIPLEY**, July 18, 1719	1	41
Joseph, s. Joseph & Elizabeth, b. Aug. 26, 1723	1	41
Joseph, s. Joseph & Elizabeth, d. Dec. 23, 1726	1	83
Joseph, s. Nath[anie]ll & Mehetabel, b. May 5, 1735	1	74
Joseph, s. Joseph & Elizabeth, b. Dec. 22, 1736; d.		
Oct. 12, 1760	1	83
Joseph, Dea., d. Dec. 29, 1747, in the 85th y. of his		
age	1	220
Joseph, Dea., d. Dec. 29, 1747, in the 85th y. of his		
age	2	59
Joseph, s. [John & Mary], b. Jan. 14, 1775	2	23
Joseph, Dea., d. Dec. 5, 1783, in the 96th y. of his		
age	1	83
Joseph, s. [Jabez & Judeth], b [ ]	2	57
Joseph Denison, s. [Solomon & Anna], b. Oct. 28, 1778	2	75
Josephine, d. Wallace, carpenter, ae. 29, & Cynthia,		
ae. 23, b. June 26, [1847?]	4	3
Judeth, [w. Jabez], d. Sept. 24, 1786, in the 44th y.		
of her age	2	57
Lora, m. William **BUTLER**, Oct 2, 1788	3	48
Lucy, d. Col. Jabez & Sarah, b. June 16, 1744	1	126

	Vol.	Page
HUNTINGTON, (cont.)		
Lucy, d. [Jonathan, Jr. & Sarah], b. Nov. 16, 1759,		
in East Haddam	2	59
Lucy, d. [John & Mary], b. Dec. 9, 1780; d. Sept. 7,		
1782	2	23
Lidia, d. Thomas & Elizabeth, b. Feb. 12, 1702	A	9
Lydia, m. Dea. Nath[anie]ll **WALES**, Oct. 22, 1730	1	107
Lydia, d. David & Mary, b. Aug. 29, 1737; d. Aug.		
30, 1737	1	227
Lydia, d. Solomon & Mary, b. Nov. 21, 1744	1	91
Lydia, m. Elisha **TINKER**, Nov. 13, 1763	2	93
Lydia, d. [Hezekiah & Submit], b. Aug. 7, 1775	2	70
Marg[a]ret, d. Solomon & Mary, b. Apr. 8, 1730	1	91
Maria, m. James **BINGHAM**, Dec. 30, 1829, by Rev.		
Roger Bingham	3	144
Marial, d. [Daniel & Martha], b. Jan. 13, 1789; d.		
Apr. 23, 1796	3	29
Mary, d. Joseph & Rebeckah, b. Aug. 4, 1707	A	10
Mary, d. [Joseph & Rebeckah], b. Aug. 4, 1707	2	59
Mary, d. Joseph & Elizabeth, b. July 17, 1732	1	83
Mary, d. David & Mary, b Apr. 2, 1735	1	74
Mary, d. William & Mary, b. Dec. 19, 1735	1	158
Mary, d. Solomon & Mary, b. Oct. 8, 1741	1	91
Mary, w. Nathan, d. Nov. 24, 1754	1	310
Mary, m. Jabez **FITCH**, Jan. 5, 1758	2	37
Mary, d. [Abner & Mary], b. Aug. 10, 1765	2	28
Mary, m. Nehemiah **TINKER**, Dec. 31, 176[ ]	2	91
Mary, d. [William & Mery], b. Feb. 10, 1772	2	162
Mary Ann, d. [Mason & Sally], b. June 24, 1813	3	71
Mason, s. [Daniel & Martha], b. Feb. 11, 1792	3	29
Mason, m. Sally **PARSONS**, Mar. 19, 1819	3	71
Mehetabel, d. Nathaniell & Mehetabel, b. Aug. 8,		
1729	1	74
Mehetable, wid. Nath[anie]ll, d. Oct. 4, 1781	1	214
Milany, m. John **LINCOLN**, Mar. 19, 1812	3	69
Minor, s. [Solomon & Anne], b. Apr. 22, 1763	2	75
Molley, d. Elisha & Elizabeth, b. Mar. 18, 1754	1	256
Nancy, m. Samuel **PERKINS**, Feb. 24, 1793	2	234a
Nancy, m. Samuel **PERKINS**, Feb. 24, 1793	3	50
Nancy, of Windham, m. Zalmon A. **CHURCH**, of Mans-		
field, Mar. 27, 1842, by Rev. J.E Tyler	3	201
Nathan, s. David & Mary, b. July 22, 1726	1	74
Nathan, m. Mary **BURLEY**, Oct. 2, 1752	1	310
Nathan, m. Mary **MASON**, Apr. 15, 1756	2	13
Nathan, s. Abner & Mary, b. Sept. 16, 1758; d.		
Dec. 17, 1767	2	28
Nathaniel, s. [Joseph & Rebeckah], b. Sept. [ ],		
1691, at Norwich	2	59

	Vol.	Page
HUNTINGTON, (cont.)		
Nathaniel, m. Mehetable **THURSTON**, Feb. 28, 1722/3	1	74
Nathaniel, s. Nathaniell & Mehitable, b. Dec. 25, 1724	1	74
Nath[anie]ll, s. [Eliphalet & Dinah], b. Aug. 3, 1762	2	78
Nath[anie]ll, d. Dec. 2, 1767, in the 77th y. of his age	1	214
Olive, d. Nathan & Mary, b. Nov. 8, 1752; d. July 29, 1755	1	310
Olive, d. N[athan] & Mary, b. July 19, 1757	2	13
Olive, m. Asa **ROBINSON**, Jr., Sept. 17, 1777	2	93
Philena, d. [Jabez & Judeth], b. [ ]	2	57
Philomela, d. [Daniel & Maria], b. Dec. 31, 1787	3	29
Philura, d. Elisha & Elizabeth, b. Jan. 15, 1756	1	256
Polly, d. [Solomon & Anna], b. Feb 22, 1781	2	75
Rachel, m. Joseph **BINGHAM**, Nov. 30, 1742, in Norwich	1	38
Ralph, s. [Jonathan, Jr. & Sarah], b. May 6, 1767; d. Nov. 22, 1767	2	59
Rebeckah, d. [Joseph & Rebeckah], b. Sept. 18, 1702	2	59
Rebeckah, d. Joseph & Rebeckah, b. Sept. 19, 1702	A	10
Rebeckah, m. John **CRANE**, Jan. 24, 1733/4	1	148
Rebeckah, d. Solomon & Mary, b. June 7, 1735	1	91
Rebeckah, w. [Dea. Joseph **HUNTINGTON**], d. Nov. 28, 1748, in the 83rd y. of her age	1	220
Rebeckah, w. [Dea. Joseph], d. Nov. 28, 1748, in the 83rd y. of her age	2	59
Robart Dennisson, s. Elisha & Elizabeth, b. Aug. 14, 1758	1	256
Roger, s. Jon[atha]n & Sarah, b. Dec. 3, 1757	2	9
Roger, m. Susannah **ELDERKIN**, Aug. 10, 1780	2	229
Roswell, m. Sarah **READ**, Oct. 29, 1777	2	214
Ruth, d. Thomas & Elizabeth, b. Aug. 8, 1699	A	9
Ruth, m. Ralph **WHEELOCK**, Jan. 8, 1707/8	1	27
Ruth, m. Sam[ue]ll **LINKON**, Aug. 22, 1723	1	70
Sabry, d. [Abner & Mary], b. Dec. 2, 1772	2	28
Sam[ue]ll, s. Nath[anie]ll & Mehetabel, b. July 5, 1731	1	74
Sam[ue]ll, Jr. , m. Jemima **DUNHAM**, Jan. 3, 1740	1	227
Sam[ue]ll, s. Jabez & Sarah, b. Oct. 19, 1742; d. Jan. 15, 1742/3	1	126
Sam[ue]l B., m. Lucy W. **YOUNG**, Feb. 24, 1829, by Rev. Dennis Platt	3	135
Sarah, d. Joseph & Rebeckah, b. May 2, 1705	A	10
Sarah, d. [Joseph & Rebeckah], b. May 27, 1705	2	59
Sarah, m. Thomas **BINGHAM**, Apr. 23, 1724	1	79

	Vol.	Page
HUNTINGTON, (cont.)		
Sarah, d. Jabez & Elizabeth, b. June 20, 1727	1	78
Sarah, m. Ebenezer **WRIGHT**, Mar. 28, 1728	1	124
Sarah, m. Jonathan **HUNTINGTON**, Jr., Oct. [ ], 1757	2	59
Sarah, d. [Jonathan, Jr. & Sarah], b. May 10, 1766; d. June 7, 1766	2	59
Sarah, d. [Jonathan, Jr. & Sarah], b. Oct. 26, 1768	2	59
Simon, s. [Jonathan, Jr. & Sarah], b. Apr. 15, 1762	2	59
Solomon, s. Joseph & Rebeckah, b. Feb. 6, 1699/1700	A	10
Solomon, s. [Joseph & Rebeckah], b. Feb. 6, 1700	2	59
Solomon, m. Mary **BUCKINGHAM**, Oct. 31, 1727	1	91
Solomon, s. Solomon & Mary, b. Nov. 24, 1728; d. Jan. 2, 1728/9	1	91
Solomon, s. Solomon & Mary, b. Oct 9, 1737	1	91
Solomon, d. Apr. 31, 1752	1	91
Solomon, m. Anne **DENNISON**, Mar. 28, 1762	2	75
Solomon, twin with Anna, s. Solomon & Anna, b. Apr. 7, 1770	2	75
Submit, d. [Hezekiah & Submit], b. Mar. 29, 1758; d. Oct. 18, 1759	2	70
Submit, d. [Hezekiah & Submit], b. Aug. 8, 1765	2	70
Susannah, d. Abner & Mary, b. Sept. 16, 1756	2	28
Sibbil, d. Jonathan & Elizabeth, b. June 30, 1740	1	134
Sibel, d. Jonathan & Elizabeth, d. Jan. 20, 1741/2	1	220
Sibel, d. Nath[anie]ll & Mehetable, b. Oct. 22, 1742/3	1	214
Sybel, d. [Eliphalet & Dinah], b. Feb. 8, 1766	2	78
Sibbel, d. [Hezekiah & Submit], b. Nov. 22, 1768	2	70
Sibbel, d. [Jonathan, Jr. & Sarah], b. Aug. 5, 1775, at Worthington; d. May 6, 1776	2	59
Temperance, d. Solomon & Mary, b. Oct. 6, 1739	1	91
Tryphena, d. Jabez & Elizabeth, b. Aug. 27, 1729	1	78
Wealthian, d. John & Ann, b. Jan. 6, 1757	2	23
Whitman, s. Abner & Mary, b. July 10, 1763	2	28
William, s. Simeon & Elizabeth, b. Aug. 20, 1745/6	1	206
William, m. Mary **CUTLER**, Feb. 15, 1770	2	162
William, s. [William & Mary], b. Dec. 6, 1770	2	162
William, m. Lucretia **HARRIS**, Nov. 27, 1823	3	14
Zeruiah, d. Solomon & Mary, b. Feb. 24, 1732/3	1	91
Zerviah, m. John **YOUNG**, Nov. 12, 1754	2	22
——, d. [John & Mary], b. Sept. 3, 1783; d. same day	2	23
HUNTLEY, Luther, m. Eunice **LINCOLN**, b. of Windham, Aug 19, 1833, by Stowell Lincoln, J.P.	3	188
HUNTROUS, Chester, Dr., m. Lucretia **LATHROP**, Mar. 10, 1825	3	121
HURD, John, m. Sarah **HANDY**, Sept. 16, 1725	1	65

	Vol.	Page
HURD, (cont.)		
Mary*, d. Zebulon & Judith, b. Jan. 14, 1723/4		
(*correction **"WEBB**, Mary Hurd" handwritten		
in margin of original manuscript)	1	65
Sarah, d. John & Sarah, b. June 15, 1726	1	65
HURLBUTT, HURLBURT, Abigail, d. Elijah & Abigail, b.		
Feb. 26, 1727/8	1	75
Abigail, m. David **YEOMAN**, Nov. 13, 1754	1	325
Alfred, s. [Elisha & Phebe], b. Dec. 1, 1756	1	272
Alfred, m. Lydia **BABCOCK**, Jan. 11, 1786	2	205
Ann, d. Elijah & Abigail, b. Apr. 14, 1730	1	75
Anna, d. [Elisha & Phebe], b. Aug. 13, 1764	1	272
Anne, m. James **FITCH**, May 23, 1763	2	91
Anne, d. [Lydia & Alfred], b. Dec. 6, 1786	2	205
C[h]loe, d. Elijah & Abigail, b. June 20, 1743	1	82
C[h]loe, d. Elijah & Abigail, b. June 20, 1743	1	196
Elijah, m. Abigail **BACKUS**, Aug. 18, 1725	1	75
Elijah, s. Elijah & Abigail, b. Mar. 3, 1731/2	1	75
Elisha, s. Elijah & Abigail, b. June 13, 1726	1	75
Elisha, m. Mary **SMITH**, Oct. 18, 1747	1	272
Elisha, m. Phebe **CARTER**, May 3, 1750	1	272
Elisha, m. Phebe **CARTER**, May [ ], 1750	1	302
Elisha, d. Aug. 3, 1771	1	272
Enoch, s. Elisha & Phebe, b. Nov. 21, 1754	1	272
Jerusha, d. Elijah & Abigail, b. Aug. 8, 1741	1	82
Jerusha, d. Elijah & Abigail, b. Aug. 8, 1741	1	196
Lydia, d. Elisha & Phebe, b. Feb. 1, 1750/51	1	272
Lydia, d. Elisha & Phebe, b. Feb. 1, 1750/51	1	302
Martha, d. Elisha & Phebe, b. Jan. 6, 1753	1	272
Martha, m. Jonathan **CAREY**, Sept. 21, 1775	2	145
Mary, d. Elijah & Abigail, b. Nov. 14, 1737	1	75
Mary, m. Phinehas **CARY**, Feb. 26, 1769	2	151
Mary Smith, [d. Elisha &] Mary, b. Sept. 4, 1748;		
d. Sept. 23, 1748	1	272
Nathaniel, s. Elijah & Abigail, b. Sept. 16,		
1739	1	196
Phebe, d. [Elisha & Phebe], b. Nov. 14, 1759	1	272
Phebe, m. Capt. Thomas **FANNING**, Jan. 16, 1772	2	181
Prudence, s. Elijah & Abigail, b. Sept. 3, 1734	1	75
Tabitha, of Windham, m. Samuel **MEADE**, of Geneva,		
N.Y., Oct. 18, 1836, by Rev. Edward Harris	3	179
Thomas, s. [Elisha & Phebe], b. May 24, 1762	1	272
Winthrop, s. [Elisha & Phebe], b. Dec. 24, 1769	1	272
HUTCHINS, HUCHENS, George, m. Mary **NEFF**, Oct. 22, 1826,		
by Abner Robinson, J.P.	3	129
Lucy, housekeeper, black, June 1, 1849, ae. 21	4	154
Mary, of Windham, m. Henry M. **CONANT**, of Hampton,		
Sept. 28, 1845, by John Crocker, Willimantic	3	223

	Vol.	Page
HUTCHINS, HUCHENS, (cont)		
Sally, of Windham, m. Gilbert **SIMON**, of Coventry,		
July 10, 1831, by John Baldwin, J P	3	154
Tryphenia C., of Windham, m. Elijah M. **NICHOLS**,		
of Mansfield, Dec. 2, 1834, by Rev L H		
Corson	3	172
HUTCHISON, Eleazer, s Joseph & Ruth, b. Feb 12, 1744/5	1	274
Elisha, s. Joseph & Ruth, b. Aug. 22, 1746	1	274
Eunice, m. Thomas **DENISON**, Dec. 4, 1766	2	163
Joseph, s. Sam[ue]ll & Rachel, b. Feb. 25, 1719/20	1	13
Joseph, m Ruth **READ**, Nov 11, 1742	1	274
Rachel, d. Joseph & Ruth, b. Aug. 15, 1749	1	274
Rachel, [w. Sam[ue]ll], d. May 6, 1750	1	13
Sam[ue]ll, m. Rachel **ALLYN**, June 14, 1715	1	13
Sam[ue]ll, s Sam[ue]ll & Rachel, b Apr 18, 1718	1	13
Sarah, d. Sam[ue]ll & Rachel, b. May 12, 1716	1	13
Sarah, m. John **CRANE**, Nov. 11, 1742	1	173
HYDE, HIDE, Adaline, of Windham, m. Ichabod Perry **LEWIS**,		
of Exeter, R I , Oct 3, 1831, by Joel W White,		
J.P.	3	154
Almira, of Franklin, m Samuel **MANNING**, of Lebanon,		
June 20, 1838, by Rev. John E. Tyler	3	186
Asahel, s [Ichabod & Abigail], b Apr 18, 1775	2	177
Benjamin, m. Anna **ELDRIDGE**, Jan. 30, 1766	2	124
Caleb, s. Samuell & Elizabeth, b. Apr. 9, 1699	A	22
Daniel, s. Samuell & Elizabeth, b. Aug. 16, 1694	A	22
Gustavus Stoughton, s. Mat[t]h[ew] & Roxalania, b		
Sept. 27, 1758; d. Nov. 17, 1759	2	12
Ichabod, m Abigail **BURNAM**, Jan 24, 1771	2	177
Joseph, of Lebanon, m. Julia **SMITH**, of Windham, Sept.		
12, 1825, by Rev C B Everest	3	115
Joshua, s. [Ichabod & Abigail], b. Oct. 6, 1771	2	177
Mary, m Oliver **DURKEE**, June 21, 1764	2	104
Matthew, m. Roxalania **STOUGHTON**, June 15, 1756	2	12
Pamela, d [Ichabod & Abigail], b July 4, 1773	2	177
Samuel, s Samuell & Elizabeth, b. Sept. 10, 1691	A	22
Samuel, s [Benjamin & Anna], b Dec 25, 1766	2	124
Sarah, d. Samuell & Elizabeth, b. Dec. 20, 1696	A	22
W[illia]m A., s. W[illia]m H., operative, ae 40, of		
Willimantic, b. Nov. 10, 1850	4	12
IDE, Emily E , d. Dec 2, [1849], ae. 17	4	155
Mary, of Griswold, Conn., m. Warren **HUMES**, of Burrill-		
ville, R.I., July 2, 1846, by Rev John E Tyler	3	229
IDEY, S. E., ae. 21, m. W[illia]m **COBBES**, operative, ae. 19,		
July 9, 1848	4	111
INGALLS, Asa, s. [Peter & Sarah], b. Apr. 30, 1776	2	205
Malinda, of Windham, m Zapparah S **LYON**, of Union,		
Nov. 27, 1842, by Rev. Alfred Burnham	3	206

	Vol.	Page
INGALLS, (cont.)		
Peter, m. Sarah **ASHLEY**, Apr. 20, 1775	2	205
Sarah, d. [Peter & Sarah], b. Dec. 15, 1777	2	205
INGERSOLL, Mary, m. Amos **UTLEY**, Oct. 22, 1777	2	44
INGHAM, Matilda, of Windham, m. Ariel **SPARKS**, of Vernon,		
Jan. 15, 1829, by Rev. Dennis Platt	3	134
INGRAHAM, Catharine, m. Jonathan **JENNINGS**, June 3, 1804	3	56
Ellen B., d. Jehiel, miller, of Willimantic, b.		
May 13, [1850]	4	10
Lareances, of Lebanon, m. Eliphalet **MANNING**, of		
Windham, Nov. 23, 1846, by Elder Henry Greenslit	3	232
Nathan, s. Joseph & Mary, b. Feb. 24, 1723/4	1	52
INGRAM, Julia Ann, m. John **BINGHAM**, 2d, July 4, 1830, by		
Rev. Chester Tilden, Willimantic	3	147
Lucius, of Columbia, m. Jerusha **BATES**, of Windham,		
Aug. 27, 1843, by Rev. Henry Greenslit	3	211
JACKSON, Albert, black, b. Chapin, res. Willimantic, d.		
May 1, 1851, ae. 6 m.	4	157
Bennett, black, b. Lebanon, res. Windham, d. May		
[ ], 1848, ae. 17	4	151
Sarah, m. Elijah **BINGHAM**, July 19, 1752	1	154
JACOBS, Aboiza, b. Mansfield, res. Willimantic, d. July		
20, [1849], ae. 34	4	153
Elizabeth, m. Samuel **LINKHORN**, June 2, 1692	1	31
Elizabeth, m. Samuel **LINKON**, June 20, 1692	A	24
George W., of Mansfield, m. Amelia **WILBUR**, of Willi-		
mantic, Mar. 27, 1836, by Rev. Moseley Dwight,		
Willimantic	3	177
Jerusha, m. Stephen **BROWN**, Jr., Dec. 12, 1790	3	6
Julia M., d. July 18, [1849], ae. 9	4	155
L.W., merchant, ae. 32, m. 2d w. Elizabeth **HATCH**, ae.		
21, May 10, [1850], by Rev. J. Cady	4	116
Lafayette, weaver, ae. 22, b. Mansfield, res. Willi-		
mantic, m. Pattie **JORDAN**, operative, ae. 17, b.		
Plainfield, res. Willimantic, Dec. 29, 1850, by		
Rev. J. Cady	4	117
Luther A., m Ann Clarissa **WEBB**, b of Willimantic,		
Mar. 30, 1846, by John Cooper	3	228
Mary, m. Stephen **BROWN**, Nov. [ ], 1734	1	135
Seth, of Boston, Mass., m. Nancy **HOWE**, of Windham,		
Apr. 26, 1829, by John Baldwin, J.P	3	135
Susannah, m. Jonathan **BADCO[C]K**, Sept. 16, 1741	1	125
William W., of Mansfield, m. Sophronia **NEWCOMB**, of		
Columbia, Mar. 30, 1830, at her mother's, in		
Windham, by Henry Brown	3	141
JAGGER, Amey, m. John **CROSS**, Nov. 26, 1818	3	53
Silas, m. Delight A. **BILL**, b. of Windham, Aug. 27,		
1837, by Rev. Silas Leonard	3	183

	Vol.	Page
JAMES, Betsey M., m. Isaac T **POTTER**, Oct 21, 1833, by		
Rev. Alva Gregory, Willimantic	3	166
Emily, m. Enoch M. **DANIELS**, June 20, 1830, by Rev.		
Chester Tilden, Willimantic	3	146
JEAROM, Timothy, s. Timothy & Abigail, b. Oct. 17, 1713	1	14
Zerubbabel, s. Timothy & Abigail, b. Apr. 3, 1715	1	14
JENNER, Elias B., m. Laura **YOUNG**, Jan. 9, 1833, by Rev.		
Roger Bingham	3	163
Elias B., m. Amy **PAGE**, Aug. 30, 1845, by Andrew		
Sharp	3	222
Mary E., m. Samuel B. **GAGER**, b. of Windham (Scotland		
Society) Mar. 21, 1836, by Rev. Ben[a]jah Cook,		
Jr., at Willimantic Falls	3	177
Jenner, Nancy S., m. Nelson H. **AVERY**, b. of Willimantic		
Village, June 25, 1837, by Rev. B. Cook, Jr.	3	182
JENNINGS, GINNINGS, GENNINGS, GININGS, GENINGS,		
JENNING, Abel, s. Ebenezer & Jemima, b. Mar. 29,		
1728	1	54
Abel, s. Ebenezer & Jemima, d Jan. [ ], 1747, at		
Cape Breton	1	164
Abi, d. [Ebenezer & Susannah], b. Sept. 6, 1792	2	213
Abigail, m. Nathaniel **HOUEY**, Nov. 25, 1712	1	14
Abigail, d. Jonathan & Susannah, b. Jan. 14, 1693	A	5
Abigail, d. Joseph, Jr. & Sarah, b. Nov. 13, 1736	1	169
Agrippa Anna, d. [John, Jr. & Anna], b. Jan. 13, 1772	2	46
Alice, d. Manoah, b. Aug. 20, 1772	2	198
Amelia, m. Jonathan **SMITH**, Oct 28, 1832, by Rev.		
Roger Bingham	3	162
Ann, d. Ebenezer & Martha, b. Sept. 15, 1740	1	206
Ann, w. John, Jr., d. Aug. 20, 1778	2	46
Anna, d. Joseph, Sr. & Hannah, b. Aug. 21, 1735	1	143
Anna, m. Gideon **SIMONDS**, [ ]	2	78
Asenath, m. John **HUNT**, Jr., Oct. 21, 1792	3	45
Bethiah, d. Ebenezer & Mary, b. Mar. 11, 1720	1	39a
Bethiah, m. Daniel **WARNER**, Dec. 6, 1739	1	199
David, s. Jonathan & Susannah, b. Feb. 25, 1699	A	6
David, m. Elizabeth **MILLAND**, Jan. 4, 1720/21	1	37
David, s. David & Elizabeth, b. Jan. 27, 1725/6;		
d. Jan. 27, 1725/6	1	64
Deborah, d. Joseph & Sarah, b. Feb. 20, 1731/2	1	59
Deborah, m. David **CANADA**, Jan. 10, 1749/50	1	301
Ebennezer, s. Jonathan & Susannah, b. Feb. 18, 1691	A	5
Ebenezer, m. Mary **BIDLOCK**, Dec. 16, 1713	1	39a
Ebenezer, s. Ebenezer & Mary, b. June 14, 1715	1	39a
Ebenezer, m. Jemima **BINGHAM**, Aug. 10, 1726	1	54
Ebenezer, m. Martha **MUNSON**, Oct. 30, 1737	1	54
Ebenezer, s. [Capt. Joseph & Tameezen], b. Sept.		
14, 1776	2	194

	Vol.	Page

JENNINGS, GINNINGS, GENNINGS, GININGS, GENINGS,
  JENNING, (cont.)

Mary, m. Richard **ABBE**, Nov. 16, 1703	1	227
Mary, d. Ebenezer & Mary, b. Nov. 24, 1717	1	39a
Mary, d. Joseph & Sarah, b. Oct. 24, 1722/3	1	59
Mary, w. Ebenezer, d. Feb. 22, 1735* (*correction		
the 3 in 1735 is crossed out and 1725 is hand-		
written at the end of the entry in the original		
manuscript)	1	39a
Mary, m. Thomas **SNELL**, Mar. 9, 1736/7	1	159
Mary, d. Joseph, Jr. & Sarah, b. Nov. 7, 1738; d.*		
Aug. 13, 1753, in the 11th y. of her age		
(*arrow drawn in original manuscript concludes		
that the entire death entry for this Mary belongs		
to the next Mary)	1	169
Mary, d. Joseph, 3rd & Sarah, b. Aug. 24, 1742	1	169
Mary, m. Robert **COBURN**, Jr., Nov. 7, 1749	1	297
Mary Ann, of Windham, m. Charles **SQUIRES**, of Ashford,		
Sept. 22, 1839, by Elder Henry Greenslit	3	190
Milton, s. [Jonathan & Mindwell], b. Feb. 3, 1795	2	245
Nathan, s. Ebenezer & Jemima, b. Feb. 11, 1729/30	1	54
Nathan, s. Ebenezer & Jemima, d. Feb. 29, 1751	1	164
Nathan Tileston, s. [Jonathan & Mindwell], b. July		
10, 1786	2	245
Ne[h]amiah, s. Joseph, Sr. & Hannah, b. Dec. 11,		
1740	1	143
Nelson, s. [Jonathan & Mindwell], b. July 25, 1807	2	245
Phebe, m. Samuel **KINGSBURY**, Feb. 10, 1778	2	242
Phebe, m. Jehiel **SPAFFORD**, Nov. 29, 1781	2	241
Ransford, s. [Ebenezer & Abi], b. Apr. 9, 1789	2	213
Robert, s. Joseph & Sarah, b. July 11, 1719	1	47
Royal, s. [Jonathan & Mindwell], b. Mar. 3, 1791	2	245
Royal, m. Desire **DAVIS**, May 27, 1816	3	89
Royal Davis, s. [Royal & Desire], b. Nov. 29, 1817	3	89
Samuel, s. [Joseph, Jr. & Ruth, Jr.], b. Apr. 4,		
1789	2	69
Sarah, d. Joseph & Sarah, b. Jan. 1, 1722	1	47
Sarah, d. Joseph, 3rd, & Sarah, b. July 17, 1746; d.		
Aug. 10, 1753, ae. 8 y.	1	169
Sarah, d. Joseph, Jr. & Sarah, b. May 16, 1755	1	222
Sarah, d. [John, Jr. & Anna], b. July 20, 1759	2	46
Sarah, m. Manning **FRANCIS**, Apr. 1, 1772	2	184
Sarah, w. Capt. Joseph, d. Oct. 8, 1772, in the 57th		
y. of her age	1	222
Sarah, of Windham, m. David **WHEELER**, of Plainfield,		
Apr. 9, 1778	2	203
Sibel, d. Joseph, Jr. & Sarah, b. Feb. 8, 1740/41; d.		
Nov. [ ], 1741	1	169

	Vol.	Page

JENNINGS, GINNINGS, GENNINGS, GININGS, GENINGS, JENNING, (cont.)

Sibel, d. Joseph & Sarah, b. July 14, 1752 — 1 — 169

Silas, s. Ebenezer & Mary, b. June 20, 1725; d.
June 20, 1725 — 1 — 54

Simon, s. Ebenezer & Jemima, b. May 16, 1734; d.
May 17, 1734 — 1 — 54

Susan, m. Worthington **LADD**, May 8, 1836, by
Samuel Perkins, J.P. — 3 — 178

Susannah, w. Jonathan, d. Nov. 28, 1700 — A — 6

Susannah, d. Joseph & Sarah, b. Nov. 28, 1708 — 1 — 47

Sybil, see under Sibel

Tamazene, d. [Capt. Joseph & Tameezen], b. Apr. 22,
1778 — 2 — 194

Tamezen, w. Capt. Joseph, d. May 26, 1778 — 2 — 194

Zebulon, m. Abigail **DEANS**, Nov. 16, 1772 — 2 — 101

Zeruiah, d. David & Elizabeth, b. July 11, 1735 — 1 — 64

JEPSON, JAPSON, Anson, of Springfield, Mass., m. Eliza
HEB[B]ARD, of Windham, Mar. 11, 1834, by Rev.
Alva Gregory — 3 — 168

Eliza, m. Horace **SMITH**, b. of Springfield, Mass.,
Mar. 12, 1838, by Rev. John E. Tyler — 3 — 185

Mary Ann, b. England, res. Willimantic, d. May 20,
1860, ae. 23 — 4 — 159-0

JEWELL, Elizabeth, d. Benj[ami]n & Hannah, b. Oct. 17,
1753 — 1 — 137

Joseph Millan, s. Benj[ami]n & Hannah, b. Feb. 7,
1763 — 1 — 137

Lucy, d. Benj[amin] & Hannah, b. May 26, 1760 — 1 — 137

Sam[ue]ll, s. Benja[mi]n & Hannah, b. Sept. 20, 1754 — 1 — 137

Thomas, s. Benj[amin] & Hannah, b. Mar. 2, 1757 — 1 — 137

JEWETT, Elizabeth, d. [Thomas & Prudence], b. Sept. 29,
1785 — 2 — 204

Thomas, m. Prudence **RUDE**, Feb. 3, 1785 — 2 — 204

JILLSON, Asa, manufacturer, b. Cumberland, res. Windham,
d. Apr. 7, 1848, ae. 64 — 4 — 151

Charles, s. Asa W., manufacturer, ae. 25, & Hannah E.,
ae. 25, of Willimantic, b. [   ], 1848 — 4 — 1

El[i]za Ann, m. Ahab **WILKINSON**, b. of Windham, June
[ ], 1833, by Rev. John Storrs — 3 — 167

Eunice H., of Pelham, Mass., m. Newton **FITCH**, Apr. 20,
1834, by Rev. Jesse Fisher — 3 — 169

John S., of Willimantic, m. Lydia K. **STONE**, of Guil-
ford, Nov. 23, 1834, by Rev. Philo Judson, at
Willimantic — 3 — 171

Sally Ann, ae. 36, m. H.A. **GEER**, farmer, ae. 37, Nov
22, 1848, by Rev. J.R. Arnold — 4 — 113

Thomas, s. Asa W., manufacturer, ae. 27, b. Nov. 5,

	Vol.	Page
JILLSON, (cont.)		
[1849]	4	9
William S., Capt., m. Caroline **CURTIS**, b. of		
Windham, Dec. 26, 1831, by Rev. R.T. Crampton	3	157
JOHNSON, Abigail, d. Caleb & Lydia, b. Mar. 11, 1733/4	1	106
Alice, d. Caleb & Lydia, b. Dec. 27, 1730	1	106
Anne, w. Joseph, d. June 19, 1777	2	25
Avis, m. William **TRIM**, Mar. 20, 1832, by Rev. Alva		
Gregory, Willimantic	3	158
Bela, s. [Joseph & Mehitable], b. Feb. 17, 1786	2	25
Betsey, m. Joseph D. **FITCH**, Oct. 25, 1807	3	59
Caleb, Jr., m. Esther **BUGBEE**, Feb. 6, 1745/6	1	258
Charles C., of Franklin, m. Lucy A. **FLINT**, of		
Windham, Mar. 22, 1847, by Rev. J.E. Tyler	3	234
Cha[rle]s L., s. Cha[rle]s, farmer, & Lucy, ae. 25,		
b. Jan. 13, 1851	4	13
Dan, s. [Joseph & Mehitable], b. July 9, 1789; d		
July 5, 1790	2	25
Dan, s. [Joseph & Mehitable], b. Apr. 16, 1791	2	25
Earl W., s. Charles, farmer, ae. 24, & Lucy Ann,		
ae. 26, b. Aug. 17, 1849	4	9
Elizabeth, m. Thomas **LINKION**, Jr., May 17, 1769	2	155
Elizabeth, d. [Joseph & Anne], b. Apr. 21, 1776; d.		
June 11, 1777	2	25
Emily, d. [Levi & Anne], b. Feb. 21, 1811	3	85
Emily, m. John Abijah **PERKINS**, b. of Windham, Mar.		
26, 1834, by L.S. Corson, Rector	3	170
Esther, d. Caleb & Esther, b. Jan. 10, 1746/7	1	258
George Clinton, s. [Levi & Anne], b. Feb. 3, 1813	3	85
Guy, s. [Joseph & Mehitable], b. Feb. 23, 1799	2	25
Harry, s. [Joseph & Mehitable], b. July 5, 1793	2	25
Isaac, s. Caleb & Lydia, b. Dec. 9, 1735	1	106
James, s. Levi, b. Aug. 21, 1768	2	143
James Monroe, [s. Levi & Anne], b. [ ]	3	85
Joseph, m. Anne **WARNER**, June 21, 1775	2	25
Joseph, m. Mehitable **BARROWS**, June 19, 1783	2	25
Levi, m. Anne **MARTIN**, Sept. 19, 1804	3	85
Lydia, m. John **FRAME**, Oct. 19, 1746	1	265
Marcy, d. Caleb & Esther, b. Feb. 15, 1747/8	1	258
Mary, m. David **THOMAS**, Oct. 10, 1739	1	199
Mary, m. John Carey **GEER**, Sept [ ], 1815	3	81
Mehitable, m. Joseph **SPARKS**, Apr. 29, 1747	1	275
Olive, d. [Levi & Anne], b. Nov. 16, 1806	3	85
Olive, m. Elisha G. **HAMMOND**, Nov. 25, 1830, by Rev.		
Roger Bingham	3	150
Pretsy, d. [Joseph & Mehitable], b. Jan. 21, 1784	2	25
Rhoda, m. Benjamin **LINKON**, Nov. 25, 1773	2	185
Rosannah, d. Owen, dyer, ae. 43, & Catharine, ae. 33,		

	Vol.	Page
JOHNSON, (cont.)		
of Willimantic, b. Jan. 7, [1848]	4	5
Sally, d. [Levi & Anne], b. Dec. 3, 1808	3	85
Sarah, d. Caleb & Lydia, b. July 29, 1729	1	106
Sarah, of Windham, m. Edward **SPAULDING**, of Brooklyn,		
May 5, 1835, by Rev. L.H. Corson	3	173
Sarah, d. Owen, dyer, ae. 40, & Parthenia, ae. 37,		
b. July 20, 1851	4	12
Stephen, s. Caleb & Lydia, b. Dec. 26, 1737	1	106
William, s. Caleb & Lydia, b. Aug. 20, 1732	1	106
William Martin, s. [Levi & Anne], b. Apr. 18, 1805	3	85
JONES, Charlotte, d. [John & Diadama], b. Feb. 1, 1792	2	47
Christian, d. [John & Diadama], b. Apr. 20, 1780	2	47
George, s. [John & Diadama], b. Dec. 4, 1794	2	47
James s., [John & Diadama], b. May 8, 1782, in		
Stonington; d. May 26, 1786	2	47
John, m. Diadama **READ**, Dec. 19, 1778	2	47
John, s. [John & Diadama], b. July 21, 1789	2	47
Lucy, m. Nehemiah **RIPLEY**, Aug. 13, 1815	2	57
Lucy F., of Windham, m. Lucius **CADY**, of Canterbury,		
Apr. 3, 1834, by Rev. Jesse Fisher	3	169
Mary, m. Rufus **FFLINT**, Mar. 13, 1739/40	1	211
Nancy, d. [John & Diadama], b. May 2, 1784, in		
Coventry	2	47
Nancy had child Mary **ELLIOTT**, b. Jan. 12, 1806	3	73
Polly, d. [John & Diadama], b. Jan. 13, 1787	2	47
Sarah, d. July 9, 1850, ae. 21	4	155
JORDAN, Charles, s. Lyman, laborer, ae. 30, & Susan, ae.		
30, b. June 14, 1848	4	2
Elisha, painter, ae. 18, b. Brooklyn, res. Rockville,		
R.I., m. Nancy **WHITE**, operative, ae. 21, b.		
Haddam, res. Rockville, R.I., Nov. 21, 1850, by		
Rev. J. Cady	4	117
Emeline, of Willimantic, m. Geo[rge] W. **LYMAN**, of		
Norwich, [ ], by Rev. John Cooper	3	223
Gertrude, b. Windham, res. Willimantic, d. Sept. 11,		
1859, ae. under 1 y.	4	159-0
Julia Ann, twin with Julius, d. Lyman, stonemason,		
ae. 33, & Julia Ann, ae. 33, of Willimantic, b.		
Nov. 11, 1850	4	12
Julius, twin with Julia Ann, s. Lyman, stonemason,		
ae. 33, & Julia Ann, ae. 33, of Willimantic, b.		
Nov. 11, 1850	4	12
Lyman, m. Louisa **KENYON**, b. of Willimantic, Windham,		
Oct. 11, 1835, by Rev. Benajah Cook, Jr.	3	174
Nancy Ann, m. Henry **BOND**, b. of Windham, July 12, 1846,		
by Rev. John Cooper, Willimantic	3	229
Pattie, operative, ae. 17, b. Plainfield, res. Willi-		

	Vol	Page
JORDAN, (cont)		
mantic, m Lafayette **JACOBS**, weaver, ae. 22, b.		
Mansfield, res Willimantic, Dec 29, 1850, by		
Rev. J Cady	4	117
JUDD, John F , m. Olive **FULLER**, Sept 6, 1825, by Elisha		
Frink, Elder	3	71
JUDGE, W[illia]m, laborer, ae 26, b. Ireland, res Willi-		
mantic, m. Kate **CURRY**, operative, ae. 23, b.		
Ireland, res Willimantic, July 9, 1851, by Rev		
Smith	4	117
KARTWRIGHT, [see under **CARTWRIGHT**]		
KASSON, Olive, m. Elijah **BAKER**, Nov. 4, 1779	3	47
KEACH, Benjamin, of Mansfield, m Tryphosa **COBURN**, of		
Windham, Feb. 24, 1822, by Elder Elias Sharp	3	66
KEATS, John, of Windham, d July 16, 1697	A	8
KEENE, Cha[rle]s F., s. H.F., mason, b. Dec. 9, 1850	4	13
KEIGWIN, KEGWIN, Cornelia, ae 20, of Windham, m Edwin C		
MAHONEY, carpenter, ae. 27, b. Providence, Dec.		
30, [1849], by Rev. J M. Phillips	4	114
Mary J., d. John G., ae. 24, b. May 1, [1849]	4	6
KEIRER, Henry H , of Hampton, m Abby **DAVIS**, of Willimantic,		
Jan. 22, 1837, by Rev. P. Judson, at Willimantic	3	181
KELLEY, Henry, m. Caroline **SLY**, Mar 21, 1833, by Rev.		
Alva Gregory	3	164
Simeon C., m. Caroline U **VERGISON**, b of Willi-		
mantic, Feb. 20, 1837, by Rev. Philo Judson, at		
Willimantic	3	182
KEMPTON, Phebe, ae. 19, m. [ ] **GRAVES**, farmer, ae.		
23, May [1850], by Rev. Calhoun	4	115
KENNEDY, KENNADY, KENEDY, Algernon Sidney, d. Feb 18,		
1800, at Port Antonio, Jamaica	2	60
Harriet, d. July 23, 1783	2	60
James, s. [Samuel & Amelia], b Aug 31, 1773; d Jan.		
11, 1774	2	180
John, s. [Jonathan & Theodore], b. July 19, 1771	2	132
Jonathan, m. Theodore **FLINT**, Dec. 10, 1767	2	132
Meriam, w Isaac, d June 5, 1799	2	60
Patrick, s. [Jonathan & Theodore], b. Apr. 18, 1769	2	132
Polly, d. [Samuel & Amelia], b Jan 22, 1777	2	180
Samuel, m Amelia **LARRABEE**, Jan. 7, 1773	2	180
Thomas, s [Samuel & Amelia], b Nov 22, 1774	2	180
——, d. Sept. 15, 1847, ae. 2 m.	4	151
KENNEY, [see also **KINNE**], Huntington F , m Delia C. **FITCH**,		
b. of Windham, Nov. 21, 1843, by Rev. Giles H.		
Desham	3	212
Sarah A., ae. 24, m. Dr. Henry **GRAY**, physician, ae.		
24, Oct 4, 1849, by Rev J E Tyler	4	114
KENYON, Amelia, ae. 16, m. Frederick **HARVEY**, laborer, ae.		

	Vol.	Page

KENYON, (cont.)

24, b. N.Y., res. Windham, Feb. 6, 1848, by
Daniel Dorchester — 4 111

Betsey O.C., m. Freeman **SMALL**, Feb. 6, 1844, by
Rev. Andrew Sharp — 3 213

Caroline, d. Aug. 4, 1850, ae. 9 — 4 157

Celia L., m. Anson A. **AVERY**, b of Willimantic, May
8, 1837, by Philo Judson, at Willimantic — 3 182

Emyline, ae. 22, b. Franklin, res. Columbia, m
Joseph **TRACY**, machinist, ae. 34, of Fanklin,
May 8, 1848, by Rev John Tyler — 4 111

Henry, m. Nancy **BACKUS**, Aug. 3, 1840, by Rev. John
B. Guilde, Willimantic — 3 196

Henry, d. Nov. 25, [1849], ae. 1 — 4 155

Lewis H., s. Henry, operative, ae. 28, b. Nov. 14,
[1848] — 4 6

Louisa, m. Lyman **JORDAN**, b. of Willimantic, Windham,
Oct. 11, 1835, by Rev. Benajah Cook, Jr. — 3 174

Lucy, d. Apr. 3, [1850], ae. 19 — 4 155

Martha R. (?)*, carpenter, ae. 20, b. Griswold,
res. Norwich, m Lydia **STETSON**, operative, ae.
21, b. Lisbon, res. Norwich, Jan. 5, 1851, by
Elder Bromley (*Perhaps Matthew?) — 4 117

W[illia]m F., farmer, b. Windham, res. Chaplin, m.
Lucy A. **WEBSTER**, July 4, 1848, by James M.
Phelps — 4 112

KIBBEE, Elizabeth, [w. John], d. Nov. 5, 1731 — 1 106

John, s. John & Elizabeth, b. Mar. 9, 1728/9; d. Aug.
23, 1730, ae. 1 y. 5 m. — 1 106

John, m. Hannah **LOMBARD**, Mar. 21, 1732/3 — 1 106

KIDDER, Luther, m Phebe **CHURCH**, Sept. 25, 1789 — 2 51

Phebe, d. [Luther & Phebe], b. Feb. 23, 1790 — 2 51

Rachel Joanna, d. [Luther & Phebe], b. Oct 15, 1791 — 2 51

KIES, [see under **KYES**]

KILLEY, Mary, m. Delauna **MILLARD**, Mar. 29, 1818 — 3 87

KILLIAM, Sam[ue]ll, m. Elizabeth **ROSE**, Nov. 11, 1714 — 1 4

KIMBALL, **KIMBAL**, Abigail, d. [Richard & Abigail], b. Sept.
27, 1761 — 1 301

Andrew, m. Eliabeth **KIMBALL**, Sept. 19, 1749 — 1 307

Andrew, s. [Andrew & Elizabeth], b. Dec. 14, 1750 — 1 307

Anna, d. [Peletiah & Mary], b. Dec. 25, 1765 — 2 97

Anne, d. [Sam[ue]ll & Ann], b Nov. 9, 1758 — 1 324

Asael, s. [Peletiah & Mary], b. Aug. 11, 1775 — 2 97

Caroline, m. Sumner **LINCOLN**, Oct. 16, 1842, by Rev.
Alfred Burnham — 3 205

Charles, s. Sam[ue]ll & Ann, b. Feb. 25, 1755 — 1 324

Ebenezer, s. [Richard & Abigail], b. June 24, 1771 — 1 301

Elijah, s. Richard & Abigail, b. Sept. 19, 1754 — 1 301

	Vol.	Page

KIMBALL, KIMBAL, (cont.)

	Vol.	Page
Elijah, of Windham, m. Deliverance **BABCOCK**, of Richmond, Mar. 8, 1780	2	233
Elijah, s. [Elijah & Deliverance], b. Jan. 14, 1781	2	233
Elizabeth, m. Andrew **KIMBALL**, Sept. 19, 1749	1	307
Ellen, tailoress, b. Chester, res. Windham, d. Jan. 10, 1848, ae. 25	4	151
Enoch, s. [Richard & Abigail], b. Dec. 20, 1765	1	301
Eugene, s. Albert, farmer, ae. 40, & Melissa, ae. 36, b. Aug. 13, 1847	4	4
Eunice, d. [Richard & Abigail], b. Nov. 30, 1756	1	301
Irena, d. [Peletiah & Mary], b. Mar. 2, 1770; d. Nov. 16, 1775	2	97
Irena, d. [Peletiah & Mary], b. Nov. 22, 1777	2	97
Irena, m. Joseph **MEACHAM**, Jan. 1, 1809	3	13
James, s. [Peletiah & Mary], b. Feb. 15, 1772	2	97
Jedediah, s. [Andrew & Elizabeth], b Dec. 1, 1749	1	307
Jesse, s. [Richard & Abigail], b. Feb 5, 1759	1	301
Joanne, m. Othniel **LUCE**, Feb. 16, 1786	2	176
Lucy, m. Asher **FLINT**, Sept. 14, 1755	1	314
Lucy, d. [Peletiah & Mary], b. Dec. 25, 1774; d. Aug. 3, 1775	2	97
Lucy, d. [Peletiah & Mary], b. Feb. 4, 1780	2	97
Lydia, d. [Richard & Abigail], b. Aug. 6, 1763	1	301
Mary, d. Richard & [Abigail], b. Nov. 10, 1752	1	301
Mary, of Preston, m. Oliver **PARRISH**, of Windham, Dec. 22, 1756	2	34
Maryann, d. [Peletiah & Mary], b. May 10, 1768	2	97
Mary L., of Windham, m. Lyman **HEBBARD**, of Canterbury, Oct. 30, 1831, by Rev. Jesse Fisher	3	158
Peletiah, m. Mary **CROWELL**, Dec. 13, 1763	2	97
Peletiah, s. [Peletiah & Mary], b. Sept. 12, 1766	2	97
Richard, Jr., m. Abigail **HUNTINGTON**, Nov. 7, 1750	1	301
Richard, s. [Richard & Abigail], b. July 16, 1768	1	301
Samuel, m. Ann **MUDGE**, Apr. 18, 1754	1	324
Samuel, s. [Sam[ue]ll & Ann], b. Feb. 1, 1761	1	324
Sarah, m. Samuell **ROBINSON**, Jan. 2, 1748/9	1	285
Sarah, m. Daniel **STOUGHTON**, June 2, 1752	1	224
Sarah, d. [Andrew & Elizabeth], b. Mar. 31, 1753	1	307
Sarah, d. [Sam[ue]ll & Ann], b. Nov. 9, 1756	1	324
Sarah, mother of Peletiah, d. July 3, 1788	2	97
Stephen H., m. Lucy **ALLEN**, b. of Willimantic, Oct. 10, 1836, by Rev. Philo Judson, at Willimantic	3	179
——, child of Gurdon, shop-keeper, ae. 28, & [ ], ae. 23, b. July 6, 1848	4	2
——, child of Gurdon, laborer, ae. 42, of Willimantic, b. Jan. 28, [1850]	4	10

	Vol.	Page
KIMPTON, Caroline, of Willimantic, m. Alfred **LINCOLN**, of Coventry, Sept. 22, 1834, by Rev. Philo Judson	3	170
KINDEL, KINDALL, Abiga[i]l, d. David & Abiga[i]l, b. Oct. 21, 1742	1	249
Alice, d. David & Abigail, b. Jan. 18, 1746/7	1	249
David, m. Abigail **HOLT**, Nov. 5, 1741	1	249
David, s. David & Abiga[i]l, b. Nov. 13, 1744	1	249
KING, Elizabeth, w. [Walter], d. [ ], at Utica, N.Y.	3	24
Eunice W., of Windham, m. Daniel T. **RAMSDELL**, of Lyon, Mass., Dec. 29, 1839, by Reuben Ransom	3	191
Sarah, of Windham, m. William E. **TINCKOM**, of Windham, Oct. 20, 1833, by Rev. Alva Gregory, Willimantic	3	166
Walter, of Utica, N.Y., m. Elizabeth **CLARK**, d. Jabez, Nov. 13, 1810	3	24
KINGSBURY, KINGSBERY, [see also **KINGSLEY**], Abigail, d. David & Ruth, b. June 26, 1724	1	57
Abigail, d. Jonathan & Abigail, b. Mar. 17, 1742	1	181
Abigail, d. [Jonathan & Abigail], b. Mar. 17, 1742	2	127
Abigail, w. Jonath[an], d. Nov. 3, 1749	1	181
Abigail, w. Jon[a]t[ha]n, d. Nov. 3, 1749	2	127
Abigail, m. John **GOLD**, Nov. 13, 1759	2	82
Alice, d. [Sanford & Elizabeth], b. Apr. 24, 1767	2	118
Amey, d. Capt. Joseph, b. Mar. 17, 1761	1	101
Anna, d. [Jonathan, Jr. & Anna], b. Nov. 21, 1768	2	134
Anna, m. Ezra **KINGSLEY**, June 18, 1772	2	181
Anne, w. Jon[a]th[an], d. Oct. 23, 1773, in the 28th y. of her age	2	134
Arenah, d. John & Deborah, b. July 24, 1731	1	125
Artimece, d. [Jonathan & Lodema], b. June 15, 1776	2	134
Betsey, d. [Sanford & Elizabeth], b. Oct. 18, 1779	2	118
Charles, s. [Sanford & Elizabeth], b. Apr. 19, 1773	2	118
C[h]loe, m. Ebenezer **FITCH**, May 4, 1760	2	68
Daniel, s. Jonath[an] & Hannah, b. Apr. 14, 1753; d. Oct. 3, following	1	309
Daniel, s. [Jon[a]th[an] & Hannah], b. Apr. 14, 1753; d. Oct. 3, 1753	2	127
Daniel, s. [Col. Jonathan & Sarah], b. Nov. 23, 1761; d. Aug. 4, 1767	2	95
Daniel, s. [Lieut. Jon[a]th[a]n & Sarah, b. Nov. 23, 1761; d. Aug. 4, 1767	2	127
Deliverance, d. [Capt. Joseph & Deliverance], b. Aug. 12, 1755	1	101
Elizabeth, d. Jon[a]th[an] & Hannah, b. Mar. 14, 1758	1	309
Elizabeth, d. [Jon[a]th[an] & Hannah], b. Mar 14, 1758	2	127
Esther, d. [Col. Jonathan & Sarah], b. Apr. 4, 1764	2	95

	Vol.	Page
KINGSBURY, KINGSBERY, (cont.)		
Easther, d. [Lieut. Jon[a]th[a]n & Sarah], b. Apr.		
4, 1764	2	127
Eunice, d. Jos[eph] & Deliverance, b. Apr. 27, 1753	1	101
Eunice, m. Josiah **READ**, Jan. 2, 1755	2	8
Eunice, d. Capt. Joseph [& Deliverance], d. Oct. 28,		
1766	1	101
Eunice, d. [Samuel & Phebe], b. Nov. 19, 1782	2	242
Eunice, m. Barzillai **RUD[D]**, Nov. 26, 1810	3	39
Fanny, d. [Thomas & Patience], b. Apr. 28, 1790	3	24
Hannah, d. Nath[anie]l & Hannah, b. Jan. 23, 1718/9	1	4
Han[n]ah, d. Jonath[an] & Hannah, b. Oct. 2, 1754;		
d. same day	1	309
Hannah, d. [Jon[a]th[an] & Hannah], b. Oct. 2, 1754;		
d. same day	2	127
Hannah, d. Jon[a]th[an] & Hannah, b. Sept. 29, 1755	1	309
Hannah, d. [Jon[a]th[an] & Hannah], b. Sept. 29, 1755	2	127
Hannah, w. Jonathan, d. May 6, 1760	1	309
Hannah, w. Jon[a]th[an], d. May 6, 1760	2	127
Hannah, d. [Thomas & Patience], b. July 8, 1785	3	24
Irena, d. Capt. Joseph & Deliverance, b. Feb. 24, 1758;		
d. Aug. 9, 1759	1	101
Jabez, s. Nathaniel & Hannah, b. Jan. 21, 1717	1	4
Jerusha, d. Capt. Joseph & Deliverance, b. Apr. 3, 1751	1	101
John, m. Deborah **SPAULDING**, Oct. 21, 1730	1	125
Jonathan, m. Abigail **HOLT**, Dec. 3, 1736	2	127
Jonathan, s. Jonathan & Abigail, b. Apr. 25, 1745	1	181
Jonathan, s. [Jonathan & Abigail], b. Apr. 25, 1745	2	127
Jonathan, m. Hannah **CLARK**, Jan. 9, 1750/51	1	309
Jon[a]th[an], m. Hannah **CLARK**, Jan. 9, 1754	2	127
Jonathan, Col., m. Sarah **BALLARD**, Jan. 14, 1761	2	95
Jon[a]th[a]n, Lieut., m. Sarah **BALLARD**, Jan. 14, 1761	2	127
Jonathan, Jr., m. Anna **GEER**, Jan. 14, 1768	2	134
Jonathan, Sr., d. Dec. 28, 1770	2	127
Jonathan, m. Lodema **RANSOM**, June 21, 1775	2	134
Joseph, s. Nath[anie]l & Hannah, b. June 7, 1723	1	4
Joseph, s. Capt. Joseph [& Deliverance], d. Jan 12,		
1759	1	101
Lodema, d. [Jonathan & Lodema], b. Feb. 24, 1780	2	134
Lora, d. [Jonathan, Jr. & Anna], b. Sept. 8, 1771	2	134
Lucy, d. [Thomas & Patience], b. Feb. 13, 1784; d.		
Mar. 13, 1798	3	24
Lucy, d. [Thomas & Patience], b. Nov. 28, 1797	3	24
Margaret, w. Thomas, d. Feb. 10, 1753, ae. 70 y.	1	12
Mary, m. Stephen **BINGHAM**, Dec. 11, 1712	1	34
Mary, m. James **UTLEY**, Jr., Aug. 10, 1742	1	291
Mary, d. Jonathan & Han[na]h, b. Apr. 24, 1760	1	309
Mary, d. [Jon[a]th[an] & Hannah], b. Apr. 24, 1760	2	127

	Vol.	Page
KINGSBURY, KINGSBERY, (cont.)		
Mason, s. [Samuel & Phebe], b. June 18, 1788	2	242
Mercy, d. [Jonathan, Jr. & Anna], b. Oct 9, 1773;		
d. May 12, 1774	2	134
Olive, d. [Sanford & Elizabeth], b. Nov 22, 1775	2	118
Oliver, s. [Sanford & Elizabeth], b. July 27, 1770;		
d. Nov. 21, 1772	2	118
Phila, d. [Thomas & Patience], b. Dec. 29, 1778; d.		
Mar. 2, 1779	3	24
Phila, 2d, d. [Thomas & Patience], b. Apr. 5, 1780	3	24
Phila, m. Erastus **BIBBINS**, Jan. 1, 1799	3	94
Priscilla, d. Nathaniel & Hannah, b. Mar. 22, 1720	1	4
Royal, s. [Thomas & Patience], b. Nov. 24, 1781	3	24
Rhode, d. [Jonathan & Lodema], b. Mar. 31, 1778	2	134
Sam[ue]ll, s. Thomas & Sarah, b. Apr. 3, 1750	1	304
Samuel, m. Phebe **GINNINGS**, Feb. 10, 1778	2	242
Sanford, m. Elizabeth **FITCH**, Jan. 9, 1766	2	118
Sanford, s. [Samuel & Phebe], b. Nov. 7, 1791	2	242
Sarah, m. John **GENNINGS**, Jr., Jan. 10, 1749/50	1	297
Sarah, d. [Samuel & Phebe], b. Aug. 20, 1778	2	242
Sarah, w. Thomas, d. [ ]	1	304
Simon, s. Nathaniel & Hannah, b. July 25, 1715	1	4
Tabatha, m. Zacheas **WALDO**, Feb. 3, 1746/7	2	119
Thomas, m. Sarah **PRESTON**, Nov. 24, 1749	1	304
Thomas, father of [Jonathan], d. Apr. 20, 1751	1	309
Thomas, s. [Thomas & Sarah], b. Apr. 24, 1752	1	304
Thomas, m. Content **NEFF**, Mar. 1, 1759; d. Nov. 13,		
1767	1	304
Thomas, m. Patience **STOEL**, Apr. 2, 1778	3	24
KINGSLEY, KINGSLY, Abel, s. [John & Mary], b. Jan. 10,		
1758	1	322
Abigail, [d. John & Elizabeth], b. Oct. 14, 1725	1	62
Abigail, d. Isaac & Abigail, b. Nov. 22, 1753	1	268
Abigail, [twin with Jacob, s. John & Mary], b. Dec.		
19, 1775	1	322
Abigail, twin with Jacob, d. [John & Mary], b. Dec.		
19, 1775	2	212
Abner, s. Eldad & Priscilla, b. Jan. 27, 1733/4	1	121
Abner, s. [Eliphas & Tryphenia], b. Mar. 10, 1767	2	110
Adams, s. [John & Mary], b. June 12, 1768	1	322
Adams, s. [John & Mary], b. June 12, 1768	2	212
Adonijah, s. [Josiah & Dorothy], b. Apr. 3, 1734	1	198
Adonijah, m. Bethiah **BAKER**, Sept. 23, 1756	2	19
Alfred, s. [Eben[ezer] & Margaret], b. Jan. 7, 1765	2	38
Alice, d Ezra & Mary, b. Sept. 4, 1746	1	107
Alvin, s. [Elisha & Susanna], b. Oct. 20, 1770	2	147
Amos, m. Ruth **ADAMS**, June 12, 1723	1	64
Ann, [d. John & Elizabeth], b. Nov. 9, 1731	1	62

	Vol.	Page
KINGSLEY, KINGSLY, (cont.)		
Anne, d. [Ezra & Anne], b. Feb. 3, 1778	2	181
Asael, s. [John & Mary], b. Jan. 10, 1758	2	212
Asahel, m. Elizabeth **LUCE**, Nov. 26, 1789	2	52
Charity, d. [Jeremiah & Hannah], b. July 29, 1764	2	28
Chloe, d. [John & Mary], b. Dec. 17, 1770	1	322
Chloe, d. [John & Mary], b. Dec. 17, 1770	2	212
David, s. Isaac & Abigail, b. Jan. 22, 1748/9	1	268
Doratha, d. [Josiah & Dorothy] b. Sept 17, 1729	1	198
Dorathea, d. Elip[hale]t & Eliza, b. June 11, 1754	1	296
Dorothy, m. William **PARRISH**, Jr., May 11, 1749	1	288
Ebenezer, s. John & Elizabeth, b. Apr. 5, 1714	1	15
Ebenezer, s John & Elizabeth, d. July 22, 1714	1	16
Ebenezer, s. John & Elizabeth, b. Oct. 17, 1720	1	62
Ebenezer, s. Salmon & Lydia, b. Apr. 26, 1747	1	240
Eben[ezer], m. Margaret **PARRISH**, May 24, 1761	2	38
Eldad, s. John & Sarah, b. Jan. 8, 1707	1	15
Eldad, m. Priscilla **BASS**, June 20, 1733	1	121
Eleanor Maria, d. [Jonathan, Jr. & Eleanor], b.		
Jan. 28, 1813	3	97
Eleanor Maria, d. [Jonathan, Jr. & Eleanor], b.		
Jan. 28, 1813	3	99
Eliphalet, s. John & Sarah, b. Feb. 2, 1704	A	28
Eliphalet, s. John & Sarah, d. May 9, 1721	1	15
Eliphalet, s. Josiah & Dorothy, b. Dec. 3, 1721	1	28
Eliphalet, m. Elizabeth **WHITE**, Dec. 9, 1749	1	296
Eliphas, s. [Josiah & Dorothy], b. Feb. 8, 1740	1	198
Eliphaz, m. Tryphenia **PALMER**, Nov. 24, 1762	2	110
Elisha, s. Eldad & Prescilla, b. Apr 1, 1742	1	219
Elisha, s. [Josiah & Dorothy], b. Aug. 7, 1743	1	198
Elisha, m. Susanna **BAKER**, Nov. 4, 1767	2	147
Elizabeth, d. Ezra & Elizabeth, b. June 18, 1727	1	7
Elizabeth, w. Ezra, d. Mar. 19, 1735	1	7
Elizabeth, d. [Josiah, Jr. & Elizabeth], b. Feb. 24,		
1743/4 (sic) [Probably 1753/4]	1	264
Elizabeth, m. Gideon **HEB[B]ARD**, Dec. 14, 1749	1	294
Elizabeth, d. Salmon & Lydia, b. Feb. 7, 1749/50	1	240
Eno[c]k, [s. John & Elizabeth], b. Oct. 10, 1730	1	62
Enoch, s. [John & Mary], b. Dec. 2, 1755	1	322
Enoch, s. [John & Mary], b. Dec. 2, 1755	2	212
[E]unice, d. Eldad & Priscilla, b. May 20, 1736	1	121
[E]unice, d. Salmon & Lydia, b. July 9, 1745	1	240
Eunice, m. Jonathan **BREWSTER**, Feb. 12, 1767	2	135
Eunice, [twin with Joseph], d. [Eben[ezer] &		
Margaret], b. Sept. 5, 1767	2	38
Ezra, m. Elizabeth **WIGHT**, Dec. 31, 1719	1	7
Ezra, s. Ezra & Elizabeth, b. Aug. 15, 1721	1	7
Ezra, s. Ezra & Elizabeth, d. Nov. 1, 1733	1	107

	Vol.	Page
KINGSLEY, KINGSLY, (cont.)		
Ezra, m. Mary **FOLLET,** Nov. 10, 1743	1	7
Ezra, s. Ezra & Mary, b. Aug. 13, 1744	1	107
Ezra, m. Anna **KINGSBURY,** June 18, 1772	2	181
Ezra, s. [Ezra & Anna], b. Nov. 11, 1775	2	181
Hannah, d. Ezra & Mary, b. Nov. 21, 1751	1	107
Hannah, d. [Jeremiah & Hannah], b. Dec. 4, 1766	2	28
Harriet, d. [Jonathan, Jr. & Eleanor], b. Mar. 3, 1814	3	97
Harriet, d. [Jonathan, Jr. & Eleanor], b. Mar. 3, 1814	3	99
Ireniah, [d. John & Elizabeth], b. May 20, 1734	1	62
Isaac, m. Abigail **PALMER,** Jan. 20, 1746	1	268
Isaac, s. Isaac & Abigail, b. Sept. 2, 1747	1	268
Isaiah, s. Amos & Ruth, b. June 11, 1725	1	64
Jabez, s. Josiah & Dorothy, b. Aug. 19, 1726	1	198
Jabez, m. Irena **MANNING,** Mar. 7, 1749/50	1	299
Jabez, s. Jabez & Irena, b. Oct. 5, 1750	1	299
Jacob, [twin with Abigail], [s. John & Mary], b. Dec. 19, 1775	1	322
Jacob, twin with Abigail, s. [John & Mary], b. Dec. 19, 1775	2	212
James, s. Adonijah & Bethiah, b. May 8, 1757	2	19
James Luce, s. [Jonathan & Zillah], b. Aug. 28, 1778	2	216
Jane D., m. Francis S. **AMEDOWN,** Nov. 3, 1845, by Andrew Sharp	3	225
Jason, s. [John & Mary], b. Nov. 14, 1765	1	322
Jason, s. [John & Mary], b. Nov. 14, 1765	2	212
Jeremiah, s. Nath[anie]ll & Hannah, b. Dec. 2, 1726	1	62
Jeremiah, s. [Josiah & Dorothy], b. Apr. 3, 1738	1	198
Jeremiah, m. Hannah **LILLIE,** Jan. 9, 1757	2	28
Jerusha, d. John & Elizabeth, b. Sept. 17, 1723	1	62
Jerusha, m. Simeon **ROBINSON,** Feb. 2, 1742/3	1	244
Jerusha, d. Salmon & Lydia, b. Sept. 29, 1762	1	240
Jerusha, d. [Eliphaz & Tryphenia], b. Mar. 20, 1765	2	110
Joannah, [d. John & Elizabeth], b. Sept. 3, 1729	1	62
John, m. Elizabeth **BASS,** Dec. 25, 1717	1	46
John, d. Mar. 17, 1732/3, ae. about 68 y.	1	15
John, m. Mary **BURNAP,** Feb. 19, 1755	1	322
John, m. Mary **BURNAP,** Feb. 19, 1755	2	212
John, d. [1850], ae. 60	4	157
Jonathan, s. John & Elizabeth, b. Dec. 24, 1718	1	46
Jonathan, Sr., d. Sept. 12, 1732	2	216
Jonathan, m. Abigail **HOLT,** Dec. 3, 1736	1	181
Jonathan, s. Salmon & Lydia, b. May 15, 1753	1	240
Jonathan, m. Zillah **LUCE,** Jan. 22, 1777	2	216

	Vol.	Page
KINGSLEY, KINGSLY, (cont.)		
Jonathan, s. [Jonathan & Zillah], b. July 22, 1786	2	216
Jonathan, Jr., m. Eleanor **HOWARD**, Dec. 12, 1811	3	97
Jonathan, Jr., m. Eleanor **HOWARD**, Dec. 12, 1819		
(Probably 1811)	3	99
Joseph, [twin with Eunice], s. [Eben[ezer] &		
Margaret], b. Sept. 5, 1767	2	38
Josiah, m. Dorothy **BINGHAM**, Dec. 10, 1718	1	28
Josiah, s. Josiah & Dorothy, b. Mar. 31, 1724	1	28
Josiah, Jr., m. Elizabeth **PALMER**, Nov. 11, 1752	1	264
Lathrop, s. [Ezra & Anna], b. Apr. 2, 1773; d.		
May 10, 1782	2	181
Lathrop, s. [Ezra & Ann], b. June 18, 1782	2	181
Lemuel, d. [s.][Eliphalet & Elizabeth], b. Oct. 24,		
1764	1	296
Lewis, s. [Jonathan, Jr. & Eleanor], b. June 21, 1829	3	97
Lucretia, d. Ezra & Mary, b. June 4, 1748	1	107
Lydia, d. John & Elizabeth, b. July 20, 1717	1	15
Lydia, m. Samuel **HEB[B]ARD**, Jan. 17, 1738/9	1	185
Lydia, d. Eldad & Prescilla, b. May 17, 1739	1	219
Lydia, d. Eliphalet & Elizabeth, b. Feb. 3, 1749/50	1	296
Lydia, d. Salmon & Lydia, b. Apr. 24, 1760	1	240
Margaret, d. [Eben[ezer] & Margaret], b. Jan. 3, 1763	2	38
Martha, d. [Eliphalet & Elizabeth], b. Feb. 22, 1752	1	296
Mary, d. John & Sarah, d. Mar. 7, 1706	A	28
Mary, d. Josiah & Dorothy, b. Oct. 11, 1719	1	28
Mary, d. Ezra & Elizabeth, b Aug. 6, 1730	1	7
Mary, m. Samuel **STODDARD**, Mar. 12, 1753	1	320
Mary, d. [John & Mary], b. May 25, 1773	1	322
Mary, d. [John & Mary], b. May 25, 1773	2	212
Mary, d. [Ezra & Anne], b. June 5, 1780	2	181
Molly Whiting, d. [Jonathan & Zillah], b. Mar. 12, 1781	2	216
Nathan, s. Salmon & Lydia, b. Jan. 23, 1744/5	1	240
Nathaniel, m. Sarah **WALDEN**, Mar. 16, 1748/9	1	289
Oliver, Dr., m. Martha **WILKINSON**, b. of Willimantic,		
May 19, 1835, by Rev. Philo Judson	3	173
Oren, s. [Salmon & Lydia], b. Aug. 21, 1764	1	240
Patty, d. [Jonathan & Zillah], b. Jan. 20, 1784; d.		
July 19, 1788	2	216
Phinehas, s. Isaac & Abigail, b. Dec. 21, 1750	1	268
Rhoda, m. John P. **WEBB**, farmer, Feb. 20, 1850, by		
Mr. Hazen	4	114
Ruby, m. Isaac **PALMER**, Dec. 10, 1795	2	186
Rufus, s. [John & Mary], b. Apr. 11, 1763	1	322
Rufus, s. [John & Mary], b. Apr. 11, 1763	2	212
Salmon, s. Ezra & Elizabeth, b. Sept. 27, 1723	1	7
Salmon, m. Lydia **BURGEE**, Jan. 24, 1743	1	240
Salmon, s. Salmon & Lydia, b. Sept. 17, 1755	1	240

	Vol.	Page
KNIGHT, (cont.)		
Rachel, m. Jonathan **HANDY**, Mar. 20, 1718	1	16
Sarah, m. Elisha **LILLY**, May 25, 1721	1	58
Sarah, m. Solomon **ABBE**, June 17, 1751	1	313
Sarah, m. John **WALDEN**, Jr., Nov. 12, 1752	1	240
KNOWLES, Mary, d. Nathaniell & Mary, b. Sept. [ ], 1713	1	32
Mary, w. Nath[anie]ll, d. June 10, 1716	1	32
Mattatiah, d. Nathaniell & Mary, b. Jan. 4, 1716	1	32
Nathaniell, m. Elizabeth **BACON**, Apr. 25, 1717	1	32
Rebeckah, d. Nathaniell & Mary, b. Jan. 30, 1710/11	1	32
Ruth, d. Nath[anie]ll & Elizabeth, b. Apr. 5, 1718	1	32
KNOWLTON, Hannah, m. Nathaniel **FARNAM**, Nov. 18, 1762	2	107
KUBB, Mary A., d. Michael A., spinner, ae. 22, b. Dec. 14, [1849]	4	10
KYES, Lucy, d. James & Tabathy, b. May 4, 1747	1	79
LADD, Frances A., of Franklin, m. Jabez C. **HUNT**, of Norwich, Oct. 21, 1850, by Rev. Jno. Cady	4	118
Ginda, m. Betsey **ROBINSON**, Mar. 29, 1835, by Rev. Roger Bingham	3	172
Worthington, m. Susan **JENNINGS**, May 8, 1836, by Samuel Perkins, J.P.	3	178
Worthington, of Coventry, m. Maryan **WELLS**, of Windham, Apr. 19, 1846, by Elder Thomas Jones	3	228
——, child of Zaccheas, merchant, ae. 27, & Eliza, ae. 25, b. Dec. 20, 1847	4	3
LAFFERTY, ——, d. John, blacksmith, ae. 35, & Hannah, ae. 48, b. Feb. 16, 1851	4	13
LAINYER, Emma, b. Canaan, res. Willimantic, d. Apr. 7, 1851, ae. 5	4	157
LAMB, Eben[eze]r, m. Mary **BIGBEE**, Jan. 17, 1748/9	1	288
Hannah A., of Franklin, m. Charles W. **CHAPPELL**, of Lebanon, Oct. 3, 1837, by Rev. B. Cook, Jr., at Willimantic Falls	3	183
Marcy, m. Thomas **LINKON**, July 7, 1747	1	176
Mary, m. Ebenezer **LINKION**, Mar. 4, 1761	2	133
Rebeckah, m. Thomas **DURGEE**, June 26, 1728	1	92
LAMBERT, LAMBART, Margaret, m. David **CANADA**, Nov. 5, 1718	1	21
Sarah, m. John **MANNING**, Jr., June 10, 1744	1	265
LAMPHERE, Anne, m. John **BROUGHTON**, Sept. 23, 1745	1	255
Mary, m. Sam[ue]ll **FFLINT**, Apr. 13, 1736	1	157
LANCY, Pat, laborer, ae. 20, m. Catharine **RONA**, ae. 20, Dec. [ ], [1850], by Rev. Brady	4	115
LANFEAR, Prudence, m. Thomas **LINKON**, Sept. 12, 1738	1	176
LARKHAM, Cha[rle]s A., s. Alfred, house carpenter, ae. 32, & Julia, ae. 25, b. Dec. 31, 1850	4	13
Joseph, s. Alfred, ae. 29, & Julia, ae. 24, b. Aug. [ ], 1848	4	7

	Vol.	Page

LARKHAM, (cont.)
Lamey L., of Voluntown, m. Mary L. **REED**, of Windham,
Sept. 30, 1832, by Rev. Alva Gregory ... 3 ... 161
LARRABEE, LARRABE, [see also **CARRABEE**], Abigail, d.
John & Sarah, b. June 20, 1694 ... A ... 7
Amelia, m. Samuel **KENNEDY**, Jan. 7, 1773 ... 2 ... 180
Amey, twin with Lucy, d. Libbeas & Lucy, b. Apr. 3,
1789 ... 2 ... 46
Charles, s. [Timothy & Abigail], b. Sept. 30, 1763 ... 1 ... 305
Charles, m. Amanda **BINGHAM**, Mar. 23, 1846, by Rev.
J.E. Tyler ... 3 ... 109
Charles, m. Amanda **BURNHAM**, b. of Windham, Mar. 23,
1846, by Rev. J.E. Tyler ... 3 ... 227
Frederick, s. [Timothy & Abigail], b. Feb. 16, 1760 ... 1 ... 305
Hannah, d. Aug. 22, 1757 ... 1 ... 109
John, m. Sarah **MORGIN**, Apr. 15, 1689 ... A ... 7
John, s. John & Sarah, b. Jan. 16, 1690 ... A ... 7
John, m. Mary **HATCH**, May 22, 1711 ... 1 ... 28
John, s. John & Hannah, b. Nov. 29, 1732 ... 1 ... 109
John, d. Mar. [ ], 1746 ... 1 ... 109
John, s. [Timothy & Abigail], b. Jan. 8, 1757; d.
Mar. 15, 1757 ... 1 ... 305
John, twin with Timothy, s. [Timothy & Abigail], b.
Mar. 11, 1758 ... 1 ... 305
John, m. Mehetable **HARE**, Nov. 18, 1779, by Samuel Gray,
J.P. ... 2 ... 224
Joseph, s. John & Sarah, b. Mar. 27, 1692 ... A ... 7
Julia, m. Eliphalet **RIPLEY**, Nov. 19, 1818 ... 3 ... 91
Libeas, s. [Timothy & Abigail], b. Oct. 15, 1765 ... 1 ... 305
Leb[b]eus, m. Marcy **WEBB**, Sept. 27, 1799 ... 3 ... 96
Libbeas, m. Lucy **FITCH**, Oct. 5, 1788 ... 2 ... 46
Lebbeus, of Windham, m. Lucy **FITCH**, d. Col. Eleazer,
of Windham, Oct. 5, 1788 ... 3 ... 43
Lucie, d. John & Sarah, b. June 10, 1697 ... A ... 7
Luce, d. Tim[othy] & Abigail, b Aug. 26, 1751 ... 1 ... 305
Lucy, w. Libbeas, d. Apr. 9, 1789 ... 2 ... 46
Lucy, twin with Amey, d. Libbeas & Lucy, b. Apr. 3,
1789; d. July 25, 1793 ... 2 ... 46
Mary, d. [Charles & Amanda], b. Oct. 9, 1851 ... 3 ... 109
Pamphlia, d. [Timothy & Abigail], b. Mar. 18, 1753 ... 1 ... 305
Sarah, d. [Timothy & Abigail], b. Aug. 17, 1767 ... 1 ... 305
Thankfull, d. John & Sarah, b. June 26, 1701 ... A ... 7
Timothy, s. John & Hannah, b. Oct. 8, 1730 ... 1 ... 109
Timothy, m. Abigail **WOOD**, Feb. 20, 1750/51 ... 1 ... 305
Timothy, twin with John, s. [Timothy & Abigail], b.
Mar. 11, 1758; d. [ ] ... 1 ... 305
Timothy, s Timothy & Abigail, b. Jan. 17, 1769;
d. Aug. [ ], 1790 ... 1 ... 305

	Vol.	Page
LARRABEE, LARRABE, (cont.)		
Timothy had negro Corydon, b. Mar. 4, 1784	1	305
Timothy, s. [Marcy & Leb[b]eus], b. July 1, 1802	3	96
—, [d. Timothy & Abigail], b. Mar. 13, 1755;		
lived about 8 hours	1	305
—, d. [Charles & Amanda], b. Jan. 19, 1850;		
d. Jan. 23, 1850	3	109
LARRANCE, [see also **TARRANCE** and **DORRANCE**], Deborah,		
m. Paul **HEB[B]ARD**, Jan. 6, 1735/6	1	152
Rose, m. Nero **GARDINER**, Apr. 9, 1797	3	27
LASSELL, LASELL, LASEL, LASSAL, LASELE, CASSAL,		
CASSEL, CASSALL, CASAL, Abigail, d. Thomas &		
Mary, b. Jan. 26, 1707/8	A	31
Abigail, d. Isaac & Bethiah, b. Apr. 6, 1740	1	159
Abigail, m. Joseph **PALMER**, Apr. 27, 1758	2	41
Abigail, m. Amasa **PALMER**, May 13, 1762	2	19
Athniel, s. John & Jeal, b. Jan. 18, 1741/2	1	220
Bethiah, d. Isaac & Bethiah, b. May 10, 1742/3 (sic)	1	159
Bethiah, m. Henry **SILSBY**, Apr. 5, 1744	1	246
Chester, s. [Josiah & Lydia], b. Feb. 23, 1784	2	141
Cloye, d. James & [E]unice, b June 26, 1740		
[Chloe?]	1	189
C[h]loe, m. Benj[ami]n **SMITH**, Sept. 10, 1759	2	48
Enoch, s. [Josiah & Lydia], b. Dec. 20, 1774	2	141
Eunice, w. Capt. James, d. July 20, 1757	1	189
Isaac, s. Joshua & Mary, b. Sept. 10, 1715	1	10
Isaac, m. Bethiah **WOODARD**, Oct 12, 1738	1	159
Isaac, d. Jan. 20, 1791	1	159
James, s. Thomas & Mary, b. Jan. 23, 1704	A	31
James, Capt., m. Jerusha **CARY**, Jan. 19, 1758; d.		
[ ]	2	40
James, s. [Josiah & Lydia], b. Aug. 22, 1781; d.		
Jan. 25, 1785	2	141
James, s. [Josiah & Lydia], b. Oct. 10, 1786	2	141
James, Capt., d. [ ]	2	40
Jeal, d. John & Jeal, b. Mar. 12, 1743/4	1	220
Jerusha, Wid., m. Jeremiah **WELSH**, May 25, 1785	2	20
Jerusha A., of Windham, m. Horace **ENSWORTH**, of		
Hartford, Apr. 19, 1840, by Rev. Otis C Whiton	3	193
John, s. Thomas & Mehitable, b. Mar. 20, 1737/8	1	162
John, s. [Josiah & Lydia], b. Feb. 24, 1777	2	141
Joshua, m. Mary **BURNUP**, Dec. 14, 1714	1	10
Joshua, m. Elizabeth **SKIFF**, Jan. 16, 1739/40	1	212
Joshua, s. Joshua & Elizabeth, b. Dec. 20, 1740	1	212
Joshua, Jr., m. Susannah **WALDEN**, Feb. 6, 1750/51	1	302
Joshua, m. Hannah **BINGHAM**, Jan. 20, 1757	2	33
Joshua, s. Joshua & Hannah, b. Oct. 16, 1757	2	33
Josiah, m. Lydia **BINGHAM**, Sept. 29, 1768	2	141

	Vol.	Page
LASSELL, LASELL, LASEL, LASSAL, LASELE, CASSAL,		
CASSEL, CASSALL, CASAL, (cont.)		
Josiah, s. [Josiah & Lydia], b. Apr. 21, 1771;		
d. Dec. [ ], 1771	2	141
Josiah, s. [Josiah & Lydia], b. Sept. 28, 1772	2	141
Laben, s. [Joshua & Hannah], b. June 16, 1791;		
d. Sept. 20, 1761	2	33
Laura M., of Windham, m. Pliney **ABBOTT**, of		
Vienna, N.Y., [ ], by Rev. Jesse Fisher	3	167
Lemuel, s. Joshua & Hannah, b. June 24, 1759	2	33
Lucy, d. [Josiah & Lydia], b. Aug. 11, 1791	2	141
Lucy, m. James L. **SMITH**, June 18, 1823	3	114
Lydia, d. [Josiah & Lydia], b. May 10, 1779	2	141
Martha, d. [Joshua & Hannah], b. Mar. 25, 1765	2	33
Mary, d. [Josiah & Lydia], b. Jan. 15, 1769	2	141
Mehetable, d. Thomas & Mehetable, b. May 21, 1740;		
d. June 5, 1740	1	162
Mehetable, d. Thomas & Mehetable, b. June 30, 1742	1	228
Nathaniel, s. Thomas & Mehitable, b. May 4, 1741;		
d. May 4, 1741	1	228
Patience, m. Abner **FLINT**, July 1, 1756	2	12
Ruth, d. Thomas & Mary, b. May 12, 1711	1	17
Susan M., m. Ja[me]s R. **ALLEN**, b. of Windham, Oct. 4,		
1846, by Rev. Thomas L. Greenwood	3	230
Susannah, w. Josh[ua], Jr., d. July 29, 1753	1	302
Susannah, d. [Joshua & Hannah], b. Oct. 3, 1762	2	33
Thomas, m. Mehetable **SMITH**, Sept. 23, 1734	1	162
Thomas, s. Thomas & Mehitable, b. July 20, 1736; d.		
June 2, 1740	1	162
——, s. [Joshua, Jr.] & Susannah, b. Mar. 16, 1753;		
d. in about 2 hrs.	1	302
LATHROP, LOTHROP, Abigail, d. [Eben[eze]r & Deborah], b.		
May 5, 1780	2	20
Abner, s. Benjamin & Mercy, b. Mar. 22, 1737; d. Aug.		
5, 1741	1	113
Abner, s. Benj[ami]n & Sybel, b. Feb. 15, 1758	1	306
Abner, s. [Benjamin, Jr. & Sybbel], b. Feb. 15, 1758	2	120
Abner, m. Betsey **ABBE**, Oct. 1, 1796	3	46
Abner, s. [William A. & Jerusha], b. Oct. 6, 1826	3	119
Ama E., d. [Oliver & Harriet], b. [ ]	3	63
Ann D., m. John L. **WHEELER**, Nov. 27, 1840, by Rev		
John B. Guild, Willimantic	3	196
Annah, d. Benjamin & Mercy, b. Feb. 15, 1732/3	1	113
Anna, m. Joseph **WARNER**, Jr., Dec. 31, 1754	2	6
Anne, d. [Eben[eze]r & Deborah], b. Oct. 14, 1774	2	20
Aseriah, m. Lucy **FISH**, June 8, 1845, by Andrew Sharp	3	223
Benj[amin], Jr., m. Sybel **BACKUS**, July 8, 1751	1	306
Benjamin, Jr., m. Sybbel **BACKUS**, July 8, 1751	2	120

	Vol.	Page
LATHROP, LOTHROP, (cont.)		
Benjamin Harvey, s. [Roswell & Sarah], b. Dec. 22, 1773	2	187
Edward, m. Charlotte D. **LEE**, b. of Windham, Sept. 5, 1841, by Rev. Henry Beers Sherman	3	198
Eliza, d. Benj[ami]n & Sybel, b. Feb. 11, 1754, at Ashford	1	306
Elizabeth, m. Bowle **ARNOLD**, Sept. 24, 1702	A	33
Elizabeth, m. Joshua **RIPLEY**, Jr., Mar. 26, 1740	1	290
Elizabeth, d. [Benjamin, Jr. & Sybbel], b. Feb. 11, 1754, at Ashford	2	120
Ellmarnce W., s. Edmond, laborer, black, ae. 31, & Delintha, ae. 21, b. Jan. 31, 1851	4	13
Erastus, s. [Eben[eze]r & Deborah], b. May 28, 1772	2	20
Frank, s. Lee, stage proprietor, b. Mar. 7, 1851	4	13
George Earl, s. [Oliver & Harriet], b. June 29, 1817	3	63
Gurdon, s. Eben[eze]r & Deborah, b May 23, 1770	2	20
Jedediah, s. Jed[ediah] & Sarah, b. Aug. 18, 1768	2	138
John, s. Benjamin & Mercy, b. Apr 4, 1738	1	113
John, s. [Benjamin, Jr. & Sybbel], b. Aug. 10, 1768	2	120
Laura, m. Thomas **WELCH**, [ ]	3	55
Lib[b]eas, s. Benj[ami]n & Sybel, b. Dec. 27, 1755; d. July 10, 1761 (Lebbeus)	1	306
Lib[b]eas, s. [Benjamin, Jr. & Sybbel], b. Dec. 27, 1755; d. July 10, 1761	2	120
Lee, m. Francis R. **DEVOTION**, Oct. 16, 1831, by Rev. Rich[ar]d F. Cleveland (Scotland)	3	155
Leonetta, d. Ella, ae. 28, & Dianna, ae. 22, b. May 16, 1849	4	7
Lorain, s. Benj[ami]n & Sybel, b. Aug. 21, 1763; d. Sept. 13, 1765	1	306
Lorain, s. [Benjamin, Jr. & Sybbel], b. Aug. 21, 1763; d. Sept. 13, 1765	2	120
Louisa, m. Benjamin **GREAVES**, May 10, 1831, by Rev. Rich[ar]d F. Cleveland	3	153
Lucretia, m. Dr. Chester **HUNTROUS**, Mar. 10, 1825	3	121
Lucy, b. June 8, 1799; m. Justin **SWIFT**, Nov. 8, 1819	3	122
Lydia, d. Benjamin & Mercy, b. Aug. 15, 1742	1	113
Lydia, m. James C. **STAMFORD**, Sept. 21, 1829, by Rev. Dennis Platt	3	137
Marcy, m. John **FITCH**, Jr., Nov. 7, 1753	1	326
Martha, m. Ebenezer **DEVOTION**, July 25, 1738	1	216
Nathaniell, s. Benjamin & Mercy, b Dec. 29, 1734	1	113
Oliver, s. [Eben[eze]r & Deborah], b. May 8, 1778	2	20
Oliver, m. Harriet **CAREY**, Feb. 23, 1817	3	63
Rosewell, s. Benj[ami]n, Jr. & Sybel, b. Feb. 22, 1752	1	306
Roswell, s. [Benjamin, Jr. & Sybbel], b. Feb. 22, 1752	2	120
Roswell, m. Sarah **BADGER**, Oct. 22, 1772	2	187

	Vol.	Page
LATHROP, LOTHROP, (cont.)		
Sarah, m. Joseph **FRINK**, [ ], 1763	2	93
Sarah, d. Jed[ediah], & Sarah, b. Jan. 19, 1771	2	138
Solomon, s. Benjamin & Mercy, b. Feb. 23,		
1739/40	1	113
Solomon, [s. Benjamin & Mercy], d. Sept. 1, 1740	1	113
Sibbel, d. [Benjamin, Jr. & Sybbel], b. Mar. 1,		
1761; d. Aug. 2, 1764	2	120
Sybel, d. Benj[ami]n & Sybel, b. Mar. 1, 1761; d.		
Aug. 2, 1764	1	306
Sibbel, d. [Benjamin, Jr. & Sybbel], b. July 17, 1771	2	120
Wealthie, d. [Benj[ami]n & Sybel], b. July 29, 1766	1	306
Wealthe, d. [Benjamin, Jr. & Sybbel], b. July 29,		
1766	2	120
William A., m. Jerusha **BIBBONS**, Mar. 28, 1824	3	119
W[illia]m A., m. Nancy **YORK**, b. of Preston, May 3,		
1845, by Rev. J.E. Tyler	3	221
William Abner, s. [Abner & Betsey], b. Oct, 28, 1797	3	46
LAVELL, Josiah, Jr., of Quincy, Mass., m. Mary **SIMPSON**,		
of Windham, Dec. 16, 1830, by Rev. R.T. Crampton	3	149
LAW, Barbara, m. James **SPAULDING**, Sept. 3, 1795	3	34
LEACE, Erastus, s. [John & Sarah], b. Feb. 4, 1790	2	60
Gurdon, s. [John & Sarah], b. Jan. 18, 1799	2	60
Hervey, s. [John & Sarah], b. Oct. 15, 1796	2	60
John, m. Sarah **BURNHAM**, Nov. 3, 1789	2	60
John, s. [John & Sarah], b. Feb. 28, 1794	2	60
LEACH, Amos, m. Mercy **MARTIN**, May 16, 1728	1	126
Amos, s. Amos & Mercy, b. Dec. 8, 1730	1	126
Ebenezer, s. Amos & Mercy, b. Jan. 16, 1741	1	113
Ephraim, s. Amos & Mercy, b. July 8, 1744	1	113
Eunice, m. Jedediah **STORY**, Sept. 14, 1800	3	62
James, d. Sept. 12, 1726, ae. about 72 y.	1	60
James, s. Amos & Mercy, b. Mar. 12, 1728/9; d.		
Sept. 19, 1747, in the 19th y. of his age	1	126
James, [s. Amos & Mercy], b. Aug. 12, 1748	1	113
Jemima, d. Amos & Mercy, b. Aug. 22, 1743	1	113
Johanna, d. Amos & Mercy, b. May 24, 1739	1	126
John, s. Amos & Mercy, b. Aug. 10, 1735	1	126
Joseph, s. James & Mary, b. Oct. 27, 1719	1	34
Joseph, s. James & Mary, b. Oct. 29, 1720	1	60
Luther D., m. Lucy **SMITH**, Oct. 24, 1811	3	30
Mary, d. James & Mary, b. May 9, 1719	1	60
Mary, d. Amos & Mercy, b. Oct. 1, 1732	1	126
Mary, m. Timothy **PEARL**, Nov. 15, 1737	1	241
Mary, w. James, d May 12, 1745	1	60
Samuel, weaver, b. England, res. Willimantic, d.		
Mar. 4, 1860, ae. 55	4	159-0
Sarah, d. Amos & Mercy, b. Jan. 19, 1736/7	1	126

	Vol.	Page
LEACH, (cont.)		
Sarah, m. Jonathan **FISH**, Mar. 18, 1762	2	206
Simeon, s. Amos & Mercy, b. Mar. 28, 1746	1	113
Thomas, of Willimantic, d. Mar. 14, 1860, ae.		
10 d.	4	159-0
LEARNED, [see also **LEONARD**], Bathsheba, m. Augustus		
HEB[B]ARD, Mar. 19, 1796	2	63
Elizabeth Church, m. Jonathan **HEB[B]ARD**, June 19,		
1781	2	175
Maria, m. George **WOODWORTH**, Sept. 6, 1825, by Rev.		
Jesse Fisher	3	116
LEARY*, James C., s. John, ae. 32, & Margaret, ae. 35,		
of Willimantic, b. July 14, 1850 (***LEAVY**?)	4	12
LEAVENS, Elizabeth, m. David **HEB[B]ARD**, Sept. 15, 1743	1	239
LEDLIE, Amelia, d. [Hugh & C[h]loe], b Nov. 13, 1765;		
d. Dec. 6, 1765	1	317
Elizabeth, d. Hugh & C[h]loe, b. Jan. 13, 1755	1	317
Hugh, m. C[h]loe **STOUGHTON**, June 10, 1739	1	317
Margaret, d. Hugh & C[h]loe, b. Oct 24, 1752	1	317
Mary, d. Hugh & C[h]loe, b. [ ]	1	317
Timothy, s. Hugh & C[h]loe, b. [ ]	1	317
William, s. [Hugh & C[h]loe], b. July 25, 1763	1	317
LEE, Andrew Frink, s. [Jonathan & Jerush[a], b. Mar. 4,		
1811	3	2
Cha[rle]s, hatter, ae. 22, m. Abby S. **BROWN**, ae. 18,		
Nov. 29, [1850], by Rev. Bromley	4	115
Charlotte D., m. Edward **LATHROP**, b. of Windham,		
Sept. 5, 1841, by Rev. Henry Beers Sherman	3	198
George, s. [Jonathan & Jerush[a], b. May 2, 1813	3	2
Harriet, d. [Jonathan & Jerush[a], b. Jan. 17, 1800	3	2
Harriet, of Windham, m. Geo[rge] **DRAPER**, of Attleboro,		
Mass., June 3, 1829, by Rev. Jesse Fisher	3	136
John D., colored, d. Feb 20, 1851, ae 8	4	157
Jonathan, s. [Samuel & Sarah], b. Jan. 26, 1774	2	154
Jonathan, m. Jerush[a] **FLINT**, Apr. 19, 1795	3	2
Jonathan, d. June 3, 1822	3	2
Julia Sumner, d. [Jonathan & Jerush[a], b. Nov. 24,		
1795	3	2
Lucretia, d. [Jonathan & Jerush[a], b. Mar. 22, 1808	3	2
Lucy, m. Simeon Palmer **DOWNER**, Apr. 8, 1830, by Rev.		
Roger Bingham	3	144
Lydia, d. [Jonathan & Jerush[a], b. Nov. 22, 1797, at		
Walpole, N.H.	3	2
Mary, d. [Jonathan & Jerush[a], b. Apr. 2, 1802	3	2
Polly, m. George W. **WEBB**, Mar. [ ], 1806	3	78
Samuel, m. Sarah **MARSH**, Mar. 23, 1769	2	154
Samuel, s. [Samuel & Sarah, b. Jan. 17, 1773	2	154
Samuel, s. [Jonathan & Jerush[a], b. July 14, 1805	3	2

	Vol.	Page
LEE, (cont.)		
Samuel, m. Laura M. **YOUNG**, June 27, 1830, by Rev.		
Richard F. Cleveland	3	146
Sarah, d. [Samuel & Sarah], b. Jan. 29, 1771	2	154
LEFFINGWELL, Henry, m. Betsey **BABCOCK**, Oct. 19, 1831, by		
Roger Bingham	3	155
Mary, m. Isaac **GROSS**, May 22, 1712	1	39
LEONARD, LENARD, [see also **LEARNED**], Ellen, ae. 16, m.		
John **MAUREY**, laborer, ae. 23, Dec. [ ], [1849],		
by Rev. Willard	4	115
Geo[rge], m. Susan **POTTER**, b. of Windham, Aug. 6,		
1843, by Rev. Henry Bromley	3	210
Malinda, m. Leonard **WELDEN**, May 4, 1846, at Willi-		
mantic, by Rev. John Cooper	3	229
Phebe, m. Isaac **CANADA**, Jan. 21, 1729/30	1	94
LEWIS, Albert E., d. Mar. 31, [1850], ae. 1 1/2	4	155
Ann A., d. T., operative, ae. 41, b. Sept. 30, [1848]	4	6
Catharine, twin with Eugene, d. Sheffield, merchant,		
ae. 43, & Julia, ae. 36, of Willimantic, b. May		
11, [1851]	4	12
Edna, d. Timo[thy] & Sarah, b. July 27, 1760	2	61
Elizabeth, d. [Timo[th] & Sarah], b. Feb. 27, 1762	2	61
Erastus F., b. Mansfield, res. Willimantic, d. Aug.		
17, [1838], ae. 2 1/2	4	153
Eugene, twin with Catharine, s. Sheffield, merchant,		
ae. 43, & Julia, ae. 36, of Willimantic, b. May		
11, [1851]	4	12
Ichabod Perry, of Exeter, R.I., m. Adaline **HYDE**, of		
Windham, Oct. 3, 1831, by Joel W. White, J.P.	3	154
Isaac, s. Timo[thy] & Sarah, b. May 20, 1755	2	61
John, s. Timo[thy] & Sarah, b. Nov. 19, 1752	2	61
Judeth, d. Timo[thy] & Sarah, b. July 25, 1756	2	61
Martha, d. Timo[thy] & Sarah, b. Dec. 18, 1758	2	61
Mary, d. Shubael & Mary, b. Jan. 27, 1746/7	1	291
Mary E., d. Frank C., carpenter, ae. 40, b. Dec. 18,		
[1849]	4	9
Samuel, s. Shubael & Mary, b. July 30, 1748	1	291
Sarah, d. Timo[thy] & Sarah, b. Mar. 11, 1754	2	61
Sheffield, m. Julia **FITCH**, Nov. 30, 1837, at Willi-		
mantic, by Rev. Philo Judson	3	184
——, child of Samuel A., manufacturer, ae. 33, of		
Willimantic, b. May 27, [1850]	4	10
LEVERY, ——, w. John, d. Jan. 19, 1851	4	158
LILLIE, LYLIE, LILLY, LILLEY, Abigail, d. Elisha & Sarah,		
b. Oct. 19, 1725; d. Apr. 1, 1728	1	58
Abigail, s. Elisha & Sarah, b. Sept. 13, 1738	1	146
Abigail, d. [John & Jerusha], b. Feb. 28, 1772	2	77
Abner, s. [George & Mary], b. June 3, 1759	2	27

	Vol.	Page
LILLIE, LYLIE, LILLY, LILLEY, (cont.)		
Anne, d. Jacob & Phebe, b. Jan. 10, 1736/7	1	72
Benj[ami]n, s. Benj[ami]n & Marcy, of Stafford,		
b. Feb. 27, 1756, in Windham	1	255
Benjamin, s. [Jonathan & Sarah], b. June 25, 1759	2	79
Benj[amin] Holt, s. [Ezra & Esther], b. Nov. 30,		
1809	2	14
Bethiah, d. George & Sarah, b. June 8, 1712	1	35
Betsey, d. [Ezra & Esther], b. June 18, 1796	2	14
Charles, m. Almira **BINGHAM**, Feb. 13, 1825, by		
Alfred Young, Esq.	3	60
Charles, m. Sarah L. **BOON**, b. of Willimantic, Feb.		
15, 1846, by H. Slade	3	226
Charles Harvey, s. [Orrin & Olive], b. Oct. 5, 1822	3	94
Charlotte, m. Lyman **ALLEN**, Dec. 1, 1835, by Rev.		
Jesse Fisher	3	176
Charlotte, d. Charles, ae. 24, b. July 16, [1849]	4	6
Charlotte Augusta, d. [Ezra & Esther], b. July 15,		
1813	2	14
Daniel, s. [John & Jerusha], b. Mar. 28, 176[ ]	2	77
David, s. Elisha & Sarah, b. Sept 1, 1736	1	146
Elijah, s. Jonath[an] & Hannah, b. Dec. 26, 1756	2	3
Elijah, m. Ama **SMITH**, June 7, 1781	2	239
Elisha, m. Sarah **KNIGHT**, May 25, 1721	1	58
Elisha, s. Elisha & Sarah, b. Mar. 19, 1731/32*		
(*correction Mar. 19, 1731/32 crossed out and		
1729 was handwritten in original manuscript)	1	58
Elisha, Jr., m. Huldah **TILDEN**, of Norwich, Mar. 19,		
1755	1	321
Elisha, Jr., m. Hildah **TILDEN**, Mar. 19, 1755	2	4
Elisha, s. Elisha & Huldah, b. May 21, 1764	2	4
Elisha, d. July 5, 1767, in the 69th y. of his age	1	146
Elizabeth, m. Joseph **MEACHAM**, Jan. 16, 1722/3	1	66
Elizabeth, d. Jacob & Phebe, b. Aug. 28, 1726	1	72
Esther, d. [Ezra & Esther], b. Oct. 22, 1799; d.		
Mar. 15, 1811	2	14
Eunice, d. Jonath[an] & Hannah, b. Mar. 26, 1758	2	3
Eunice, m. Ebenezer **HEB[B]ARD**, Sept. 30, 1790	2	124
Ezra, s. Elisha & Huldah, b. Sept. 5, 1765	2	4
Ezra, m. Esther **HOLT**, May 29, 1788	2	14
George, m. Rebeckah **PALMER**, Apr. 28, 1714	1	35
George, d. Oct. 10, 1719	1	18
George, s. Elisha & Sarah, b. Sept. 2, 1723	1	58
George, d. Sept. 2, 1723	1	58
George, m. Mary **BURGE**, Nov. 12, 1751	2	27
George, m. Harriet **ROBINSON**, Jan. 2, 1825, by Abner		
Robinson, Esq.	3	59
George Henry, s. [Orrin & Olive], b. Dec. 19, 1819	3	94

	Vol	Page
LILLIE, LYLIE, LILLY, LILLEY, (cont.)		
Hannah, d. Jacob & Phebe, b. Feb. 16, 1738/9	1	72
Hannah, m. Jeremiah **KINGSLEY**, Jan. 9, 1757	2	28
Hannah, d. Elisha & Huldah, b. Sept. 23, 1760	2	4
Harriet A., m. Zaccheas **WALDO**, b. of Windham,		
Aug. 18, 1841, by Rev. Richard Woodruff, of		
Scotland Society	3	197
Harriet Adaline, d. [Ezra & Esther], b. Oct. 17,		
1805	2	14
Huldah, d. Elisha, Jr. & Huldah, b. May 20, 1757	2	4
Jacob, m. Phebe **THURSTON**, Oct. 23, 1723	1	72
Jacob, d. May 26, 1751	1	212
Jane, d. Jacob & Phebe, b. May 10, 1741	1	212
Jared, s. Elisha, Jr. & Huldah, b. Mar. 27, 1759	2	4
Jared, m. Susannah **TUCKERMAN**, Mar. 18, 1784	2	253
Jerusha, d. Elisha, Jr. & Huldah, b. Oct. 20, 1755	2	4
Jerusha, m. James **FLINT**, 3rd, Apr. 22, 1773	2	191
Jerusha, d. [John & Jerusha], b. Apr. 20, 17[ ]	2	77
Joel, s. Elisha & Sarah, b. Mar. 4, 1739/40	1	146
John, s. Elisha & Sarah, b. Sept. 20, 1734	1	146
John, s. [George & Mary], b. June 7, 1756	2	27
John, m. Jerusha [ ], Apr. 15, 1762	2	77
*Jonathan, s. of Elisha & Sarah, b. Mar. 19, 1731/2		
(*correction entire entry handwritten at bottom		
of page in the original manuscript)	1	58
Jonathan, s. George & Sarah, b. June 24, 1711; d.		
July 4, 1711	1	35
Jonathan, m. Sarah **KINGSLEY**, Aug. 26, 1752	2	79
Jonath[an], m. Hannah **TILDEN**, of Norwich, Dec. 12,		
1754	1	320
Jonathan, m. Hannah **TILDEN**, Dec. 12, 1754	2	3
Lemira, d. [Elisha & Huldah], b. Sept. 7, 1768	2	4
Lemuel, [triplet with Lucy & Leonard], s. Jonath[an]		
& Hannah, b. Feb. 22, 1761; d. Apr. 13, 1762	2	3
Leonard, [triplet with Lucy & Lemuel], s. Jonath[an]		
& Hannah, b. Feb. 22, 1761	2	3
Lester, s. [Jonathan & Sara], b. Apr. 27, 1761	2	79
Lettice, d. [Elisha & Huldah], b. Mar. 16, 1767	2	4
Lucinda, d. [Ezra & Esther], b. Nov. 28, 1788	2	14
Lucy, d. Jonathan & Hannah, b. Aug. 28, 1759; d. Sept.		
26, 1759	2	3
Lucy, [triplet with Lemuel & Leonard], d. Jonath[an]		
& Hannah, b. Feb. 22, 1761	2	3
Lucy, m. Jeremiah **ORMSBY**, May 14, 1778	2	28
Lydia, m. Daniel **MEACHAM**, Dec. 18, 1729	1	98
Lidea, d. Elisha & Huldah, b. June 12, 1763	2	4
Lydia, m. Dr. Vine **SMITH**, Mar. 10, 1822	3	101-2
Martha, m. Sam[ue]ll **BROUGHTON**, May 2, 1711	1	24

	Vol	Page
LILLIE, LYLIE, LILLY, LILLEY, (cont)		
Marvin, m. Lydia **ROBINSON**, Aug. 29, 1825, by Rev.		
Jesse Fisher	3	114
Mary, m. Eleiser **PALMER**, Mar. 28, 1723	1	73
Mary, d. Jacob & Phebe, b. June 11, 1734	1	72
Mary, d. R[e]uben & Mary, b. July 4, 1736	1	139
Mary, m. Jeremiah **BINGHAM**, Sept. 25, 1740	1	208
Mary, had s. Elan **MOLISON**, b. May 13, 1766	2	122
Nancy Ann, m. Elisha **YORK**, July 11, 1824	3	119
Nathan, s. Jacob & Phebe, b. May 14, 1729	1	72
Nath[aniel] R , m. Emily M **BALDWIN**, b of		
Windham, June 8, 1836, by Rev. Philo Judson		
at Willimantic	3	178
Nathaniel Rudd, s. [Ezra & Esther], b. Aug. 21,		
1802	2	14
Orrin, m. Olive **SMITH**, Nov. 27, 1817	3	94
Phebe, d Jacob & Phebe, b Jan. 4, 1724/5	1	72
Phebee, m. Joseph **MANNING**, Oct. 29, 1745	1	254
Pollidver, s. [John & Jerusha], b. June 19, 1769	2	77
Polly Webb, d. [Ezra & Esther], b. May 5, 1793; d.		
July 25, 1831	2	14
Prince, s. [George & Mary], b. Jan. 8, 1762; d.		
Mar. [ ], 1778, in the army	2	27
Rebecka, d. George, d. Jan. 18, 1719	1	18
Rebeckah, d Elisha & Sarah, b Mar 4, 1721/22	1	58
Rebeckah, m. Benjamin **HOLDING**, Feb. 3, 1757	2	25
R[e]uben, s. George & Sarah, b. May 18, 1709	1	35
R[e]uben, m. Mary **BREWSTER**, Feb. 14, 1733/4	1	139
R[e]uben, d May 28, 1737	1	139
R[e]uben, s. [George & Mary], b. Mar. 28, 1752; d.		
Jan 24, 1754	2	27
R[e]uben, s. [George & Mary], b. May 3, 1754	2	27
Roswell, s [Elijah & Ama], b Nov. 8, 1781	2	239
Sarah, w. George, d. June 8, 1713	1	35
Sarah, d. Elisha & Sarah, b Sept. 8, 1727	1	58
Sarah, [w. Elisha], d. Feb. 1, 1779, in the 84th y.		
of her age	1	146
Silas, s. R[e]uben & Mary, b. Oct. 25, 1734	1	139
Silas, m Mehetable **FOSTER**, Nov 10, 1763	2	95
Sibel, d. Jacob & Phebe. b. May 7, 1745; d. Aug. 2,		
1745	1	212
Sibbel, m. Elias **ROBINSON**, Aug. 26, 1779	3	12
Thomas, s [Jared & Susannah], b Mar. 24, 1785	2	253
Turner, s. Jona[than] & Hannah, b. Oct. 8, 1755	2	3
Warren S., farmer, ae 23, of Windham, m Julia A.		
FORD, ae. 17, b. Hampton, res. Windham, [ ],		
1851, by Rev Henry Greenslit	4	118
William, s. [John & Jerusha], d. Nov. 4, 1772	2	77

	Vol.	Page
LILLIE, LYLIE, LILLY, LILLEY, (cont.)		
William, s. [John & Jerusha], b. Mar. 13, 17[ ]	2	77
——, d. [Jonathan & Sarah], b. Oct. 20, 1753	2	79
——, s. [Jonathan & Sarah], b. May 26, 1755	2	79
——, d. [Jonathan & Sarah], b. July 30, 1757	2	79
LINCOLN, LINKON, LINKION, LINKHORN, LINKORN,		
Abigail, d. Jacob & Abigail, b. June 22, 1741	1	155
Abigail, m. George **AIM**, July 6, 1770	2	157
Achsah, d. [Sam[ue]l, Jr. & Phillis], b. Jan. 23,		
1766	1	271
Albert, s. [Jonah & Lucy], b. Sept. 9, 1802	2	254
Alfred, of Coventry, m. Caroline **KIMPTON**, of Willi-		
mantic, Sept. 22, 1834, by Rev. Philo Judson	3	170
Alma, m. William L. **DEXTER**, b. of Windham, June 6,		
1836, by Rev. Dexter Bullard	3	178
Alma Roxania, d. [Jabez & Abby], b. Oct. 25, 1811	3	62
Ann, d. Jacob & Abigail, b. Apr. 24, 1750; d. May 16,		
[1750]	1	155
Ann, d. [Jacob & Abigail], b. Jan. 26, 1756	1	155
Anner, d. John & Anner, b. Jan. 21, 1759	2	3
Anne, Wid., m. Mitchell **RICHARDS**, Mar. [ ], 1796	2	202
Asena, d. [Jonah & Eunice], b. Mar. 23, 1778	2	200
Asenath, m. William **RUMFORD**, b. of Windham, Oct. 21,		
1835, by John Baldwin, J.P.	3	174
Benj[amin], s. Tho[ma]s & Marcy, b. Dec. 9, 1750	1	176
Benjamin, m. Rhoda **JOHNSON**, Nov. 25, 1773	2	185
Benja[mi]n, s. [Benjamin & Rhoda], b. Apr. 10, 1776	2	185
Betsey, d. [David & Clarissa], b. Feb. 15, 1797	3	55
Betsey, d. July 24, 1851, ae. 70	4	158
Betsey Cannada, d. [Jacob & Betsey], b. Aug. 15, 1808	3	21
Burr, b. Chaplin, res. Windham, d. Aug. 8, [1851],		
ae. 45 [Burt?]	4	158
Burt, m. Elmira **WOOD**, Sept. 30, 1827	3	148
Caroline M., m. George **LINCOLN**, Nov. 9, 1846, by Rev.		
Frederick P. Coe	3	231
Caroline Matilda, d. [Jabez & Abby], b. Dec. 27, 1809	3	62
Carr, s. [Jonah & Lucy], b. Oct. 2, 1804 (Perhaps		
"Case")	2	254
Charles, s. Thomas & Elizabeth, b. Sept. 13, 1788	2	155
Charles, m. Mary Ann **BOND**, b. of Windham, Feb. 5, 1837,		
by John Baldwin, J.P.	3	181
Charles T., s. [Ralph & Almira], b. Mar. 10, 1824	3	70
Clarissa, m. David **LINCOLN**, Sept. 1, 1796	3	55
Clarissa, of Windham, m. Edwin **HOLLINGSWORTH**, of		
Woodstock, Nov. 24, 1839, by Rev. R. Ransom	3	191
Dan, s. [Jonah & Lucy], b. July 27, 1786	2	254
Daniel, s. Sam[ue]ll & Ruth, b. Apr. 5, 1736; d. Apr.		
20, 1736	1	70

	Vol.	Page

LINCOLN, LINKON, LINKION, LINKHORN, LINKORN,
(cont.)

Daniel, s. Jacob & Abigail, b. Aug. 31, 1738	1	155
Daniel, m. Mary **PRESTON**, June 22, 1763	2	85
Daniel, father of Jacob, d. Aug. 31, 1808	3	21
Daniel, m. Betsey **CROSS**, Nov. 11, 1833, by Rev. Roger Bingham	3	166
David, m. Clarissa **LINCOLN**, Sept. 1, 1796	3	55
David, farmer, d. May 12, 1860, ae. 86 y. 3 m.	4	159-0
Dwight, manufacturer, ae. 23, m. Eliza D. **WEBB**, ae. 24, Nov. 3, 1847, by Holmes Slade	4	111
Ebenezer, m. Mary **LAMB**, Mar. 4, 1761	2	133
Ebenezer (?), s. [Sam[ue]l, Jr. & Phillis], b. Jan. 25, 1768	1	271
Edgar S., [s. Jared W. & Joanna], b. Aug. 2, 1847	3	214
Edeth M., d. Frank M., merchant, ae. 34, & Mary A., ae. 25, b. Jan. 11, 1850	4	10
Edmond S., s. Samuel S., ae. 28, & Cordelia, ae. 31, b. June 15, [1848]	4	8
Eleizar, s. Sam[ue]ll & Ruth, b Mar. 7, 1732/3; d. Nov. 13, 1754	1	70
Eleazer, s. John & Rebeck[a]h, b. Dec. 9, 1755; d. Dec. 21, 1755	2	3
Eleazer, s. John & Rebeck[a]h, b. Nov. 30, 1757; d. Nov. 7, 1759	2	3
Elihu, s. Sam[ue]l, Jr. & Phebe, b. July 31, 1749; d. Nov. 7, 1754	1	271
Elihu, s. Sam[ue]l, Jr. & Phillis, b. July 25, 1760	1	271
Elijah, s. [Jacob & Abigail], b. Jan. 23, 1752	1	155
Elisha, s [Jonah & Lucy], b. Jan. 12, 1795	2	254
Eliza, twin with Janette, d. Allen, farmer, ae. 33, & Selinda, ae. 30, of Willimantic, b. Dec. 22, [1849]	4	10
Elizabeth, d Samuell & Elizabeth, b. Dec. 18, 1707	1	31
Elizabeth, d. [Sam[ue]l, Jr. & Phillis], b. Apr. 8, 1764	1	271
Elizabeth, d. [Thomas, Jr. & Elizabeth], b. Feb. 5, 1772	2	155
Elizabeth, w. Jacob, d. Dec. 24, 1804	3	21
Elizabeth Scott, [d. Jacob & Elizabeth], b. June 19, 1804; d. Feb. 19, 1805	3	21
Emily, m. Andrew J. **CONGDON**, b. of Willimantic, Sept. 23, 1839, by Rev. B. Cook, Jr., of Willimantic	3	190
Eunice, m. Luther **HUNTLEY**, b. of Windham, Aug. 19, 1833, by Stowell Lincoln, J.P.	3	188
Fanny, d. [John, Jr. & Mary], b. May 9, 1780	2	251
Frank M., s. [Ralph & Almira], b. Dec. 24, 1816	3	70
Frank M., m. Mary A. **BURNHAM**, Nov. 22, 1846, by Rev.		

	Vol	Page
LINCOLN, LINKON, LINKION, LINKHORN, LINKORN, (cont.)		
Issac H. Coe	3	232
George, m. Caroline M. **LINCOLN**, Nov. 9, 1846, by Rev. Frederick P. Coe	3	231
George, s Geo[rge], manufacture, ae. 26, & Amelia M. ae. 24, b. Aug. 6, 1847	4	3
George H., s. Charles, farmer, ae. 34, & Mary E., ae. 31, b. Dec. [ ], 1847	4	3
Giles Earl, [s. Burt & Elmira], b. Apr. 10, 1834	3	148
Gurdon, twin with Reuben, s. [Samuel 3rd & Prudence], b. Jan. 25, 1787	2	238
Hall, s. [Jonah & Lucy], b. Oct. 20, 1788	2	254
Hannah, d. [Daniel & Mary], b. June 10, 1774	2	85
Hannah, d. [Jonah & Eunice], b. June 17, 1786	2	200
Harry, s. [David & Clarissa], b. Sept. 30, 1798	3	55
Herbert S., b. Oct. 28, 1837	3	72
Herbert S., s. [Marvin & Asenath], b. Oct. 28, 1837	3	181
Hezekiah, s. Jacob & Abigail, b. May 7, 1748	1	155
Hezekiah, m. Hannah **SIMONS**, Feb. 6, 1771	2	161
Irene, d. [Jeremiah & Anne], b. Apr. 5, 1779	2	202
Isaac, s. [Jeremiah & Anne], b. Dec. 13, 1781	2	202
Jabez, b. May 18, 1784	2	155
Jabez, m. Abby **SCOTT**, of Franklin, Sept. 6, 1807	3	62
Jabez N., m. Mary **CLARK**, Jan. 4, 1846, by Rev. Abel Nichols	3	226
Jacob, s. Samuel & Elizabeth, b. May 10, 1696	A	24
Jacob, s. Samuell & Elizabeth, b. May 10, 1696	1	31
Jacob, m. Abigail **MASON**, Apr. 28, 1736	1	155
Jacob, s. Jacob & Abigail, b. Jan. 31, 1736/7	1	155
Jacob, Jr., m. Abigail **CARTER**, Jan. 24, 1758	2	38
Jacob, Jr., d. Apr. 21, 1760	2	38
Jacob, s. [Daniel & Mary], b. Apr. 8, 1765; d. Dec. 31, 1766	2	85
Jacob, s. [Daniel & Mary], b. July 26, 1767	2	85
Jacob, m. Elizabeth **SCOTT**, Mar. 12, 1797	3	21
Jacob, m. Betsey **CANNADA**, Nov. 26, 1805	3	21
James, s. [Jonah & Lucy], b. May 31, 1784	2	254
Jane W., d. [Ralph & Almira], b. Apr. 27, 1819	3	70
Janette, twin with Eliza, d. Allen, farmer, ae. 33, & Selinda, ae. 30, of Willimantic, b. Dec. 22, [1849]	4	10
Jared W., m. Joanna **SPAFFORD**, b. of Windham, Apr. 21, 1844, by Rev H. Slade, Scotland	3	214
Jeremiah, s. Tho[ma]s & Marcy, b. Nov. 14, 1751	1	176
Jeremiah, m. Anne **ABBE**, Sept. 20, 1775	2	202
Jeremiah, s. [Jeremiah & Anne], b. Mar. 18, 1789	2	202
Jeremiah, d. Apr. 30, 1794	2	202

	Vol.	Page
LINCOLN, LINKON, LINKION, LINKHORN, LINKORN, (cont.)		
Luther, s. Jacob, Jr. & Abigail, b. Dec. 21, 1758	2	38
Lyman, s. [David & Clarissa], b. Apr. 1, 1802	3	55
Marcelia, m. Luther **BURNHAM**, Apr. 29, 1827, by Rev. Alfred Burnham	3	130
Marcy, d. Samuel & Elizabeth, b. Dec. 4, 1698	A	24
Marcy, d. Samuell & Elizabeth, b. Dec. 4, 1698	1	31
Margaret, of Windham, m. Sheldon **STORRS**, of Mansfield, Nov. 24, 1839, by Rev. Reuben Ransom	3	191
Maria, d. [Jonah & Lucy], b. Nov. 23, 1799	2	254
Maria, m. Abel P. **WYLLIS**, Jan. 29, 1838, at Willimantic, by Rev. Philo Judson	3	185
Marvin, m. Asenath **BROOKS**, b. of Windham, Jan. 1, 1837, by Rev. Alfred Burnham	3	181
Mary, d. Sam[ue]l, Jr. & Phillis, b. May 16, 1762	1	271
Mary, b. Mansfield, res. Windham, d. Sept. [ ], 1847, ae. 21	4	152
Mary E., of Windham, m. Thomas **WIGGIN**, of Greenport, N.Y., Nov 26, 1844, by Erastus Dickenson	3	217
Mercy, m. George **MARTIN**, Nov. 5, 1736; d. Aug. 4, 1760	1	116
Mercy, w. Tho[ma]s, d. Apr. 5, 1758	1	176
Nancy, d. [Jeremiah & Anne], b. Mar. 18, 1785	2	202
Nathan, s. Jacob & Abigail, b. May 11, 1746	1	155
Nathan, farmer, ae. 60, b. Windham, res. Chaplin, m 2d w. Elizabeth **LUCE**, ae. 57, Dec. [ ], 1848, by P.B. Peck, Esq.	4	112
Nathaniel, s. Sam[ue]ll & Elizabeth, b. Apr. 11, 1705; d. Apr. 18, 1705	1	31
Nathaniell, s. Sam[ue]ll & Ruth, b. Nov. 18, 1728	1	70
Nath[anie]l, m. Agnes **AUSTIN**, Dec. 21, 1757	2	37
Nathaniel, s. [Nath[anie]l & Anges], b. Feb. 4, 1771	2	37
Nathaniel, Jr., m. Anna **STEEL**, June 10, 1792	2	67
Nathaniel, m. Huldah **WARNER**, b. of Windham, Jan. 3, 1836, by Rev. Edward Harris	3	176
Nicholas E., s. Lorin, ae. 29, & Elizabeth, ae. 24, b. Feb. 23, [1848]	4	8
Olive, d. John & Anner, b. June 24, 176[ ]	2	3
Oliver, s. Tho[ma]s & Marcy, b. Apr. 28, 1756	1	176
Orrymell, s. [Thomas, Jr. & Elizabeth], b. Feb. 25, 1770	2	155
Oshea, s. [Sam[ue]ll, Jr. & Phillis], b. Jan. 3, 1772	1	286
Pameta, d. [Jonah & Eunice], b. Sept. 4, 1782	2	200
Phebe, d. Sam[ue]l, Jr. & Phebe, b. June 8, 1751	1	271
Phebe, w. Sam[ue]l, d. Feb. 2, 1754	1	271
Phebe, d. [Jonah & Eunice], b. Sept. 20, 1790	2	200
Phillis, w. Sam[ue]ll, Jr , d. Feb. 25, 1776	1	286

	Vol.	Page
LINCOLN, LINKON, LINKION, LINKHORN, LINKORN, (cont.)		
Prudence, w. Thomas, d. Feb. 24, 1741	1	176
Prudence, d. Tho[ma]s & Marcy, b. Feb 20, 1754	1	176
Prudence, m. Samuel **LINKON**, 3rd, Nov. 29, 1781	2	238
Prudence, d. [Jacob & Elizabeth], b. Dec. 18, 1797	3	21
Pubuah (?), d. [Jacob & Elizabeth], b. Jan. 7, 1803; d. Oct. 1, 1803	3	21
Ralph, s. [Jonah & Lucy], b. Dec. 22, 1792	2	254
Ralph, m. Almira **TRUMBULL**, Mar. 28, 1816	3	70
Rebeckah, w. [John], d. Mar. 26, 1758	2	3
Reuben, twin with Gurdon, s. [Samuel, 3rd & Prudence], b. Jan. 25, 1787	2	238
Royal, s. [David & Clarissa], b. July 8, 1804	3	55
Royal, m. Phila **BIBBENS**, Oct. 12, 1823	3	71
Ruth, w. Sam[ue]ll, d. Oct. 6, 1757	1	70
Ruth, d. Sam[ue]ll, Jr. & Phillis, b. Jan 1, 1759	1	271
Ruth, w. Jonah, d. Aug. 19, 1775	1	94
Samuel, m. Elizabeth **JACOBS**, June 2, 1692	1	31
Samuel, m. Elizabeth **JACOBS**, June 20, 1692	A	24
Sam[ue]ll, s. Sam[ue]ll & Elizabeth, b. Jan. 20, 1693; d. Jan. 28, 1693	1	31
Samuell, s. Samuell & Elizabeth, b. Nov. 29, 1693	A	24
Samuel, s. Samuel & Elizabeth, b. Nov. 29, 1693	1	31
Sam[ue]ll, m. Ruth **HUNTINGTON**, Aug. 22, 1723	1	70
Sam[ue]ll, s. Sam[ue]ll & Ruth, b. Dec. 27, 1724	1	70
Sam[ue]ll, Jr., m. Phebe **FENTON**, Oct. 1, 1747	1	271
Sam[ue]l, s. Sam[ue]l, Jr. & Phebe, b. June 21, 1753	1	271
Sam[ue]l, Jr., m. Phillis **AUSTEN**, Mar. 9, 1758	1	271
Sam[ue]ll, m. Mary **AUSTIN**, Mar. 14, 1758	1	83
Samuel, 3rd, m. Prudence **LINKON**, Nov. 29, 1781	2	238
Shubael, s. Sam[ue]ll, Jr & Phillis, b. Mar. 6, 1770	1	286
Sophia, d. [Jacob & Elizabeth], b. Jan. 20, 1801	3	21
Sophia, m. Ira **PRESTER**, painter, Jan. 22, 1850, by J.M. Phillips	4	114
Stephen, s. [Jeremiah & Anne], b. Mar. 4, 1777	2	202
Stowell, Jr., s. Geo[rge], manufacturer, ae. 27, & Mariah, ae. 24, b. [　　], 1850	4	13
Sumner, m. Caroline **KIMBALL**, Oct. 16, 1842, by Rev. Alfred Burnham	3	205
Sylvester, m. Sarah **FULLER**, Aug. 28, 1836, by Elias Sharpe, Elder	3	179
Sylvester, s. [David & Clarissa], b. [　　]	3	55
Temperance, d. Thomas & Prudence, b. Sept. 5, 1740	1	176
Theodore, d. Sept. [　], 1847, ae. 2 m.	4	151

	Vol	Page
LINCOLN, LINKON, LINKION, LINKHORN, LINKORN, (cont.)		
Theodore, s. Samuel A., farmer, ae. 45, b. July 16, 1850	4	11
Thomas, s. Samuell & Elizabeth, b. Oct. 24, 1701	A	24
Thomas, s. Samuell & Elizabeth, b. Oct. 24, 1701	1	31
Thomas, m. Prudence **LANFEAR**, Sept. 12, 1738	1	176
Thomas, s. Thomas & Prudence, b. July 27, 1739	1	176
Thomas, m. Marcy **LAMB**, July 7, 1747	1	176
Thomas, Jr., m. Elizabeth **JOHNSON**, May 17, 1769	2	155
Tho[ma]s E., of Willimantic, d Feb. 22, 1851, ae. 20	4	157
Warner, m. Triphenia **YOUNG**, Mar. 23, 1830, by Rev. Roger Bingham	3	143
W[illia]m Earle, s. [Burt & Elmira], b. July 23, 1828	3	148
——, s. Tho[ma]s & Marcy, b. Feb. 12, 1747/8	1	176
——, child of Samuel, ae. 48, & Jean, b. July 6, [1848]	4	8
——, child of Charles, farmer, ae. 28, of Willimantic, b. Jan. 19, [1850]	4	10
——, st. b. female, b. Apr. 11, 1860	4	161
——, st. b. child b. May 6, 1860	4	159-0
LINDALL, Abigail, m. Joseph **HEB[B]ARD**, Apr. 20, 1698	A	21
LINDSEY, James, m. Lydia **DYER**, Dec. 31, 1836, by Rev. Philetus Greene	3	180
LITCHFIELD, Andrew M., of Hampton, m. Caroline **FULLER**, of Windham, Dec. 30, 1829, by Rev. Jesse Fisher	3	140
Elisha, physician, b. Hampton, res. Windham, d. Aug. 14, 1848, ae 43	4	154
Thomas J., of Hartford, m. Marcia P. **ROBINSON**, of Windham, Sept. 14, 1831, by Rev. Jesse Fisher	3	154
LITTLE, Philemon, m. Nancy **ABBE**, June 29, 1799, by Hezekiah Bissell, J.P ; d. Jan. 13, 1840	3	67
Philamon, d. Jan. 13, 1840	3	67
Sophia, m. John **MOODEY**, Mar. 28, 1830, by Rev Roger Bingham	3	144
LITTLEFIELD, LITTLEFIELDS, Alathear Ann, [d. Jairus & Alatheah], b. [ ]	3	54
Albert G., s. [Jairus & Alatheah], b. Jan. 22, 1810	3	54
Alice, d. [Ebenezer & Beulah], b. Apr. 6, 1778	2	182
Alice Antoinette, [d. Jairus & Alatheah], b. [ ]	3	54
Ebenezer, m. Beulah **SAWYER**, Dec. 24, 1769	2	182
Ebenezer Henry, [s. Jairus & Alatheah], b. [ ]	3	54
Elizabeth, d. [Ebenezer & Beulah], b. Apr. 7, 1774	2	182
Elizabeth Jane, [d. Jairus & Alatheah], b [ ]	3	54
Harriet C., m. John **THOMPSON**, b. of Willimantic, Nov. 14, 1841, by Rev. Andrew Sharp, Willimantic	3	199
Jairus, s. [Ebenezer & Beulah], b. Jan. 14, 1783	2	182

	Vol.	Page
LITTLEFIELD, LITTLEFIELDS, (cont.)		
Jairus, m. Alatheah **ELDERKIN**, Nov. 23, 1805	3	54
James, m Catharine A. **PATT**, b. of Willimantic,		
Oct. 18, 1835, by Rev. Philo Judson, at		
Willimantic	3	174
John, merchant, ae. 31, m. 2d w. Elizabeth **DURANT**,		
ae. 29, Sept. 1, 1849, by Rev. Hicks	4	115
Lora, d. [Ebenezer & Beulah], b. Nov. 11, 1780	2	182
Lora, m. James **PALMER**, Oct. 8, 1801	3	75
Lucretia, d. [Jairus & Alatheah], b. Dec. 2, 1808;		
d. Feb. 24, 1809	3	54
Luther, s. [Ebenezer & Beulah], b. June 25, 1770	2	182
Luther, s. [Jairus & Alatheah], b. Apr. 24, 1807	3	54
Lydia Elderkin, d. [Jairus & Alatheah], b. July 29,		
1812	3	54
Mary, [d. Jairus & Alatheah], b. [ ]	3	54
LOBDILL, LOBDIL, Sarah, m. Nathanial **BINGHAM**, July 25,		
1705	A	26
Sarah, m. Nathaniell **BINGHAM**, July 25, 1705	1	37
LOCKWOOD, Henry, s. Delight **WARNER**, b. Aug. 10, 1780	3	44
LOMBARD, Hannah, m. John **KIBBEE**, Mar. 21, 1732/3	1	106
Zenas O., of Lebanon, m. Lydia W. **SMITH**, of Willi-		
mantic, Windham, June 26, 1837, by Rev. B. Cook,		
Jr.	3	182
LONG, Abigail, of Windham, m. Henry **SHELDON**, of Mansfield,		
Sept. 6, 1829, by Rev. Jesse Fisher	3	137
William, of Canterbury, m. Lucy **FARNUM**, of Hampton,		
Mar. 4, 1833, by Rev. Jesse Fisher	3	165
——, child of Stephen, laborer, ae. 23, & Mary, ae.		
28, of Willimantic, b. Oct. 22, 1849	4	5
LOOMIS, LUMMIS, A.M.C., farmer, d. Oct. 17, [1849], ae. 33	4	155
Asher M. C., m. Phebe W. **WILSON**, Dec. 14, 1843, by		
Rev. Andrew Sharpe	3	212
Charlotte, m. Joseph B. **BLIVIN**, b. of Windham, July 3,		
1839, by Rev Windslow Ward	3	189
Charlotte Elizabeth, m. Joseph Barber **BLIVEN**, July 3,		
1839, in Willimantic, by Rev. Windsor Ward; d.		
Sept. 29, 1855	4	23-4
Daniel, s. John & Mary, b. Aug. 18, 1772	2	173
Elizabeth, d. [John & Ruth], b. Jan. 17, 1766	1	228
George, m. Charlotte **WARNER**, Mar. 7, 1832, by Rev.		
Rich[ar]d F. Cleveland	3	158
John, m. Mary **FULLER**, Dec. 10, 1747	1	228
John, s. John & Mary, b. Dec. 4, 1754	1	228
John, m. Ruth **AVEREL**, Jan 20, 1758	1	228
John, m. Eunice **SESSIONS**, Jan. 5, 1775	2	173
Jonathan, s [John & Ruth], b. July 31, 1759	1	228
Laura, b. Dec. 5, 1790; m. Luther P. **SMITH**, Sept. 12,		

	Vol	Page
LOOMIS, LUMMIS, (cont.)		
1814	3	139
Margaret, d. John & Mary, b. Aug. 17, 1756	1	228
Mary, d. John & Mary, b. Jan. 23, 1748/9	1	228
Mary, w. John, d. Sept. 9, 1756	1	228
Ruth, d. [John & Ruth], b. Sept. 16, 1761	1	228
Ruth, w. Rev John, d. Dec. 3, 1773	2	173
Sarah, d. John & Mary, b. Apr. 14, 1751	1	228
Sarah, m. Henry **DURKEE**, Jr., Apr. 23, 1778	2	148
William, s. [John & Ruth], b. Aug. 30, 1763	1	228
William, s. John, d. Jan. 18, 1778	2	173
LORD, Betty, d. [Solomon & Meriam], b. May 16, 1769, at		
Coventry	2	165
Caroline, m. Frederick **PRENTICE**, Jan. 23, 1823, by		
Rev. Jesse Fisher	3	107
Charlotta, d. [Solomon & Merian], b. Dec. 2, 1772	2	165
Eliza, of Norwich, m. John **PRENTICE**, of Griswold,		
Feb. 15, 1826	3	121
Gertenia(?), child of Tretus & Eliza, b. Mar 2,		
[1849]	4	7
Joshua B., m. Lucretia T **HOWES**, Nov 2, 1841, by		
Rev. Andrew Sharp	3	198
Nathan, s. [Solomon & Merian], b. Mar. 9, 1774	2	165
Peggy, m. Jacob **HAZEN**, Feb. 24, 1785	2	160
Prudence M., d. Aug 27, 1849, ae. 29	4	155
Solomon, m. Marian **COLEMAN**, Apr. 3, 1766	2	165
Zelotes, s. [Solomon & Merian], b. Aug. 24, 1771	2	165
——, child of Daniel, manufacturer, ae. 35, &		
Prudence, ae. 30, of Willimantic, b July 21, 1849	4	5
LORDEN, Lyman, m. Laura **BECKWITH**, Aug. 11, 1844, by Rev.		
Cha[rle]s Noble, Willimantic	3	216
LOTHROP, [see under **LATHROP**]		
LOURA, ——, b. Ireland, res Willimantic, d. [Dec] 25,		
[1849], ae. 2	4	153
LOVET, Sarah J , m. W[illia]m H. **ROBINSON**, Sept 26, 1847,		
by Rev. Andrew Sharp	3	236
LUCE, Abigail, d. [David & Eliza[bet]h], d. Apr 14, 1759	2	9
Abigail, d. David & Mehetable, b. Mar. 22, 1760	2	9
Alice, d. David & Mehetable, b. Oct. 3, 1775	2	9
Amy, d. [Ebenezer & Anna], b. Aug. 7, 1757	1	293
Amie, m. Elias **ROBINSON**, June 4, 1795	3	12
An[n], d. Israel & Grace, b. Aug. 14, 1721	1	22
Anna, d. Israel & Grace, b. Aug. [ ], 1721	1	128
Annah, d. [Ebenezer & Anna], b. Aug. 9, 1764; d. Sept.		
2, 1764	1	293
Annah, d. [Ebenezer & Anna], b. Oct. 17, 1767	1	293
Azubah, d. [Ebenezer & Anna], b. May 12, 1753	1	293
Benjamin, s. Israel & Grace, b. Nov. 26, 1709	1	22

	Vol.	Page
LUCE, (cont.)		
David, d. May 13, 1752, in the 70th y. of his age	2	9
David, m. Mehitable **DIMMICH**, May 24, 1759	2	9
David, s. [David & Mehetable], b. Dec. 3, 1766; d.		
Sept. 14, 1775	2	9
David, s. David & Mehetable, b. Dec. 9, 1777	2	9
Ebenezer, m. Anna **ROBINSON**, Oct 26, 1749	1	293
Ebenezer, s. [Ebenezer & Anna], b. Dec. 9, 1759	1	293
Eleazer, s. Israel & Grace, b. Feb. 21, 1712; d.		
May 12, 1727	1	22
Elizabeth, d. Joseph & Elizabeth, b. July 18, 1731	1	128
Eliza[bet]h, w. [David], d. Nov. 10, 1754, in the		
70th y. of her age	2	9
Elizabeth, d. [David & Mehetable], b. May 24, 1762	2	9
Elizabeth, m. Asahel **KINGSLEY**, Nov. 26, 1789	2	52
Elizabeth, ae. 57, m. Nathan **LINCOLN**, farmer, ae.		
60, b. Windham, res. Chaplin, Dec. [ ], 1848,		
by P.B. Peck, Esq.	4	112
[E]unice, d. Nathaniel & Mary, b. July 13, 1741	1	164
Grace, [w. Israel], d. May 18, 1730	1	128
Hannah, [d. Israel & Grace], d. Nov. 10, 1715	1	22
Israel, s. Israel & Grace, b. Apr. 8, 1714; d.		
May 3, 1727	1	22
Israel, d. May 20, 1727	1	22
James, Jr., m. Zillah **CARY**, May 13, 1762	2	89
James, d. Jan. 17, 1765, in the 56th y. of his		
age	1	274
Jemima, wid. [Jonathan], d. June 15, 1778	1	267
Jerusha, d. Eb[enezer] & Anna, b. Oct. 26, 1750	1	293
Jonathan, s. Josiah & Sarah, b. Aug. 8, 1710	1	2
Jonathan, d. Apr. 1, 1777	1	267
Joseph, m. Elizabeth **ROOD**, July 18, 1727	1	128
Joseph, s. Joseph & Elizabeth, b. Dec. 25, 1729;		
d. Dec. 25, 1729	1	128
Joseph, s. Joseph & Elizabeth, b. Oct. 28, 1733	1	128
Joshua, m. Mercy **BISHOP**, Oct. 17, 1733	1	116
Josiah, s. Josiah & Sarah, b. Dec. 18, 1707	1	2
Josiah, s. [Ebenezer & Anna], b. Aug. 27, 1765	1	293
Judah, d. Josiah & Sarah, b. Sept. 30, 1705	1	2
Lucretia, d. Nathaniel & Mary, b. Apr. 5, 1748	1	164
Mary, d. Israel & Grace, b. May 9, 1718	1	22
Mehetable, d. [David & Mehetable], b. Dec. 18, 1768	2	9
Nathan, s. Nathaniell & Mary, b Oct. 16, 1736	1	164
Nathaniell, s. Josiah & Sarah, b. Dec. 31, 1712	1	2
Nath[anie]ll, m. Mary **PRENTICE**, Dec. 25, 1735	1	164
Othniel, m. Joanne **KIMBALL**, Feb. 16, 1786	2	176
Rebecka, [d. Israel & Grace], d Mar. 28, 1722	1	22
Rebeckah, d. Joseph & Elizabeth, b. Sept. 14, 1728;		

	Vol.	Page
LUCE, (cont.)		
d. Sept. 28, 1728	1	128
Remember, d. [David & Mehetable], b. May 6, 1772	2	9
R[h]ode, d. Joshua & Mercy, b. Nov. 26, 1734	1	116
Sarah, d. [Ebenezer & Anna], b. June 22, 1752; d.		
next day	1	293
Sarah, d. [Ebenezer & Anna], b. Mar. 1, 1762	1	293
Susannah, d. [David & Mehetable], b. Aug. 26, 1764	2	9
Susannah, m. Nathan **FULLER**, Mar. 8, 1788	2	212
Thankfull, d. Israel & Grace, b. Nov. 28, 1715	1	22
Thankfull, m. Thomas **BUTLER**, June 19, 1749	1	250
Zillah, m. Jonathan **KINGSLEY**, Jan. 22, 1777	2	216
Zilpha, d. [Ebenezer & Anna], b. May 22, 1755	1	293
——, s. Jonath[an] & Jemima, b. July 5, 1744; d.		
July 18, 1744	1	267
LUCKEY, Samuel, of New York City, m. Caroline M.		
NEWCOMB, of Windham, Feb. 21, 1847, by H. Slade	3	234
LUDDINGTON, LUDINGTON, [see also **DUDINGTON**], David,		
s. James & Eliner, b. Mar. 19, 1739	1	215
Elizabeth, d. James & Elizabeth, b. Apr. 23, 1737	1	215
Elizabeth, m. Zachariah **DEANS**, June 18, 1760	2	64
Ellenor, m. Eben[eze]r **PALMITER**, Aug. 6, 1764	2	129
LYMAN, Betsey, m. Luther **BACKUS**, [ ]	3	4
Elizabeth F., m. Henry M. **PRENTICE**, b. of Windham,		
Aug. 22, 1842, by Rev. A.C. Wheat	3	203
Geo[rge] W., of Norwich, m. Emeline **JORDAN**, of		
Willimantic, [ ], by Rev. John Cooper	3	223
Malinda, m. Luther **BACKUS**, [ ]	3	4
Nancy A., m. Joseph **BROWN**, Jr., Nov. 2, 1826, by Rev		
Cornelius B. Everest	3	74
William, m Elizabeth **SAWYER**, Dec. 2, 1832, by Rev		
Roger Bingham	3	162
LYNCH, John, s. John, laborer, ae. 35, & Joanna, ae. 40, b.		
Aug. 27, 1850	4	12
LYNN, Arthur H., s. W[illia]m F , farmer, ae 39, &		
Elizabeth, ae. 39, of Willimantic, b. Apr. 19, 1851	4	12
LYON, Abigail, m. Edward **CHAPPELL**, Sept. 25, 1831, by Rev.		
Rich[ar]d F. Cleveland	3	154
Alice, d. [Robert & Alice], b. June 14, 1769	2	102
Amelia B., b. Willimantic, res. Windham, d. Dec. 18,		
1847, ae. 5 w	4	151
Casper L., m. Sarah **STEBBINS**, b. of Willimantic, Oct		
13, 1839, at Willimantic, by Rev B. Cook, Jr., of		
Willimantic	3	190
Charles, of Lisbon, m Harriet **GURLEY**, of Windham,		
Sept. 23, 1829, by Rev. Dennis Platt	3	138
Chester, s. [Robert & Alice], b. May 25, 1772	2	102
Elizabeth B., d. Apr. 12, 1848, ae. 58	4	152

	Vol.	Page
LYON, (cont.)		
Harriet, of Canterbury, m. Henry P. **PALMER**, of		
Windham, Aug. 11, 1834, by Rev. Jesse Fisher	3	169
Robert, m. Alice **HOLT**, Nov. 13, 1764	2	102
Robert, s. [Robert & Alice], b Dec 23, 1765	2	102
Roswell, s. [Robert & Alice], b. Oct. 2, 1770	2	102
Rufus, s [Robert & Alice], b. Apr. 24, 1767	2	102
Samantha L., m. Hollis A. **SNOW**, Mar. 28, 1842, by		
Rev. Andrew Sharp	3	201
Sarah, of Lisbon, m. Elijah A. **WILLIAMS**, of		
Canterbury, Sept. 30, 1832, by Rev. Levi Nelson	3	96
Zapparah S., of Union, m. Malinda **INGALLS**, of		
Windham, Nov. 27, 1842, by Rev Alfred Burnham	3	206
Zerviah, m. Joseph **ASHLEY**, Apr. 25, 1764	1	223
MAGUNE, Elizabeth, d. Isaac & Elizabeth, b Apr. 1, 1699	A	28
Isaac, s. Isaac & Elizabeth, b. Mar. 22, 1706	A	30
MAEONEY, MAHONY, Caroline A., d. Edwin, carpenter, ae 27,		
& Caroline, ae. 21, b. May 10, 1851	4	14
Edwin C., carpenter, ae. 27, b. Providence, m		
Cornelia **KEGWIN**, ae. 20, of Windham, Dec. 30,		
[1849], by Rev. J.M. Phillips	4	114
MAINARD, MAINAR, MANARD, MAINOR, Abigail, m. Joshua		
BURNHAM, Apr. 19, 1740	1	298
Amos, [s. Elnathan & Bial], b. June 14, 1743	1	242
Amos, m. Elizab[et]h **BUTTON**, Apr. 20, 1769	2	144
Amy, [d. Elnathan & Bial], b. July 29, 1759	1	242
Cyrus, s. [Elnathan & Bial], b. Sept. 6, 1745	1	242
Elizabeth, m. Ephraim **UPTON**, Apr. 14, 1757	2	112
Elnathan, d. Dec. 6, 1777	1	300
Hannah, d. [Elnathan & Bial], b. Apr. 27, 1747	1	242
Mary, d. Elnathan & Bial, b. May 2, 1741	1	242
Moses, [s. Elnathan & Bial], b. Nov. 3, 1756	1	242
Reuben, s [Elnathan & Bial], b. Feb. 22, 1752	1	242
Susannah, w. Zach[ariah], d. Oct. 18, 1753	1	146
Thankful, d. [Elnathan & Bial], b. Nov 9, 1749	1	242
Zach[ariah], m. Mary **NEFF**, Jan. 28, 1754	1	146
Zilpha, [d. Elnathan & Bial], b. Sept. 3, 1754	1	242
MAINE, MAIN, Albert N., of Bolton, m. Susan **HARVEY**, Aug.		
21, 1843, at Willimantic, by Rev. J.B. Guild	3	211
Almira, of Willimantic, m. Ira **WINSOR**, of Sterling,		
Nov. 27, 1836, by Rev. Philo Judson, at		
Willimantic	3	181
Andrew, s. Jonathan W., farmer, ae 32, b. Feb. 6,		
[1850]	4	10
Elvira Lovina, d Lorry, farmer, & Harriet C , b.		
Nov. 2, 1847	4	3
Harriet, m. Lemuel **STANTON**, Dec. 19, 1830, by Rev		
Roger Bingham	3	150

	Vol	Page

MAINE, MAIN, (cont)

Jonathan W., m. Lydia C. **ROBINSON**, b. of Windham,
Nov. 25, 1841, by Rev. J.E. Tyler   3   199

Laura S., ae. 24, m. John P. **AYERS**, merchant, ae.
22, Mar 1849, by Rev. Mr. Robinson   4   113

Lavina G., of Norwich, m. Charles **WOOD**, of South
Woodstock, [Mar.] 25, 1838, by Rev. John E.
Tyler   3   185

Oliver Fenner, d. Mar. 28, 1848, ae. 5 m   4   151

MAL[L]ORY, Norman, of Canterbury, m. Sophia **BECKWITH**, of
Windham, Sept. 10, 1845, by John Crocker   3   223

MANNIHAN, Geo[rge], s. G. W., ae. 34, b. July 23, [1849]   4   6

Sarah B., b. Woodstock, res. Willimantic, d Nov. 23,
1850, ae. 31   4   157

MANNING, Abigail, d. Sam[ue]ll & Iverna, b. Nov. 25, 1722   1   3

Abigail, d. John & Abigail, b. Sept. 4, 1728   1   100

Abigail, m. John **WELCH**, Oct. 27, 1745   1   251

Abigail, d. John & Sarah, b. Oct. 10, 1749; d. July
6, 1750   1   265

Abigail, d. [Joseph & Phebee], b. June 25, 1766   1   254

Abigail, d. [Joel], b. Feb. 12, 1798   3   32

Alathear, d. Josiah & Mary, b. Feb. 23, 1753   1   234

Alathear, s. [John, Jr. & Sarah], b. Jan. 25, 1760   1   265

Alitha, m. Erastus **PALMER**, May 28, 1822   3   104

Alfred, s. [Joel & Abigail], b. Dec. 16, 1782   2   194

Alice, d. Phineas & Sarah, b. Sept. 16, 1755; d.
Oct. 2, 1755   1   304

Alice, m. Seth **PALMER**, Jr., June 14, 1756; d. Nov.
26, 1794   2   14

Alice, see also Ellis

Amelia, m. Benjamin **SMITH**, Oct. 3, 1792   3   123

Andrew, s. [John, Jr. & Sarah], d. July 8, 1755   1   265

Anna, d. John & Sarah, b. Aug. 20, 1745   1   265

Asenath, m. Dr William **ROBINSON**, Nov. 10, 1774   2   209

Barnabus, s. John & Sarah, b. Sept. 14, 1768   2   139

Benj[ami]n, twin with John, [s John, Jr. & Sarah],
b. Mar. 30, 1753; d. Jan. 18, 1755   1   265

Benjamin, s. [John, Jr. & Sarah], b Oct. 16, 1757   1   265

Benjamin, m. Sarah **MANSELL**, Nov. 11, 1787   2   56

Calvin, s. Hez[ekiah] & Mary, b. May 4, 1746   1   229

Charles, d. Sept. 9, [1849], ae. 4   4   156

Charles F., m. Lydia A. **HEBBARD**, b of Windham, Oct
10, 1842, by Rev. J.E. Tyler   3   204

Cyrus, s. Josiah & Mary, b. May 15, 1743; d. Dec 14,
1776   1   234

Cyrus, m. Mary **BAKER**, Dec. 12, 1771   2   170

Cyrus, d. Dec. 14, 1776, at New Haven, returning from
the Army, in the 34th y. of his age   2   170

	Vol.	Page
MANNING, (cont.)		
Dan, s. Joseph & Phebee, b. Sept. 29, 1753	1	254
Dan, m. Lydia **PETERS**, Mar. 2, 1775	2	201
David, s. Sam[ue]ll & Irena, b. Jan. 14, 1726/7	1	77
Deborah, d. Sam[ue]ll & Deborah, d. Jan. 30, 1723/4	1	58
Deborah, w. Sam[ue]ll, d. Aug. 8, 1727	1	77
Delia, d. Cha[rle]s, blacksmith, ae. 29, & Lydia,		
ae. 28, b. Sept. 10, 1847	4	4
Eleazer, s. Josiah & Mary, b. July 25, 1749	1	234
Elijah, s. Josiah & Mary, b. Apr. 3, 1755	1	234
Elijah, s. Josiah & Mary, d. the latter part of		
1777 or the beginning of 1778, in the Army	1	234
Eliphalet, s. John & Sarah, b. May 17, 1747	1	265
Eliphalet, s. [Benjamin & Sarah], b. June 12, 1791	2	56
Eliphalet, of Windham, m. Lareances **INGRAHAM**, of		
Lebanon, Nov. 23, 1846, by Elder Henry Greenslit	3	232
Elizabeth, m. Samuel **BINGHAM**, Nov. 23, 1721	1	3
Elizabeth, d. Hez[ekiah] & Mary, b. July 7, 1755	1	229
Elizabeth, m. John **BAKER**, Jr., Dec. 14, 1775	2	208
Elizabeth, d. [Joel & Abigail], b. Jan. 26, 1789	2	194
Ellis, d. John & Abigail, b. Aug. 1, 1732	1	100
Ellis, see also Alice		
Eunice, m. Marshall **PALMER**, Oct. 9, 1783	2	227
Fanny, d. [Benjamin & Sarah], b. June 18, 1789	2	56
Frederick, m. Anne **YOUNG**, July 19, 1781	2	73
Hannah, d. Josiah & Mary, b. May 22, 1751; d. Oct		
[ ], 1753	1	234
Hannah, d. [Josiah & Mary], b. May 18, 1757	1	234
Henry, m. Eunice N. **DEVOTION**, Nov. 30, 1823	3	114
Henry Louis, s [Henry & Eunice N.], b. Sept. 22, 1824	3	114
Hezekiah, s. Sam[ue]ll & Iverna, b. Aug. 8, 1721	1	3
Hezekiah, m. Mary **WEBB**, Sept. 22, 1745	1	229
Increase, s. Josiah & Mary, b. Jan. 18, 1761	1	234
Irena, [w. Sam[ue]ll], d. Jan. 20, 1726/7	1	77
Irene, d. Josiah & Mary, b. Apr. 18, 1747	1	234
Irena, m. Jabez **KINGSLEY**, Mar. 7, 1749/50	1	299
Irena, m. William **CARY**, Jr. May 16, 1771	2	169
Jacob, s. Joseph & Phebe, b. Oct. 5, 1750	1	254
James, s. Cyrus & Mary, b. July 14, 1772	2	170
Jane, m Horace **HALL**, June 28, 1829, by Rev. Roger		
Bingham	3	142
Jane, d Sept. 2, [1849], ae. 2	4	156
Jerusha, d. Hez[ekiah] & Mary, b. Dec. 19, 1750	1	229
Joel, s. [Joseph & Phebee], b. Apr. 1, 1756	1	254
Joel, m. Abigail **BUNDY**, Mar. 1, 1782	2	194
Joel, m. [ ] **BUNDY**, [ ]	3	32
John, Jr., m. Sarah **LAMBERT**, June 10, 1744	1	265
John, Jr., m. Sarah **SEABURY**, Jan. 27, 1752	1	265

	Vol.	Page
MANNING, (cont.)		
Sally, d. [Joel], b. Dec. 20, 1793	3	32
Sam[ue]ll, m. Iverna **RYPLEY**, Apr. 27, 1719	1	3
Sam[ue]ll, s. John & Abigail, b. Nov. 3, 1723, at Cambridge	1	100
Sam[ue]ll, s. Sam[ue]ll & Irena, b. Oct. 22, 1725; d. June 3, 1727	1	77
Samuel, Sr., d. Feb. 20, 1755	1	77
Samuel, of Lebanon, m. Almira **HYDE**, of Franklin, June 20, 1838, by Rev. John E. Tyler	3	186
Samuel, d. July [1850], ae. 86	4	157
Sarah, d. Sam[ue]ll & Irena, b. Feb. 22, 1723/4	1	77
Sarah, d. John & Abigail, d. Feb. 13, 1736/7	1	100
Sarah, w. Sam[ue]ll, d. Oct. 11, 1746	1	77
Sarah, d. Phinehas & Sarah, b. Dec. 20, 1749	1	304
Sarah, w. Phinehas, d. Apr. 20, 1750	1	304
Sarah, w. John, d. Apr. 28, 1751	1	265
Sare, d. John & Abigail, b. Oct. 28, 1837 [1737?]	1	100
Seabury, s. [John, Jr. & Sarah], b. July 3, 1762	1	265
Seth, s. [Dan & Lydia], b. Dec. 27, 1775	2	201
Sophia, d. [Frederick & Anne], b. June 2, 1784	2	73
Susannah, d. John & Abigail, b. Oct. 8, 1734	1	100
Tryphenia, m. Daniel **BUCK**, Jan. 15, 1766	2	120
——, d. Joseph & Phebee, b. Feb. 22, 1745/6	1	254
——, child of Charles & Lydia, b. May 14, [1849]	4	8
MANSELL, [see also **MANSON** and **MUNSELL**], Sarah, m Benjamin **MANNING**, Nov. 11, 1787	2	56
MANSON, Lois, m. John **ABBE**, Jr. [ ]	1	319
MAPLES, Olive, m. Charles **PIERCE**, Aug. 29, 1829, by Chester Tilden, Willimantic	3	137
MARKHAM, Anne, d. Israel & Anne, b. July 19, 1734	1	143
Israel, m. Anne **SPENCER**, May 11, 1733	1	143
Israel, s. Israel & Anne, b. Jan. 21, 1735/6	1	143
MARSH, [see also **MASH**], Abigail, m. John **RIPLEY**, June 7, 1769	2	155
Anna, d. Joseph & Anne, b. Nov 14, 1745	1	226
Anne, w. Joseph, d. Aug. 26, 1753	1	226
Daniel, s. Joseph & Anne, b. Apr. 5, 1744; d Apr. 26, 1753	1	226
Daniell, s. [Joseph & Lydia], b. Apr. 3, 1764	1	230
Eben[ezer], s. Joseph & Lydia; b. Aug. 1, 1755	1	230
Elihu, m. Zeruiah **ABBE**, May 10, 1736	1	170
Elihu, s. Elihu & Zeruiah, b. Sept. 17, 1737	1	170
Elizabeth, d. Joseph & Anne, b. Dec. 5, 1749; d. Apr. 29, 1753	1	226
Esther, d. John & Sarah, b. Sept. 20, 1738	1	175
Hannah, m. Dr. Joshua **SUMNER**, July 2, 1788	2	249

	Vol.	Page
MARSH, (cont.)		
John, m. Sarah **MARTIN**, Sept. 29, 1736	1	175
Jonathan F., s. J.P., cabinet manufacturer, ae. 40,		
& Prudence, ae. 36, of Willimantic, b. May 15,		
[1849]	4	5
Joseph, m. Anne **STEDMAN**, Apr. 27, 1743	1	226
Joseph, s. Jos[eph] & Anne, b. Dec. 20, 1747; d		
June 12, 1753	1	226
Joseph, m. Lydia **BENNET[T]**, June 20, 1754	1	230
Joseph, s. Joseph & Lydia, b. Feb. 1, 1759	1	230
Joseph, Jr., of Norwich, m. Lora M. **FITCH**, Dec. 28,		
1823	3	116
Lois, d. Joseph & Lydia, b. Apr. 15, 1762	1	230
Luce, d. John & Sarah, b. Apr. 9, 1742	1	175
Mary, m. Dr. Benjamin **DYER**, Mar. 13, 1783	2	250
Phebe, m. Joseph **CARY**, July 1, 1747	1	269
Phineas, s. John & Sarah, b. June 29, 1737	1	175
Phinehas, s. Joseph & Lydia, b. Sept. 29, 1760	1	230
Sarah, d. John & Sarah, b. Mar. 20, 1740	1	175
Sarah, m. Samuel **LEE**, Mar. 23, 1769	2	154
Stephen, s. Joseph & Anne, b. Feb. 5, 1752; d. May 8,		
1753	1	226
Susannah, d. John & Sarah, b. Dec. 1, 1743	1	175
Thomas, s. [Joseph & Lydia], b. Dec. 29, 1765	1	230
MARTIN, Aaron, s. George, Jr. & Sarah, b. July 30, 1742	1	150
Aaron, m. Eunice **FLINT**, Nov. 13, 1766	2	126
Aaron, s. [Aaron & Eunice], b. Feb. 25, 1772	2	126
Abel, s. [Shubael & Abigail], b. July 19, 1779	2	220
Abigail, d. Jonathan & Jemima, b. Jan. 14, 1733/4	1	114
Alfred, m. Julia E. **SAFFORD**, Nov. 26, 1846, by Rev.		
Isaac H. Coe	3	232
Amasa, s. Ebenezer & Jerusha, b. Oct. 7, 1740	1	163
Amasa, s. [Joseph & Elizabeth], b July 31, 1764	1	307
Anna, d. George & Mercy, b. July 15, 1725	1	80
Anna Marsh, d. [Gideon & Rachal], b. May 18, 1767	2	124
Anne, m. Levi **JOHNSON**, Sept. 19, 1804	3	85
Ashbell, s. [Jonathan, Jr. & Jerusha], b. Apr 19,		
1791	2	166
Benjamin, s Ebenezer & Jerusha, b. Feb. 28, 1744/5	1	163
Betsey, m. John **BASS**, Apr. 25, 1821	3	74
Betsey, m. John **BASS**, Apr. 25, 1821	3	103
Betty, d. [Aaron & Eunice], b. Nov. 16, 1784	2	126
C[h]loe, d [David & Elizabeth], b. Mar. 14, 1764	2	15
Cornelia, d. [Erastus & Julia], b. Sept. 29, 1821	3	125
Cinthia, d. [Joseph & Zerviah], b. Mar 15, 1784	2	202
Cyrel, s. [George, 3rd, & Sarah], b. Mar. 5, 1779	2	101
Daniel, s. [Aaron & Eunice], b. June 12, 1770	2	126
Daniel B., of Chaplin, m. Sarah R. **FULLER**, of Windham,		

	Vol.	Page
MARTIN, (cont.)		
Feb. 20, 1833, by Rev. L.S. Hough, of Chaplin	3	163
David, s. George, Jr. & Grace, b Feb. 22, 1735/6	1	150
David, m. Elizabeth **HENDE[E]**, May 27, 1756	2	15
David, m. Dinah **UTLEY**, Jan. 25, 1775	2	15
David, s. [Aaron & Eunice], b. July 26, 1790	2	126
Deborah, d. John & Sarah, b. Jan 1, 1750/51	1	280
Dicey, d. Sarah **SMITH**, b. Jan. 5, 1769	2	171
Dolle, d. [George, Jr & Dorothy], b. Aug. 13, 1771	2	109
Ebenezer, m. Mary **MILLARD**, Oct. 4, 1724	1	76
Ebenezer, m. Jerusha **DURGE**, Apr. 1, 1729	1	76
Ebenezer, s. Ebenezer & Jerusha, b. Mar. 31, 1732	1	76
Ebenezer, s. John & Hannah, b. Aug. 28, 1752	1	280
Ebenezer, s. [George, & Dorothy], b. July 19, 1773	2	109
Ebenezer, d. July 13, 1775, in the 79th y. of his age	1	163
Edwin, s. [Erastus & Julia], b. Jan. 5, 1824	3	125
Elijah, s. [George, 3rd, & Sarah], b. Feb. 11, 1789	2	101
Eliphalet, s. John & Hannah, b. Sept. 12, 1754	1	280
Eliphalet, m. Eunice **CLARK**, May 15, 1799	2	87
Elisha, s. [Joseph, Jr. & Abigail], b. Sept. 16, 1776	2	203
Elizabeth, d. George, Jr. & Anne, b Jan. 17, 1707	1	116
Elizabeth, d. George & Anne, b. Jan. 17, 1707/8	1	80
Elizabeth, m. David **PRESTON**, Aug. 2, 1726	1	85
Elizabeth, d. Ebenezer & Jerusha, b. Aug. 1, 1738	1	163
Eliz[abeth], m. Ebenezer **GRIFFEN**, Jr., Feb. 2, 1757	2	52
Eliz[abeth], d. [David & Elizabeth], b. Oct. 23, 1759; d. Nov. 8, 1759	2	15
Elizabeth, d. [Joseph & Elizabeth], b. Dec. 24, 1761	1	307
Elizabeth, d. [David & Elizabeth], b. Jan. 14, 1767	2	15
Elizabeth, w. David, d. June 12, 1771, in the 38th y. of her age	2	15
Elizabeth, d. [Joseph, Jr. & Abigail], b. Mar. 28, 1779	2	203
Emelia, d. [William & Naomi], b. June 4, 1775	2	54
Erastus, s. [George, 3rd, & Sarah], b. Sept. 11, 1785; d. Feb 22, 1786	2	101
Erastus, s. [George, 3rd, & Sarah], b. Dec. 14, 1786	2	101
Erastus, b. Dec. 14, 1786; m Julia **ASHLEY**, Jan. 11, 1816	3	125
Esther, d. [Gideon & Rachal], b. Mar. 30, 1771	2	124
Eunice, d. [Joseph & Elizabeth], b. Dec. 26, 1756	1	307
Eunice, d. [Aaron & Eunice], b. Mar. 2, 1774	2	126
Eunice, m. Ebenezer **CLARK**, Jan. 12, 1778	2	218
Eunice, d. [Eliphalet & Eunice], b. Nov 19, 1799	2	87
George, Jr., m. Anne **CHOATE**, of Chebacco in Ipswich, Nov. 29, 1706	1	116
George, s. George & Mercy, b. Apr. 19, 1712	1	80
George, Jr., m. Grace **HOWARD**, Oct. 23, 1733	1	150
George, m. Mercy **LINKON**, Nov. 5, 1736	1	116

	Vol.	Page
MARTIN, (cont.)		
Jonathan, s. Jonathan & Jemima, b. Apr. 13, 1743	1	114
Jonathan, s. George [Jr. & Sarah], d. Sept. 24, 1744	1	247
Jonathan, s. George, Jr. & Sarah, b. May 24, 1746; d.		
Sept. 3, 1746	1	247
Jonathan, s. [David & Elizabeth], b. Mar. 4, 1762; d.		
Jan. 24, 1763	2	15
Jonathan, s. [Aaron & Eunice], b. Aug. 8, 1767	2	126
Jonathan, Jr., m. Jerusha **WELCH**, Mar. 9, 1769	2	166
Jonathan, s. [Jonathan, Jr. & Jerusha], b. Jan. 23,		
1776	2	166
Joseph, s. Ebenezer & Jerusha, b. Mar. 29, 1730	1	76
Joseph, s. Jonathan & Jemima, b. Nov. 7, 1738	1	114
Joseph, father of Jonathan, d. May 13, 1750, in the		
66th y. of his age	1	116
Joseph, m. Elizabeth **FORD**, Oct. 17, 1751	1	307
Joseph, s. Joseph & Elizabeth, b July 24, 1752; d.		
Dec. 22, 1752	1	307
Joseph, s. Joseph & Elizabeth, b. May 6, 1754	1	307
Joseph, m. Elizabeth **COY**, Jan. 3, 1765	2	116
Joseph, Jr., m. Abigail **BUTLER**, June 2, 1774	2	203
Joseph, m. Zerviah **DAYLEY**, Apr. 11, 1776	2	202
Juliana, d. [Jonathan, Jr. & Jerusha], b. Feb. 2,		
1783	2	166
Lemuel, s. John & Hannah, b. Sept. 15, 1756	1	280
Lora, d. [George, 3rd & Sarah], b. Mar. 4, 1782; d.		
Mar. 1, 1786	2	101
Lora, m. Benjamin **DURKEE**, Aug. 26, 1804	3	55
Lora, d. [Erastus & Julia], b. Mar. 4, 1817	3	125
Lucinda, d. [Gideon & Rachal], b. Apr. 16, 1769	2	124
Lucy, d Eben[eze]r & Jerusha, b. May 8, 1747	1	163
Lucy, d. George, Jr. & Sarah, b. May 6, 1749	1	189
Lucy, m. Sam[ue]ll **FLINT**, Jr., Dec. 17, 1767	2	139
Lucy, m. Nath[anie]ll **FLINT**, 3rd, May 23, 176[ ]	2	123
Luther, s. Jonathan & Jemima, b Apr 10, 1752	1	116
Lydia, d. [Aaron & Eunice], b. Mar. 26, 1793	2	126
Lydia Maria, d. [Erastus & Julia], b. Nov 28, 1829	3	125
Marcy, d. George, Jr. & Sarah, b. Apr. 18, 1744	1	247
Martha, d. Jonathan & Jemima, b May 28, 1741	1	114
Martha, d. [Jonath[an] & Jemima], d. Apr. 25, 1750	1	116
Mary, d. Ebenezer & Mary, b. Feb 11, 1726	1	76
Mary, w. Ebenezer, d. Oct. 1, 1728	1	76
Mary, d. Jonathan & Jemima, b. Apr. 21, 1732	1	114
Mary, mother of Jonathan & w. Joseph, d. Jan. 25,		
1745/6, in the 63rd y. of her age	1	116
Mary, m. Stephen **PARKER**, Mar. 22, 1748/9	1	290
Mary, d. John & Sarah, b. May 9, 1749	1	280
Mary, d. [George, Jr. & Dorothy], b. July 18, 1769	2	109

	Vol.	Page
MARTIN, (cont.)		
Mary, d. [Aaron & Eunice], b. Oct. 8, 1777	2	126
Mary, see under Mary **TICKNOR**	1	116
Mary Dingley, d. [William & Naomi], b. July 12, 1770	2	54
Melane, d. [Jonathan, Jr. & Jerusha], b. Apr. 16, 1771	2	166
Mercy, d. George & Mercy, b. June 25, 1710	1	80
Mercy, m. Amos **LEACH**, May 16, 1728	1	126
Mercy, w. George, d. Aug. 1, 1730	1	80
Mercy, wid. George, d. Aug. 4, 1760	1	116
Nathaniel Ford, s. [Joseph & Elizabeth], b. Oct. 27, 1759	1	307
Nathaniel Ford, m. Jerusha **LINKON**, Dec. 1, 1783	2	255
Olive, d. [Nathaniel Ford & Jerusha], b. Sept. 27, 1784	2	255
Olive, d. [Aaron & Eunice], b. Oct. 10, 1788	2	126
Olive, m. John **BROWN**, Jr., Oct. 10, 1793	3	19
Orson, s. [Joseph & Zerviah], b. June 26, 1782	2	202
Phebe, d. [David & Elizabeth], b. Oct. 15, 1769	2	15
Phebe, d. [William & Naomi], b. Jan. 31, 1780	2	54
Phebe H., of Windham, m. Seth **BALDWIN**, of Brooklyn, Conn., Nov. 27, 1845, by Rev. Henry Coe	3	225
Polly, m. Joel **BASS**, Dec. 22, 1796	2	112
Rachal M., of Windham, m. Kingsbury **CADY**, of Hartford, Jan. 10, 1847, by H. Slade	3	233
Ralph, s. [George, 3rd & Sarah], b. Oct. 11, 1793; d. Aug. 18, 1795	2	101
Rebecca, d. George, Jr. & Sarah, b. July 3, 1747	1	247
Rufus, s. [Gideon & Rachal], b. May 25, 1773	2	124
Sabrina, m. Morris **BAKER**, Feb. 20, 1827, by Rev. Cornelius B. Everest	3	25
Sally, d. [George, 3rd & Sarah], b. Jan. 9, 1797	2	101
Samuel, s. [George, Jr. & Dorothy], b. July 3, 1765	2	109
Samuel, s. [Jonathan, Jr. & Jerusha], b. Jan. 7, 1781	2	166
Samuel, s. [Aaron & Eunice], b. Feb. 7, 1783	2	126
Sarah, d. George & Mercy, b. Mar. 31, 1721	1	80
Sarah, m John **MARSH**, Sept 29, 1736	1	175
Sarah, d. George, Jr. & Sarah, b. May 1, 1739	1	150
Sarah, d. Jonathan & Jemima, b. May 5, 1745	1	114
Sarah, w. John, d. May 25, 1751	1	280
Sarah, m. Henry **BROWN**, May 5, 1762	2	101
Sarah, d. [Aaron & Eunice], b. Aug. 9, 1779	2	126
Sarah, d. [Gideon & Rachal], b. May 27, 1780	2	124
Sarah, wid. George, d. Dec. 5, 1807	1	189
Sarah, d [Erastus & Julia], b. June 9, 1833	3	125
Shubael, s. William & Naomi, b. Dec. 3, 1757	2	54
Shubael, m. Abigail **FLINT**, Apr. 20, 1779	2	220
Stephen, s. [William & Naomi], b. Mar. 10, 1772; d.		

	Vol.	Page
MARTIN, (cont.)		
Sept. 10, 1772	2	54
Susannah, d. [Joseph & Elizabeth], b. Dec. 19, 1765	2	116
Sybel, d. [Joseph & Zerviah], b. May 3, 1780	2	202
Thomas Brown, s. [George, Jr. & Dorothy], b. Mar 16, 1767	2	109
Timothy, s. [Gideon & Rachal], b. Jan. 8, 1776; d. July 4, 1777	2	124
Timothy, s. [Gideon & Rachal], b. Apr. 9, 1778	2	124
William, s. Ebenezer & Jerusha, b. Mar. 11, 1736	1	163
William, twin with George, s. George & Sarah, b. Apr. 7, 1751	1	247
William, Dea., m. Naomi **UPTON**, Mar. 3, 1757	2	54
Zalmon, s. [George, 3rd & Sarah], b. June 14, 1791	2	101
----, child of James, laborer, ae. 38, & Sophronia, ae. 37, b. June 4, 1848	4	2
MASEALLE(?), Zabee, d. June 1, 1848, ae. 88	4	152
MASH, [see also **MARSH**], [E]unice, m. Nathan **ABBOT[T]**, Nov. 24, 1742 (Perhaps "**MARSH**"?)	1	223
MASON, Abigail, m. Jacob **LINKON**, Apr. 28, 1736	1	155
Ann, w. Hezekiah, d. Aug. 2, 1724	A	15
Anne, d. Jonathan & Hannah, b. Nov. 23, 1738	1	157
Augustus, ae. 22, m. [ ], May 19, [1848], by Rev. H. Brownley	4	113
Hannah, d. Hezekiah & Ann, b. June 14, 1702	A	32
Hezekiah, m. Ann **BINGHAM**, June 7, 1699	A	32
Hez[ekiah], m. Sarah **ROBINSON**, Nov. 15, 1725; d. Dec. 15, 1726	1	79
Jonathan, s. Hezekiah & Ann, b. July 30, 1715	A	32
Jonathan, m. Hannah **PARSON**, Dec. 7, 1737	1	157
Jonathan, s. Jonathan & Hannah, b. Aug. 29, 1740	1	157
Lydia, m. Bartholomew **FLINT**, Dec. 22, 1754	1	325
Lydia, m. Bartholomew **FLINT**, Dec 22, 1754	1	328
Lydia, m. Bartholo[me]w **FLINT**, Dec. 22, 1754	2	5
Mary, m. David **HUNTINGTON**, June 30, 1725	1	74
Mary, m. Nathan **HUNTINGTON**, Apr. 15, 1756	2	13
Rachel, d. Hezekiah & Ann, b. Apr. 12, 1701; d. Apr 14, 1701	A	32
Rachel, m. Charles **MUDGE**, Oct. 3, 1727	1	87
Theodore, s. Andrew, farmer, ae. 21, & Emily, ae. 40, of Willimantic, b. Jan. 29, 1848	4	1
Theodore W., d. Aug. 28, 1848, ae. 3 m.	4	153
MATSON, Washburn N., of South Glastonbury, m. Harriet **FRANKLIN**, of Willimantic, Mar. 24, 1844, by Rev. Ziba Loveland	3	213
MATTHEWS, Frederick A., of Hartford, m. Mary S. **TYLER**, of Andover, Sept. 28, 1828, by Rev. Jesse Fisher	3	131
MAUREY, John, laborer, ae. 23, m. Ellen **LEONARD**, ae. 16,		

	Vol.	Page
MAUREY, (cont.)		
Dec. [ ], [1849], by Rev. Willard	4	115
MAXWELL, Joshua, m Azubah **WARNER**, Apr. 15, 1779; d		
Apr. 2, 1799	2	250
MAY, Julia E., ae. 22, b. Westerly, res. Willimantic,		
m. John N. **BLIVEN**, merchant, ae. 23, b. Westerly		
res. Willimantic, Oct. [ ], 1851, by Rev. J.H.		
Farnsworth	4	117
——, child of James, operative, ae. 40, b. Oct. 1,		
[1848]	4	5
MAYHEW, Catharine A., ae. 21, m. Royal B **CROSS**, ae. 30,		
June 17, [1849], by Tho[ma]s Bond	4	113
MAYNARD, [see under **MAINARD**]		
McCALL, Anna, m. Eliphalet **MURDOCK**, Mar. 25, 1778	2	226
Molly, m. Joseph **BADCOCK**, Jr., May 1, 1782	3	37
McCALLUM, Henry, m. Nancy Merrick **BINGHAM**, Dec. 25,		
1845, by Rev. Abel Nichols	3	226
McCARTY, M., ae. 22, m. Mat[t]hew **COSTELLO**, paper maker,		
ae. 24, Sept. [ ], [1850], by Rev. Brady	4	115
McCRACKEN, ——, d. Jan. 31, [1849], ae. 2 d.	4	155
——, twins of W[illia]m, laborer, ae. 41, of		
Willimantic, b. July 29, [1850]	4	10
McCURDY, Sarah, m. Ebenezer **BASS**, Jr., Mar. 27, 1811	3	71
McDANIELS, Andrew, m. Eliza **TRACY**, Dec. 10, 1826, by Rev.		
Cornelius B. Everest	3	18
McGOENTY, Betsey, d. [Capt. John & Jerusha], b. Mar. 15,		
1804	3	53
Elisha Abbe, s. [Capt. John & Jerusha], b. June 18,		
1807	3	53
Emma, d. [Capt. John & Jerusha], b. June 16, 1814	3	53
Jerusha Abby, d. [Capt. John & Jerusha], b. Jan. 28,		
1812	3	53
John, Capt , m. Jerusha **ABBE**, Aug. 30, 1801	3	53
John, s. [Capt. John & Jerusha], b. Oct. 25, 1809	3	53
McGOUTY, Elizabeth, m. John **BALDWIN**, Jr., July 7, 1822, by		
Samuel Perkins, Esq.	3	105
Emma, m. Edwin G. **BALCOM**, b. of Windham, Apr. 5, 1835,		
by Rev. L.H. Corson	3	172
McGOVERN, Cha[rle]s, s. Pat, laborer, ae. 30, of Willi-		
mantic, b. Mar. 20, [1850]	4	10
McNALLY, Abby Everest, d. Burnard, b. June 29, 1822	3	105
Isabella D., ae. 25, b. Windham, res. Windham, m.		
Sam[ue]l A. **FOSTER**, carpenter, ae. 42, b. Hebron,		
res. Hebron, Nov. 25, 1850, by Rev. Sam[ue]l G.		
Williams	4	117
McTHURSTON, Clark, farmer, ae. 24, of Stafford, m. Harmey		
BALDWIN, ae. 24, Aug. 20, 1847, by Rev. Daniel		
Dorchester	4	111

	Vol.	Page
MEACHAM, [see also **MEACKIM**], Abigail, d [Seth & Ruth],		
b. Oct. 16, 1752	1	315
Abigail, m. Abijah **FULLER**, May 15, 1777	2	236
Annline Fuller, d. [Joseph & Irena], b. Feb. 10,		
1810	3	13
Benjamin, s. Jeremiah & Deborah, b. May 16, 1714	1	49
Benjamin, s. Daniel & Lydia, b. Mar. 2, 1742/3	1	192
Benjamin, d. Dec. 7, 1762	1	192
Charles, s. [Enoch & Peggy], b. Feb. 28, 1797	2	164
Charles Lewis, s. [Joseph & Irena], b. Sept. 12,		
1817	3	13
Daniel, m. Lydia **LILLEY**, Dec. 18, 1729; d. Apr. 16,		
1758	1	98
Daniel, s. Daniel & Lydia, b. Apr. 18, 1731	1	98
Daniel, d. Apr. 16, 1758	1	98
Deborah, w. Jeremiah, d. Dec. 3, 1721	1	49
Deborah, d. Daniel & Lydia, b. Sept. 22, 1735	1	98
Deborah, d. Daniel & Lydia, d. Oct. 5, 1742	1	192
Deborah, m. Thomas **BUTLER**, Feb. 7, 1744/5; d. Mar. 3,		
1748/9	1	250
Deborah, d Daniel & Lydia, b. Nov. 3, 1749	1	192
Elijah, s. [Joseph, Jr. & Lydia], b. July 13, 1779;		
d. Apr. 23, 1786	2	65
Elijah, s. [Enoch & Peggy], b. Aug. 14, 1794	2	164
Eliza, d. [Joseph, Jr. & Elizabeth Stansborough], b.		
May 30, 1802	3	13
Elizabeth, d. Joseph & Elizabeth, b. May 12, 1728	1	66
Elizabeth, w. Joseph, d. Mar. 28, 1779	1	66
Elizabeth, w. Joseph, d. Mar. 11, 1808	3	13
Enoch, s. [Joseph, Jr. & Lydia], b. Sept. 9, 1764; d.		
Mar. 23, 1765	2	65
Enoch, s. [Joseph, Jr. & Lydia], b. Mar. 7, 1768	2	65
Enoch, m. Peggy **GILES**, Apr. 11, 1793	2	164
Esther, m. Hope **ROGERS**, Nov. 14, 1715	1	48
[E]unis, d. Joseph & Elizabeth, b. Feb. 1, 1725/6	1	66
Jared Kimball, s. [Joseph & Irena], b. Nov. 15, 1815	3	13
Jemima, d. Joseph & Elizabeth, b. Oct. 2, 1741; d.		
Nov. 26, 1742	1	181
Jemima, d. Joseph, Jr. & Lydia, b. Nov. 17, 1761; d.		
May 28, 1777	2	65
Jemima, d. [Joseph, Jr. & Lydia], b. Sept. 19, 1781;		
d. Apr. 28, 1786	2	65
Jeremiah, d. Apr. 14, 1743, ae. 99 y.	1	181
Jeremiah, s. [Seth & Ruth], b. Jan. 28, 1759	1	315
Jerusha, d. Joseph & Elizabeth, b. July 29, 1735	1	66
Jonathan, s. Joseph & Elizabeth, b. Nov. 15, 1723	1	66
Jon[atha]n, s. Joseph & Elizabeth, d. Aug. 24, 1738	1	181
Jonathan, s. [Seth & Ruth], b. May 16, 1757	1	315

	Vol.	Page
MEACHAM, (cont.)		
Jonathan, s. [Joseph, Jr. & Lydia], b. Mar. 17, 1777;		
d. May 22, 1788	2	65
Joseph, m. Elizabeth **LILLY**, Jan. 16, 1722/3	1	66
Joseph, s. Joseph & Elizabeth, b. June 13, 1732	1	66
Joseph, Jr., m. Lydia **DIMMICK**, Nov. 27, 1760	2	65
Joseph, s. [Joseph, Jr. & Lydia], b. Sept 14, 1772	2	65
Joseph, d. Aug. 11, 1789	1	66
Joseph, Jr., m. Elizabeth Stansborough **SNOW**, Nov. 19,		
1795	3	13
Joseph, d. Apr. 3, 1798	2	65
Joseph, m. Irena **KIMBALL**, Jan. 1, 1809	3	13
Joseph Dimmick, s. [Joseph & Irena], b. Sept. 9, 1811	3	13
Lois, d. [Seth & Ruth], b. Mar. 6, 1761	1	315
Lucinda, d. [Joseph, Jr. & Elizabeth Stansborough],		
b. Sept. 5, 1806	3	13
Luce, [twin with Lydia], d. Daniel & Deborah, b. May		
4, 1738	1	98
Luce, d. Daniel & Lydiah, d. Dec. 28, 1741	1	192
Lucy, d. Daniel & Lydia, b. Sept. 18, 1745	1	192
Lucy, d. Daniel & Lydia, d. Oct. 11, 1754	1	192
Lydia, d. Jeremiah & Deborah, b. Nov. 28, 1709	1	49
Lydia, [twin with Luce], d. Daniel & Deborah, b. May 4,		
1738	1	98
Lydia, w. Daniel, d. Nov. 18, 1754	1	192
Lydia, d. [Joseph, Jr. & Lydia], b. Jan. 11, 1766; d.		
Apr. 28, 1768	2	65
Lydia, d. [Joseph, Jr. & Lydia], b. Feb. 19, 1770	2	65
Lydia, d. [Joseph, Jr. & Elizabeth Stansborough], b.		
June 14, 1796	3	13
Mary, d. Joseph & Elizabeth, b. Apr. 22, 1738	1	66
Mary, d. [Joseph, Jr. & Elizabeth Stansborough], b.		
Aug. 13, 1800	3	13
Nancy, d. [Joseph & Irena], b. Apr. 27, 1821	3	13
Rachel, d. Jere[miah] & Deborah, b. July 20, 1716	1	49
Rachel, m. Ebenezer **WOODWARD**, June 19, 1744	1	248
Remember, d. [Joseph, Jr. & Lydia], b. Jan. 18, 1775;		
d. June 22, 1777	2	65
Remember, d. [Joseph, Jr. & Lydia], b. Mar. 21, 1785	2	65
Ruth, d. Seth & Ruth, b. July 30, 1754	1	315
Samuell, s. Jeremiah & Deborah, b. July 22, 1712	1	49
Sarah, d. Daniel & Lydia, b. May 7, 1733	1	98
Sarah, m. Moses **PHE[L]PS**, May 29, 1745	1	260
Seth, s. Jeremiah & Deborah, b. Oct. 5, 1718	1	49
Seth, m. Ruth **SIMONS**, Dec. 19, 1751	1	315
Sophronia, d. [Joseph, Jr. & Elizabeth Stansborough],		
b. Sept. 15, 1804	3	13
Vine, s. [Joseph, Jr. & Elizabeth Stansborough], b.		

	Vol.	Page
MEACHAM, (cont.)		
May 19, 1798; d. Aug. 10, 1798	3	13
Vine Ansel, s. [Joseph & Irena], b. July 23, 1813	3	13
Zeruiah, d. Daniel & Deborah, b. Apr. 10, 1741	1	98
MEACKIM, [see also **MEACHAM**], Leander, of Hebron, m.		
Elisa **BURNHAM**, of Windham, Sept. 28, 1842, by		
Rev. A.C. Wheat	3	203
MEADE, Samuel, of Geneva, N.Y., m. Tabitha **HURLBURT**, of		
Windham, Oct. 18, 1836, by Rev. Edward Harris	3	179
MEDBURY, David, m. Lucy **HARVEY**, Mar. 14, 1824	3	118
MELLIN, Catharine, ae. 19, m. Peter **CRAGIN**, paper maker,		
ae. 26, of Dublin, Aug, 29, [1848], by Rev. And.		
Robinson	4	113
MELONEY, Geo[rge] W., s. Norman, machinist, ae. 33, of		
Willimantic, b. Feb. 15, [1850]	4	10
MENNIREAU, Albert W., s. W[illia]m P., farmer, ae. 27, &		
Cornelia A., ae. 20, b. Oct. 10, 1847	4	4
MERCY, Rebeckah, m. William **RIPLEY**, Jr., Mar. 10, 1757	2	27
MERRICK, Justina L., of Willimantic, d. June 16, 1860, ae.		
29	4	161
MERRY, Lydia, m. Jacob **WATTERS**, Feb. 13, 1737/8	1	176
MESSENGER, MESENGER, Benoni, s. Return & Sarah, b. Sept.		
4, 1718	1	4
Mary, d. Return & Sarah, b. May 10, 1714	1	4
Mary, m. John **RIPLEY**, Jan. 15, 1734/5	1	141
Nathan, s. Return & Sarah, b. Mar. 16, 1716	1	4
Nathan, s. Benoni & Mary, b. Sept. 25, 1743	1	240
Return, m. Sarah **BEFINGS***, Apr. 16, 1713 (*correction		
the f in **BEFINGS** was crossed out and **BEVINS** was		
handwritten in margin of original manuscript)	1	4
Sarah, w. Return, d. Sept. 25, 1718	1	4
METCHER*, Ceyton, laborer, ae. 21, b. Bozrah, res. Willi-		
mantic, m. Lydia A. **TERRINGTON**, ae. 21, b. Bozrah,		
res. Willimantic, June [ ], 1851, by Rev. R.K.		
Brush (*Perhaps "**MITCHELL**"?)	4	117
MICHEAL, [see also **MITCHELL**], Katurah, of Windham, m. Job		
PRIMUS, of Canterbury, Sept. 25, 1792	3	51
MILLARD, Abigail, d. Benjamin & Lydia, b. July 19, 1710;		
d. Jan. 23, 1741/42	1	8
Anne, d. David & Susannah, b. Mar. 23, 1744	1	114
Asenath, d. [Joseph & Rebeckah], b. Dec. 4, 1758	2	88
Asenath, m. Ahimaz **HEB[B]ARD**, May 24, 1781	2	251a
Benj[ami]n, s. Joseph & Rebeckah, b. Mar. 30, 1756	1	322
Benjamin, s. [Joseph & Rebeckah], b. Mar. 30, 1756	2	88
Benjamin, m. Lucretia **BINGHAM**, Jan. 19, 1784	2	71
Charles, s. [Benjamin & Lucretia], b. Jan. 14, 1785	2	71
Delauna, m. Mary **KILLEY**, Mar 29, 1818	3	87
Elijah, s. [Joseph & Rebeckah], b. Nov. 14, 1760	2	88

	Vol	Page
MILLARD, (cont.)		
Elijah, s. [Benjamin & Lucretia], b. Oct. 30, 1787	2	71
Elizabeth, d. Benjamin & Lydia, b. Apr. 20, 1702	A	1
Elizabeth, m. David GEN[N]INGS, Jan. 4, 1720/21	1	37
Irena, d. [Joseph & Rebeckah], b. Oct. 26, 1766; d.		
June 7, 1768	2	88
John, s. [Joseph & Hannah], b. Jan. 16, 1793	2	100
Joseph, m. Rebeckah **SAWYER**, Aug. 28, 1753	2	88
Joseph, s. [Joseph & Rebeckah], b. Mar. 7, 1763	2	88
Joseph, m. Hannah **FISK**, Nov. 24, 1791	2	100
Julia S., m. James M. **HAWKINS**, b. of Willimantic,		
[Oct.] 28, 1838, by Rev. J.E. Tyler	3	187
Julia Sophronia, d. [Delauna & Mary], b. Apr. 13,		
1819	3	87
Luther, s. [Joseph & Rebeckah], b. Sept. 2, 1770	2	88
Lydia, d. Benjamin & Lydia, b. May 1, 1698	A	1
Lydia, d. Jan. 7, 1756, ae. 84 y.	1	8
Lydia, d. [Joseph & Rebeckah], b. Aug. 5, 1757	2	88
Lydia Louisa, d. [Delauna & Mary], b. Feb. 25,		
1823	3	87
Mary, d. Benjamin & Lydia, b. July 1, 1699	A	1
Mary, m. Ebenezer **MARTIN**, Oct. 4, 1724	1	76
Mary, d. [Joseph & Rebeckah], b. Sept. 7, 1754	2	88
Mary, m. John **LINKON**, Jr., July 9, 1782	2	251
Mary, m. George **TRAIN**, b. of Windham, July 17,		
[1831], by [Rev. Alva Gregory], at Willimantic	3	156
Nathan, [twin with -----], s. [Joseph & Rebeckah],		
b. Feb. 1, 1765; d. June 16, 1767	2	88
Nathan, s. [Joseph & Rebeckah], b. June 6, 1768	2	88
Rebeckah, d. David & Susannah, b. May 5, 1738	1	114
Sarah, d. David & Susannah, b. Jan. 16, 1734/5	1	114
Sarah, d. [Benjamin & Lucretia], b. Aug. 14, 1786	2	71
Shubael, s. [Joseph & Rebeckah], b. Jan. 16, 1773	2	88
Solomon, s. David & Susannah, b. June 6, 1737	1	114
Susan Lucretia, d. [Delauna & Mary], b. Oct. 17,		
1820	3	87
Susannah, d. David & Susannah, b. Mary 8, 1742	1	114
-----, [twin with Nathan], s. [Joseph & Rebeckah], b.		
Feb. 1, 1765; d. Feb. 6, 1765	2	88
MILLER, Asenath, d. [Joseph & Rebeckah], b. Dec. 4, 1758	1	322
Elisha, s. [Joseph & Rebeckah], b. Nov. 14, 1760	1	322
Joseph, m. Rebeckah **SAWYER**, Aug. 28, 1753	1	322
Julia Ann, m. Alfred B. **PALMER**, Jan. 1, 1834, at		
Plainfield, by Rev. Charles S. Weaver	3	167
Lydia, d. [Joseph & Rebeckah], b. Aug. 5, 1757	1	322
Mary, d. Jo[seph] & Rebeck[ah], b. Sept. 7, 1754	1	322
MILLS, Tyler, d. Oct. 1, [1849], ae. 2	4	156
MINER, Eliza, ae. 48, m. Gardiner **CRANSTON**, farmer, ae. 38,		

	Vol.	Page
MINER, (cont.)		
b. R.I., res. Windham, Nov. 24, 1847, by Rev.		
A. Sharp	4	111
Fanny, d. Betsey, b. Nov. 1, 1786	3	42
Noyce, b. Mar. 31, 1778	3	42
MITCHEL, MICHELL, [see also **MICHEAL**, Abraham, m. Mary		
ABBE, Apr. 27, 1699	A	8
Daniel, s. Abraham & Mary, b. & d. Dec. 10, 1700	A	29
MOFFETT, Michael, ae. 21, m. Jan. 4, [1848], [ ],		
by And. Roberts	4	113
MOLISON, Elan, s. Mary **LILLIE**, b. May 13, 1766	2	122
MOODEY, John, m. Sophia **LITTLE**, Mar. 28, 1830, by Rev.		
Roger Bingham	3	144
MOON, Nancy, m. Nathaniel **ABBE**, Sept. 20, 1784, by		
Hezekiah Bissell, J.P.	3	67
MOORE, Polly, m. Dudley **HOVEY**, Oct. 8, 1795	3	44
MORE, Abigail, m. Caleb **BADCO[C]K**, Jan. 21, 1712/13	1	28
David, m. Sally **TRIM**, Jan. 4, 1835, by Rev. Philo		
Judson, at Willimantic	3	171
Elizabeth, m. Daniel **EDWARDS**, Feb. 27, 1700	A	8
Joshua, m. Dorothy **BADCO[C]K**, Mar. 3, 1774*		
(*correction 1774 crossed out and 1714 hand-		
written next to it in original manuscript)	1	19
Mary, w. William, d. Apr. 3, 1700	A	12
Mary, w. William, d. Sept. 18, 1727	1	69
William, s. William & Mary, d. Jan. 23, 1700	A	12
William, m. Mary **ALLIN**, July 17, 1700	A	10
William, m. Tamar **SIMONS**, June 10, 1728	1	69
MOREY, [see also **MAUREY**], Havilah, of Bozrahville, m.		
Esther B. **CAREY**, of Windham, Aug. 30, 1836,		
by Rev. Jesse Fisher	3	179
MORGAN, Alice, d. [Sam[ue]ll, Jr. & Bethia], b. Aug. 20,		
1777	2	13
Asher, s. [Sam[ue]ll, Jr. & Bethia], b. Aug. 30,		
1762	2	13
Bethiah, w. Capt. Sam[ue]ll, d. Feb. 12, 1800	2	13
Ebenezer, m. Desire **BRANCH**, June 24, 1745. Certified		
by Hez[ekiah] Lord	1	254
Elisha, s. [Sam[ue]ll, Jr. & Bethia], b. Jan. 28, 1773	2	13
Eunice, d. [Sam[ue]ll, Jr. & Bethia], b. Mar. 14, 1770	2	13
James, s. [Sam[ue]ll, Jr. & Bethia], b. July 23, 1779	2	13
Jerusha G., m. Erastus **FULLER**, Mar. 24, 1816	3	79
Loisa, d. [Sam[ue]ll, Jr. & Bethia], b. Aug. 18, 1766	2	13
Lucy, d. [Sam[ue]ll, Jr. & Bethia], b. Feb. 3, 1756	2	13
Margaret, m. Ebenezer **HIB[B]ARD**, Mar. 16, 1709	1	47
Martha, d. [Sam[ue]ll, Jr. & Bethia], b. Jan. 7, 1775	2	13
Martha, m. Zuriel **PALMER**, Oct. 27, 1796	3	20
Matilda, d. [Sam[ue]ll, Jr. & Bethia], b. Oct. 6, 1764	2	13

	Vol	Page
MORGAN, (cont.)		
Matilda, m. Nathaniel **MANNING**, Sept. 4, 1783	3	112
Nathan, s. [Sam[ue]ll, Jr. & Bethia], b. Sept. 6, 1758	2	13
Nathan, m. Abigail **PALMER**, Oct. 14, 1780	2	244
Nathan, s. [Nathan & Abigail], b. Oct. 14, 1781	2	244
Nathaniel, s. Ebenezer & Desire, b. June 2, 1746	1	254
Rachall M., of Windham, m. John D. **MARTIN**, of Hartford, Jan. 25, 1844, by Rev. Holmes Slade, Scotland	3	212
Sam[ue]ll, Jr., of Preston, m. Bethia **PARRISH**, of Windham, Oct. 2, 1755	2	13
Sam[ue]ll, s. [Sam[ue]ll, Jr. & Bethia], b. Dec. 27, 1760	2	13
Samuel, Capt., m. Hannah **ASPINWALL**, Apr. 28, 1802	2	13
Sarah, m. John **LARRABE**, Apr. 15, 1689	A	7
William, s. [Sam[ue]ll, Jr. & Bethia], b. June 22, 1768	2	13
Zerviah, m. Solomon **PETTINGALE**, Dec. 23, 1761	2	77
——, s. [Sam[ue]ll, Jr. & Bethia], b. July [ ], 1781; d. same day	2	13
MORRISEY, Ellen, b. Hebron, Ct., res. Willimantic, d. Apr. 29, 1860, ae. 4	4	159-0
MORRISON, F.G., child of W[illia]m, carpenter, ae. 44, b. Sept 14, [1848]	4	6
Francis M., s. W[illia]m, mechanic, ae. 41, b. June 17, [1849]	4	11
William, m. Mary Ann **TRACY**, Nov. 29, 1832, by Rev. Alva Gregory	3	162
William, m. Harriet **FITCH**, May 3, 1847, by Rev. Andrew Sharpe	3	235
MORSE, Asaph, s. Benj[ami]n & Polly, b. Nov. 18, 1760	2	60
Nathan, of Woodstock, m. Eunice **BASS**, of Windham, Aug. 25, 1844, by Rev. Thomas Tallman, Scotland	3	216
Prescilla, m. William **GROW**, May 30, 1776	2	215
MOSELEY, MOSLEY, Abigail, d. Sam[ue]ll & Mary, b. May 3, 1754; d. Aug. 17, 1754	1	328
Abigail, m. Dr. John **CLARK**, Dec. 13, 1781	2	240
Anna, d. [Nath[anie]l, Jr. & Rosannah], b. July 17, 1769	2	146
Anne, d. Samuel & Bethiah, b. May 23, 1746	1	158
Bethiah, w. Samuell, d. May 29, 1750	1	158
B[e]ulah, d. Nath[anie]ll & Sarah, b. Mar. 2, 1752	1	249
Beulah, d. [Nath[anie]l & Sarah], b. Mar. 2, 1752	2	66
Ebenezer, s. Samuell & Bethyah, b. Feb. 19, 1740/41	1	144
Ebenezer, s. [Nath[anie]l & Sarah], b. Feb. 11, 1759	1	249
Ebenezer, s. [Nath[anie]l & Sarah], b. Feb. 11, 1759	2	66
Ebenezer, m. Martha **STRONG**, Sept. 14, 1773	2	249

	Vol.	Page
MOSELEY, MOSLEY, (cont.)		
Ebenezer, s. [Ebenezer & Martha], b. Nov. 21,		
1782	2	249
Elisha, s. [Nath[anie]l & Sarah], b. Jan. 9, 1766	2	66
Elizabeth, d. Samuell & Bethyah, b. Nov. 15, 1737	1	144
Elizabeth, d. [Nath[anie]l & Sarah], b. Jan. 11,		
1753; d. Oct. 16, 1754	2	66
Elizabeth, d. Nath[anie]ll & Sarah, b. June 11,		
1753; d. Oct. 16, 1754	1	249
Elizabeth, d. Sam[ue]ll & Mary, b. Nov. 19, 1756	1	328
Elizabeth, d. [Nath[anie]l & Sarah], b. July 11, 1757	1	249
Elizabeth, d. [Nath[anie]l & Sarah], b. July 11, 1757	2	66
Elizabeth, m. Josiah **HAMMOND**, Jr., Sept. 28, 1780	2	231
Emma F., ae. 22, m. Newton M. **HOLT**, harness maker,		
ae. 24, of Hampton, Nov. 25, 1847	4	111
Emmy M., m. Newton M. **HOLT**, Nov. 5, 1847	4	112
Easther, d. [Nath[anie]l & Sarah], b. Apr. 23, 1760	1	249
Easther, d. [Nath[anie]l & Sarah], b. Apr. 23, 1760	2	66
Fanny L., m. Delos **FISH**, b. of Willimantic, Nov. 16,		
1846, by Rev. John E. Tyler	3	231
Flavell, s. Nath[anie]ll & Sarah, b. Feb. 4, 1747/8	1	249
Flaval, s. [Nath[anie]ll & Sarah], b. Feb. 4, 1747/8	2	66
Hannah, d. Samuell & Bethiah, b. Mar. 31, 1735/6	1	144
Hannah, d. Nicholas & Sarah, b. July 20, 1746	1	157
Hannah, d. Nath[anie]ll & Sarah, b. July 20, 1746	1	249
Hannah, d. [Nath]anie]l & Sarah], b. July 20, 1746	2	66
Hannah, m. Hezekiah Augustus **RIPLEY**, Nov. 3, 1793	2	72
Jared A., of Chaplin, m. Eunice **SPENCER**, of Windham,		
Mar. 24, 1845, by Rev. John E. Tyler	3	220
John, s. Sam[ue]ll & Bethiah, b. Feb. 27, 1747/8	1	158
Joseph, s. Nath[anie]ll & Sarah, b. Mar. 12, 1744/5	1	249
Joseph, s. [Nath[anie]l & Sarah], b. Mar. 12, 1744/5	2	66
Marsilva, d. [Nath[anie]l, Jr. & Rosannah], b. Oct.		
12, 1773	2	146
Mary, m. Seth **PALMER**, June 14, 1739	1	165
Mary, d. Samuell & Bethyah, b. Nov. 13, 1743	1	144
Mary, d. Samuel & Bethiah, b. Nov. 13, 1743	1	158
Mary C., of Chaplin, m. Eliph[ale]t **RICE**, of Windham,		
[Sept.] 26, 1845, by Rev. John E. Tyler	3	224
Nat[anie]l, b. Dec. 4, 1715, in Dorchester; m. Sarah		
CAPEN, Aug. 17, 1742	2	66
Nath[anie]l, s. [Nath[anie]l & Sarah], b. Dec. 22, 1743	1	249
Nathaniel, s. [Nath[anie]l & Sarah], b. Dec. 22, 1743,		
in Stoughton	2	66
Nath[anie]l, Jr., m. Rosannah **ALLWORTH**, Sept. 29, 1768	2	146
Nathaniel, s. [Nath[anie]l, Jr. & Rosannah], b. June		
20, 1771	2	146
Nath[anie]l, m. Sarah **CAPRON** [ ]	1	249

	Vol.	Page
MOSELEY, MOSLEY, (cont.)		
Patty, d. [Ebenezer & Martha], b. Oct. 12, 1774	2	249
Ruth, d. [Nath[anie]l & Sarah], b. Sept. 15, 1761;		
d. Feb. [ ], 1762	2	66
Samuell, Rev., m. Bethyah **BILLINGS**, July 4, 1734	1	144
Samuell, s. Samuell & Bethyah, b. Apr. 27, 1739	1	144
Sam[ue]ll, Rev., m. Mary **GAYLORD**, Apr. 1, 1752	1	328
Sarah, d. [Nath[anie]ll & Sarah], b. Aug. 21, 1750	1	249
Sarah, d. [Nath[anie]l & Sarah], b. Aug. 21, 1750	2	66
Sarah, d. Sam[ue]ll & Mary, b. Apr. 1, 1759	1	328
Sophia, d. [Ebenezer & Martha], b. Oct. 16, 1776	2	249
Thomas, s. Nath[anie]ll & Sarah, b. May 7, 1749	1	249
Thomas, s. [Nath[anie]ll & Sarah], b. May 7, 1749	2	66
Uriel, s. Nath[anie]l & Sarah, b. Feb. 1, 1756	1	249
Uriel, s. [Nath[anie]l & Sarah], b. Feb 1, 1756	2	66
William, s. Sam[ue]ll & Mary, b. Jan. 1, 1753; d.		
Aug. 17, 1754	1	328
William, s. Sam[ue]ll & Mary, b. June 20, 1755	1	328
----, s. [Ebenezer & Martha], b. Apr. 18, 1779;		
d. [Apr.] 22, [1779]	2	249
MOTTE, Sarah, d. Sam[ue]ll & Sarah, b. Dec. 11, 1746	1	177
MOULTON, MOLTON, MOULTEN, MOLTEN, Abigail, m. Abel		
BINGHAM, Mar. 1, 1725/6	1	73
Abigail, d. [James, Jr. & Abigail], b. Jan. 7, 1752	2	49
Abigail, m. John **HAMMOND**, Apr. 7, 1761	2	96
Albert, [s. John], b. Sept. 6, 1820	3	128
Alice, d. [James, Jr. & Abigail], b. Apr. 27, 1757	2	49
Amanda Harriet, d. [John & Celinda], b. Oct. 21,		
1794	2	242
Amos, s. [James, Jr. & Abigail], b. Apr. 14, 1764	2	49
Benjamin, s. [James, Jr. & Abigail], b. Mar. 14, 1755	2	49
Celinda, d. [John & Celinda], b. Dec. 29, 1807	2	242
Cha[rle]s, farmer, ae. 24, b. Chaplin, res. Chaplin,		
m. Susan M. **BROWN**, ae. 23, b. Mansfield, res.		
Chaplin, Oct. 25, 1850, by Rev. Knight	4	118
Daniel, s. [Samuel & Sarah], b. Dec. 24, 1774	2	87
Ebenezer, s. Robert & Hannah, b. Dec. 25, 1709	1	49
Edward E., d. Apr. 16, [1849], ae. 1 1/2	4	155
Edward F., m. Mary A. **BENCHLEY**, June 21, 1846, by Rev.		
Andrew Sharp	3	229
Edward Lee, [s. John], b. July 12, 1824	3	128
Freeborn, s. Robert & Hannah, b. Apr. 3, 1717	1	49
Hannah, m. Stephen **FFULLER**, Jan. 1, 1723/4	1	80
Harriet Amanda, [d. John], b. Feb. 7, 1827	3	128
James, Jr., m. Mary **CARY**, July 2, 1745	2	49
James, Jr., m. Abigail **WOODWARD**, Dec. 18, 1749	2	49
James, s. [James, Jr. & Abigail], b. Oct 25, 1750	2	49
James, Jr. m. Prudence **WALES**, Mar. 22, 1780	2	247

	Vol.	Page
MOULTON, MOLTON, MOULTEN, MOLTEN, (cont.)		
James, s. [James, Jr. & Prudence], b. May 13, 1781	2	247
James, Jr., d. Jan. 28, 1782	2	247
Jerusha, d. [John & Celinda], b. June 11, 1792	2	242
Jerusha, m. Lewis **TINKER**, Sept. 17, 1815	3	79
John, s. Robert & Hannah, b. Feb. 5, 1720/21	1	49
John, m. Celinda **SPAFFORD**, Mar. 3, 1785	2	242
John, s. [John & Celinda], b. Apr. 11, 1801	2	242
John H., druggist, ae. 21, of Windham, m. Charlotte **FREEMAN**, ae. 22, May 12, 1850, by Rev. J.H. Farnsworth	4	115
Joseph, s. Robert & Hannah, b. Aug. 24, 1716	1	49
Leroy Davis, s. Alfred, mason, ae. 34, & Julia, ae. 35, b. May 7, [1851]	4	13
Lois, d. Robert & Hannah, b. Apr. 3, 1706	1	49
Lois, m. Stephen **DURGEY**, Mar. 19, 1729/30	1	118
Lucy, d. [James, Jr. & Abigail], b. May 14, 1759	2	49
Lucy, m. Oliver **BINGHAM**, Nov. 13, 1783	2	140
Lydia, d. Robert & Hannah, b. Jan. 13, 1708	1	49
Lydia, d. [James, Jr. & Mary], b. Sept. 25, 1748	2	49
Lydia Juliette Howes, [d. John], b. Oct. 27, 1818	3	128
Mary, m. John **BINGHAM**, Dec. 6, 1721	1	79
Mary, w. James, Jr., d. Oct. 5, 1748	2	49
Mehetabel, d. Robert & Hannah, b. Mar. 24, 1712	1	49
Mehetable, m. Elkannah **SPRAGUE**, Dec. 9, 1754	2	74
Nancy, d. [John & Celinda], b. Sept. 13, 1787	2	242
Polly, d. [John & Celinda], b. Sept. 15, 1785	2	242
Roswell, s. [William & Keziah], b. Dec. 31, 1755	2	29
Roswell, s. [John & Celinda], b. Jan 1, 1797	2	242
Sam[ue]l, [twin with Susannah], s. Robert & Hannah, b. June 15, 1714	1	49
Samuel, m. Sarah **RINGE**, Dec. 17, 1767	2	87
Sam[ue]ll, s. [Samuel & Sarah], b. July 18, 1768	2	87
Samuel, d. Feb. 17, 1777	2	87
Susannah, [twin with Sam[ue]l], d. Robert & Hannah, b. June 15, 1714; d. Oct. 8, 1714	1	49
Wealthy, d. [John & Celinda], b. Apr. 27, 1790	2	242
William, s. William & Jane, b. May 31, 1696; d. Oct. 10, 1696	A	29
William, s. William & Jane, b. Nov. 5, 1697	A	29
William, m. Keziah **CROWEL**, July 4, 1753	2	29
William, s. [William & Keziah], b. Apr. 17, 1754	2	29
William, s. [Samuel & Sarah], b. Mar. 8, 1771	2	87
William, [s. John], b. Dec. 25, 1831	3	128
——, st. b. child of A.K , & Eliza, b. July 25, [1848]	4	6
——, s. Edward L., merchant, ae. 27, & Mary A., ae. 27, of Willimantic, b. Dec. 28, 1850	4	12

	Vol.	Page
MUDGE, Ann, m. Samuel KIMBALL, Apr. 18, 1754	1	324
Charles, m. Rachel MASON, Oct. 3, 1727	1	87
Charles, s. [William & Mary], b. Mar. 30, 1763	2	82
Charles, d. Feb. 11, 1778	1	87
Ichabod, s. [William & Mary], b. Aug. 31, 1767	2	82
Lydia, d. Charles & Rachel, b. Dec. 31, 1728	1	87
Lydia, m. Sam[ue]ll BINGHAM, Jr., Nov. 10, 1748	1	282
Lidia, d. [William & Mary], b. Jan. 14, 1773	2	82
Mary, d. Charles & Rachel, b. Mar. 5, 1731/2	1	87
Mary, m. Napthali WEBB, Oct. 2, 1751	1	309
Prudence, d. [William & Mary], b. Nov. 22, 1764	2	82
Prudence, m. Jared WEBB, June 3, 1790	2	188
Rachel, d. Charles & Rachel, b. June 26, 1738	1	87
William, s. Charles & Rachel, b. Feb. 9, 1740/41	1	87
William, m. Mary SPENCER, June 10, 1762	2	82
MULLIN, James, operative, b. Ireland, res. Willimantic,		
d. July 3, 1851, ae. 17	4	157
MUNSEAR, Mary M., ae 23, m. Allen CARPENTER, farmer,		
ae. 20, of Windham, Mar. 12, 1847, by Alfred		
Brewster	4	111
MUNSELL, [see also MANSELL, MANSON and MUNSON],		
Lois, m. Bethuel WALDO, May 25, 1743	1	207
MUNSON, [see also MANSON, MANSELL and MUNSELL],		
Martha, m. Ebenezer GEN[N]INGS, Oct. 30, 1737	1	54
MURDOCK, Amos, m. Sybel FLINT, Oct. 24, 1751	1	308
Anne, d. [Eliphalet & Anna], b. Feb. 14, 1786	2	226
Betsey, d. [Eliphalet & Anna], b. May 16, 1794	2	226
Betsey, m. Nathan BROWN, Apr. 3, 1831, by Geo[rge]		
T. Catlin, J.P.	3	152
Clar[r]isa, d. [Eliphalet & Anna], b. Dec. 16, 1778	2	226
Dan, s. Sam[ue]ll & Submit, b. Feb. 24, 1741/2	1	175
Dan, s. [Samuel, Jr. & Mary], b. Mar. 23, 1767	1	303
Dan, s. [Samuell & Mary], b. Mar. 23, 1767	2	160
Deborah, d. [Eliphalet & Anna], b. Dec. 30, 1781	2	226
Debba, m. Aaron GAGER, June 20, 1805	3	99
Eli, s. [Samuel, Jr. & Mary], b. June 9, 1765	1	303
Eli, s. [Samuell & Mary], b. June 9, 1765	2	160
Eliphalet, s. Sam[ue]ll & Submit, b. Oct. 5, 1748	1	175
Eliphalet, m. Anna McCALL, Mar. 25, 1778	2	226
Elizabeth, d. [Samuell & Mary], b. June 15, 1770	2	160
[E]unice, d. Sam[ue]ll & Submit, b. Jan. 29,		
1750/51	1	175
Eunice, d. [Samuell & Mary], b. Feb. 26, 1774	2	160
Hannah, m. Moses HEB[B]ARD, May 31, 1744	1	270
Hannah, m. Moses HIBBARD, May 31, 1744	2	5
Hezekiah, s. Sam[ue]ll & Mary, b. May 10, 1752	1	303
Hezekiah, s. Sam[ue]ll & Mary, b. May 10, 1752	2	160
Jerusha, d. [Ephalet & Anna], b. Nov. 1, 1789	2	226

	Vol.	Page
MURDOCK, (cont.)		
John, s. Samuel, Jr. & Mary, b. Dec. 1, 1756/7; d.		
Apr. 25, 1758	1	303
John, s. Sam[ue]ll & Mary, b. Dec. 1, 1756; d.		
Apr. 25, 1758	2	160
John, s. [Samuel, Jr. & Mary], b. Oct. 23, 1760	1	303
John, s. [Samuell & Mary], b. Oct. 23, 1760	2	160
Joshua, s. Sam[ue]ll & Mary, b. Sept. 27, 1753	1	303
Joshua, s. Sam[ue]ll & Mary, b. Sept. 27, 1753; d.		
May 29, 1761, in the 8th y. of his age	2	160
Joshua, s. [Samuel, Jr. & Mary], d. May 29, 1761, in		
the 8th y. of his age	1	303
Joshua, s. [Samuel, Jr. & Mary], b. Oct. 9, 1763	1	303
Joshua, s. [Samuell & Mary], b. Oct. 9, 1763	2	160
Lucy, d. [Eliphalet & Anna], b. Sept. 30, 1787; d.		
Apr. 6, 1791	2	226
Lucy, d. [Eliphalet & Anna], b. Feb. 25, 1792	2	226
Lydia, d. Sam[ue]ll & Submit, b. June 27, 1745	1	175
Lydia, m. William **WARNER,** Nov. 1, 1769	2	159
Mary, d. Sam[ue]ll & Mary, b. Jan. 24, 1750/51	1	303
Mary, d. Sam[ue]ll & Mary, b. Jan. 4, 1750/51	2	160
Philena, d. [Eliphalet & Anna], b. July 14, 1780	2	226
Sam[ue]ll, Jr., m. Mary **WIGHT,** Mar. 15, 1749/50	1	303
Samuel, Jr., m. Mary **WIGHT,** Mar. 15, 1749/50	2	160
Sam[ue]ll, s. Sam[ue]ll & Mary, b. Feb. 11, 1755	1	303
Samuell, s. Sam[ue]ll & Mary, b. Feb. 11, 1755	2	160
Submit, m. Maj. Hezekiah **HUNTINGTON,** Nov. 28, 1754	2	70
Submit, d. [Samuel, Jr. & Mary], b. Jan. 10, 1759	1	303
Submit, d. [Samuell & Mary], b. Jan. 10, 1759	2	160
Throop, s. [Samuel, Jr. & Mary], b. Oct. 15, 1768	1	303
Throop, s. [Samuell & Mary], b. Oct. 15, 1768	2	160
William, s. Sam[ue]ll & Sibmit, b. Jan. 2, 1738	1	175
——, s. [Eliphalet & Anna], b. Jan. 8, 1754; d.		
Feb. 1, 1784(?)	2	226
MURPHY, Catharine, d. Sept. [ ], [1849], ae. 40	4	156
Elizabeth, twin with May, d. Ja[me]s, farmer, b.		
Mar. 24, [1850]	4	11
May, twin with Elizabeth, d. Ja[me]s, farmer, b.		
Mar. 24, [1850]	4	11
MURR[A]Y, John, farmer, b. Ireland, res. Windham, d. Apr.		
17, 1860, ae. 72	4	159-0
Margaret, ae. 25, m. John **CARR,** laborer, ae. 29, Jan.		
29, [1850], by Rev. Brady	4	115
NACY, Mary, of Willimantic, m. Zaccheas D. **CLARK,** of Spring-		
field, Mass., Nov. 16, 1845, by B.M. Alden,		
Willimantic	3	224
NEAL, Ann, m. Richard F. **CLEVELAND,** Sept. 16, 1829, by Rev		
Nelson Read, in the Methodist Episcopal Church,		

	Vol.	Page
NEAL, (cont.)		
Baltimore, Md.	3	153
Henry C., b. Ireland, res. Windham, d. Nov. 15,		
1847, ae. 5	4	151
Patrick E., ae. 24, m. Ann **GORMLEY**, ae. 21, Apr. 22,		
[1849], by Mr. Robinson	4	113
Phebe C., d. Phineas C., laborer, ae. 35, & Mort(?)		
C., ae. 40, b. June 20, 1848	4	2
Royal C., operative, ae. 22, b. Ireland, res.		
Windham, m. Catharine **CORGALL**, ae. 21, Feb. 4,		
1848, by a Catholic Priest	4	111
NEFF, NEEFF, KNEFF, Ann, d. Clement & Mary, b. Aug. 3,		
1723	1	127
Ann, twin with Mary, d. Clement & Patience, b. Aug.		
12, 1736	1	311
Benjamin, s. William & Grace, b. May 16, 1734	1	145
Clement, s. Clement & Mary, b. May 17, 1711	1	127
Clement, m. Patience **BROWN**, Dec. 12, 1735	1	311
Clement, s Clem[ent] & Patience, b. Apr. 29, 1738	1	311
Content, d. Clem[ent], & Patience, b. Aug. 15, 1740	1	311
Content, m. Thomas **KINGSBURY**, Mar. 1, 1759	1	304
Daniel, s. [William & Mary], b. July 1, 1763	2	72
Deborah, d. Clem[ent] & Patience, b. Aug. 30, 1750	1	311
Dorcas, m. Jonathan **GINNINGS**, Feb. 7, 1793	2	216
Hannah, d. Clem[ent] & Patience, b. July 6, 1743;		
d. Sept. 13, 1752	1	311
John, twin with Matthew, s. Clem[ent] & Patience, b.		
May 6, 1746	1	311
Joseph, s. Will[ia]m & Grace, b. July 27, 1746	2	126
Lucy, d. [William, Jr. & Lucy], b. Jan. 25, 1784	2	240
Martha, d. W[illia]m & Grace, b. Oct. 4, 1742	2	126
Martha, m. John **SESSIONS**, Nov. 20, 1766	2	143
Mary, d. Clement & Mary, b. June 7, 1707	1	127
Mary, twin with Ann, d. Clement & Patience, b. Aug. 12,		
1736	1	311
Mary, m. Zach[ariah] **MAINOR**, Jan. 28, 1754	1	146
Mary, m. George **HUCHENS**, Oct. 22, 1826, by Abner		
Robinson, J.P.	3	129
Matthew, twin with John, s. Clem[ent] & Patience, b.		
May 6, 1746; d. Sept. 15, 1752	1	311
Ruth, d. William & Grace, b. May 31, 1737	1	145
Salathiel, s. [William & Mary], b. Mar. 20, 1765	2	72
Stephen, cooper, d. Sept. 20, [1849], ae. 76	4	156
Thomas, s. Clement & Mary, b. Mar. 12, 1713/14	1	127
Thomas, s. [William & Grace], b. July 31, 1744	1	145
William, s. Clement & Mary, b. Mar. 16, 1708/9	1	127
William, m. Grace **WEBSTER**, June 11, 1733	1	145
William, s. William & Grace, b. May 14, 1739	1	145

	Vol.	Page

NEFF, NEEFF, KNEFF, (cont.)

	Vol.	Page
William, m. Mary **COBURN**, Aug. 28, 1761	2	72
William, s. William & Mary, b. Jan. 12, 1762	2	72
William, Jr., m. Lucy **FORD**, Nov. 1, 1781	2	240
William, s. [William, Jr & Lucy], b. June 7, 1782	2	240
NEWCOMB, Caroline M., of Windham, m. Samuel **LUCKEY**, of New York City, Feb. 21, 1847, by H. Slade	3	234
Elizabeth, m. Ebenezer **WRIGHT**, Apr. 20, 1721	1	68
May Ann, m. William **SMITH**, Oct. 24, 1830, by Henry Hall, J.P.	3	148
Ruth, d. Apr. [ ], 1851, ae. 69	4	158
Sophronia, of Columbia, m. William W. **JACOBS**, of Mansfield, Mar. 30, 1830, at her mother's, in Windham, by Henry Brown	3	141
William, m. Harriet **COOK**, b. of Windham, Nov. 27, 1828, by Rev. Dennis Platt	3	133
NEWTON, Calvin, m. Mary H. **SPENCER**, Oct. 2, 1843, by Rev. Andrew Sharp	3	211
NICHOLS, [see also **NICLAS**], Elijah M., of Mansfield, m. Tryphenia C. **HUCHENS**, of Windham, Dec. 2, 1834, by Rev. L.H. Corson	3	172
Eliza B., m. Richard S. **PEASE**, Mar. 14, 1843, by Rev. Andrew Sharp	3	208
John, s. Elijah M., farmer, ae. 38, by Nov. 19, [1849]	4	9
John, d. Jan. [ ], 1851, ae. 14 m.	4	157
Lydia, of Mansfield, m. Charles A. **GALLUP**, of Windham, [Sept.] 4, 1839, by Rev. John E. Tyler	3	191
Maleta, Mrs., d. Mar. 20, [1849], ae 42 (Entered among births)	4	6
Matild[a], d. Mar. 20, [1849], ae. 53	4	154
Rebecca, m. Averell H.C. **CARD**, Dec. 24, 1826, by Rev. Jesse Fisher	3	126
Warren, of Providence, R.I., m. Matilda **PARRISH**, of Windham, Mar. 17, 1822	3	98
NICLAS, [see also **NICHOLS**], Marg[a]ret, m Benjamin **PHILLIPS**, Dec. 17, 1744	1	180
NILES, Abel, b Hampton, res. Windham, d. Oct. 2, 1847, ae. 15 m.	4	151
NIMOCK, Walter, of Carthage, Jefferson County, N.Y., m. Calistia H. **BIRCHARD**, of Norwich, Apr. 27, 1843, by Rev. Henry Bromley	3	208
NORTON, Huldah, m. William **COBB**, Dec. 22, 1768	2	176
Sarah, m. Jonathan **HUNTINGTON**, Aug. 7, 1754	1	220
Sarah, m. Jonathan **HUNTINGTON**, Aug. 7, 1754	2	9
Sarah, m. Eleazer **WALES**, Dec. 4, 1757, by Jonath[an] Huntington, Assist.	2	34
NORWOOD, Zerviah had s. Jonathan **ARMS**, 3rd, b. Oct. 20, 1764	2	74
Zerviah, m. James **DAILEY**, Aug. 19, 1766	2	74

	Vol.	Page
NOTT, James W., of Willimantic, d. Jan. 27, 1860, ae.		
6 mo.	4	161
NOYES, Alexander, m. Angeline **WHITING**, July 4, 1830,		
by Rev. Chester Tilden, Willimantic	3	147
Amanda, m. David **CROWELL**, b. of Windham, May 2,		
1833, by Rev. Alva Gregory	3	164
OLDS, Melessa, of Canterbury, m. George Anson **TRACY**,		
Apr. 14, 1833	3	219
ONEHUW, Solomon, d. June 11, 1748, at Kinderhook; was		
killed by Indians	1	170
O'NEIL, Falam(?), laborer, d. Dec. 27, [1849], ae. 37	4	155
Felix, d. July 10, 1850, ae. 1 1/2	4	155
John, blacksmith, ae. 30, m. Bridget **BOAB**, ae. 22,		
Nov. 29, [1850], by Rev. Brady	4	155
Mary, d. Roger, laborer, ae. 25, b. Apr. 1, [1849]	4	11
——, child of Roger, d. June [ ], 1849	4	153
ORDWAY, Daniel, s. Jacob & Rebeckah, b. June 3, 1719/20	1	5
John, s. Jacob & Rebeckah, b. Dec. 7, 1725	1	14
Sarah, d. Jacob & Rebeckah, b. Nov. 5, 1723	1	14
ORMS, [see also **ARMS**], Elizabeth, d. Jon[a]th[an] & Hannah,		
b. Jan. 5, 1750/51; d. July 8, 1750	1	312
Jonathan, m. Hannah **CANADA**, Jan. 17, 1749/50	1	312
Patience, m. Ebenezer **WOODWARD**, Oct. 14, 1770	2	169
ORMSBY, ORMSLY, [see also **ARMSBEE**], Abner, s. [Abner], b.		
Nov. 12, 1792	3	47
Alethea Marina, d. [Owen & Alethea], b. June 19, 1805	3	58
Alathea Marina, of Windham, Conn., m. Capt. Frederick		
WOODS, of New York, N.Y., Oct. 21, 1828, by Rev.		
Henry Chase. Witnessed by Elizabeth S. **DISBROW**	3	161
Amos, s. Sam[ue]ll & Dinah, b. Nov. 5, 1749	1	211
Apama, d. [Abner], b. Oct. 5, 1794	3	47
Bela, s. [Ephraim & Ruth], b. June 17, 1767	2	76
Betsey, d. [Royal & Sally M.], b. Mar. 20, 1828	3	131
Elijah, s. John & Deb[orah], b. Feb. 15, 1763	2	6
Elijah, s. [Eliphalet & Sarah], b. June 9, 1786	2	73
Eliphalet, m. Sarah **ROBINSON**, July 4, 1781	2	73
Elisha, s. John & Deb[orah], b. Jan 5, 1759	2	6
Eliza, d. [Owen & Alethea], b. July 24, 1801	3	58
Eliza, m. James **ADAMS**, Feb. 10, 1828, by Rev. Jesse		
Fisher	3	152
Elizabeth, d. John & Susan[n]ah, b. Mar. 6, 1706	1	7
Emma, d. [Owen & Alethea], b. May 10, 1793	3	58
Ephraim, m. Ruth **HIBBARD**, [ ] 16, 1762	2	76
Fanny, d. [Eliphalet & Sarah], b. July 25, 1784	2	73
George, s. [Stephen & Phebe], b. May 3, 1791	2	252
Hannah, d. Sam[ue]ll & Dinah, b. June 17, 1747	1	211
Hannah, d. [Jeremiah & Lucy], b. May 2, 1781; d.		
Oct. 10, 1782	2	28

	Vol.	Page
ORMSBY, ORMSLY, (cont.)		
Hannah, d. [Jeremiah & Lucy], b. Aug. 25, 1785	2	28
Harriet, d. [Stephen & Phebe], b. Mar. 9, 1795	2	252
Henry B., s. [Royal & Sally M.], b. Aug. 21, 1837	3	131
Ichabod, s. Jonathan & Mercy, b. Apr. 15, 1704	A	28
Isaac, s. [John & Deb[orah], b. Apr. 20, 1771	2	6
Jemima, d. [Stephen & Jemima], b. Feb. 23, 1784	2	252
Jemima, w. Stephen, d. Mar. 22, 1784	2	252
Jeremiah, m. Lucy **LILLIE**, May 14, 1778	2	28
John, s. John & Susannah, b. Feb. 29, 1704	A	28
John, s. John & Deb[orah], b. Nov. 14, 1760	2	6
John, Jr., m. Lydia **REED**, Oct. 28, 1784	2	231
John, s. [Royal & Sally M.], b. Mar. 15, 1831	3	131
Jonathan, m. Mercy **ABBE**, June 8, 1703	A	26
Keziah, d. John & Susannah, b. Feb. 24, 1710/11	1	7
Lauritta Maria, d. [Owen & Alethea], b. July 11, 1809	3	58
Leonard, s. [Jeremiah & Lucy], b. July 9, 1780; d. same day	2	28
Leonard, s. [Jeremiah & Lucy], b. July 7, 1783	2	28
Lucinda, d. [Ephraim & Ruth], b. July 10, 1763	2	76
Lucy, d. [Jeremiah & Lucy], b. Dec. 25, 1778; d. Feb. 4, 1786	2	28
Lucy, d. [Stephen & Phebe], b. Oct. 21, 1787	2	252
Lucy, d. [Royal & Sally M.], b. July 20, 1834; d. Apr. 17, 1853	3	131
Luther Parkus, s. [Royal & Sally M.], b. Aug. 8, 1839	3	131
Lydia, d. [Ephraim & Ruth], b. July 8, 1765	2	76
Lydia M., d. [Royal & Sally M.], b. Sept. 29, 1845	3	131
Marion, s. [Owen & Alethea], b. Jan. 28, 1803	3	58
Nathan, s. Sam[ue]ll & Dinah, b. July 13, 1745	1	211
Norman, s. [Owen & Alethea], b. Mar. 7, 1798	3	58
Oliver, [twin with Orrin], s. John & Deb[orah], b. Aug. 14, 1766	2	6
Oliver, machinist, of Willimantic, d. June 10, [1849], ae. 55	4	153
Oliver P., s. [Royal & Sally M.], b. Sept. 4, 1826	3	131
Orrin, [twin with Oliver], s. John & Deb[orah], b. Aug. 14, 1766	2	6
Owen, m. Alethea **BIBBINS**, Jan. 5, 1793	3	58
Permelia, d. [John, Jr. & Lydia], b. Feb. 2, 1792	2	231
Parmela, m. Samuel **DAVIS**, Apr. 30, 1820	3	90
Polly, d. [Eliphalet & Sarah], b. July 13, 1782	2	73
Ralph, farmer, d May 22, 1860, ae. 58	4	159-0
Royal, m. Sally M. **WILBUR**, Dec. 18, 1825, by Amhurst Scoville, J.P.	3	131
Samuell, s. John & Susan[n]ah, b. May 8, 1708	1	7

	Vol	Page
ORMSBY, ORMSLY, (cont.)		
Sam[ue]ll, s. Sam[ue]ll & Dinah, b. Sept. 17, 1740	1	211
Sanford, s. [Eliphalet & Sarah], b. Apr. 20, 1788	2	73
Sophronia French, d. [Owen & Alethea], b. Oct. 26, 1795	3	58
Stephen, m. Jemima **SNELL**, Dec. 6, 1781	2	252
Stephen, m. Phebe **COLLINS**, Nov. 9, 1786	2	252
Susannah, d. [Sam[ue]ll & Dinah], b. May 27, 1752	1	211
Susannah, d. John & Deb[orah], b. Nov. 1, 1768	2	6
Tabatha, d. Sam[ue]ll & Dinah, b. Feb. 27, 1742	1	211
Tryphena, d. [John, Jr. & Lydia], b. Jan. 21, 1788	2	231
William, s. [Abner], b. July 25, 1796	3	47
William, s. [Royal & Sally M.], b. Feb 28, 1842	3	131
OSBORN, Leman, engraver, ae. 31, res. Albany, m. Julia **CHILDS**, operative, ae. 26, b. Keene, N.H., res. Albany, Jan. 13, 1851, by Rev. Miner	4	117
W[illia]m H., of Columbia, m. Mary R. **HERVIE**, of Windham, Apr. 28, 1844, by Comfort D. Fillmore, Local Deacon	3	214
OTIS, Dorcas, m. George P. **BATES**, Jan. 31, 1830, by Rev. Roger Bingham	3	143
Lofton H., s. W[illia]m K., physician, ae. 25, & Mary C., ae. 30, of Willimantic, b. Sept 10, 1847	4	1
Uriah H., ae. 26, m. [ ], Feb. 10, 1848, by Rev. Gay	4	113
W[illia]m L., of Willimantic, d. Nov. 19, 1850, ae. 3	4	157
OWEN, Abigail, d. [Frederick & Peggy], b. Jan. 16, 1782	2	224
David, s. [Frederick & Peggy], b. Jan. 14, 1786	2	224
David K., merchant, ae. 32, b. Ashford, res. Hartford, m. Martha B. **WHIPPLE**, tailoress, ae. 28, b. Norwich, res Hartford, his 2d w., May 4, 1851, by Rev. S.G. Williams	4	117
Eliphalet, s. [Frederick & Peggy], b. May 9, 1784	2	224
Frederick, m. Peggy **HIBBARD**, Sept. 10, 1778, by Samuel Gray, J.P.	2	224
Mary J., d. Thomas, laborer, ae. 35, of Willimantic, b. Apr. [1850]	4	10
Polly, d. [Frederick & Peggy], b. July 21, 1788	2	224
Raimer, [child of Frederick & Peggy], b. Dec. 20, 1779	2	224
Zerviah, d. [Frederick & Peggy], b. Feb. 13, 1779	2	224
PAGE, Amy, m. Elias B. **JENNER**, Aug. 30, 1845, by Andrew Sharp	3	222
Charles Henry, s. Henry, farmer, ae. 31, & Mary, ae. 32, b. Oct. 12, [1849]	4	9
Charlotte M., m. Henry **SMITH**, Oct. 7, 1844, by Rev. Andrew Sharp, Willimantic	3	217
Henry, m. Mary **STODDARD**, b. of Windham, June 27, 1844, by Rev. J.E. Tyler	3	215

	Vol.	Page
PAGE, (cont.)		
Laura, m. Whitman **POTTER**, Mar. 5, 1837, by Rev.		
Philo Judson	3	182
Lucy N., m. Luther **RIXFORD**, Mar. 7, 1825, by John		
Baldwin, Esq.	3	37
Marcy, m. Alfred B. **FRINK**, Apr. 8, 1822, by John		
Baldwin, Esq.	3	34
Tryphena, m. Henry W. **GRISWOLD**, b. Feb. 22, 1824	3	18
W[illia]m, d. Apr. 9, [1851], ae. 80	4	157
PAINE, PAIN, PAYNE, PAYN, Ann, m. Jeremiah **ROSS**, Oct. 31,		
1744	1	253
Anna, d. Joseph & Anna, b. Apr. 2, 1727	1	81
Dorothy, d. Joseph & Sarah, b. Feb. 9, 1728/9	1	105
Hannah, m. Jonathan **BASS**, June 2, 1761	2	101
James, m. Frances Ann **ABBE**, b. of Windham, May 25,		
1835, by Rev. L.H. Corson	3	173
James, of Astatan(?), Wis., m. Abby **BURNHAM**, of		
Windham, Sept. 25, 1845, by Rev. J.E. Tyler	3	222
John, s. Joseph & Anna, b. Apr. 26, 1725	1	81
Joseph, m. Anna **BADCO[C]K**, Feb. 26, 1723/4	1	81
Joseph, s. Joseph & Anna, b. Apr. 23, 1729	1	81
Lyma, m. Thomas **BINGHAM**, Jr., Nov. 29, 1809	3	68
Margaret, m. Dr. Isaac **BENNET**, Sept. 9, 1784	2	90
Mary, m. John **BASS**, Dec. 23, 1751	1	312
Nathan H., of Brooklyn, m. Marcia M. **FULLER**, of		
Windham, May 7, 1838, by Rev. O.C. Whiton	3	186
Nathaniel C., of Lebanon, m. Anna A. **GAVITO**, of		
Willimantic, Oct. 4, 1846, by Rev. John Cooper	3	233
PALMER, Aaron, s. Samuell & Hipzabeth, b. Mar. 12,		
1722/23	1	8
Abiah, d. [Jonah & Abiah], b. Oct. 11, 1769	2	171
Abigail, d. Seth & Elizabeth, b. Jan. 9, 1725	1	5
Abigail, d. Elihu & Abigail, b. Jan. 9, 1729/30;		
d. Mar. 12, 1729	1	51
Abigail, d. Elihu & Abigail, b. Mar. 25, 1733	1	124
Abigail, m. Isaac **KINGSLEY**, Jan. 20, 1746	1	268
Abigail, m. Peter **ROBINSON**, Jr., Nov. 13, 1755	2	1
Abigail, [twin with Joseph], d. Joseph & Abigail,		
b. Jan. 13, 1761	2	41
Abigail, d. [Jonah & Abiah], b. June 25, 1765; d.		
Nov. 26, 1765	1	324
Abigail, d. [Jonah & Abiah], b. June 25, 1765; d.		
Nov. 26, 1765	2	171
Abigail, [wid. Elihu], d. Dec. 29, 1765, ae. about		
65 y.	1	124
Abigail, d. [Jonah & Abiah], b. Jan. 6, 1768	2	171
Abigail, m. Nathan **MORGAN**, Oct. 14, 1780	2	244
Abigail, w. Joseph, d. Apr. 14, 1809	2	41

	Vol.	Page
PALMER, (cont.)		
Abigail, m. Asa **SHEPARD**, Aug. 17, 1826, by Rev.		
Jesse Fisher; d. Jan. 27, 1852	3	127
Abner, of Norwich, made affidavit in Norwich		
Oct. 17, 1844, before Ebenezer Fuller, J.P.,		
"Cyrus Tracy, s. Cyrus & Elizabeth, b. July		
12, 1784; m. Hannah **SNOW**, d. Samuel, of		
Ashford, Mar. 3, 1808, by William Perkins,		
Esq., at the house of Samuel **SNOW** in Ashford	3	218
Alfred, s. [Ephraim & Bethiah], b. Nov. 9, 1806	3	40
Alfred B., m. Julia Ann **MILLER**, Jan. 1, 1834, by		
Rev. Charles S. Weaver, at Plainfield	3	167
Alice, w. Seth, d. Nov. 26, 1794	2	14
Alice, d. [Naniah & Cynthia], b. Dec. 10, 1797	2	62
Alice, m. Marcus **SMITH**, Feb. 17, 1825, by Rev.		
Jesse Fisher	3	118
Allethea, d. Joseph & Abigail], b, June 24, 1769	2	41
Amasa, s. Elihu & Abigail, b. July 13, 1726; d.		
Apr. 30, 1727	1	51
Amasa, s. Elihu & Abigail, b. Aug. 29, 1737	1	124
Amasa, m. Abigail **LASSELL**, May 13, 1762	2	19
Amos, s. Ich[abod] & Phebe, b. Sept. 30, 1742	1	174
Amos, m. Laura **BURNHAM**, b. of Willimantic Falls,		
Dec. 11, 1836, by Rev. Benajah Cook, Jr.	3	180
Amos, m. Artless **PHIL[L]IP**, b. of Windham, Apr. 7,		
1839, at Willimantic, by Rev. Benajah Cook, of		
Willimantic	3	188
Andrew, s. [Josiah & Phebe], b. Oct. 19, 1774	2	86
Ann, d. Samuell & Hipzabeth, b. July 19, 1730	1	8
Ann Elizabeth, d. Barrows, manufacturer, ae. 26, &		
Elizabeth, ae. 25, of Willimantic, b. June 14,		
1848	4	1
Anna, wid. Samuel, d. Feb. 7, 1761, ae. about 80 y.	1	84
Asenath, d. Shubael & Sybel, b. Mar. 25, 1755	1	314
Azel, s. [Eleazer & Mary], b. Aug. 12, 1777	2	10
Benjamin Webb, s. [James & Lora], b. Nov. 11, 1808	3	75
Beriah, s. [Eleazer & Mary], b. Mar. 24, 1773; d.		
Apr. 5, 1773	2	10
Kalven, s. [Jos[eph] & Abigail, b Sept. 1, 1766	2	41
Calvin, m. Hannah **HARTSHORN**, Oct. 6, 1791	3	59
Charles, s. [Marshall & Eunice], b. Mar 12, 1784;		
d. July 14, 1786	2	227
Charles, s. [Marshall & Eunice], b. June 23, 1787	2	227
Charles N., m. Maria **WOODWORTH**, Feb. 25, 1830, by		
Rev. Jesse Fisher	3	140
Charlotte, d. [Charles N. & Maria], b. July 4, 1832	3	140
Charlotte, ae. 18, m. John **STANTON**, teamster, ae. 25,		
Nov. 29, 1849, by Rev. Tho[ma]s Tallman	4	114

	Vol.	Page

PALMER, (cont.)

Charlotte Eliza, d. [John & Charlotte Y.], b.		
Jan. 2, 1837	3	116
Chloe, d. [Naniah & Cynthia], b. Dec. 19, 1792	2	62
Cynthia, d. [Naniah & Cynthia], b. May 9, 1784	2	62
Cynthia, m. Abner W. **ALLEN**, Oct. 18, 1807	3	61
Cyrus, m. Eliza **HUNTINGTON**, Mar. 24, 1844, by Rev.		
Andrew Sharp	3	213
David, s. [John & Lydia], b. Apr. 20, 1769	2	105
David, s. [Calvin & Hannah], b. June 26, 1798	3	59
Deborah, m. Darius **WEBB**, Oct. 8, 1767	2	203
Delight, d. Shubael & Sybel, b. Oct. 28, 1760	1	314
Delight, m. Daniel **BENNET**, of Preston, Feb. 28,		
1782	2	95
Desire, d. [Jenah & Abiah], b. Nov. 5, 1761	1	324
Desire, d. [Jonah & Abiah], b. Nov. 5, 1761	2	171
Ebenezer, s. Samuell & Hipzabeth, b. Jan. 25, 1714	1	8
Ebenezer, m. Mary **WEBB**, Mar. 11, 1741	1	215
Ebenezer, s. [James & Lora], b. Feb. 28, 1806	3	75
Ebenezer Fitch, s. [Naniah & Cynthia], b. Jan. 29,		
1791; d. Aug. 31, 1791	2	62
Edna, d. Zeb[ulon] & Lois, b. Apr. 19, 1747	1	258
Eleizer, m. Mary **LILLY**, Mar. 28, 1723	1	73
Eleizer, s. Eleizer & Mary, b. July 7, 1726	1	73
Eleazer, Jr., m. Mary **BINGHAM**, May 5, 1756	2	10
Eleazer, Jr., m. Mary **EATON**, Nov. 8, 1770	2	10
Eleazer, s. [Eleazer & Mary], b. Sept. 1, 1785	2	10
Eli, s. [Jonah & Abiah], b. Apr. 4, 1772; d. Nov. 30,		
1775	2	171
Elias, s. [Josiah & Phebe], b. July 7, 1780	2	86
Elihu, m. Abigail **ROBINSON**, Sept. 30, 1725	1	51
Elihu, s. Elihu & Abigail, b. Feb. 9, 1727/8	1	51
Elihu, Jr., m. Lois **FOSTER**, Aug 11, 1752	1	319
Elihu, d. July 22, 1764, in the 64th or 65th y. of		
his age	1	124
Elihu, s. [Elihu & Lois], b. Aug. 7, 1764	1	319
Elijah, s Sam[ue]ll, 3rd & Lydia, b. Mar. 21, 1739/40	1	186
Eliphalet, s. Eleizer & Mary, b. May 25, 1725	1	73
Eliphalet, s. [Enos & Jerusha], b. Dec. 11, 1764	2	98
Elisha, m. Mary **BARSTOW**, Oct. 22, 1807	3	100
Eliza, d. [James & Lora], b. Sept. 30, 1813	3	75
Elizabeth, m. John **SPENCER**, Aug. 29, 1711	1	45
Elizabeth, d. Seth & Elizabeth, b. Aug. 15, 1721	1	5
Elizabeth, w. Sam[ue]ll, Sr., d. May 10, 1725, in the		
81st y. of her age	1	8
Elizabeth, w. Jonah, d. Aug. 5, 1725, ae. 63	A	30
Elizabeth, w. Seth, d. Jan. 8, 1738/9	1	165
Elizabeth, d. Ich[abod] & Phebe, b. June 4, 1747	1	174

	Vol	Page
PALMER, (cont.)		
Elizabeth, m. Josiah **KINGSLEY**, Jr., Nov. 11, 1752	1	264
Elizabeth, d. Shubael & Sybel, b. June 25, 1753	1	314
Elizabeth, d. Eleazer, Jr. & Mary, b. Jan. 16, 1759	2	10
Elizabeth, m. Jared **HEBBARD**, Oct. 19, 1774	2	210
Elizabeth, d. [Joseph & Abigail], b. June 12, 1778	2	41
Elizabeth, of Windham, m. Cyrus **TRACY**, of Preston, Nov. 8, 1783	3	3
Ellen, b. Ireland, res. Windham, d. Jan. 28, 1860, ae. 32	4	159-0
Emily, m. Elijah **CLARK**, b. of Windham, [ ], 1833, by Rev. John Storrs	3	167
Emily, m. Henry A. **BENCHLEY**, b. of Willimantic, Apr. 28, 1839, at Willimantic by Rev. B. Cook, Jr., of Willimantic	3	189
Emily Curtis, d. [John & Charlotte Y.], b. Dec. 4, 1821	3	116
Enos, s. Eleizer & Mary, b. July 12, 1732	1	73
Enos, m. Jerusha **WEBB**, Mar. 21, 1764	2	98
Ephriam, s. [Joseph & Abigail], b. Jan. 15, 1776	2	41
Ephraim, s. [Calvin & Hannah], b. Dec. 2, 1795	3	59
Ephraim, m. Bethiah **BARSTOW**, Feb. 4, 1806	3	40
Erastus, s. Josiah & Phebe, b. July 29, 1772	2	86
Erastus, m. Alitha **MANNING**, May 28, 1822	3	104
Esther, d. Seth & Elizabeth, b. June 1, 1730	1	95
Esther, m. Reuben **ROBINSON**, Jan. 12, 1748/9	1	285
Esther, [w. John], d. Oct. 28, 1754	1	294
Est[h]er, m. Jeremiah **BINGHAM**, Jr. Jan. 15, 1772	2	167
Esther, d. [Joseph & Abigail], b. Aug. 8, 1783	2	41
[E]unice, d. Ichabod & Phebe, b. Aug. 19, 1740	1	174
[E]unice, d. [Elihu, Jr. & Lois], b. June 4, 1753; d. Oct. 18, 1754	1	319
Eunice, d. Elizhu and Lois, b. Aug. 25, 1755	1	319
Eunice, m. Josiah **SMITH** Jr., Dec. 25, 1776	2	214
Eunice, d. [Eleazer & Mary], b. Feb 27, 1781	2	10
Eunice, d. [Marshall & Eunice], b. Jan. 18, 1789	2	227
Eunice, Wid., m. David **FOX**, May 22, 1814, by Rev. Jesse Fisher	3	54
Eunice, m. Abner **ROBINSON**, b. of Windham, Mar. 23, 1843, by Rev. Isaac H. Coe	3	207
Ezekiel, s. Samuel, 3rd, & Lydia, b. Dec. 15, 1744	1	186
Fanny T., of Windham, m. Charles **CUMMINGS**, of Plainfield, Jan. 1, 1840, by Rev. Reuben Ransom, Willimantic	3	192
Fitch, m. Harriet G. **WILLIAMS**, Nov. 23, 1842, by Rev. Andrew Sharp, Willimantic	3	206
Gershom, m. Hannah **SPENCER**, June 28, 1715	1	38a

	Vol.	Page
PALMER, (cont.)		
Gershom, s. [Shubael & Sybel], b. Dec. 29, 1766	1	314
Gershom, m. Naomi **ALLEN**, of Coventry, June 23, 1772	2	171
Gurdon, s. [Calvin & Hannah], b. May 2, 1802	3	59
Hannah, d. Gershom & Hannah, b. May 16, 1720	1	38a
Hannah, m John **READ**, Apr. 27, 1721	1	45
Hannah, d. Seth & Elizabeth, b. Mar. 1, 1727/8; d. Dec. 19, 1792	1	95
Hannah, d. Eleazer & Mary, b. Apr. 23, 1743	1	198
Hannah, m. Joshua **READ**, Aug. 7 1754	1	255
Hannah, d. [Elihu & Lois], b. July 1, 1757	1	319
Hannah, m. Sam[ue]ll **DODGE**, May 18, 1767	2	64
Hannah, w. Gershom, d. Nov. 22, 1769, in the 79th y. of her age	1	38a
Hannah, d. [Joseph & Abigail], b. Dec. 30, 1780	2	41
Henry, s. [Calvin & Hannah], b. Feb. 7, 1793	3	59
Henry P., s. [Elisha & Mary], b. Nov. 27, 1808	3	100
Henry P., of Windham, m. Harriet **LYON**, of Canterbury, Aug. 11, 1834, by Rev. Jesse Fisher	3	169
Henry Wolcott, s. [John & Charlotte Y.], b. June 10, 1826	3	116
Hezekiah B., s. [Elisha & Mary], b. Sept. 17, 1810	3	100
Hezekiah B., m. Susan E. **TRACY**, Oct. 5, 1835, by Rev. Jesse Fisher	3	174
Ichabod, s. Samuel & Hipzabeth, b. Apr. 17, 1716	1	8
Ichabod, m. Phebe **BROUGHTON**, Nov. 22, 1738	1	174
Irena, d. [Enos & Jerusha], b. Nov. 7, 1770; d. May 27, 1771	2	98
Irena, d. Enos & Jerusha, b. June 8, 1772	2	98
Isaac, s. Joseph & Abigail, b. Apr. 19, 1759; d. Jan. 24, 1767	2	41
Isaac, s. [Joseph & Abigail], b. Aug. 10, 1773	2	41
Isaac, m. Ruby **KINGSLEY**, Dec. 10, 1795	2	186
Isaac L., m. Sarah A. **BABCOCK**, b. of Windham, Sept. 26, 1841, by Rev. John E. Tyler	3	198
Isaac Lazell, s. [Isaac & Ruby], b. Sept. 16, 1807	2	186
James, s. [Enos & Jerusha], b. Oct. 4, 1767; d. Feb. 14, 1773	2	98
James, m. Lora **LITTLEFIELD**, Oct. 8, 1801	3	75
James L., [s. Elisha & Mary], b. May 12, 1812	3	100
James L., [s. Elisha & Mary], b. Dec. 5, 1816	3	100
James Miller, s. [Alfred B. & Julia Ann], b. Jan. 27, 1835	3	167
James Nelson, s [James & Lora], b. July 19, 1803	3	75
Jane A., d. Alfred & Sarah, b. Sept. 27, [1849]	4	8
Jehoadan, d. Seth & Elizabeth, b. Apr. 20, 1733; d. Apr. 20, 1733	1	95

	Vol.	Page
PALMER, (cont.)		
Jeremiah, s. Ich[abod], & Phebe, b. July 19, 1744	1	174
Jerusha, d. Eleizer & Mary, b. Apr. 9, 1737	1	73
Jerusha, m. Nathan **ROBINSON**, Jan. 15, 1764	2	99
Jerusha, d. [Enos & Jerusha], b. July 17, 1774	2	98
John, s. Samuell & Hipzabeth, b. Mar. 6, 1720/21	1	8
John, m. Esther **CLEVELAND**, May 18, 1749	1	294
John, m. Lydia **EAMES**, Oct. 28, 1755	2	105
John, s. [John & Lydia], b. Sept. 12, 1756	2	105
John, s. [Naniah & Cynthia], b. Mar. 12, 1795	2	62
John, b. Mar. 12, 1795; m. Charlotte Y. **BINGHAM**,		
Nov. 8, 1820, by C.B. Everest	3	116
John B., [s. Elisha & Mary], b. Jan. 9, 1819	3	100
John Pitt, s. [John & Charlotte Y.], b. Aug. 18,		
1834	3	116
Jonah, s. Gershom & Hannah, b. July 18, 1716; d.		
Nov 14, 1719	1	38a
Jonah, d. Sept. 19, 1730, ae. 68	A	30
Jonah, d. Elihu & Abigail, b. July 23, 1731	1	124
Jonah, m. Abiah **ROBINSON**, Oct. 31, 1754	1	324
Jonah, m. Abiah **ROBINSON**, Oct. 31, 1754	2	171
Jonah, s. Jonah & Abigail, b. Nov. 18, [1755]; d.		
Nov. 24, 1755	1	324
Jonah, s. [Jonah & Abiah], b. Nov. 18, 1755; d.		
Nov. 24, 1755	2	171
Jonah, s. Shubael & Sybel, b. June 2, 1758	1	314
Joseph, s. Seth & Elizabeth, b. Jan. 22, 1736/7	1	165
Joseph, s. Eleizer & Mary, b. Feb. 16, 1744/5	1	198
Joseph, m. Abigail **LAS[S]EL**, Apr. 27, 1758	2	41
Joseph, [twin with Abigail], s. Joseph & Abigail,		
b. Jan. 13, 1761	2	41
Josiah, s. [Shubael & Sybel], b. Apr. 1, 1763	1	314
Josiah, m. Phebe **MANNING**, May 22, 1770	2	86
Julia, d. [Zuriel & Martha], b. Nov. 18, 1799; d.		
Nov. 18, 1802	3	20
Julia Ann, d. Feb. 3, 1835	3	167
Kalven, see under Calvin		
Levi, s. John & Esther, b. Feb. 9, 1749/50	1	294
Lewis Copeland, s. [John & Charlotte Y.], b. Jan. 16,		
1829	3	116
Lois, d. Elihu & Lois, b. Apr. 20, 1761	1	319
Lois, d. [Zuriel & Martha], b. Feb. 3, 1804	3	20
Lora Glice*, d. [James & Lora], b. Dec. 6, 1804		
(*Alice?)	3	75
Lucius, s. [Zuriel & Martha], b. Jan. 12, 1802	3	20
Luce, d. Ebenezer & Mary, b. Apr. 24, 1742	1	215
Lucy, d. [Calvin & Hannah], b. Dec. 6, 1792	3	59
Lucy, m. John **SMITH**, Nov. 6, 1842, by Rev. John B.		

	Vol.	Page
PALMER, (cont.)		
Guild, Willimantic	3	206
Lydia, d. Samuel, 3rd, & Lydia, b. Jan. 11, 1748/9	1	186
Lydia, d. [John & Lydia], b. Dec. 16, 1764	2	105
Marshall, s. [John & Lydia], b. Dec. 24, 1758	2	105
Marshall, m. Eunice **MANNING**, Oct. 9, 1783	2	227
Marshall, d. July 7, 1812	2	227
Martha, d. Sam[ue]ll & Hipzabeth, b. Apr. 25, 1710;		
d. Apr. 26, 1710	1	8
Mary, m. John **ABBE**, Mar. 12, 1723	1	37
Mary, d. Seth & Elizabeth, b. Oct. 17, 1723	1	5
Mary, d. Eleizer & Mary, b. May 19, 1728	1	73
Mary, d. Eleizer & Mary, b. June 20, 1743; d. June 20,		
1843* (*probably 1743)	1	198
Mary, d. Eb[enezer] & Mary, b. June 20, 1743; d. same		
day	1	215
Mary, d. Eb[enezer] & Mary, b. June 11, 1744	1	215
Mary, m. Elisha **HEB[B]ARD**, Aug. 16, 1744	1	237
Mary, w. Eliazer, Jr., d. Sept. 9, 1760	2	10
Mary, w. Eleazer, d. July 9, 1768, in the 66th y. of		
her age	2	8
Mary, d. [Eleazer & Mary], b. June 6, 1775; d. Sept.		
12, 1800	2	10
Mary A., m. Jefferson **CAMPBELL**, b. of Windham, Mar. 3,		
1839, by Rev. Otis C. Whiton, of Scotland Society	3	189
Mary H., d. [Elisha & Mary], b. Sept. 18, 1814	3	100
Mason, of Canterbury, m. Olive **ROBINSON**, of Windham,		
Feb. 11, 1826	3	120
Mehetable, d. Eleizer & Mary, b. Sept. 8, 1739	1	198
Mahitable, m. Abner **ROBINSON**, Apr. 7, 1763	2	132
Mercy, d. Eleizer & Mary, b. Feb. 24, 1734/5	1	73
Moses, s. Samuell & Hipzabeth, b. Aug. 24, 1726	1	8
Naniah, m. Cynthia **FITCH**, May 23, 1782	2	62
Namiah, d. Feb. 24, 1829	2	62
Naomi, w. Gershom, d. Aug. 15, 1773	2	171
Nathan, s. [Elihu & Lois], b. Apr. 6, 1769	1	319
Nathaniel, s. Samuel, 3rd, & Lydia, b. Mar. 2, 1742	1	186
Nehemiah, see under Naniah and Namiah		
Olive, d. [Elihu & Lois], b. Oct. 22, 1766	1	319
Parmelia, d. [Amasa & Abigail], b. June 3, 1764	2	19
Pamela, d. [Naniah & Cynthia], b. Oct. 3, 1786	2	62
Perram, s. [Amasa & Abigail], b. Dec. 21, 1762	2	19
Phebe, d. Gershom & Hannah, b. Nov. 20, 1718	1	38a
Phebe, d. Ich[abod], & Phebe, b. May 23, 1749	1	174
Phebe, d. [Josiah & Phebe], b. Jan. 15, 1777	2	86
Rebeckah, m. Thomas **READ**, Feb. 22, 1711/12	1	40
Rebeckah, m. George **LILL[E]Y**, Apr. 28, 1714	1	35
Rhode, d. Elihu & Abigail, b. Sept. 6, 1735; d.		

	Vol.	Page
PALMER, (cont.)		
Mar. [ ], 1735/6	1	124
Ruth, d. Jonathan & Elizabeth, d. Nov. 16, 1711	1	18
Sally, ae. 26, b. Voluntown, res. Willimantic, m. Edwin **SIMMONS**, merchant, ae. 30, b. Foster, res. Willimantic, Oct. 3, 1850, by Rev. Henry Bromley	4	117
Samuell, m. Hipzabeth **ABBE**, Apr. 8, 1707	1	8
Samuell, s. Samuell & Hipzabeth, b. Sept. 18, 1711	1	8
Samuel, m. Anna **DURGE**, Dec. 6, 1827 [1727?]; d. Nov. 18, 1743, ae. about 84 y.	1	84
Sam[ue]ll, 3rd, m. Lydia **SIBLEY**, Jan. 18, 1738/9	1	186
Sam[ue]ll, d. Nov. 18, 1743, ae. about 84 y.	1	84
Samuel, s. [John & Lydia], b. Jan. 6, 1762	2	105
Samuel Morgan, s. [Zuriel & Martha], b. Oct. 12, 1797	3	20
Sanford, s. [Naniah & Cynthia], b. May 5, 1800	2	62
Sanford Kingsbury, s. [John & Charlotte Y.], b. July 1, 1831	3	116
Sarah, d. Sam[ue]ll & Hipzabeth, b. Feb. 2, 1707/8	1	8
Sarah, d. Eb[enezer] & Mary, b. July 24, 1749	1	215
Seth, m. Elizabeth **CARY**, Apr. 19, 1720	1	5
Seth, s. Seth & Elizabeth, b. May 14, 1734	1	95
Seth, m. Mary **MOSELEY**, June 14, 1739; d. Aug. 1, 1772, in the 79th y. of his age	1	165
Seth, Jr., m. Alice **MANNING**, June 14, 1756	2	14
Seth, s. [Joseph & Abigail], b. May 12, 1771	2	41
Seth, d. Aug. 1, 1772, in the 79th y. of his age	1	165
Seth, d. July 14, 1804	2	14
Seth, d. Oct. 12, 1848, ae. 77	4	151
Shubael, s. Gershom & Hannah, b. Jan. 14, 1720/21	1	38a
Shubael, m. Sybel **BINGHAM**, Aug. 20, 1752	1	314
Shubael, d. Sept. 5, 1771, in the 51st y. of his age	2	1
Sophia, d. [Ephraim & Bethiah], b. Dec. 1, 1814	3	40
Sophia, m. Lewis A. **SMITH**, b. of Windham, [ ], by Rev. Daniel G. Sprague	3	181
Susan B., m. Oliver F **WOOD**, [ ], by Rev. Jesse Fisher	3	127
Susan Barstow, d. [Ephraim & Bethiah], b. Feb. 11, 1809	3	40
Sibel, d. Eb[enezer] & Mary, b. Jan. 1, 1746/7	1	215
Sybel, d. [Shubael & Sybel], b. Nov. 29, 1768	1	314
Sybel, w. Shubael, d. May 2, 1771	1	314
Thaddeus, s. Elihu & Lois, b. Aug. 16, 1754; d. Sept. 5, 1754	1	319
Thaddeas, s. Elihu & Lois, b. June 22, 1759	1	319
Tryphenia, d. Eleizer & Mary, b. May 1, 1741	1	198
Tryphenia, m. Eliphaz **KINGSLEY**, Nov. 24, 1762	2	110

	Vol.	Page
PALMER, (cont.)		
Vaniah, d. [Jonah & Abiah], b. Feb. 17, 1758	1	324
Vaniah, s. [Jonah & Abiah], b Feb 17, 1758	2	171
Wealthia, d. [Jonah & Abiah], b. Nov. 4, 1763	1	324
Weltha, d. [Jonah & Abiah], b. Nov. 4, 1763	2	171
William, s. Zeb[ulon] & Lois, b. Sept. 4, 1749	1	258
William, s. [Jonah & Abiah], b. Oct. 15, 1759	1	324
William, s. [Jonah & Abiah], b. Oct. 15, 1759;		
d. Mar. 12, 1773	2	171
William, s. [Naniah & Cynthia], b. Nov. 1, 1788;		
d. Aug. 31, 1791	2	62
William, s. [Calvin & Hannah], b. Mar. 31, 1808	3	59
W[illia]m F., shoemaker, ae. 28, b. Windham, res.		
Springfield, m. Susan **WEBB**, ae. 24, b. Windham,		
Oct. [ ], [1850], by Rev. Henry Coe	4	118
W[illia]m Fitch, s. [John & Charlotte Y.], b. June		
29, 1824	3	116
Zebulon, s. Samuell & Hipzabeth, b. May 19, 1718	1	8
Zeb[ulon], m. Lois **CARPENTER**, Apr. 25, 1746	1	258
Zinas, s. Joseph & Abigail, b. May 25, 1764	2	41
Zuruiah, d. Eleiser & Mary, b. Feb. 12, 1723/4; d.		
Mar. 20, 1728	1	73
Zuriah, d. Eleizer & Mary, b. Feb. 24, 1730/31	1	73
Zuriah, m. Experience **ROBINSON**, Feb. 14, 1748/9	1	287
Zuriel, s. [Eleazer & Mary], b. Nov. 14, 1771	2	10
Zuriel, m. Martha **MORGAN**, Oct. 27, 1796	3	20
——, twin daughters, Eleazer, Jr. & Mary, b.		
Nov. 30, 1756	2	10
——, twin daughters, Eleazer, Jr. & Mary, d.		
Nov. 30, 1756	2	10
——, s. [Shubael & Sybel], b. Feb. [ ], 1757;		
d. same day	1	314
——, s. Eleazer & Mary, b. Aug. 24, 1757; d.		
Aug. 24, 1757	2	10
——, s. [Elihu & Lois], b. June 4, 1763; d. same		
day	1	319
——, d. Shubael & Sybel, b. Feb. 4, 1765; d. same		
day	1	314
——, child of Amos, laborer, ae. 35, & Julia A.,		
ae. 40, of Willimantic, b. [ ], 1848	4	1
——, d. in child birth, Jan 28, 1860	4	159-0
PALMITER, Eben[eze]r, m. Ellenor **LUDDINGTON**, Aug. 6, 1764	2	129
Hannah, m. Joshua **HEBBARD**, Dec. 2, 1772	2	176
PANKIS(?), Freelove, m. Uriah R. **TRACY**, b. of Windham,		
Jan. 8, 1840, by Rev. Otis C. Whiton	3	193
PARK, Elizabeth S., of Willimantic Falls, m. Joshua **PORTER**,		
of Columbia, Oct. 8, 1837, by Rev. B. Cooke, Jr.,		
at Willimantic Falls	3	183

	Vol	Page
PARKER, Amanda A., of Mansfield, m. Christopher G		
CHAMPLAIN, of Willimantic Falls, Aug. 8, 1836,		
by Rev. B. Cook, Jr., at Willimantic Falls	3	178
Ebenezer, s. [Stephen & Mary], b. Sept. 28, 1758	1	290
Edwin (sic), ae. 23, b. Ashford, res. Illinois, m.		
Edward **HOLDEN**, min[ister], ae. 35, b. Dorchester,		
res. Illinois, July 28, [1850], by E. W. Barrows	4	118
Elizabeth, m. John **CLARK**, Nov. 12, 1747	1	280
Hannah, m. Daniel **BUTLER**, Dec. 5, 1744	1	257
Hannah H., of Windham, m. Zephaniah **HERRINGTON**, of		
Mansfield, Mar. 11, 1827, by Rev. Cornelius B.		
Everest	3	125
Jane, ae. 19, m. James B. **WEEDEN**, carpenter, ae. 22,		
Nov. 28, [1849], by Rev. Burgess	4	115
John, s. [Stephen & Mary], b. Nov. 15, 1756	1	290
John, d. Oct. 16, 1766, ae. about 78	1	63
Mary, m. Jonathan **HOLT**, Apr. 12, 1738	1	189
Mary, d. [Stephen & Mary], b. Jan. 1, 1755	1	290
Ruth, m. Nath[anie]ll **HOVEY**, Jr., Jan. 21, 1747/8	1	292
Sarah, m. John **MARTIN**, June 16, 1748	1	280
Stephen, m. Mary **MARTIN**, Mar. 22, 1748/9	1	290
Stephen, s. [Stephen & Mary], b. Oct. 28, 1752	1	290
Watson M., m. Olive **ROBERTS**, b of Coventry, Conn.,		
May 24, 1840, by Rev. Ella Dunham	3	193
Zaccheas, of Mansfield, m. Rhoda **CRANSTON**, of Willi-		
mantic, Mar. 8, 1846, by John Cooper	3	228
PARKHURST, Adelaide, d. Elias, ae. 44, & Hannah, ae. 33, b		
June 17, [1847]	4	3
Ann E., ae. 17, of Windham, m. Daniel S. **CARTER**,		
farmer, ae. 23, b. S. Kingstown, R.I., res.		
Windham, Mar. 11, 1851, by Rev. H. Greenslit	4	118
Eldora, d. Ja[me]s, farmer, ae. 28, & Lucy Ann, ae.		
25, b. Sept. 17, [1849]	4	9
Jane M., of Scotland, Conn., m. Danforth **BROWN**, of		
Worcester, Mass., Sept. 6, 1846, by Rev. Thomas		
Tallman, of Scotland	3	230
——, child of Elias, farmer, ae. 46, b. July 19,		
1850	4	11
PARKIS, James, m Lucy A. **POLLARD**, b. of Windham, Mar. 4,		
1844, by Rev. Henry Greenslit	3	213
PARRISH, PARISH, Abigail, d. [Archippus & Abigail], b Dec.		
25, 1763	2	81
Abraham, s. [Zebulon & Hannah], d. Jan. 23, 1772	2	4
Abraham, s. [Zebulon & Hannah], b. Mar. 30, 1772	2	4
Abraham, s Zebulon & Han[na]h, b. Feb. 14, 1757	2	4
Alice, d. [John, Jr. & Tammey], b. May 31, 1773	2	16
Almy, d. [Archippus & Abigail], b. Oct. 12, 1765	2	81
Altheah, m. Michael **DEVINEY**, b. of Windham, July 28,		

	Vol.	Page
PARRISH, PARISH, (cont.)		
1844, by Rev. Alfred Burnham	3	215
Anna, d. [John, Jr. & Tammey], b. Dec. 31, 1767	2	16
Archiup, [twin with Marg[a]ret], s. Isaac &		
Marg[a]ret, b. Oct. 10, 1735	1	57
Archippus, m. Abigail **BURNAP**, Mar. 10, 1763	2	81
Asa, s. William & Jerusha, b. Jan. 27, 1722/3	1	67
Asa, s. [John & Hannah], b. Mar. 25, 1766	2	30
Asael, s. John, Jr. & Tammey, b. Aug. 28, 1765	2	16
Bethiah, d. William & Bethiah, b. Sept. 26, 1739	1	67
Bethiah, w. William, d. Feb. 26, 1741/2	1	67
Bethia, of Windham, m. Sam[ue]ll **MORGAN**, Jr., of		
Preston, Oct. 2, 1755	2	13
Chester, s. [Oliver & Mary], b. Nov. 2, 1757; d.		
Feb. 8, 1758	2	34
Cinthia, d. [John & Hannah], b. Oct. 8, 1770	2	30
Dan, s. Oliver & Mary, b. Jan. 15, 1759	2	34
Daniel, s. [Jacob & Mehetable], b. Oct. 29, 1775	2	194
Deborah, d. [Stephen & Mary], b. Oct. [ ], 1764	1	290
Dorothy, m. Thomas **BASS**, Nov. 9, 1726	1	82
Dorothy, d. William, Jr., d. Sept. 22, 1753	1	288
Eliphaz, s. [William, Jr. & Dorothy], b. Sept. 2,		
1749	1	288
Eliphas, m. Dorothy **BURNHAM**, Nov. 1, 1770	2	178
Ephraim, s. John & Hannah, b. Mar. 27, 1755	2	30
Esther, d. Isaac & Marg[a]ret, b. June 15, 1738	1	57
Esther, m. Joseph **SESSIONS**, Jr., Jan. 26, 1758	2	45
Eunice, d. [William, Jr. & Dorothy], b. May 2, 1751	1	288
Eunice, d. [Eliphas & Dorothy], b. Aug. 22, 1773	2	178
Eunice, m. Roger **CARY**, Jan. 27, 1780	2	239
Hannah, d. [John & Hannah], b. Jan. 31, 1764	2	30
Hannah, w. John, d. Feb. 9, 1777	2	30
Irena, d. [Zebulon & Hannah], b. Oct. 27, 1761	2	4
Isaac, m. Marg[a]ret **SMITH**, Mar. 31, 1720/21	1	57
Isaac, s. Isaac & Marg[a]ret, b. Dec. 16, 1723	1	57
Jacob, m. Mehetable **FLINT**, Feb. 2, 1772	2	194
Jerusha, [w. William], d. Mar 23, 1726/7	1	67
Jerusha, d. Isaac & Marg[a]ret, b. Nov. 6, 1727	1	57
Jerusha, d. William & Bethyah, b. Feb. 1, 1740/41	1	229
Jerusha, d. William & Bethyah, b. Feb. 1, 1740/41; d.		
Feb. 14, 1740/41	1	214
Jerusha, d. William & Bethia[h], d. Feb. 14, 1741/2	1	67
Jerusha, d. William & Jerusha, b. Aug. 29, 1744; d.		
Mar. 24, 1745/6	1	229
Jerusha, m. Jacob **SIMONS**, Apr. 21, 1747	1	273
Jerusha, m. Jacob **SIMONS**, 3rd, Apr. 21, 1747	2	207
Jerusha, d. [John & Hannah], b. Dec. 12, 1768	2	30
Jesper, s. [Zebulon & Hannah], b. Mar. 9, 1767	2	4

PARRISH, PARISH, (cont.)	Vol.	Page
Jesse, s. John, Jr. & Tammey, b. Mar. 11, 1761	2	16
John, s. Isaac & Margaret, b. Mar. 1, 1721/22;		
d. Dec. 23, 1724	1	57
John, s. William & Jerusha, b. Mar. 10, 1726/7	1	67
John, s. Isaac & Marg[a]ret, b. July 24, 1732	1	57
John, Jr., m. Tammey **PRESTON**, May 27, 1756	2	16
John, m. Hannah **HEBBARD**, Apr. 16, 1778	2	30
John, s. [John & Hannah], b. June 23, 1779	2	30
Lucy, d. John & Hannah, b. Dec. 6, 1757	2	30
Lucy, d. [Zebulon & Hannah], b. June 18, 1764	2	4
Lucy, d. [Eliphas & Dorothy], b. Feb. 27, 1771	2	178
Lydia, d. William & Jerusha, b. Sept. 16, 1719	1	67
Marg[a]ret, [twin with Archiup], d. Isaac &		
Marg[a]ret, b. Oct. 10, 1735	1	57
Margaret, w. Isaac, d. Dec. 20, 1753, in the 55th y.		
of her age	1	57
Margaret, m. Eben[ezer] **KINGSLEY**, May 24, 1761	2	38
Mary, d. [Zebulon & Hannah], b. Apr. 18, 1759	2	4
Mary, d. [Jacob & Mehetable], b. May 30, 1774	2	194
Matilda, d. [John, Jr. & Tammey], b. Apr. 12, 1770	2	16
Matilda, m. Eleazer **CAREY**, Nov. 21, 1792	3	34
Matilda, of Windham, m. Warren **NICHOLS**, of Providence,		
R.I., Mar. 17, 1822	3	98
Nathan, s. [Zebulon & Hannah], b. June 30, 1769	2	4
Nath[aniel], s. [Stephen & Mary], b. Feb. 20, 1767	1	290
Olive, d. Oliver & Mary, b. May 12, 1761	2	34
Oliver, s. Isaac & Marg[a]ret, b. July 29, 1730	1	57
Oliver, of Windham, m. Mary **KIMBALL**, of Preston,		
Dec. 22, 1756	2	34
Oliver, s. [John & Hannah], b. Apr. 15, 1762	2	30
Patte, d. [John, Jr. & Tammey], b. Feb. 24, 1776	2	16
Rosel, s. [William, Jr. & Dorothy], b. Oct. 2, 1752	1	288
Sarah, m. John **WALDEN**, Jr., Sept. 26, 1751	2	79
Sarah, d. John, Jr. & Tammey, b. Mar. 2, 1757	2	16
Sarah, d. Stephen & Mary, b. Dec. 11, 1760	1	290
Stephen, s Zebulon & Hannah, b. Jan. 28, 1755	2	4
Susannah, d. Isaac & Margaret, b. Oct. 20, 1742	1	57
Susannah, m. John **SPAFFORD**, Feb. 18, 1762	2	85
Tammey, d. John, Jr. & Tammey, b. May 27, 1759	2	16
Truman, s. [John, Jr. & Tammey], b. Sept. 20, 1779	2	16
Welthian, d. John, Jr. & Tammey, b. Aug. 18, 1763	2	16
William, m. Jerusha **SMITH**, Nov. 8, 1716	1	67
William, s. William & Jerusha, b. Aug. 11, 1717; d.		
Mar. 15, 1724	1	67
William, s. William & Jerusha, b. Jan. 15, 1724/5	1	67
William, m. Bethiah **BREWSTER**, May 23, 1738	1	67
William, m. Jerusha [ ], Apr. 13, 1742	1	229
William, Jr., m. Dorothy **KINGSLEY**, May 11, 1749	1	288

	Vol.	Page
PARRISH, PARISH, (cont.)		
William, s. John & Hannah, b. May 25, 1760	2	30
William, Jr., d. Oct. 23, 1762, ae. 38	1	288
William, d. Oct. 21, 1763, ae. 68	1	229
Zebulon, s. Isaac & Marg[a]ret, b. Feb. 12, 1725/6	1	57
PARSONS, PARSON, Asenath, m. Elizer **DEMING,** Jan. 2, 1826	3	122
Hannah, m. Jonathan **MASON,** Dec. 7, 1737	1	157
R.C., s. Peter L., accountant, b. Mar. 16, 1850	4	13
Sally, m. Mason **HUNTINGTON,** Mar. 19, 1819	3	71
PATT, Catharine A., m. James **LITTLEFIELD,** b. of Willimantic, Oct 18, 1835, by Rev. Philo Judson, at Willimantic	3	174
Sarah A., dressmaker, ae. 26, b. Scituate, R.I., res. Willimantic, m. H.L. **FISK,** doctor, ae. 27, b. Stafford, res Willimantic, May 11, 1851, by Rev. S.G. Williams	4	117
PATTEN, Mary, d. Nathaniell & Mary, b. Mar. 26, 1735	1	154
PAYNE, [see under **PAINE**]		
PEABODY, PABODY, Asa, m. Mary **PRINTICE,** July 13, 1742	1	233
Lucie, d. Asa & Mary, b. Jan. 30, 1743	1	233
Polly, m. Festus **REED,** Feb. 3, 1807	3	58
PEARL, Abigail, d. Timothy & Mary, b. June 30, 1745; d. Sept. 19, 1769	1	241
Alice, d. Timothy & Dinah, b. July 6, 1743	1	274
Alice, d. Timothy & Dinah, b. Sept. 6, 1747; d. 10th day of same month	1	274
David, s. Timothy & Mary, b. Feb. 9, 1743	1	241
Elizabeth, d. Timothy & Elizabeth, b. Jan. 18, 1729/30	1	87
Elizabeth, w. Timothy, d Aug. 29, 1736	1	87
Hannah, d. Timothy & Dinah, b. May 17, 1751	1	274
Hannah, d. Tim[othy] & Mary, b. [ ]	1	241
James, s. Timothy & Mary, b. Mar. 24, 1738	1	241
James, s. Timothy & Mary, b. Mar. 24, 1739	1	192
James, s. Nathan & Elizabeth, b. Oct. 27, 17[ ]	2	1
John, s. Timothy & Elizabeth, b. Jan. 20, 1725	1	87
Lydia, d. Timothy & Elizabeth, b. July 31, 1734	1	87
Lydia, m. Daniel **DENISON,** Nov. 27, 1753	1	320
Mary, d. Timothy & Mary, b. Jan. 24, 1742	1	241
Nathan, s. Timothy & Elizabeth, b. Nov 22, 1727	1	87
Nathan, m. Elizabeth **WILEY,** Mar. 7, 1748	2	1
Phebe, d. Timothy & Elizabeth, b. May 12, 1732	1	87
Philip, s. Tim[othy] & Mary, b. June 30, 1747	1	241
Phinehas, s. Tim[othy] & Mary, b. Aug. 2, 1753	1	241
Phinehas, [s. Timothy & Dinah], b. Aug. 2, 1753	1	274
Richard, s. Timothy & Mary, b. Feb. 4, 1740	1	241
Ruth, d. Timothy & Dinah, b. Aug. 31, 1749	1	274
Ruth, d. Tim[othy] & Mary, b. [ ]	1	241

	Vol	Page
PEARL, (cont.)		
Stephen, s. Nathan & Eliz[abeth], b. Apr. 28, 174[ ]	2	1
Timothy, s. Timothy & Elizabeth, b. Oct. 24, 1723	1	87
Timothy, m. Mary **LEACH**, Nov. 15, 1737	1	241
Timothy, m. Dinah **HOLT**, Nov. 6, 1746	1	274
Timothy, d. Oct. 9, 1773, in the 79th y. of his age	1	87
PEASE, Anna, housekeeper, b. R.I., res. Windham, d. Jan.		
22, 1860, ae. 65	4	159-0
Esther M., of Windham, m. Jesse F. **DANIELS**, of		
Lebanon, Jan. 5, 1845, by Rev. Charles Noble	3	219
Martha, m. Robert **PRENTICE**, Mar. 25, 1832, by Rev		
Alva Gregory	3	159
Richard S., m. Elisa B. **NICHOLS**, Mar. 14, 1843, by		
Rev. Andrew Sharp	3	208
PECK, Anna, d. June 12, [1850], ae. 15 m.	4	156
Julia A., d. Terrill, papermaker, ae. 26, & Almira,		
ae. 26, b. Feb. 2, 1849	4	5
Lydia, of Franklin, m. Capt. Ebenezer **HUNTINGTON**,		
Sept. 10, 1810	3	50
——, child of Pease L., ae. 34, & Emeline, ae. 34,		
b. July 2, [1848]	4	8
PECKAM, Richard W., of Franklin, m. Mary **WALES**, of		
Windham, Dec. 2, 1844, by Rev. J.E. Tyler	3	218
PENRE, Lydia, of Willimantic, m. Seth **COLLINS**, of Columbia,		
Feb. 10, 1846, at Willimantic, by John Cooper	3	227
PENVER, Sarah, m. Joseph **ALLEN**, 3rd, Feb. 15, 1813	3	70
PERKINS, PIRKENS, Almira J., of Windham, m. Alexander F.		
ADIE, of Providence, R.I., Dec. 2, 1840, by Rev.		
J.E. Tyler	3	195
Caroline E., b. Sterling, res. Windham, d. July 31,		
[1849], ae. 27	4	153
Cha[rle]s H., s. Mason, laborer, ae. 24, & Althear,		
ae. 21, of Willimantic, b. Nov. 1, 1850	4	13
Cha[rle]s W., papermaker, ae. 27, b. Manchester, res.		
Willimantic, m. Elizabeth **AVERY**, ae. 27, b. Volun-		
town, res. Willimantic, Sept. 8, 1850, by Rev.		
J. H. Farnsworth	4	117
Deborah, m. Benajah **CARY**, Feb. 11, 1741/2	1	223
Eliza Maria, of Lisbon, m. Mason **CLEVELAND**, Feb. 19,		
1822	3	97
Elizabeth, m. Joseph **WOODWARD**, May 19, 1748	1	296
Elizabeth, m. Joseph **WOODWARD**, May 19, 1748	2	33
Ellen Eliza, [d. John Abijah & Emily], b. Dec. 17, 1840	3	170
Francis, s. Jacob & Mary, b. Aug. 27, 1758	1	230
Hannah, m. Lemuel **BINGHAM**, Apr. 28, 1737	1	162
Hannah, m. Job **CARROLL**, Nov. 28, 1844, by Rev. J.B.		
Guild, Willimantic	3	218
Harriet, d. [Samuel & Nancy], b. Apr. 19, 1802	3	50
Harriet, m. Edward **CLARKE**, May 28, 1823	3	113

	Vol.	Page
PERKINS, PIRKENS, (cont.)		
Henrietta, of Windham, m. Charles **WHITMAN**, of Hart-		
ford, Nov. 13, 1833, by L.S. Corson, Rector	3	170
Hezekiah, of Norwich, m. Sarah **FITCH**, d. Col.		
Eleazer, of Windham, Mar. 4, 1784	3	43
Horatio Nelson, s. [Samuel & Nancy], b. Feb. 13,		
1799; d. Sept. 9, 1800	3	50
Jacob, s. Jacob & Mary, b. Apr. 28, 1745	1	230
Jerusha, m. Jabez **FOX**, Feb. 26, 1777	2	212
John Abijah, m. Emily **JOHNSON**, b. of Windham, Mar.		
26, 1834, by L.S. Corson, Rector	3	170
Judeth, m. Gamaleel **RIPLEY**, Jan. 23, 1772	2	84
Mary, d. Jacob & Mary, b. Mar. 30, 1751; d. Apr. 12,		
1753	1	230
Mary Ann, [d. John Abijah & Emily], b. Apr. [ ], 1836	3	170
Mary Ann, m. Thomas **SPENCER**, Jr., Oct. 6, 1845, by		
Andrew Sharp	3	224
Minor, laborer, ae. 22, m. Athea **BROWN**, ae. 26, Jan. 1,		
[1850], by Rev. Bromley	4	115
Nancy Huntington, d. [Samuel & Nancy], b. Dec. 24, 1793	2	234a
Nancy Huntington, d. [Samuel & Nancy], b. Dec. 24, 1793	3	50
Samuel, m. Nancy **HUNTINGTON**, Feb. 24, 1793	2	234a
Samuel, m. Nancy **HUNTINGTON**, Feb. 24, 1793	3	50
Samuel, s. [Samuel & Nancy], b. Feb. 16, 1797	3	50
Samuel, b. Lisbon, res. Windham, d. Sept. 22, 1850, ae.		
84	4	158
Samuel H., m. Charlotte E. **CLARKE**, [ ]	3	120
Sarah, d. Jacob & Mary, b. Nov. 25, 1747	1	230
Silas, s. Ann **WEBB**, b. July 15, 176[ ]	2	1
Willey, s. Jacob & Mary, b. Oct. 7, 1761	1	230
William, m. Dorcas **WILLIAMS**, Feb. 11, 1762, by Rev. Mr.		
Cogswell	2	72
----, s. Cha[rle]s W., papermaker, ae. 27, & Elizabeth,		
ae. 22, of Willimantic, b. Sept. 8, 1851	4	12
PERRIGO, Warren, farmer, d. Apr. 6, 1848, ae. 26	4	152
PERRY, [see also **PEVEY**], Albert L., carpenter, ae. 27, m.		
Mary A. **WHEELER**, ae. 18, Apr. 24, [1850], by Rev.		
J. Brewster	4	114
Albert Lincoln, s. [Benjamin & Lucy], b. Nov. 12, 1822	3	96
Ann, m. Benj[amin] **HEWITT**, June 3, 1829, by Elder Esek		
Brown	3	157
Anna H., d. George & Sarah, b. Mar. 12, [1849]	4	8
Benjamin, m. Lucy **SINCLAIR**, Nov. [ ], 1821, by Rev.		
C.B. Everest	3	96
Charles B., [s. Wanton G. & Eliza Ann], b. May 1, 1838	3	113
Esther Annie, [d. Wanton G. & Eliza Ann], b. Sept. 6,		
1846	3	113
George, of Lisbon, m. Sarah Ann **GAGER**, of Windham,		

	Vol.	Page
PERRY, (cont.)		
Mar. 12, 1842, by Rev. Joseph Ayer, Jr., of Lisbon	3	201
George S., [s. Wanton G. & Eliza Ann], b. Jan. 15, 1844	3	113
Henry Benjamin, s. [Benjamin & Lucy], b. May 8, 1826	3	96
Jane, [d. Wanton G. & Eliza Ann], b. Feb. 10, 1840	3	113
Loisa W., m. William **CORBEN**, Jan. 11, 1847, by Rev. John Cooper	3	234
Lucy, d. [Benjamin & Lucy], b. Mar. 1, 1828	3	96
Lucy L., d. Nov. 29, 1850, ae. 53	4	157
Lucy L., d. Albert L., house carpenter, ae 28, & Mary, ae. 19, b. June 9, 1851	4	14
Mancia* Emily, d. [Benjamin & Lucy], b. Apr. 30, 1833 (*Perhaps "Marrcia")	3	96
Martha, m. Walter **ASHLEY**, Feb. 15, 1829, by Rev. Roger Bingham	3	142
Mary Ann, m. Asa N. **BURGESS**, b. of Windham, Nov. 29, 1841, by Rev. Nathan Wildman	3	200
Mary E., of Windham, m. James H. **FULLER**, of Mansfield, Apr. 29, 1839, by Rev. Winslow Ward	3	189
Ransom, m. Abigail **FOX**, Jan. 13, 1833, by Henry Hall, J.P.	3	163
Richard, operative, ae. 26, b. Mansfield, res. Windham, m. Roxana **THOMPSON**, ae. 25, Nov. 28, 1847, by Tho[ma]s Dowling	4	111
Richard H., clerk, of Willimantic, d. Jan. 18, 1860, ae. 37	4	161
Sally, m. Peter **WELLS**, Jan. 15, 1824	3	116
Sarah Maria, d. [Benjamin & Lucy], b. Aug. 9, 1830	3	96
Wanton G., m. Eliza Ann **WELLS**, June 19, 1837, at Brooklyn	3	113
PETERS, Lydia, m. Dan **MANNING**, Mar. 2, 1775	2	201
Margaret, m. Josiah **REED**, Aug. 23, 1781	2	246
PETTINGILL, PETTINGALE, Abigail, d. [Solomon & Zerviah], b. Feb. 14, 1767	2	77
Abner(?), s. [Solomon & Zerviah], b. June 30, 1769	2	77
Asaph, s. [Lemuel & Easter], b. May 8, 1762	2	65
Hannah, d. [Solomon & Zerviah], b. Oct. 25, 1762	2	77
Lemuel, m. Easter **BURNAM**, Jan. 26, 1758	2	65
Lydia, d. [Lemuel & Easter], b. Mar. 13, 1760	2	65
Martha, d. [Solomon & Zerviah], b. Jan. 18, 1772	2	77
Permilia, d. [Solomon & Zerviah], b. Apr. 18, 1776	2	77
Solomon, m. Zerviah **MORGAN**, Dec. 23, 1761	2	77
Uriah, s. [Lemuel & Easter], b. Oct. 26, 1758; d. May 31, 1759	2	65
Zerviah, d. [Solomon & Zerviah], b. [ ]	2	77

	Vol.	Page
PETTINGILL, PETTINGALE, (cont.)		
—, s. [Solomon & Zerviah], b. Nov. 30, 1764	2	77
PEVEY, Joanna, of Willimantic, m. Aaron **BIGALOW,** of		
Colchester, Sept. 27, 1846, by Rev. John		
Cooper (Perhaps "**PERRY**")	3	230
PHELPS, PHEPS, Betty, m. Abel **BINGHAM,** Oct. 13, 1752	1	148
Moses, m. Sarah **MEACHAM,** May 29, 1745	1	260
Naomi, m. Bela **ALLEN,** May 19, 1793	2	83
Sarah, d. Moses & Sarah, b. Sept. 8, 1746	1	260
W[illia]m A., ae. 26, m. Sarah J. **WILDER,** ae. 20,		
July 7, [1850]	4	114
PHILLIPS, PHILIP, Alpheas, s. Sam[ue]ll & Alice, b.		
Mar. 24, 1746	1	125
Andrew, of Hebron, m. Maria **CHAMPLAIN,** of Lebanon,		
June 6, 1847, by Rev. Daniel Dorchester,		
Willimantic	3	235
Ann, d. John & Elizabeth, b. June 29, 1743	1	180
Artless, m. Amos **PALMER,** b. of Windham, Apr. 7.		
1839, at Willimantic, by Rev. Benajah Cook, of		
Willimantic	3	188
Benjamin, s. Benony & Mary, b. Apr. 12, 1713	1	43
Benjamin, m. Mary **CANNAWAY,** Feb. 2, 1737/8	1	180
Benjamin, m. Marg[a]ret **NICLAS,** Dec 17, 1744	1	180
Benony, m. Mary **BARRADEL,** June 12, 1712	1	43
Elihu, manufacturer, ae. 24, m. Martha **HARRIS,** ae.		
19, Apr. 14, 1850, by [Rev.] Bromley	4	116
Elizabeth, d. John & Elizabeth, b. July 2, 1744	1	180
George, farmer, b. Hampton, res. Willimantic, m.		
Elizabeth J. **HARVEY,** b. Hampton, res. Willi-		
mantic, Feb. 27, 1851, by Rev. S.G. Williams	4	118
Harkness, c. spinner, b. Griswold, Ct., res. Willi-		
mantic, d. Feb. 17, 1860, ae. 60	4	159-0
James, s. Benony & Mary, b. Mar. 17, 1721	1	43
Jeremiah, m. Anna **EDWARDS,** Sept. 29, 1821, by Rev.		
C.B. Everest	3	120
John, s. Benony & Mary, b. Apr. 6, 1715	1	43
John, m. Elizabeth **BOURN,** Feb. 2, 1737/8	1	180
John, s. John & Elizabeth, b. Sept. 22, 1747	1	180
Josiah F., of Canterbury, m. Emily **SMITH,** of Scot-		
land, Nov. 26, 1846, by Rev. T. Tallman, of		
Scotland	3	232
Judeth, d. [Samuell & Mary], b. Jan. 14, 1756	1	125
Lydia, d. John & Elizabeth, b. Mar. 12, 1739/40	1	180
Marg[a]ret, w. [Benjamin], d. Nov. 12, 1745	1	180
Martha, d. [Samuell & Mary], b. Sept. 4, 1761	1	125
Mary, d. Benony & Mary, b. May 12, 1718	1	43
Mary, d. [Samuell & Mary], b. Feb. 2, 1754	1	125
Sam[ue]ll, s. Benony & Mary, b. Aug. 20, 1716	1	43

	Vol.	Page
PHILLIPS, PHILIP, (cont.)		
Samuell, s. Benj[ami]n & Mary, b. Nov. 2, 1738	1	180
Sam[ue]ll, m. Alice **BOURN**, Feb. 20, 1745	1	125
Sam[ue]ll, s. Benj[ami]n & Marg[a]ret, b. July		
24, 1745	1	180
Samuell, m. Martha **DECKER**, Mar. 27, 1751	1	125
Sam[ue]ll, s. [Samuell & Mary], b. Jan. 25, 1758	1	125
Sarah, d. John & Elizabeth, b. June 18, 1738	1	180
Sarah, of Willimantic, m. Charles **HARDING**, of		
Mansfield, May 27, 1839, at Willimantic, by		
Rev. B. Cook, Jr., of Willimantic	3	189
Silence, d. [Samuell & Mary], b. June 19, 1764	1	125
PHINEY, [see also **PINNEY**], Edwin S., of Canterbury, m.		
Henrietta **SPAFFORD**, of Windham, Apr. 3, 1836,		
by Rev. Jesse Fisher	3	177
PIERCE, PEIRCE, Charles, m. Olive **MAPLES**, Aug. 29, 1829,		
by Chester Tilden, Willimantic	3	137
Hannah T., of Scotland, m. Anson A. **SNOW**, of Hampton,		
Dec. 14, 1845, by H. Slade	3	225
Maria, m. Orrin **GREENE**, Sept. 24, 1828, by Alfred		
Young, J.P.	3	130
PINNEY, [see also **PHINEY**], Waterman, of Griswold, m. Mary		
Ann **APLEY**, of Chaplin, Aug. 17, 1842, by Rev.		
N.C. Wheat	3	202
PLACE, Olive S., m. Lewis **WORDEN**, Sept. 6, 1847, by Rev.		
Andrew Sharp	3	236
Solomon F., m. Olive S. **BENCHLEY**, June 9, 1844, by		
Rev. Andrew Sharp	3	215
POLK, Julia, ae. 37, m. Mason **CHURCH**, ae. 46, b. Mansfield,		
res. Chaplin, Feb. 13, 1848, by W[illia]m Lamb	4	112
POLLARD, Barnabus H., m. Julia A. **SCOTT**, July 4, 1844, by		
Rev. Andrew Sharp	3	215
John, farmer, ae. 53, b. Griswold, res. Windham, m.		
Lucy **MANNING**, ae. 41, Aug. 1, [1848], by Rev.		
Tho[ma]s Sullivan (His 2d marriage)	4	112
Lucy A., m. James **PARKIS**, b. of Windham, Mar. 4, 1844,		
by Rev. Henry Greenslit	3	213
POLLOCK, Susan, d. May [ ], [1849]	4	153
POLLY, Fitch, of New London, m. Mary Abbe **CROSS**, of		
Windham, Jan. 26, 1840, by Rev. John E. Tyler	3	192
Harriet M., d. Fitch, manufacturer, ae. 34, b. Feb. 5,		
1850	4	11
John, farmer, d. Nov. 11, 1848, ae. 8	4	154
POND, George Gilbert, s. [Charles], b. Nov. 29, 1833	3	72
POOL, Nancy, m. Timothy **WARREN**, Jan. 2, 1794	3	7
PORTER, A.D., laborer, ae. 20, m. H.A. **COBB**, ae. 21, Nov.		
29, [1848], by Mr. Bray	4	113
Anna M., d. Austin, laborer, ae. 21, of Willimantic, b.		

	Vol.	Page
PORTER, (cont.)		
Feb. 8, [1850]	4	10
David, of Lebanon, m. Abby **SHEFFIELD**, of Windham, Oct. 18, 1841, by Rev. Nathan Wildman, of Lebanon	3	199
Jesse, m. Betsey **SNOW**, b. of Windham, Nov. 11, 1833, by Rev. A. Gregory	3	166
Joshua, of Columbia, m. Elizabeth S. **PARK**, of Willimantic Falls, Oct. 8, 1837, by Rev. B. Cooke, Jr., at Willimantic Falls	3	183
Martha E., of Willimantic, m. John A. **WARNER**, of Brooklyn, Sept. 20, 1841, by Rev. Andrew Sharpe, Willimantic	3	198
Mary E., d. Selden, painter, ae. 23, b. Oct. 16, [1849]	4	9
Mary E., b. Woodstock, res. Willimantic, d. Sept. 3, 1850, ae. 11 m.	4	157
Sally, b. Franklin, res. Willimantic, d. Aug. [ ], 1850, ae. 62	4	157
Sarah A., d. Selden T., painter, ae. 24, & Sarah, ae. 20, of Willimantic, b. Aug. 11, 1850	4	12
Sophia S., m. Thomas W. **CUNNINGHAM**, June 5, 1843, by Rev. Andrew Sharp	3	209
——, Miss, operative, ae. 27, b. Lisbon, res. Mansfield, m. Edward **HARRIS**, farmer, ae. 27, b. Windham, res. Mansfield, Oct. 15, 1850, by Rev. Wallace	4	117
POTT, [see under **PATT**]		
POTTER, Alpheas W., [s. Whitman & Laura], b. Jan. 28, 1838	3	182
Caroline, m. Chester **DEAN**, b. of Willimantic, Oct. 1, 1838, at Willimantic, by Rev. P. Judson	3	187
Daniel, m. Hannah B. **DUNHAM**, Dec 9, 1841, by Rev Andrew Sharp	3	199
Ellen, m. John B. **SCOVILLE**, b. of Columbia, Mar. 8, 1841, by Rev. J.E. Tyler	3	196
Isaac T., m. Betsey M. **JAMES**, Oct. 21, 1833, by Rev. Alva Gregory, Willimantic	3	166
Lydia, m. James **WILLSON**, June 24, 1818	3	86
Niles, m. Amey B. **DORRANCE**, b. of Willimatnic, Nov. 17, 1833, by Rev. A. Gregory	3	166
Susan, m. Geo[rge] **LEONARD**, b. of Windham, Aug. 6, 1843, by Rev. Henry Bromley	3	210
Thomas, m. Susan **STANIFORD**, Mar. 26, 1834, by Rev. Roger Bingham	3	168
Whitman, m. Laura **PAGE**, Mar. 5, 1837, by Rev. Philo Judson	3	182
Willard A., [s. Whitman & Laura], b. May 13, 1841	3	182
POWERS, Anne, b. Apr. 22, 1762; m John **BYRNE**, Nov. 14, 1784	3	3

	Vol.	Page
POWERS, (cont.)		
Hazard, s. Hazard, b. Mar. 28, 1803	3	31
William, s. [Hazard], b. Mar. 8, 1805	3	31
PRENTICE, PRINTICE, PRENTIS, Ab[b]y, m. Ira. W.		
VAUGHAN, b. of Windham, Oct. 24, 1842, by		
Rev. A.C. Wheat	3	205
Caroline, m. Philip **WILLSON**, Sept. 14, 1845, by John		
Crocker, Willimantic	3	223
Frederick, m. Caroline **LORD**, Jan. 23, 1823, by Rev.		
Jesse Fisher	3	107
Henry M., m. Elizabeth F. **LYMAN**, b. of Windham, Aug.		
22, 1842, by Rev. A.C. Wheat	3	203
John, of Griswold, m. Eliza **LORD**, of Norwich, Feb.		
15, 1826	3	121
Lama*, m. Rensalaer C. **HOVEY**, b of Willimantic, Oct.		
2, 1836, by Rev. Philo Judson, at Willimantic		
(*Laura?)	3	179
Mary, m. Nath[anie]ll **LUCE**, Dec. 25, 1735	1	164
Mary, m. Asa **PAYBODY**, July 13, 1742	1	233
Mary A., m. Henry S. **SMITH**, Mar. 8, 1841, by Rev.		
And[rew] Sharpe, Willimantic	3	196
Robert, m. Martha **PEASE**, Mar. 25, 1832, by Rev. Alva		
Gregory	3	159
Robert, mechanic, d. May 15, [1850], ae. 43	4	155
Sophronia, m. James **MARTIN**, b. of Windham, Dec. 8,		
1840, by Rev. Andrew Sharpe, Willimantic	3	195
Susan, m. Robert W. **HOOPER**, b. of Willimantic, July 19,		
1837, by Rev. Philo Judson, at Willimantic	3	183
PRESTER, Ira, painter, m. Sophia **LINCOLN**, Jan. 22, 1850, by		
J.M. Phillips	4	114
PRESTON, PRESSON, Abiah, s. Jacob & Sarah, b. Apr. 1, 1735	1	118
Abraham, s. Jacob & Sarah, b. Jan. 1, 1748/9	1	241
Alfred, s. [Stephen & Lois], b. Oct. 23, 1779	2	225
Amos, s. Benj[amin] & Deborah, b. Jan. 27, 1738/9; d.		
Nov. 5, 1756	1	90
Anna, d. [William, Jr. & Desire], b. May 15, 1768	2	96
Anne, d. David & Elizabeth, b. Sept. 22, 1736; d.		
June 25, 1737	1	85
Asa, s. John & Elerner, b. June 8, 1732	1	146
Benjamin, m. Deborah **HALL***, May 5, 1727 (*correction		
HALL is crossed out and **HOLT** is handwritten at		
end of entry in original manuscript)	1	90
Benj[amin], s. Benj[amin] & Deborah, b. Dec. the last,		
1727	1	90
Daniel, s. Benj[ami]n & Deborah, b. Mar. 16, 1729/30	1	90
Daniel, s. Benj[ami]n & Deborah, b. Mar. 3, 1731/2	1	90
Daniel, m. Dinah **FORD**, Mar. 4, 1756	2	14
David, m. Elizabeth **MARTIN**, Aug. 2, 1726	1	85

	Vol.	Page

PRESTON, PRESSON, (cont.)

David, s. David & Elizabeth, b. June 20, 1731	1	85
Deborah, d. Benj[ami]n & Deborah, b. Dec. 10, 1740	1	90
Desire, w. Will[ia]m, d. Apr. 3, 1814	2	96
Ebenezer, s. David & Elizabeth, b. May 28, 1727	1	85
Eliphalet, s. William & Lois, b. Feb. 15, 1745; d. Feb. 25, 1758	1	136
Eliphalet, s [William, Jr. & Desire], b. Apr. 7, 1764	2	96
Eliphalet, m. Clarinda **SPAFFORD**, Jan. 25, 1787	2	204
Elizabeth, d. David & Elizabeth, b. Oct. 30, 1733	1	85
Elizabeth, d. Joseph & Elizabeth, b. Nov. 3, 1739	1	141
Elizabeth, d. [William, Jr. & Desire], d. Mar. 14, 1792	2	96
Easther, d. [William, Jr. & Desire], b. Nov. 27, 1776	2	96
Eunice, d. Jacob & Sarah, b. Apr. 20, 1741	1	118
[E]unice, d. Theodore & [E]unice, b. Sept. 29, 1743	1	232
Eunice, d. [Stephen & Lois], b. June 4, 1773, in Canterbury	2	225
Fanny, d. [William, Jr. & Desire], b. Apr. 19, 1778	2	96
Hannah, d. Joseph & Elizabeth, b. Jan. 1, 1734/5	1	141
Hannah, [twin with Isaac], d. Jacob & Sarah, b. Apr. 19, 1744	1	241
[H]enery, s. Jacob & Sarah, b. June 7, 1737	1	118
Henry, d. Dec. 20, 1759	1	173
Henry, s. [William, Jr. & Desire], b. Feb. 1, 1784; d. Jan. 20, 1789	2	96
Isaac, [twin with Hannah], s. Jacob & Sarah, b. Apr. 19, 1744	1	241
Jacob, Jr., m. Sarah **FFOSTER**, Sept. 21, 1730	1	118
Jacob, s. Jacob & Sarah, b. Feb. 24, 1732/3	1	118
Jacob, m. Mary **HOLMES**, Jan. 1, 1752	1	241
Jerusha, d. Benj[amin] & Deborah, b. July 29, 1736	1	90
John, m. Elerner **STILES**, Mar. 18, 1730/31	1	146
John, d. July 26, 1733	1	83
John, s. John & Elerner, b. Apr. 12, 1735	1	146
John, Jr., m. Mary **FORD**, Dec. 9, 1736	1	179
John, s. John & Mary, b. Sept. 9, 1737	1	179
Joseph, m. Elizabeth **ROBINS**, Apr. 23, 1734	1	141
Joseph, husband, of Phebe **FFARNUM**, d. Feb. 24, 1737/8	1	180
Joseph, 2d, m. Mary **FFRAME**, Apr. 8, 1738	1	173
Lois, d. William & Lois, b. Feb. 16, 1737/8	1	136
Lois, m. James **SMITH**, Apr. 30, 1766	2	125
Mary, d. Benj[amin] & Deborah, b Apr 2, 1734; d. Aug. 31, 1742	1	90
Mary, m. Stephen **SMITH**, Dec. 28, 1736	1	182
Mary, d. Jacob & Sarah, b. Aug. 18, 1739	1	118

	Vol	Page
PRESTON, PRESSON, (cont.)		
Mary, m. Daniel **LINKION**, June 22, 1763	2	85
Mary had s. Avery **AVEREL**, b. Dec. 3, 1771	2	181
Mehetabel, d. William & Lois, b. Mar. 22, 1740	1	136
Mehetable, m. Jacob **SIMONDS**, Jr , Sept. 28, 1760	1	273
Mehetable, m. Jacob **SIMONS**, Jr., Sept. 28, 1760	2	207
Nathaniell, s. Joseph & Elizabeth, b. Mar. 26,		
1737	1	141
Nath[anie]ll, s. William & Lois, b. Dec. 31, 1748;		
d. Apr. 8, 1749	1	136
Oliver, s. [William, Jr. & Desire], b. July 27,		
1766	2	96
Ruamah, d. William & Lois, b. June 22, 1736	1	136
Ruamah, m. Daniel **CANADA**, Nov. 16, 1763	2	154
Sally, d William, d. May 19, 1823	2	96
Sam[ue]ll, s. John & Mary, b. Aug. 20, 1727	1	83
Sarah, d. David & Elizabeth, b. Sept. 5, 1728	1	85
Sarah, d. John & Mary, b. Feb. 6, 1729/30; d. Mar.		
18, 1730/31	1	83
Sarah, d. Jacob & Sarah, b. Aug. 20, 1731	1	118
Sarah, d. Theodore & [E]unice, b. Apr. 6, 1747	1	232
Sarah, m. Thomas **KINGSBURY**, Nov. 24, 1749	1	304
Sarah, w. Jacob, d. Apr. 14, 1751	1	241
Sarah, d. William & Lois, b. Dec. 17, 1753; d.		
Jan. 6, 1754	1	136
Stephen, s. William [& Lois], b. Jan. 17, 1749	1	136
Stephen, m. Lois **HAMMOND**, Jan. 4, 1773	2	225
Susannah, d. Theodore & [E]unice, b. Mar. 20,		
1748/9	1	232
Sybel, d. [William & Lois], b. Nov. 30, 1750	1	136
Tamme, d. William & Lois, b. Jan. 18, 1734/5	1	136
Tammey, m. John **PARRISH**, Jr., May 27, 1756	2	16
Theodore, m. [E]unice **BUNDE**, Jan. 29, 1741/2	1	232
William, m. Lois **SIMONS**, Feb. 28, 1733/4	1	136
William, s. William & Lois, b. Dec. 7, 1742	1	136
William, Jr., m. Desire **WILLIAMS**, Aug. 18, 1763	2	96
William, d. May 20, 1778, in the 67th y. of his age	1	136
William, s. [Eliphalet & Clarinda], b. Sept. 10, 1787	2	204
PRICE, Mary, of Stafford, m. John **GENNINGS**, Jr., Nov. 9,		
1779	2	46
PRIMUS, Job, of Canterbury, m. Katurah **MICHEAL**, of Windham,		
Sept. 25, 1792	3	51
PRIOR, Issac N., of Hartford, m. Susan D. **AVERY**, of Windham,		
Aug. 20, 1833, by Rev. S.H. Corson	3	165
PURRINGTON, PURINGTON, PURINTON, Benjamin, m. Jane		
RIDER, Apr. 13, 1835, by Rev. Roger Bingham	3	173
-----, child of Benj[ami]n, carpenter, ae. 35, & Jane,		
ae. 34, b. July 20, 1848	4	5

	Vol.	Page
PURRINGTON, PURINGTON, PURINTON, (cont.)		
——, s. Benj[amin], of Willimantic, d. Aug. [ ],		
1850, ae 2 w.	4	157
——, s. Benj[amin], carpenter, ae. 42, & [ ],		
ae. 38, of Willimantic, b. Oct. [ ], 1850	4	12
PUTNAM, Eunice, m. William **BURGESS**, Dec. 23, 1756	2	56
QUINN, Ann A., d. Thomas, operative, ae. 40, b. Nov. 24,		
[1848]	4	6
Emily, d. Thomas, spinner, ae. 47, of Willimantic, b.		
Dec. 2, 1849	4	10
Susan, d. Thomas, operative, ae. 40, b. Nov. 21, [1848]	4	6
RAMSDELL, Daniel T., of Lyon, Mass., m. Eunice W. **KING**, of		
Windham, Dec. 29, 1839, by Rev. Reuben Ransom	3	191
RAND, Electa, m. Ce[a]sar **CHEETS**, Nov. 14, 1793	2	71
RANDALL, ——, s. W[illia]m, mule spinner, ae. 26, & Lucy,		
ae. 24, b. May 21, [1851]	4	13
RANSOM, David, s. Robert & Hannah, b. May 22, 1748	1	248
Hannah, d. Robert & Hannah, b. Jan. 4, 1744/5	1	248
Lodema, m. Jonathan **KINGSBURY**, June 21, 1775	2	134
Sarah, d. Robert & Hannah, b. Apr. 23, 1746	1	248
RATHBURN, RATHBONE, Amelia, m. Amos **BRALEY**, Dec. 9,		
1829, by Rev. Chester Tilden, Willimantic	3	140
Sarah, m. Israel **HAIL**, Nov. 16, 1752	1	318
RAY, Emery B., of Haddam, m. Eliza Abby **CONGDON**, of Willi-		
mantic Falls, Nov. 26, 1835, by Rev. Benajah Cook	3	175
READ, REED, REID, Abby, d. [Festus & Polly], b. May 16,		
1808	3	58
Abijah, s. David & Hannah, b. Jan. 12, 1747/8	1	246
Abner, s. David & Mary, b. Aug. 19, 1749	1	263
Abner, s. [E]lephalet & Sybel], b. Aug. 24, 1792	2	76
Abner, m. Sally M. **BECKWITT**, [ ]	3	83
Amasa, s. John & Hannah, b. May 15, 1729	1	109
Beriah, s. Josh[ua] & Hannah], b Dec. 4, 1749	1	255
Christian, m. John **FFLINT**, May 5, 1709	1	6
David, s. Thomas & Rebeckah, b. Sept. 8, 1722	1	40
David, m. Mary **ELICE**, Dec. 28, 1746	1	263
Diadama, m. John **JONES**, Dec. 19, 1778	2	47
Dinah, m. Eliphalet **HUNTINGTON**, Nov. 4, 1762	2	78
Dorothy, w. Joshua, d. Dec. 26, 1753	1	255
Edeth, d. [Joshua & Edeth], b. Feb. 17, 1763	2	36
Edeth, m. Samuel **SPENCER**, Apr. 2, 1784	2	214
Elihue, s. John & Hannah, b. June 16, 1725; d.		
July 11, 1726	1	45
Eliphalet, s. [David & Mary], b. July 29, 1762	1	263
[E]lephalet, m. Sybel **TRACY**, Apr. 1, 1784	2	76
Eliphalet, s. Abner & Sally M., b. Sept. 22, 1820	3	83
Elisa, m. Allen **CLARK**, b. of Windham, Nov. 15,		
1842, by Rev. J.E. Tyler	3	205

	Vol.	Page
READ, REED, REID, (cont.)		
Elizabeth, d. John & Mary, b. Sept. 18, 1715	1	45
Ella, shoemaker, of Windham, d. Mar. 2, 1848, ae.		
82	4	151
Ellee, s. [Joshua & Edeth], b. Jan. 27, 1766	2	36
Esther, d. Thomas & Esther, b. Nov. 13, 1737	1	109
[E]unice, d. [David & Mary], b. July 17, 1753	1	263
Eunice, d. [Josiah & Margaret], b. June 3, 1782	2	246
Festus, m. Polly **PEABODY**, Feb. 3, 1807	3	58
Hannah, d. John & Hannah, b. Apr. 7, 1722	1	45
Hannah, m. Hezekiah **FOLLETT**, Jan. 8, 1743/4	1	239
Hannah, w. Joshua, d. Dec. 26, 1750	1	255
Hannah, [w. Joshua], d. June 13, 1755	1	255
Hannah, d. Josiah & Eunice, b. Sept. 27, 1755	2	8
Hannah, [w. John], d. Oct. 12, 1755, in the 60th y.		
of her age	1	109
Hannah, d. [Joshua & Edeth], b. Jan. 17, 1759	2	36
Hannah, d. Joshua [& Edeth], d. Sept. 8, 1759	2	36
Hannah, m. Daniel **BUTLER**, Feb. 24, 1774	2	204
Irena, d. John & Hannah, b. Feb. 4, 1730	1	109
Jeremiah, d. Thomas & Esther, b. May 8, 1740	1	117
John, m. Mary **BRANCH**, Mar. 14, 1711	1	45
John, s. John & Mary, b. Jan 10, 1716/17	1	45
John, s. John & Mary, d. Nov. 10, 1717	1	46
John, m. Hannah **PALMER**, Apr. 27, 1721	1	45
John, s. John & Hannah, b. Aug. 4, 1723	1	45
John, d. Mar. 4, 1727/8, ae. 81 y.	1	46
John, d. Mar. 5, 1735, ae. 50 y.	1	109
John, m. Rebecca **TURNER**, Mar. 6, 1745	1	256
John Thompson, m. Sarah Louisa **CLACK***, b. of Washing-		
ton, D.C., [Oct.] 8, 1845, by Rev. Abel Nichols		
(*Perhaps **CLARK**?)	3	224
Jonathan, s. John & Rebecca, b. Mar. 18, 1746	1	256
Joshua, s. Thomas & Rebeckah, b. Aug. 27, 1716	1	40
Joshua, m. Hannah **FOLLET**, Dec. 26, 1745	1	255
Joshua, m. Dorothy **WOODWARD**, July 2, 1751	1	255
Joshua, m. Hannah **PALMER**, Aug. 7, 1754	1	255
Joshua, m. Edeth **BIDLAKE**, Apr. 7, 1756	2	36
Josiah, s. Thomas & Esther, b. Nov. 21, 1731	1	109
Josiah, s. David & Hannah, b. Apr. 17, 1744	1	246
Josiah, m. Eunice **KINGSBURY**, Jan. 2, 1755	2	8
Josiah, d. in the year of 1756. "Killed by Indians		
in his march from Fort Edward to [ ]		
with Lieut. Grant and party"	2	8
Josiah, s. [David & Mary], b. July 6, 1760	1	263
Josiah, m. Margaret **PETERS**, Aug. 23, 1781	2	246
Julius A., s. Benj[ami]n, ae. 24, b. Apr. 1, [1849]	4	6
Lauretta, d. [Festus & Polly], b. Mar. 22, 1811	3	58

	Vol.	Page
READ, REED, REID, (cont.)		
Lephalet, see under Eliphalet		
Lucy, d. [Joshua & Edeth], b. Mar. 23, 1770	2	36
Lydia, d. [David & Mary], b. July 31, 1758; d.		
Apr. 29, 1760	1	263
Lydia, d. [David & Mary], b. May 25, 1764	1	263
Lydia, m. John **ORMSBY**, Jr., Oct. 28, 1784	2	231
Mary, m. Robert **HIB[B]ARD**, Dec. 3, 1702; d. Mar.		
7, 1763	1	20
Mary, m. Robard **HIB[B]ARD**, Dec. 22, 1702	A	1
Mary, d. John & Mary, b. Aug 8, 1713	1	45
Mary, w. John, Jr., d. Oct. 8, 1718	1	46
Mary, d. David & Mary, b. Sept. 2, 1751	1	263
Mary, m. Jabez **GILBERT**, June 8, 1769	2	147
Mary Ann, m. John C. **HOOPER**, b. of Willimantic		
Village, Windham, Apr. 11, 1826, by Rev. Benajah		
Cook, Jr., at Willimantic	3	177
Mary E., m. Eli C. **WYLLYS**, Feb. 1, 1843, by Rev.		
Henry Beers Sherman	3	207
Mary L., of Windham, m. Lamey L. **LARKHAM**, of		
Voluntown, Sept. 30, 1832, by Rev. Alva Gregory	3	161
Mary O., d. Benj[amin], laborer, ae. 25, b. July 28,		
[1850]	4	11
Mehetable, d. Thomas & Rebeckah, b. Aug. 10, 1714	1	40
Mehetable, m. Joseph **ROBINSON**, July 17, 1735	1	168
Nathan, s. John & Mary, b. Sept. 1, 1718	1	45
Nathan, s. John & Mary, d. Nov. 11, 1718	1	46
Nathaniel, s. John & Sarah, b. Mar. 9, 1696; d.		
Apr. 3, 1696	A	12
Nathaniell, s. John & Mary, b. Mar. 2, 1712	1	45
Nathaniell, s. John & Mary, d. Mar. 12, 1712	1	46
Nath[anie]l, s. John & Han[n]ah, b. Dec. 22, 1726	1	46
Phinehas, s. [Joshua & Edeth], b. Feb. 24, 1768	2	36
Rachel, m. John **DEAN**, Jan. 22, 1745/6	1	266
Rebeckah, d. Thomas & Rebeckah, b. Feb. 23, 1720/21	1	40
Rebeckah, w. Thomas, d. Mar. 7, 1725/6	1	40
Rebeckah, d Thomas & Esther, b. June 15, 1728; d.		
July 25, 1728	1	109
Rebeckah, d. Thomas & Esther, b. Jan. 17, 1729/30	1	109
Roxana, d. [E]lephalet & Sybel], b. Jan. 22, 1788	2	76
Ruth, d. Thomas & Rebeckah, b. Dec. 12, 1712	1	40
Ruth, m. Joseph **HUTCHINSON**, Nov. 11, 1742	1	274
Ruth, d. [Joshua & Edeth], b. Mar. 18, 1761	2	36
Sally M., m. John **SPENCER**, Feb. 13, 1825, by Samuel		
Perkins, Esq.	3	84
Sama[n]tha, m. Newton **ROBINSON**, Dec. 26, 1830, by		
Rev. Roger Bingham	3	150
Sarah, m. Isaac **HALLET**, Apr. 24, 1700	A	8

	Vol	Page
READ, REED, REID, (cont)		
Sarah, d. Thomas & Esther, b. Nov. 15, 1733	1	109
Sarah, d [Joshua & Edeth], b July 3, 1757	2	36
Sarah, m. Roswell **HUNTINGTON**, Oct. 29, 1777	2	214
Seth, s John & Hannah, d Feb. 6, 1733/4	1	109
Seth, s. Thomas & Esther, b. Mar. 28, 1735	1	109
Solomon, s Thomas & Rebeckah, b Aug 19, 1718	1	40
Susannah, d. John & Hannah, b. Feb. 24, 1733/4;		
d Apr. 16, 1735	1	109
Thomas, m. Rebeckah **PALMER**, Feb. 22, 1711/12	1	40
Thomas, s Thomas & Rebeckah, b May 5, 1725; d		
May 5, 1725	1	109
Thomas, m Easther **WEBB**, Nov 9, 1726	1	40
Thomas, s. Thomas & Esther, b July 15, 1736; d.		
Sept 12, 1736	1	109
Thomas, s. David & Mary, b. Nov. [ ], 1747	1	263
Titus, s. [Lephalet & Sybel], b Aug 24, 1786	2	76
Tryphena, d [David & Mary], b Oct. 19, 1756	1	263
W[illia]m, m Dorothy **WARREN**, Sept. 20, 1835, by		
Rev. Benajah Cook, Jr., in Willimantic Village	3	174
REED, [see under **READ**]		
REID, [see under **READ**]		
RICE, Almira, of Worcester, Mass , m. Robert B. **STANTON**,		
of Brooklyn, Jan 6, 1841, by Rev. J.E. Tyler	3	195
Eliph[ale]t, of Windham, m. Mary C **MOSELEY**, of		
Chaplin, [Sept.] 26, 1845, by Rev. John E.		
Tyler	3	224
Reuben A., of Mansfield, m. Lucy A. **GEER**, of Chaplin,		
Aug 10, 1845, by Rev. Henry Greenslit	3	222
RICH, Susan, of Plainfield, m. John **ROOD**, of Windham, Nov.		
15, 1846, by Thomas Gray, J.P	3	231
RICHARDS, Lucy, d. [Mitchell & Wid. Anne], b. Aug. 21, 1796	2	202
Mitchell, m. Wid. Anne **LINKON**, Mar. [ ], 1796	2	202
RICHARDSON, Catharine, m. Lucius **HEBBARD**, Jan. 12, 1823	3	107
John, Jr., m. Martha **HOLT**, Jan 1, 1754	1	322
Lillian J., ae. 26, m. A G. **TUDOR**, merchant, ae. 28,		
Apr 11, [1849], by Rev J E Tyler	4	114
Mary, m. Peter **SIMPSON**, b. of Windham, Sept. 30, 1832,		
by Rev. Alva Gregory	3	161
Mary A., m. Henry R. **TRACY**, b. of Windham, Sept. 27,		
1842, by Rev J E Tyler	3	204
Mercy, m. Sam[ue]ll **BLANCHER**, Mar. 27, 1727	1	121
Reuben, s. John & Martha, b Dec. 7, 1754	1	322
Sophronia, of Windham, m. Jonathan W. **HOOKER**, of Nor-		
wich, Nov 11, 1838, by Oliver Kingsley, Jr , J P	3	187
RICHMOND, Charles, of Killingly, m. Olive **WILLSON**, of Plain-		
field, Nov 7, 1830, by Henry Hall, J P ,		
Willimantic	3	148

	Vol.	Page
RIDER, Henrietta, m. Christopher C. **STRONG**, Apr. 13,		
1835, by Rev. Roger Bingham	3	173
Jane, m. Benjamin **PURINTON**, Apr. 13, 1835, by Rev.		
Roger Bingham	3	173
Laura A., ae. 22, m. Alfred F. **SIMONS**, laborer,		
ae. 34, May 26, [1850], by Tho[ma]s Tallman	4	114
Mary M., m. John S. **SMITH**, Apr. 15, 1832, by Rev.		
Rich[ar]d F. Cleveland	3	160
RIDINGTON, Anna, m Stephen **GREENLEAF**, Sept. 19, 1772	2	186
RILEY, Margaret, ae. 20, m. James **GRAY**, laborer, ae. 20,		
Oct. [ ], [1850], by Rev. Brady	4	115
Mary, m. W[illia]m B. **THOMPSON**, farmer, Dec. 9,		
[1849], by Rev. J. E. Tyler	4	114
Pat, laborer, ae. 35, m. Bridget **BROWN**, ae. 20,		
May 10, [1850], by Rev. Brady	4	115
Tho[ma]s, Jr., s. Thomas, laborer, ae. 39, of		
Willimantic, b. Apr. [ ], 1848	4	5
RINGE, RENDGE, Daniel, m. Amy **ROBINSON**, Apr. 16, 1755	1	327
Daniel, s. Isaac & Marcy, b. Mar. 10, 1761	1	288
Eunice, d. [Isaac & Marcy], b. June 24, 1765; d.		
June 15, 1766	1	288
Isaac, s. [Issac & Marcy], b. May 28, 1773	1	288
John, s. [Isaac & Marcy], b. Aug. 9, 1768	1	288
Lucy, d. Isaac & Marcy, b. Feb. 5, 1759	1	288
Martha, d. Isaac & Mary, b. Sept. 11, 1756	1	288
Sarah, d. Isaac & Mary, b. May 7, 1752	1	288
Sarah, m. Samuel **MOLTON**, Dec. 17, 1767	2	87
William, s. Isaac & Mary, b. Oct. 10, 1754	1	288
RIPLEY, RYPLEY, Abby Lucretia, d. [Zephaniah & Lucretia],		
b. Jan. 15, 1805	3	52
Abiah, d. [Eben[ezer] & Mehitable], b. Dec. 12, 1762	2	11
Abigail, d. Jeremiah & Abigail, b. Mar. 11, 1730/31;		
d. Feb. 18, 1732/3	1	75
Abigail, m. John **ABBE**, Apr. 23, 1757	1	148
Abigail, d. [John & Abigail], b. Sept. 28, 1773; d.		
Nov. 24, 1777	2	155
Abigail A., d. [Nehemiah & Lucy], b. Jan. 24, 1819	2	57
Abigail A., of Windham, m. William P. **ADAMS**, of		
Brooklyn, Oct. 7, 1844, by Rev. John E. Tyler	3	217
Abraham, s. [Eben[ezer] & Mehitable], b. Feb. 25,		
1761	2	11
Alitheah, d. David & Lydia, b. Apr. 24, 1738	1	149
Alethea, d. [W[illia]m & Lydia], b. Aug. 23, 1759;		
d. Sept. 5, 1759	2	24
Alethea, d. [W[illia]m & Lydia], b. Jan. 11, 1761	2	24
Alice, [d. Joshua & Hannah], b. Sept. 17, 1683, at		
Hingham	A	16
Allice, d. John & Mary, b. Sept. 30, 1744	1	141

	Vol.	Page
RIPLEY, RYPLEY, (cont.)		
Alma H., s. [Jeremiah & Olive], b. Sept. 24, 1842	3	92
Ama, d. Nathaniel & Anne, b. Nov. 20, 1751	1	273
Ann, [d. Joshua & Hannah], b. Nov. 1, 1704	A	17
Ann, d. David & Lydia, b. Aug. 24, 1726	1	61
Ann, m. Capt. Sam[ue]ll **BINGHAM,** May 17, 1769	2	148
Anna, m. Nath[anie]ll **RIPLEY,** Oct. 31, 1745	1	273
Anna, d. [Eben[ezer] & Mehitable], b. June 20, 1770	2	11
Anne, d. Nath[anie]ll & Anna, b. Aug. 20, 1749	1	273
Anne, m. Dan **HIBBARD,** Jan. 2, 1772	2	183
Anne, w. Nehemiah, d. Nov. [ ], 1813	2	57
Benj[ami]n, s. Jere[miah] & Abigail, b. Mar. 5, 1734/5; d. Nov. 20, 1736	1	75
Benjamin, s. [Charles & Tabitha], b. Jan. 28, 1761	2	34
Bradford, s. David & Lydia, b. Dec. 26, 1744	1	248
Bradford, s. [Ralph & Eunice], b. Mar. 18, 1776; d. Sept. 12, 1823, in the Island of Trinidad	2	195
Calvin, s. [Charles & Tabitha], b. Feb. 16, 1772	2	34
Charles, s. Jeremiah, Jr. & Abigail, b. Feb. 25, 1732/3	1	75
Charles, m. Tabitha **ABBE,** Nov. 16, 1758	2	34
Charles, s. [Charles & Tabitha], b. Aug. 19, 1762	2	34
Charles, s. [Nehemiah & Amie], b. Apr. 29, 1794	2	57
Charles, s. [Jeremiah & Olive], b. Mar. 19, 1833	3	92
Charles, Lieut., d. [ ] "in captivity with the British Army at Philadelphia"	2	34
Christopher, s. [Ralph & Eunice], b. Dec. 12, 1781	2	195
David, [s. Joshua & Hannah], b. May 20, 1697	A	16
David, m. Lydia **CARY,** Mar. 21, 1720	1	61
David, s. David & Lydia, b. Feb. 7, 1730/31	1	61
David, s. William, Jr. & Rebeckah, b. Jan. 18, 1761; d. June 11, 1782	2	27
David, d. Feb. 16, 1781, in the 84th y. of his age	1	248
David, s. [Hezekiah Augustus & Hannah], b. Apr. 5, 1797	2	72
David B., m. Mary **ROBINSON,** Feb. 6, 1800	3	40
David B., d. May 12, 1812. "Was drowned in the River Ohio"	3	40
David Bradford, s. [Gamaleel & Judeth], b. Apr. 19, 1778	2	84
Dolly, d. [Hezekiah Augustus & Hannah], b. Oct. 25, 1794	2	72
Dolly, m. James **WEBB,** May 7, 1817	3	82
Dwight, s. [Eben[ezer] & Mehitable], b. Aug. 7, 1764	2	11
Eben, m. Mehitable **BURBANK,** June 11, 1752	2	11
Ebenezer, s. Joshua & Mary, b. June 27, 1729	1	39
Eben[eze]r, s. [Eben[ezer] & Mehitable], b. Mar. 26, 1766	2	11

	Vol.	Page

RIPLEY, RYPLEY, (cont.)

	Vol.	Page
Eleanor, d. [Eben[ezer] & Mehitable], b. Aug. 16, 1754	2	11
Elbridge, s. [Eleazer, Jr. & Ann], b. Oct. 31, 1809	3	69
Eleara*, s. [Jeremiah & Olive], b Nov. 13, 1834 (*Eleaza?)	3	92
Eleazer, s. Jeremiah & Abigail, b. Apr. 21, 1724	1	75
Eleazer, m. Meriann **WEBB**, Mar. 23, 1757	2	39
Eleazer, s. [Eleazer & Meriann], b. [ ], 1767	2	39
Eleazer Jr., m. Anne **HUNTINGTON**, Mar. 28, 1802	3	69
Eleazer, d. July 26, 1823, ae. 55 y.	3	69
Elijah, s. John [& Mary], b. May 24, 1747	1	141
Eliphalet, s. Joshua, Jr & Elizabeth, b. Oct. 28, 1749	1	290
Eliphalet, s. [Ralph & Eunice], b. Oct. 31, 1784	2	195
Eliphalet, m. Julia **LARRABEE**, Nov. 19, 1818	3	91
Elisha Paine, s. [John & Abigail], b. Dec. 12, 1771; d. May 26, 1773	2	155
Elizabeth, d. Jeremiah & Mary, b. Mar. 17, 1691	A	27
Elizabeth, m. Joseph **HUNTINGTON,** July 18, 1719	1	41
Elizabeth, d. Joshua & Mary, b. Nov. 4, 1724	1	39
Elizabeth, d. [Joshua, Jr. & Elizabeth], b. May 22, 1754	1	290
Eliz[abe]th, w. Gam[alie]l, d. Jan. 10, 1765	2	84
Elizabeth, m. Thomas **DYER**, May 6, 1771	2	166
Elizabeth, d. [Gamaleel & Judeth], b. Mar. 19, 1776	2	84
Elizabeth, w. Joshua, Jr., d. July 1, 1778	1	290
Elizabeth, d. [Ralph & Eunice], b. Aug. 9, 1778	2	195
Elizabeth, m. Capt. William **YOUNG**, Jr., Dec. 26, 1801	3	70
Elizabeth Ann, d. [Eleazer, Jr. & Anne], b. Mar. 10, 1808	3	69
Epafras, s. [Charles & Tabitha], b. Feb. 13, 1759	2	34
Erastus, s. [Joshua, Jr. & Elizabeth], b. June 17, 1770	1	290
Eunice, d. [Ralph & Eunice], b. Nov. 12, 1786	2	195
Eunice, d. [Hezekiah & Eunice], b. June 6, 1789	2	253
Eunice, d. [Hezekiah & Eunice], b. June 6, 1789	3	1
Eunice, m. Frederick **TRACY**, June 11, 1816	3	79
Eunice, w. Hezekiah, d. May 4, 1823	3	1
Eunice, d. [Jeremiah & Olive], b. Nov. 11, 1828	3	92
Ffaith, [d. Joshua & Hannah], b. Sept. 20, 1686, at Hingham	A	16
Ffaith, m. Samuell **BINGHAM**, Jan. 5, 1708	1	3
Ffaith, d. David & Lydia, b. May 6, 1722	1	61
Ffaith, m. James **BREWSTER**, Mar 15, 1738/9	1	160
Faith, d. W[illia]m & Lydia, b. Oct. 13, 1757	2	24
Francis, d. [Jeremiah & Olive H.], b. Mar 12, 1827	3	92
Frank W., s. Jeremiah, ae. 50, & Olive, ae. 46, b.		

	Vol	Page
RIPLEY, RYPLEY, (cont.)		
Sept. 8, [1849]	4	7
Gamaleel, s. David & Lidiah, b. Apr. 19, 1736	1	61
Gamaleel, s. David & Lydia, d. May 29, 1737	1	60
Gamaleel, s. David & Lydia, b. Oct. 24, 1740	1	149
Gamaliel, m. Eliz[abe]th **HIBBARD**, Dec. 15, 1764	2	84
Gamaleel, m. Judeth **PERKINS**, Jan. 23, 1772	2	84
Gamiel, s. [Gamaleel & Judeth], b. Feb. 8, 1774;		
d. July 11, 1795, ae. 21 y. 5 m.	2	84
Gamaleel, d. Apr. 15, 1799	2	84
George, s. [Hezekiah & Eunice], b. Mar. 7, 1792	2	253
George, s. [Hezekiah & Eunice], b. Mar. 7, 1792;		
d. May 19, 1817	3	1
Hannah, [d. Joshua & Hannah], b. Mar. 2, 1685, at		
Hingham	A	16
Hannah, d. Jeremiah & Mary, b. June 21, 1707	A	17
Hannah, m. Sam[ue]ll **WEBB**, Oct. 8, 1711	1	7
Hannah, d. Joshua & Mary, b. Jan. 12, 1718/19	1	39
Hannah, w. Joshua, d. May 28, 1738, ae. about 75 y.	1	188
Hannah, d. David & Lydia, b. Feb. 23, 1750	1	248
Hannah, d. [Joshua], d. Nov. 8, 1750	1	55
Hannah, d. [Eben[ezer] & Mehitable], b. Apr. 28, 1753	2	11
Hannah, d. [John & Abigail], b. Oct. 7, 1777; d. Oct.		
10, 1777	2	155
Harriet, d. [Eleazer, Jr. & Anne], b. June 15, 1812	3	69
Harriet Elizabeth, d. [Zephaniah & Lucretia], b.		
Mar. 30, 1810	3	52
Henriette, d. [John & Abigail], b. May 13, 1770; d.		
Oct. 23, 1795	2	155
Henry, s. [David B. & Mary], b. June 20, 1801; d.		
June 24, 1801	3	40
Hervey, twin with Judeth, s. [Gamaleel & Judeth], b.		
Oct. 25, 1772	2	84
Hezekiah, [s. Joshua & Hannah], b. June 10, 1695	A	16
Hezekiah, m. Meriam **FFITCH**, Oct. 16, 1740	1	205
Hezekiah, s. David & Lydia, b. Feb. 3, 1742/3	1	149
Hezekiah, m. Mary **SKINNER**, Nov. 25, 1746	1	262
Hezekiah, s. Hezekiah & Mary, b. Sept. 25, 1748	1	262
Hezekiah, d. Feb. 7, 1779, in the 84th y. of his age	1	262
Hezekiah, m. Eunice **DUNN**, Apr. 29, 1784	2	253
Hezekiah, m. Eunice **DUMONT**, Apr 29, 1784	3	1
Hezekiah, s. [Hezekiah & Eunice], b. May 17, 1785	2	253
Hezekiah, s. [Hezekiah & Eunice], b. May 17, 1785	3	1
Hez[ekiah], d. Nov. 11, 1836	3	1
Hezekiah Augustus, m. Hannah **MOSELEY**, Nov. 3, 1793	2	72
Horace, s. [Eben[ezer] & Mehitable], b. Aug. 20, 1772	2	11
Irenia, [d. Joshua & Hannah], b. Aug. 28, 1700	A	16
Irena, d. David & Lydia, b. Feb. 11, 1728/9	1	61

	Vol.	Page

RIPLEY, RYPLEY, (cont.)

Irena, m. Dr. Timothy **WARNER**, Jan. 11, 1749/50	1	300
Iverna, m. Sam[ue]ll **MANNING**, Apr. 27, 1719	1	3
Jabez, s. John & Mary, b. Mar. 28, 1752; d. Mar. 28, 1753	1	141
Jabez, s. [John & Mary], b. Apr. 10, 1754, in Preston	1	141
Jabez, s. [John & Abigail], b. May 24, 1786	2	155
Jabez Perkins, s. [Gamaleel & Judeth], b. Mar. 25, 1788; d. Feb. 18, 1790	2	84
James, s. [Ralph & Eunice], b. Dec. 10, 1794	2	195
Jeremiah, m. Mary **GAGER**, Apr. 7, 1690	A	27
Jeremiah, s. Jeremiah & Mary, b. Apr 15, 1696	A	27
Jeremiah, m. Abigail **CARY**, Jan. 9, 1722/3	1	75
Jeremiah, Lieut., m. Ann **DENISON**, July 16, 1734	1	100
Jeremiah, s. John & Mary, b. June 24, 1741	1	141
Jeremiah, s. Eliazer & Meriann, b. Oct. 31, 1758	2	39
Jeremiah, m. Olive H. **BYRNE**, Sept. 15, 1825	3	92
Jeremiah, [s. Nehemiah & Amie], b. [ ]	2	57
Jerusha, d. [Joshua & Hannah], b. Nov. 1, 1704	A	17
Jerusha, m. Edward **BROWN**, Sept. 9, 1744	1	253
Jerusha, d. [Eben[ezer] & Mehitable], b. May 28, 1756	2	11
John, s. Jeremiah & Mary, b. Nov. 13, 1698	A	27
John, m. Mary **MES[S]ENGER**, Jan. 15, 1734/5	1	141
John, s. Joshua & Mary, b. Mar. 31, 1738	1	39
John, m. Abigail **MARSH**, June 7, 1769	2	155
John, s. [Jeremiah & Olive], b. Oct. 25, 1841	3	92
John Abbe, s. [Charles & Tabitha], b. Apr. 3, 1764	2	34
John Bradford, s. [John & Abigail], b. July 6, 1780	2	155
John H., m. Eliza L. **SPAULDING**, b. of Windham, Oct. 8, 1829, by Rev. Dennis Platt	3	138
John Huntington, s. [Eleazer, Jr. & Anne], b. Jan. 25, 1803	3	69
Joshua, m. Hannah **BRADFORD**, Nov. 28, 1682	A	16
Joshua, [s. Joshua & Hannah], b. May 13, 1688, at Hingham	A	16
Joshua, m. Mary **BACKUS**, Dec. 8, 1712	1	39
Joshua, s. Joshua & Mary, b. Oct. 30, 1725	1	39
Joshua, d. May 18, 1739, ae. about 80 y.	1	188
Joshua, Jr., m. Elizabeth **LATHROP**, Mar. 26, 1740	1	290
Joshua, s. [Joshua, Jr. & Elizabeth], b. May 16, 1761	1	290
Joshua, d. Nov. 18, 1773, in the 85th y. of his age	1	55
Josiah, s. Jeremiah & Mary, b. Apr. 14, 1703	A	28
Josiah, s. [Eleazer & Meriann], b. May 4, 1771	2	39
Judeth, twin with Hervey, d. [Gamaleel & Judeth], b. Oct. 25, 1772; d. same day	2	84
Judeth, m. George **BINGHAM**, Feb. 20, 1825, by Rev.		

RIPLEY, RYPLEY, (cont.)   Vol.   Page

Jesse Fisher	3	119
Judeth Perkins, d. [David B. & Mary], b. June 9, 1803	3	40
Julia, d. [John & Abigail], b. May 16, 1792	2	155
Julia, d. Jan. 29, 1850, ae. 61	4	156
Julia L., d. Nov. [ ], 1849, ae. 31	4	156
Julia Larrabee, d. [Eliphalet & Julia], b. Jan. 19, 1820	3	91
Julia Larrabee, [d. Eliphalet & Julia], d. Nov. [ ], 1849	3	91
Juliania, d. [Eben[ezer] & Mehitable], b. July 31, 1757	2	11
Juliania, d. Eben[ezer] & Mehetable, d. July 18, 1759	2	11
Justin, s. [Eben[ezer] & Mehitable], b. Jan. 1, 1759	2	11
Justin, s. Eben[ezer] & Mehetable, d. Oct. 25, 1761	2	11
Justus, s. [Eleazer, Jr. & Anne], b. Oct. 18, 1817	3	69
Laura, d. [Ralph & Eunice], b. July 4, 1792	2	195
Laura, m. Earl **SWIFT**, Apr. 18, 1810	3	64
Leah, [d. Joshua & Hannah], b. Apr. 17, 1693	A	16
Leah, m. Sam[ue]ll **COOK**, Mar. 14, 1716	1	38
Lucretia, d. [Hezekiah Augustus & Hannah], b. Oct. 25, 1803	2	72
Lucy, d. [John & Abigail], b. Sept. 12, 1778	2	155
Lucy, d. [Hezekiah & Eunice], b. May 10, 1794	2	253
Lucy, d. [Hezekiah & Eunice], b. May 10, 1794	3	1
Lucy, of Windham, m. Elijah Worthington **BLISS**, of Sharbourne, N.Y., May 24, 1815	3	26
Luther, s. [Nehemiah & Amie], b. Dec. 14, 1791	2	57
Lydia, d. David & Lydia, b. Feb. 24, 1723/4	1	61
Lydia, d. [Joshua, Jr. & Elizabeth], b. July 30, 1763	1	290
Lydia, d. [Gamaleel & Judeth], b. Dec. 4, 1780; d. May 10, 1789	2	84
Lydia, m. Christopher **FITCH**, Apr. 29, 1784	2	149
Margaret, [d. Joshua & Hannah], b. Nov. 4, 1690, at Norwich	A	16
Marian, d. [Hezekiah & Eunice], b. Dec. 29, 1786	2	253
Mary, d. Jeremiah & Mary, b. Mar. 15, 1693; d. Apr. 7, 1693	A	27
Mary, d. Jeremiah & Mary, b. May 12, 1694; d. Sept. 26, 1695	A	27
Mary, d. Joshua & Mary, b. Nov. 18, 1714	1	39
Mary, w. Lt. [Jeremiah], d. Dec. 4, 1721	A	17
Mary, d. Jeremiah & Abigail, b. Apr. 16, 1728; d. July 24, 1758	1	75
Mary, m. Joshua **ABBE**, Apr. 14, 1736	1	161
Mary, d. John & Mary, b. Sept. 2, 1743; d. Oct. 31, 1743	1	141
Mary, d. John & Mary, b. [ ], 1749	1	141
Mary, d. [Joshua, Jr. & Elizabeth], b. Oct. 4, 1774	1	290

	Vol.	Page

RIPLEY, RYPLEY, (cont.)

	Vol.	Page
Mary, w. Hezekiah, d. Nov. 17, 1787, in the 84th y. of her age	1	262
Mary, d. [Eleazer, Jr. & Anne], b. Aug. 24, 1804; d. Aug. 9, 1806	3	69
Mary, d. [Jeremiah & Olive H.], b. Apr. 12, 1831	3	92
Mary Ann, d. [Hezekiah & Eunice], b. Dec. 29, 1786	3	1
Mary Ann, m. Erastus **WILCOX**, Mar. 26, 1809, by Rev. Mr. Welles	3	54
Mary Leonard, d. [Zephaniah & Lucretia], b. Sept. 5, 1814	3	52
Meriam, w. Hezekiah, d. Dec. 19, 1744	1	205
Nathaniell, s. Joshua & Mary, b. June 30, 1721	1	39
Nath[anie]ll, m. Anna **RIPLEY**, Oct. 31, 1745	1	273
Nath[anie]ll, s. [Joshua, Jr. & Elizabeth], b. Feb. 14, 1768	1	290
Nathaniel, of Middlebury, Vt., m. Philena **WALES**, of Windham, Nov. 7, 1824, by Rev. Erastus Ripley	3	88
Nehamiah, s. Jeremiah & Mary, b. July 9, 1705	A	17
Nehemiah, m. Marcy **ALLEN**, June 17, 1736	1	149
Nehemiah, s. Jeremiah & Abigail, b. Mar. 7, 1736/7; d. Jan. 15, 1756	1	75
Nehemiah, s. Eleazer & Meriann, b Mar. 7, 1761	2	39
Nehemiah, m. Amie **GOULD**, Feb. 24, 1791	2	57
Nehemiah, m. Lucy **JONES**, Aug. 13, 1815	2	57
Olive, d. [Joshua, Jr. & Elizabeth], b. Sept. 13, 1756	1	290
Olive, m. Jabez **FITCH**, Jr., Oct. 7, 1773	2	186
Oliver, s. [John & Abigail], b. Nov. 12, 1788	2	155
Peter, s. Jeremiah & Mary, b Mar. 11, 1701	A	28
Peter, s. Lieut. Jeremiah, d. June 6, 1742, ae. about 41 y.	1	41
Phineas, s. Joshua & Mary, b. Nov. 25, 1716	1	39
Phinehas, s. Joshua, d. Aug. 4, 1746	1	55
Phinehas, s. Nath[anie]ll & Anna, b. Mar. 20, 1746/7	1	273
Polly, d. [John & Abigail], b. Nov. 2, 1775; d. Nov 22, 1777	2	155
Rachel, [d. Joshua & Hannah], b. Apr. 17, 1693	A	16
Ralph, s. Joshua, Jr. & Elizabeth, b. Oct. 25, 1751	1	290
Ralph, m. Eunice **HUNTINGTON**, Dec. 8, 1774	2	195
Ralph Huntington, s. [Ralph & Eunice], b. Nov. 16, 1789; d. [ ]	2	195
Roger, s. [Joshua, Jr. & Elizabeth], b. Apr. 10, 1759	1	290
Roswell, s. [Gamaliel & Eliz[abe]th, b. Dec. 31, 1764; d. Oct. 4, 1791	2	84
Sarah, d. Jeremiah & Abigail, b. June 5, 1726	1	75
Sarah, d. [Charles & Tabitha], b. May 9, 1767	2	34
Selina, of Windham, m. Zachi **CURTIS**, of Chaplin, Feb. 10, 1845, by Rev. J.E. Tyler	3	220

	Vol.	Page
RIPLEY, RYPLEY, (cont.)		
Thaddeus, s. [Eben[ezer] & Mehitable], b. Oct. 22, 1767	2	11
Vine, s. [Charles & Tabitha], b. Nov. 30, 1769	2	34
William, s. Joshua, Jr & Mary, b. Feb. 12, 1733/4	1	39
William, s. David & Lydia, b. July 12, 1734	1	61
William, m. Lydia **BREWSTER**, Jan. 11, 1757, by Rev. Eben[eze]r Devotion	2	24
William, Jr., m. Rebeckah **MERCY**, Mar. 10, 1757	2	27
William, s. [Gamaleel & Judeth], b. May 27, 1782	2	84
William, s. [Eleazer, Jr. & Anne], b. May 1, 1806	3	69
William Bradford, s. [John & Abigail], b. Aug. 14, 1784; d. Sept. 15, 1785	2	155
Zelina, d. [Eleazer & Meriann], b. Jan. 27, 1764; d. Dec. 3, 1775	2	39
Zelima, d. [Nehemiah & Amie], b. May 24, 1796	2	57
Zephaniah, s. [Gamaleel & Judeth], b. Oct. 17, 1779	2	84
Zephaniah, m. Lucretia **ABBE**, Apr. 12, 1804	3	52
Zeruiah, d. Jeremiah & Mary, b. Oct. 31, 1711	A	17
Zerviah, m. Joseph **DINGLEY**, Jr., Apr. 25, 1739	1	210
RISING, Lucy, of Windham, m. Card M. **CRAIN**, of Mansfield, Jan. 3, 1833, by Henry Hall, J.P.	3	162
RISLEY, Mary, m. Stephen **BROWN**, June [ ], 1729	1	135
RIXFORD, Luther, m. Lucy N. **PAGE**, Mar. 7, 1825, by John Baldwin, Esq.	3	37
ROACH, Ellen, d. John, laborer, b. Dec. 10, [1849]	4	9
Ellen, d. Dec. 26, 1849 (infant)	4	155
Frances, d. Thomas, laborer, ae. 41, b. June 5, [1849]	4	11
ROATH, [see under **ROUTH**]		
ROBBINS, ROBINS, Abigail, d. [John & Rebeckah], b. Dec. 13, 1767	1	293
Abigail had s. John **COOK**, b. June 9, 1777; d. Sept. 9, 1778	2	17
Abigail, m. James **COOK**, July 16, 1778	2	17
Alice, d. John & Rebeckah, b. Dec. 31, 1749	1	293
Diantha, d. [Ephraim & Abigail], b. May 28, 1772; d. May 29, 1772	2	190
Diantha, d. [Ephraim & Abigail], b. Apr. 22, 1774	2	190
Eben[eze]r, s. John & Rebeckah, b. Feb. 24, 1758	1	293
Elijah, m. [ ] **HALL**, [ ], 1762	2	76
Elizabeth, m. Joseph **PRESTON**, Apr. 23, 1734	1	141
Enos, s. [Jehiel & Hannah], b. & d. [Between 1744 & 1748]	2	63
Enos, s. [Jehiel & Mary], b. Feb. 1, 1764	2	63
Ephraim, m. Abigail **CALKINS**, May 5, 1771	2	190
Frances A., of Windham, m. Rev. John N. **SHUTTS**, of New Brunswick, N.J , Aug. 12, 1843, by Rev. John E. Tyler	3	210

	Vol.	Page
ROBBINS, ROBINS, (cont.)		
Hannah, d. [Jehiel & Hannah], b. & d. [between 1744 & 1748]	2	63
Hannah, w. Jehiel, d. May [ ], 1748	2	63
Hannah, d. [John & Rebeckah], b. Feb. 10, 1760	1	293
Hannah, d. Jehiel & Mary], b. Mar. 13, 1761	2	63
Jehiel, m. Hannah **FARNAM**, Jan. 31, 1744	2	63
Jehiel, m. Wid. Mary **BENNET**, Nov. 18, 1758	2	63
Jeremiah, s. [John & Rebeckah], b. Jan. 17, 1762	1	293
John, m. Rebeccah **FARNAM**, Jan. 21, 1748/9	1	293
John, s. John & Rebeckah, b. Mar. 21, 1754	1	293
Lemuel, m. Rachel **BASS**, Apr. 30, 1769	2	192
Martha E., d. John W., farmer, ae. 52, & Ann E., ae. 47, b. Sept. 13, 1848	4	3
Mary, d. Robert* & Rebeckah, b May 2, 1748 (*John?)	1	293
Mary, m. Jonathan **UTLEY**, May 1, 1766	2	149
Mary, d. [Jehiel & Mary], b. Feb. 21, 1768	2	63
Nathaniel, s. [Jehiel & Hannah], b. & d. [between 1744 & 1748]	2	63
Nath[anie]ll, father of John, d. Apr. 7, 1753	1	293
Nath[anie]ll, s. [John & Rebeckah], b. Dec 17, 1766	1	293
Olive, d. John & Rebeckah, b. June 1, 1769	2	164
Pamela, d. [Lemuel & Philena], b. Jan. 25, 1771	2	192
Patience, d. John & Rebeckah, b. Jan. 10, 1752	1	293
Philena, d. [Lemuel & Rachel], b. Nov. 25, 1769	2	192
Rebecca, d. [John & Rebeckah], b. June 11, 1764	1	293
Rufus, s. [John & Rebeckah], b. Mar. 27, 1771	2	164
Solomon, s. John & Rebeckah, b. Mar. 3, 1756	1	293
Sophia, m. John **FLINT**, Nov. 5, 1829, by Rev Roger Bingham	3	142
Thomas Bass, s. [Lemuel & Philena], b. Oct. 9, 1772	2	192
[ ]ena, d. [Elijah], b. Aug. 18, 1763; d. Dec. 17, 1764	2	76
[ ]in, s. [Elijah], b. May 10, 1765	2	76
ROBERTS, Amelia, m Scott **SMITH**, Dec. 12, 1836, by Rev. Philo Judson at Willimantic	3	180
Celey, b. Coventry, R.I , res Windham, d. Mar. 30, 1851, ae. 67	4	157
James, a transient person, m. Anne **YOUNG**, July 30, 1769	2	2
Olive, m. Watson M. **PARKER**, b. of Coventry, Conn., May 24, 1840, by Rev. Ella Dunham	3	193
Ruba Anne, m. James **GORDON**, Apr. 29, 1844, by Rev. John B. Guild, Willimantic	3	214
ROBERTSON, Susan, m. Elijah H. **DUNHAM**, b. of Windham, Jan. 1, 1833, by Dexter Bullard	3	163
Warren, m. Lucy **RUSSELL**, Oct. 5, 1828, by Rev. Chester Tilden	3	130

	Vol.	Page
ROBINSON, Abel, s. Sam[ue]ll & Sarah, b. Sept. 15, 1761	1	285
Abel, m. Eunice **WOODWARD**, Mar. 17, 1795	3	10
Abiah, s. Thomas & Annah, b. May 16, 1727	1	115
Abiah, m. Jonah **PALMER**, Oct. 31, 1754	1	324
Abiah, m. Jonah **PALMER**, Oct. 31, 1754	2	171
Abiah, d. [Simeon & Jerusha], b. Dec. 20, 1762	1	244
Abigail, m. Elihu **PALMER**, Sept. 30, 1725	1	51
Abigail, d. Israel & Sarah, b. Feb. 22, 1736/7	1	81
Abigail, m. Silas **FLINT**, Apr. 19, 1762	2	34
Abigail, d. [Peter, Jr. & Abigail], b. Aug. 8, 1772	2	1
Abigail, w Peter, d. Sept. 25, 1774, in the 42nd y.		
of her age	2	1
Abner, s. Peter & Ruth, b. Feb. 22, 1738	1	77
Abner, m. Mahitable **PALMER**, Apr. 7, 1763	2	132
Abner, s. [Abner & Mahitable], b. Mar. 1, 1770	2	132
Abner, s. [Abner, Jr. & Clarissa], b. July 15, 1817	3	66
Abner, Jr., m. Clarissa **WEBB**, Mar. 2, 1806	3	66
Abner, d. Nov. 24, 1815	2	132
Abner, m. Eunice **PALMER**, b. of Windham, Mar. 23, 1843,		
by Rev. Isaac H. Coe	3	207
Achsah, d. Isaac & Deborah, b. July 1, 1742	1	203
Adrian, s. [Nathan & Jerusha], b. Aug. 27, 1770	2	99
Adrian, m. Elizabeth **SMITH**, Apr. 18, 1793	2	144
Alathear, d. [Experience & Zurviah], b. July 17, 1760	1	287
Alithea, d. [Eliphaz & Jemima], b. Oct. 27, 1785	2	220
Albigence, s. [Andrew & Olive], b. Dec. 21, 1785; d.		
July 15, 1788	3	28
Albigence, s. [Andrew & Olive], b. Oct. 12, 1789	3	28
Alfred Augustus, s. [Septimies & Sarah], b. Oct. 3,		
1815	3	85
Ama, d. Thomas & An[n]ah, b. May 1, 1733	1	115
Amy, m. Daniel **RENDGE**, Apr. 16, 1755	1	327
Amey, d. [Jacob & Anna], b. Oct. 17, 1774	2	17
Andrew, s. [Experience & Zurviah], b. Aug. 1, 1762	1	287
Andrew, m. Olive **HOVEY**, Mar. 10, 1785	3	28
Andrew, m. Lydia **CHURCH**, Mar. 17, 1813	3	28
Andrew, m. Bethiah **CHURCH**, Apr. 16, 1820	3	28
Andrew, d. June 10, 1849, ae. 22 (Entered among		
births)	4	6
Andrew, farmer, d. June 10, 1849, ae. 89	4	154
An[n]ah, d. Thomas & An[n]ah, b. Mar. 17, 1730	1	115
Anna, d. Isaac & Deborah, b. June 18, 1746	1	203
Anna, m. Ebenezer **LUCE**, Oct. 26, 1749	1	293
Anna, d. Simeon & Jerusha, b. July 3, 1752; d. Oct. 25,		
1754	1	244
Anna, d. [Simeon & Jerusha], b. July 17, 1760	1	244
Anna, d. Jacob & Anna, b. Nov. 4, 1761	2	17
Anna, m. David **HOVEY**, Aug. 28, 1783	2	133

	Vol.	Page

ROBINSON, (cont.)

	Vol.	Page
Asa, s. Thomas & Annah, b. Oct. 17, 1726	1	115
Asa, m. Mary **FRENCH**, Oct. 25, 1749	1	292
Asa, s. Asa & Mary, b. June 6, 1757	1	292
Asa, Jr., m. Olive **HUNTINGTON**, Sept. 17, 1777	2	93
Asa, [s. Thomas], b. Apr. 5, 1827	3	58
Asa Aspinwall, s. [Gurdon & Lydia], b. May 14, 1814	3	62
Asenath, d. [Reuben & Esther], b. June 26, 1766	1	285
Asher, s. Sam[ue]ll & Sarah, b July 5, 1752	1	285
Asher, m. Sarah **WEST**, Sept. 3, 1778	2	211
Bathsheba, d. Peter & Ruth, b. July 31, 1746	1	231
Bela, s. [James & Chloe], b. Jan. 19, 1789	2	234
Benj[amin], m. Jerusha **BINGHAM**, Mar. 4, 1728/9	1	110
Benjamin Franklin, s. [Abner, Jr. & Clarissa], b. Mar. 9, 1808	3	66
Betsey, d. [Jonathan & Elizabeth], b. June 23, 1785	2	107
Betsey, d. [Asa, Jr. & Olive], b. Dec. 26, 1793	2	93
Betsey, m. Gamaleel **BINGHAM**, Aug. 5, 1800	3	46
Betsey, m. Bradford **BUCK**, Feb 11, 1806	3	53
Betsey, m. Ginda **LADD**, Mar. 29, 1835, by Rev. Roger Bingham	3	172
Calvin, s. [Nath[anie]ll & Charlotte], b. May 9, 1787; d. Dec. [ ], 1788	2	20
Calvin, s. [Nath[anie]ll & Charlotte], b. Sept. 4, 1804	2	20
Calvin, of Windham, m. Sophronia **CLAP[P]**, of South Hampton, Mass., Apr. 1, 1832, by Rev. Anson S. Atwood, Mansfield	3	159
Calvin Newcomb, s. [Ebenezer & Zilpha], b. Feb. 26, 1824	3	25
Caroline A., school teacher, d. July 14, [1849], ae. 29	4	155
Charity, d. [Asa & Mary], b. June 16, 1772	1	292
Charity, m. Elias **UPTON**, Apr. 29, 1800	3	56
Charles, [s. Thomas], b. Oct. 12, 1820	3	58
Chloe, w. James, d. Jan. 26, 1811	2	234
Clayburn, s. Sam[ue]ll & Sarah, b. Apr. 4, 1754	1	285
Clifford, s. Reuben & Esther, b. Jan. 8, 1756	1	285
Cynthia, d. [Abner, Jr. & Clarissa], b. Apr. 8, 1823	3	66
Daniel, s. Israel & Sarah, b. Jan. 18, 1732/3	1	81
Daniel, m. Mary **FLINT**, Mar. 29, 1758	2	81
Darius, s. [Andrew & Olive], b. July 15, 1795	3	28
Deborah, [twin with Susannah], d. Joseph & Mehetable, b. Mar. 14, 1735/6	1	168
Deborah, [triplet with Nathaniell & Isaac], d. [Isaac & Deborah], b. Apr. 15, 1752	1	203
Deborah, d. Isaac & Deborah, b. Apr. 8, 1744	1	203
Deborah, d. [Sam[ue]l, Jr. & Sarah], b. Mar. 5, 1774	2	95
Deborah, d. [Isaac, Jr. & Joanna], b July 20, 1780, in Mansfield	2	172

	Vol.	Page
ROBINSON, (cont.)		
Dorcas, d. Sam[ue]ll & Sarah, b. Apr. 2, 1749	1	285
Dorcas, m. Archibald **BATES**, Nov. 20, 1826, by		
Elder Allen Barnes	3	128
Dorcas Dwight, d. [Andrew & Olive], b. Dec 15,		
1801	3	28
Ebenezer, s. Simeon & Jerusha, b. Apr 18, 1744	1	244
Ebenezer, s. [Andrew & Olive], b. Feb. 21, 1788	3	28
Ebenezer, m. Zilpha **WEST**, Jan. 5, 1814	3	25
Eber, s. Jacob & Anna, b. Oct. 7, 1759	2	19
Eleizer, s. Israel & Sarah, b. July 8, 1734	1	81
Eleazer, s. Eunice **BROUGHTON**, b. Jan. 5, 1762	2	9
Eliab, s. Peter & Ruth, b. Aug. 22, 1742	1	231
Eliab, m. Lucy **WILLIAMS**, Jan. 30, 1777	2	256
Eliab, m. Lucy **WILLIAMS**, Jan. 30, 177[ ]	2	218
Eliab, s. [Eliab & Lucy], b. Jan. 15, 1785; d.		
Jan. 26, 1785	2	218
Eliab, s. [Eliab & Lucy], b. Jan. 15, [178[ ]; d.		
[Jan.] 26, 178[ ]	2	256
Elias, s. [Experience & Zurviah], b. Apr. 14, 1757;		
in Norwich	1	287
Elias, m. Sibbel **LILLIE**, Aug. 26, 1779	3	12
Elias, s. [Elias & Sibbel], b. Nov. 13, 1780	3	12
Elias, m. Amie **LUCE**, June 4, 1795	3	12
Elias, d. Feb. last day, 1805	3	12
Eliel, s. [Reuben & Esther], b. Sept. 24, 1768	1	285
Elijah, s. Benj[ami]n & Jerusha, b. Oct. 1, 1735	1	110
Eliphalet, s. Benj[ami]n & Jerusha, b. Dec. 5, 1739	1	110
Eliphalet, s. Simeon & Jerusha, b. Mar. 23, 1756	1	244
Eliphalet, s. [Abel & Eunice], b. July 12, 1795	3	10
Eliphaz, s. Simeon & Jerusha, b. May 19, 1750	1	244
Eliphaz, m. Jemima **ROGERS**, Oct. 21, 1780	2	220
Eliphaz, d. Oct. 9, 1785, ae. 34 y. "Was instantly		
killed by the falling of a stick of timber"	2	255a
Eliphaz, d. Dec. 9, 1785, ae. 34 y. "Was instantly		
killed by the falling of a stick of timber"	2	220
Eliphaz, m. Jemima **ROGERS**, Oct. 21, [ ]	2	255a
Elisha, s. Israel & Sarah, b. Feb. 7, 1724/5	1	81
Elisha, s. Elisha **ROBINSON** & Ann **SQUIER**, b. May 30,		
1745	1	78
Elisha, s. [Andrew & Olive], b. Dec. 4, 1791	3	28
Elisha T., [d. Thomas], b. Feb. 9, 1825	3	58
Elizabeth, d. Peter 7 Ruth, b. Nov. 6, 1732	1	77
Elizabeth, m. Josiah **SMITH**, Nov. 13, 1746	1	267
Elizabeth, d. [Abner & Mahitable], b. Aug 6, 1774	2	132
Emeline, m. Nelson D. **WEAVER**, b. of Willimantic, Oct.		
2, 1836, by Rev. Philo Judson, at Willimantic	3	179
Ephraim, s. Josiah & Elizabeth, b. May 24, 1749	1	267

	Vol.	Page

ROBINSON, (cont.)

	Vol.	Page
Ephraim, s. Sam[ue]ll & Sarah, b. May 13, 1760	1	285
Esther, d. Reuben & Esther, b. Feb. 18, 1749; d		
July 19, [1749]	1	285
Easther, m Lieut. Benj[amin] **FOLLETT**, Feb. 2, 1758	2	39
Easther, d. [Reuben & Esther], b. Feb. 6, 1764	1	285
Eunice, d. Benj[ami]n & Jerusha, b. Nov. 16, 1731	1	110
Eunice, w. Abel, d. Feb. 2, 1796	3	10
Experience, s. Peter & Ruth, b. Apr. 22, 1728	1	77
Experience, m. Zuriah **PALMER**, Feb. 14, 1748/9	1	287
Experience, d. Sept. 10, 1807	1	287
Fanny, d. [Asher & Sarah], b. June 14, 1779	2	211
Fanney, d. [Nath[anie]l & Phebe, b. Oct. 22, 1779	2	20
Fanny, d. [James & Chloe], b. Sept. 2, 1797	2	234
Fanny, d. [James, Jr. & Fanny], b. July 26, 1811	3	51
Fanny R., of Windham, m. Leonard R. **DUNHAM**, of		
Mansfield, Apr. 2, 1833, by Rev. Henry Mayo,		
Windsor	3	164
Florence L , d. Miner S., carpenter, ae 40, b. Nov		
17, [1849]	4	9
George, s. [Jonathan & Elizabeth], b. Apr. 26, 1780	2	107
George Edward, s. [Septimies & Sarah], b. Apr. 6,		
1823	3	85
George Washington, s. [Sam[ue]l, Jr. & Sarah], b.		
Sept. 13, 1776	2	95
Gurdon, s. [James & Chloe], b. Oct. 10, 1783	2	234
Gurdon, m. Lydia **ASPINWALL**, Nov. 9, 1809	3	62
Hannah, d. Reuben & Esther, b. Feb. 27, 1761	1	285
Hannah, d. [Eliphaz & Jemima], b. Mar. 3, 1783	2	220
Hannah, d. [Eliphaz & Jemima], b. Mar. 3, 1783	2	255a
Hannah F., of Windham, m. Caleb **EATON**, of Norwich,		
Oct. 9, 1842, by Rev. Isaac H. Coe	3	204
Hannah Francis, d. [Ebenezer & Zilpha], b. Dec. 16,		
1818	3	25
Harriet, m. George **LILLIE**, Jan. 2, 1825, by Abner		
Robinson, Esq.	3	59
Harriet, m Thomas **ROBINSON**, Oct. 13, 1833, by Joel		
W. White, J.P.	3	165
Henry Webb, s. [Septimies & Sarah], b. June 6, 1807		
[sic]	3	85
Huldah, d. [Jacob & Anna], b. Aug. 22, 1769	2	17
Irena, d. Benj[ami]n & Jerusha, b. Nov. 1, 1733	1	110
Irenia, d. [Jacob & Anna], b. Jan. 15, 1764	2	17
Isaac, m. Deborah **HEB[B]ARD**, Dec. 15, 1737	1	203
Isaac, s. Isaac & Deborah, b. Oct. 12, 1748	1	203
Isaac, [triplet with Nathaniell & Deborah], s. [Isaac		
& Deborah], b. Apr. 15, 1752	1	203
Isaac, Jr., m. Joanna **COLEMAN**, Oct. 26, 1775	2	172

	Vol.	Page
ROBINSON, (cont.)		
Isaac, s. [Isaac, Jr. & Joanna], b. June 2, 1787,		
in Coventry	2	172
Isaac N., m. Louisa H. **WALDEN**, Sept. 9, 1832, by		
Rev. Rich[ar]d F. Cleveland	3	161
Israel, m. Sarah **SABIN**, May 12, 1724	1	81
Israel, m. Deborah **CHAPMAN**, Feb. 21, 1748/9	1	81
Israel, d. Jan. 12, 1775, in the 80th y. of his age	1	81
Isreal G., m. Huldah **BABCOCK**, b. of Windham, Feb. 2,		
1840, by Rev. John E. Tyler	3	192
Jabez, s. [Jonathan & Elizabeth], b. Oct. 27, 1790	2	107
Jacob, s. Peter & Ruth, b. Aug. 14, 1734	1	77
Jacob, m. Anna **TRACY**, Nov. 4, 1756	2	17
Jacob, s. [Jacob & Anna], b. Mar. 7, 1772	2	17
James, s. Experience & Zuriah, b. Nov. 21, 1749/50;		
d. same day	1	287
James, s. Experience & Zurviah, b. Nov. 30, 1752	1	287
James, m. Chloe **WELCH**, Feb. 8, 1781	2	234
James, s. [James & Chloe], b. Oct. 8, 1781	2	234
James, Jr., m. Fanny **BRONSTON**, of Mass., Oct. 28, 1810	3	51
James, m. Sallinda **ROBINSON**, of Tolland, June 2, 1812	2	234
Jane, b. Lisbon, res. Windham, m. Elisha **GREEN**, farmer,		
ae. 21, b. Lisbon, res. Windham, Sept. [ ], 1850,		
by Rev. Henry Greenslit	4	118
Jane F., m. Chandler **SMITH**, Jan. 15, 1837, by Rev.		
William A. Curtis	3	181
Jemina, d. Sam[ue]ll & Sarah, b. Oct. 2, 1750	1	285
Jerusha, d. Simeon & Jerusha, b. June 23, 1754	1	244
John, s. Isaac & Deborah, b. Dec. 31, 1739	1	203
John, s. [Elias & Sibbel], b. Oct. 23, 1791	3	12
John Newton, s. [Andrew & Bethiah], b. Apr. 27, 1809		
[sic]	3	28
John Williams, s. [Eliab & Lucy], b. Apr. 23, 1782	2	218
John Williams, s. [Eliab & Lucy], b. Apr. 23, 1782	2	256
Jonathan, s. [Daniel & Mary], b. Apr. 26, 1760	2	81
Jonathan, m. Elizabeth **ROUSE**, Dec. 9, 1779	2	107
Joseph, m. Mehetable **READ**, July 17, 1735	1	168
Joseph, s. Joseph & Mehetable, b. Feb. 17, 1742/3	1	168
Joshua, s. Peter & Ruth, b. Sept. 24, 1748	1	231
Josiah, s. Joseph & Mehetable [sic], b. Feb. 5, 1758;		
d. Feb. 11, 1758	1	169
Julia, m. Henry **FARNAM**, Jan. 10, 1830, by Rev. Roger		
Bingham	3	141
Laura E., d. Andrew K., clergyman, ae. 28, & Louisa,		
ae. 27, of Willimantic, b. July 27, 1848	4	1
Levi, s. Tho[ma]s & Annah, b. Mar. 18, 1736; d. Mar. 9,		
1739	1	115
Levi, s. Asa & Mary, b. Oct. 26, 1750	1	292

	Vol.	Page
ROBINSON, (cont.)		
Levi, m. Levina **SPAFFORD**, Dec. 1, 1780	3	32
Levina, d. [Levi & Levina], b. Aug. 31, 1795	3	32
Levina, w. Levi, d. Jan. 23, 1814	3	32
Lewis, s. [Asa, Jr. & Olive], b. Dec. 14, 1790	2	93
Lois, d. [Abner & Mahitable], b. Nov. 15, 1765	2	132
Lois, d. [Abner, Jr. & Clarissa], b. Feb. 10, 1815	3	66
Lois, m. Eleazar **CAREY**, Apr. 13, [ ], by Rev. Roger Bingham	3	173
Lucinda, d. [Andrew & Olive], b. July 22, 1798	3	28
Lucinda, m. Aaron **HILL**, June 3, 1832, by Rev. Roger Bingham	3	160
Lucius, s. [Elias & Amie], b. July [ ], 1798; at Mansfield	3	12
Luce, d. Joseph & Mehetable, b. Mar. 28, 1740/1; d. Mar. 16, 1742	1	168
Lucy, d. Joseph & Mary [sic], b. Feb. 25, 1746/7	1	168
Lucy, d. [Eliab & Lucy], b. Feb. 12, 1778	2	218
Lucy, d. [Eliab & Lucy], b. Feb. 12, 1778	2	256
Lucy, d. [Isaac, Jr. & Joanna], b. Sept. 11, 1782	2	172
Lucy, d. [Levi & Levina], b. Dec. 2, 1785	3	32
Lucy, d. [James & Chloe], b. May 15, 1786	2	234
Luther, s. [Nath[anie]ll & Charlotte], b. June 27, 1793	2	20
Luther, s. [Gurdon & Lydia], b. June 5, 1811	3	62
Lydia, d. Benj[ami]n & Jerusha, b. Feb. 5, 1741/2	1	110
Lydia, d. [Experience & Zurviah], b. Jan. 3, 1768	1	287
Lydia, d. [Elias & Sibbel], b. Mar. 12, 1789	3	12
Lydia, m. Bela **FRINK**, Apr. 15, 1795	2	192
Lydia, w. Andrew, d. Oct. 12, 1819	3	28
Lydia, d. [Andrew & Bethiah], b. Mar. 1, 1821	3	28
Lydia, m. Marvin **LILLIE**, Aug. 29, 1825, by Rev. Jesse Fisher	3	114
Lydia C., m. Jonathan W. **MAINE**, b. of Windham, Nov. 25, 1841, by Rev. J.E. Tyler	3	199
Marah, [twin with William], d. Joseph & Mary, b. Aug. 24, 1749	1	168
Marcia P., of Windham, m. Thomas J. **LITCHFIELD**, of Hartford, Sept. 14, 1831, by Rev. Jesse Fisher	3	154
Marcus Tullins, s. [James & Sallinda], b. Feb. 22, 1813	2	234
Mariah, of Windham, m. Darius **BACON**, of Southbridge, Mass., Mar. 26, 1844, by Rev. Isaac H. Coe	3	313
Martha, d. [Dr. William & Asenath], b. Aug. 12, 1780	2	209
Martha Permelia, d. [Septimies & Sarah], b. Aug. 19, 1807	3	85
Mary, d. Simeon & Jerusha, b. Oct. 28, 1745	1	244
Mary, d. [Asa & Mary], b. June 15, 1764	1	292

	Vol.	Page
ROBINSON, (cont.)		
Mary, d. [Abner & Mahitable], b. Apr. 10, 1772;		
d. Nov. 22, 1775	2	132
Mary, d. [Eliphaz & Jemima], b. Oct. 27, 1781	2	220
Mary, d. [Eliphaz & Jemima], b. Oct. 27, 1781	2	255a
Mary, d. [Jonathan & Elizabeth], b. Mar. 15, 1798	2	107
Mary, m. Israel **BIBBONS**, Sept. 12, 1799	3	38
Mary, m. David B. **RIPLEY**, Feb. 6, 1800	3	40
Mary, m. Roswell Randal **CASEY**, July 22, 1828, by		
Hon. John Baldwin	3	130
Mehetable, d. Joseph & Mehetable, b. Nov. 3, 1739	1	168
Mehittable, d. [Abner & Mahitable], b. Jan. 29, 1768	2	132
Merial, d. Jacob & Anna, b. Nov. 9, 1757; d. Apr. 16,		
1759	2	17
Moses, s. Joseph & Mehetable, b. Dec. 9, 1744	1	168
Nancy, d. [Jonathan & Elizabeth], b. Dec. 16, 1787	2	107
Nancy, m. Edwin **DYER**, b. of Windham, Feb. 28, 1841,		
by Rev. J.E. Tyler	3	196
Nancy M., of Windham, m. Henry T. **BENNING**, of Meriden,		
Sept. 22, 1833, by Rev. Ella Dunham	3	165
Nathan, s. Peter & Ruth, b. July 19, 1736	1	77
Nathan, m. Jerusha **PALMER**, Jan. 15, 1764	2	99
Nathan, s. [Nathan & Jerusha], b. Aug. 5, 1772	2	99
Nathan, s. [Asa, Jr. & Olive], b. Aug. 15, 1796	2	93
Nathan Leach, s. [Septimies & Sarah], b. Dec. 13, 1810	3	85
Nathaniell, [triplet with Isaac & Deborah], s. [Isaac		
& Deborah], b. Apr. 15, 1752	1	203
Nathaniel, m. Phebe **COLEMAN**, Aug. 13, 1778	2	20
Nathaniel, s. [Nath[anie]l & Phebe], b. June 20, 1785,		
at South Hampton	2	20
Nath[anie]ll, m. Charlotte **SHELDON**, Jan 12, 1786	2	20
Newell, s. [Nathan & Jerusha], b. Mar. 24, 1767	2	99
Newton, m. Sama[n]tha **REED**, Dec. 26, 1830, by Rev.		
Roger Bingham	3	150
Olive, d. [Asa, Jr. & Olive], b. Mar. 19, 1788	2	93
Olive, d. [Adrian & Elizabeth], b. Feb. 23, 1794	2	144
Olive, d. Adrian, b. Feb. 23, 1794	2	193
Olive, w. Andrew, d. Mar. 15, 1812	3	28
Olive, of Windham, m. Mason **PALMER**, of Canterbury,		
Feb. 11, 1826	3	120
Olive H., m. Leonard **ROSWELL**, b. of Willimantic, July		
19, 1839, by Elder Thomas Jones	3	189
Olive Hovey, d. [Ebenezer & Zilpha], b. Feb. 2, 1815	3	25
Oliver, s. [Sam[ue]ll & Sarah], b. Sept. 15, 1766; d.		
Dec. 14, 1767	1	285
Oliver, s. [Asa, Jr. & Olive], b. Apr. 21, 1785	2	93
Orinda, d. [Isaac, Jr. & Joanna], b. Mar. 4, 1776	2	172
Orran, s. [Nath[anie]ll & Charlotte], b. Apr. 10, 1791	2	20

	Vol.	Page
ROBINSON, (cont.)		
Permilia, d. [Andrew & Olive], b. Aug. 18, 1793	3	28
Parmelia, d. [Ebenezer & Zilpha], b. July 15, 1822	3	25
Patrick, s. [Peter, Jr. & Abigail], b. Apr. 7, 1768	2	1
Permelia, see under Parmelia		
Peter, m. Ruth **FFULLER**, June 30, 1725	1	77
Peter, s. Peter & Ruth, b. May 19, 1730	1	77
Peter, Jr., m. Abigail **PALMER**, Nov. 13, 1755	2	1
Peter, s. [Peter, Jr. & Abigail], b. May 15, 1766	2	1
Peter, Jr., d. July 18, 1778	2	1
Peter, d. Mar. 22, 1785	1	231
Phebe, d. Asa & Mary, b. Oct. 2, 1752	1	292
Phebe, d. [Dr. William & Asenath], b. July 17, 1776	2	209
Phebe, d. [Isaac, Jr. & Joanna], b Apr. 24, 1785, in Coventry	2	172
Phebe, w. Nathaniel, d. June 15, 1785, at South Hampton	2	20
Phebe, d. [Nath[anie]ll & Charlotte], b. Jan. 24, 1789	2	20
Phebe, b. S. Hampton, Mass., res. Willimantic, d. Aug. 6, 1850, ae. 62 y.	4	157
Phelena, d. [Abner & Mahitable], b. Mar 24, 1764	2	132
Philomelia, d. [Isaac, Jr. & Joanna], b. Mar. 8, 1778	2	172
Polly, d. [Abner & Mahitable], b. Mar. 30, 1780	2	132
Polly, d. [Asa, Jr. & Olive], b. Feb. 25, 1800	2	93
Prudence, d. Joseph & Mary, b. May 25, 1753	1	168
Rachel, d. Peter & Ruth, b. Mar. 30, 1744	1	231
Rachal, m. Cornelius **COBURN**, Apr. 5, 1780	2	227
Ralph, s. [Eliab & Lucy], b. Mar. 12, 1780	2	218
Ralph, s. [Eliab & Lucy], b. Mar. 12, 1780	2	256
Ralph, [s. Thomas], b. Dec. 2, 1822	3	58
Ralph Webb, s. [Abner, Jr. & Clarissa], b. Oct. 5, 1811	3	66
Rebeckah, d. Joseph & Mehetable, b. Dec. 1, 1737	1	168
Rebeckah, m. Joseph **ALLEN**, Jr., Mar. 11, 1761	2	75
R[e]uben, s. Thomas & Annah, b. Jan. 17, 1725	1	115
Reuben, m. Esther **PALMER**, Jan. 12, 1748/9	1	285
Reuben, s. Reuben & Esther, b. Jan. 13, 1759	1	285
Reuben, m. Hannah **SNELL**, Oct. 26, 1846, by Rev. Andrew Sharp	3	232
Rhoda, d. [Peter, Jr. & Abigail], b. Apr. 25, 1761; d. Nov. 19, 1761	2	1
Richard, s. Sam[ue]ll & Sarah, b. May 13, 1763	1	285
Rob[er]t W., m. Maria **BASS**, b. of Windham, Sept. 18, 1837, by Rev. Otis C. Whiton, of Scotland Society, Windham	3	184
Robert Waterman, s. [Abner, Jr. & Clarissa], b. Apr. 26, 1809	3	66
Rosannah, black, b. Charleston, R.I., res. Windham, d. Mar. 29, 1848, ae. 71	4	151

	Vol.	Page

ROBINSON, (cont.)

	Vol.	Page
Rosemond, d. [Peter, Jr. & Abigail], b. Aug. 26, 1756	2	1
Rosamond, m. Nathan **WALES**, June 29, 1780	2	67
Rosewell, s. [Nathan & Jerusha], b. Jan. 17, 1776	2	99
Rowenna, d. [Nathan & Jerusha], b. Jan. 2, 1769	2	99
Rowenna, d. [Nathan & Jerusha], d. Oct. 2, 1775	2	99
Roxey, d. [Jonathan & Elizabeth], b. July 27, 1782	2	107
Rufus, s. [Nathan & Jerusha], b. Sept. 18, 1774	2	99
Ruth, d. Peter & Ruth, b. Dec 14, 1740	1	231
Ruth, d. Jan. 9, 1795	1	231
Sallinda, of Tolland, m. James **ROBINSON**, June 2, 1812	2	234
Sallinda, w. James, d. July 13, 1813	2	234
Salome, d. [Nathan & Jerusha], b. June 12, 1764	2	99
Sam[ue]ll, s. Peter & Ruth, b. July 6, 1726	1	77
Samuell, m Sarah **KIMBALL**, Jan. 2, 1748/9	1	285
Sam[ue]ll, s. Israel & Deborah, b. June 3, 1750	1	81
Sam[ue]ll, s. Sam[ue]ll & Sarah, b. Sept. 16, 1757	1	285
Sam[ue]l, Jr., m. Sarah **SCOT[T]**, Apr. 13, 1773	2	95
Sam[ue]ll, s. [Sam[ue]ll & Sarah], d. Sept. 23, 1776, in New York	1	285
Samuel Johnson, s. [Sam[ue]l, Jr. & Sarah], b. May 20, 1775	2	95
Samuel Newel, s. [Ebenezer & Zilpha], b. May 12, 1817	3	25
Sarah, m. Hez[ekiah] **MASON**, Nov. 15, 1725	1	79
Sarah, w. Israel, d. May 3, 1737	1	81
Sarah, d. Isaac & Deborah, b. Sept. 10, 1738	1	203
Sarah, d. [Daniel & Mary], b. Dec. 2, 1758	2	81
Sarah, d. [Sam[ue]ll & Sarah], b. June 22, 1768	1	285
Sarah, m. Eliphalet **ORMSBY**, July 4, 1781	2	73
Sarah, b. Groton, res. Windham, d. Mar. 16, 1851, ae. 61	4	158
Septimeas, s. [Abner & Mahitable], b. Apr. 14, 1777	2	132
Septimies, m. Sarah **WEBB**, Feb. 5, 1803	3	85
Sibbel, d. Sam[ue]ll & Sarah, b. Sept. 14, 1755	1	285
Sibbel, w. Elias, d Dec. 15, 1794	3	12
Simeon, m. Jerusha **KINGSLEY**, Feb. 2, 1742/3	1	244
Simeon, s. Simeon & Jerusha, b. Feb. 25, 1747	1	244
Sophia, d. [Eliphaz & Jemima], b. Oct. 27, 1785	2	255a
Sophia, d. [James & Chloe], b , Sept. 4, 1791	2	234
Sophronia, d. [Nath[anie]l & Phebe], b. Nov. 21, 1781	2	20
Susannah, [twin with Deborah], d. Joseph & Mehetable, b. Mar. 14, 1735/6; d. July 26, 1737	1	168
Sybil, see under Sibbel		
Tho[ma]s, s. Asa & Mary, b. Jan. 2, 1755	1	292
Thomas, s. [Asa & Mary], d. Nov. 13, 1776, at Stamford	1	292
Thomas, s. [Asa, Jr. & Olive], b. Aug. 7, 1779	2	93
Thomas, d. Mar. 28, 1783, in the 85th y. of his age	1	115

	Vol.	Page

ROBINSON, (cont.)

Thomas, m. Harriet **ROBINSON**, Oct. 13, 1833, by Joel

 W. White, J.P. 3 165

Tho[ma]s, laborer, black, d. Aug. 10, 1860, ae. 48 4 161

Thomas M., [s. Thomas], b. Jan. 5, 1833 3 58

Tophar, s. Reuben & Esther, b. Feb. 19, 1753 1 285

Tracy, s. [Jacob & Anna], b Mar. 1, 1778 2 17

Tryphenia, d. Exper[ience] & Zurviah, b. Feb. 21,

 1750/51; d. Jan. 10, 1755 1 287

Tryphenia, d. Exp[erience] & Zurviah, b. July 20, 1755 1 287

Tryphena, m. John **BURNAM**, Oct. 23, 1777 2 211

Tryphenia, d. [Andrew & Olive], b. Feb. 18, 1800 3 28

Urban, s. [Andrew & Olive], b. Sept. 14, 1804 3 28

Vienna, d. [Nathan & Jerusha], b. Feb. 4, 1766 2 99

Vine, s. [Jacob & Anna], b. July 25, 1767 2 17

Wad, s. Peter, Jr., d. July 16, 1778 2 1

Waterman, s. [Abner, Jr. & Clarissa], b. Jan. 15, 1807 3 66

Whiting, s. [Asa, Jr. & Olive], b. Sept. 21, 1782 2 93

William, [twin with Marah], s. Joseph & Mary, b. Aug.

 24, 1749 1 168

William, Dr., m. Asenath **MANNING**, Nov. 10, 1774 2 209

William, s. [Dr. William & Asenath], b. June 20, 1783 2 209

W[illia]m, operative, ae. 25, of Thompson, m. Sarah

 GAVIT, ae. 19, Sept. 26, 1847, by Rev. A. Sharp 4 111

William Andrew, s. [Ebenezer & Zilpha], b. July 30,

 1820 3 25

W[illia]m H., m. Sarah J. **LOVET**, Sept 26, 1847, by

 Rev. Andrew Sharp 3 236

W[illia]m H., s. W[illia]m H., store, ae. 27, & Mary

 BATTELLE, ae. 18, b. Apr. 25, 1848 4 2

William Pitt, s. [Septimies & Sarah], b. Nov. 20, 1813 3 85

William T., m. Julian **HAZARD**, Aug. 5, 1832, by Rev.

 Roger Bingham 3 160

Zerviah, w. Experience, d. June 9, 1806 1 287

Zilpah, d. [Asa & Mary], b. Aug. 12, 1767 1 292

Zimran, s. [Asa & Mary], b. Mar. 30, 1761 1 292

Zip[p]orah, d. Reuben & Esther, b. Jan. 31, 1750/51 1 285

Zipporah, m. John **WEBB**, Jr., Nov. 12, 1772 2 180

——, s. [Peter, Jr & Abigail], b Dec 23, 1762 2 1

——, s. [Dr. William & Asenath], b. Sept. 23, 1778;

 d. same day 2 209

ROCKWELL, Elizabeth, m. Jonathan **HUNTINGTON**, Nov. 7,

 1734 1 134

RODMAN, Robert, of Lebanon, m. Celinda **STARK**, of Mansfield,

 Nov. 10, 1830, by Rev. R.T. Crampton 3 149

ROGEN, [see under **ROGERS**]

ROGERS, Anne, d. Jeduthan & Anne, b. Dec. 10, 1749 1 281

Anne, w. Jeduthan, d. Dec. 30, 1762 1 281

	Vol.	Page
ROGERS, (cont.)		
Asa, s. [Jeduthan & Hannah], b. Mar. 14, 1769	2	103
Benoni, d. Apr. 10, [1849], ae. 89 (Entered among births)	4	6
Bixbee, s. Jethro & Hannah, b Dec. 18, 1749; d. Dec. 27, 1749	1	271
Cynthia, d. [Oliver & Hannah], b. Apr. 20, 1774	2	211
Daniel, s. [Oliver & Hannah], b. Nov. 19, 1776	2	211
Esther, d. Jed[uthan] & Anne, b. Mar. 6, 1750/51; d. Sept. 6, 1753	1	281
Esther, d. [Jeduthan & Anne], b Jan 7, 1755; d. Jan. 22, 1756	1	281
Hannah, d. Josiah & Hannah, b. July 15, 1748	1	276
Hannah, d. [Jeduthan & Hannah], b. Aug. 31, 1764	2	103
Hannah, w. Jeduthan, d. Aug. 13, 1771	2	103
Hannah, d. [Oliver & Hannah], b. May 26, 1785	2	211
Hope, m. Esther **MEACHAM**, Nov. 14, 1715	1	48
Ichabod, s. Hope & Esther, b. Jan. 19, 1718/19	1	48
Ic[h]abod, m. Presilla **HOLT**, Nov. 10, 1743	1	235
Isaiah, s. [Jeduthan & Anne], b. Feb. 26, 1760; d. Apr. 22, 1763	1	281
Ishmael, s. Hope & Esther, b. July 7, 1717	1	48
Jeduthan, s. Hope & Esther, b. Feb. 16, 1723/4	1	66
Jeduthan, m. Anne **FARNAM**, Oct. 21, 1747	1	281
Jeduthan, s. Jeduthan & Anne, b. May 24, 1748; d. June 24, 1750	1	281
Jeduthan, s. Jed[uthan] & Anne, b. Mar. 4, 1753	1	281
Jeduthan, m. Hannah **KNIGHT**, Oct. 12, 1763	2	103
Jeduthan, m. Eunice **BURGE**, Oct. 4, 1772	2	69
Jemima, m. Eliphaz **ROBINSON**, Oct. 21, 1780	2	220
Jemima, m. Eliphaz **ROBINSON**, Oct. 21, [ ]	2	255a
Jerusha, d. [Jeduthan & Anne], b. July 19, 1758	1	281
Jethro, s. Hope & Esther, b. Apr. 14, 1722	1	66
Jethro, m. Hannah **HOLT**, Oct. 8, 1747	1	271
Joel, s. Hope & Esther, b. Oct. 14, 1729	1	66
Jonah, s. Josiah & Hannah, b. Dec. 15, 1743	1	276
Joseph, s. Hope & Esther, b. Aug. 5, 1716; d Aug. 9, 1716	1	48
Josiah, s. Hope & Esther, b. Oct. 7, 1720	1	48
Josiah, m. Hannah **FORD**, Mar. 1, 1742/3	1	276
Josiah, s. Josiah & Hannah, b. Aug. 2, 1747; d. Sept. 7, 1748	1	276
Lovewell, s. [Oliver & Hannah], b. Jan. 17, 1772	2	211
Lucy, d. [Jeduthan & Anne], b. Oct. 24, 1756	1	281
Mary, d. Hope & Esther, b. Oct. 6, 1727	1	66
Oliver, s. Jethro & Hannah, b. Apr. 14, 1748	1	271
Oliver, m. Hannah **COBURN**, Feb. 11, 1770	2	211
Philora, d. [Oliver & Hannah], b. Sept. 23, 1778	2	211

	Vol.	Page
ROGERS, (cont.)		
Rufus, s. [Jeduthan & Hannah], b. Jan. 16, 1767	2	103
Ruth, d. Hope & Esther, b. Aug. 23, 1732	1	66
Sarah, d. Hope & Esther, b. Feb. 21, 1725/6	1	66
Tabitha, d. [Jeduthan & Anne], b. Nov 19, 1761	1	281
Tryphena, d. [Oliver & Hannah], b. Dec. 7, 1788	2	211
W[illia]m, Dea., of Norwich, m. Abby **BYRNE**, of		
Windham, [ ], by Rev. John Storrs	3	166
RONA, Catharine, ae. 20, m. Pat **LANCY**, laborer, ae 20,		
Dec. [1850], by Rev. Brady	4	115
ROOD, [see also **RUDE**], Elizabeth, m. Joseph **LUCE**, July		
18, 1727	1	128
John, of Windham, m. Susan **RICH**, of Plainfield,		
Nov. 15, 1846, by Thomas Gray, J.P.	3	231
Wellington, s John, painter, ae. 28, & Susan,		
ae. 28, b. Jan 25, 1850	4	13
----, d. Rufus, blacksmith, ae 34, & Amy, ae. 28,		
b. Oct. 17, 1850	4	13
ROOT, David, m. Elizabeth **WILLIAMS**, Feb. 15, 1846, by		
Andrew Sharp	3	227
Stephen, m. Lucinda **CLARK**, Nov. 24, 1835, at Willi-		
mantic, by Rev. S.R. Cook	3	175
ROSE, Elizabeth, m. Sam[ue]ll **KILLIAM**, Nov. 11, 1714	1	4
ROSELE, Leonard, farmer, ae. 30, b. Windham, res. Rock-		
ville, m. Huldah **DONE**, ae. 25, b. Coventry, res.		
Rockville, his 2d w., Sept. 15, [1850], by Rev.		
E.W. Barrows	4	118
ROSS, Aleph, d. Jerem[iah] & Ann, b. Dec. 17, 1745	1	253
Ann, d. Jerem[iah] & Ann, b. Jan. 5, 1746/7	1	253
Austin, of Great Barrington, Mass., m. Chartola		
WHITE, of Willimantic, Aug. 23, 1846, by Rev.		
John Cooper	3	230
Daniel, m. Marg[a]ret **HOUES**, June 5, 1716	1	46
Daniel, s. Daniel & Mary, b. June 13, 1719; d. July		
4, 1720	1	46
Daniel, s. Joseph & Sarah, b. June 26, 1736	1	177
Daniel, m. Judith **WARNER**, Mar. 30, 1741	1	46
Diana, d. Jer[emiah] & Ann, b. Nov. 18, 1751	1	253
Elizabeth, d. [Jere[miah] & Ann], b. June 10, 1764,		
in New London	1	253
Jemima, d. Daniel & Margaret, b. Aug. 31, 1721; d.		
Dec. 11, 1721	1	46
Jeremiah, s. Joseph & Sarah, b. July 26, 1721	1	30
Jeremiah, m. Ann **PAIN[E]**, Oct. 31, 1744	1	253
Jerrem[iah], s. Jerem[iah] & Ann, b. July 4, 1748	1	253
Jeremiah, s. Jere[miah] & Ann, b. Jan. 6, 1759	1	253
John, s. Joseph & Sary, b. July 6, 1723	1	30
John S., of Chaplin, m. Harriet S. **DEVOTION**, of		

	Vol.	Page
ROSS, (cont.)		
Windham, Dec. 23, 1833, by Rev. Jesse Fisher	3	168
Joseph, m. Sarah **UTLEY**, Sept. 16, 1716	1	30
Joseph, s. Joseph & Sarah, b. Dec. 8, 1716	1	30
Lucy, d. Jere[miah] & Ann, b. Oct. 14, 1755	1	253
Lydia, d. Joseph & Sarah, b. Mar. 22, 1728	1	30
Marg[a]ret, w. Daniel, d. June 19, 1724	1	46
Mary, w. Daniel, d. July 7, 1709	1	46
Mary, d. Nov 5, 1725, ae. about 79 y.	1	30
Mary, d. Joseph & Sarah, b. June 6, 1734	1	177
Mary, d. Jer[emiah] & Ann, b. Dec. 21, 1753	1	253
Payne, m. Miranda **FULLER**, May 3, 1835, by Rev.		
Roger Bingham	3	175
Ruth, d. Daniel & Marg[a]ret, b. May 7, 1717	1	46
Ruth, m. Joshua **HIB[B]ARD**, Oct. 4, 1733	1	127
Sarah, d. Joseph & Sarah, b. Apr. 13, 1732	1	177
Simeon, s. Joseph & Sarah, b. Feb. 13, 1718/19	1	30
William, s. Joseph & Sarah, b. Mar. 31, 1730	1	177
William, s. Jere[miah] & Ann, b. Mar. 29, 1761	1	253
Zebulon, s. Joseph & Sary, b. Aug. 25, 1725	1	30
ROSWELL, Leonard, m. Olive H. **ROBINSON**, b. of		
Willimantic, July 19, 1839, by Elder Thomas		
Jones	3	189
ROUNDY, ROUNDYE, ROUNDING, Alyin, s. [Samuel & Anna],		
b. Apr. 20, 1766	2	26
Amey, d. [Samuel & Anna], b. Mar. 31, 1759	2	26
Anne, d. [Samuel & Anna], b. May 15, 1771	2	26
Asael, s. [Samuel & Anna], b. Jan. 27, 1756	2	26
Ede, d. [Samuel & Anna], b. July 14, 1761	2	26
John, s. Robert & Elizabeth, b. Aug. 23, 1726	1	27
John, s. Robert & Elizabeth, b. Aug. 23, 1726	1	195
Robert, m. Elizabeth **GREEN**, Feb. 15, 1726	1	27
Robert, m. Elizabeth **GREEN**, Feb. 15, 1725/6	1	195
Robert, s. Robert & Elizabeth, b. Jan. 23, 1737/8	1	195
Samuel, s. Robert & Elizabeth, b. June 6, 1733	1	195
Samuel, m. Anna **HUNTINGTON**, Dec. 23, 1755	2	26
Samuel, s. [Samuel & Anna], b. Dec. 19, 1768	2	26
ROUSE, Elizabeth, m. Jonathan **ROBINSON**, Dec. 9, 1779	2	107
John, m. Zerviah **BACKUS**, Mar. 13, 1763	2	80
John, farmer, ae. 27, m. Mary Ann **WELCH**, ae. 21,		
[1849]	4	113
Nancy, m. John **COREY**, Jan. 1, 1837, by Rev. Philetus		
Greene	3	180
Roxalany, d. [John & Zerviah], b. Oct. 25, 1773; d.		
Aug. 9, 1778	2	80
Zerviah, d. [John & Zerviah], b. Feb. 3, 1772; d.		
Apr. 28, 1772	2	80
ROUTH, Cynt[hi]a, of Windham, m. John M. **FULLER**, of Kent,		

	Vol.	Page
ROUTH, (cont.)		
Aug. 27, 1825, by Rev. Jesse Fisher (Perhaps		
"**ROATH**")	3	115
ROYAL, Nabby, ae. 37, b. Mansfield, res. Willimantic, m.		
Ephraim **HERRICK**, cabman, ae. 37, b. Preston,		
res. Willimantic, Jan. 20, 1851, by Rev. John		
Cady	4	117
ROYCE, Aaron, s. John & Sarah, b. Feb. 17, 1695	A	23
Daniel, s. John & Sarah, b. May 27, 1697	A	23
Ebenezer, s. John & Sarah, b. Mar. 31, 1699	A	23
James, s. John & Sarah, b. Aug. 13, 1691	A	23
John, s. John & Sarah, b. July 23, 1686	A	23
John, s. John & Sarah, b. Dec. 11, 1699	A	23
Moses, s. John & Sarah, b. June 6, 1689	A	23
Patience, d. John & Sarah, b. Sept. 4. 1693	A	23
RUDD, RUD, Abigail, m. Barnard **CASE**, May 22, 1712	1	32
Abigail, d. Jonathan & Easther, b. Dec. 13, 1748; d.		
Aug. 13, 1760	1	266
Abigail, d. [Zeb[ulon] & Jerusha], b. Sept. 29, 1762	1	217
Abigail, d. [Jonathan, Jr. & Mary], b. June 13, 1767	2	127
Bazaleel, s. Zeb[ulon] & Jerusha, b. July 13, 1751	1	217
Barzillai, m. Eunice **KINGSBURY**, Nov. 26, 1810	3	39
Caroline, d. [Barzillai & Eunice], b. June 5, 1809	3	39
Dinah, d. Jonathan & Esther, b. Feb. 12, 1744/5	1	185
Elizabeth, d. [Jonathan, Jr. & Mary], b. Mar. 13, 1772	2	127
Elle, m. Susannah **COBURN**, Sept. 9, 1789	3	42
Esther, d. Jonathan & Esther, b. Sept. 4, 1739	1	185
Esther, wid. Nath[anie]l, d. Mar. 22, 1766, in the 84th		
y. of her age	1	48
Easther, w. Lieut. Jonathan, d. Nov. 8, 1777, in the		
65th y. of her age	1	266
Henry, s. [Elle & Susannah], b. May 8, 1798	3	42
Hezekiah, s [Jonathan, Jr. & Mary], b. Feb. 2, 1781	2	127
James, s. Jonath[an] & Easther, [b.] Nov. [ ], 1750	1	266
Jerusha, d. Zebulon & Jerusha, b. Apr. 23, 1744	1	217
Jerusha, m. Andrew **FRINK**, May 26, 1762	2	45
Jonathan, s. Nathaniell & Rebeckah, b. Nov. 27, 1710	1	48
Jonathan, m. Esther **TYLER**, Dec. 6, 1738	1	185
Jonathan, s. Jonathan & Esther, b. Apr. 29, 1743	1	185
Jonathan, Jr., m. Mary **TRACY**, Oct. 1, 1766	2	127
Jonathan, d. Dec. 6, 1771, in Kent, in the 60th y. of		
his age	1	266
Jonathan, s. [Jonathan, Jr. & Mary], b. Aug. 16, 1774	2	127
Jonathan, m. Amie **TYLER**, Mar. 1, 1804	3	58
Lucy, d. [William & Eunice], b. Dec 15, 1773; d.		
[ ]	2	166
Lydia, d. [Jonathan, Jr. & Mary], b. May 6, 1785	2	127
Martha, d. Zeb[ulon] & Jerusha, b. Sept. 1, 1756; d.		

	Vol.	Page
RUDD, RUD, (cont.)		
Sept. 13, 1758	1	217
Martha, d. [Zeb[ulon] & Jerusha], b. Aug. 26, 1759	1	217
Mary, d. Zeb[ulon] & Jerusha, b. May 24, 1748	1	217
Mary, d. [Jonathan, Jr. & Mary], b. Aug 22, 1770	2	127
Mary, w. Jonathan, d. June 7, 1803	2	127
Nathaniel, m. Rebeckah **WALDO**, Dec. 27, 1709	1	48
Nathaniell, s. Nathaniell & Rebeckah, b. May 30, 1713	1	48
Nath[anie]l, Ens., m. Esther **BURMAN**, Apr. 18, 1728;		
d. Feb. 20, 1760, in the 76th y. of his age	1	48
Nathaniel, s. Zebulon & Jerusha, b. Sept. 8, 1742	1	217
Nath[anie]l, s. Jonath[an] & Easther, b. Feb. 22, 1753	1	266
Nath[anie]l, Capt., d Feb. 20, 1760, in the 76th y.		
of his age	1	48
Orren, s. [Elle & Susannah], b. Jan. 13, 1795	3	42
Polly, d. [Elle & Susannah], b. Apr. 20, 1790	3	42
Rebeckah, d. Nathaniel & Rebeckah, b. Nov. 17, 1714	3	48
Rebeckah, w. Nathaniel, d. Sept. 27, 1727	1	48
Rebeckah, m. John **CARY**, Jr., Nov. 13, 1740	1	209
Rebeckah, d. Jonathan & Esther, b. July 12, 1741	1	185
Rebecca, d. Oct. 19, 1771, in the 31st y. of her age	1	266
Sarah, m. Philemon **WOOD**, Nov. 26, 1761	2	74
Sarah, d. [Jonathan, Jr. & Mary], b. Dec. 17, 1776	2	127
Simon Tracy, s. [Jonathan, Jr. & Mary], b. Sept. 1,		
1768	2	127
William, Capt., d. Aug. 21, 1735	2	166
William, s. Jonathan & Easther, b. Jan. 20, 1746/7	1	266
William, m. Eunice **WALDO**, Dec. 23, 1771	2	166
Zavest, d. Zeb[ulon] & Jerusha, b. May 21, 1746	1	217
Zebulon, s. Nathaniel & Rebeckah, b. July 26, 1717	1	48
Zebulon, m. Jerusha **BREWSTER**, June 4, 1741	1	217
RUDE, [see also **ROOD**], Abigail, Jr., m. Ebenezer **WEBB**, Jr.,		
Aug. 28, 1777	2	246
Prudence, m. Thomas **JEWETT**, Feb. 3, 1785	2	204
RUMFORD, William, m. Asenath **LINCOLN**, b. of Windham, Oct.		
21, 1835, by John Baldwin, J.P.	3	174
RUSS, Amelia, m. Henry **FITCH**, Jan. 8, 1843, by Rev. Andrew		
Sharp, Willimantic	3	206
Edgar, s. Lewis, stone-mason, ae. 24, & Julia, ae. 20,		
b. July 1, 1847	4	1
Julia A., m. Hardin H. **FITCH**, Nov. 9, 1842, by Rev.		
Andrew Sharp, Willimantic	3	205
Julia Etta, m. Daniel C. **SESSIONS**, Apr. 21, 1844, by		
Andrew Sharp	3	215
RUSSELL, Eliza, m. Nathaniel P.P. **BROWN**, b. of Windham,		
Mar. 24, 1835, by Rev. Philo Judson, at Willimantic	3	172
Lucy, m. Warren **ROBERTSON**, Oct. 5, 1828, by Rev.		
Chester Tilden	3	130

	Vol.	Page
RUSSELL, (cont.)		
Phebe, m. Henry **FFARNUM**, June 12, 1712	1	131
Sophia L , m Calvin **BACKUS**, b. of Chaplin, Nov 4,		
1840, by Rev. John E. Tyler	3	194
RYAN, Elizabeth, ae. 25, m Geo[rge] **FIELD**, manufacturer,		
ae. 25, Sept. 25, 1849, by Rev. J E. Tyler	4	114
SABIN, SABEN, Abigail, d Daniell & Abigail, b Jan. 20,		
1702; d. Mar. 26, 1702	A	30
Anna, m. Jabez **HEBBARD**, Dec 6, 1779	2	226
Daniell, m. Abigail **ABBE**, Mar. 18, 1701	A	30
Sarah, d Daniell & Abigail, b. Mar 27, 1703	A	30
Sarah, m. Israel **ROBINSON**, May 12, 1724	1	81
Susannah, m William **DURKEE**, Mar 3, 1725/6	1	55
SAFFORD, Epaphras, m. Lydia **BASS**, Apr. 3, 1836, by Rev.		
Jesse Fisher	3	177
Jaeng[ ]m Thompson, s. Ad[d]ison, blacksmith, ae.		
34, & Mary A., ae. 33, b Jan. 4 , 1848	4	1
Julia E., m. Alfred **MARTIN**, Nov. 26, 1846, by Rev.		
Isaac H Coe	3	232
Martin, m. Harriet **BUSHNELL**, Nov. 7, 1831, by Henry		
Hall, J P	3	155
Morgan, of Canterbury, m. Mary Ann **HEWITT**, of		
Windham, Dec 2, 1832, by Rev Alva Gregory	3	162
SALSBEY, [see under **SILSBY**]		
SAMPSON, Anne, d. [Zephaniah & Tamar], b Aug 22, 1787	3	27
Asenath, d. [Zephaniah & Tamar], b. Mar. 26, 1780	3	27
Catharine, d. [Zephaniah & Tamar], b Feb. 12,		
1782	3	27
Jennett, d [Zephaniah & Tamar], b. Mar 7, 1792	3	27
Zephaniah, m. Tamar [ ], Apr. 12, 1779	3	27
SANDERS, Herbert O , s. Clark M., manufacturer, ae 35,		
b. Nov. 29, [1849]	4	9
SAUNDERS, Clark M , weaver, ae 32, b. Smithfield, res.		
Windham, m. Caroline **HOVEY**, ae. 30, Jan. 2,		
1848, by Thomas Dowling	4	111
SAVAGE, Abigail, m. Ebenezer **ABBE**, Feb. 22, 1729/30	1	121
SAWYER, Abigail, d [Jacob], b. Dec 29, 1742	2	157
Abigail, [d. Jacob & Prudence], b. [ ]	1	123
Abner, s. [Jacob & Jemime], b. Nov 24, 1787	2	141
Ann, d. Elijah & Hannah, b. Feb. 28, 1734/5	1	94
Ann, m. Abisha **BINGHAM**, Feb. [ ], 1755	2	161
Asahel, s. Elijah & Hannah, b. May 21, 1751	1	193
Azariah, s. Elij[ah] & Hannah, b Sept 11, 1755	1	193
Benjamin, s. Jonathan & Sarah, b Mar. 19, 1752; d.		
Oct 6, 1772 "Was drowned at sea"	1	164
Beulah, d. Joshua & Sarah, b. Nov. 18, 1744	1	149
Beulah, m Ebenezer **LITTLEFIELDS**, Dec 24, 1769	2	182
Charlotte E., m. Henry C. **FITCH**, Feb. 16, 1823	3	110

	Vol	Page
SAWYER, (cont.)		
Charlotte Elderkin, d. [Dan & Charlotte], b. July		
18, 1803	3	23
Cornelius, s. Jacob & Prudence, b. July 6, 1751	1	123
Cornelius, s. [Jacob], b. July 1, 1752	2	157
Cornelius, s. [Jacob & Jemime], b. May 5, 1783	2	141
Dan, s. James & Lucy, b. Oct. 17, 1770	2	161
Dan, m. Charlotte **DENISON**, Feb. 4, 1795	3	23
Deborah, d. Elijah & Hannah, b. June 29, 1749	1	193
Deborah, m. Jonathan **HIBBARD**, July 18, 1772	2	175
Delight, w. Matthais, d. Sept. 10, 1800	2	231
Dinah, d. [Jacob], b. Apr. 20, 1744	2	157
Dinah, [d. Jacob & Prudenct], b. [ ]	1	123
Elijah, m. Hannah **TERRELL**, Mar. 7, 1732/33	1	94
Elijah, s. Elijah & Hannah, b. Apr. 20, 1734; d.		
Apr. 20, 1734	1	94
Elizabeth, d. [Jacob], b. Jan. 18, 1733	2	157
Elizabeth, d. Joshua & Sarah, b. Dec. 28, 1746	1	149
Elizabeth, m. Daniel **SMITH**, Jan. 25, 1767	2	123
Elizabeth, m. William **LYMAN**, Dec. 2, 1832, by Rev.		
Roger Bingham	3	162
Elizabeth, [d. Jacob & Prudence], b. [ ]	1	123
Ephraim, s. [Jacob], b. Feb. 10, 1740	2	157
Ephraim, [s. Jacob & Prudence], b. [ ]	1	123
Erastus, s. [Jacob & Jemime], b. Feb. 3, 1781	2	141
Eunice, d. [Jacob], b. May 22, 1736	2	157
Eunice, [d. Jacob & Prudence], b. [ ]	1	123
Hannah, d. Elijah & Han[na]h, b. July 7, 1758	1	255
Hannay, m. Robert **CUNNINGHAM**, Sept. 10, 1783	2	55
Irena, d. Elijah & Hannah, b. Sept. 3, 1746	1	193
Jacob, m. Prudence **STANDISH**, Sept. 3, 1730	1	123
Jacob, d. Aug. 22, 1758, in the 51st y. of his age	2	157
Jacob, m. Jemime **BROUGHTON**, June 22, 1778	2	141
Jacob, [s. Jacob & Prudence], b. [ ]	1	123
Jacob, d. [ ]	1	123
Jacob Standish, [s. Jacob], b. Apr. 10, 1754	2	157
James, s. Joshua & Sarah, b. Oct. 28, 1749	1	149
James, m. Lucy **WARNER**, July 9, 1770	2	161
James Denison, s. [Dan & Charlotte], b. Sept. 17, 1713		
[1813]	3	23
Jany, factory, b. W. Greenwich, R.I., res. Willimantic,		
d. Apr. 3, [1849], ae. 15	4	153
Jemima, d. Jacob & Prudence, b. July 6, 1731	1	123
Jemima, d. [Jacob], b. July 6, 1731; d. June 23, 1747	2	157
Jemima, d. [Jacob], b. Mar. 7, 1749	2	157
Jemima, m. Stephen **WOODWARD**, Jan. 8, 1772	2	167
Jemima, d. [Jacob & Jemime], b. May 19, 1785	2	141
Jemima, [d. Jacob & Prudence], b. [ ]	1	123

	Vol.	Page
SAWYER, (cont.)		
Jeremiah, s. [Jacob], b. July 26, 1746	2	157
Jeremiah, [s. Jacob & Prudence], b. [ ]	1	123
Jerusha, d. Elijah & Hannah, b. Dec. 16, 1739	1	193
Jerusha, m. Joseph **COY**, Dec. 31, 1767	2	130
Joshua, m. Sarah **FFLINT**, Nov. 5, 1735	1	149
Julette, d. [Dan & Charlotte], b. Jan. 26, 1796; d.		
Oct. 11, 1796	3	23
Kezia, d. Joshua & Sarah, b. Jan. 11, 1738/9	1	149
Keziah, m. Daniel **FOSTER**, Apr. 1, 1765	2	112
Lucy Warner, d. [Dan & Charlotte], b. Aug. 17, 1800	3	23
Lydia, d. Elijah & Hannah, b. Apr. 17, 1742	1	193
Lydia, m. Andrew **FRINK**, Oct. 9, 1770	2	45
Mary, d. Joshua & Sarah, b. Feb. 28, 1742	1	149
Mallathias, s Elijah & Hannah, b. June 10, 1744		
(Matthias?)	1	193
Matthais, m. Delight **HILL**, Apr. 5, 1778	2	231
Matthais, m. Jerusha **FITCH**, July 11, 1802	2	231
Nancy Manning, d. [Dan & Charlotte], b. May 5, 1809	3	23
Prudence, d. [Jacob], b. Apr. 30, 1738	2	157
Prudence, m. John **BOND**, Aug. 29, 1759; d. Dec. 25,		
1769, in the 59th y. of her age	2	151
Prudence, [d. Jacob & Prudence], b. [ ]	1	123
Prudence, see under Prudence **BOND**	2	157
Prudence, Davis, d. [Dan & Charlotte], b. Oct. 10, 1805	3	23
Rachel, d. Elijah & Han[na]h, b. Mar. 22, 1761	1	255
Rachal, m. Shubael **CROSS**, [ ]	3	78
Ralph, s. [Jacob & Jemime], b. Dec. 21, 1778	2	141
Rebeccah, d. Elijah & Hannah, b. May 21, 1737	1	94
Rebeckah, m. Joseph **MILLER**, Aug. 28, 1753	1	322
Rebeckah, m. Joseph **MILLARD**, Aug. 28, 1753	2	88
Rhoda, d. Joshua & Sarah, b. Jan. 23, 1740/41	1	149
Ruth, d. Joshua & Sarah, b. Feb. 24, 1736/7	1	149
Susan D., m. Henry **BACKUS**, Jan. 3, 1819, by Rev. C.B.		
Everest	3	86
Susannah Denison, d. [Dan & Charlotte], b. Dec. 4,		
1798	3	23
[SCOLFIELD], **SCHOLFIELD**, ——, b. Norwich, res. S. Windham,		
d. Mar. 3, 1860, ae. 16 m.	4	159-0
SCOTT, SCOT, Abby of Franklin, m. Jabez **LINCOLN**, Sept. 6,		
1807	3	62
Abigail, m. Joseph **BINGHAM**, Dec. 14, 1710	1	38
Abigail, d. Benjamin & Mary, b. Aug. 22, 1712; d. Jan.		
24, 1719/20	1	38a
Abigail, d. Benjamin & Mary, b Feb. 8, 1720/21	1	38a
Ebenezer, d. Apr. 19, 1700	A	12
Elizabeth, m. Jonathan **FISKE**, Aug. 9, 1750	1	302
Elizabeth, m. Jacob **LINKON**, Mar. 12, 1797	3	21

	Vol.	Page
SCOTT, SCOT, (cont.)		
Hannah, d. Benjamin & Mary, b. May 11, 1711	1	38a
Ichabod, s. Benjamin & Mary, b. Sept. 27, 1717	1	38a
Joseph, s. Ichabod & Phebe, b. Oct. 16, 1745	1	256
Julia A., m. Barnabus H. **POLLARD**, July 4, 1844, by		
Rev. Andrew Sharp	3	215
Mary, d. Benjamin & Mary, b. May 13, 1715	1	38a
Mary, d. Ich[abod] & Phebe, b. Sept. 10, 1745 [sic]	1	256
Sarah, m. Sam[ue]l **ROBINSON**, Jr., Apr. 13, 1773	2	95
Seymour, m. Sally **BENNET[T]**, Jan. 7, 1833, by Rev.		
A. Gregory, Willimantic	3	163
William, s. Benjamin & Mary, b. Sept. 9, 1708; d.		
Nov. 22, 1708	1	38a
William, s. Benjamin & Mary, b. Sept. 29, 1716	1	38a
Zebadiah, s. Benjamin & Mary, b. Feb. 14, 1713/14	1	38a
SCOVILLE, John B., m. Ellen **POTTER**, b. of Columbia, Mar.		
8, 1841, by Rev. J.E. Tyler	3	196
Temperance, of Bozrah, m. Philip A. **CAPEN**, of Windham,		
Apr. 25, 1841, by Rev. John E. Tyler	3	197
SCRANTON, W[illia]m N., painter, b. Voluntown, res. Willi-		
mantic, d. July 19, [1849], ae. 31	4	153
SCRIPTURE, John, s. John & Abigail, b. Apr. 25, 1716	1	12
Simeon, s. John & Abigail, b. Dec. 11, 1717	1	12
SEABURY, Sarah, m. John **MANNING**, Jr., Jan. 27, 1752	1	265
SEARLES, SEARL, SARLES, Abigail, d. Ebenezer & Martha,		
b. Feb. 7, 1721/2	1	60
Ebenezer, s. Ebenezer & Martha, b. May 8, 1716	1	60
Elisha, s. Ebenezer & Martha, b. May 20, 1718	1	60
Elisha, s. [Philip & Hannah], b. Nov. 4, 1775; d.		
May 6, 1778	2	199
Elisha, s. [Philip & Olive], b. Jan. 9, 1782	2	199
Gideon, s. Ebenezer & Martha, b. July 4, 1720	1	60
Hannah, w. Philip, d. Jan. 9, 1778	2	199
Hannah, d. [Philip & Olive], b. Aug. 18, 1785	2	199
Joel W., shoemaker, ae. 50, of Hampton, m. Lydia		
H. **FLINT**, ae. 42, tailoress, of Hampton,		
Jan. 21, 1851, by Rev. Henry Greenslit	4	118
John, s. Ebenezer & Martha, b. May 6, 1711	1	60
Mary, d. Ebenezer & Martha, b. Nov. 13, 1712	1	60
Philip, m. Hannah **TROWBRIDGE**, Dec. 29, 1774	2	199
Philip, m. Olive **FARNAM**, Oct. 25, 1780	2	199
Philip, s. [Philip & Olive], b. Aug. 19, 1783	2	199
Rufus, s. [Philip & hannah], b. Oct. 23, 1777;		
d. Jan. 9, 1778	2	199
William, s. Ebenezer & Martha, b. Oct. 13, 1728	1	60
SEARS, Sarah, m. George **YOUNG**, Mar. 29, 1823	3	112
SEAS, Mary, m. John **FFORD**, Aug. 5, 1735	1	163
SEGAR, Abigail, of Lebanon, m. Edward **ALLEN**, of Windham,		

	Vol.	Page
SEGAR, (cont.)		
Feb. 7, 1847, by Rev. John Cooper, Willimantic	3	234
Alice, d. [William], b. Oct. 4, 1796	2	176
Anne, d. William, b. June 25, 1794	2	176
Benjamin, s. [William], b. June 12, 1800	2	176
Benjamin, m. Martha **CONGDON**, Mar. 29, 1830, by		
Elder Babcock, at Pomfret	3	157
William, s. [William], b. June 1, 1798	2	176
William Penn, s. [Benjamin & Martha], b. Aug. 27, 1831	3	157
SELDEN, Charles, s. [Ezra & Mary], b. Oct. 18, 1807	3	41
Elijah, s. [Ezra & Mary], b. Aug. 11, 1809	3	41
Elijah, m. Wealthy **HALL**, of East Haddam, Apr. 17, 1811	3	41
Ezra, m. Mary **CONGDON**, Dec. 7, 1806	3	41
Ezra, d. June 30, 1813	3	41
Hannah, w. Elijah, d. Apr. 2, 1810	3	41
Mary, w. Ezra, d. Nov. 7, 1815	3	41
Sarah, d. [Ezra & Mary], b. June 6, 1811	3	41
SENVANTO, Julia M., ae. 21, b. S. Coventry, res. Willi-		
mantic, m. Addison A. **GODFREY**, merchant, ae. 20, b.		
S. Coventry, res. Willimantic, Oct. 13, 1850, by		
Rev. Henry Bromley	4	117
SESSIONS, SESIONS, Abiah, m. Ezekiel **HOLT**, May [ ], 1748	1	287
Asael, s. [John & Martha], b. June 12, 1769	2	143
Daniel C., m. Julia Edda **RUSS**, Apr. 21, 1844, by		
Andrew Sharp	3	215
Elisha, s. [John & Martha], b. Sept. 17, 1773	2	143
Esther, d. Joseph, Jr. & Esther, b. June 6, 1758	2	45
[E]unice, d. Joseph & Elizabeth, b. Feb. 25, 1731	1	143
Eunice, m. John **LOOMIS**, Jan. 5, 1775	2	173
Eunice, d. [John & Martha], b. Oct. 29, 1776	2	143
Isabella, ae. 28, b. Mansfield, res. Willimantic, m.		
Harry **BOSS**, spinner, ae. 37, b. Hampton, res.		
Willimantic, Mar. 3, 1851, by Rev. S.G. Williams	4	118
John, s. Joseph & Elizabeth, b. Apr. 8, 1741	1	143
John, m. Martha **NEFF**, Nov. 20, 1765	2	143
John, s. [John & Martha], b. Jan. 23, 1768	2	143
Joseph, s. Joseph & Elizabeth, b. Sept. 12, 1734	1	143
Joseph, Jr., m. Esther **PARRISH**, Jan. 26, 1758	2	45
Josiah, s. [John & Martha], b. June 28, 1771	2	143
SEYMOUR, Fanny, m. James **GEER**, Oct. 5, 1813	3	82
SHALLIESS, Francis, m. Ann **BARROWS**, Aug. 19, 1781	2	243
Joseph, s. [Francis & Ann], b. Oct. 24, 1783	2	243
William, s. [Francis & Ann], b. Dec. 14, 1781	2	243
SHARP, George, operative, ae. 19, m. Jerusha **CHILDS**, ae.		
17, Aug. 10, 1848	4	111
George, ae. 22, m. [ ], Aug. [1848],		
by Priest Magenty (?)	4	113
Martha L., d. Geo[rge], ae. 22, & Jerush[a], ae. 20,		

	Vol.	Page
SHARP, (cont.)		
of Willimantic, b. Aug. 10, 1850	4	12
SHATTUCK, SHATTOCK, Hannah, d. Nath[anie]ll & Ruth, b.		
Feb. 12, 1751	1	252
Hannah, m. Ralph **BINGHAM**, June 26, 1776	2	244
Mary, d. Nath[anie]ll & Ruth, b. Sept. 8, 1743	1	252
Mary, m. Stephen **BROWN**, Jr., Dec. 3, 1760	2	58
Nathaniel, m. Ruth **HEB[B]ARD**, Feb. 16, 1741/2	1	252
Nathaniell, s. Nathaniel & Ruth, b. June 30, 1748	1	252
SHAW, Abigail, d. William & Elizabeth, b. May 7, 1734	1	104
Benjamin, [twin with Joseph], s. William & Elizabeth,		
b. June 28, 1743	1	104
Elizabeth, d. William & Elizabeth, b. May 18, 1726	1	104
Ephraim, s. William & Elizabeth, b. Nov. 21, 1738	1	104
Esther, d. [William J. & Lydia], b. Feb. 15, 1756	2	20
Eunice, d. [William, Jr. & Lydia], b. Sept. 10,		
1750	2	20
Ezra, s. Israel & Mary, b. May 3, 1746	1	171
George, m. Martha **GATES**, Dec. 2, 1726	1	97
Hannah, d. [William, Jr. & Lydia], b. May 10, 1753	2	20
Israel, s. William & Johannah, b. Mar. 5, 1713	1	34
Israel, m. Mary **DANIEL**, Sept. 20, 1734	1	171
Johan[n]ah, d. George & Martha, b. Aug 19, 1732	1	97
John, s. George & Martha, b. Mar. 7, 1727/8; d.		
Jan. 11, 1730/31	1	97
John, s. George & Martha, b. Mar. 3, 1737/8	1	97
Joseph, [twin with Benjamin], s. William & Elizabeth,		
b. June 28, 1743	1	104
Lydia, d. William & Elizabeth, b. July 20, 1736	1	104
Mary, d. William & Elizabeth, b. Nov. 4, 1731	1	104
Mary, d. George & Martha, b. Apr. 20, 1735	1	97
Mary, d. Israel & Mary, b. Aug. 9, 1741; d. July 26,		
1742	1	171
Mehetable, d. Israel & Mary, b. May 5, 1736	1	171
Nath[anie]ll, s. George & Martha, b. Mar. 6, 1729/30;		
d. Feb. 6, 1740/41	1	97
Nathaniel, s. George & Martha, b. May 23, 1741	1	229
Samuel, m. Philena **CROSS**, Nov. 11, 1833, by Rev. Roger		
Bingham	3	166
Thomas, s. Israel & Mary, b. Apr. 21, 1738; d. July 19,		
1742	1	171
Thomas, s. Israel & Mary, b. Apr. 9, 1744	1	171
William, d. Mar. 13, 1715	1	34
William, m. Elizabeth **DAVICE**, Oct. 9, 1725	1	104
William, s. William & Elizabeth, b. Oct. 31, 1727; d.		
June 10, 1729	1	104
William, s. William & Elizabeth, b. Aug. 27, 1729	1	104
William, Jr., m. Lydia **FRAME**, Oct. 15, 1749	2	20

	Vol.	Page
SHEFFIELD, Abby, of Windham, m. David **PORTER**, of Lebanon, Oct. 18, 1841, by Rev. Nathan Wildman, of Lebanon	3	199
Elizabeth Straght, d. George H. & Sarah, b. Dec. 30, 1826	3	128
SHELDON, Charles S., s. W[illia]m H., miller, ae. 37, b. Mar. 22, 1849	4	11
Charlotte, m. Nath[anie]ll **ROBINSON**, Jan. 12, 1786	2	20
Henry, of Mansfield, m. Abigail **LONG**, of Windham, Sept. 6, 1829, by Rev. Jesse Fisher	3	137
Nelson, of Canterbury, m. Phebe E. **SHELDON**, of Palmer, Mass., Feb. 21, 1847, by Rev. T. Tallman, Scotland	3	234
Phebe E., of Palmer, Mass., m. Nelson **SHELDON**, of Canterbury, Feb. 21, 1847, by Rev. T. Tallman, Scotland	3	234
Samuel, m. Ruth **FAY**, July 26, 1829, by E. Lee Brown, Willimantic	3	137
SHEPARD, Abigail, [w. Asa], d. Jan. 27, 1852	3	127
Asa, m. Abigail **PALMER**, Aug. 17, 1826, by Rev. Jesse Fisher	3	127
Isaac, s. Chester, ae. 43, b. Mar. 28, [1849]	4	6
SHEPPARDSON, Abby, d. Otis, farmer, b. Mar. 9, [1850]	4	11
SHERMAN, Sarah Ann, m. Royal S. **COLBURN**, Mar. 18, 1833, by Rev. Alva Gregory	3	164
SHIFFT, Jemima, d. Jan. 29, 1786	1	202
Ruth, d. Dec. 3, 1784	1	202
William, s. Silas & Abigail, b. Dec. 14, 1751	1	202
SHIPPEY, Albert C., d. Hasara, woolen manufacturer, ae. 40, & Phelene, ae. 35, b. Mar. 16, [1851]	4	13
SHUTTS, John N., Rev., of New Brusnwick, N.J., m. Frances A. **ROBINS**, of Windham, Aug. 12, 1843, by Rev. John E. Tyler	3	210
SIBLEY, Lydia, m. Sam[ue]ll **PALMER**, 3rd, Jan. 18, 1738/9	1	186
SILSBRY, [see also **SILSBY** and **SILSBURY**], Elizabeth, d. Samuel & Elizabeth, b. Aug. 15, 1747	1	262
Sam[ue]l, m. Elizabeth **WOODWARD**, Dec. 5, 1746	1	262
Sarah, d. Sam[ue]l & Elizabeth, b. Mar. 1, 1748/9	1	262
SILSBURY, **SILSBERY**, [see also **SILSBY** and **SILSBRY**], Chloe, d. John & Huldah, b. Aug. 11, 1748	1	257
John, m. Huldah **CARPENTER**, May 12, 1746	1	257
Jonathan, d. Dec. 1714	1	44
Jonathan, s. John & Huldah, b. Jan. 30, 1746/7	1	257
SILSBY, **SILLSBEY** [see also **SILSBURY** and **SILSBRY**], Bethyah, d. June 6, 1725	1	54
Bridget, d. Sam[ue]l & Elizabeth, b. Aug. 3, 1754; d. Feb. 4, 1755	1	262
C[h]loe, m. Sam[ue]l **BAKER**, Jr., Sept. 27, 1774	2	92
Eliphas, s. Henry & Bethiah, b. Apr. 22, 1759	1	246

	Vol.	Page
SILSBY, SILLSBEY, (cont.)		
Elizabeth, d. Sam[ue]l & Elizabeth, d. May 12, 1757	1	262
Eurebius, s. Sam[ue]l & Eliza, b. Feb. 9, 1758	1	262
Hannah, m. Samuell **ABBE**, Mar. 15, 1710 (Written		
"**SALSBEY**")	1	22
Hannah, d. Henry & Bethiah, b. May 17, 1745	1	246
Henery, s. Jonathan & Lydia, b. Mar. 11, 1718	1	44
Henry, m. Bethiah **LASELL**, Apr. 5, 1744	1	246
Henry, s. Henry & Bethiah, b. Apr. 29, 1751; d.		
Nov. 22, 1752	1	246
Henry, s. Henry & Bethiah, b. May 31, 1753	1	246
John, s. Jonathan & Lydia, b. Apr. 4, 1723	1	54
Jonathan, m. Lydia **ALLEN**, Mar. 1, 1715	1	44
Jonathan, s. Henry & Bethiah, b. June 2, 1749	1	246
Jonathan, d. May 14, 1751	1	54
Julius, s. Sam[ue]l & Elizabeth, b. Oct. 7, 1752	1	262
Kerenhappack(?), d. Sam[ue]l & Elizabeth, b. Oct. 14,		
1751	1	262
Lasel, s. Henry & Bethiah, b. Mar. 30, 1755	1	246
Lydia, d. Jonathan & Lydia, b. Apr. 11, 1716	1	44
Lydia, d. Henry & Bethiah, b. Sept. 22, 1747	1	246
Mary, d. Jonathan & Lydia, b. Dec. 28, 1720	1	44
Ozias, s. Henry & Bethiah, b. June 15, 1761	1	246
Sam[ue]ll, s. Jonathan & Lydia, b. Apr. 4, 1726	1	54
Sam[ue]ll, s. Sam[ue]ll & Elizabeth, b. Nov. 4,		
1755	1	262
Sarah, m. Moses **COLLSON**, Apr. 10, 1766	2	121
SIMMONS, Edwin, merchant, ae. 30, b. Foster, res. Willi-		
mantic, m. Sally **PALMER**, ae. 26, b. Voluntown,		
res. Willimantic, Oct. 3, 1850, by Rev. Henry		
Bromley (His 2d marriage)	4	117
Sarah, m. George **MARTIN**, 3rd, May 7, 1778	2	101
SIMMS, Samuel, ae. 36, b. Ashford, m. Julia A. **WELDIN**, ae.		
19, Oct. 10, 1847, by Daniel Dorchester	4	111
SIMONS, SIMONDS, Abel, s. [Jacob, Jr. & Mehetable], b.		
Feb. 8, 1774; d. Sept 29, 1776	2	207
Abigail, d. Joshua & Mary, b. Apr. 13, 1740; d. Apr.		
22, 1740	1	112
Abigail, d. [Joshua & Mary], b. Feb. 14, 1743	1	112
Abigail, d. Jacob & Ruth, b. Dec. 15, 1749; d. July		
26, 1750	1	192
Ada, d. [Nathan & Prudence], b. June 26, 1787	2	197
Adriel, m. Sarah **BINGHAM**, Mar. 8, 1781	2	241
Adroyal, s. [Jeduthan & Rebeckah], b. Feb. 2, 1757	2	24
Alfred F., laborer, ae. 34, m. Laura A. **RIDER**, ae. 22,		
May 26, [1850], by Tho[ma]s Tallman	4	114
Ama, d. Jacob, 3rd, & Jerusha, b. Mar. 21, 1756	1	273
Ama, d. [Jacob, 3rd, & Jerusha], b. Mar. 21, 1756	2	207

	Vol.	Page
SIMONS, SIMONDS, (cont.)		
Amelia, d. [Gideon & Anna], b. Aug. 29, 1767	3	78
Amhurst, s. [Shubael & Tamma], b. Apr. 1, 1775	2	156
Ann, d. Jonathan & Meriam, b. Dec. 19, 1718; d.		
Jan. 12, 1720/21	1	9
Ann, d. Jonathan & Meriam, b. May 12, 1721	1	9
Ann, m. Lues **COVEL**, May 30, 1745	1	140
Anna, d. [Jacob, Jr. & Mehetable], b. Feb. 16,		
1776	2	207
Anson, s. [Jeduthan & Rebeckah], b. Oct. 18, 1768	2	24
Arad, s. Nathan & Sarah, b. Aug. 27, 1754	1	203
Babcock, twin with Jonathan, s. [Gideon & Anna],		
b. Dec. 26, 1782; d. 3 weeks after birth	2	78
Betsey, d. [Nathan & Prudence], b. Feb. 25, 1774;		
d. Dec. 25, 1777	2	197
Betsey, d. [Nathan & Prudence], b. Dec. 12, 1777	2	197
Billie, twin with Shubael, s [Shubael & Tamma],		
b. Mar. 14, 1770	2	156
C[h]loe, d. [Jacob, Jr. & Mehetable], b. Aug. 18,		
1761	1	273
Chloe, d. [Jacob, Jr. & Mehetable], b. Aug. 18, 1761	2	207
C[h]loe, d. [Gideon & Anna], b. July 28, 1763; d.		
[ ] 19, [ ]	2	78
Clarre, d. [Jacob, Jr. & Mehetable], b. Mar. 3, 1782	2	207
Darius, s. Nathan & Sarah, b. July 24, 1742	1	203
David, s. Jacob & Ruth, b. July 12, 1745	1	192
David, s. [Elijah & Margaret], b. Jan. 11, 1781	2	232
Elijah, s. Jacob & Mary, b. Aug. 29, 1723	1	44
Elijah, s. Jacob & Jerusha, b. Dec. 2, 1753; d. Oct.		
8, 1754	1	273
Elijah, s. [Jacob, 3rd, & Jerusha], b. Dec. 2, 1753;		
d. Oct. 8, 1754	2	207
Elijah, m. Margaret **CANNADA**, Apr. 6, 1780	2	232
Elijah, m. Mary **STANDFORD**, b. of Windham, Feb. 28,		
1842, by Rev. John E. Tyler	3	200
Eliphalet, s. Joshua & Mary, b. June 5, 1737	1	112
Elizabeth, [d. Jeduthan & Rebeckah], b. May 2, 1771	2	24
[E]unis, d. Jonathan & Meriam, b. May 16, 1713	1	9
Eunice, d. [Jacob, 3rd, & Jerusha], b. Oct. 29, 1751,		
in Norwich	2	207
Eunice, d. Jacob, 3rd, & Jerusha, b. Oct. 29, 1757,		
in Norwich	1	273
Eunice, m. Samuel **CUTLER**, Nov. 23, 1769	2	177
Ezekiel, s. Joshua & Mary, b. June 13, 1733	1	112
Fanny, d. [Elijah & Margaret], b. Apr. 21, 1783	2	232
Gideon, s. Joshua & Mary, b. Feb. 7, 1734/5	1	112
Gideon, m. Anna **GENNINGS**, [ ]	2	78
Gilbert, of Coventry, m. Sally **HUCHENS**, of Windham,		

	Vol	Page
SIMONS, SIMONDS, (cont.)		
July 10, 1831, by John Baldwin, J.P.	3	154
Hannah, d. Nathan & Sarah, b. May 2, 1752	1	203
Hannah, m. Hezekiah **LINKON**, Feb. 6, 1771	2	161
Jacob, s. Jonathan & Miriam, b. Sept. 11, 1708	1	9
Jacob, m. Mary **CRANE**, Apr. 4, 1710	1	44
Jacob, s. Jacob & Mary, b. Jan. 22, 1719/20	1	44
Jacob, Jr., m. Ruth **GRAY**, May 2, 1728	1	103
Jacob, m. Jerusha **PARRISH**, Apr. 21, 1747	1	273
Jacob, 3rd, m. Jerusha **PARISH**, Apr. 21, 1747	2	207
Jacob, Jr., m. Mehetable **PRESTON**, Sept. 28, 1760	1	273
Jacob, Jr., m. Mehetable **PRESTON**, Sept. 28, 1760	2	207
Jacob, s. [Jacob, Jr. & Mehetable], b. Dec. 29, 1768	1	273
Jacob, s. [Jacob, Jr. & Mehetable], b. Dec. 29, 1768	2	207
Jacob, d. [ ]	1	132
James, twin with [ ], s. [Gideon & Anna], b. Aug. 6, 1771	2	78
Jeduthan, [twin with Jemima], s. Jacob & Mary, b. Apr. 6, 1729	1	44
Jeduthan, m. Rebeckah **DIMMICK**, Oct. 19, 1756	2	24
Jeduthan, s. [Jeduthan & Rebeckah], b. Sept. 20, 1763	2	24
Jeduthan, farmer, d. July 8, [1850], ae. 87	4	156
Jemima, [twin with Jeduthan], d. Jacob & Mary, b. Apr. 6, 1729	1	44
Jemima, m. Zebediah **HOLT**, Jr., Feb. 16, 1758	2	47
Jemima, d. [Jeduthan & Rebeckah], b. July 29, 1761; d. Jan. 23, 1764	2	24
Jemima, d. [Jeduthan & Rebeckah], b. Nov. 11, 1765	2	24
Jerusha, d. [Jacob, 3rd & Jerusha], b. Nov. 2, 1747	2	207
Jerusha, d. Jacob & Jerusha, b. Nov. 23, 1747	1	273
Jerusha, w. Jacob, d. Apr. 10, 1760	1	273
Jerusha, w. Jacob, 3rd, d. Apr. 10, 1760	2	207
Jerusha, m. Stephen **DURKEE**, May 15, 1766	2	153
John, s. Jacob, Jr. & Ruth, b. Nov. 8, 1737; d. Jan. 2, 1737/8	1	103
John, s. Jacob, Jr. & Ruth, b. Mar. 27, 1739	1	192
John, s. Nathan & Sarah, b. Oct. 10, 1760	1	217
Jonathan, m. Miriam **ALLYN**, Dec. 10, 1702	1	9
Jonathan, m. Wealth[e]an **ALLEN**, Dec. 16, 1702	A	1
Jonathan, s. Jonathan & Miriam, b. Mar. 29, 1707	1	9
Jonathan, s. Jonathan & Meriam, d. Oct. 3, 1707	1	10
Jonathan, s. Jonathan & Mariam, b. July 26, 1723	1	55
Jonathan, d. Sept. 14, 1727, ae. 46 y. 5 m.	1	10
Jonathan, m. Elizabeth **WILLIAMS**, Nov. 21, 1744	1	247
Jonathan, twin with Babcock, s. [Gideon & Anna], b. Dec. 26, 1782	2	78
Joshua, s. Jonathan & Miriam, b. Mar. 24, 1705	1	9
Joshua, m. Mary **BADCO[C]K**, Mar. 27, 1733	1	112

	Vol.	Page

SIMONS, SIMONDS, (cont.)

Lama, m. Charles **GALLUP**, Feb. 11, 1838, by Rev.
Alfred Burnham — 3 — 184

Lama, see also Lima

Levi, s. [Adriel & Sarah], b. Dec. 21, 1785 — 2 — 241

Lima, d. [Adriel & Sarah], b. Nov. 22, 1781 — 2 — 241

Lima, see also Lama

Lois, d. Jonathan & Meriam, b. Mar. 15, 1711 — 1 — 9

Lois, m. William **PRESTON**, Feb. 28, 1733/4 — 1 — 136

Lois, d. [Jacob, Jr. & Mehetable], b. Mar. 1,
1767 — 2 — 207

Loue, d. Nathan & Sarah, b. Jan. 8, 1745 — 1 — 203

Louisa, m. William **BIBBINS**, Apr. 23, 1769 — 2 — 158

Louisa, d. Alfred & Laura, b. Sept. 1, 1850 — 4 — 13

Louisa, d. Elijah, farmer, ae. 34, & Laura, ae. 27,
b. Sept. 10, 1850 — 4 — 14

Lucian, s. [Gideon & Anna], b. Jan. 17, 1778 — 2 — 78

Lucius, twin with Lucy, [s. Gideon & Anna], b. Mar.
27, 1775; d. Jan. 23, 1781 — 2 — 78

Lucy, d. [Jacob, Jr. & Mehetable], b. Aug. 23, 1763 — 1 — 273

Lucy, d. [Jacob, Jr. & Mehetable], b. Aug. 23, 1763 — 2 — 207

Lucy, twin with Lucius, [d. Gideon & Anna], b. Mar.
27, 1775; d. Sept. 26, 1778 — 2 — 78

Lucy, d. [Nathan & Prudence], b. July 31, 1780 — 2 — 197

Lucy, m. Jerome **BROWN**, Mar. 14, 1802 — 3 — 60

Lydia, d. Nathan & Sarah, b. Nov. 21, 1757 — 1 — 203

Lydia, d. [Gideon & Anna], b. Mar. 8, 1780 — 2 — 78

Lydia, d. [Nathan & Prudence], b. Feb. 18, 1783 — 2 — 197

Martha, d. Jacob & Ruth, b. Sept. 29, 1741; d. Dec.
12, 1741 — 1 — 192

Martha, d. Jacob & Ruth, b. Jan. 15, 1743/2; d. Oct.
19, 1744 — 1 — 192

Mary, d. Jacob & Mary, b. Aug. 1, 1726 — 1 — 44

Mary, d. [Joshua & Mary], b. Dec. 10, 1744 — 1 — 112

Mary, m. John **SPENCER**, Nov. 5, 1746 — 1 — 272

Mary, d. Jacob & Jerusha, b. Mar. 28, 1760 — 1 — 273

Mary, d. [Jacob, 3rd, & Jerusha], b. Mar. 28, 1760 — 2 — 207

Mary, d. [Gideon & Anna], b. Oct. 15, 1773; d. Sept.
26, 1775 — 2 — 78

Mary, w. [Jacob], d. Sept. 30, 1776 — 1 — 132

Meriam, m. Caleb **BADCO[C]K**, May 7, 1728 — 1 — 92

Meriam, d. Jacob & Ruth, b. Sept. 1, 1730; d. Aug. 26,
1733 — 1 — 103

Meriam, d. Jacob, Jr. & Ruth, b. Mar. 6, 1734/5 — 1 — 103

Mille, d. [Jacob, Jr. & Mehetable], b Apr. 27, 1778 — 2 — 207

Minor, s. [Gideon & Anna], b. Feb. 5, 1766; d. Feb.
20, 17[ ] — 2 — 78

Nancy, d. [Shubael & Tamma], b. Aug. 31, 1783 — 2 — 156

	Vol.	Page
SIMONS, SIMONDS, (cont.)		
Nathan, s. Jonathan & Miriam, b. Sept. 10, 1715	1	9
Nathan, m. Sarah **BALCOM**, Oct. 29, 1741	1	203
Nathan, s. Nathan & Sarah, b. Apr. 2, 1749	1	203
Nathan, m. Prudence **BROUGHTON**, Apr. 15, 1773	2	197
Nathan, s. [Nathan & Prudence], b. May 31, 1785;		
d. Nov. 15, 1788	2	197
Nathaniel Thomas, s. [Nathan & Prudence], b. Feb.		
8, 1792	2	197
Olive, d. [Jacob, Jr. & Mehetable], b. Feb. 24,		
1765	1	273
Olive, d. [Jacob, Jr. & Mehetable], b. Feb. 5, 1765	2	207
Olive, of Hampton, m. Dilauna **BACKUS**, Jan 5, 1811	3	54
Prudence, d. [Nathan & Prudence], b. Jan. 25, 1776	2	197
Rebeckah, d. [Jeduthan & Rebeckah], b. May 18, 1759	2	24
Richard, s. Jacob & Mary, b. Oct. 18, 1731	1	44
Robert, d. Aug. 29, 1724, ae. nearly 79 y.	1	10
Royal, s. [Gideon & Anna], b. Oct. 9, 1764	2	78
Rufus, s. Jacob & Mary, d. Jan. 24, 1731/2	1	132
Rufus, s. [Shubael & Tamma], b. Sept. 29, 1773; d.		
Apr 2, 1774	2	156
Rufus, s. [Shubael & Tamma], b. Sept. 17, 1777	2	156
Ruth, d. Jacob & Ruth, b. Mar. 15, 1728/9	1	103
Ruth, m. Seth **MEACHAM**, Dec. 19, 1751	1	315
Sally, d. [Nathan & Prudence], b. July 10, 1789; d.		
Aug. 20, 1792	2	197
Sarah, d. Nathan & Sarah, b. Mar. 10, 1746/7	1	203
Sarah, d. [Jacob, Jr. & Mehetable], b. Mar. 31, 1771	1	273
Sarah, d.]Jacob, Jr. & Mehetable], b. Mar. 30, 1771	2	207
Sempter, s. [Jeduthan & Rebeckah], b. May 22, 1773	2	24
Septer, s. [Adriel & Sarah], b. Nov. 19, 1782	2	241
Shubael, s. Jacob & Jerusha, b. May 6, 1749	1	273
Shubael, s. [Jacob, 3rd, & Jerusha], b. May 6, 1749	2	207
Shubael, m. Tamma **DURKEE**, Apr. 6, 1769	2	156
Shubael, twin with Billie, s. [Shubael & Tamma], b.		
Mar. 14, 1770	2	156
Tamar, m. William **MORE**, June 10, 1728	1	69
Tamarsin, d. Jonathan & Miriam, b. July 22, 1703	1	9
Tamarson, d. Jonathan & Meriam, d. Jan. 27, 1706	1	10
Tamazin, d. Jacob & Mary, b. Nov. 30, 1710	1	44
Tamarsen, m. Mary **WILLIAMS**, June 20, 1728	A	1
Tammey, d. [Shubael & Tamma], b. Aug. 15, 1772; d.		
Sept. 18, 1772	2	156
Tammey, d. [Shubael & Tamma], b. May 3, 1780	2	156
Tammey, d. [Adriel & Sarah], b. July 7, 1784	2	241
Theodore, s. Jacob, Jr. & Ruth, b. Jan. 27, 1732/3	1	103
William, s. [Gideon & Anna], b. Mar. 8, 1769	2	78
——, twin with James, d. [Gideon & Anna], b.		

	Vol.	Page
SIMONS, SIMONDS, (cont.)		
Aug. 6, 1771; d. same day	2	78
SIMPSON, Fanny, m. Benj[amin] P. **BUSHNELL**, Nov. 28, 1839,		
by Rev. Reuben Ransom	3	191
Laura, of Willimantic, m. Harvey **CRANE**, of Hartford,		
Dec. 2, 1834, by Rev. Philo Judson	3	171
Mary, of Windham, m. Josiah **LAVELL**, Jr., of Quincy,		
Mass., Dec. 16, 1830, by Rev. R.T. Crampton	3	149
Peter, m. Mary **RICHARDSON**, b. of Windham, Sept 30,		
1832, by Rev. Alva Gregory	3	161
SINCLAIR, Lucy, m. Benjamin **PERRY**, Nov. [ ], 1821, by		
Rev. C.B. Everest	3	96
SKIFF, SKIFFE, SKEFFE, Abigail, d. Nathaniell & Hannah, b.		
Oct. 16, 1727	1	90
Elizabeth, d Nathaniell & Hannah, b. Nov. 27, 1729	1	90
Elizabeth, m. Joshua **LASSAL**, Jan. 16, 1739/40	1	212
Hannah, d. Nath[anie]ll & Hannah, b. Apr. 14, 1725	1	29
Hannah, d. Nathaniell & Hannah, d. Sept. 14, 1737	1	90
Hannah, d. Aug. 22, 1775, in the 83rd y. of her age	1	90
Jemima, d. Nathaniell & Hannah, b. May 25, 1722	1	29
Jemima, d. Dea. Nath[anie]l, d. Jan. 29, 1786	2	53
Joseph, s. Nathaniell & Hannah, b. Mar. 20, 1719/20	1	29
Nathaniell, m. Hannah [ ]*, April. 24, 1716		
(*correction "Her surname was **CARY**; she was dau.		
Joseph & Hannah, b. Mar. 7, 1693. Parentage proved		
by will of her father. (Correction noted by		
Kendall P. Hayward, Aug. 9, 1946." Entry typed and		
affixed to original manuscript.)	1	29
Nathaniell, d. Apr. 24, 1723, ae. 78 y.	1	29
Nath[anie]ll, Dea., d. Mar. 23, 1761	1	90
Ruth, d. Nathaniel & Hannah, b. Mar. 31, 1718	1	29
Ruth, d. Dec. 31, 1741, ae. 90 y.	1	90
Ruth, d. Dr. Nath[anie]ll, d. Dec. 3, 1784, ae. 66	1	287
Ruth, d. Dea. Nath[anie]l, d. Dec. 3, 1784	2	53
Zerviah, d. Nathaniell & Hannah, b. Jan. 13, 1733/4	1	90
Zerviah, m. Ezekiel **CARY**, Mar. 15, 1764	2	97
SKINNER, Eliza H., ae. 19, b. Bolton, res. Springfield, m		
John D. **BARBER**, merchant, ae. 31, b. W. Spring-		
field, res. Springfield, Nov. 19, 1850, by Rev.		
Jno. Cady	4	118
Elizabeth, m. Jasper **GIDDENS**, Oct. 9, 1765	2	111
Mary, m. Hezekiah **RIPLEY**, Nov. 25, 1746	1	262
SLADE, Dean, m. Mariot **FELCH**, Aug. 12, [1832], by Rev. Alva		
Gregory	3	160
SLATE, Anne, d William & Elizabeth, b. Apr. 29, 1710	1	43
Daniel, s. William & Elizabeth, b. Mar. 30, 1708	1	43
Ebenezer, s. William & Elizabeth, b. Jan. 19, 1717/18	1	43
Elizabeth, d. William & Elizabeth, b. Aug. 29, 1705	1	43

	Vol.	Page
SLATE, (cont.)		
Ezek[i]el, s. William & Elizabeth, b. Dec. 26, 1719	1	43
John, s. William & Elizabeth, b. June 7, 1715	1	43
Mary, m. Luke **FLINT**, June 6, 1776	2	135
Mehetable, m. Daniel **CLARK**, Oct. 19, 1780	2	250
Samuell, s. William & Elizabeth, b. Nov. 8, 1711	1	43
William, s. W[illia]m & Elizabeth, b. Dec. 7, 1703	A	28
SLY, Caroline, m. Henry **KELLEY**, Mar. 21, 1833, by Rev. Alva Gregory	3	164
SMALL, Alvin C., m. Laura **BALCOM**, Feb. 1, 1846, at Willimantic, by John Cooper	3	227
Freeman, m. Betsey O.C. **KENYON**, Feb. 6, 1844, by Rev. Andrew Sharp	3	213
SMITH, Abigail, m. Daniel **HOLT**, Mar. 31, 1730	1	120
Abijah, s. Daniel & Rebeckah, b. June 29, 1729	1	151
Abner, m. [ ] **TRACY**, [ ]	3	101-2
Alethea, d. [Nathaniel & Hannah], b. Mar. 14, 1757	2	18
Alitheah, d. [James & Lois], b. Apr. 5, 1767	2	125
Almira, d. [Joshua & Lora], b. Apr. 3, 1797	3	39
Ama, m. Elijah **LILLIE**, June 7, 1781	2	239
Amelia, w. Benj[amin], d. Apr. 25, 1846	3	123
Amey, d. Josiah & Amey, b. Sept. 23, 1737	1	178
Amey, w. Josiah, d. July 13, 1746	1	178
Amey, d. [Nathaniel & Hannah], b. Oct. 22, 1762	2	18
Amy, m. Thomas **BINGHAM**, Feb. 13, 1766	2	117
Anna, m. Capt. Hez[ekiah] M. **BAKER**, Mar. 30, 1830, by Walter Williams, J.P. Canterbury	3	159
Asa, s. [Matthew & Annas], b. Feb. 20, 1792	3	9
Benj[ami]n, s. Stephen & Mary, b. Feb. 25, 1748	1	182
Benj[ami]n, m. C[h]loe **LASSEL**, Sept. 10, 1759	2	48
Benjamin, s. [Benj[ami]n & Cloe], b. Feb. 28, 1764	2	48
Benjamin, m. Amelia **MANNING**, Oct. 3, 1792	3	123
Benjamin, d. Apr. 24, 1834	3	43
Benjamin, d. Apr. 24, 1834	3	123
Calleb, s. Josiah & Elizabeth, b. Dec. 14, 1751	1	267
Caroline, d. [Benjamin & Amelia], b. Dec. 8, 1793	3	123
Caroline, res. Scotland, d. [Apr.] 10, [1849], ae. 56	4	153
Caroline Francis, d. David F., farmer, ae. 49, & Caroline, ae. 43, b. Oct. 26, [1849]	4	9
Chandler, m. Jane. F. **ROBINSON**, Jan. 15, 1837, by Rev. William A. Curtis	3	181
Charles s. [Benjamin & Amelia], b. June 25, 1797	3	123
Charles, s. Joshua & Ann, b. Sept. 14, 1807	3	143
Charles, m. Mary **ABBE**, Nov. 3, 1835, at North Windham. "Obtained from the Parish Register of the St. Paul's Church, Windham."	3	143
Charles L., m. Sophia **BURNHAM**, Sept. 11, 1826, by Rev.		

	Vol.	Page
SMITH, (cont.)		
Jesse Fisher	3	127
Charles Lucas, s. [Josiah, Jr. & Eunice], b. Mar. 12, 1802	2	214
Charlotte Ann, d. [Jairus & Nancy], b. Aug. 2, 1819	3	92
Charlotte Ann, m. Christopher **FERGUSON**, b. of Windham, May 28, 1838, by Rev. John E. Tyler	3	186
Charlotte Augusta, d. [Abner], b. Nov. 10, 1818	3	101-2
Chauncey Martin, s. [David F. & Caroline], b. Oct. 26, 1837	3	197
C[h]loe, d. [Benj[ami]n & C[h]loe], b. Aug. 16, 1766	2	48
Clarisse, d. [Jonah & Alathea], b. Nov. 16, 1766	2	55
Clinton, s. [Marcus & Alice], b. Feb. 25, 1835	3	118
Cornelia, of Windham, m. David **BENJAMIN**, of Preston, Mar. 23, 1835, by Rev. Jesse Fisher	3	173
Daniel, s. Daniel & Rebeckah, b. Dec. 7, 1733	1	151
Daniel, d. [s.] Josiah & Amey, b. Feb. 2, 1743/4	1	178
Daniel, m. Elizabeth **SAWYER**, Jan. 25, 1767	2	123
David Augustus, s. [Luther P. & Laura], b. July 8, 1827	3	139
David F., m. Caroline **TYLER**, May 11, 1829	3	197
Dorcas, m. Joel **DODGE**, June 18, 1753	1	322
Dwight, [s. Charles L. & Sophia], b. May 9, 1827	3	127
Edwin, m. Amanda **FRINK**, Oct. 16, [1828], by Rev. Dennis Platt, Willimantic Falls	3	132
Edwin Tyler, s. [David F. & Caroline], b. Sept. 6, 1835	3	197
Eleazer, s. Jonah & Alathea, b. Jan. 14, 1762	2	55
Eleazer, of Canterbury, m. Joanna **FOX**, of Windham, Dec. [ ], 1832, by Rev. John Storrs	3	162
Elias, s Josiah & Elizabeth, b. June 10, 1750; d. Oct. 21, 1771	1	267
Elijah, s. [Matthew & Annas], b. July 20, 1789	3	9
Elisha, Lieut., d. May 1, 1714	1	17
Elisha Palmer, s. [Josiah, Jr & Eunice], b. Oct. 20, 1789	2	214
Elisha Tracy, s [Abner], b. Dec. 12, 1820	3	101-2
Elisha, d. [Josiah & Elizabeth], d. Nov. 3, 1771	1	267
Elizabeth, w Elisha, d. Jan. 20, 1703	A	13
Elizabeth, d. Josiah & Elizabeth, b. Mar. 24, 1753	1	267
Elizabeth, m. Adrian **ROBINSON**, Apr. 18, 1793	2	144
Elmira, d. [Marcus & Alice], b. Nov. 5, 1831	3	118
Emily, [d. Abner], b. Apr. 10, 1827	3	101-2
Emily, m. Harvey **WINCHESTER**, b. of Windham, Oct. 10, 1836, by Rev William A. Curtis	3	180
Emily, of Windham, m. Isaac **GOODSPEED**, of Southbridge, Mass., June 12, 1837, by Rev. Philo Judson, at Willimantic Village	3	183

	Vol.	Page
SMITH, (cont.)		
Emily, of Scotland, m. Josiah F. **PHILLIPS**, of Canterbury, Nov. 26, 1846, by Rev. T. Tallman, of Scotland	3	232
Emma, d. John, merchant, ae. 45, & Laura, ae. 32, of Willimantic, b. Oct. [ ], 1850	4	12
Esther, d. Elisha & Elizabeth, b. Nov. 24, 1702	A	13
Easther, m. Ebenezer **WALES**, Oct. 20, 1719	1	34
Eunice, d. Benj[ami]n & C[h]loe, b. Mar. 13, 1762	2	48
Eunice, d. [Solomon & Eunice], b. July 8, 1770	2	63
Eunice, d. [Josiah, Jr. & Eunice], b. Feb. 24, 1780	2	214
Fanny, d. [Matthew & Annas], b. Aug. 7, 1790	3	9
Frank Howard, [s. William & Hannah W.], b. Jan. 3. 1841	3	203
George, s. [Benjamin & Amelia], b. July 24, 1805	3	123
George, s. [Luther P. & Laura], b. May 31, 1824	3	139
George, [s. Charles L. & Sophia], b. Dec. 31, 1831	3	127
Guilford, s. Charles & Mary, b. May 12, 1839	3	143
Harriet A., d. A.B., watchmaker, ae. 38, & Ann M., ae. 22, of Willimantic, b. Mar. 20, 1851	4	12
Harriet Augusta, d. [David F. & Caroline], b May 21, 1830	3	197
Helen Elizabeth, d. [David F. & Caroline]., b. July 2, 1832	3	197
Henry, s. [Luther P. & Laura], b. Aug. 3, 1815	3	139
Henry, m. Charlotte M. **PAGE**, Oct. 7, 1844, by Rev. Andrew Sharp, Willimantic	3	317
Henry, merchant, ae. 21, b. N. Scituate, res. California, m. Emelya **WITHERELL**, operative, ae. 19, b. So. Glocester, res. Willimantic, Jan. 12, 1851, by Rev. Blush	4	117
Henry S., m. Mary A. **PRENTIS**, Mar. 8, 1841, by Rev. And[rew] Sharpe, Willimantic	3	196
Horace, m. Eliza **JAPSON**, b. of Springfield, Mass., Mar. 12, 1838, by Rev. John E. Tyler	3	185
Jarius, s. [Josiah & Elizabeth], b. June 22, 1759	1	267
Jarius, m. Nancy **BINGHAM**, Oct. 18, 1818	3	92
Jairus, s. [Jairus & Nancy], b. Dec. 31, 1823	3	92
James, s. Stephen & Mary, b. Jan. 6, 1744/5	1	182
James, m. Lois **PRESTON**, Apr. 30, 1766	2	125
James, s. John, machinist, ae. 42, & Lucy, ae. 29, of Willimantic, b. Mar. 3, 1848	4	1
James L., m. Lucy **LASELL**, June 18, 1823	3	114
James M., d. Mar. 28, [1850], ae. 3	4	155
Jerusha, m. William **PARRISH**, Nov. 8, 1716	1	67
John, s. Stephen & Mary, b. May 18, 1738	1	182
John, m. Lucy **PALMER**, Nov. 6, 1842, by Rev. John B Guild, Willimantic	3	206

	Vol.	Page
SMITH, (cont.)		
John H., s. L[o]uis, ae. 33, & Sophy, ae. 33, b.		
May 19, [1847]	4	3
John S., m. Mary M. **RIDER**, Apr. 15, 1832, by Rev.		
Rich[ar]d F. Cleveland	3	160
Jonah, s. Josiah & Elizabeth, b. Dec. 6, 1747	1	267
Jonah, m. Alathea **CARY**, Nov. 15, 1759	2	55
Jonathan, m. Amelia **JENNINGS**, Oct. 28, 1832, by		
Rev. Roger Bingham	3	162
Joseph, of Willimantic, d. Aug. 15, 1860, ae. 2 m.	4	161
Joseph Josiah, [s Charles L. & Sophia], b. Nov 2,		
1835	3	127
Joshua, s. [Solomon & Eunice], b. Jan. 4, 1766	2	63
Joshua, m. Lora **ALLEN**, Jan. 29, 1790	3	39
Joshua, d. July [ ], 1821, ae. 51	3	89
Joshua, d. Sept. 1, 1821	3	39
Josiah, m. Elizabeth **ROBINSON**, Nov. 13, 1746	1	267
Josiah, Jr., m. Eunice **PALMER**, Dec. 25, 1776	2	214
Julia, of Windham, m. Joseph **HYDE**, of Lebanon, Sept.		
12, 1825, by Rev. C.B. Everest	3	115
Julia Elizabeth, d. William, b. May 3, 1832	3	161
Laura, d. [Luther P. & Laura], b. Apr. 11, 1822	3	139
Lewis A., m. Sophia **PALMER**, b. of Windham, [ ],		
by Rev. Daniel G. Sprague	3	181
Lora, [w. Joshua], d. Apr. 14, 1800	3	39
Luceanna, d. Daniel & Rebeckah, b. Feb. 7, 1732/3	1	151
Lucy, d. [Josiah, Jr. & Eunice], b. Oct. 3, 1783	2	214
Lucy, m. Luther D. **LEACH**, Oct. 24, 1811	3	30
Luther P., b. Jan. 4, 1790; m. Laura **LOOMIS**, Sept. 12,		
1814	3	139
Lydia, d. Josiah & Amey, b. Jan. 18, 1741/2	1	178
Lydia, m. Sam[ue]ll **BAKER**, Jr., Dec. 8, 1763	2	92
Lydia, d. [Nathaniel & Hannah], b. May 21, 1765	2	18
Lydia W., of Willimantic, Windham, m. Zenas O.		
LOMBARD, of Lebanon, June 26, 1837, by Rev B.		
Cook, Jr.	3	182
M. Annette, d. Noah A., ae 28, & Laura, ae. 27, b.		
Nov. 12, 1848	4	6
Marcus, s. [Josiah, Jr. & Eunice], b. Aug. 15, 1798	2	214
Marcus, s. [Abner], b. Sept. 10, 1822	3	101-2
Marcus, m. Alice **PALMER**, Feb. 17, 1825, by Rev Jesse		
Fisher	3	118
Marcus, m. Deborah **WEBB**, Feb. 21, 1845, by Rev. Andrew		
Sharp	3	220
Marcus, farmer, d. May 3, [1849], ae. 50	4	154
Marcus, d. Aug. 3, [1849], ae. 63 (Entered among		
births)	4	6
Marg[a]ret, m. Isaac **PARRISH**, Mar. 31, 1720/21	1	57

	Vol.	Page
SMITH, (cont.)		
Marian, d. [Marcus & Alice], b. Mar. 28, 1826	3	118
Martha, d. Elisha & Elizabeth, b. Apr. 26, 1713	1	17
Martha, d. [Josiah & Elizabeth], b. Aug. 30, 1757	1	267
Martha, m. Daniel **BARNAM**, Apr. 20, 1780	2	14
Martin, of Vernon, Conn., m. Clarissa **HUNT**, of Bolton, Conn., Apr. 2, 1845, by Rev. Charles Noble, Willimantic	3	221
Mary, d. Elisha & Elizabeth, b. May 23, 1714	1	17
Mary, d. Josiah & Amey, b. Nov 19, 1739	1	178
Mary, d. Stephen & Mary, b. July 25, 1741	1	182
Mary, m. Elisha **HURLBURT**, Oct. 18, 1747	1	272
Mary, m. Joshua **WIGHT**, Jr., Nov. 16, 1762	2	89
Mary, d. [Solomon & Eunice], b Dec. 4, 1763	2	63
Mary, w. Stephen, d. Apr. 13, 1766	1	182
Mary, m. Alfred **KINNE**, b. of Windham, Apr. 10, 1839, by Rev. John E. Tyler	3	188
Mary, d. Charles & Mary, b. Feb 20, 1842	3	143
Mary F., d. Lyman F., laborer, ae. 39, & Jane, ae. 39, of Willimantic, b. Mar. 25, 1851	4	12
Mary P., m. Enoch G. **BOONE**, b. of Windham, Jan. 31, 1841, by Rev. P.T. Kenney, Willimantic	3	196
Matthew, m. Annas **STRICKLAND**, Mar. 20, 1788	3	9
Ma[t]thew, of Chaplin, m. Emma **KINNE**, of Windham, Oct. 18, 1828, by Samuel Perkins, J.P.	3	131
Mehetable, m. Thomas **CASSAL**, Sept. 23, 1734	1	162
Mehitable, d. [Stephen & Mary], b. Nov. 3, 1754	1	182
Minor, s. Nath[anie]l & Hannah, b. June 21, 1760	2	18
Nancy P., d. Apr. 12, [1850], ae. 7 m.	4	155
Nathaniel, m. Hannah **WALDEN**, Oct. 21, 1756	2	18
Noah A., m. Laura A. **HOVEY**, b. of Willimantic, Sept. 7, 1846, by Rev. John Cooper	3	230
Olive, d. [Josiah, Jr. & Eunice], b. Dec. 20, 1793	2	214
Olive, m. Orrin **LILLIE**, Nov. 27, 1817	3	94
Oliver, m. Zerviah **BINGHAM**, Sept. 27, 1764	2	200
Oliver, m. Patience **BIBBONS**, June 23, 1791	3	35
Orrin, s. [Matthew & Annas], b. Aug. 27, 1797	3	9
Palmer, s. Isaac, mechanic, ae. 26, & Sabra S., ae. 22, b. Feb. 11, 1851	4	13
Pattey, d. [Josiah, Jr. & Eunice], b. Oct. 14, 1787	2	214
Peabody, s. Stephen & Mary, b. July 27, 1749	1	182
Peter, s. Stephen & Mary, b. July 28, 1743	1	182
Phebe, d. Daniel & Rebeckah, b. Aug. 7, 1735	1	151
Phebe, d. Josiah & Amey, b. Jan. 31, 1745/6	1	178
Phebe, d. [Oliver & Zerviah], b. Feb. 20, 1774	2	200
Phebe, m. Wightman **WILLIAMS**, Feb. 22, 1825, at Hampton	3	106

	Vol.	Page

SMITH, (cont.)

	Vol.	Page
Polly, d. [James & Lois], b. Jan. 9, 1771	2	125
Polly, m. Aaron **GAGER**, May 5, 1803; d. May 10, 1804	3	99
Rockwell, s. [Daniel & Elizabeth], b. May 13, 1769	2	123
Roger, s. Benj[ami]n & C[h]loe, b. Apr. 9, 1760	2	48
Roswell, s. [Daniel & Elizabeth], b. July 28, 1767	2	123
Rufus, s. [Matthew & Annas], b. Apr. 26, 1795	3	9
Sarah, m. Richard **HENDE[E]**, Mar 1, 1693	A	6
Sarah, d. Stephen & Mary, b. Dec. 11, 1751	1	182
Sarah, d. [Josiah & Elizabeth], b. Feb. 4, 1755	1	267
Sarah had d. Dicey **MARTIN**, b. Jan. 5, 1769	2	171
Sarah, m. Luther **MANNING**, Nov. 11, 1779	2	225
Sarah, m. Cuff **BASS**, Sept. 1, 1785	2	15
Sarah, [d. Charles L. & Sophia], b. Mar. 18, 1829	3	127
Sarah, d. Sept. 4, [1849], ae. 83	4	156
Sarah Paine, d. [Luther P. & Laura], b. Feb. 5, 1818	3	139
Scott, m. Amelia **ROBERTS**, Dec. 12, 1836, by Rev. Philo Judson, at Willimantic	3	180
Seth, d. June 24, [ ]	1	17
Seymour W., of Springfield, Mass., m. Elizabeth H. **WAITE**, of Windham, Sept. 30, 1839, by Rev. R. Ransom, Willimantic	3	190
Solomon, m. Eunice **BENNETT**, Nov. 27, 1760	2	63
Solomon, s. Solomon & Eunice, b. Aug. 31, 1761	2	63
Sophia, d. [Josiah, Jr. & Eunice], b. Jan. 1, 1792	2	214
Sophia, d. [Matthew & Annas], b. Oct. 2, 1793	3	9
Sophronia, d. [Oliver & Patience], b. Oct. 14, 1791	3	35
Stephen, m. Mary **PRESTON**, Dec. 28, 1736	1	182
Stephen, s. Stephen & Mary, b. June 19, 1739	1	182
Stephen, d. [ ], 1760	1	182
Stephen, s. [James & Lois], b. Oct. 19, 1768	2	125
Susan Ann, d. [David F. & Caroline], b. Apr. 5, 1840	3	197
Susan[n]ah, m. Nehemiah **TRACY**, June 19, 1744	1	245
Susannah, d. [Jonah & Alathea], b. May 21, 1764	2	55
Uriah T., s. [Abner], b. Jan. 28, 1825	3	101-2
Vine, s. [Josiah, Jr. & Eunice], b. Jan. 5, 1796	2	214
Vine, Dr., m. Lydia **LILLIE**, Mar. 10, 1822	3	101-2
Warren, s. [Josiah, Jr. & Eunice], b. Nov. 28, 1777	2	214
William, m. Mary Ann **NEWCOMB**, Oct. 24, 1830, by Henry Hall, J.P.	3	148
William, m. Hannah W. **WEST**, Apr. [ ], 1835	3	203
William C., m. Clarissa **CHILD**, Feb. 19, 1812, by Isaac Ticknor, J.P.	3	42
Zerviah, d. [Oliver & Zerviah], b. Nov. 4, 1765	2	200
SNELL, Bette, d. Thomas & Abigail, b. Nov. 10, 1705	1	3
Betty, d. Thomas & Mary, b. May 6, 1749	1	159
[E]unice, d. Thomas & Mary, b. Mar. 3, 1742/3	1	159

	Vol	Page
SNELL, (cont)		
Hannah, m. Reuben **ROBINSON**, Oct. 26, 1846, by		
Rev Andrew Sharp	3	232
Hannah S., m. Zelotes E. **CHAFFEE**, Mar. 8, 1841,		
by Rev. Andrew Sharpe, Willimantic	3	196
Jemima, m. Stephen **ORMSBY**, Dec. 6, 1781	2	252
Lois, m. W[illiam] L , **WEAVER**, June 26, 1842, by		
Andrew Sharp, Willimantic	3	202
Mary, d Thomas & Mary, b Sept. 6, 1741, d Nov.		
2, 1741	1	159
Mary, d. Thomas & Mary, b. Aug 27, 1746	1	159
Thomas, s. Thomas & Abigail, b Dec. 29, 1707	1	3
Thomas, m Mary **GEN[N]INGS**, Mar 9, 1736/7	1	159
Thomas, s. Thomas & Mary, b Aug. 22, 1751	1	159
William, s. Thomas & Mary, b Dec. 25, 1737	1	159
SNOW, Abigail, d. [Thomas & Lucy], b. Dec. 13, 1790	2	215
Anson A , of Hampton, m Hannah T **PIERCE**, of		
Scotland, Dec. 14, 1845, by H Slade	3	225
B.F , ae 40, m [ ], June 7, 1848, by		
Mr Osborn	4	113
Betsey, m. Jesse **PORTER**, b. of Windham, Nov 11,		
1833, by Rev. A. Gregory	3	166
Cynthia, m. Charles **TUCKER**, b of Windham, May 10,		
1840, by Rev. Otis C. Whiton	3	194
Darius, s. [Thomas & Lucy], b Mar. 15, 1788	2	215
Elijah, s. [Thomas & Lucy], b. Sept. 17, 1796	2	215
Elizabeth Stansborough, d. [Thomas & Lucy], b. Mar		
22, 1776	2	215
Elizabeth Stansborough, m Joseph **MEACHAM**, Jr ,		
Nov. 19, 1795	3	13
Hannah, m William **ABBOT**, July 8, 1777	2	228
Hannah, m. Amhurst **WILLES**, Mar. 22, 1795	2	52
Hannah, d Samuel, of Ashford, m Cyrus **TRACY**, s		
Cyrus & Elizabeth, of Windham, Mar. 3, 1808, by		
William Perkins, Esq , at the house of Samuel		
SNOW in Ashford. Witnessed: Abner **PALMER**, of		
Norwich	3	218
Hollis A., m. Samantha L. **LYON**, Mar. 28, 1842, by		
Rev Andrew Sharp	3	201
Huldah, d. [Thomas & Lucy], b. June 11, 1784	2	215
L[e]Roy, s. Augustus, dancing master, & Hannah, b		
Feb. 26, [1850]	4	10
Levina, d [Thomas & Lucy], b June 3, 1782	2	215
Mary E., d. Horace, shoe-maker, ae. 22, & Elizabeth,		
ae. 21, of Willimantic, b. May 13, 1847	4	5
Mary Jane, m. John H. **SPENCER**, laborer, of Windham,		
July 23, 1851, by Rev. H Baker	4	118
Salome, of Ashford, m. William B. **BADGE**, of		

	Vol.	Page
SNOW, (cont.)		
Hartford, May 10, 1831, by Rev. Alva Gregory, Willimantic	3	156
Sophia, d. [Thomas & Lucy], b. Feb. 8, 1778	2	215
Sybel, d. [Thomas & Lucy], b. July 27, 1780	2	215
Thomas, m. Lucy **SPAFFORD**, Mar. 27, 1769	2	215
Thomas, s. [Thomas & Lucy], b. Mar. 9, 1794	2	215
SOUTHGATE, Isaac, m. Maria **WEBB**, July 1, 1830, by Rev. Richard F. Cleveland	3	146
SOUTHWORTH, Jane, ae. 29, b. Mansfield, m. Daniel F. **TERRY**, cabinet maker, ae. 28, b. Hartford, res. Willimantic, Jan. 16, 1851, by Rev. S.G. Williams	4	117
SPAFFORD, Abel, s. [John & Susannah], b. July 31, 1766	2	85
Abel, m. Lois **SPENCER**, Oct. 15, 1792	2	56
Almyra, d. Charles, paper maker, ae. 26, & Celia, ae. 23, of Willimantic, b. Jan. 2, 1848	4	1
Asa, m. Huldah **FLINT**, Dec. 16, 1746	1	275
Asa, s. [Jehiel & Phebe], b. July 2, 1792	2	241
Caroline, d. [Darius], b. Nov. 1, 1823	3	9
Celinda, m. John **MOULTON**, Mar. 3, 1785	2	242
Clarinda, m. Eliphalet **PRESTON**, Jan. 25, 1787	2	204
Clarissa, d. [Jehiel & Phebe], b. June 9, 1782	2	241
Darius, s. Asa & Huldah, b. Jan. 4, 1749/50; d. July 3, 1778	1	275
Elijah, s. Asa & Huldah, b. Nov. 1, 1754	1	275
Elijah, s. [Jehiel & Phebe], b. Mar. 4, 1786	2	241
Eliphalet, s. [Asa & Huldah], b. July 16, 1763	1	275
Eliphaz, s. [Asa & Huldah], b. July 7, 1761; d. Mar. 7, 1782	1	275
Elisha, s. [Jehiel & Phebe], b. Mar. 18, 1784	2	241
Francis Henrietta, d. Darius, b. Apr. 24, 1817	3	9
Gamiel, s. [Asa & Huldah], b. Nov. 22, 1766	1	275
George, s. Mary **DICKENS**, black, ae. 23, b. May 6, 1848	4	3
George, papermaker, d. Nov. 5, [1849], ae. 55	4	153
Hannah, m. John **MARTIN**, Nov. 6, 1751	1	280
Henrietta, of Windham, m. Edwin S. **PHINEY**, of Canterbury, Apr. 3, 1836, by Rev. Jesse Fisher	3	177
Henry, s. [Phinehas & Susannah], b. Aug. 30, 1786	2	225
Huldah, d. Asa & Huldah, b. Jan. 18, 1747/8	1	275
Jehiel, s. [Asa & Huldah], b. Mar. 25, 1759	1	275
Jehiel, m. Phebe **JENNINGS**, Nov. 29, 1781	2	241
Joanna, m. Jared W. **LINCOLN**, b. of Windham, Apr. 21, 1844, by Rev. H. Slade, Scotland	3	214
John, m. Susannah **PARRISH**, Feb. 18, 1762	2	85
John, s. [Abel & Lois], b. Dec. 18, 1796	2	56
Julia, m. John B. **HOSMORE**, Oct. 15, 1826, by Rev.		

	Vol.	Page
SPAFFORD, (cont.)		
Cornelius B. Everest	3	123
Lester, s. [John & Susannah], b. Mar. 20, 1764	2	85
Lester, s. [Abel & Lois], b. July 10, 1794	2	56
Levina, m. Levi **ROBINSON**, Dec. 1, 1780	3	32
Lucy, d. Asa & Huldah, b. Aug. 16, 1751	1	275
Lucy, m. Thomas **SNOW**, Mar. 27, 1769	2	215
Lydia, d. [John & Susannah], b. June 6, 1768	2	85
Marvin, of Spaffordville, m. Caroline **ABBE**, of		
Windham, Jan. 6, 1839, in St. Paul's Church,		
by Rev. John W. Woodward	3	188
Meriam, m. Aaron **GEER**, Oct. 19, 1755	1	281
Minor, s. [John & Susannah], b. Mar. 19, 1770	2	85
Miner, of Windham, m. Nancy **ADAMS**, of Gotham,		
Nov. 11, 1835, by Rev. Jesse Fisher	3	176
Moses, m. Abigail **BEBINS**, May 24, 1763	2	90
Oliver, s. [John & Susannah], b. Aug. 27, 1762	2	85
Phinehas, s. Asa & Huldah, b. Dec. 16, 1756	1	275
Phinehas, m. Susannah **HEB[B]ARD**, Mar. 28, 1782	2	225
Sally, d. [Phinehas & Susannah], b. Jan. 9, 1783	2	225
Selende, d. [Moses & Abigail], b. Mar. 9, 1764	2	90
Susan, ae. 22, m. Joel R. **ARNOLD**, lawyer, ae. 26,		
Oct. 23, [1849], by Mr. Brownley	4	113
Vine, s. [Asa & Huldah], b. Feb. 5, 1769	1	275
Wealthy, d. Sept. 12, 1849, ae. 77	4	154
William, s. [Moses & Abigail], b. May 3, 1765	2	90
William, s. [Jehiel & Phebe], b. Aug. 25, 1790	2	241
SPARKS, Ariel, of Vernon, m. Matilda **INGHAM**, of Windham,		
Jan. 15, 1829, by Rev. Dennis Platt	3	134
John B., of Willimantic, d. Oct. 10, 1859, ae. 2 y.		
4 m.	4	159-0
Joseph, m. Mehitable **JOHNSON**, Apr. 29, 1747	1	275
Lemuel, s. Joseph & Mehetable, b. Sept. 11, 1747	1	275
SPAULDING, SPALDEN, Anne, d. [James & Hannah], b. June		
22, 1781	2	62
Benjamin, s. [James & Hannah], b. Aug. 8, 1786	2	62
Clyana, d. [James & Hannah], b. June 6, 1773	2	62
Content, d. [James & Hannah], b. Sept. 30, 1782	2	62
Deborah, m. John **KINGSBURY**, Oct. 21, 1730	1	125
Edeth, m. Benjamin **BIDLAKE**, Nov. 11, 1742	1	238
Edward, of Brooklyn, m. Sarah **JOHNSON**, of Windham,		
May 5, 1835, by Rev. L.H. Corson	3	173
Eliza L., m. John H. **RIPLEY**, b. of Windham, Oct. 8,		
1829, by Rev. Dennis Platt	3	138
[E]unice, d. Jonathan & [E]unice, b. Feb. 18,		
1736/7	1	164
Frances, s. [James & Hannah], b. Aug. 31, 1778	2	62
Hannah, d. [James & Hannah], b. June 4, 1772	2	62

	Vol.	Page
SPAULDING, SPALDEN, (cont.)		
Hannah, w. James, d. Aug. 24, 1790, in the 35th		
y. of her age	2	62
James, m. Hannah [ ], Oct. 22, 1771	2	62
James, s. [James & Hannah], b. Sept. 18, 1776	2	62
James, m. Barbara **LAW**, Sept. 3, 1795	3	34
James, m. Experience **DEANS**, May 22, 1797	3	31
James, of Norwich, m. Catharine **COOK**, of Windham,		
Jan. 5, 1829, by Rev. Dennis Platt	3	133
Jonathan, s. [James & Hannah], b. Dec. 6, 1779	2	62
Joseph, s. [James & Hannah], b. Jan. 15, 1788	2	62
Julia G., of Windham, m. Levi **DURKEE**, of Norwich,		
Oct. 8, 1829, by Rev. Dennis Platt	3	138
Lucy, d. [James & Hannah], b. Apr. 24, 1785	2	62
Lydia, d. [James & Hannah], b. Oct. 8, 1783	2	62
Nabby, d. [James & Experience], b. June 13, 1798	3	31
Rufus Payne, m. Lucretia **SWIFT**, [ ]	3	120
Ruth, d. [James & Hannah], b. Sept. 30, 1774	2	62
William, s. [James & Hannah], b. Sept. 8, 1789	2	62
SPENCER, Anne, d. John & Elizabeth, b. May 6, 1717	1	45
Anne, m. Israel **MARKHAM**, May 11, 1733	1	143
Anne, d. [David & Mary], b. May 29, 1773	2	24
Benjamin, s. Benj[ami]n & Sarah, b. Feb. 16, 1747/8;		
d. July 27, 1748/9	1	152
David, [twin with Deborah], s. John & Elizabeth, b.		
May 27, 1731	1	102
David, m. Mary **HILL**, June 16, 1762	2	24
Deborah, [twin with David], d. John & Elizabeth, b.		
May 27, 1731; d. Oct. 16, 1735	1	102
Deborah, d. Ebenezer & Sarah, b. Oct. 9, 1739	1	153
Ebenezer, s. John & Elizabeth, b. May 8, 1714	1	45
Ebenezer, m. Sarah **HEB[B]ARD**, Sept. 29, 1736	1	153
Ebenezer, d. Apr. 28, 1748	1	152
Elias, s. [Jeduthan & Abigail], b. Jan. 18, 1793	2	218
Elijah, s. [John, Jr. & Mary], b. Feb. 14, 1758	1	272
Elisha, s. [Jeduthan & Abigail], b. June 1, 1779	2	218
Elizabeth, d. John & Elizabeth, b. July 22, 1719	1	45
Elizabeth, d. John & Elizabeth, d. Dec. 18, 1742	1	102
Elizabeth, d. Eben[eze]r & Sarah, b. Oct. 27, 1745	1	152
Elizabeth, w. John, d. July 1, 1750	1	102
Elizabeth, d. [Jeduthan & Abigail], b. Aug. 27,		
1785; d. Oct. 2, 1785	2	218
Emily D., d. Simeon, farmer, ae. 22, & Emeline, ae.		
25, b. Jan. 23, 1851	4	14
Eunice, of Windham, m. Jared A. **MOSELEY**, of Chaplin,		
Mar. 24, 1845, by Rev. John E. Tyler	3	220
Freeman D., m. Lucinda **UTLEY**, Mar. 19, 1845, by Rev.		
Andrew Sharp	3	220

	Vol.	Page
SPENCER, (cont.)		
George, s. [Jeduthan & Abigail], b. Apr. 29,		
1795; d. May 17, 1795	2	218
Gershom, s. Eb[enezer] & Sarah, b. Apr. 28, 1744;		
d. June 8, 1744	1	153
Gideon, s. Ebenezer & Sarah, b. Sept. 14, 1741	1	153
Hannah, m. Gershom **PALMER**, June 28, 1715	1	38a
Henry A., s. John, farmer, ae. 18, & Mary, ae. 17,		
b. Apr. 19, 1851	4	14
Huldah, of Willimantic, m. Edward T. **COBB**, of		
Lebanon, Apr. 19, 1846, by Jacob Bakin	3	229
Ichabod, s. John & Mary, b. July 16, 1764; d. Oct.		
13, 1780	1	272
Ichabod, s. [Jeduthan & Abigail], b. July 16, 1781	2	218
James H., s. [Jeduthan & Abigail], b. Jan. 16, 1787	2	218
Jeduthan, m. Abigail **BROWN**, Aug. 13, 1776	2	218
Jerusha, d. John & Elizabeth, b. July 19, 1721	1	45
Jerusha, d. John, d. June 23, 1744	1	102
Jerusha, d. John & Mary, b. Aug. 2, 1748; d. Dec. 4,		
1749	1	272
Jerusha, d. [John & Mary], b. July 11, 1760	1	272
Jerusha, m. Nath[anie]l **HODGKINS**, Jan. 1, 1784	2	254
Jesse, s. [David & Mary], b. June 26, 1771; d. May 26,		
1771	2	24
John, m. Elizabeth **PALMER**, Aug. 29, 1711	1	45
John, s. John & Elizabeth, b. Jan. 24, 1723/4; d. Mar.		
6, 1766	1	45
John, m. Mary **SIMONS**, Nov. 5, 1746	1	272
John, m. Eleanor **ARNOLD**, Jan. 24, 1750/51; d. Apr. 5,		
1772	1	102
John, s. John, Jr. & Mary, b. June 4, 1751	1	272
John, Jr., d. Mar. 6, 1766	1	272
John, d. Apr. 5, 1772	1	102
John, m. Sally M. **REED**, Feb. 13, 1825, by Samuel		
Perkins, Esq.	3	84
John, shoemaker, ae. 27, b. Montville, res. New Jersey,		
m. Eliza **CLARK**, ae. 22, Mar. 15, 1848, by Tho[ma]s		
Dowling	4	111
John H., laborer, of Windham, m. Mary Jane **SNOW**, July		
23, 1851, by Rev. H. Baker	4	118
John L., s. [Jeduthan & Abigail], b. Oct 3, 1783	2	218
Jonathan, s. John & Mary, b. Aug. 19, 1753	1	272
Lemuel, s. [John & Mary], b. July 14, 1762	1	272
Louis, d. [David & Mary], b. Sept. 16, 1767	2	24
Lois, m. Abel **SPAFFORD**, Oct. 15, 1792	2	56
Lucius W., m. Mary A. **COX**, b. of Windham, Feb. 19,		
1838, at. Willimantic, by Rev. B. Cook, Jr.	3	185
Lucy, d. [Samuel & Edeth], b. May 2, 1787	2	214

	Vol.	Page
SPENCER, (cont.)		
Lucy, m. Charles W. H. **WARREN**, June 20, 1826	3	106
Mary, m. William **MUDGE**, June 10, 1762	2	82
Mary, d. [John & Mary], b. Sept. 13, 1766; d.		
Oct. 23, 1775	1	272
Mary, m. Paul **HOLT**, Jan. 4, 1774	2	187
Mary, d. [Jeduthan & Abigail], b. Sept. 3, 1777;		
d. Jan. 29, 1781	2	218
Mary E., m. Zadoc D. **BABCOCK**, b. of Windham, Nov		
14, 1841, by Rev. Nathan Wildman, of Lebanon	3	199
Mary H., m. Calvin **NEWTON**, Oct. 2, 1843, by Rev.		
Andrew Sharp	3	211
Nathaniel, s. Ebenezer & Sarah, b. Oct. 22, 1737	1	153
Orran, s. [Samuel & Edeth], b. Apr. 7, 1785	2	214
Phineas, s. [David & Mary], b. Nov. 22, 1764	2	24
Polly, d. [David & Mary], b. Sept. 16, 1776	2	24
Prudence, m. Rodman **BASS**, Apr. 29, 1844, by Rev.		
John B. Guild, Willimantic	3	214
Sam[ue]ll, d. Jan. 8, 1726/7, ae. about 88 y.	1	54
Sam[ue]ll, s. John & Elizabeth, b. June 15, 1729;		
d. Apr. 12, 1748	1	102
Samuel, s. John & Mary, b. July 14, 1762	1	272
Samuel, m. Edeth **READ**, Apr. 2, 1784	2	214
Sarah, m. John **CRANE**, Sept. 16, 1708	1	24
Sarah, d. Apr. 15, 1733, ae. about 73 y.	1	102
Silas, s. John & Mary, b. June 20, 1747; d. Sept.		
17, 1747	1	272
Silas, s. John, Jr. & Mary, b. Dec. 14, 1755	1	272
Tabitha, m. Moses **CLEVELAND**, May 31, 1759	2	99
Thomas, Jr., m. Mary Ann **PERKINS**, Oct. 6, 1845, by		
Andrew Sharp	3	224
Zaccheas, s. [David & Mary], b. Jan. 31, 1763	2	24
——, child of F.D., ae. 28, & Lucinda, ae. 36, b.		
July 22, [1848]	4	8
——, male, d. July 12, 1860, ae. 3 m.	4	161
SPICER, Harriet P., d. John A., spinner, ae. 35, b. Mar.		
4, [1849]	4	11
SPRAGUE, Abigail, d. [Elkannah & Mehetable], b. July 18,		
1755, in Lebanon	2	74
Elkannah, m. Mehetable **MOULTON**, Dec. 9, 1754	2	74
Elkannah, s. [Elkannah & Mehetable], b. Dec. 19, 1760	2	74
Frances A., d. Samuel A., operative, ae. 23, b. Nov.		
12, [1848]	4	6
Ignatius, s. [Elkannah & Mehetable], b. Nov. 17, 1758	2	74
James B., farmer, ae. 23, of Windham, m. Emma **GALLUP**,		
ae. 20, Nov. 25, 1848, by Rev. B.M. Allen	4	112
Vine, s. [Elkannah & Mehetable], b. Oct. 31, 1756, in		
Lebanon	2	74

	Vol.	Page
SPRAGUE, (cont.)		
William Fuller, s. Willaim B., b. Apr. 17, 1820	3	39
SQUIRES, SQUIRE, SQUIERS, SQUIER, Ann had s. Elisha		
ROBINSON, reputed f. Elisha **ROBINSON**, b.		
May 30, 1745	1	78
Ann P., m. Warren B. **ELLIOT**, b. of Windham, Aug.		
18, 1844, by Rev. S.B. Paddock, of Norwich	3	216
Anna, of Willimantic, d. Apr. 27, 1860, ae. 2	4	159-0
Charles, of Ashford, m. Mary Ann **JENNINGS**, of		
Windham, Sept. 22, 1839, by Elder Henry		
Greenslit	3	190
James, m. Mariet **JENNINGS**, of Windham, Jan. 15,		
1843, by Rev. J. E. Tyler	3	206
Philomela, b. Windham, res. Willimantic, d. Jan.		
16, 1860, ae. 73	4	159-0
——, child of Cha[rle]s, laborer, ae. 40, & Mary,		
ae. 38, b. July 10, 1851	4	13
STAMFORD, [see also **STANFORD**], Daniel, s. [John & Jerusha],		
b. Jan. 21, 1769	2	58
Ebenezer, m. Susannah **TRESCOT**, Mar. 2, 1806	3	36
Henry E., [s. James C. & Lydia], b. Feb. 10, 1834	3	137
James.C., m. Lydia **LATHROP**, Sept. 21, 1829, by Rev.		
Dennis Platt	3	137
John, m. Jerusha **STOUGHTON**, July 5, 1760	2	58
John, s. [John & Jerusha], b. Jan. 18, 1761	2	58
John L., [s. James C. & Lydia], b. June 26, 1831	3	137
Mary, d. [John & Jerusha], b. Dec. 7, 1765	2	58
Mary, d. [Ebenezer & Susannah], b. Nov. 14, 1806	3	36
Sarah, d. John & Jerusha], b. Mar. 30, 1763	2	58
Susan, [d. Ebenezer & Susannah], b. [ ]	3	36
Thomas, s. [John & Jerusha], b. Apr. 24, 1771; d.		
Nov. 24, 1771	2	58
STANDISH, Arastus, m. Lydia **CLARK**, Nov. 24, 1835, by Rev.		
S.R. Cook, at Willimantic, Windham	3	175
Mercy, m. Ralph **WHEELOCK**, Sept. 30, 1726	1	27
Prudence, m. Jacob **SAWYER**, Sept. 3, 1730	1	123
STANFORD, STANDFORD, STANIFORD, STANIFOR, [see also		
STAMFORD], Daniel, s. [John & Jerusha], b. Jan.		
21, 1769	3	65
James, s. [Timothy & Julia], b. July 25, 1800	3	29
Jerusha, d. [John & Jerusha], b. Jan. 26, 1781	3	65
John, m. Jerusha **STAUGHTON**, [ ], 1760	3	65
John, s. [John & Jerusha], b. Jan. 18, 1761	3	65
John, late Jr., m. Mary **BROWN**, wid. Col. Thomas, &		
d. Rev. Elijah **LATHROP**, of Hebron, May 9, 1805	3	65
John, d. Aug. 12, 1811, ae. 74 y. 2 m. 9 d.	3	65
John, m. Lydia **BINGHAM**, Jan. 21, 1816	3	65
Mary, d. [John & Jerusha], b. Dec. 7, 1765	3	65

	Vol.	Page
STANFORD, STANDFORD, STANIFORD, STANIFOR, (cont.)		
Mary, w. John, d. Oct. 19, 1813	3	65
Mary, m. Elijah **SIMONDS**, b. of Windham, Feb. 28,		
1842, by Rev. John E. Tyler	3	200
Sarah, d. [John & Jerusha], b. Mar. 30, 1763	3	65
Sarah, m. Ebenezer **GRAY**, Mar. 30, 1786	2	215
Sarah, m. Ebenezer **GRAY**, b. of Windham, Mar. 30,		
1786, by Rev. Stephen White; d. Sept. 29,		
1835	3	110
Staughton, s. [John & Jerusha], b. Jan. 8, 1779	3	65
Susan, m. Thomas **POTTER**, Mar. 26, 1834, by Rev.		
Roger Bingham	3	168
Thomas, s [John & Jerusha], b. Apr. 24, 1771; d.		
Nov. following	3	65
Thomas, s. [John & Jerusha], b. Feb. 12, 1788	3	65
Timothy, s. [John & Jerusha], b. Jan. 27, 1773	3	65
Timothy, m. Julia **ELDERKIN**, Nov. 14, 1795	3	29
STANLEY, Julia, d. Frederick & Sabra, b. Feb. 6, 1794	2	56
STANTON, [see also **STAUNTON**], Hannah E., m. Prosper		
HAZEN, of Franklin, Mar. 14, 1825	3	5
Hannah E., m. Prosper **HAZEN**, Mar. 14, 1825, by Rev.		
C.B. Everest	3	112
John, teamster, ae. 25, m. Charlotte **PALMER**, ae. 18,		
Nov. 29, 1849, by Rev. Tho[ma]s Tallman	4	114
John L., of Norwich, m. Rhoda Ann **HOLMES**, of Windham,		
Jan. 1, 1846, by Rev. R.V. Lyon	3	226
Lemuel, m. Harriet **MAIN**, Dec. 19, 1830, by Rev. Roger		
Bingham	3	150
Robert B., of Brooklyn, m. Almira **RICE**, of Worcester,		
Mass., Jan. 6, 1841, by Rev. J.E. Tyler	3	195
STAPLETON, John, s. John, ae. 24, & Mary J., ae. 30, b		
June 24, [1849]	4	7
——, Mrs., housekeeper, b. Ireland, res. Willimantic,		
d. Oct. 29, 1848, ae. 35	4	153
STARK, Celinda, of Mansfield, m. Robert **RODMAN**, of Lebanon,		
Nov. 10, 1830, by Rev. R.T. Crampton	3	149
Fitch, m. Lucinda P **GRIFFIN**, b. of Lyme, Sept. 14,		
1830, by Rev. Chester Tilden	3	148
STARKWEATHER, Abel Fitch, [s. Elisha & Elizabeth], b. [ ]	3	108
Elisha, m. Elizabeth **FITCH**, Sept. 1, 1822, by Rev.		
Cornelius B. Everest	3	108
Emily Amanda, [d. Elisha & Elizabeth], b. [ ]	3	108
Ezra, m. Mary E. **FLINT**, May 1, 1833, by Rev. Roger		
Bingham	3	164
Henry, m. Eliza A. **GALLUP**, Aug. 27, 1844, at Willi-		
mantic, by Rev. J.B. Guild	3	216
Henry Clark, [s. Elisha & Elizabeth], b.[ ]	3	108
Julia Elizabeth, [d. Elisha & Elizabeth], b. [ ]	3	108

	Vol.	Page
STAUNTON, [see also STANTON], Sally, m. Thomas		
BECKWITH, Feb. 2, 1823	3	109
STEARNES, STEARNS,Ann M., d. N.A., harness maker,		
ae. 24, b. Oct. 13, [1849]	4	9
Diana, m. John BINGHAM, Dec. 31, 1822, by Samuel		
Perkins, Esq.	3	106
STEAVENS, [see also STEPHENS], Est[h]er, m. Zaccheas		
WALDO, Jr., Apr. 12, 1781	2	235
STEBBINS, Sarah, m. Casper L. LYON, b. of Willimantic,		
Oct. 13, 1839, at Willimantic, by Rev. B.		
Cook, Jr., of Willimantic	3	190
STEDMAN, STEADMAN, Anne, m. Joseph MARSH, Apr. 27,		
1743	1	226
Anne, d. [Thomas, Jr. & Mehetable], b. Aug. 7,		
1764	2	113
Daniel, s. Thomas & Anna, b. Dec. 9, 1745	1	212
Elizabeth, d. Thomas & Anna, b. Apr. 30, 1739	1	200
Esther, d. Tho[ma]s & Anna, b. Sept. 25, 1748	1	212
Hannah, d. [James & Hannah], b. Nov. 23, 1769	1	305
James, m. Hannah GRIFFIN, Apr. 11, 1751	1	305
Luce, d. Thomas & Anna, b. Mar. 8, 1740	1	200
Mary, d. Thomas & Anna, b. Aug. 15, 1734	1	200
Mary, d. Tho[ma]s & Anna, d. Apr. 20, 1753	1	212
Mary, d. [Thomas, Jr. & Mehetable], b. Apr. 14,		
1762	2	113
Mary, d. [James & Hannah], b. Jan. 16, 1772	1	305
Patience, d. Thomas & Anna, b. Apr. 17, 1743	1	200
Pruda, m. John CROSS, b. of Windham, Sept. 8,		
1844, by Stowell Lincoln, J.P.	3	217
Sarah, d. Thomas & Anna, b. Oct. 30, 1736	1	200
Sarah, m. Joseph CHAPLIN, June 13, 1754	1	317
Sarah, m. Joseph CHAPLIN, [ ]	2	10
Thomas, m. Anna [ ], Apr. 9, 1724. (Arnold		
Copy says "Perhaps 1734")	1	200
Thomas, Jr., m. Mehetable GRIFFEN, Sept. 23, 1760	2	113
Thomas, s. James & Hannah, b. Nov. 6, 1761	1	305
Thomas, Dea., d. Apr. 9, 1773, in the 75th y. of his		
age	1	212
STEEL*(Correction STEEL crossed out and STOWELL, STOEL		
written in original manuscript. Additionally, a		
note was added on Connecticut State Library,		
Hartford, notepaper that states: "All STEEL entries		
in Windham Vital Records should probably be STOEL		
(STOWELL). See STOWELL Genealogy, and Jonathan		
Clark's "Windham Families" (photostat of manuscript		
in Vault 1), page 214." Entry was signed "MBC		
3/23/37".		
Anna, d. Eben[eze]r, d. Sept. 30, 1754	1	188

	Vol.	Page

STEEL, [STOWELL, STOEL], (cont.)

Anner, m. John **LINKION**, May 30, 1758 — 2 — 3

Anna, m. Nathaniel **LINKON**, Jr., June 10, 1792 — 2 — 67

Eunice, m. Ma[t]thew **WARNER**, Apr. 10, 1769 — 2 — 145

Josiah, s. Eben[eze]r & Annah, b. Mar. 20, 1750 — 1 — 140

Patience, d. Eben[eze]r & Annah, b. Nov. 24, 1753 — 1 — 140

STEPHENS, [see also **STEAVENS**], Harriet E., d. Henry, laborer, & Harriet, b. Oct. 8, 1850 — 4 — 13

Mary Ann, m. Lafayette **ARNOLD**, b. of Providence, R.I., Feb. 20, 1842, by Rev. Andrew Sharp — 3 — 200

Phebe had d. [E]unice **GEN[N]INGS**, b. July 13, 1732. Reputed father Joseph **GEN[N]INGS** — 1 — 87

STETSON, Lydia, operative, ae. 21, b. Lisbon, res. Norwich, m. Martha (?) R. **KENYON**, carpenter, ae. 20, b. Griswold, res. Norwich, Jan. 5, 1851, by Elder Bromley (Matthew?) — 4 — 117

STEWART, Charles, of Fishkill, N.Y., m. Salome B. **YOUNG**, of Windham, May 12, 1834, by Rev. L.H. Corson — 3 — 171

Martha, d. Robert K., teacher, ae. 27, & Susan C. ae. 25, b. Aug. 13, 1849 — 4 — 9

Sarah, of Norwich Landing, m. Benjamin **BINGHAM**, Oct. 15, 1754 — 1 — 324

Sarah, of Norwich, m. Benjamin **BINGHAM**, Oct. 15, 1754 — 2 — 49

STILES, Asa, s. Sam[ue]l & Huldah, b. Mar. 10, 1752 — 2 — 29

Elerner, m. John **PRESTON**, Mar. 18, 1730/31 — 1 — 146

Goold, s. Sam[ue]l & Huldah, b. Mar. 12, 1750 — 2 — 29

Han[n]ah, d. [Isaac & Mary], b. Nov. 23, 1754 — 1 — 313

Huldah, d. Sam[ue]ll & Huldah, b. Sept. 18, 1736 — 1 — 142

Huldah, m. James **HOLT**, Dec. 31, 1769 — 2 — 149

Isaac, s. Sam[ue]l & Huldah, b. Sept. 26, 1747 — 2 — 29

Isaac, m. Mary **BRADLEY**, Apr. 17, 1751 — 1 — 313

Leah, d. Sam[ue]l & Huldah, b. Mar. 27, 1743 — 2 — 29

Lucy, d. Sam[ue]l & Huldah, b. Oct. 22, 1758 — 2 — 29

Mary, d. [Isaac & Mary], b. June 9, 1752 — 1 — 313

Mehetabel, d. Sam[ue]ll & Huldah, b. Nov. 15, 1740 — 1 — 142

Rachel, d. Sam[ue]l & Huldah, b. Apr. 5, 1745 — 2 — 29

Sam[ue]ll, m. Huldah **DURGEY**, Oct. 7, 1735 — 1 — 142

Samuell, s. Sam[ue]ll & Huldah, b. Nov. 6, 1738 — 1 — 142

William, s. Sam[ue]l & Huldah, b. July 31, 1755 — 2 — 29

STIMPSON, Stephen, of Coventry, m. Hannah Matilda **JENNINGS**, of Windham, Jan. 27, 1828, by Thomas Gray, J.P. — 3 — 132

W[illia]m H., s. W[illia]m, farmer & Mary, ae. 24, b. Sept. 16, 1850 — 4 — 13

STODDARD, Andrew, s. [Samuel & Hannah], b. June 4, 1789 — 2 — 236

Azariah, s. [Samuel & Mary], b. Feb. 1, 1758 — 1 — 320

Elizabeth, d. [Samuel & Mary], b. Nov. 16, 1753 — 1 — 320

George E., s. [Wait & Sarah], b. Dec. 25, 1800 — 3 — 63

	Vol.	Page
STODDARD, (cont.)		
Hannah, d. [Samuel & Hannah], b. Aug. [ ], 1784	2	236
Isaac A., m. Mary L. **WHITE**, b. of Windham, Nov.		
6, 1837, by Rev. Charles J. Todd	3	184
Lemuel, s. [Samuel & Mary], b. Nov. 1, 1755	1	320
Lucy, d. [Samuel & Hannah], b. June 6, 1786	2	236
Marion Wait, s. [Wait & Sarah], b. Aug. 4, 1796,		
at Groton	3	63
Mary, m. Henry **PAGE**, b. of Windham, June 27, 1844,		
by Rev. J.E. Tyler	3	215
Park Allen, s. [Wait & Sarah], b. Sept. 22, 1798	3	63
Sally, d. [Samuel & Hannah], b. Aug. 12, 1782	2	236
Sally Maria, [d. Wait & Sarah], b. Apr. 16, 1793,		
at Groton	3	63
Samuel, m. Mary **KINGSLEY**, Mar. 12, 1753	1	320
Samuel, m. Hannah **FULLER**, Dec. 2, 1778	2	236
Samuel, s. [Samuel & Hannah], b. Oct. 10, 1780; d.		
July [ ], 1782	2	236
Tabitha F., of Windham, m. George **CAPRON**, of Palmyra,		
N.Y., Oct. 20, 1841, by Rev. J.E. Tyler	3	198
Wait, m. Sarah **ALLEN**, Dec. 4, 1791	3	63
STOEL, [see under **STEEL**, also **STOWELL** (Entire entry hand-		
written in original manuscript.)		
STONE, Emily, d. of Obadiah, of Thompson, Conn., m.		
Frederick Palmer **TRACY**, [ ]	3	219
Lydia K., of Guilford, m. John S. **JILLSON**, of Willi-		
mantic, Nov. 23, 1834, by Rev. Philo Judson, at		
Willimantic	3	171
STORRS, Sam[ue]ll, m. Martha **BURGE**, Oct. 31, 1700	A	32
Sam[ue]l, s. Sam[ue]ll & Martha, b. Aug. 22, 1701	A	32
Sarah A., m. Samuel A. **BOTTOM**, b. of Mansfield, Mar.		
10, 1842, at North Windham, by Elder R.V. Lyon,		
of Ashford	3	201
Sheldon, of Mansfield, m. Margaret **LINCOLN**, of Windham,		
Nov. 24, 1839, by Rev. Reuben Ransom	3	191
STORY, George, s. [Jedediah & Eunice], b. Nov. 19, 1803	3	62
Henry, s. [Jedediah & Eunice], b. Sept. 8, 1801	3	62
Jedediah, m. Eunice **LEACH**, Sept. 14, 1800	3	62
Mary, d. [Jedediah & Eunice], b. Nov. 27, 1806	3	62
Mary A., ae. 19, m. Michael **COBBES**, operative, ae. 21,		
b. East Lyme, res. Windham, Jan. 7, 1848, by Abel		
Nelson	4	111
STOUGHTON, STAUGHTON, C[h]loe, m. Hugh **LEDLIE**, June		
10, 1739	1	317
Daniel, m. Jerusha **BACKUS**, Oct. 20, 1742	1	224
Daniel, m. Sarah **KIMBALL**, June 2, 1752	1	224
Gustavus, d. May 6, 1757, in New York	1	224
Jerusha, d. Daniel & Jerusha, b. Sept. 14, 1744	1	224

	Vol.	Page

STOUGHTON, STAUGHTON, (cont.)

Jerusha, w. Daniel, d. Sept. 24, 1744 — 1 — 224

Jerusha, m. John **STAMFORD**, July 5, 1760 — 2 — 58

Jerusha, m. John **STANIFORD**, [ ], 1760 — 3 — 65

Roxalania, m. Matthew **HIDE**, June 15, 1756 — 2 — 12

Sarah, w. Daniel, d. Mar. 24, 1759 — 1 — 224

STOWELL, STOEL*, Elizabeth, m. Oliver **FOLLETT**, Mar. 29, 1798 (*Correction "see also under **STEEL**" handwritten in original manuscript.) — 3 — 30

Mary, m. Silas **FRINK**, Nov. 11, 1804 — 3 — 44

Patience, m. Thomas **KINGSBURY**, Apr. 2, 1778 — 3 — 24

Phila, m. Andrew **FRINK**, Oct. 12, 1801 — 3 — 51

STRICKLAND, Annas, m. Matthew **SMITH**, Mar. 20, 1788 — 3 — 9

STRONG, Christopher C., m. Henrietta **RIDER**, Apr. 13, 1835, by Rev. Roger Bingham — 3 — 173

Elener, m. Stephen **FITCH**, Jan. 25, 1736/7 — 1 — 172

Lois, m. William **WEBB**, May 16, 1782 — 2 — 247

Martha, m. Ebenezer **MOSELEY**, Sept. 14, 1773 — 2 — 249

Tryphenia, m. Aaron **ALLEN**, Mar. 30, 1809 — 3 — 24

STUBBS, Betsey, d. [Samuel & Marian], b. Jan. 28, 1775 — 2 — 72

Samuel, m. Marian **CROSS**, Apr. 16, 1774 — 2 — 72

SUFFORD, Hannah, m. James **GLASS**, Oct. 28, 1767 — 2 — 135

SULLIVAN, B., laborer, ae. 30, m. Mary **HENDERSON**, ae. 23, Jan. 1, [1850], by Rev. Brady — 4 — 115

Bridget, of Willimantic, d. Feb. 8, 1860, ae. 9 m. — 4 — 159-0

Daniel, b. Colchester, res. Willimantic, d. Apr. 28, 1860, ae. 4 — 4 — 159-0

Ellen, of Willimantic, d. Apr. 1, 1860, ae. 1 y. 2 m. — 4 — 159-0

——, housekeeper, b. Ireland, res. Willimantic, d. Aug. 21, [1849], ae. 26 — 4 — 153

——, of Willimantic, d. Apr. 28, 1860, ae. 3 — 4 — 159-0

SUMNER, Harriet, m. William **GOFF**, Oct. 22, 1835, by Rev. Roger Bingham — 3 — 175

Joshua, Dr., m. Hannah **MARSH**, July 2, 1788 — 2 — 249

Nancy E., m. David H. **FISKE**, Oct. 22, 1835, by Rev. Roger Bingham — 3 — 175

SWEENEY, John, s. John, laborer, ae. 31, b. Dec. 29, 1850 — 4 — 13

SWEET, Ann, of Hampton, m. William **BARBER**, of Hebron, Feb. 26, 1839, at Willimantic, by Rev. Philo Judson — 3 — 188

SWEETLAND, SWETLAND, Abi, m. Ebenezer **GINNINGS**, Oct. 22, 1783 — 2 — 213

John C., m. Lydia **GOODSPEED**, May 13, [ ], by Rev. Cornelius B. Everest — 3 — 80

Susan, ae. 23, m. Alonzo **GREEN**, laborer, ae. 24, Mar. [ ], [1849], by Mr. Bray — 4 — 113

SWIFT, Abby Maria, d. [Justin & Lucy], b. Jan. 22, 1821 — 3 — 122

Alathea, [d. Earl & Laura], b. June [ ], 1815 — 3 — 64

Albert E., [s. Earl & Laura], b. Jan. 27, 1811 — 3 — 64

	Vol.	Page
SWIFT, (cont.)		
Earl, m. Laura **RIPLEY**, Apr. 18, 1810	3	64
Eliza, of Franklin, m. Charles C. **HAYWARD**, of		
Windham, Dec. 24, 1835, by Rev. L.H. Corson,		
Willimantic	3	176
Emily C., of Windham, m. Elijah **CHAPMAN**, of		
Tolland, June 23, 1830, by Rev. Richard F.		
Cleveland	3	146
Harriet, [d. Earl & Laura], b. Oct. 17, 1813	3	64
James Doliver Jackson [s. Earl & Laura], b.		
Oct. 19, 1825	3	64
Julia, [d. Justin & Lucy], b. [ ]	3	122
Julia P., m. Charles **BABCOCK**, b. of Windham,		
Jan. 20, 1829, by Rev. Dennis Platt	3	134
Justin, b. Nov. 3, 1793, at Lebanon; m. Lucy		
Lathrop, Nov. 8, 1819	3	122
Laura Ripley, [d. Earl & Laura], b. Mar. 8, 1818	3	64
Lucretia, m. Rufus Payne **SPAULDING**, [ ]	3	120
Ralph R., [s. Earl & Laura], b. Sept. 29, 1822	3	64
Sarah, [d. Justin & Lucy], b. [ ]	3	122
Sarah Fearing, [d. Earl & Laura], b. Aug. [ ],		
1824	3	64
William, s. [Justin & Lucy], b. Mar. 16, 1823	3	122
William, m. Harriet G. **BYRNE**, b. of Windham, May 3,		
1847, by Rev. J.E. Tyler	3	235
W[illia]m F., s. W[illia]m, merchant, ae. 26, &		
Harriet, ae. 23, b. Mar. 5, 1848	4	3
——, d. W[illia]m, merchant, ae. 28, b. June 29,		
1851	4	13
TAINTOR, Mary Abbie, d. Aug. 27, 1860, ae. 87	4	161
TAMBLING, Abigail, d. Elisha & Martha, b. Mar. 20, 1736	1	169
Abijah, s. Elisha & Martha, b. Mar. 25, 1733	1	169
Stephen, s. Elisha & Martha, b. Apr. 1, 1738	1	169
TARBOX, ——, child of W[illia]m, blacksmith, b. Dec. 30,		
[1849]	4	9
TARRANCE, [see also **LARRANCE**], Sam[ue]ll, m. Mary		
HEB[B]ARD, Nov. 6, 1733	1	135
TAVERNER, Charles H., cigar maker, b. Lisbon, res. Windham,		
d. July 6, 1849, ae. 38	4	154
TAYLOR, Ammi, s. [John & Rhoda], b. Sept. 7, 1773	2	30
Frank W., of N. Stonington, m. Lucy **BENTLEY**, of		
Windham, [Sept.] 5, 1830, by Rev. Chester Tilden,		
Willimantic	3	147
Hezekiah, s. John & Rhoda, b. Mar. 22, 1770	2	30
John, s. John & Rhoda, b. Oct. 19, 1766	2	30
John, harnessmaker, d. June 18, [1850], ae. 59	4	155
Miranda, m. Moses B. **HOPKINS**, Aug 22, 1825	3	119
Polly, d. [John & Rhoda], b. Mar. 20, 1777	2	30

	Vol.	Page
TAYLOR, (cont.)		
Rhoda, d. John & Rhoda, b. Feb. 7, 1765	2	30
Zach[ariah], b. May 13, [1848]	4	8
TEMPLE, Amie, wid. William, late of Boston, & d.		
Col. Eleazer **FITCH**, m. Isaac **CLARK**, of		
Vermont, Mar. 29, 1790	3	43
Anne, of Windham, m. Gen. Isaac **CLARK**, of		
Castleton, Mar. 25, 1790	2	59
William, of Boston, m. Anne **FITCH**, d. Col.		
Eleazer, of Windham, Apr. 12, 1781	3	43
TERRELL, **TEREL**, Hannah, m. Elijah **SAWYER**, Mar. 7,		
1732/3	1	94
Mary, m. Daniel **DIMUCK**, Nov. 23, 1732	1	140
Mehetable, d. Lewis & Mehetable, b. Mar. 11,		
1736/7	1	160
Mehitable, w. Lewis, d. Dec. 3, 1744	1	160
Tryphenia, d. Lewis & Mehetable, b. Oct. 23, 1739	1	160
TERRINGTON, [see also **YERRINGTON**], Lydia A., ae. 21,		
b. Bozrah, res. Willimantic, m. Ceyton		
METCHER (**MITCHELL**?), laborer, ae. 21, b.		
Bozrah, res. Willimantic, June [ ], 1851,		
by Rev. R. K. Brush	4	117
TERRY, Daniel F., cabinet maker, ae. 28, b. Hartford,		
res. Willimantic, m. Jane **SOUTHWORTH**, ae. 29,		
b. Mansfield, Jan 16, 1851, by Rev. S. G.		
Williams	4	117
THATCHER, Asa, m. Hannah **HUNT**, July 22, 1779	2	131
Asa, s. [Asa & Hannah], b. Oct. 3, 1790	2	131
Benjamin, s. [Asa & Hannah], b. Apr. 9, 1783	2	131
Betsey, d. [Asa & Hannah], b. Feb. 27, 1789	2	131
Hannah, d. [Asa & Hannah], b. Apr. 14, 1785	2	131
Harriet, d. [Asa & Hannah], b. Feb. 28, 1797	2	131
Henry, s. [Asa & Hannah], b. Apr. 10, 1795	2	131
Jerusha, d. [Asa & Hannah], b. Feb. 24, 1792	2	131
Melissa, d. [Asa & Hannah], b. Aug. 31, 1793	2	131
Tryphenia, d. [Asa & Hannah], b. Apr. 21, 1787	2	131
THAYER, Horace, of Thompson, m. Sarah L. **BARSTOW**, of		
Windham, May 7, 1840, by Rev. Otis C. Whiton	3	194
THOMAS, David, m. Mary **JOHNSON**, Oct. 10, 1739	1	199
Edwin, manufacturer, ae. 20, m. Maria L. **HARP**,		
ae. 19, June [ ], [1850], by Rev. J. Cady	4	116
Hannah, d. David & Mary, b. July 1, 1744	1	199
Jonathan, s. David & Mary, b. Sept. 10, 1742	1	199
Mary, d. David & Mary, b. Apr. 10, 1740; d. May		
20, 1741	1	199
Mary, d. David & Mary, b. Apr. 20, 1746	1	199
THOMASTON, Hannah, m. John **CARY**, Jan. 15, 1726	1	13
THOMPSON, Ann E., d. Hezekiah, laborer, ae. 27, of		

	Vol.	Page
THOMPSON, (cont.)		
Willimantic, b. Aug. 16, [1850]	4	10
Ebenezer, of Charlestown, R.I., m. Amanda **TORREY**,		
Mar. 28, 1824	3	17
John, m. Harriet C. **LITTLEFIELD**, b. of Willi-		
mantic, Nov. 14, 1841, by Rev. Andrew Sharp,		
Willimantic	3	199
Marilla, m. Mason **HARTSHORN**, of Hampton, May 4,		
1826	3	124
Mary, m. Philip **WILLSON**, b. of Windham, [ ],		
1833, by Rev. John Storrs	3	167
Mary M., d. Cha[rle]s, sheriff, ae. 33, & Nancy		
G., ae. 25, b. Aug. 25, 1850	4	12
Roxana, ae. 25, m. Richard **PERRY**, operative, ae. 26,		
b. Mansfield, res. Windham, Nov. 28, 1847, by		
Tho[ma]s Dowling	4	111
W[illia]m B., farmer, m. Mary **RILEY**, Dec. 9, [1849],		
by Rev. J.E. Tyler	4	114
THORN[E], Malantha T., ae. 25, b. Mansfield, res. Willi-		
mantic, m. Eliza A. **WILLSON**, ae. 17, of Willi-		
mantic, Nov 19, 1850, by Rev. Jno. Cady	4	118
——, child of James, mason, ae. 36, b. May [ ],		
1850	4	11
THROOP, Dorcas, m. David **HEB[B]ARD**, June 26, 1763, by		
Rev. Peter Reynolds	2	86
THURSTON, Clark, see under Clark **McTHURSTON**		
Mehetabel, m. Nathaniel **HUNTINGTON**, Feb. 28, 1722/3	1	74
Phebe, m. Jacob **LILLY**, Oct. 23, 1723	1	72
TICKNOR, David, s. Isaac & Mary, b. Dec. 3, 1758	1	116
Mary, d. Jona[than] **MARTIN**, & mother of David **TICKNOR**	1	116
TILDEN, TILDON, Hannah, of Norwich, m. Jonath[an] **LILLIE**,		
Dec. 12, 1754	1	320
Hannah, m. Jonathan **LILLIE**, Dec. 12, 1754	2	3
Hildah, m. Elisha **LILLIE**, Jr., Mar. 19, 1755	2	4
Huldah, of Norwich, m. Elisha **LILLIE**, Jr., Mar. 19,		
1755	1	321
Lydia, d. Ithamar & Lydia, b. Apr. 18, 1768	2	122
Mary, d. Ithamer & Lydia, b. May 26, 1766	2	122
Sarah, of Norwich, m. John **FLINT**, Dec. 30, 1772	2	190
TINCKOM, [see also **TINKER**], William E., m. Sarah **KING**,		
b. of Windham, Oct. 20, 1833, by Rev. Alva		
Gregory, Willimantic	3	166
TINGLEY, TINGSLEY, Abby C., of Windham, m. Dr. E B. Allen,		
of Belchartown, Mass., Oct. 25, 1840, by Rev.		
John E. Tyler	3	194
Cotea, child of W[illia]m S., laborer, ae. 24, &		
Catharine, ae. 33, of Willimantic, b. Nov. 20,		
[1848 or 1849]	4	5

	Vol.	Page
TINGLEY, TINGSLEY, (cont.)		
Geo[rge] B., m. Mary **BABCOCK**, of Willimantic		
Village, Apr. 3. 1836, by Rev. Philo Judson,		
at Willimantic	3	177
Mary M., m. Geo[rge] Smith **CATLIN**, b. of Windham,		
June 12, 1834, by Rev. L.H. Corson	3	171
William L., m. Catharine P. **HEBBARD**, May 24, 1843,		
by Rev. Andrew Sharp	3	209
TINKER, [see also **TINCKOM**], Abigail Griswold, d. [Elisha		
& Lydia], b. Aug. 20, 1764	2	93
Alexander, s. [Nehemiah & Mary], b. July 16, 1772	2	91
Almarine, s. [Nehemiah & Mary], b. May 22, 1768	2	91
Bela, s. [Nehemiah & Mary], b. Sept. 3, 1778; d.		
Oct. [ ], 1778	2	91
Elisha, m. Lydia **HUNTINGTON**, Nov. 13, 1763	2	93
Elisha, s. [Elisha & Lydia], b. Oct. 30, 1766	2	93
Joel, s [Nehemiah & Mary], b. Sept. 2, 1774	2	91
John, s. [Nehemiah & Mary], b. July 14, 1764	2	91
Joseph Buckingham, s. [Nehemiah & Mary], b. Dec. 21,		
1779	2	91
Lamon, s. [Nehemiah & Mary], b. June 24, 1770	2	91
Lewis, m. Jerusha **MOULTON**, Sept. 17, 1815	2	79
Lydia, d. [Nehemiah & Mary], b. July 27, 1782; d.		
Oct. 4, 1783	2	91
Nehemiah, s. [Nehemiah & Mary], b. May 17, 1766	2	91
Nehemiah, m. Mary **HUNTINGTON**, Dec. 31, 176[ ]	2	91
Nehemiah, Capt., d. Mar. 17, 1783	2	91
Polly, d. [Nehemiah & Mary], b. July 12, 1776	2	91
Sarah, d. [Nehemiah & Mary], b. July 5, 1763	2	91
Sarah, m. William **WALES**, Apr. 24, 1779	2	93
TOPLIFF, Calvin, of Coventry, m. Harriet **ABBE**, Nov. 24,		
1825, by Rev. Cornelius B. Everest	3	31
TOPP, John, s. John, operative, ae 39, & Sarah, ae. 39,		
of Willimantic, b. Feb. 28, 1850	4	12
TORREY, Amanda, m. Ebenezer **THOMPSON**, of Charlestown,		
R.I., Mar. 28, 1824	3	17
Delia A., d. Peter, farmer, colored, ae. 35, & Sarah,		
ae. 16, b. Mar. 25, 1851	4	14
TOURS, Elizabeth, m. Stephen **CALSE**, Nov. 1, 1782, by Mr		
Justice Belnap, at Newburgh, N.Y.	2	252
TRACY, Abigail Elizabeth, [d. George Anson & Melissa], b.		
[ ]	3	219
Ada, [d. Erasmus Darwin & Maria Isabella], b. Feb. 18,		
1844, at Nassau Co., Fla.	3	219
Andrew, s. Thomas & Elizabeth, b. Aug. 1, 1754	1	315
Andrew, m. Fidelia **CADY**, Mar. 25, [1849], by Mr. Bray	4	113
Anna, m. Jacob **ROBINSON**, Nov. 4, 1756	2	17
Caroline, m. Sanford **CAREY**, May 16, 1811	3	77

	Vol.	Page
TRACY, (cont.)		
Caroline Olivia, [d. John & Delia], b. Nov. 16,		
1838; d. Nov. 16, 1857	4	22
Selia, [d. Erasmus Darwin & Maria Isabella], b.		
Apr. 14, 1842, at Nassau Co., Fla.	3	219
Cora, [d. John & Delia], b. July 12, 1855; d.		
Feb. 24, 1858	4	22
Cynthia, m. Charles **HUNTINGTON**, Mar. 15, 1809	3	22
Cyrus, of Preston, m. Elizabeth **PALMER**, of		
Windham, Nov. 8, 1783	3	3
Cyrus, s. Cyrus & Elizabeth, b. July 12, 1784	3	3
Cyrus, s. Cyrus & Elizabeth, b. July 12, 1784,		
Windham; m. Hannah **SNOW**, d. Samuel, of Ashford,		
Mar. 3, 1808, by William Perkins, Esq., at the		
house of Samuel **SNOW**, Ashford. Witnessed by		
Abner **PALMER**, of Norwich	3	218
Cyrus Mason, [s Cyrus & Hannah], b. May 7, 1824,		
at Norwich	3	219
Daniel, s. [Zebediah & Eunice], b. Sept. 17, 1790	2	222
Daniel, m. Julia **WILKINSON**, b. of Windham, Mar. 14,		
1838, at Willimantic, by Rev. Philo Judson	3	186
Deborah, d. Stephen & Deborah, b. Jan. 8, 1714	1	11
Deborah, w. Stephen, d. Dec. 6, 1735, in the 52nd		
y. of her age	1	159
Deborah, d. Tho[ma]s & Eliza[be]th, b. Mar. 10, 1756	1	315
Delia Maria, [d. John & Delia], b. May 17, 1844	4	22
Diah, s. [Zebediah & Eunice], b. Oct. 26, 1802	2	222
Dolly Ann, m. Simon L. **KINGSLEY**, of Bozrah, June 4,		
1826	3	124
Eliza, m. Andrew **McDANIELS**, Dec. 10, 1826, by Rev.		
Cornelius B Everest	3	18
Elizabeth, d. [Tho[ma]s & Elizabeth], b. Apr. 15,		
1765	1	315
Elizabeth, d. [Phineas & Elizabeth], b. July 16, 1770	2	118
Erasmus Darwin, [s. Cyrus & Hannah], b. Sept. 22, 1800	3	219
Erasmus Darwin, m. Maria Isabella **TURNER**, of N. Caro-		
lina, [ ], 1835	3	219
Erasmus Darwin, [s. George Anson & Melissa], b.		
[ ]	3	219
Eunice, m. John **BASS**, Sept. 18, 1814	3	74
Eunice, of Windham, m. Cha[rle]s **ARMSTRONG**, of Frank-		
lin, May 28, 1843, by Rev. J.E. Tyler	3	209
Eunice C., of Windham, m. Thomas S. **WILLIAMS**, of		
Hampton, Oct. 10, 1833, by Rev. Jesse Fisher	3	167
Fanning, of Canterbury, m. Pamela **CUSHMAN**, of Windham,		
May 11, 1829, by Rev. Jesse Fisher	3	136
Frederick, m. Eunice **RIPLEY**, June 11, 1816	3	79
Frederick Augustus Eugene, [s. Frederick Palmer &		

	Vol.	Page
TRACY, (cont)		
Emily], b. July 18, 1838, at Lynn, Mass.;		
d. Feb. 23, 1839, at Lynn Mass.	3	219
Frederick Palmer, [s. Cyrus & Hannah], b. Feb.		
22, 1815	3	219
Frederick Palmer, m. Emily **STONE**, d. Obadiah,		
of Thompson, Conn. [ ]	3	219
Frederick William, [s. Frederick Palmer & Emily],		
b. Feb. 9, 1842, at Concord, N.H.	3	219
George, s. [Frederick & Eunice], b. Feb. 17, 1819	3	79
George Anson, [s. Cyrus & Hannah], b. July 16,		
1809	3	219
George Anson, m. Melessa **OLDS**, of Canterbury, Apr.		
14, 1833	3	219
Grace Emeline, [d. Frederick Palmer & Emily], b.		
Mar. 2, 1844, at Cambridge, Mass.	3	219
Gurdon, res. Scotland, d. July 6, [1849], ae. 76	4	153
Harriet Newell, [d. George Anson & Melissa], b.		
[ ]	3	219
Henry, s. [Frederick & Eunice], b. Apr. 22, 1817	3	79
Henry R., m. Mary A. **RICHARDSON**, b. of Windham,		
Sept. 27, 1842, by Rev. J.E. Tyler	3	204
Henry W., s [Uriah R & Sophronia], b. Aug. 21,		
1828	3	128
James, s. Stephen & Deborah, b. June 15, 1720	1	11
James, m. Susannah **BISHOP**, May 26, 1748	1	278
James, Lieut., d. Sept. 21, 1756, at Fort Edward	1	278
James, s. Thomas & Elizabeth, b. Jan. 28, 1760	1	315
John, s. Stephen & Deborah, b. Apr. 25, 1718	1	11
John, Lieut., d. May 30, 1718, in the 85th y. of		
his age	1	11
John, s. [Zebadiah & Asenath], b. Feb. 21, 1812	3	68
John, b. Feb. 21, 1812; m. Delia **BARROWS**, Apr. 14,		
1835, in Mansfield, by Rev. S.S. Atwood	4	22
John Cushman, s. Fanning & Pamela, b. Feb. 25,		
1830	3	136
John Theodore, [s. John & Delia], b. July 2, 1842	4	22
Joseph, s. Tho[ma]s & Elizabeth, b. July 18, 1763	1	315
Joseph, machinist, ae. 34, of Franklin, m. Emyline		
KENYON, ae. 22, b. Franklin, res. Columbia,		
May 8, 1848, by Rev. John Tyler	4	111
Julia, d. [Thomas C.], b. Oct. 11, 1823	3	75
Julia, m. Oliver F. **HARRIS**, b. of Windham, Apr. 7,		
1845, by Rev. Tho[ma]s Tallman, Scotland	3	221
Julia Ida, [d. John & Delia], b. Aug. 12, 1847	4	22
Julius Augustus, [s. George Anson & Melissa], b.		
[ ]	3	219
Lois, m. Eliphalet **COBURN**, Oct. 28, 1781	2	153

	Vol	Page
TRACY, (cont.)		
Louisa, m. Joseph **ALLEN**, Jr., Jan. 12, 1786	2	87
Lucian, [s. Erasmus Darwin & Maria Isabella],		
b. Dec. 6, 1835, at Centreville, Ga.	3	219
Luce, m. William **CASE**, Nov. 11, 1736	1	187
Lucy, d. [Phineas & Elizabeth], b. May 31, 1772	2	118
Lucy Ann, d. Thomas C., b. Aug. 29, 1822	3	75
Lydia, m. Amos D. **ALLEN**, Aug. 18, 1796	2	26
Lydia, m. Amos D. **ALLEN**, Aug. 18, 1796	3	76
Maria, m. Daniel **HUNTINGTON**, Apr. 19, 1786	3	29
Maria, m. John **BASS**, b. of Windham, Feb. 11,		
1838, by Rev. Otis C. Whiton	3	185
Maria Jane, [d. George Anson & Melissa], b.		
[ ]	3	219
Mary, d. Stephen & Deborah, b. Aug. 26, 1708	1	11
Mary, d. [Thomas & Elizabeth], b. Nov. 12, 1752	1	315
Mary, m. Jonathan **RUDD**, Jr., Oct. 1, 1766	2	127
Mary, m. Jedediah **BINGHAM**, Sept. 12, 1810	2	228
Mary Ann, m. William **MORRISON**, Nov. 29, 1832, by		
Rev. Alva Gregory	3	162
Mary Ann, d. John H., manufacturer, ae. 40, &		
Hannah, ae. 37, b. Jan. 24, [1850]	4	10
Mary Louisa, [d. Frederick Palmer & Emily], b.		
Dec. 8, 1839, at Thompson, Conn.	3	219
Meriel, d. [Perez & Deidamia], b. Nov 27, 1765	2	130
Nathan, s. James & Susannah, b. Oct. 31, 1750	1	278
Nathaniel, s. Stephen & Deborah, b. June 21, 1722	1	11
Nathaniel, s. Stephen & Deborah, d. Oct. 11, 1750	1	159
Nehemiah, m. Susan[n]ah **SMITH**, June 19, 1744	1	245
Orrin*, s. Stephen & Deborah, b. Jan. 27, 1710/11		
(*correction Orrin crossed out and Prince		
handwritten in margin of original manuscript		
along with notation: "K.B. Brainerd. In probate		
files".)	1	11
Perez, m. Deidamia **DIMMICK**, Mar. 31, 1765	2	130
Phineas*, m. Elizabeth **HOLBROOK**, May 29, 1766		
(*correction Phineas crossed out and Prince		
handwritten in margin of original manuscript.)	2	118
Portia Lucretia, [d. George Anson & Melissa], b.		
May 7, 1851	3	219
Prince, s. [Phineas & Elizabeth], b. July 8, 1767	2	118
Samuel, s. [Zebediah & Eunice], b. Jan. 30, 1789	2	222
Sarah, d. John, Jr. & Luce, of Dixbury, d. June 18,		
1773	1	123
Stephen, m. Deborah **BINGHAM**, Jan. 26, 1707	1	11
Stephen, s. James & Susannah, b. Apr. 27, 1749	1	278
Stephen, d. Dec. 19, 1769	1	159
Susan, of Windham, m. Isaac **CLARKE**, of Canterbury,		

	Vol.	Page
TRACY, (cont.)		
Apr. 12, 1826	3	121
Susan E., m. Hezekiah B. **PALMER**, Oct. 5, 1835,		
by Rev. Jesse Fisher	3	174
Susan Elizabeth, d. [Sylvester & Lucy], b. June		
15, 1815	3	77
Susan[n]ah, d. Nehemiah & Susan[n]ah, b. Mar. 14,		
1744/5	1	245
Susannah, w. James, d. Nov. 24, 1750	1	278
Susannah, d. Tho[ma]s & Elizabeth, b. July 2, 1758	1	315
Sybel, m. [E]lephalet **REED**, Apr. 1, 1784	2	76
Sylvester, m. Lucy **FULLER**, Feb. 27, 1814	3	77
Thomas, s. Stephen & Deborah, b. Aug 19, 1725	1	11
Thomas, m. Elizabeth **WARNER**, Oct. 28, 1751	1	315
Thomas, s. Tho[ma]s & Elizabeth, b Sept. 4, 1761	1	315
Thomas, s. [Zebediah & Eunice], b. Sept. 1, 1793;		
d. May 10, 1795	2	222
Thomas Chaplin, s. [Zebediah & Eunice], b. Nov. 27,		
1797	2	222
Timo[thy], s. [Perez & Deidamia], b. Oct. 22, 1767	2	130
Uriah R., m. Sophronia **GAGER**, May 16, 1826, by		
Rev. Jesse Fisher	3	128
Uriah R., m. Freelove **PANKIS**(?), b. of Windham,		
Jan. 8, 1840, by Rev. Otis C. Whiton	3	193
Washington Irving, [s. Erasmus Darwin & Maria		
Isabella], b. Mar. 27, 1838, at Centreville, Ga.	3	219
William H., s. Jabez, manufacturer, ae. 38, &		
Hannah, ae. 34, b. Dec. 15, 1847	4	4
William Henry Harrison, [s. Erasmus Darwin & Maria		
Isabella], b. Aug. 8, 1840, at Centreville, Ga.	3	219
Zebediah, m. Eunice **CHAPLIN**, Jan. 10, 1788	2	222
Zebadiah, m. Asenath **HUNTINGTON**, Dec. 14, 1808	3	68
----, m. Abner **SMITH**, [ ]	3	101-2
TRAIN, George, m. Mary **MILLARD**, b. of Windham, July 17,		
[1831], by [Rev. Alva Gregory], at Willimantic	3	156
TREADWAY, TREDWAY, Dyer, m. Jerusha **HOVEY**, Sept. 28,		
1810	3	57
Jenette F., m. Joseph **ABEL**, b. of Willimantic, May		
6, 1838, by Rev. Silas Leonard	3	186
Lucy Manning, d. [Dyer & Jerusha], b. Aug. 11, 1801		
(sic)	3	57
TRESCOT, Susannah, m. Ebenezer **STAMFORD**, Mar. 2, 1806	3	36
TRIM, TRIMM, Alvin, m. Harriet **CHAPPELL**, Apr. 11, 1830,		
by Rev. Roger Bingham	3	144
Sally, m. David **MORE**, Jan. 4, 1835, by Rev. Philo		
Judson, at Willimantic	3	171
William, m. Avis **JOHNSON**, Mar. 20, 1832, by Rev.		
Alva Gregory, Willimantic	3	158

	Vol.	Page
TRIPP, Samuel, m. Laura **BIBBONS**, Mar. 28, 1830, by		
Rev. Roger Bingham	3	141
TROWBRIDGE, TROBRIDGE, Hannah, m. Philip **SEARL**, Dec.		
29, 1774	2	199
James, of Ashford, m. Abigail **WELCH**, of Windham,		
May 5, 1830, by Rev. Rich[ard] F. Cleveland	3	145
TRUMBULL, Almira, m. Ralph **LINCOLN**, Mar. 28, 1816	3	70
Joseph, Col., m. Emelia **DYER**, Mar. 12, 1778; d.		
July 23, 1778, in Lebanon	2	206
TUBBS, Deborah, of Norwich, m. Joseph **WOOD**, Jr., of		
Windham, Apr. 8, 1756	2	7
TUCKER, Charles, m. Cynthia **SNOW**, b. of Windham, May		
10, 1840, by Rev. Otis C. Whiton	3	194
Erastus, of Windham, m. Eliza **HOVEY**, of Windham,		
May 21, 1829, by Rev. Jesse Fisher	3	136
Joseph, s. Cha[rle]s, manufacturer, ae. 35, b.		
Apr. 23, 1850	4	11
Richard, m. Delia **WALDO**, b. of Windham, Nov. 13,		
1831, by Rev. Alva Gregory, Willimantic	3	156
TUCKERMAN, Susannah, m. Jared **LILLIE**, Mar. 18, 1784	2	253
TUDOR, A.G., merchant, ae. 28, m. Lillian J. **RICHARDSON**,		
ae. 26, Apr. 11, [1849], by Rev. J.E. Tyler	4	114
TURNER, Ashley, s. C.W., butcher, ae. 33, b. Aug. 29,		
1849	4	11
Jonathan A., m. Mary M. **BOONE**, Dec. 15, 1844, by		
Rev. Andrew Sharp, Willimantic	3	218
Maria Isabella, of N. Carolina, m. Erasmus Darwin		
TRACY, [ ], 1835	3	219
Rebecca, m. John **READ**, Mar. 6, 1745	1	256
TYLER, Amie, m. Jonathan **RUDD**, Mar. 1, 1804	3	58
Caroline, m. David F. **SMITH**, May 11, 1829	3	197
Daniel, farmer, d. Oct. 13, [1849], ae. 76	4	156
Esther, m. Jonathan **RUDD**, Dec. 6, 1738	1	185
Julia, d. John E., ae. 39, & Mary W., ae. 36, b.		
Nov. 11, [1848]	4	7
Mary Ann, m. Calvin B. **BROMLEY**, b. of Windham, Oct.		
11, [1837], by Rev. Otis C. Whiton, of Scotland		
Society, Windham	3	184
Mary S., of Andover, m. Frederick A. **MATTHEWS**, of		
Hartford, Sept. 28, 1828, by Rev. Jesse Fisher	3	131
UPTON, Asa*, s. [Elias & Charity], b. Mar. 20, 1803		
(*correction, entire entry for Asa affixed to		
original manuscript on slip of paper.)	3	56
Elias, s. Ephraim & Mary, b. Apr. 19, 1745	1	154
Elias, s. Elias & Lucy, b. Jan. 18, 1778	3	56
Elias, m. Charity **ROBINSON**, Apr. 29, 1800	3	56
Elias Lyman, s. [Elias & Charity], b. Apr. 18, 1810	3	56
Ephraim, m. Mary **DINGLEY**, Dec. 31, 1731	1	154

	Vol.	Page
UPTON, (cont.)		
Ephraim, m. Elizabeth **MAINARD**, Apr. 14, 1757	2	112
John, m. Zerviah **WRIGHT**, Jan. 8, 1740/41	1	222
John*, s. [Ephraim & Elizabeth], b. May 27, 1758 (*correction, entire entry for John affixed to original manuscript on slip of paper.)	2	112
Joseph, s. Eph[raim] & Mary, b. May 14, 1747	1	154
Julia, d. [Elias & Charity], b. Mar. 30, 1801	3	56
Mary, d. Ephraim & Mary, b. Oct. 1, 1736	1	154
Mary, d. [Ephraim & Elizabeth], b. June 14, 1761	2	112
Naomy, d. Ephraim & Mary, b. Apr. 29, 1741	1	154
Naomi, m. Dea. William **MARTIN**, Mar. 3, 1757	2	54
Sarah, d. John & Zerviah, b. Oct. 17, 1741	1	222
Sarah, d. [Ephraim & Elizabeth], b. July 15, 1764	2	112
UTLEY, UTLY, Abigail, d. Jeremiah & Mary, b. Sept. 26, 1733	1	96
Abigail, d. [Samuel & Hannah], b. Nov. 19, 1749	1	269
Abigail, m. Amos **CLARK**, Oct. 23, 1755	2	31
Alice, d. [Nathan & Hannah], b. Nov. 1, 1762	2	140
Amasa, s. Japheth & Anna, b. Feb. 3, 1746/7	1	197
Amos, s. James & Annah, b. Nov. 5, 1735	1	51
Amos, m. Grace **MARTIN**, Mar. 2, 1757	2	44
Amos, s. [Amos & Grace], b. Aug. 22, 1764	2	44
Amos, m. Mary **INGERSOLL**, Oct. 22, 1777	2	44
Anna, d. [James, Jr. & Mary], d. Oct. 19, 1754, in the 10th y. of her age	1	291
Anna, d. [Samuel & Hannah], b. Jan. 6, 1755	1	269
Antipas, s. [Sam[ue]l], b. Feb. 16, 1770	1	269
Asa*, s. [Elias & Charity], b. Mar. 20, 1803 (*correction **UPTON** surname handwritten in margin of original manuscript)	3	56
Assnah, d. [Thomas & Abigail], b. July 2, 1785	2	242
Bridget, d. James & Annah, b. Nov. 3, 1733	1	117
Bridget, d. [Amos & Grace], b. Jan. 27, 1759	2	44
Cyrus, s. [Sam[ue]l], b. Mar. 11, 1767	1	269
Daniel, s. Jeremiah & Mary, b. Feb. 11, 1739/40	1	221
Dicea, d. [Joseph & Jerusha], b. Sept. 12, 1767	2	16
Dinah, m. David **MARTIN**, Jan. 25, 1775	2	15
Ebenezer, s. [Joseph & Jerusha], b. Dec. 2, 1770	2	16
Ede, d. [Nathan & Hannah], b. Dec. 26, 1763	2	140
Elijah, s. [Sam[ue]l], b. Feb 15, 1778	1	269
Elizabeth, d. James & Annah, b. Apr. 22, 1729	1	51
Elizabeth, d. [Samuel & Hannah], b. Jan. 18, 1757	1	269
Esther, d. Jere[mia]h & Mary, b. Mar. 9, 1747	1	221
Esther, d. [Joseph & Jerusha], b. Apr. 12, 1780	2	16
Eunice, d. [Joseph & Jerusha], b. Jan. 16, 1774	2	16

	Vol.	Page

UTLEY, UTLY, (cont.)

Grace, w. Amos, d. Aug. 12, 1775, in the 38th
    y. of her age   2   44

Hannah, d. James & Annah, b. Apr. 17, 1727; d.
    May 30, 1731   1   51

Hannah, d. James & Annah, b. June 15, 1731   1   51

Hannah, d. [Samuel & Hannah], b. Jan. 5, 1753   1   269

Hannah, m. Aaron **GEER**, July 8, 1755   1   281

Hancock, s. [Amos & Grace], b. Aug. 12, 1774   2   44

Hannah, d. [Sam[ue]l], d. Feb. 25, 1778   1   269

James, s. James & Annah, b. Mar. 17, 1721   1   51

James, Jr., m. Mary **KINGSBURY**, Aug. 10, 1742   1   291

James, s. James, Jr. & Mary, b. Dec. 10, 1751;
    d. Oct. 16, 1754   1   291

James, s. James & Mary, b. Aug. 15, 1756   1   291

James, d. Sept. 22, 1774, in the 54th y. of his
    age   1   291

James, s. [Thomas & Abigail], b. Sept. 2, 1781   2   242

Japheth, s. Japheth & Anna, b. Feb. 9, 1745/6   1   197

Jeremiah, s. Jeremiah & Mary, b. July 15, 1730   1   96

Jeremiah, s. [Joseph & Jerusha], b Nov. 29,
    1775, in Pomfret   2   16

Jerusha, d. [Joseph & Jerusha], b. Mar 26, 1758   2   16

Joel, m. Abigail **DURKEE**, Jan. 7, 1768   2   131

John, s. Jeremiah & Mary, b. June 5, 1738   1   221

John*, s. [Ephraim & Elizabeth], b. May 27, 1758
    (*correction **UPTON** surname handwritten in margin
    of original manuscript)   2   112

Jonathan, s. Jeremiah & Mary, b. June 26, 1741   1   221

Jonathan, m. Mary **ROBINS**, May 1, 1766   2   149

Jonathan, s. [Jonathan & Mary], b. Apr. 1, 1770   2   149

Joseph, s. Jeremiah & Mary, b. Mar. 6, 1732   1   96

Joseph, m. Jerusha **MARTIN**, May 29, 1754   2   16

Joseph, s. [Joseph & Jerusha], b. Apr. 8, 1762   2   16

Lucinda, m. Freeman D. **SPENCER**, Mar 19, 1845, by
    Rev. Andrew Sharp   3   220

Lucy, d. [Joseph & Jerusha], b. May 18, 1760   2   16

Lydia, d. [Stephen & Zip[p]orah], b. Jan. 21, 1760   2   51

Mary, m. Joseph **ALLEN**, Jan. [ ], 1723/4   1   134

Mary, d. Jeremiah & Mary, b. June 23, 1726   1   96

Mary, d. James & Mary, b. Oct. 30, 1747; d. Nov. 8,
    [1747]   1   291

Mary, d. James, Jr. & Mary, b. June 29, 1749; d. Oct
    20, 1754   1   291

Mary, d. [Joseph & Jerusha], b. Apr. 15, 1756   2   16

Mary, d. [Jonathan & Mary], b. Feb. 1, 1767   2   149

Nathan, s. Jerem[iah] & Mary, b. Feb. 15, 1743   1   221

Nathan, m. Hannah **DURKEE**, Apr. 27, 1762   2   140

	Vol.	Page
UTLEY, UTLY, (cont.)		
Oliver, s. [Stephen & Zip[p]orah], b. Sept. 14, 1758	2	51
Parsy, d. [Jonathan & Mary], b. Aug. 10, 1768	2	149
Phebe, d. [Joseph & Jerusha], b. Oct. 24, 1778	2	16
Phil[l]ip, s. [Samuel & Hannah], b. July 26, 1751; d. May 18, 1754	1	269
Phillip, s. [Samuel & Hannah], b. Feb. 26, 1760	1	269
Prescillah, d. Jeremiah & Mary, b. Dec. 21, 1727	1	96
Rufus, s. [Sam[ue]l], b. May 25, 1773	1	269
Samuel, s. James & Annah, b. May 28, 1723	1	51
Samuel, m. Hannah **ABBOT[T]**, Aug. 1, 1748	1	269
Sam[ue]ll, s. James & Mary, b. Nov. 8, 1758	1	291
Samuel, s. [Samuel & Hannah], b. Feb. 2, 1759	1	269
Samuel, d. Nov. 15, 1782	1	269
Sarah, m. Joseph **ROSS**, Sept. 16, 1716	1	30
Sarah, d. Jere[miah] & Mary, b. Oct. 25, 1746	1	221
Sarah, d. [Amos & Grace], b. Nov. 4, 1757	2	44
Sarah, d Jeremiah, Jr. & Elizabeth, b. Aug. 10, 1760	2	2
Sarah, m. Isaac **DODGE**, Oct. 28, 1762	2	84
Stephen, s. Jeremiah & Mary, b. Mar. 28, 1736	1	96
Stephen, m. Zip[p]orah **HASTINGS**, Apr. 28, 1757	2	51
Stephen, s. [Samuel & Hannah], b. Nov. 21, 1762	1	269
Thomas, s. James, Jr. & Mary, b. Apr. 20, 1754	1	291
Thomas, m. Abigail **HODGKINS**, May 25, 1780	2	242
Thomas, s. [Thomas & Abigail], b. July 30, 1783	2	242
Timothy, s. James & Annah, b. May 3, 1739	1	198
Timothy, s. [Samuel & Hannah], b. Mar. 22, 1765	1	269
Ursula, d. [Amos & Grace], b. May 17, 1762	2	44
Wilkes, s. [Amos & Grace], b. Apr. 13, 1769	2	44
William, s. James & Annah, b. Feb. 5, 1724/5	1	51
VALENTINE, Elliott, of Boston, Mass., m. Jane Ann **GRAY**, of Lebanon, Nov. 6, 1823	3	115
VAUGHAN, Ira W , m. Ab[b]ly **PRENTICE**, b. of Windham, Oct 24, 1842, by Rev. A.C. Wheat	3	205
VEAZEY, Eleazer, m. Mary **BROWN**, Feb. 18, 1771	2	193
Elizabeth, d. [Eleazer & Mary], b. May 5, 1777	2	193
Mary, d. [Eleazer & Mary], b. Nov. 18, 1773	2	193
VERGISON, Caroline U., m. Simeon C. **KELLEY**, b. of Willimantic, Feb. 20, 1837, by Rev. Philo Judson, at Willimantic	3	182
VINING, Colaty, m. Ephraim **BACKUS**, Oct. 10, 1734	1	142
VINTON, Sarah, d. Malaliah & Sarah, b. Dec. 8, 1733	1	144
Sarah, m. Jonathan **BINGHAM**, June 7, 1735/6	1	144
WADE, Carlton W., s. Henry S., shoemaker, ae. 37, b. May 1, [1850]	4	11
WAITE, Elizabeth H., of Windham, m. Seymour W. **SMITH**, of		

	Vol.	Page
WAITE, (cont.)		
Springfield, Mass., Sept. 30, 1839, by Rev.		
R. Ransom, Willimantic	3	190
[WALBRIDGE], **WALLBRIDGE**, Sarah, m. Phineas **MANNING**,		
Jan. 22, 1750/51	1	304
WALCOTT, [see under **WOLCOTT**]		
WALDEN, Abigail, d. John & Abigail, b. Feb. 13, 1718/19	1	59
Abigail, w. [John], d. Mar. 29, 1773, in the 74th		
y. of her age	1	168
Asa, s. [John, Jr. & Sarah], b. Apr. 9, 1759; d.		
Feb. 3, 1760	2	79
Asa, s. [John, Jr. & Sarah], b. Jan. 26, 1761	2	79
David, s. [John, Jr. & Sarah], b. Feb. 3, 1764	2	79
Dorcas, mother of Joseph, d. Apr. 9, 1748, in the		
88th y. of her age	1	76
Ebenezer, s. John & Abigail, b. Mar. 8, 1738/9	1	168
Hannah, d. John & Abigail, b. May 5, 1735	1	168
Hannah, m. Nathaniel **SMITH**, Oct. 21, 1756	2	18
Irena, d. [John, Jr. & Sarah], b. Feb. 27, 1754	2	79
John, s. John & Abigail, b. Aug. 10, 1720; d.		
Dec. 24, 1726	1	59
John, s. John & Abigail, b. Jan. 22, 1733/4	1	168
John, Jr., m. Sarah **PARRISH**, Sept. 26, 1751	2	79
John, s. [John, Jr. & Sarah], b. Aug. 24, 1752	2	79
John, Jr., m. Sarah **KNIGHT**, Nov. 12, 1752	1	240
John, d. June 12, 1759, in the 77th y. of his age	1	168
Jonathan, s. John, Jr. & Prudence, b. Sept. 12, 1728	1	99
Joseph, m. Sarah **BINGHAM**, Jan. 16, 1723/4; d. May 30,		
1755, in the 61st y. of his age	1	76
Joseph, s. [John, Jr. & Sarah], b. Nov. 12, 1752	1	240
Joseph, s. [John, Jr. & Sarah], b. Nov. 12, 1752	2	79
Joseph, d. May 30, 1755, in the 61st y. of his age	1	76
Louisa H., m. Isaac N. **ROBINSON**, Sept. 9, 1832, by		
Rev. Rich[ar]d F. Cleveland	3	161
Mary, d. John & Abigail, b. Aug. 4, 1726; d. Jan.		
[sic] 3, 1726/7	1	59
Minor, s. [John, Jr. & Sarah], b. Dec. 16, 1770	2	79
Sarah, d. John & Abigail, b. May 24, 1728	1	59
Sarah, m. Nathaniel **KINGSLEY**, Mar. 16, 1748/9	1	289
Sarah, d. [John, Jr. & Sarah], b. Dec. 22, 1762; d.		
Mar. 4, 17[ ]	2	79
Sarah, d. [John, Jr. & Sarah], b. Oct. 12, 1765	2	79
Sarah, m. Col. Thomas **DYAR**, Oct. 5, [ ]	2	1
Susannah, d. John & Abigail, b. May 24, 1724; d.		
Dec. 4, 1726	1	59
Susannah, d. John & Abigail, b. Mar. 12, 1731	1	59
Susannah, m. Joshua **LASSELL**, Jr., Feb 6, 1750/51	1	302
Susannah, d. [John, Jr. & Sarah], b. July 2, 1768	2	79

	Vol.	Page
WALDEN, (cont.)		
——, s. [John, Jr. & Sarah], b. June 22, 1775	2	79
WALDO, WALDOW, WALDOE, Abigail, m Cornelius **WALDO**,		
Oct. 30, 1735	1	165
Abigail, d. Cornelius & Abigail, b. July 17, 1745	1	165
Ann, d. [John & Jemima], b. Nov. 24, 1758	1	306
Anne, d. Edward & Thankfull, b. Nov. 8, 1714	1	29
Betheul, s. Edward & Thankfull, b. June 10, 1719	1	29
Bethuel, m. Lois **MUNSELL**, May 25, 1743	1	207
Caroline Lovett, twin with Catharine Bailey, d.		
Zaccheas, Jr., b. Jan. 1, 1824	3	95
Catharine, m. Joseph **DINGLEY**, Nov. 2, 1702	A	33
Catharine Bailey, twin with Caroline Lovett, d.		
Zaccheas, Jr., b. Jan. 1, 1824	3	95
Charles, s. [Ebenezer & Eunice], b. May 23, 1802;		
d. Nov. 2, 1802	3	17
Charles Backus, s. [Ebenezer & Eunice], b. Oct. 22,		
1803	3	17
Cornelius, s. Edward & Thankfull, b. Feb. 18,		
1711/12	1	29
Cornelius, m. Abigail **WALDOW**, Oct. 30, 1735	1	165
Cornelius, s. Cornelius & Abigail, b. Mar. 21, 1741	1	165
Dalithe, s. [Zacheas & Tallathe], b. Aug. 5, 1760	1	268
Dalithe, see also Tabitha & Talitha		
Daniel, s. [Zacheas & Tabitha], b. Sept. 10, 1762	2	119
Delia, m. Richard **TUCKER**, b. of Windham, Nov. 13,		
1831, by Rev. Alva Gregory, Willimantic	3	156
Eben[eze]r, s. [Zacheas & Tabitha], b. Aug. 15, 1766	2	119
Ebenezer, m. Eunice **DEVOTION**, Aug. 22, 1797	3	17
Ebenezer, s. [Ebenezer & Eunice], b. June 9, 1798	3	17
Edward, m. Thankfull **DEMMUCK**, June 28, 1706	1	29
Edward, s. Edward & Thankful, b. July 27, 1709	1	29
Edward, Dea., d Aug. 3, 1767, ae. 84	1	29
Elizabeth, d. Zacheas & Tallathe, b. Oct. 11, 1754	1	268
Elizabeth, d. [Zacheas & Tabitha], b. Oct. 11, 1754	2	119
Elizabeth, d. [Ebenezer & Eunice], b. Sept. 25, 1807	3	17
Est[h]er, d. [Zaccheas, Jr. & Est[h]er], b. July 14,		
1786	2	235
Esther, m. Jason **GAGER**, Jr., Nov. 3, 1806	3	57
Est[h]er, w. Zaccheas, d. Aug. 22, 1825	2	235
Eunice, d. Zac[c]heas & Tallathe, b. Feb. 12, 1753	1	268
Eunice, d. [Zac[c]heas & Tabitha], b. Feb. 12, 1753	2	119
Eunice, m. William **RUDD**, Dec. 23, 1771	2	166
Eunice, d. [Ebenezer & Eunice], b. Dec. 23, 1799	3	17
Ezra, s. Bethuel & Lois, b. Mar. 23, 1745/6	1	207
Gamaleel, s. John & Jemima, b. Aug. 28, 1755	1	306
George, [s. Ebenezer], b. Apr. 14, 1816	3	17
Giles, s. Ebenezer, b. May 25, 1814	3	17

	Vol.	Page
WALDO, WALDOW, WALDOE, (cont.)		
Irena, d. Cornelius & Abigail, b. Apr. 18, 1738	1	165
Jenna, m. Jonah **BREWSTER**, Jan. 25, 1743/4	1	243
Joanna, d. Bethuel & Lois, b. May 10, 1748	1	207
Joannah, d. Ed[ward] & Thankfull, b. Apr. [ ],		
1823 (1723?)	1	29
John, d. Apr. 14, 1700	A	12
John, m. Elizabeth **FFENNO**, Oct. 3, 1706	1	19
John, s. John & Elizabeth, b. Oct. 10, 1707	1	19
John, s. Edward & Thankfull, b. Apr. 19, 1717; d.		
Aug. 29, 1726	1	29
John, s. Edw[ar]d & Thankfull, b. Sept. 18, 1728	1	29
John, s. Zac[c]heas & Tallathe, b. Apr. 22, 1750	1	268
John, s. Zac[c]heas & Tabitha, b. Apr. 22, 1750	2	119
John, m. Jemima **ABBOTT**, Mar. 14, 1750/51	1	306
John, s. [John & Jemima], b. Feb. 16, 1762	1	306
John Devotion, s. [Ebenezer & Eunice], b. Feb. 6,		
1801	3	17
Joseph, s. [Zac[c]heas & Tabitha], b. Oct. 5, 1758	2	119
Josiah, s. [Zac[c]heas & Tallathe], b. Oct. 5, 1758	1	268
Levi, s. [Zaccheas, Jr. & Est[h]er, b. Feb. 14, 1782	2	235
Lewis, of Windham, m. Alice S. **BALDWIN**, of Canterbury,		
Feb. 26, 1834, by Rev. Otis C. Whiton	3	169
Louis, s. [Ebenezer & Eunice], b. Mar. 4, 1806	3	17
Nancy, d. [Zaccheas, Jr. & Est[h]er], b. Oct. 7, 1784	2	235
Nancy, m. Roger **BINGHAM**, Sept. 1, 1815	3	87
Nathaniel, s. Cornelius & Abigail, b. Nov. 6, 1743	1	165
Olive, d. [John & Jemima], b. Nov. 23, 1753	1	306
Ozias, s [Zac[c]heas & Tabitha], b. Apr. 21, 1768	2	119
Phillip, s. John & Jemima, b. Jan. 21, 1752	1	306
Polly, d. [Zaccheas, Jr. & Est[h]er], b. Oct. 4, 1795	2	235
Rebeckah, d. John & Elizabeth, b. Apr. 5, 1709	1	19
Rebeckah, m. Nathaniel **RUDD**, Dec. 27, 1709	1	48
Ruth, m. Isaac **CRANE**, Aug. 12, 1716	1	132
Ruth, d. Zac[c]h[eas] & Tallathe, b. Nov. 28, 1748	1	268
Ruth, d. Zac[c]heas & Tabitha, b. Nov. 28, 1748	2	119
Ruth, m. Ebenezer **BASS**, Dec. 13, 1769	2	150
Samuel Lovit[t], s. [Zaccheas, Jr. & Est[h]er], b.		
Apr. 6, 1783	2	235
Shuball, s. Edward & Thankfull, b. Apr. 7, 1707	1	29
Sophia, d. [Zaccheas, Jr. & Est[h]er, b. Aug. 27,		
1791	2	235
Tabitha, d. [Zac[c]heas & Tabitha], b. Aug. 5, 1760	2	119
Tabitha, w. Zaccheas, d. Jan. 18, 1789, in the 63rd		
y. of her age	2	119
Tabitha, see also Dalithe and Talitha		
Talitha, d. [Zaccheas, Jr. & Est[h]er], b. Mar. 10,		
1789	2	235

	Vol.	Page
WALDO, WALDOW, WALDOE, (cont.)		
Talitha, m. Moses **ABBE**, Feb. 2, 1808. Record from		
First Church in Windham.	3	19
Talitha, see also Dalithe & Tabitha		
Temperance, d Bethuel & Lois, b. July 20, 1744	1	207
Thankfull, d. Ed[ward] & Thankfull, b. July 3, 1726;		
d Aug. 25, 1726	1	29
Thankfull, w. Dea. Edward, d. Dec. 13, 1757	1	29
Zac[c]heus, s Edward & Thankfull, b. July 19, 1725	1	29
Zac[c]heas, m. Tallathe **KINGSLEY**, Feb. 3, 1746/7	1	268
Zac[c]heas, m. Tabatha **KINGSBURY**, Feb. 3, 1746/7	2	119
Zac[c]heas, s. [Zac[c]heas & Tallathe], b. Nov. 20,		
1756	1	268
Zaccheas, s. [Zac[c]heas & Tabitha], b. Nov. 20, 1756		
Zaccheas, Jr , m. Est[h]er **STEAVENS**, Apr. 12, 1781	2	119
Zaccheas, s. [Zaccheas, Jr. & Est[h]er], b. May 21,	2	235
1793		
Zaccheas, father of Ebenezer, d. Sept. 10, 1810	2	235
Zaccheas, m. Harriet A. **LILLIE**, b of Windham, Aug.	3	17
18, 1841, by Rev. Richard Woodruff, of Scotland		
Society		
Zerviah, d. [John & Jemima], b. Feb. 2, 1760	3	197
Ziporan, s. Zac[c]heas & Tallathe, b. Nov 13, 1747	1	306
Ziporan, s. [Zac[c]heas & Tabatha], b. Nov. 13, 1747	1	268
-----, d [Zac[c]heas & Tabitha], b Dec [ ], 1765;	2	119
d. soon		
WALES, Abigail, d. Nath[anie]ll & Prudence, b. June 21,		
1748	2	119
Abigail, m Thomas **GRAY**, Apr. 9, 1771	1	84
Abigail, d. [Nathaniel, 3rd & Grace], b. Apr. 19, 1773;	2	179
d. Dec 15, 1774		
Abner, s. Nath[anie]ll & Prudence, b. Mar. 9, 1730/31	1	326
Abner, s Nath[anie]ll, Jr & Prudence, d June 10,	1	85
1733		
Abner, s. Nath[anie]ll, Jr. & Prudence, b. June 25,	1	84
1735; d June 7, 1736/7		
Amelia, d. [Nathaniel, 3rd, & Grace], b. Mar. 6, 1766	1	84
Ann, d. Ebenezer & Easther, b. Sept. 17, 1720; d May	1	326
13, 1721		
Asahael, s. [Jonathan & Ziba], b. Mar. 7, 1764	1	34
Blake, s [Nathaniel, 3rd, & Grace], b Sept 22, 1775	2	40
Caroline, m. Joel **WEBB**, Oct. 31, 1781	1	326
Caroline, [d. W[illia]m & Nancy P.], b Feb 14, 1842	2	32
Charles, [s. W[illia]m & Nancy P.], b. Feb. 17, 1840	3	182
Clarissa, m. John **FITCH**, Feb. 24, 1780	3	182
Clerice, d. Seth & Jemima, b. Nov. 1, 1769	2	230
Ebenezer, m. Easther **SMITH**, Oct. 20, 1719	2	55
Ebenezer, s Ebenezer & Easther, b. Dec. 10, 1729	1	34

	Vol.	Page
WALES, (cont.)		
Ebenezer, m. Deborah **WARD**, Oct. 13, 1741	1	138
Eleizer, s. Ebenezer & Esther, b. Apr. 20, 1732	1	93
Eleazer, m. Sarah **NORTON**, Dec. 4, 1757, by		
Jonath[an] Huntington, Assist.	2	34
Elihal, s. [Nathaniel, 3rd, & Grace], b. June 22,		
1761	1	326
Eliel, m. Anne **EDGERTON**, June 28, 1792	2	108
Elijah, s. Eben[ezer] & Deb[orah], b. Jan. 26,		
1747/8	1	261
Elisha, s. Ebenezer & Esther, b. Mar. 18, 1728	1	93
Elisha, m. Mary **ABBE**, Apr. 23, 1747	1	260
Elizabeth, d. Ebenezer & Esther, b. Nov. 28, 1730	1	93
Esther, w. Ebenezer, d. Oct. 10, 1737	1	138
Esther, d. Eben[ezer] & Deborah, b. Mar. 8, 1745/6	1	261
Fanny, twin with Philena, d. Nathan & Rosamond, b.		
Mar. 25, 1784	2	67
Frederick, s. [Nathaniel, Jr. & Mary], b. Mar. 9,		
1758; d. Jan. 17, 1759	2	42
George, s. Seth & Jemima, b. Nov. 1, 1759	2	55
George, s. [William & Sarah], b. May 12, 1787	2	93
Harriet, d. [Jonathan, Jr. & Jerusha], b. May 30,		
1792	2	132
Isaac, s. Ebenezer & Esther, b. July 27, 1735	1	138
Jerusha, d. Nathaniell & Mercy, b. Nov. 27, 1717	1	11
Jerusah, m. Eleizer **CARY**, Jr., Jan. 29, 1735/6	1	156
Jerusha, d. [Nathaniel, 3rd, & Grace], b. Aug. 22,		
1768	1	326
Jerusha, d. [Nathan & Rosamond], b. Dec. 11, 1798	2	67
Jerusha, m. Thomas **GROW**, Apr. 20, 1831, by Rev. Roger		
Bingham	3	153
John, s. Ebenezer & Esther, b. Apr. 12, 1734	1	138
Jonathan, s. Nath[anie]ll, Jr. & Prudence, b. Apr. 11,		
1738	1	84
Jonathan, m. Ziba **ABBE**, May 19, 1757	2	40
Jonathan, Jr., m. Jerusha **BADCOCK**, Apr. 13, 1794	2	132
Joseph Denison, s. [Nathaniel, 3rd, & Grace], b. Jan.		
27, 1771	1	326
Laura, d. [William & Sarah], b. Apr. 13, 1792	2	93
Lucretia, d. [Nathaniel, 3rd, & Grace], b. Dec. 9, 1779	1	326
Lucy, d. [William & Sarah], b. Jan. 9, 1795	2	93
Lydia, d. [William & Sarah], b. Apr. 28, 1784	2	93
Mary, of Windham, m. Richard W. **PECKHAM**, of Franklin,		
Dec. 2, 1844, by Rev. J.E. Tyler	3	218
Mercy, w. Nathaniell, d. Jan. 22, 1725/6	1	11
Nancy, d. [Nathan & Rosamond], b. Mar. 15, 1781	2	67
Nathan, s. Nathaniell & Prudence, d. Jan. 28, 1748/9	1	103
Nathan, m. Rosamond **ROBINSON**, June 29, 1780	2	67

	Vol.	Page
WALES, (cont.)		
Nathaniell, m. Mercy **WEST**, Feb. 14, 1715/16	1	11
Nathaniel, s. Ebenezer & Easther, b. Mar. 20,		
1722	1	34
Nathaniell, Jr., m. Prudence **DENISON**, Dec. 27,		
1726	1	85
Nath[anie]ll, s. Nath[anie]ll, Jr. & Prudence, b.		
Feb. 14, 1727/8; d. July 15, 1728	1	85
Nath[anie]ll, Dea., m. Lydia **HUNTINGTON**, Oct. 22,		
1730; d. June 22, 1744	1	107
Nath[anie]ll, s. Nath[anie]ll, Jr. & Prudence, b.		
June 1, 1733	1	84
Nathaniel, Jr., m. Mary **WETMORE**, Mar. 15, 1741	2	42
[Nath[anie]ll], Dea., d. June 22, 1744	1	107
Nathaniel, 3rd, m. Grace **BREWSTER**, Feb. 9, 1755	1	326
Nath[anie]ll, Dea., d. Nov. 5, 1782	1	86
Nathaniel, s. [Nathan & Rosamond], b. Jan. 16, 1786	2	67
Nathaniel, Capt., d. Nov. 13, 1810	3	62
Oliver, s. Ebenezer & Deborah, b. Feb. 27, 1744	1	138
Peter, s. [Nathan & Rosamond], b. Sept. 28, 1791	2	67
Philena, twin with Fanny, d. [Nathan & Rosamond], b.		
Mar. 25, 1784	2	67
Philena, of Windham, m. Nathaniel **RIPLEY**, of Middle-		
bury, Vt., Nov. 7, 1824, by Rev. Erastus Ripley	3	88
Polly, d. [William & Sarah], b. July 5, 1789	2	93
Prudence, d. Nath[anie]ll, Jr. & Prudence, b. June		
12, 1729/30; d. same day	1	85
Prudence, d. Nath[anie]ll, Jr. & Prudence, b. Mar.		
20, 1746	1	84
Prudence, d. Nathaniell & Prudence, d. Nov. 30, 1748	1	103
Prudence, d. [Nathaniel, 3rd, & Grace], b. Dec. 31,		
1758	1	326
Prudence, m. James **MOULTON**, Jr., Mar. 22, 1780	2	247
Prudence, [w. Dea. Nath[anie]ll], d. May 15, 1792	1	86
Roger, s. Jonathan & Ziba, b. Feb. 7, 1759	2	40
Rosamond, d. Mar. 14, 1849, ae. 92 y. 7 m.	4	154
Sally, d. [William & Sarah], b Jan. 24, 1782	2	93
Shuba[e]l, s. Nath[anie]ll, Jr. & Prudence, b. Nov. 3,		
1740	1	84
Shubael, s. Nath[anie]ll & Prudence, d. Dec. 25, 1748	1	103
Solomon, s. Ebenezer & Esther, b. Nov. 19, 1729	1	93
Stephen, s. [Nathaniel, 3rd & Grace], b. Aug. 22, 1756	1	326
Susannah, d. Nathaniell & Mercy, b. Feb. 5, 1723	1	11
Susan[n]ah, w. Dea. Nathaniel, d. Feb. 5, 1729/30, ae.		
about 67 y.	1	10
Susannah, d. Mar. 7, 1736/7. "Perhaps d. Nath[anie]ll,		
Jr. & Prudence"	1	84
Susannah, d. Ebenezer & Deborah, b. July 2, 1742	1	138

	Vol.	Page
WALES, (cont.)		
Susannah, d. [Nathaniel, 3rd, & Grace], b. Aug. 2, 1763	1	326
Susannah, m. Nathan **BADCOCK**, Mar. 21, 1780	2	37
Susannah, d. [Eliel & Anne], b. Dec. 16, 1794	2	108
Timothy, s. Nathaniel & Susanna, d. Aug. 15, 1719	1	10
Timothy, s. Nathaniell & Mercy, b. Sept. 6, 1725; d. Dec. 19, 1728	1	11
Timothy, s. Ebenezer & Esther, b. Oct. 7, 1737	1	138
William, s. Dea. Nathan[ie]ll & Prudence, b. June 20, 1750; d. Nov. 6, 1761	1	86
William, s. [Jonathan & Ziba], b. Mar. 1, 1762	2	40
William, m. Sarah **TINKER**, Apr. 24, 1779	2	93
W[illia]m, m. Nancy P. **CLARK**, b. of Windham, Apr. 8, 1837, by Rev. W[illia]m A. Curtis	3	182
W[illia]m Henry, [s. W[illia]m & Nancy P.], b. Aug. 12, 1850	3	182
Zeruiah, d. Nathaniell & Mercy, b. Nov. 11, 1719	1	11
Zerviah, m. Eleizer **FFITCH**, May 11, 1738	1	183
——, d. [Nathaniel, Jr. & Mary], b. June 22, 1760; d. July 1, 1760	2	42
——, s. [Nathaniel, Jr. & Mary], b. Sept. 20, 1761; d. same day	2	42
——, child [Nathaniel, Jr. & Mary], b. Apr. 22, 1765	2	42
——, d. W[illia]m, mason, b. Aug. 12, 1850	4	13
WALKER, Betsey, d. [Hez[ekiah] & Jerusha], b. Sept. 6, 1783	2	198
Jesse, s. Hez[ekiah] & Jerusha, b. Oct. 12, 1779	2	198
Lois, d. Hez[ekiah] & Jerusha, b. May 9, 1781	2	198
WALLIS, Abia, w. Joshua, d. May 17, 1696	A	24
Joshua, m. Hannah **WELLS**, Nov. 11, 1697	A	24
WALTON, Joseph, s. [Joseph] & Abigail, b. Apr. 26, 1782	2	168
WARD, Amanda A., of Willimantic, Windham, m. Geo[rge] W. **FAY**, of Marlborough, Mass., Oct. 5, 1835, by Rev. Benajah Cook, Jr.	3	174
Deborah, m. Ebenezer **WALES**, Oct. 13, 1741	1	138
Edwin, b. Marlborough, res. Willimantic, d. Sept. 17, [1848], ae. 83	4	153
WARNER, Andrew, s. Joseph & Elizabeth, b. Nov. 25, 1725; d. Dec. 23, 1726	1	166
Andrew, s. Joseph & Elizabeth, b. Mar. 29, 1731	1	166
Andrew, s. Isaac & Anne, b. Oct. 6, 1758	1	197
Anna, d. Joseph, Jr. & Anna, b. Oct. 5, 1755; d. Oct. 29, 1755	2	6
Anne, d. Isaac & Anne, b. Jan. 19, 1741/2; d. Nov. 14, 1760	1	197
Anne, m. Joseph **JOHNSON**, June 21, 1775	2	25
Azuba, d. [Nathaniel & Elizabeth], b. July 27, 1758	1	289

	Vol.	Page
WARNER, (cont.)		
Azubah, m. Joshua **MAXWELL**, Apr. 15, 1779	2	250
Bela, s. [Mathew & Eunice], b. Oct. 25, 1771	2	145
Bethiah, d. Daniel & Bethiah, b. Mar. 18, 1745/6;		
d. Apr. 19, 1746	1	199
Betsey, d. [Ichabod & Hannah], b. Feb. 9, 1799	3	49
Betsey, of Windham, m. Thomas **WINDSHIP**, of Hartford,		
June 30, 1822	3	105
Charles, s. [Elnathan & Lydia], b. Aug. 2, 1798	2	248
Charles, m. Margaret **HALL**, Apr. 11, 1827, by Rev.		
Cornelius B. Everest	3	126
Charlotte, d. [Elnathan & Lydia], b. Dec. 4, 1801	2	248
Charlotte, m. George **LOOMIS**, Mar. 7, 1832, by Rev.		
Rich[ar]d F. Cleveland	3	158
Daniel, m. Bethiah GEN[N]INGS, Dec. 6, 1739	1	199
Daniel, s. Daniel & Bethiah, b. Aug. 15, 1740	1	199
Delight had s. Henry **LOCKWOOD**, b. Aug. 10, 1780	3	44
Earl, s. [Ichabod & Hannah], b. Aug. 15, 1806	3	49
Elisha, s. Andrew & Deborah, b. Apr. [ ], 1707	1	40
Elizabeth, d. Joseph & Elizabeth, b. Nov. 9, 1728	1	166
Elizabeth, m. Thomas **TRACY**, Oct. 28, 1751	1	315
Elizabeth, d. Nathaniel & Elizabeth, b. Dec. 29, 1751	1	289
Elizabeth, w. Lieut. Joseph, d. Feb. 26, 1767, in the		
69th y. of her age	1	166
Elizabeth, d. [Elnathan & Lydia], b. Apr. 9, 1782	2	248
Elizabeth, d. Nov. 27, 1812	1	289
Elnathan, s. Nathaniel & Elizabeth, b. Nov. 1, 1753	1	289
Elnathan, m. Lydia **BEAMONT**, May 9, 1781	2	248
Elnathan, m. Philena **DUNHAM**, Feb. 5, 1815	2	248
Emily, d. [Ichabod & Hannah], b. June 25, 1809	3	49
Erastus, s. [Elnathan & Lydia], b. Mar. 23, 1790; d.		
July 24, 1800	2	248
Euliga* Ichabod, d. Jan. 18, 1767 (*correction Euliga		
crossed out and "Ensign" handwritten in margin of		
original manuscript)	2	122
Eunice, d. Isaac & Anne, b. Nov. 3, 1756	1	197
Eunice, m. John **BINGHAM**, May 1, 1777	2	45
George, s. [Ichabod & Hannah], b. Nov. 29, 1811; d.		
June 20, [1811], ae. 7 m.	3	49
Geo[rge] Erastus, s. [Ichabod & Hannah], b. July 7,		
1823	3	49
Hannah, d. [Euliga* Ichabod & Mary], d. Sept. 28, 1750		
(*correction Euliga crossed out in original manu-		
script)	2	122
Hannah, d. Timo[thy] & Irena, b. Nov. 23, 1751	1	300
Harry, s. [Elnathan & Lydia], b. Feb. 23, 1794; d.		
Aug. 17, 1794	2	248
Huldah, d. [Nathaniel & Elizabeth], b. Aug. 28, 1756	1	289

	Vol.	Page
WARNER, (cont.)		
Huldah, m. Jesse **FITCH**, Apr. 29, 1779	2	230
Huldah, d. [Elnathan & Lydia], b. Dec. 29, 1795	2	248
Huldah, m. Nathaniel **LINCOLN**, b. of Windham, Jan. 3, 1836, by Rev. Edward Harris	3	176
Ichabod*, m. Hannah **COLLINS**, Apr. 2, 1798 (*correction Ichabod d. Jan. 18, 1767 hand-written in margin of original manuscript)	3	49
Irenay, d. Timo[thy] & Irena, b. Nov. 30, 1753	1	300
Irena, m. Nathan **HIBBARD**, Dec. 4, 1764	2	103
Isaac, m. Ann **DAVIS**, Oct. 11, 1739	1	197
Isaac, s. Isaac & Anne, b. Apr. 20, 1750	1	197
Jared, s. Tim[othy] & Irena, b. Sept. 10, 1754; d. Oct. 15, 1755	1	300
Jared, s. Timo[thy] & Irena, b. Sept. 17, 1756	1	300
John, m. Priscilla **WOOD**, Feb. 28, 1762	2	92
John, s. [Ichabod & Hannah], b. Feb. 12, 1819	3	49
John A., of Brooklyn, m. Martha E. **PORTER**, of Willimantic, Sept. 20, 1841, by Rev. Andrew Sharpe, Willimantic	3	198
Jonathan, s. Daniel & Bethiah, b. Aug. 25, 1742	1	199
Joseph, s. Andrew & Deborah, b. Apr. 27, 1701/2	1	40
Joseph, m. Elizabeth **ALLEN**, June 4, 1722	1	166
Joseph, s. Joseph & Elizabeth, b. Apr. 2, 1724	1	166
Joseph, Jr., m. Anna **LATHROP**, Dec. 31, 1754	2	6
Joseph, Lieut., d. Sept. 13, 1767, in the 66th y. of his age	1	166
Judith, m. Daniel **ROSS**, Mar. 30, 1741	1	46
Lucia, d. [Ichabod & Hannah], b. Aug. 25, 1803	3	49
Lucy, d. Isaac & Anne, b. June 12, 1748	1	197
Lucy, m. James **SAWYER**, July 9, 1770	2	161
Lucy, d. [Elnathan & Lydia], b. Mar. 20, 1788	2	248
Lydia, d. Timo[thy] & Irena, b. Mar. 1, 1759; d. Dec. 6, 1764	1	300
Lydia, d. [William & Lydia], b. Aug. 4, 1770	2	159
Lydia, w. W[illia]m, d. Aug. 8, 1770	2	159
Lydia, d. [Elnathan & Lydia], b. Feb. 19, 1792	2	248
Lydia, w. Elnathan, d. Feb. 28, 1814	2	248
Lydia, d. Joseph & Elizabeth, b. [ ]	1	166
Maria, m. Thomas L. **ADAMS**, b. of Windham, Nov. 9, 1840, by Rev. O.C. Whiton, of Scotland Society	3	195
Maria W., d. [Ichabod & Hannah], b. June 29, 1816	3	49
Mary, d. Andrew & Deborah, b. Apr. [ ], 1703	1	40
Mary, d. Joseph & Elizabeth, b. Apr. 7, 1733	1	166
Mary, d. [Euliga* Ichabod & Mary], d. Jan. 29, 1747 (*correction Euliga crossed out in original manuscript)	2	122
Mary, w. Euliga* Ichabod, d. April 26, 1747		

	Vol.	Page
WARNER, (cont.)		
(*correction Euliga crossed out in original		
manuscript)	2	122
Mary, d. Daniel & Bethiah, b. May 4, 1747	1	199
Mary, d. John & Priscilla, b. June 8, 1765	2	116
Marthew, s. Isaac & Ann, b. June 28, 1743	1	197
Ma[t]thew, m. Eunice **STEEL**, Apr. 10, 1769	2	145
Milan, s. [Mat[t]hew & Eunice], b. Feb. 8, 1770	2	145
Nathan, s. Daniel & Bethiah, b. June 6, 1744	1	199
Nathaniel, m. Elizabeth **WEBB**, June 19, 1749	1	289
Nathaniel, s. [Elnathan & Lydia], b. Sept. 26,		
1784; d. Dec. 21, 1784	2	248
Nathaniel, d. Apr. 12, 1807	1	289
Noama, d. Joseph & Elizabeth, b. July 6, 1736	1	166
Rosewell, s. Isaac & Anne, b. Sept. 18, 1753; d.		
Apr. 15, 1754	1	197
Roxana, d. [Ichabod & Hannah], b. Feb. 17, 1801;		
d. May 17, 1802	3	49
Ruth, m. Gideon **BINGHAM**, Nov. 15, 1761	2	46
Samuel, s. [Euliga* Ichabod & Mary], d. June 21,		
1747 (*correction Euliga crossed out in original		
manuscript)	2	122
Sam[ue]l, s. Nathaniel & Elizabeth, b. May 6, 1750	1	289
Sam[ue]ll, s. Nathaniel [& Elizabeth], d. Nov. 6, 1754	1	289
Sarah, d. [Elnathan & Lydia], b. Oct. 10, 1785	2	248
Thankful, d. Andrew & Deborah, b. May 1, 1698	1	40
Thomas, s. Andrew & Deborah, b. Apr. [ ], 1705	1	40
Timothy, Dr., m. Irena **RIPLEY**, Jan. 11, 1749/50	1	300
Timothy, Dr., d. Apr. 8, 1760	1	300
Timothy, s. [John & Priscilla], b. Nov. 13, 1763	2	92
Timothy, s. John & Priscilla, b. Nov. 13, 1763	2	116
Tryphenia, d. [Nathaniel & Elizabeth], b. Sept. 10,		
1768	1	289
William, s. Joseph & Elizabeth, b. Apr. 7, 1729	1	166
William, m. Lydia **MURDOCK**, Nov. 1, 1769	2	159
William, s. William & [2d w. Mary, b. Oct. 18, 1777	2	159
William L., s. [Ichabod & Hannah], b. May 17, 1814	3	49
——, s. [Nathaniel & Elizabeth], b. June 1, 1761;		
d. same day	1	289
——, d. George & Sarah, b. July 1, [1849]	4	8
WARREN, Charles W. H., m. Lucy **SPENCER**, June 20, 1826	3	106
David, d. Oct. [ ], 1738	1	94
Delight, d. David & Patience, b. May 29, 1733	1	94
Dorothy, m. W[illia]m **READ**, Sept. 20, 1835, by Rev.		
Benajah Cook, Jr., in Willimantic Village	3	174
Elizabeth, d. [John & Elizabeth], b. Sept. 20, 1763,		
in Ashford	2	108
Hannah M., m. Benjamin **FOLLETT**, Nov. 16, 1828, by		

	Vol.	Page
WARREN, (cont.)		
Rev. Roger Bingham	3	143
Heastar, m. Robert **DURKE**, Apr. 25, 1738	1	191
John, m. Elizabeth **BURNAP**, Mar. 6, 1760	2	108
Luce, d. David & Patience, b. June 18, 1730	1	94
Lucy, d. [Nathaniel & Mary], b. Mar. 27, 1767	2	111
Lydia, d. [John & Elizabeth], b. Feb. 1, 1761	2	108
Nathaniel, m. Mary **HIBBARD**, Jan. 9, 1763	2	111
Patience, d. David & Patience, b. Aug. 20, 1727	1	94
Rebecca, d. [Timothy & Nancy], b. Mar. 2, 1795	3	7
Sarah, d. David & Patience, b. July 7, 1738	1	94
Timothy, s. [Nathaniel & Mary], b. Dec. 4, 1763	2	111
Timothy, m. Nancy **POOL**, Jan. 2, 1794	3	7
——, child of George A., laborer, ae. 22, of		
Willimantic, b. July 23, [1850]	4	10
WATERMAN, WATTERMAN, Elijah, Rev., m. Lucy **ABBE**, Nov.		
18, 1795	2	54
Elijah, Rev., m. Lucy **ABBE**, Nov. 18, 1795	3	1
Elizabeth, m. Lt. John **FFITCH**, July 10, 1695	A	15
Elizabeth, m. John **FFITCH**, [s. James & Prescilla],		
July 10, 1695	1	33
Julia, d. [Rev. Elijah & Lucy], b. Jan. 12, 1799	3	1
Mary, d. [Rev. Elijah & Lucy], b. Apr. 5, 1797	2	54
Mary, d. [Rev. Elijah & Lucy], b. Apr. 5, 1797	3	1
WATERS, WATTERS, Elizabeth, d. Jacob & Lydia, b. Aug. 6,		
1738	1	176
Hezekiah, s. Jacob & Lydia, b. Oct. 15, 1740	1	176
Jacob, m. Lydia **MERRY**, Feb. 13, 1737/8	1	176
Lydia, w. Jacob, d. July 6, 1744	1	176
Moses, s. Jacob & Lydia, b. Sept. 21, 1742	1	176
WEARE, [see also **WEAVER**], John, m. Lydia **CAREY**, July 13,		
1823	3	113
WEAVER, [see also **WEARE**], Ann, m. Jesse **CURTIS**, of Coven-		
try, Oct. 6, 1825, by Rev. C.B. Everest	3	114
Denison P., of Windham, m. Harriet **YOUNG**, of Ashford,		
Nov. 9, 1840, by Rev. Henry Greenslit	3	194
George L., m. Submit M. **DUNHAM**, July 11, 1835, by		
Rev. Ella Dunham	3	173
Hannah J., d. F.B., machinist, b. Sept. 10, [1849]	4	9
Horatio Bulkley, s. John, b. July 30, 1823	3	48
Howard, s. Edward, clerk, ae. 33, & Almira, ae. 33,		
of Willimantic, b. Feb. 16, 1851	4	12
John, of Windham, m. Lucinda **HOW**, of Coventry, R.I.,		
June 12, 1843, by Calvin Hebbard, J.P.	3	209
Joseph E., m. Almira **DUNHAM**, b. of Windham, Oct. 6,		
1839, by Rev. Ella Dunham, Willimantic	3	191
Lathrop P., s. Palmer, ae. 30, & Harriet, ae. 36, b.		
Sept. 12, [1848]	4	7

	Vol.	Page
WEAVER, (cont.)		
Lois A., d. W[illia]m L., book-seller, ae. 29, &		
[ ], ae. 27, b. Feb. 20, 1848	4	2
Lucinda, m. Job T. **YOUNG**, Nov. 26, 1846, by Rev.		
Tho[ma]s Tallman, of Scotland	3	232
Marvin B., m. Sarah A. **DUNHAM**, b. of Willimantic		
Falls, July 3, 1836, by Rev. Benajah Cook, Jr.	3	178
Nelson D., m. Emeline **ROBINSON**, b. of Willimantic,		
Oct. 2, 1836, by Rev. Philo Judson, at		
Willimantic	3	179
W[illia]m L., m. Lois **SNELL**, June 26, 1842, by		
Andrew Sharp, Willimantic	3	202
WEBB, Abigail, d. Zebulon & Judeth, b. June 12, 1738	1	129
Abner, s. Zebulon & Judeth, b. Sept. 12, 1733	1	129
Abner, s. Napthali & Mary, b. June 26, 1759	1	309
Abner, m. Prudence **BAKER**, Nov. 2, 1780	2	237
Abner, s. [Abner & Prudence], b. Mar. 5, 1783	2	237
Adin, s. [Christopher & Olive], b. Mar. 31, 1780	2	220
Allice, d. Eb[enezer] & Ruth, b. Aug. 3, 1749	1	210
Ann, d. Nathaniell & Elizabeth, b. June 13, 1728	1	33
Ann, d. Eb[enezer] & Ruth, b. Mar. 13, 1745/6	1	210
Ann, d. John & Ann, b. June 11, 1747	1	261
Ann had s. Silas **PERKINS**, b. July 15, 176[ ]	2	1
Ann Clarissa, m. Luther A. **JACOBS**, b. of Williman-		
tic, Mar. 30, 1846, by John Cooper	3	228
Anne, d. [Nathaniel & Zerviah], b. Nov. 5, 1772	2	137
Azariah, s. Joshua & Hannah, b. Oct. 11, 1748	1	244
Benjamin, s. [Stephen & Content], b. July 28, 1780	2	152
Bethiah, d. Zebulon & Judeth, b. May 13, 1736	1	129
Betsey, b. Brooklyn, res. Windham, d. Mar. 21, 1849,		
ae. 40	4	154
Caroline, d. [Joel & Caroline], b. Aug. 14, 1782	2	32
Catharine L., of Windham, m. Jonathan **BENNET**, of		
Pomfret, Apr. 12, 1829, by Rev. Jesse Fisher	3	135
Charles, s. [Abner & Prudence], b. May 20, 1800	2	237
Charles, s. [William & Amanda], b. Mar. 11, 1833	3	117
Charles Lee, s. [Nathaniel & Zerviah], b. Oct. 8,		
1781	2	137
Christopher, s. Eb[enezer] & Ruth, b. June 14, 1755	1	210
Christopher, m. Olive **BROWN**, Jan. 8, 1778	2	220
Clarissa, d. [John, Jr. & Zipporah], b. Aug. 14, 1783	2	180
Clarissa, m. Abner **ROBINSON**, Jr., Mar. 2, 1806	3	66
Daniel, s. [Christopher & Olive], b. Apr. 13, 1778, in		
Canterbury	2	220
Darius, s. Ebenezer & Ruth, b. July 28, 1742	1	210
Darius, m. Deborah **PALMER**, Oct. 8, 1767	2	203
David, s. [Stephen & Content], b. Sept. 8, 1785 (1786)	2	152
Deborah, d. [Joel & Caroline], b. Feb. 6, 1784	2	32

	Vol.	Page
WEBB, (cont.)		
Deborah, m. Marcus **SMITH**, Feb. 21, 1845, by Rev.		
Andrew Sharp	3	220
Ebenezer, s. Samuell & Hannah, b. Apr. 26, 1712;		
d. Jan. 8, 1713	1	7
Ebenezer, s. Sam[ue]ll & Hannah, b. Jan. 12,		
1718/19	1	7
Ebenezer, m. Ruth **CRANE**, Dec. 3, 1740	1	210
Ebenezer, s. Eb[enezer] & Ruth, b. May 29, 1757	1	210
Ebenezer, Jr., m. Abigail **RUDE**, Jr., Aug. 28, 1777	2	246
Edwin B., [s. Benj[ami]n], b. Dec. 26, 1806	3	90
Eleazer, s. [Joel & Caroline], b. Aug. 29, 1791;		
d. Apr. 14, 1794	2	32
Eleazer Wales, s. [Joel & Caroline], b. Oct. 2, 1798	2	32
Eliphalet, s. Zebulon & Judeth, b. Feb. 20, 1742/3	1	129
Elisha, s. [Stephen & Content], b. Feb. 4, 1785	2	152
Eliza D., ae. 24, m. Dwight **LINCOLN**, manufacturer,		
ae. 23, Nov. 3, 1847, by Holmes Slade	4	111
Elizabeth, d. Nathaniell & Elizabeth, b. June 3,		
1723	1	33
Elizabeth, d. John [& Ann], b. Oct. 1, 1748; d. Feb.		
5, 1752	1	261
Elizabeth, m. Nathaniel **WARNER**, June 19, 1749	1	289
Elizabeth, d. Eb[enezer] & Ruth, b. Feb. 19, 1753	1	210
Elizabeth, d. John & Ann, b. Feb. 18, 1755	1	261
Elizabeth, m. Jedediah **BINGHAM**, Apr. 29, 1779	2	228
Elizabeth, wid. Nathaniel, d. July 3, 1780, ae. 84	1	259
Elizabeth Dorrance, [d. John, Jr. & Nabby], b. May 18,		
1823	3	83
Elizabeth W., [d. Benj[ami]n], b. May 15, 1805	3	90
Emily, ae. 27, m. W[illia]m S. **ARMSTRONG**, painter, ae.		
48, Dec. 30, [1849], by Rev. J.M. Phillips	4	114
Erastus, s. [Abner & Prudence], b. June 16, 1781	2	237
Easther, m. Thomas **READ**, Nov. 9, 1726	1	40
Esther, d. [John, Jr. & Zipporah], b. May 7, 1786; d.		
Feb. 23, 1788	2	180
Eunice, [twin with Jerusha], d. Nath[anie]l & Eliza-		
beth, b. Jan. 12, 1733/4	1	33
[E]unice, m. Samuell **COOK**, Mar. 31, 1751	1	311
Eunice, m. William **CARY**, Feb. 19, 1754	1	323
Eunice, m. William **CARY**, Feb. 19, 1754	2	32
Eunice, d. John & Ann, b. June 4, 1756	1	261
Eunice, twin with Lois, d. John, Jr. & Zipporah, b.		
Oct. 26, 1775	2	180
Eunice, m. Uriah **BINGHAM**, Apr. 26, 1781	2	235
Frank, [s. Benj[ami]n], b. Nov. 19, 1809	3	90
Frank, of Hartford, m. Henrietta **HEBBARD**, of Windham,		
Sept. 17, 1837, by Rev. Dexter Bullard	3	183

	Vol.	Page
WEBB, (cont)		
Frederick, s. [Abner & Prudence], b. Aug. 22, 1785	2	237
George, s [Peter & Tamerin], b. Apr 22, 1800	2	50
George, m. Eliza A. **WHITE**, of Meriden, Nov. 7, 1824, by Rev. Mr Hinsdale	3	125
George W., m. Polly **LEE**, Mar. [ ], 1806	3	78
George Washington, s [Nathaniel & Zerviah], b Aug 6, 1779	2	137
Hannah, d Sam[ue]ll & Hannah, b Jan 29, 1715	1	7
Hannah, w. Sam[ue]ll, d. Mar. [ ], 1751	1	7
Hannah, d Joshua & Hannah, b. June 19, 1753	1	244
Hannah, d. Eb[enezer] & Ruth, b. Aug. 31, 1759	1	210
Harriet, d. [Ralph & Eunice], b Dec 29, 1816	3	83
Harriet, d. [Henry & Hannah], b. [ ]; d [ ]	3	2
Harriet D., m. James **BENNET**, Oct. 18, 1835, by Rev. Jesse Fisher	3	176
Henry, s. [Nathaniel & Zerviah], b. Sept. 2, 1768	2	137
Henry, m Hannah **CLIFT**, June 1, 1794	2	55
Henry, m. Hannah **CLIFT**, June 1, 1794	3	2
Henry, s. [Joel & Caroline], b July 23, 1796	2	32
Henry, s. [Ralph & Eunice], b. Nov. 9, 1818	3	83
Henry, m. Sarah E. **BINGHAM**, b of Windham, Feb 13, 1842, by Rev. John E. Tyler	3	200
Horatio, s. [Joel & Caroline], b Feb. 21, 1794	2	32
Horatio, ae. 55, of Windham, m 3rd w. Jerusha A. **KINNEY**, ae. 44, b Lebanon, Dec. 13, 1849, by Rev. Joseph Bunter (?)	4	114
Jabez, s John & Ann, b Apr 18, 1753	1	261
James, s. Sam[ue]ll & Deb[orah], b. Aug. 9, 1758	1	259
James, s [John & Ann], b Feb. 19, 1767	1	261
James, s. [Stephen & Content], b. Apr. 26, 1778	2	152
James, s. [John, Jr & Zipporah], b June 5, 1793	2	180
James, m. Dolly **RIPLEY**, May 7, 1817	3	82
Jared, s. John & Ann, b. June 10, 1759	1	261
Jared, m. Prudence **MUDGE**, June 3, 1790	2	188
Jared, s [John, Jr & Nabby], b. July 9, 1818, d Sept. 30, 1820	3	83
Jehiel, s Joshua & Hannah, b Jan 23, 1744/5	1	244
Jemima, d. Zeb[ulo]n & Judah, b. Apr. 20, 1745	1	129
Jerusha, [twin with Eunice], d Nath[anie]l & Elizabeth, b. Jan. 12, 1733/4; d. Sept. 18, 173[ ]	1	33
Jerusha, d. Ebenezer & Ruth, b Apr 17, 1744	1	210
Jerusha, d. Sam[ue]ll & Deborah, b. May 19, 1747	1	259
Jerusha, m Enos **PALMER**, Mar 21, 1764	2	98
Jerusha, m. Elisha **ABBE**, Oct. 27, 1774	2	195
Joel, s. Samuel, Jr. & Deborah, b Nov 29, 1748	1	259
Joel, m. Caroline **WALES**, Oct. 31, 1781	2	32

	Vol.	Page
WEBB, (cont.)		
Joel Wales, s. [John, Jr. & Nabby], b. Sept. 15, 1834	3	83
John, s. Nathaniell & Elizabeth, b. June 14, 1719	1	33
John, m. Ann **DEVOTION**, July 30, 1746	1	261
John, s. John & Ann, b. Nov. 12, 1749	1	261
John, Jr., m. Zipporah **ROBINSON**, Nov. 12, 1772	2	180
John, s. [John, Jr. & Zipporah], b. Aug. 3, 1773;		
d. June 29, 177[ ]	2	180
John, s. [John, Jr. & Zipporah], b. Aug. 2, 1781;		
d. Mar. 7, 178[ ]	2	180
John, d. Feb. 27, 1787	1	261
John, s. [Jared & Prudence], b. May 8, 1791	2	188
John, Jr., m. Nabby **FOSTER**, Oct. 2, 1817	3	83
John P., farmer, m. Rhoda **KINGSLEY**, Feb. 20, 1850,		
by Mr. Hazen	4	114
John Pascal, [s. John, Jr. & Nabby], b. Dec. 8, 1820	3	83
Jonathan, s. Eb[enezer] & Ruth, b. Oct. 2, 1747	1	210
Jonathan, s. [John, Jr. & Zipporah], b. Sept. 10, 1779	2	180
Jonathan, s. [Stephen & Content], b. Dec. 12, 1790	2	152
Joseph, s. Joshua & Hannah, b. May 8, 1746	1	244
Joseph Baker, s. [Abner & Prudence], b. Apr. 7, 1805	2	237
Joshua, s. Sam[ue]ll & Hannah, b. Feb. 2, 1721/22	1	7
Joshua, m. Hannah **ABBE**, May 28, 1744	1	244
Judeth, d. Zebulon & Judeth, b. Dec. 28, 1727	1	65
Julia, d. [George W. & Polly], b. Feb. 17, 1809	3	78
Larin, s. [Darius & Deborah], b. Aug. 13, 1770		
(Lorin?)	2	203
Laura, d. [Peter & Tamerin], b. May 15, 1794	2	50
Lavina, twin with Zibbeas, d. [Napthali & Mary],		
b. Feb. 12, 1762; d. Feb. 28, 1762	1	309
Lois, d. Sam[ue]ll, Jr. & Deb[orah], b. May 15, 1752;		
d. Jan. 11, 1754	1	259
Lois, d. Sam[ue]ll, Jr. & Deb[orah], b. Feb. 16, 1753	1	259
Lois, twin with Eunice, d. John, Jr. & Zipporah, b.		
Oct. 26, 1775	2	180
Lorin, see under Larin		
Louis, m. Elisha **WHITE**, Nov. 4, 1779	2	227
Lucia, d. [Henry & Hannah], b. Mar. 23, 1809	3	2
Lucia C., m. Charles A. **WOODWORTH**, Oct. 15, 1829, by		
Rev. Richard F. Cleveland	3	138
Lucretia, d. [Nathaniel & Zerviah], b. May 8, 1775	2	137
Lucretia, d. [Henry & Hannah], b. Oct. [ ], 1802	3	2
Lucretia, m. Thomas **GRAY**, May 11, 1824, by Rev. C.B.		
Everest	3	117
Lucy, d. [John & Ann], b. May 30, 1762	1	261
Lucy, m. Jonah **LINKON**, May 1, 1783	2	254
Lucy, d. [Abner & Prudence], b. Jan. 29, 1798	2	237
Lucy, d. [George W. & Polly], b. Nov. 24, 1806	3	78

	Vol	Page

WEBB, (cont)

	Vol	Page
Lucy, of Windham, m. Ebenezer **GREENSLIT**, of Hampton, June 1, 1826	3	124
Lucy L., m. Reuben G. **FAIRBANKS**, Mar. 11, 1831, by Rev Rich[ar]d F. Cleveland	3	152
Lydia, d. [John & Ann], b Apr. 29, 1765	1	261
Maria, d. [Peter & Tamerin], b. June 17, 1789	2	50
Maria, m. Isaac **SOUTHGATE**, July 1, 1830, by Rev. Richard F Cleveland	3	146
Mary, m. Amos **DODGE**, Oct. 14, 1713	1	42
Mary, d. Nathaniell & Elizabeth, b. Dec 23, 1725	1	33
Mary, m. Ebenezer **PALMER**, Mar. 11, 1741	1	215
Mary, d. Dec. 21, 1744, in the 81st y of her age	1	139
Mary, m. Hezekiah **MANNING**, Sept. 22, 1745	1	229
Mary, d. Hez[ekiah] & Mary, b Feb. 25, 1752	1	309
Mary, m. Barnabus **ANNIBALL**, Dec. 27, 1759	2	61
Mary, d [Nathaniel & Zerviah], b Sept. 23, 1770	2	137
Mary, d. [Stephen & Content], b. Nov. 26, 1772	2	152
Mary, m. Henry **DOWNING**, Aug 15, 1774	2	196
Mary, d. [Abner & Prudence], b. Feb. 13, 1795	2	237
Mary, m Christopher T. **HUNTINGTON**, Sept 9, 1823	3	112
Mary Ann, d. [Jared & Prudence], b. Feb. 2, 1800	2	188
Mary C., d. [Henry & Hannah], b. Jan. [ ], 1800	3	2
Mary C., m. Tho[ma]s **GAGE**, Sept. 30, 1821, by Rev. Cornelius B Everest	3	117
Mary Hurd*, d. Zebulon & Judith, b. Jan. 14, 1723/4 (*correction entire entry handwritten at bottom of page in original manuscript–see **HURD**)		
Matilda C., [d. Benjamin], b June 24, 1813	3	90
Miriann, d. Nathaniell & Elizabeth, b. Oct. 17, 1730	1	33
Meriann, m. Eleazer **RIPLEY**, Mar 23, 1757	2	39
Nancy, m. Andrew **EDGARTON**, Oct. 16, 1794	3	35
Napthah, s. Zebulon & Judeth, b July 30, 1729	1	65
Napthali, m. Mary **MUDGE**, Oct. 2, 1751	1	309
Napthali, s. Napthali & Mary, b Dec 3, 1753	1	309
Nathan, s. Zebulon & Judeth, b. Oct. 9, 1731	1	129
Nathan, s. [Stephen & Content], b. Apr 7, 1767	2	152
Nathan, s. [Darius & Deborah], b. June 13, 1768	2	203
Nathaniell, m. Elizabeth **FFITCH**, Apr 24, 1718	1	33
Nathaniell, s. Nathaniell & Elizabeth, b. Aug. 1, 1735	1	33
Nathaniel, s Sam[ue]l, Jr. & Deb[orah], b Sept. 3, 1750	1	259
Nathaniel, d. Sept. 19, 1750	1	259
Nathaniel, m. Zerviah **ABBE**, May 15, 1768	2	137
Nathaniel, s. [Stephen & Content], b. Jan 15, 1770	2	152
Nath[anie]l, s. [Joel & Caroline], b. May 25, 1787	2	32
Nathaniel, Jr., of Windham, m. Charlotte **CLEVELAND**, of Mansfield, Apr. 15, 1792	2	129

	Vol.	Page
WEBB, (cont.)		
Nathaniel, Capt., d. Jan. 25, 1814, ae. 77 y.	2	137
Permela, d. [Stephen & Content], b. May 26, 1789	2	152
Peter, s. Sam[ue]ll & Deb[orah], b. Nov. 14, 1755	1	259
Peter, of Windham, m. Tamerin **DENNY**, of Leicester,		
June 5, 1783	2	50
Polly, d. [William & Lois], b. May 17, 1783	2	247
Prudence, d. [Abner & Prudence], b. Dec. 22, 1787	2	237
Prudence, 2d, d. [Abner & Prudence], b. July 15,		
1792	2	237
Ralph, s. [John, Jr. & Zipporah], b. Oct. 12, 1788	2	180
Ralph, m. Eunice **DORRANCE**, Dec. 31, 1815	3	83
Reuben, s. [Ebenezer, Jr. & Abigail, Jr.], b. Feb.		
12, 1780	2	246
Ruby, d. [Darius & Deborah], b. May 26, 1774	2	203
Rufus, s. [Stephen & Content], b. May 8, 1768	2	152
Ruth, d. Eb[enezer] & Ruth, b. Feb. 22, 1750/51	1	210
Ruth, w. Ebenezer, d. Feb. 28, 1796	1	210
Sam[ue]ll, m. Hannah **RYPLE**, Oct. 8, 1711	1	7
Sam[ue]ll, s. Nathaniell & Elizabeth, b. Mar. 5,		
1720/21	1	33
Samuel, d. Feb. 20, 1738/9, in the 79th y. of his age	1	139
Sam[ue]ll, m. Deborah **DAVISON**, July 2, 1746	1	259
Samuell, m. Eliza[be]th **FISK**, May 14, 1752	1	15
Sam[ue]l, s. [Joel & Caroline], b. Mar. 16, 1789	2	32
Sarah, d. Zebulon & Judeth, b. Apr. 2, 1741	1	129
Sarah, d. Nap[t]h[ali] & Mary, b. Nov. 16, 1755	1	309
Sarah, d. [Ebenezer, Jr. & Abigail, Jr.], b. Feb. 19,		
1778	2	246
Sarah, d. [Stephen & Content], b. Jan. 31, 1782	2	152
Sarah, d. [Joel & Caroline], b. Sept. 5, 1785	2	32
Sarah, m. Septimies **ROBINSON**, Feb. 5, 1803	3	85
Sarah, d. [George & Eliza A.], b. July 31, 1825	3	125
Stephen, s. Zeb[ulo]n & Judah, b. Mar. 17, 1746/7	1	129
Stephen, m. Content **HEWETT**, May 22, 1766	2	152
Stephen, s. [Stephen & Content], b. June 27, 1774	2	152
Susan, ae. 24, b. Windham, m. W[illia]m F. **PALMER**,		
shoemaker, ae. 28, b. Windham, res. Springfield,		
Oct. [ ], [1850], by Rev. Henry Coe	4	118
Thomas, s. [Darius & Deborah], b. June 29, 1772	2	203
Thomas, s. [Jared & Prudence], b. Feb. 25, 1795	2	188
Thomas, m. Mary **DORRANCE**, Jan. 20, 1822	3	93
Thomas Denny, s. [Peter & Tamerin], b. May 10, 1784	2	50
Timothy, m. Sarah **HAYWARD**, May 26, 1728	1	92
William, m. Dorothy **BURNAM**, Oct. 16, 1750	1	313
William, s. [William & Dorothy], b. July 6, 1751	1	313
William, s. Napthali & Mary, b. Apr. 26, 1758	1	309
William, m. Lois **STRONG**, May 16, 1782	2	247

	Vol.	Page
WEBB, (cont.)		
William, s. [Henry & Hannah], b. May 19, 1797	3	2
William, m. Amanda **WOLCOTT**, Jan. 6, 1824, by		
Rev. Cornelius B. Everest	3	117
William H., s. [William & Amanda], b. Dec. 7, 1825	3	117
William Ripley, s. [James & Dolly], b. July 29,		
1818	3	82
Zebulon, m. Judith **HOWARD**, Dec. 19, 1722	1	65
Zebulon, s. Zebulon & Judith, b. July 30, 1725	1	65
Zerviah, [wid. Capt. Nathanial], d. May 17, 1825	2	137
Zibbeas, twin with Lavina, s. [Napthali & Mary],		
b. Feb. 12, 1762	1	309
——, s. [Napthali & Mary], b. Feb. 27, 1757; d.		
same day	1	309
WEBSTER, Grace, m. William **NEEFF**, June 11, 1733	1	145
Judeth, m. Sam[ue]ll **COBURN**, Jr., Jan. 29, 1750/51	1	308
Lester, of Rochester, N.Y., m. Prudence **CHAMPLAIN**,		
of Windham, Jan. 24, 1830, by Rev. Richard F.		
Cleveland	3	140
Lucy A., m. W[illia]m F. **KENYON**, farmer, b. Windham,		
res. Chaplin, July 4, 1848, by James. M. Phelps	4	112
Triphena, m. Sylvanus **BARROWS**, Jr., Sept. 14, 1786	2	231
WEDGE, Lucy, d. Thomas & Mary, b. Oct. 14, 1764	2	9
Lucy, m. David **CANNADA**, Mar. 11, 1784	2	65
Thomas A., m. Sophronia A. **BRADFORD**, Dec. 10, 1826,		
by Rev. Jesse Fisher	3	127
WEEDEN, Benjamin, Jr., of Hopkinton, R.I., m. Mary **YOUNG**,		
Mar. 23, 1825	3	35
Consider S., farmer, ae. 20, b. Hopkinton, res.		
Willimantic, m. Hannah J. **FOX**, operative, ae. 18,		
b. Hopkinton, res. Willimantic, Mar. 29, 1851,		
by Rev. Brush	4	117
Francis M., s. Benj[ami]n, gatekeeper, b. July 7,		
[1850]	4	11
James B., carpenter, ae. 22, m. Jane **PARKER**, ae. 19,		
Nov. 28, [1849], by Rev. Burgess	4	115
WEEKLY, Prudence, m. Edward **COBURN**, Oct. 17, 1751	1	258
WEEKS, Marcia, of Windham, m. Benjamin **COLE**, of Warwick,		
R.I., Oct. 18, 1832, by Rev. Ella Denham	3	161
Tho[ma]s J., Jr., s. Tho[ma]s, J., laborer, ae. 29,		
of Willimantic, b. Aug. 9, [1850]	4	10
WELCH, [see also **WELSH**], Abigail, d. Jerem[ia]h &		
Marg[are]t, b. June 4, 1754; d. Apr. 7, 1755	1	187
Abigail, d. [John, Jr. & Olive], b. Nov. 18, 1783	2	251
Abigail, w. John, d. Jan. 6, 1794	1	251
Abigail, of Windham, m. James **TRO[W]BRIDGE**, of		
Ashford, May 5, 1830, by Rev. Rich[ard] F.		
Cleveland	3	145

	Vol.	Page
WELCH, (cont.)		
Alletheah, d. [R[e]uben & Jerusha], b. Nov. 27,		
1793	2	219
Ann, d. Jerem[iah] & Marg[are]t, b. Apr. 4, 1749	1	187
Anna, d. [R[e]uben & Jerusha], b. Oct. 7, 1782	2	219
Anne*, m. Sanford **BIBBON**, Oct. 27, 1796 (*correction		
a note attached to page of original manuscript		
states: "Anne **WELCH** married Sanford **BIBBON** should		
be Fanny b. 9-9-1776 married Sanford **BIBBINS**")	3	21
Asenath, d. John & Abigail, b. Apr. 4, 1753	1	251
Asenath, m. Shubael **FITCH**, July 4, 1793	2	197
Ashaell, s. [John & Abigail], b. Mar. 21, 1764	1	251
Ashbell, m. Margaret **DORRANCE**, Oct. 15, 1795	3	38
Betsey, m. Lewis **WELCH**, Mar. 8, 1840, by Thomas Gray,		
J.P.	3	192
Cary, s. [R[e]uben & Jerusha], b. Jan. 13, 1799	2	219
Charles, s. Tho[ma]s, stone cutter, ae. 29, of Willi-		
mantic, b. Sept. 15, 1849	4	9
C[h]loe, d. Jer[emiah] & Marg[are]t, b. July 5, 1756	1	187
Chloe, m. James **ROBINSON**, Feb. 8, 1781	2	234
Chloe, d. [R[e]uben & Jerusha], b. Nov. 5, 1788	2	219
Daniel, s. Thomas & Hannah, b. Mar. 20, 1726	1	12
Eleazer, s. Jerem[iah] & Marg[are]t, b. Dec. 12, 1750	1	187
Eleazer, see under Eleazer Welch **CONTER**	3	49
Elijah, s. Jeremiah & Margaret, b. July 6, 1745	1	161
Eliphalet, s. Jeremiah & Margaret, b. May 15, 1747; d.		
Nov. 4, 1772	1	161
Eliphalet, s. [R[e]uben & Jerusha], b. Aug. 7, 1796	2	219
Elisha, s. [R[e]uben & Jerusha], b. Jan. 27, 1787	2	219
Ellice, d. [Hopestill & Allice], b. June 15, 1764	2	95
Fanny, d. [R[e]uben & Jerusha], b. Sept. 9, 1776	2	219
Gamaleel M., m. Sally C. **WILLOBY**, Mar. 4, 1831, by Rev.		
Rich[ar]d F. Cleveland	3	151
Gurdon, m. Mary **MANNING**, Dec. 9, 1789	3	56
Gurdon, s. [Gurdon & Mary], b. Sept. 1, 1797	3	56
Hannah, d. Jeremiah & Margaret, b. Mar. 2, 1737/8	1	161
Hannah, [w. Thomas], d. [ ]	1	12
Henry, s. [Gurdon & Mary], b. Sept. 26, 1790	3	56
Hopestill, m. Allice **WOODWARD**, May 12, 176[ ]	2	95
Irenah, d. John & Abigail, b. Sept. 7, 1746	1	251
Jane C., m. Albert H. **BACKUS**, b. of Windham, Mar.		
12, 1847, by Rev. B.M. Alden, Jr.	3	234
Jeremiah, s. Thomas & Hannah, b. Nov. 14, 1714	1	12
Jeremiah, m. Margaret [ ], Dec. 15, 1736	1	161
Jeremiah, s. Jeremiah & Margaret, b. Dec. 10, 1741;		
d. Dec. 26, 1741	1	161
Jerusha, d. Jeremiah & Margaret, b. May 13, 1743	1	161
Jerusha, d. John & Abigail, b. Sept. 4, 1748	1	251

	Vol.	Page

WELCH, (cont.)

	Vol.	Page
Jerusha, m. Jonathan **MARTIN**, Jr., Mar. 9, 1769	2	166
Jerusha, d. [John, Jr. & Olive], b. Feb. 24, 1787	2	251
John, s. Thomas & Hannah, b. July 8, 1717	1	12
John, m. Abigail **MANNING**, Oct. 27, 1745	1	251
John, s. John & Abi[gai]l, b. Feb. 3, 1750/51	1	251
John, Jr., m. Olive **FITCH**, Sept. 19, 1782	2	251
John, s. [John, Jr. & Olive], b. Oct. 6, 1791	2	251
John, s. Tho[ma]s, farmer, ae. 35, & [ ], ae. 30, b. Feb. 15, 1851	4	14
Julia, d. [Thomas & Laura], b. [ ]	3	55
Julia C., of Windham, m. Elijah D. **HUNTINGTON**, of Norwich, Mar. 6, 1843, by Rev. J.E. Tyler	3	207
Lewis, twin with Lucius, s. [Gurdon & Mary], b. June 14, 1794	3	56
Lewis, m. Betsey **WELCH**, Mar. 8, 1840, by Thomas Gray, J.P.	3	192
Lucius, twin with Lewis, s. [Gurdon & Mary], b. June 14, 1794	3	56
Lucy, d. [R[e]uben & Jerusha], b. Feb. 24, 1779	2	219
Lydia T., d. [R[e]uben & Jerusha], b. Aug. 11, 1791	2	219
Margaret, w. Jeremiah, d. Sept. 9, 1784, in the 72nd y. of her age	1	187
Maria, d. [John, Jr. & Olive], b. May 28, 1789	2	251
Mary, d. Jeremiah & Margaret, b. Nov. 4, 1739	1	161
Mary Ann, ae. 21, m. John **ROUSE**, farmer, ae. 27, [1849]	4	113
Mira, d. [R[e]uben & Jerusha], b. Jan. 17, 1802	2	219
Olive, d. [John, Jr. & Olive], b. June 14, 1795	2	251
Polly, d. [R[e]uben & Jerusha], b. Dec. 16, 1784	2	219
Reuben, s. Jerem[iah] & Marg[are]t, b. Aug. 21, 1752	1	187
R[e]uben, m. Jerusha **CARY**, May 1, 1776	2	219
Sarah, m. Paul **HOLT**, Jr., Aug. 20, 1767	2	145
Sarah, d. [R[e]uben & Jerusha], b. Dec. 16, 1777	2	219
Sylvester, s. [Ashbell & Margaret], b. Jan. 11, 1798	3	38
Thomas, d. Aug. 14, 1781, in the 87th y. of his age	1	12
Thomas, s. [John, Jr. & Olive], b. Apr. 14, 1785	2	251
Thomas, m. Laura **LOTHROP**, [ ]	3	55
Thomas Henry, s. [Thomas & Laura], b. Sept. 5, 1822	3	55
Vine, s. [Hopestill & Allice], b. Feb. 15, 1765	2	95
William, s. [Ashbell & Margaret], b. Dec. 11, 1800	3	38
WELDEN, WELDIN, Julia A., ae. 19, m. Samuel **SIMMS**, ae. 36, b. Ashford, Oct. 10, 1847, by Daniel Dorchester	4	111
Leonard, m. Malinda **LEONARD**, May 4, 1846, in Willimantic, by Rev. John Cooper	3	229
——, child of Leonard, laborer, ae. 47, of Willimantic, b. May 24, [1850]	4	10

	Vol.	Page
WELLS, Eliza Ann, m. Wanton G. **PERRY**, June 19, 1837,		
at Brooklyn	3	113
Hannah, m. Joshua **WALLIS**, Nov. 11, 1697	A	24
Lucy A., d. Apr. 21, [1849], ae. 24	4	155
Margaret, m. Elijah **BIBBONS**, Aug. 16, 1819, at		
Colchester	3	8
Maryan, of Windham, m. Worthington **LADD**, of Coventry,		
Apr. 16, 1846, by Elder Thomas Jones	3	228
Peter, m. Sally **PERRY**, Jan. 15, 1824	3	116
W[illia]m M., of Lyme, m. Orrilla **DENISON**, of Windham,		
July 6, 1831, by Henry Huntington, J.P.	3	153
WELSH, [see also **WELCH**], David, s. David & Anstress, b.		
Apr. 18, 1743	1	234
Eleazer, m. Abigail **BROWN**, May 20, 1784	2	14
Jeremiah, m. Wid. Jerusha **LAS[S]EL**, May 25, 1785	2	20
John, d. Apr. 12, 1743	1	234
Mary, m. Bartholomew **FLINT**, June 3, 1761	2	5
Thomas, s. [Eleazer & Abigail], b. Mar. 8, 1785	2	14
WEST, Hannah, m. Israel **EVERET**, Jr., Feb. 11, 1739/40	1	202
Hannah W., m. William **SMITH**, Apr. [ ], 1835	3	203
John, d. Jan. 31, 1766	2	10
Mary P., m. Waldo **BINGHAM**, b. of Windham, Sept. 8,		
1840, by Rev. Henry Beers Sherman	3	194
Mercy, m. Nathaniell **WALES**, Feb. 14, 1715/16	1	11
Sarah, of Tolland, m. Peter **ROBINSON**, Jr., Mar. 14,		
1775	2	1
Sarah, m. Asher **ROBINSON**, Sept. 3, 1778	2	211
Zilpha, m. Ebenezer **ROBINSON**, Jan. 5, 1814	3	25
----, child of Tho[ma]s, stonemason, ae. 27, &		
Clarissa, ae. 23, of Willimantic, b. Aug. 7,		
1850	4	12
WESTGATE, Priscelia, m. Pardon P. **CASE**, Mar. 28, 1812	3	103
WETMORE, Mary, m. Nathaniel **WALES**, Jr., Mar. 15, 1741	2	42
Rachel, m. Joshua **ELDERKIN**, July 31, 1749	2	19
Sarah, m. Jabez **HUNTINGTON**, May 21, 1735	1	126
WHEAT, Anna, d. Solomon & Anne, b. July 8, 1736	1	21
Elizabeth, d. Solomon & Margaret, b. Nov. 15, 1747	1	21
Hannah, d. Solomon & Anna, b. July 16, 1738	1	21
WHEELER, David, of Plainfield, m. Sarah **GINNINGS**, of		
Windham, Apr. 9, 1778	2	203
Elisha, s. [David & Sarah], b. Dec. 24, 1786, at		
Plainfield	2	203
John L., m. Ann D. **LATHROP**, Nov. 27, 1840, by Rev.		
John B. Guild, Willimantic	3	196
Mary A., ae. 18, m. Albert L. **PERRY**, carpenter, ae.		
27, Apr. 24, [1850], by Rev. J. Brewster	4	114
Molly, m. William **CROSS**, Jr., Oct. 24, 1767	2	172
Nathan, s. [David & Sarah], b. Oct. 10, 1779	2	203

	Vol.	Page
WHEELOCK, WHEALOCK, Abigail, d. Ralph & Ruth, b. Mar.		
3, 1717	1	27
Eleazer, s. Ralph & Ruth, b. Apr. 22, 1711	1	27
Elizabeth, d. Ralph & Ruth, b. July 18, 1709	1	27
Elizabeth, m. Joshua **HANDY**, Dec. 4, 1728	1	101
John, s. Ralph & Ruth, b. Jan. 20, 1719/20; d.		
Jan. 29, 1719/20	1	27
Mary, d. Ralph & Mercy, b. Nov. 26, 1728	1	100
Mary, m. Jabez **BINGHAM**, Jr., Dec. 29, 1746	1	264
Ralph, m. Ruth **HUNTINGTON**, Jan. 8, 1707/8	1	27
Ralph, m. Mercy **STANDISH**, Sept. 30, 1726	1	27
Ruth, d. Ralph & Ruth, b. May 25, 1713	1	27
Ruth, w. Ralph, d. Sept. 1, 1725	1	27
Ruth, m. Robert **HIB[B]ARD**, Jr., Nov. 6, 1730	1	115
Sarah, d. John & Ruth, b. July 7, 1725	1	27
Sarah, m. Joseph **BINGHAM**, Jr., Dec. 1, 1742	2	128
Sarah, m. Joseph **BINGHAM**, Jr., Dec. 21, 1742	1	233
WHIPPLE, Elisha, m. Sarah **ABBE**, Feb. 23, 1800	3	48
Henry, s. [Elisha & Sarah], b. May 30, 1800	3	48
Martha B., tailoress, ae. 28, b. Norwich, res. Hart-		
ford, m. David K. **OWEN**, merchant, ae. 32, b.		
Ashford, res. Hartford, May 4, 1851, by Rev.		
S.G. Williams	4	117
Sabina, of Willimantic, m. Ginda **BARROWS**, of Decatur,		
N.Y., Oct. 2, 1836, by Rev. Philo Judson, at		
Willimantic	3	179
WHITE, Asa, m. Hannah **CUTLER**, Apr. 7, 1805	2	45
Charles, s. [Elisha & Louis], b. June 20, 1797	2	227
Chartola, of Willimantic, m. Austin **ROSS**, of Great		
Barrington, Mass., Aug. 23, 1846, by Rev. John		
Cooper	3	230
Dyer, s. [Rev. Stephen & Mary]. b. May 20, 1762	2	174
Dyer, s. [Elisha & Louis], b. Dec. 6, 1788	2	227
Ebenezer, s. Joshua & Elizabeth, b. Sept. 17, 1740	1	97
Ebenezer, s. Joshua, Jr. & Elizabeth, d. May 27, 1744	1	177
Elisha, s. S[tephen] & Mary, b. Sept. 16, 1754	1	226
Elisha, s. [Rev. Stephen & Mary], b. Sept. 16, 1754	2	174
Elisha, m. Louis **WEBB**, Nov. 4, 1779	2	227
Elisha, s. [Elisha & Louis], b. Aug. 9, 1791	2	227
Elisha, Jr., m. Lydia **DYER**, Sept. 10, 1815	3	77
Eliza A., of Meriden, m. George **WEBB**, Nov. 7, 1824,		
by Rev. Mr. Hinsdale	3	125
Elizabeth, d. Joshua, Jr. & Elizabeth, b. July 20, 1738	1	97
Elizabeth, m. Eliphalet **KINGSLEY**, Dec. 9, 1749	1	296
Elizabeth, of Palmer, Mass., m. W[illia]m A. **FORSHEY**,		
of Ashford, June 16, 1846, by Zeph[ania]h Palmer,		
J.P.	3	229
[E]unice, d. Stephen & Mary, b. Jan. 7, 1748/9	1	226

	Vol.	Page
WHITE, (cont.)		
Eunice, d. [Rev. Stephen & Mary], b. Jan. 7, 1749	2	174
Hannah, d. Stephen & Mary, b. Dec. 20, 1742; d.		
Sept. 8, 1748	1	226
Hannah, d. [Rev. Stephen & Mary], b. Dec. 28, 1742;		
d. Sept. 8, 1748, at New Haven	2	174
Hannah, d. S[tephen] & Mary, b. Feb. 22, 1751	1	226
Hannah, d. [Rev. Stephen & Mary], b. Feb. 22, 1751	2	174
Hannah, m. Josiah **HIBBARD**, Oct. 12, 1756	2	31
Hannah, d. Rev. Stephen [& Mary], d. Dec. 19, 1793	2	174
Hannah, m. Oliver **KITRIDGE**, May 19, 1844, at Willi-		
mantic, by Rev. J.B. Guild	3	215
Harry, s. [Elisha & Louis], b. Feb. 14, 1781; d.		
Aug. 23, 1782	2	227
Harry, [s. Elisha & Louis], d. Aug. 23, 1782	2	227
Huldah, d. [Rev. Stephen & Mary], b. Apr. 17, 1760	2	174
Jemima, d. Joshua, Jr. & Elizabeth, b. Mar. 12, 1743	1	177
Jeremiah, m. Sally **BOTTON**, Oct. 1, 1801	3	20
Joel W., of Bolton, m. Sally **FOX**, June 24, 1824	3	16
John, s. Joshua & Elizabeth, b. May 3, 1731; d. Aug.		
3, 1731	1	97
John, s. Joshua & Elizabeth, b. Oct. 15, 1734; d.		
Apr. 29, 1737	1	97
John, s. S[tephen] & Mary, b. Oct. 3, 1752, N.S.	1	226
John, s. [Rev. Stephen & Mary], b. Oct. 3, 1752	2	174
Jonathan, brother of Asa, d. Jan. 29, 1789	2	45
Joshua, m. Elizabeth **CARY**, July 4, 1728	1	97
Joshua, s. Joshua & Elizabeth, b. July 1, 1736	1	97
Lydia, d. Joshua, Jr. & Elizabeth, b. Mar. 10, 1745	1	177
Lydia, d. Stephen & Mary, b. Apr. 28, 1745	1	226
Lydia, d. [Rev. Stephen & Mary], b. Apr. 28, 1745	2	174
Lydia, m. Vine **ELDERKIN**, Nov. 23, 1767	2	128
Malinda, d. [Jeremiah & Sally], b. May 21, 1803	3	20
Martha, d. Joshua, Jr. & Elizabeth, b. Oct. 11, 1749	1	177
Mary, d. Stephen & Mary, b. Dec. 23, 1743	1	226
Mary, d. [Rev. Stephen & Mary], b. Dec. 23, 1743	2	174
Mary, w. Asa, d. Mar. 25, 1804	2	45
Mary L., m. Isaac A. **STODDARD**, b. of Windham, Nov. 6,		
1837, by Rev. Charles J. Todd	3	184
Mary S., d. [Elisha, Jr. & Lydia], b. Apr. 6, 1816; d.		
Nov. 21, 1839	3	77
Mira, d. [Elisha & Louis], b. Mar. 25, 1794	2	227
Myra, of Windham, m. John **CHAMPION**, of Leroy, N.Y.,		
May 5, 1834, by L.S. Corson, Rector	3	170
Nancy, operative, ae. 21, b. Haddam, res. Rockville,		
R.I., m. Elisha **JORDAN**, painter, ae. 18, b. Brook-		
lyn, res. Rockville, R.I., Nov. 21, 1850, by Rev.		
J. Cady	4	117

	Vol.	Page
WHITE, (cont.)		
Olive Dyer, s. [Elisha & Louis], b. Feb. 17,		
1787; d. Jan. 31, 1788	2	237
Polly, m. Warner **HEB[B]ARD**, Apr. 2, 1789	3	15
Ralph, s. Asa & Mary, b. Mar. 19, 1785	2	45
Samuel, [s. Elisha & Louis], b. Sept. 22, 1782;		
d. July 31, 1796	2	227
Sarah, d. Joshua & Elizabeth, b. June 1, 1747	1	177
Sarah, d. S[tephen] & Mary, b. Nov. 10, 1757	1	226
Sarah, d. [Rev. Stephen & Mary], b. Nov. 10, 1757	2	174
Stephen, Rev., m. Mary **DYAR**, Sept. 2, 1741	1	226
Stephen, Rev., m. Mary **DYER**, Sept. 2, 1741	2	174
Stephen, s. Stephen & Mary, b. Oct. 21, 1746	1	226
Stephen, Rev., d. Jan. 9, 1794	2	174
Susannah, d. [Rev. Stephen & Mary], b. Oct. 21,		
1746	2	174
Thomas, s. [Elisha & Louis], b. Sept. 23, 1784	2	227
William, s. Joshua & Elizabeth, b. Apr. 14, 1729	1	97
——, twin sons, [Stephen & Mary], b. Mar. 6,		
1749/50; d. same day	1	226
——, twin sons, [Rev. Stephen & Mary], b. Mar. 6,		
1750; d. same day	2	174
WHITEMAN, [see also **WHITMAN**], ——, child of Geo[rge],		
laborer, ae. 33, & Sarah, ae. 29, of Willimantic,		
b. May 22, 1851	4	13
WHITING, Angeline, m. Alexander **NOYES**, July 4, 1830, by		
Chester Tilden, Willimantic	3	147
Ann, d. Samuell & Elizabeth, b. Jan. 2, 1698; d.		
Sept. 18, 1778	A	25
Ann, d. Sam[ue]ll & Elizabeth, b. Jan. 2, 1698	1	167
Anna, see Anna **FITCH**	1	54
Chester, carpenter, b. Westford, res. Mansfield, d.		
June 19, 1860, ae. 48	4	161
Dana, m. Nathan **HALL**, b. of Willimantic, Sept. 7,		
1839, by Rev. B. Cook, Jr., of Willimantic	3	190
Ebenezer, of Norwich, m. Anne **FITCH**, d. Col. Eleazer,		
of Windham, Nov. 29, 1767	3	43
Eliphalet, s. Sam[ue]ll & Elizabeth, b. Apr. 7, 1715	1	6
Eliphalet, s. Sam[ue]ll & Elizabeth, b. Apr. 8, 1715	1	167
Elisha, s. Sam[ue]ll & Elizabeth, b. Jan. 17, 1716/7	1	6
Elisha, s. Sam[ue]ll & Elizabeth, b. Jan. 17, 1717/18	1	167
Elizabeth, d. Sam[ue]ll & Elizabeth, b. Feb. 11, 1702	1	167
Elizabeth, d. Samuell & Elizabeth, b. Feb. 12, 1702	A	25
Elizabeth, d. Sept. [ ], 1730	1	167
John, s. Sam[ue]ll & Elizabeth, b. Feb. 20, 1705	1	167
John, s. Samuel & Elizabeth, b. Feb. 19, 1706	A	25
Joseph, s. Sam[ue]ll & Elizabeth, b. Mar. 1, 1722	1	167
Lidea, d. Samuell & Elizabeth, b. May 5, 1708	A	25

	Vol.	Page
WHITING, (cont.)		
Martha, d. Samuel & Elizabeth, b. Mar. 19, 1710	A	25
Martha, d. Sam[ue]ll & Elizabeth, b. Mar. 9,		
1710; d. Jan. 29, 1719	1	167
Martha, d. Sam[ue]ll & Elizabeth, d. June 29,		
1719	1	6
Mary, d. Sam[ue]ll & Elizabeth, b. Nov. 24, 1712	1	6
Mary, d. Sam[ue]ll & Elizabeth, b. Nov. 24, 1712;		
d. Aug. 9, 1736	1	167
Mary, m. Thomas **CLAP[P]**, Nov. 23, 1727	1	88
Nathan, s. Sam[ue]ll & Elizabeth, b. May 4, 1724	1	167
Samuell, m. Elizabeth **ADAMS**, Sept. 14, 1696	A	25
Sam[ue]ll, m. Elizabeth **ADAMS**, Sept. 14, 1696	1	167
Sam[ue]ll, s. Sam[ue]ll & Elizabeth, b. Feb. 20, 1700	A	25
Sam[ue]ll, s. Sam[ue]ll & Elizabeth, b. Feb. 20, 1700	1	167
Sam[ue]ll, 1st, [s. Sam[ue]ll & Elizabeth], d. Mar.		
[ ], 1718, at sea	1	167
Sam[ue]ll, s. Sam[ue]ll & Elizabeth, b. Mar. 15, 1720	1	6
Sam[ue]ll, 2d, s. Sam[ue]ll & Elizabeth, b. Mar. 15,		
1720	1	167
Sam[ue]ll, Rev., d. Sept. 27, 1725, in Enfield	1	54
Sybel, d. Sam[ue]ll & Elizabeth, b. May 6, 1708	1	167
Sibel, m. John **BACKUS**, Jr., Jan. 15, 1725	1	72
William, s. Samuell & Elizabeth, b. Jan. 22, 1704	A	25
William, s. Sam[ue]ll & Elizabeth, b. Jan. 22, 1704	1	167
——, Rev., d. Sept. 2, 1725, at Infield	1	167
WHITMAN, [see also **WHITEMAN**], Charles, of Hartford, m.		
Henrietta **PERKINS**, of Windham, Nov. 13, 1833,		
by L.S. Corson, Rector	3	170
WHITMORE, Prosper, m. Anna **HUNTINGTON**, July 23, 1747	1	269
WHITNEY, Asa, blacksmith, ae. 22, b. Stafford, res.		
Windham, m. Jane **BARROWS**, ae. 18, July 3, 1848,		
by Andrew Sharp	4	111
WHITON, ——, of Willington, m. Eliza **CLARK**, of Mans-		
field, [ ], by Rev. Henry Greenslit	3	227
WIGGIN, Thomas, of Greenport, N.Y., m. Mary E. **LINCOLN**,		
of Windham, Nov. 26, 1844, by Erastus Dickenson	3	217
WIGHT, Anna, d. Joshua, Jr. & Elizabeth, b. Sept. 6, 1755	1	177
Ebenezer, s. [Joshua, Jr. & Mary], b. Oct. 28, 1772	2	89
Elizabeth, m. Ezra **KINGSLEY**, Dec. 31, 1719	1	7
Elizabeth, w. Joshua, d. Mar. 15, 1765	1	5
Elizabeth, d. [Joshua, Jr. & Mary], b. Nov. 1, 1765	2	89
John, s. [Joshua, Jr. & Mary], b. Mar. 12, 1770	2	89
Joshua, s. Joshua & Elizabeth, b. Oct. 20, 1708	1	5
Joshua, husband of Elizabeth, d. Aug. 14, 1762	1	5
Joshua, Jr., m. Mary **SMITH**, Nov. 16, 1762	2	89
Joshua, 2d., d. Apr. 29, 1766, in the 59th y. of his		
age	1	177

	Vol.	Page
WIGHT, (cont.)		
Mary d. Joshua & Elizabeth, b. Aug. 18, 1732	1	97
Mary, m. Sam[ue]ll **MURDOCK**, Jr., Mar. 15, 1749/50	1	303
Mary, m. Samuel **MURDOCK**, Jr., Mar. 15, 1749/50	2	160
Susanna, d. [Joshua, Jr. & Mary], b. Sept. 25, 1767	2	89
William, s. [Joshua, Jr. & Mary], b. Nov. 3, 1763	2	89
WILBUR, Amelia, of Willimantic, m. George W. **JACOBS**, of Mansfield, Mar. 27, 1836, by Rev. Moseley Dwight, Willimantic	3	177
Sally M., m. Royal **ORMSBY**, Dec. 18, 1825, by Amhurst Scoville, J.P.	3	131
——, child of George G., d. July 28, [1849], ae. 1 1/2	4	153
WILCOX, Elizabeth M., of Windham, m. Charles H. **BABCOCK**, of Lebanon, [ ] 12, 1843, by Rev. Ebenezer Robinson, Willimantic	3	214
Erastus, m. Mary Ann **RIPLEY**, Mar. 26, 1809, by Rev. Mr. Welles	3	54
Mary, d. [Erastus & Mary Ann], b. June 26, 1811	3	54
WILDER, Sarah J., ae. 20, m. W[illia]m A. **PHELPS**, ae. 26, July 7, [1850]	4	114
WILEY, Elizabeth, m. Nathan **PEARL**, Mar. 7, 1748	2	1
WILKINSON, WILKENSON, Abigail, d. Ebenezer & Sarah, b. Aug. 31, 1718	1	129
Ahab, m. El[i]za Ann **JILLSON**, b. of Windham, June [ ], 1833, by Rev. John Storrs	3	167
Dorothy, d. Ebenezer & Sarah, b. Mar. 15, 1715/16	1	129
Ebenezer, s. Ebenezer & Sarah, b. Dec. 7, 1720	1	129
Ebenezer, d. July 10, 1735, ae. about 49 y.	1	129
Ebenezer, s. Ebenezer & Sarah, b. "21 y. ago Dec. last past". Affidavit of Esther, w Hope **ROGERS**, made Jan. 16, 1740/1	1	213
Ebenezer, s. Sarah & brother of Joseph, was 21 y. old "Dec. 7 last past". Affidavit of Sarah made Jan. 17, 1740/41. Witnesses: Joseph **MEACHAM**, Amos **WOODWARD**	1	213
John, s. Ebenezer & Sarah, b. June 10, 1717	1	129
Joseph, s. Ebenezer & Sarah, b. Nov. 25, 1719; d. May following	1	129
Julia, m. Daniel **TRACY**, b. of Windham, Mar. 14, 1838, at Willimantic, by Rev. Philo Judson	3	186
Marg[a]ret, d. Ebenezer & Sarah, b. June [ ], 1723	1	129
Martha, m. Dr. Oliver **KINGSLEY**, b. of Willimantic, May 19, 1835, by Rev. Philo Judson	3	173
Mary, d. Ebenezer & Sarah, b. Apr. [ ], 1722	1	129
Sam[ue]ll, s. Ebenezer & Sarah, b. Dec. [ ], 1726;		

	Vol.	Page
WILKINSON, WILKENSON, (cont.)		
d. Feb. [ ], 1727/8	1	129
WILLES, [see under **WILLIS**]		
WILLIAMS, WILLIAM, Abby Jane, d. Ja[me]s, farmer, black,		
ae. 48, & Lucy, ae. 40, b. Mar. 1, 1851	4	13
Adelia Trowbridge, d. [Wightman & Phebe], b. June		
28, 1832	3	106
Ann W., m. Amasa P. **BARROWS**, Dec. 15, 1841, by Rev.		
Andrew Sharp	3	200
Anne, d. [Prince & Marcy], b. Aug. 17, 1778	2	237
Ardelia, b. Hampton, res. Willimantic, m. Oscar L.		
FULLER, farmer, of Hampton, Jan. 13, 1851, by		
Rev. S.G. Williams	4	118
Desire, m. William **PRESTON**, Jr., Aug. 18, 1763	2	96
Dorcas, m. William **PERKINS**, Feb. 11, 1762, by Rev.		
Mr. Cogswell	2	72
Elijah, s. [Elijah A. & Sarah], b. Oct. 30, 1839	3	96
Elijah A., of Canterbury, m. Sarah **LYON**, of Lisbon,		
Sept. 30, 1832, by Rev. Levi Nelson	3	96
Elisha Hubbard, s. [Elijah A. & Sarah], b. Oct. 21,		
1835	3	96
Elizabeth, m. Jonathan **SIMONS**, Nov. 21, 1744	1	247
Elizabeth, m. David **ROOT**, Feb. 15, 1846, by Andrew		
Sharp	3	227
Eunice C., m. Joseph **CONANT**, Apr. 13, 1845, by Rev.		
James W. Woodward	3	221
Gilbert Smith, s. [Wightman & Phebe], b. Jan. 30, 1830	3	106
Harriet Chapman, d. [Wightman & Phebe], b. Nov. 3, 1835	3	106
Harriet G., m. Fitch **PALMER**, Nov. 23, 1842, by Rev.		
Andrew Sharp, Willimantic	3	206
John, ae. 21, of Willimantic, m. [ ], May 14,		
1848, by Rev. H. Brownley	4	113
John Wightman, s. [Wightman & Phebe], b. Nov. 27, 1827	3	106
Laura, of Willimantic, d. Oct. [ ], [1848], ae. 1 1/2	4	153
Laura Ann, d. [Wightman & Phebe], b. Feb. 5, 1826	3	106
Lucy, m. Eliab **ROBINSON**, Jan. 30, 1777	2	256
Lucy, m. Eliab **ROBINSON**, Jan. 30, 177[ ]	2	218
Mary, m. Tamarsen **SIMONS**, June 20, 1728	A	1
Prince, negro man, m. Marcy **GREEN**, June 12, 1777	2	237
Sarah J., ae. 19, b. Mansfield, res. Willimantic, m.		
Andrew M. **GRANT**, merchant, ae. 21, b. Ashford,		
res. Ashford, Nov. 12, 1850, by Rev. Sam[ue]l G.		
Williams	4	117
Suse, d. [Prince & Marcy], b. Mar. 12, 1780	2	237
Thomas S., of Hampton, m. Eunice C. **TRACY**, of Windham,		
Oct. 10, 1833, by Rev. Jesse Fisher	3	167
Warren, s. [Elijah A. & Sarah], b. Mar. 22, 1834	3	96
Wightman, m. Phebe **SMITH**, Feb. 22, 1825, at Hampton	3	106

	Vol.	Page

WILLIAMS, WILLIAM, (cont.)

W[illia]m Henry, s. [Elijah A. & Sarah], b. Jan.
1, 1838 — 3 — 96

——, child of James, b. Oct. 1, [1849] — 4 — 7

WILLIS WILLES, [see also **WYLLYS**], Amhurst, s. [Jacob & Zerviah], b. Mar. 22, 1772 — 2 — 44

Amhurst, m. Hannah **SNOW**, Mar. 22, 1795 — 2 — 52

Daniel, s. Jacob & Zerviah, b. Feb. 28, 1758 — 2 — 44

Dyar, s. Jacob & Zerviah, b. Feb. 13, 1754, in Norwich — 2 — 44

Henry, s. Jacob & Zerviah, b. Feb. 23, 1760 — 2 — 44

Jabez, s. Jacob & Zerviah, b. Jan. 2, 1762 — 2 — 44

Jacob, s. Jacob, d. Aug. 3, 1760, ae. about 9 y. — 2 — 44

Jacob, s. [Jacob & Zerviah], b. Aug. 16, 1766 — 2 — 44

Lydia, d. [Jacob & Zerviah], b. May 12, 1768 — 2 — 44

Nancy, d. [Amhurst & Hannah], b. Apr. 12, 1797 — 2 — 52

Polly, d. [Amhurst & Hannah], b. Dec. 12, 1795 — 2 — 52

Silvanus, s. Jacob & Zerviah, b. Mar. 26, 1756 — 2 — 44

Vine, s. [Jacob & Zerviah], b. May 2, 1770 — 2 — 44

Zerviah, d. Jacob & Zerviah, b. Oct. 23, 1764 — 2 — 44

WILLOBY, Archa, m. Lucy A. **GAGER**, Mar. 2, 1831, by Rev. Roger Bingham — 3 — 151

Eunice, m. John **YORK**, May 25, 1824 — 3 — 84

Eunice, m. Prosper **HAZEN**, of Franklin, [   ] — 3 — 3

Sally C., m. Gamaleel M. **WELCH**, Mar. 4, 1831, by Rev. Rich[ar]d F. Cleveland — 3 — 151

Sophia, m. Erastus **FOLLETT**, Jan. 2, 1825 — 3 — 109

WILSON, WILLSON, WELSON, Ann M., d. Albert, operative, ae. 36, & Olive, ae. 34, of Willimantic, b. Dec. 18, 1850 — 4 — 12

Chauncey Hammett, s. [James & Henreitta], b. May 4, 1813 — 3 — 86

David Davis, s. [James & Henrietta], b. Aug. [ ], 1816 — 3 — 86

Edwin M., s. David, farmer, ae. 27, & Almira, ae. 35, b. Feb. 10, 1851 — 4 — 14

Eliza A., ae. 17, of Willimantic, m. Malantha T. **THORN**, ae. 25, b. Mansfield, res. Willimantic, Nov. 19, 1850, by Rev. Jno. Cady — 4 — 118

George L., s. John, laborer, ae. 31, & Ann, ae. 21, of Willimantic, b. May 31, 1848 — 4 — 1

Henrietta, w. James, d. June [ ], 1817 — 3 — 86

Henry, m. Mariah **HOVEY**, b. of Willimantic, Sept. 7, 1846, by Rev. John Cooper — 3 — 230

Isaac, m. Charlotte **BACKUS**, b. of Windham, Jan. 20, 1833, by John Baldwin, J.P. — 3 — 163

James, m. Henrietta **DAVIS**, May [ ], 1812 — 3 — 86

James, m. Lydia **POTTER**, June 24, 1818 — 3 — 86

	Vol.	Page

WILSON, WILLSON, WELSON, (cont.)

John, m. Sarah F. **COX**, Mar. 15, 1846, by Andrew
Sharp — 3, 228

Julia, of Windham, m. George B. **BENNETT**, of Brook-
lyn, June 8, 1840, by Rev. Nathan Wildman, of
Lebanon — 3, 193

Mercy, m. Ezra **CASWELL**, b. of Windham, Jan. 27,
1833, by John Baldwin, J.P. — 3, 163

Olive, of Plainfield, m. Charles **RICHMOND**, of
Killingly, Nov. 7, 1830, by Henry Hall, J.P.
Willimantic — 3, 148

Phebe W., m. Asher M.C. **LOOMIS**, Dec. 14, 1843, by
Rev. Andrew Sharp — 3, 212

Philip, m. Mary **THOMPSON**, b. of Windham, [   ],
1833, by Rev. John Storrs — 3, 167

Philip, m. Caroline **PRENTICE**, Sept. 14, 1845, by
John Crocker, Willimantic — 3, 223

Sarah, ae. 19, m. John **DAVIS**, operative, ae. 22, b.
Tolland, res. Windham, Nov. 25, 1847, by Tho[ma]s
Dowling — 4, 111

Wealthy Ann, m. Thomas W. **CUNNINGHAM**, Dec. 3, 1827,
by Rev. Chester Tilden — 3, 92

William, shoemaker, b. Portland, Ct., res. Willimantic, d. Mar. 28, 1860, ae. 55 — 4, 159-0

WINCHESTER, Edgar C., s. Harvey, innkeeper, & Emily, b
Sept. 6, 1847 — 4, 2

Harvey, m. Emily **SMITH**, b. of Windham, Oct. 10, 1836,
by Rev. William A. Curtis — 3, 180

WINDSHIP, Thomas, of Hartford, m. Betsey **WARNER**, of
Windham, June 30, 1822 — 3, 105

WINDSOR, WINSOR, Abby Ann, d. Abba W.A., farmer, &
Harriet C., b. July 13, 1848 — 4, 3

Caroline, d. Alba, carriage maker, & Harriet, b.
Sept. 28, 1850 — 4, 13

Ira, of Sterling, m. Almira **MAINE**, of Willimantic,
Nov. 27, 1836, by Rev. Philo Judson, at Willimantic — 3, 181

WITHERELL, Emelya, operative, ae. 19, b. So. Glocester,
res. Willimantic, m. Henry **SMITH**, merchant, ae.
21, b. N. Scituate, res. California, Jan. 12,
1851, by Rev. Blush — 4, 117

WITTER, Amanda, of Windham, m. Leonard **BECKWITH**, of
Waterford, Jan. 3, 1847, by Rev. B.M. Alden, Jr. — 3, 233

Betsey, m. Enoch **ALLEN**, Apr. 14, 1794 — 2, 145

Josiah, s. Josiah & Mary, b. May 28, 1771 — 2, 173

Rhoda, m. Pratt **ALLEN**, Nov. 27, 1788 — 2, 232

Sarah, m. Clemence **DYER**, Nov. 1, 1829, by Rev. Chester
Tilden, Willimantic — 3, 139

William, m. Laura A. **CARD**, b. of Windham, Apr. 5, 1846,

	Vol.	Page
WITTER, (cont.)		
by Rev. B.M. Alden	3	228
W[illia]m, doctor, b. Canterbury, res. Willimantic,		
d. Apr. 9, 1850, ae. 47	4	157
WOLCOTT, WALCOT, WOLCUTT, WALCOTT, WOLCOT,		
Alma, d. [Jonathan & Abigail], b. Sept. 27, 1811	3	67
Amanda, d. [Jonathan & Abigail], b. Dec. 13, 1804	3	67
Amanda, m. William **WEBB**, Jan. 6, 1824, by Rev.		
Cornelius B. Everest	3	117
Asiel, s. [Elij[ah] & Easther], b. Sept. 12, 1766	2	41
Eleazer, s. [Elij[ah] & Easther], b. Sept. 16, 1768	2	41
Elijah, s. Stephen & Mary, b. Sept. 17, 1740	1	178
Elijah, m. Esther **BILL**, May 8, 1758	2	41
Eliphalet, s. Stephen [& Mary], b. July 1, 1750; d.		
Feb. 11, 1751/2	1	178
Eliphalet, s. Elij[ah] & Easther, b. Oct. 3, 1760	2	41
Elisha, s. [Elij[ah] & Easther], b. Nov. 26, 1770	2	41
Emily, d. [Jonathan & Abigail], b. Dec. 12, 1808	3	67
[E]unice, d. Stephen & Mary, b. Mar. 5, 1742/3	1	178
Eunice, m. Isaac **CRANE**, May 8, 1763	2	83
George W., m. Mary **KINNE**, May 16, 1824	3	118
George Washington, s. [Jonathan & Abigail], b. June		
22, 1802	3	67
Henry Slegmaker, s. [Jonathan & Abigail], b. Sept. 15,		
1813	3	67
Jabez, s. Elij[ah] & Esther, b. Dec. 10, 1758	2	41
Jonathan, d. May 25, 1745, ae. 75 y. 9 m.	1	179
Jonathan, s. [Nath[anie]l & Lydia], b. Apr. 23, 1776	2	107
Jonathan, m. Abigail **BURK[E]**, Mar. 1, 1798	3	67
Joseph, s. [Nath[anie]l & Lydia], b. Sept. 18, 1767	2	107
Lydia, d. [Nath[anie]l & Lydia], b. Oct. 18, 1771	2	107
Margaret, d. Elij[ah] & Easther, b. Sept. 20, 1762	2	41
Mary, d. [Jonathan], d. Apr. 30, 1746, ae. 51 y.	1	179
Mary, d. [Nath[anie]l & Lydia], b. Apr. 8, 1780; d.		
Dec. 23, 1783	2	107
Merriam, d. [Nath[anie]l & Lydia], b. May 4, 1774	2	107
Mos[es], s. Stephen & Mary, b. Aug. 11, 1738	1	178
Nath[anie]l, m. Lydia **FLINT**, Nov. 4, 1764	2	107
Phebe, d. [Elij[ah] & Easther], b. Sept. 18, 1764	2	41
Sam[ue]ll, s. Stephen & Mary, b. Mar. 6, 1746/7; d.		
Mar. 6, 1752	1	178
Sarah, m. Jonathan **FFRENCH**, Dec. 15, 1725	1	71
Sarah, m. Gideon **FLINT**, Nov. 5, 1753	1	321
Stephen, m. Mary **BROUGHTON**, Nov. 15, 1737	1	178
Timothy, s. [Nath[anie]l & Lydia], b. May 22, 1769	2	107
WOOD, WOODS, Abigail, m. Timothy **LARRABEE**, Feb. 20,		
1750/51	1	305
Amey, m. Ebenezer **BINGHAM**, Apr. 15, 1761	2	63

	Vol.	Page
WOOD, WOODS, (cont.)		
Anne, m. Jedediah **ELDERKIN**, Aug. 31, 1741	2	233
Augustus, s. [Isaiah & Sarah], b. May 15, 1766	2	87
Benjamin, s. Isaiah & Sarah, b. Apr. 12, 1763	2	87
Bertha, d. Joseph, Jr. & Deborah, b. May 14, 1766	2	7
Calvin, s. [Sampson & Thankfull], b. Jan. 12, 1771	2	134
Charles, of South Woodstock, m. Lavina G. **MAINE**, of Norwich, [Mar.] 25, 1838, by Rev. John E. Tyler	3	185
Deborah, d. Joseph, Jr. & Deborah, b. Mar. 16, 1764	2	7
Eliphalet, s. [Isaiah & Sarah], b. Sept. 27, 1771	2	87
Elmira, m. Burt **LINCOLN**, Sept. 30, 1827	3	148
Emma B., d. [Oliver F. & Susan B.], b. Mar. 8, 1831	3	127
Esther, d. [Sampson & Thankful], b. Sept. 5, 1763, at Tolland	2	134
Eunice, d. [Oliver F. & Susan B.], b. Aug. 15, 1828	3	127
Frederick, Capt., of New York, N.Y., m. Alathea Marina **ORMSBY**, of Windham, Conn., Oct. 21, 1828, by Rev. Henry Chase. Witnessed by Elizabeth S. **DISBROW**	3	161
Frederick William, s. [Capt. Frederick & Alathea Marina], b. June 28, 1831; d. [ ], 1832	3	161
Hannah, m. Ephraim **WRIGHT**, June 29, 1724	1	190
John, s. Joseph, Jr. & Deborah, b. Apr. 28, 1762	2	7
John P., s. [Oliver F. & Susan B.], b. May 30, 1833	3	127
Joseph, Jr., of Windham, m. Deborah **TUBBS**, of Norwich, Apr. 8, 1756	2	7
Joseph, s. Joseph, Jr. & Deb[orah], b. July 31, 1760	2	7
Joseph, d. Feb. 17, 1766, ae. about 70	1	107
Josiah, s. [Sampson & Thankfull], b. Mar. 7, 1768	2	134
Julia Ann, d. [Oliver F. & Susan B.], b. Dec. 19, 1835	3	127
Mary, m. Abner **FOLLET**, Jan. 17, 1788	2	139
Oliver F., m. Susan B. **PALMER**, [ ], by Rev. Jesse Fisher	3	127
Philemon, m. Bethiah **HOWARD**, Nov. 1, 1719	1	81
Philemon, m. Sarah **RUDD**, Nov. 26, 1761	2	74
Prescillia, d. Joseph, d. Apr. 1, 1743	1	107
Priscilla, m. John **WARNER**, Feb. 28, 1762	2	92
Ruth, m. Lemuel **BABCOCK**, Feb. 23, 1820, by Rev. Jesse Fisher	3	80
Sally, d. [Isaiah & Sarah], b. Nov. 8, 1774	2	87
Samuel, s. Joseph, Jr. & Deb[orah], b. Aug. 6, 1758	2	7
Sarah, w. Isaiah, d. May 17, 1811, ae. 74 y.	2	87
Susan, d. Clin, ae. 44, & Susan, ae. 39, b. Nov. 14, [1847]	4	3
Thankfull, d. [Sampson & Thankfull], b. Mar. 14, 1761, at Cold Spring	2	134

	Vol.	Page
WOODARD, [see under **WOODWARD**]		
WOODBURY, Daniel, m. Haddrie **DAVIS**, Nov. 24, 1775	2	188
WOODIN, Martha, m. John **DECKER**, Apr. 26, 1742.		
"Divorced".	1	230
WOODWARD, WOODARD, Abigail, d. Joseph & Elizabeth, b.		
May 13, 1715; d. May 4, 1727	1	19
Abigail, d. Benj[ami]n & Anna, b. Mar. 7, 1729/30	1	85
Abigail, d. Jacob & Abigail, b. Apr. 21, 1740	1	204
Abigail, m. James **MOLTEN**, Jr., Dec. 18, 1749	2	49
Abigail, w. Jacob, d. Aug. 1, 1753	1	204
Abigail, d. John & Synthia, b. May 7, 1757	2	6
Abigail, m. Abraham **FORD**, Nov. 8, 1763	2	94
Abijah, s. Caleb & Annah, b. Feb. 5, 1728/9	1	105
Abner, s. [Joseph & Elizabeth], b. Jan. 10, 1762	2	33
Allice, d. Jacob & Abigail, b. Apr. 10, 1746	1	204
Allice, m. Hopestill **WELCH**, May 12, 176[ ]	2	95
Amos, s. Amos & Hannah, b. Mar. 17, 1723/4; d. Sept.		
16, 1751	1	56
Amos, s. Eben[eze]r & Rachel, b. May 29, 1753	1	248
Amos, d. [ ]	1	56
Anna, d. Benj[ami]n & Anna, b. June 2, 1726	1	85
Annah, w. Benj[ami]n, d. Dec. 2, 1769	1	83
Anna, [d. Benj[ami]n & Anna], d. Aug. 18, 1785	1	85
Asa, s. Caleb & Annah, b. Aug. 11, 1732	1	105
Asa, s. Benj[ami]n & Anna, b. July 9, 1733; d. Feb.		
28, 1735/6	1	85
Benjamin, s. Benj[ami]n & Anna, b. Aug. 27, 1733	1	85
Benj[ami]n, d. Dec. 27, 1769	1	85
Bethyah, d. Joseph & Elizabeth, b. Feb. 6, 1716	1	19
Bethiah, m. Isaac **CASSALL**, Oct. 12, 1738	1	159
Caleb, m. Anna **A[N]DRAS**, July 18, 1727	1	105
Caleb, s. Caleb & Annah, b. June 16, 1738	1	105
Dorcas, d. Caleb & Annah, b. July 25, 1741	1	105
Dorrittey, d. Amos & Hannah, b. Nov. 21, 1713	1	18
Dorothy, m Joshua **READ**, July 2, 1751	1	255
Ebenezer, [s. Amos & Hannah], b. Mar. 18, 1718	1	18
Ebenezer, m. Rachel **MEACHAM**, June 19, 1744	1	248
Ebenezer, s. Eben[eze]r & Rachel, b. Mar. 25, 1751	1	248
Ebenezer, d. Feb. 15, 1754	1	248
Ebenezer, m. Patience **ORMS**, Oct. 14, 1770	2	169
Eben[ezer], s. [Ebenezer & Patience], b. Apr. 5, 1771	2	169
Elijah, s. Eb[enezer] & Rachel, b. Mar. 19, 1744/5	1	248
Elizabeth, d. Joseph & Elizabeth, b. Jan. 9, 1723	1	19
Elizabeth, w. Joseph, d. May 22, 1727	1	84
Elizabeth, d. Benj[ami]n & Anna, b. Nov. 20, 1728	1	85
Elizabeth, m. Sam[ue]l **SILSBRY**, Dec. 5, 1746	1	262
Elizabeth, d. [Joseph & Elizabeth], b. May 22, 1749	1	296
Elizabeth, d. [Joseph & Elizabeth], b. May 22, 1749	2	33

	Vol.	Page
WOODWARD, WOODARD, (cont.)		
Elizabeth, w. Jacob, d. Mar. 26, 1757	1	204
Elizabeth, [d. Benj[ami]n & Anna], d. June 4, 1772,		
ae. 43 y.	1	85
Eunice, d. Amos & Hannah, b. Oct. 16, 1721	1	56
[E]unice, d. Jacob & Abigail, b. Mar. 25, 1744	1	204
Eunice, m. Jonathan **HOVEY**, Dec. 31, 1761	2	74
Eunice, m. Abel **ROBINSON**, Mar. 17, 1795	3	10
Geo[rge] T., s. Joseph, shoemaker, & Lucy A., ae.		
39, of Willimantic, b. Apr. 8, 1848	4	1
Hannah, [d. Amos & Hannah], b. Sept. 26, 1716	1	18
Hannah, m. Benjamin **FFOLLET**, Jr., Nov. 10, 1736	1	200
Hannah, d. Eben[ezer] & Rachel, b. Mar. 17, 1747	1	248
Hannah, d. Jacob & Elizabeth, b. Feb. 23, 1755; d.		
May 26, 1755	1	204
Hannah, m. Sam[ue]ll **BASS**, Oct. 2, 1766	2	126
Hannah, w. [Amos], d. Mar. 14, 1778	1	56
Huldah, d. Caleb & Annah, b. Dec. 1, 1735	1	105
Isaiah, s. Jacob & Abigail, b. Apr. 22, 1749	1	204
Jacob, [s. Amos & Hannah], b. May 25, 1715	1	18
Jacob, m. Abigail **FFLINT**, Dec. 15, 1738	1	204
Jacob, s. Jacob & Abigail, b. Apr. 3, 1742; d. May		
18, 1748	1	204
Jacob, s. Jacob, d. Aug. 29, 1750/51	1	204
Jacob, m. Wid. Elizabeth **DURKEE**, Mar. 28, 1754	1	204
Jason, s. Joseph & Elizabeth, b. July 19, 1753	1	296
Jason, s. [Joseph & Elizabeth], b. July 19, 1753	2	33
Jemima, d. Eben[eze]r & Rachel, b. Mar. 7, 1748/9	1	248
Jeremiah, s. John & Synthia, d. Apr. 15, 1756	2	6
John, s. Caleb & Annah, b. June 2, 1744	1	105
John, s. Joseph & Elizabeth, b. June 10, 1755	1	296
John, s. [Joseph & Elizabeth], b. June 10, 1755	2	33
Joseph, s. Joseph & Elizabeth, b. Jan. 21, 1725	1	19
Joseph, d. May 30, 1727	1	84
Joseph, m. Elisabeth **PERKINS**, May 19, 1748	1	296
Joseph, m. Elisabeth **PERKINS**, May 19, 1748	2	33
Joseph, s. [Joseph & Elizabeth], b. May 26, 1751	2	33
Joseph, s. Joseph & Elizabeth, b. May 26, 1757	1	296
Joseph, of Ashford, m. Almira **GURLEY**, of Windham,		
Apr. 29, 1829, by Rev. Dennis Platt	3	136
Joshua, s. Caleb & Annah, b. July 27, 1740	1	105
Martha, d. [Joseph & Elizabeth], b. Aug. 13, 1757	2	33
Mary, d. [Amos & Hannah], b. Mar. 6, 1720	1	18
Mary, m. Daniel **CUTLER**, July 9, 1736	1	179
Othniel, s. [Joseph & Elizabeth], b. Sept. 8, 1766	2	33
Phineas, s. [Joseph & Elizabeth], b. June 3, 1764	2	33
Rebeckah, d. Caleb & Annah, b. Jan. 3, 1733/4	1	105
Sarah, d. Jacob & Abigail, b. May 13, 1751; d.		

	Vol.	Page
WOODWARD, WOODARD, (cont.)		
Oct. 9, 1751	1	204
Stephen, s. Benjamin & Hannah, b. Oct. 18, 1740	1	170
Stephen, m. Jemima **SAWYER**, Jan. 8, 1772	2	167
Stephen, d. [}	2	167
William, s. [Joseph & Elizabeth], b. Nov. 14, 1759	2	33
Zac[c]heas, s. Jacob & Abigail, b. Apr. 9, 1748; d. May 22, 1748	1	204
——, d. Jacob & Abigail, b. July 28, [ ]; d. same day	1	204
WOODWORTH, Benjamin Lord, s. [Charles A. & Lucia C.], b. July 7, 1834	3	138
Caroline Elizabeth, d. [Charles A. & Lucia C.], b. June 19, 1841	3	138
Charles A., m. Lucia C. **WEBB**, Oct. 15, 1829, by Rev. Richard F. Cleveland	3	138
Charlotte, ae. 42, m. 2d h. Sayman **DAVENPORT**, merchant ae. 43, Jan. 27, [1850], by Rev. A. H. Robinson	4	115
Courtland, d. Apr. 9, 1848, ae. 1 y. 8 m.	4	151
Elizabeth L., m. Silas F. **CLARK**, June 9, 1842, by Rev. Andrew Sharp	3	202
George, m. Maria **LEARNED**, Sept. 6, 1825, by Rev. Jesse Fisher	3	116
Hannah Webb, d. [Charles A. & Lucia C.], b. Feb. 28, 1831	3	138
Henry Chester, s. [Charles A. & Lucia C.], b. June 3, 1833	3	138
Henry Chester, s. [Charles A. & Lucia C.], d. Aug. 11, 1833	3	138
Leonard, of Coventry, m. Joanna **HOLMES**, of Willimantic, Sept. 15, 1834, by Rev. Philo Judson	3	170
Lucius, ae. 26, m. [ ], July 1, [1848], by Andrew Roberts	4	113
Lydia, b. Preston, Ct., res. Willimantic, d. Aug. 9, 1860, ae. 84	4	161
Maria, m. Charles N. **PALMER**, Feb. 25, 1830, by Rev. Jesse Fisher	3	140
Mary A., d. [Aug.] [ ], [1849]	4	153
Mira A., d. W[illia]m, ae. 27, & Maria A., ae. 24, b. Nov. 5, [1848]	4	6
Susan E., of Windham, d. Aug. 5, 1848, ae. 5 m.	4	151
W[illia]m, s. W[illia]m, laborer, ae. 37, & Mariah, ae. 29, of Willimantic, b. Mar. 14, 1848	4	1
William Chester, s. [Charles A. & Lucia C.], b. July 16, 1843	3	138
——, child of W[illia]m, laborer, ae. 36, of Willimantic, b. July 14, [1850]	4	10

	Vol.	Page
WORDEN, Lewis, m. Olive S. **PLACE**, Sept. 6, 1847, by Rev.		
Andrew Sharp	3	236
WRIGHT, Abel, s. Abel & Mary, b. Feb. 23, 1721/22	1	44
Amaziah, s. Ebenezer & Sarah, b. Feb. 11, 1738/9	1	124
Ann, m. John **HUNTINGTON**, Mar. 11, 1756	2	23
Anna, [twin with Ephraim], d. Ephraim & Hannah, b.		
Mar. 16, 1735; d. May 6, 1758	1	190
Anna, m. John **HUNTINGTON**, [ ]; d. May 6,		
1758	1	190
Beriah, s. Ephraim & Hannah, b. Feb. 22, 1737	1	190
Deborah, d. Ebenezer & Elizabeth, b. Jan. 29, 1724/5	1	68
Ebenezer, m. Elizabeth **NEWCOMB**, Apr. 20, 1721	1	68
Ebenezer, s. Ebenezer & Elizabeth, b. Jan. 2, 1726/7	1	68
Ebenezer, m. Sarah **HUNTINGTON**, Mar. 28, 1728	1	124
Eliphalet, s. Ebenezer & Sarah, b. Feb. 27, 1728/9	1	124
Elisha, s. Ebenezer & Sarah, b. Sept. 26, 1734	1	124
Elizabeth, d. Ebenezer & Sarah, b. Nov. 30, 1730	1	124
Ephraim, m. Hannah **WOOD**, June 29, 1724	1	190
Ephraim, [twin with Anna], s. Ephraim & Hannah, b.		
Mar. 16, 1735	1	190
Hannah, d. Ephraim & Hannah, b. Feb. 4, 1731	1	190
Hannah, w. Ephraim, d. Mar. 18, 1737	1	190
John, s. Ephraim & Hannah, b. Mar. 18, 1726	1	190
Martha, d. Ephraim & Hannah, b. Jan. 14, 1733	1	190
Mary d. Ebenezer & Sarah, b. Jan. 15, 1736/7; d.		
July 27, 1739	1	124
Mary Ann, of Windham, m. W[illia]m B. **ADAMS**, of Frank-		
lin, Sept. 20, 1838, by Rev. Otis C. Whiton, of		
Scotland Society	3	188
Mercy, m. Maltiah **BINGHAM**, Feb. 14, 1771	3	18
Sam[ue]ll, s. Abel, Jr. & Mary, b. May 14, 1720	1	44
Sarah, d. Abel, Jr. & Mary, b. Aug. 25, 1718	1	44
Sarah, d. Ebenezer & Sarah, b. Sept. 22, 1732	1	124
William, of Chatham, m. Julia E. **CAREY**, of Windham,		
Aug. 12, 1838, by Rev. John E. Tyler	3	187
Zerivah, m. John **UPTON**, Jan. 8, 1740/41	1	222
Zeruiah Newcomb, d. Ebenezer & Elizabeth, b. Mar. 12,		
1722	1	68
WYLLYS, WYLLIS, [see also **WILLIS**], Abel P., m. Maria		
LINCOLN, Jan. 29, 1838, at Willimantic, by Rev.		
Philo Judson	3	185
Eli C., m. Mary E. **READ**, Feb. 1, 1843, by Rev. Henry		
Beers Sherman	3	207
Frank Burnham, s. Frank, carpenter, ae. 26, & Eliza-		
beth, ae. 20, b. Apr. 8, 1849	4	5
Frank Burnham, s. Frank, ae. 26, & Elis, ae. 20, b.		
Apr. 8, [1848]	4	7
Mercy Ann, d. Abel D., ae. 35, & Mariah, ae. 20, b.		

	Vol.	Page
WYLLYS, WYLLIS, (cont.)		
Nov. 10, [1848]	4	5
Mercy Ann, d. Abel, day laborer, ae. 35, & Mariah,		
ae. 30, b. Nov. 19, [1849]	4	5
Welcome, s. Eli. C., tailor, ae. 31, & Mary E.,		
ae. 29, b. Nov. 5, [1849]	4	9
Welcome, d. July 20, [1850], ae. 8 1/2 m.	4	156
WYMAN, Sarah, m. Edward **COBURN**, Feb. 22, 1774	2	60
YEOMAN, David, m. Abigail **HURLBUTT**, Nov. 13, 1754	1	325
YERRINGTON, [see also **TERRINGTON**], Ann, d. [William &		
C[h]loe], b. [ ], on Long Island	2	102
Benjamin, [s. William & C[h]loe], b. [ ],		
on Long Island	2	102
Daniel, s. [William & C[h]loe], b. June 21, 1777	2	102
Desire, d. [William & C[h]loe], b. June 24, 1782	2	102
Frederick, [s. William & C[h]loe], b. [ ],		
on Long Island	2	102
Rebeckah, [d. William & C[h]loe, b. [ ],		
on Long Island	2	102
Uriah, s. [William & C[h]loe], b. Jan. 24, 1780	2	102
William, m. C[h]loe **CLEVELAND**, Sept. 28, 1763	2	102
William, s. William & C[h]loe], b. July 15, 1764	2	102
YORK, Collins, m. Lucretia S. **CAREY**, Dec. 8, 1822	3	109
Elisha, m. Nancy Ann **LILLIE**, July 11, 1824	3	119
John, m. Eunice **WILLOBY**, May 25, 1824	3	84
Nancy, m. W[illia]m A. **LATHROP**, b. of Preston, May 3,		
1845, by Rev. J.E Tyler	3	221
YOUNG, Anne, d. W[illia]m & Anna, b. Mar. 31, 1746	2	22
Anne, d. John & Zerviah, b. Jan. 22, 1757	2	22
Anne, m. James **ROBERTS**, a transient person, July 30,		
1769	2	2
Anne, m. Frederick **MANNING**, July 19, 1781	2	73
Betsey, m. Cranston **BOWEN**, Feb. 11, 1824	3	15
Caroline, d. [David & Freelove], b. Nov. 16, 1816	3	52
Caroline M., d. [David & Freelove], b. Oct. 26, 1814	3	52
Catharine J., d. Job T., farmer, ae. 35, b. Apr. 28,		
1850	4	11
Chipman, m. Hannah Maria **BLISH**, b. of Windham, May 16,		
1847, by Rev. Tho[ma]s Dowling, Willimantic	3	235
David, s. W[illia]m & Ann, b. Feb. 28, 1742	2	22
David, m. Freelove **ABBE**, Apr. 12, 1801	3	52
David, s. [David & Freelove], b. Jan. 10, 1819	3	52
Edward, s. [David & Freelove], b. Feb. 20, 1822	3	52
Ethelda C. L., d. W[illia]m H., mechanic, ae. 46, &		
Adah, ae. 41, b. Oct. 5, 1850	4	14
Fanny, m. Josiah **DEAN**, Jr., Apr. 11, 1831, by Rev.		
Roger Bingham	3	152
Fanny, m. Horace **FLINT**, Mar. 23, 1832, by Rev. Roger		

	Vol.	Page
YOUNG, (cont.)		
Bingham	3	159
George, m. Sarah **SEARS**, Mar. 29, 1823	3	112
Giles R., s. Ulysses, millwright, ae. 38, of Willi-		
mantic, b. Mar. 2, [1850]	4	10
Guilford Dudley, s. [David & Freelove], b. Feb. 23,		
1802	3	52
Harriet, m. George **HEB[B]ARD**, Jan. 2, 1831, by Rev.		
Roger Bingham	3	151
Harriet, of Ashford, m. Denison P. **WEAVER**, of Windham,		
Nov. 9, 1840, by Rev. Henry Greenslit	3	194
Harriet, m. Horace **YOUNG**, Feb. 5, 1843, by Rev. Andrew		
Sharp, Willimantic	3	207
Henr[i]etta, d. [David & Freelove], b. Apr. 13, 1808;		
d. May 31, 1809	3	52
Horace, m. Harriet **YOUNG**, Feb. 5, 1843, by Rev. Andrew		
Sharp, Willimantic	3	207
James Edward, s. [Capt. William, Jr. & Elizabeth], b.		
Mar. 20, 1809, at Sterling	3	70
Job T., m. Lucinda **WEAVER**, Nov. 26, 1846, by Rev.		
Tho[ma]s Tallman, of Scotland	3	232
John, m. Zerviah **HUNTINGTON**, Nov. 12, 1754	2	22
John B., d. Sept. 23, 1848, ae. 25 m.	4	151
Joseph B., s. W[illia]m H., & Adah, b. Dec. 20, 1847	4	2
Joseph B., d. Jan. 5, 1848, ae. 6 1/2 m.	4	151
Laura, m. Elias B. **JENNER**, Jan. 9, 1833, by Rev. Roger		
Bingham	3	163
Laura M., m. Samuel **LEE**, June 27, 1830, by Rev. Richard		
F. Cleveland	3	146
Laura Maria, d. [Capt. William, Jr. & Elizabeth], b.		
Apr. 9, 1807, at Providence	3	70
Lucy, d. [David & Freelove], b. Nov. 4, 1803; d. Feb.		
15, 1809	3	52
Lucy, d. [David & Freelove], b. Mar. 23, 1810	3	52
Lucy W., m. Sam[ue]l B. **HUNTINGTON**, Feb. 24, 1829, by		
Rev. Dennis Platt	3	135
Lydia, d. [Capt. William, Jr. & Elizabeth], b. Sept.		
25, 1802	3	70
Lydia Swift, of Windham, m. Henry **GARDINER**, of Hart-		
ford, Apr. 8, 1834, by L.S. Corson, Rector	3	170
Mary, d. John, & Zerviah, b. Mar. 15, 1755	2	22
Mary, d. [David & Freelove], b. July 23, 1812	3	52
Mary, m. Benjamin **WEEDEN**, Jr., of Hopkinton, R.I.,		
Mar. 23, 1825	3	35
Mary B., m Lucius **ABBE**, Jr , Apr. 18, 1813	3	72
Mary J., d. Justus, farmer, ae. 40, b. Nov. 15, [1849]	4	9
Nancy, d [David & Freelove], b. Apr. 9, 1806	3	52
Oliver, m. Elizabeth **HERRICK**, b. of Windham, Oct. 20,		

	Vol.	Page
YOUNG, (cont.)		
1836, by Rev. Benajah Cook, Jr.	3	180
Salome B., of Windham, m. Charles **STEWART**, of Fishkill, N.Y., May 12, 1834, by Rev. L.H. Corson	3	171
Samuel, s. W[illia]m & Ann, b. Mar. 14, 1740	2	22
Sarah, m. Henry **BUCK**, Nov. 30, 1791	2	208
Sarah, b. Voluntown, res. Willimantic, d. Aug. 7, [1849], ae. 56	4	153
Triphenia, m. Warner **LINCOLN**, Mar. 23, 1830, by Rev. Roger Bingham	3	143
Ulyssys, m. Sarah B. **HERRICK**, Nov. 24, 1836, by Rev. Philetus Greene	3	180
William, s. W[illia]m & Ann, b. Nov. 8, 1738	2	22
William, Jr., Capt., m. Elizabeth **RIPLEY**, Dec. 26, 1801	3	70
William, Jr., Capt., d. Oct. 29, 1809	3	70
W[illia]m H., m. Adah **DEAN**, Nov. 10, 1831, by Rev. Ralph S. Crampton	3	156
William Henry, s. [Capt. William, Jr. & Elizabeth], b. Dec. 20, 1804, at Providence	3	70
Willie C., of Willimantic, d. Apr. 24, 1860, ae. 3	4	159-0
Zerviah, m. Alfred **BINGHAM**, Nov. 24, 1787	2	50
——, child of Chipman, laborer, ae. 28, & Hannah, ae. 20, of Willimantic, b. Feb 13, 1849	4	5
——, d. [David & Freelove], b. Jan. 20, [ ]; d. next day	3	52
NO SURNAME		
A[a]ron, m. Sarah **BINGHAM**, Mar. 3, 1763	2	80
Alice, m. Benjamin **HANKS**, [ ]	2	116
Anna, m. Thomas **STEDMAN**, Apr. 9, 1724 (Arnold Copy says "Perhaps 1734")	1	200
Elizabeth, m. Asa **FISK**, Mar. 19, 1755	1	327
Elizabeth, m. Joseph **DURKEE**, [ ]	2	183
Hannah, m. Nathaniell **SKEFFE**, Apr. 24, 1716	1	29
Hannah, m. James **SPAULDING**, Oct. 22, 1771	2	62
Isabella, of Willimantic, d. Aug. 27, 1860, ae. 1	4	161
Jerusha, m. William **PARRISH**, Apr 13, 1742	1	229
Jerusha, m. John **LILLIE**, Apr. 15, 1762	2	77
Lydia, m. Ephraim **BEMIS**, Oct. 1, 1736	1	155
Margaret, m. Jeremiah **WELCH**, Dec. 15, 1736	1	161
Tamar, m. Zephaniah **SAMPSON**, Apr. 12, 1779	3	27